THE NEW TESTAMENT
IN MODERN SPEECH

Mary S. Boyd.

June. 23rd, 1929.

THE
NEW TESTAMENT
IN MODERN SPEECH

AN IDIOMATIC TRANSLATION INTO EVERY-DAY ENGLISH FROM THE TEXT OF THE RESULTANT GREEK TESTAMENT

BY THE LATE

RICHARD FRANCIS WEYMOUTH
M.A., D.Lit. (London)

Fellow of University College, London, and sometime Headmaster
of Mill Hill School, Editor of "The Resultant Greek Testament"

NEWLY REVISED BY
SEVERAL WELL-KNOWN NEW TESTAMENT SCHOLARS

FOURTH EDITION.   THIRD IMPRESSION

LONDON
JAMES CLARKE & CO., LTD., 9 ESSEX ST., STRAND, W.C.2

SCHOLARS

Printed in Great Britain

NEW TESTAMENT IN MODERN SPEECH

PREFACE TO THE FOURTH EDITION

EXCEPT for the spacing out of the conversations in the Gospels, there has been but little alteration in this translation since it was first published in 1903. During the period of more than twenty years that has since elapsed archæological and biblical researches have either modified or confirmed, and in any case have amplified, our previous knowledge ; and there is more agreement than there was formerly on many matters, particularly in regard to the origin of the different books of the New Testament.

The first edition of this book, as mentioned in the original Preface, was, at the Translator's request, edited and partly revised by the Rev. E. Hampden-Cook, M.A. He threw himself into the work with energy, made many improvements in the text, and added many notes. He also introduced side-headings, and these have been, with few alterations, retained in the present edition. The second and third editions were also supervised by him. Useful suggestions have been made by him for alterations in the text of the Gospels, or in the notes thereon, with a view to the present edition.

The task of improving the text and notes for this new edition has been largely in the hands of the Rev. S. W. Green, M.A., Professor of New Testament Exegesis at Regent's Park College and present Dean of the Faculty of Theology at the University of London, who has written all the Introductions, except that to the Apocalypse, and has given attention more particularly to the revision of the Gospels, Acts, Hebrews, and the Epistles of the Captivity. He has also, in an Appendix, contributed additional notes to some of the Epistles. He has been assisted by the Rev. Professor A. J. D. Farrer, B.A., of Regent's Park College, who has been mainly responsible for the revision of the text and notes of Romans, Corinthians, Galatians, Thessalonians, and the Pastoral and the Catholic Epistles. The

Rev. Professor H. T. Andrews, D.D., of New and Hackney Colleges, has contributed the Introduction to the Apocalypse and has revised the text and notes of that book. Also certain members of the Translator's family have assisted in the revision. Grateful acknowledgements must also be made to numerous persons who, since the third edition was published in 1909, have made suggestions for the improvement of text or notes.

In regard to the titles of the books, it has been thought better to retain with but slight variation those adopted in the Authorised Version.

Reference has been made afresh to the Translator's original manuscript. In regard to the text, the main aim has been to preserve his renderings, except where greater accuracy or greater simplicity seemed to call for change. In the case of disputed translations, if the former edition has not a footnote, one has usually been added. Special importance has been attached to the maintenance everywhere of the Translator's original conception, namely, while modernizing the English, to preserve the dignity of the language and to avoid colloquialisms. There is reason to suspect that certain passages, more particularly in the Gospels, have been misplaced. It has not been thought desirable, however, to alter the order of such passages, as any such alterations must necessarily be speculative : attention has been called in the notes to some cases of this sort.

In regard to the notes, many have been omitted, particularly those relating to the tenses of verbs, since it seems sufficient to refer the student of Greek to the Translator's pamphlet on the *Aorist* (see p. xii) ; also notes of an homiletic nature have made way for others that are more strictly explanatory ; while notes have been omitted which make reference to authorities that are now somewhat out of date.

The publishers have lent their aid, and, by the introduction of new type and in many other ways, have done their part in the production of an improved edition.

It is hoped that a translation which has been well received for many years throughout the English-speaking world may find in its new form a welcome from those who may value the results of recent scholarship.

PREFACE TO THE FOURTH EDITION

Possibly here and there some rendering or note may not be immediately acceptable to those who, quite justifiably, are jealous for tradition against the findings of recent research; but this revision has endeavoured to hold the balance even as between the traditional and the critical view of this portion of the Word of God. That 'Word' stands clear above all examination of the words. Devout scholarship may justly claim to gain for us in the New Testament a revelation even more credible and more manifestly divine than in pre-critical days. And so the revisers of this edition reverently echo the closing words of the original preface, ' and now this Translation is humbly and prayerfully commended to God's gracious blessing.'

March 1st, 1924.

FOURTH EDITION : SECOND IMPRESSION

Advantage has been taken of a new impression to correct a few misprints that escaped observation.

November, 1926.

PREFACE TO THE FIRST EDITION

THE Translation of the New Testament here offered to English-speaking Christians is a bona fide translation made directly from the Greek, and is in no sense a revision. The plan adopted has been the following :—

1. An earnest endeavour has been made (based upon more than sixty years' study of both the Greek and English languages, besides much further familiarity gained by continual teaching) to ascertain the exact meaning of every passage, not only by the light that Classical Greek throws on the language used, but also by that which the Septuagint and the Hebrew Scriptures afford ; aid being sought too from Versions and Commentators ancient and modern, and from the ample *et cetera* of *apparatus grammaticus* and theological and Classical reviews and magazines—or rather, by means of occasional excursions into this vast prairie.

2. The sense thus seeming to have been ascertained, the next step has been to consider how it could be most accurately and naturally exhibited in the English of the present day ; in other words, how we can with some approach to probability suppose that the inspired writer himself would have expressed his thoughts, had he been writing in our age and country.[1]

3. Lastly it has been evidently desirable to compare the results thus attained with the renderings of other scholars, especially of course with the Authorised and Revised Versions. But, alas, the great majority of even ' new translations,' so called, are, in reality, only Tyndale's immortal work a little—often very little—modernised !

4. But in the endeavour to find in Twentieth Century English a precise equivalent for a Greek word, phrase, or sentence, there are two dangers to be guarded against. There are a Scylla and a Charybdis. On the one hand

---

[1] I am aware of what Professor Blackie has written on this subject (*Aeschylus*, Préf., p. viii.) ; but the problem endeavoured to be solved in this Translation is as above stated.

there is the English of ' Society,' on the other hand that of
the utterly uneducated, each of these *patois* having also its
own special, though expressive, borderland which we name
' slang.' But all these salient angles (as a professor of
fortification might say) of our language are forbidden
ground to the reverent translator of Holy Scripture.

5. But again, a *modern* translation—does this imply that
no words or phrases in any degree antiquated are to be
admitted ? Not so, for great numbers of such words and
phrases are still in constant use. To be antiquated is not
the same thing as to be obsolete or even obsolescent, and
without at least a tinge of antiquity it is scarcely possible
that there should be that dignity of style that befits the
sacred themes with which the Evangelists and Apostles deal.

6. It is plain that this attempt to bring out the sense of
the Sacred Writings naturally as well as accurately in
present-day English does not permit, except to a limited
extent, the method of literal rendering—the *verbo verbum
reddere* at which Horace shrugs his shoulders. Dr.
Welldon, recently Bishop of Calcutta, in the Preface (p. vii)
to his masterly translation of the *Nicomachean Ethics* of
Aristotle, writes, ' I have deliberately rejected the principle
of trying to translate the same Greek word by the same
word in English, and where circumstances seemed to call
for it I have sometimes used two English words to represent
one word of the Greek ' ;—and he is perfectly right. With a
slavish literality delicate shades of meaning cannot be re-
produced, nor allowance be made for the influence of inter-
woven thought, or of the writer's ever shifting—not to say
changing—point of view. An utterly ignorant or utterly
lazy man, if possessed of a little ingenuity, can with the help
of a dictionary and grammar give a word-for-word rendering,
whether intelligible or not, and print ' Translation ' on his
title-page. On the other hand it is a melancholy spectacle
to see men of high ability and undoubted scholarship toil
and struggle at translation under a needless restriction to
literality, as in intellectual handcuffs and fetters, when they
might with advantage snap the bonds and fling them away,
as Dr. Welldon has done : more melancholy still, if they are
at the same time racking their brains to exhibit the result
of their labours—a splendid but idle philological *tour de
force*—in what *was* English nearly 300 years before.

7. Obviously any literal translation cannot but carry idioms of the earlier language into the later, where they will very probably not be understood ;[1] and more serious still is the evil when, as in the Jewish Greek of the N.T., the earlier language of the two is itself composite and abounds in forms of speech that belong to one earlier still. For the N.T. Greek, even in the writings of Luke, contains a large number of Hebrew idioms ; and a literal rendering into English cannot but partially veil, and in some degree distort, the true sense, even if it does not totally obscure it (and that too where *perfect* clearness should be attained, if possible), by this admixture of Hebrew as well as Greek forms of expression.

8. It follows that the reader who is bent upon getting a literal rendering, such as he can commonly find in the R.V. or (often a better one) in Darby's *New Testament*, should always be on his guard against its strong tendency to mislead.

9. One point, however, can hardly be too emphatically stated. It is not the present Translator's ambition to supplant the Versions already in general use, to which their intrinsic merit or long familiarity or both have caused all Christian minds so lovingly to cling. His desire has rather been to furnish a succinct and compressed running commentary (not doctrinal) to be used side by side with its elder compeers. And yet there has been something of a remoter hope. It can scarcely be doubted that some day the attempt will be renewed to produce a satisfactory English Bible—one in some respects perhaps (but assuredly with great and important deviations) on the lines of the Revision of 1881, or even altogether to supersede both the A.V. and the R.V. ; and it may be that the Translation here offered will contribute some materials that may be built into that far grander edifice.

10. THE GREEK TEXT here followed is that given in the Translator's *Resultant Greek Testament*.[2]

11. Of the VARIOUS READINGS, only those are here given which seem the most important, and which affect the rendering into English. They are in the footnotes, with

---

[1] A flagrant instance is the 'having in a readiness' of 2 Cor. x. 6, A.V. although in Tyndale we find ' and are redy to take vengeaunce,' and even Wiclif writes ' and we han redi to venge.'

[2] Published by Messrs. James Clarke & Co., Ltd., London. Price 4s. net.

v.L. (*varia lectio*) prefixed. As to the chief *modern* critical editions full details will be found in the *Resultant Greek Testament*, while for the *original* authorities—MSS., Versions, Patristic quotations—the reader must of necessity consult the great works of Lachmann, Tregelles, Tischendorf, and others, or the numerous monographs on separate Books.[1] In the margin of the R.V. a distinction is made between readings supported by ' a few ancient authorities,' ' some ancient authorities,' ' many ancient authorities,' and so on. Such valuation is not attempted in this work.

12. Considerable pains have been bestowed on the exact rendering of the tenses of the Greek verb ; for by inexactness in this detail the true sense cannot but be missed. That the Greek tenses do not coincide, and cannot be expected to coincide with those of the English verb ; that—except in narrative—the aorist as a rule is *more* exactly represented in English by our perfect with ' have ' than by our simple past tense ; and that in this particular the A.V. is in scores of instances more correct than the R.V. ; the present Translator has contended (with arguments which some of the best scholars in Britain and in America hold to be ' unanswerable ' and ' indisputable ') in a pamphlet [2] *On the Rendering into English of the Greek Aorist and Perfect.* Even an outline of the argument cannot be given in a Preface such as this.

13. But he who would make a truly *English* translation of a foreign book must not only select the right nouns, adjectives, and verbs, insert the suitable prepositions and auxiliaries, and triumph (if he can) over the seductions and blandishments of idioms with which he has been familiar from his infancy, but which, though forcible or beautiful with other surroundings, are, for all that, part and parcel of that other language rather than of English : he has also to beware of *connecting his sentences* in an un-English fashion.

Now a careful examination of a number of authors (including Scottish, Irish, and American) yields some interesting results. Taking at haphazard a passage from

[1] Such as McClellan's Four Gospels ; Westcott on John's Gospel, John's Epistles, and *Hebrews* ; Hackett on *Acts* ; Lightfoot, and also Ellicott, on various Epistles ; Mayor on *James* ; Edwards on 1 *Corinthians* and *Hebrews* ; Sanday and Headlam on *Romans*. Add to these Scrivener's very valuable *Introduction to the Criticism of the N.T.*

[2] Published by Messrs. James Clarke & Co., Ltd., London. Price 1s. 3d. net.

each of fifty-six authors, and counting on after some full stop till fifty finite verbs—*i.e.* verbs in the indicative, imperative, or subjunctive mood—have been reached (each finite verb, as every schoolboy knows, being the nucleus of one sentence or clause), it has been found that the connecting links of the fifty-six times fifty sentences are about one-third conjunctions, about one-third adverbs or relative and interrogative pronouns, while in the case of the remaining third there is what the grammarians call an *asyndeton*—no formal grammatical connexion at all. But in the writers of the N.T. nearly *two*-thirds of the connecting links are conjunctions. It follows that in order to make the style of a translation true idiomatic English many of these conjunctions must be omitted, and for others adverbs, etc., must be substituted.

The two conjunctions *for* and *therefore* are discussed at some length in two Appendices to the above-mentioned pamphlet on the *Aorist*, to which the reader is referred.

14. The NOTES, with but few exceptions, are not of the nature of a general commentary. Some, as already intimated, refer to the readings here followed, but the great majority are in vindication or explanation of the renderings given.

Since the completion of this new version nearly two years ago, ill-health has incapacitated the Translator from undertaking even the lightest work. He has therefore been obliged to entrust to other hands the labour of critically examining and revising the manuscript and of seeing it through the press. This arduous task has been undertaken by Rev. Ernest Hampden-Cook, M.A., St. John's College, Cambridge, of Sandbach, Cheshire, with some co-operation from one of the Translator's sons ; and the Translator is under deep obligations to these two gentlemen for their kindness in the matter. He has also most cordially to thank Mr. Hampden-Cook for making the existence of the work known to various members of the OLD MILLHILLIANS' CLUB and other former pupils of the Translator, who in a truly substantial manner have manifested a generous determination to enable the volume to see the light. Very grateful does the Translator feel to them for this signal mark of their friendship.

Mr. Hampden-Cook is responsible for the headings of the

paragraphs, and at my express desire has inserted some additional notes.

I have further to express my gratitude to Rev. Frank Ballard, M.A., B.Sc., Lond., at present of Sharrow, Sheffield, for some very valuable assistance which he has most kindly given in connexion with the Introductions to the several books.

I have also the pleasure of acknowledging the numerous valuable and suggestive criticisms with which I have been favoured on some parts of the work, by an old friend, Rev. Sydney Thelwell, B.A., of Leamington, a clergyman of the Church of England, whom I have known for many years as a painstaking and accurate scholar, a well-read theologian, and a thoughtful and devout student of Scripture.

I am very thankful to Mr. H. L. Gethin, Mr. S. Hales, Mr. J. A. Latham, and Rev. T. A. Seed, for the care with which they have read the proof sheets.

And now this Translation is humbly and prayerfully commended to God's gracious blessing.

R. F. W.

BRENTWOOD, ESSEX.
July 1902.

THE GOSPELS

The Title.—The *Greek* name (in *English* dress ' Evangel ') means ' good tidings.' If the term ' gospel ' is compounded of *good* and Anglo-Saxon *spell* (story), it exactly represents the original : if it means *God's* spell, it recalls the N.T. phrase ' the gospel of God.' Strictly speaking, there can be but one gospel, and this is indicated in the heading of the several Gospels found in the earliest manuscripts, which reads simply ' According to Matthew ' (Mark, Luke, John). The word really passes through three stages : (1) God's message to the world announced by and centring in Jesus Christ, (2) the narrative of the facts concerning Him, (3) any one written version of these facts. It is with this last, the four ' Gospels ' which stand in the front of the New Testament, that we have here to do.

The three and the one.—The four Gospels separate at a glance into these two groups : (1) Matthew, Mark, and Luke ; (2) John. The three are intimately related. The Fourth Gospel stands apart in solitary splendour. Its opening words are not the introduction to a work of history on the same plane as the three, but to a theological inter-pretation of the facts. The historical outline is almost entirely new. In the teaching of Jesus, instead of parable and homely sayings which all could understand, we have long conversations centring round the personality and mission of our Lord, expounding in mystical fashion the abstract ideas of life, light, witness, truth, and glory. Whatever the relation of the Fourth Gospel may be to its predecessors, it must be isolated in order to be understood.

THE SYNOPTIC PROBLEM

The first three Gospels, put side by side, yield a *synopsis*, or common outline of the course of the ministry. In what is at best a fragmentary record they show remarkable agreement in the *selection* of incidents, in the *order* in which these are presented, and in the *language* of those sections of the narrative which they have in common. But along with these resemblances there are differences. It is this double fact of likeness and difference which constitutes the Synoptic Problem. How are we to account for it ?

1. *The priority of Mark.*—The problem has a long history : it can only here be said that the all but unanimous judgement of modern scholarship is that the earliest account of the ministry is to be found in Mark, and that this Gospel was used as one of their sources by Matthew and by Luke. Between them they absorb practically the whole of Mark : when one of them varies the order of his sections, the other keeps to it : when they depart from his language, it is mostly for editorial reasons—modification of rough diction, toning down of expressions which might offend, curtailment under pressure of the inclusion of new material. The first of the sources used in common by Matthew and Luke is virtually our Gospel of Mark.

2. *The 'teaching-source'* (Q).—Both Matthew and Luke devote large space to teaching of Jesus which is absent from Mark. Much of this they have in common, and often in identical language. This means that they both used a second written source, now commonly called Q, from the first letter of the German word *Quelle* (source). This second source is credibly connected with the name of the Apostle Matthew, who, according to Papias, Bishop of Hierapolis c. 150 A.D., ' composed the *oracles* in the *Hebrew* language.' Matthew, himself eye-witness and companion of our Lord, can hardly be also the author of a Greek Gospel which depends so largely on the Greek work of Mark. But if tradition is right in ascribing to him a compilation of the ' oracles ' or teachings of Jesus, afterwards incorporated in a Greek translation in our first Gospel, then the three Synoptic Gospels rest upon the twin Apostolic foundation of Matthew and of Peter, to whom, according to Papias, Mark became follower and interpreter.

3. *Matter peculiar to Matthew or Luke.*—When we have detached from these Gospels what they derive from Mark and Q, each makes its own further contribution to our knowledge of the Master. Details can be best gathered

from the blank columns of a Harmony of the Gospels. Each has his separate 'birth-story,' with no points of contact except the Virgin Birth in Bethlehem, and the subsequent residence in Nazareth, differently explained. Large parts of the 'Sermon on the Mount' are peculiar to Matthew, as are three miracles and eleven parables. Luke alone records seven of the miracles and seventeen parables and parabolic stories. One notable feature in Luke's Gospel is what has been called his 'great interpolation.' From ix. 51 to xviii. 14, 'Journeyings towards Jerusalem,' he is largely alone, and it is especially from the contents of this section that his Gospel has been called ' the most beautiful book that ever was written.' ' *St. Luke*,' the Pauline Gospel, reflects Paul's great word ' *grace*.'

It is a misfortune for the understanding of the Gospels that they have been allowed to blend into a blurred portrait of their Hero. Each should be read separately as a whole, and some main impression gathered of its author's purpose in writing. The brief prefaces to the several Gospels may suggest some special characteristics to be looked for. These may be so far anticipated here as to point out that the aim of the first three Gospels is to bring us into living touch with a human-divine personality. How does a personality disclose itself? By *deeds*: read Mark's swift story of divine doing. By *words*: study Matthew's record of His teaching. By *influence*: read Luke's Gospel of grace. Tell us what a man does, says, and is: then we know him. Such is the threefold witness of our Synoptic Gospels to the Son of Man. But deeds, words, and grace are marked by a strange note of *authority*. Who then is He who has such authority to speak, to act, to forgive, and to save? It is just here that the greatest marvel of all the world's literature, *St. John*, falls into place; the ' bodily ' Gospels find their interpretation in the ' spiritual ' Gospel.

THE FOURTH GOSPEL

If *St. John* be regarded as one of the four Gospels, it raises a problem of its own, not chiefly of authorship but of contents. Mark's historical outline, adopted by Matthew and Luke, has disappeared. There are a few points of contact—the ministry of John the Baptist, the call of the first disciples, the feeding of the five thousand, the closing scenes; but when it is not a new story, it is an old story newly told, and for the most part it is absolutely new. More than any book in the New Testament this one calls aloud for isolated study, that by candid, fearless, and reverent thinking its secret may stand disclosed. At the close of the second century Clement of Alexandria, recording the judgement of the early Church, affirms that John, having observed that the *bodily* things had been exhibited in the Gospels, produced a *spiritual* Gospel; which means that while the first three were regarded as literal history, the fourth was looked upon rather as interpretation of the facts.

AUTHORSHIP

Each Gospel is anonymous: for authorship we are dependent upon early tradition, put to the test of a reasonable probability.

St. Matthew.—Uniform tradition assigns our first Gospel to the Apostle Matthew, called in *St. Mark* Levi the son of Alphaeus, and, apart from the story of his call, a mere name. The connection of his name with the Gospel, and the improbability that he was the author, have already been touched on. Papias adds to his statement that he composed the oracles in the Hebrew (or Aramaic) language, ' and each one interpreted them as he was able.' Possibly the past tense ' interpreted ' implies that by the time he wrote the difficulty had been removed by the publication of the anonymous Greek Gospel of ' Matthew.'

St. Mark.—Papias represents Mark as Peter's interpreter, and as the author of a collection of memoirs which gave the substance (' all that he remembered ') of Peter's teaching. Probably he translated Peter's catechetical sections, spoken in Aramaic, into Greek. At the close of the century Clement of Alexandria expressly states that he wrote his Gospel at the request of those who heard Peter's preaching in *Rome*. The identity of the Mark of this tradition with the John Mark of Acts and the Mark of the Epistles may be here assumed. He was the son of that Mary to whose house as a Christian centre in Jerusalem Peter betook himself on his release from prison (Acts xii. 12), and the cousin of Barnabas (Col. iv. 10). The early defection (Acts xv. 38) had been forgotten, and Mark had become Paul's fellow-worker, ' useful in ministry ' (Col. iv. 10, Philem. 24, 2 Tim. iv. 11).   Moreover, Peter writing from Rome, sends greeting from ' Mark my son ' (1 Peter v. 13 : it can hardly be doubted that ' Babylon ' stands for Rome, as in Rev. xviii. 2, etc.).   It can only be added that the general character of this Gospel amply confirms its Petrine basis and its Roman address.   Possibly Mark xiv. 51, 52 is the artist's own modest signature in a corner of his picture.

St. Luke.—Early and undisputed tradition attributes the third Gospel and Acts to Luke, the beloved physician and faithful fellow-worker of Paul (Col. iv. 14, Philem. 24, 2 Tim. iv. 11).   He is not named in Acts, but *some* travelling companion of the Apostle introduces himself in the ' *We*-sections ' of Acts beginning at xvi. 10, xx. 5, xxvii. 1. Investigation of the possible identity of this companion strongly suggests Luke, who sailed for Rome with Paul and is found with him there.   On grounds of vocabulary and style it is argued that the writer of the *We*-sections is the author of the whole book of Acts and also of the third Gospel.   The question has been and still is much in debate (see *The Beginnings of Christianity*, by Foakes Jackson and Kirsopp Lake, Part I, vol. ii, 1922).   But the traditional view is strongly defended by Professor Harnack, and still holds ground.   We may confidently attribute Luke i. 1–4 and Acts i. 1, 2 to Luke, the careful historian of the ' facts fulfilled among us ' in the ministry of Jesus and in its continuance by the Apostles throughout the Roman world.

St. John.—The authorship of the Fourth Gospel is a problem of such immense perplexity that it cannot here be discussed.   Of the five Johannine writings of the N.T. (the Gospel, 1, 2, 3 John, the Apocalypse) only the last is attributed to a John (Rev. i. 1, 4, 9; xxii. 8).   Whether the Apocalypse and the Gospel can have come from the same pen is part of the problem.   ' Nothing is better attested in early Church history than the residence and work of St. John at Ephesus.'   Of the teaching of that Ephesian school, the Gospel according to John, whether written by him or not, is the flower and crown.

DATES

To fix the dates of the Gospels is an intricate question, which cannot here be discussed. In the twenty years since this book was first published there has been no decisive correction of the dates then suggested — Mark 63–70, Matthew about 75, Luke about 80, John 80–110 A.D. Probably John is later than 80 ; and if it could be proved that Luke had read Josephus, his Gospel must be placed near the end of the century. But this is very doubtful, and the trend of recent criticism is towards the earlier dates. The teaching-source (Q) used by Matthew and Luke may well have been written before the earliest date assigned to Mark.

THE BOOKS OF THE NEW TESTAMENT

ABBREVIATIONS USED IN THE NOTES

Amer. R.V.	American Revised Version, given at the end of the English Revised Version.
A.V.	Authorized English Version, 1611.
Cf.	Compare.
ff.	And following verses.
i.e.	That is.
Lit.	Literally.
LXX	The Septuagint (Greek) Version of the Old Testament.
mg.	Margin.
n.	Note.
nn.	Notes.
N.T.	New Testament.
O.T.	Old Testament.
R.V.	Revised English Version, 1881–85.
v.L.	*Varia Lectio.* An alternative reading found in some Manuscripts of the New Testament.
vv.	Verses.

THE GOSPEL ACCORDING TO
ST. MATTHEW

CHARACTERISTICS OF ST. MATTHEW

The first words plunge us into an intensely Jewish atmosphere. Questions which may seem remote from our interest mattered greatly to the readers of this Gospel. If Jesus claimed to be Messiah was He David's son? Did He fulfil the Old Testament Scriptures? Was He the promised King? To these several questions the author answers with a confident *Yes*, especially as to the fulfilment of Old Testament prediction. Like the tolling of a bell at brief intervals we hear ' that it might be fulfilled.' Evidently a Christian Jew is writing for Christian Jews. Yet the Gospel is nobly catholic in tone and sentiment : see for example viii. 10–13. Renan's description of this Gospel as ' the most important book that ever was written ' may make appeal to the Sermon on the Mount— that great manifesto of the religion of Jesus, identifying the Kingdom of heaven with sovereignty of character. It will be observed that this is the first of five blocks into which the author groups much of our Lord's teaching, each closing with a like refrain (vii. 28, xi. 1, xiii. 53, xix. 1, xxvi. 1). Outside these blocks perhaps the most noteworthy contribution of Matthew is the parable of chapter xx. (See note there.)

THE GOSPEL ACCORDING TO
ST. MATTHEW

1 1 The Genealogy of Jesus Christ, the son of

The Ancestry of Jesus David, the son of Abraham.

2 Abraham was the father of Isaac ; Isaac of Jacob ; **3** Jacob of Judah and his brothers. Judah was the father (by Tamar) of Perez and Zerah ; Perez of Hezron ; **4** Hezron of Ram ; Ram of Amminadab ; Amminadab of Nahshon ; Nahshon of Salmon ; **5** Salmon (by Rahab) of Boaz ; Boaz (by Ruth) of Obed ; Obed of Jesse ; Jesse of **6** David—the King.

David (by Uriah's widow) was the father of Solomon ; Solomon of Rehoboam ; Rehoboam of Abijah ; Abijah of **7** Asa ; Asa of Jehoshaphat ; Jehoshaphat of Jehoram ; **8** Jehoram of Uzziah ; Uzziah of Jotham ; Jotham of Ahaz ; **9** Ahaz of Hezekiah ; Hezekiah of Manasseh ; Manasseh of **10** Amon ; Amon of Josiah ; Josiah of Jeconiah and his **11** brothers at the period of the Removal to Babylon.

After the Removal to Babylon Jeconiah had a son **12** Shealtiel ; Shealtiel was the father of Zerubbabel ; Zerub- **13** babel of Abiud ; Abiud of Eliakim ; Eliakim of Azor ; Azor **14** of Zadok ; Zadok of Achim ; Achim of Eliud ; Eliud of **15** Eleazar ; Eleazar of Matthan ; Matthan of Jacob ; and **16** Jacob of Joseph the husband of Mary, who was the mother of JESUS who is called CHRIST.

(vv. 1–17.) Cf. Luke iii. 23–38.

1. *Genealogy*] Lit. 'Book of Generation.' Or it may be rendered 'history,' as also may the corresponding expression in the Hebrew of Gen. ii. 4 ; xxxvii. 2.

3. *Perez*] Of this and other Old Testament proper names, the forms here given are those which were adopted by the O.T. revisers.

16. *Christ*] The Greek word ' *Christos* ' is an adjective meaning ' anointed,' and is the equivalent of the Hebrew ' Messiah,' also used as an adjective. It refers to the practice of instituting a priest or king to office by anointing with oil ; see *e.g.* Lev. iv. 5, 16 ; R.V. ' the anointed (LXX. *Chrislos*) priest.' Whether the personal name ' Messiah ' (Christ) is ever given in the O.T. to the vague conception of an idealised king is doubtful. It occurs twice in the A.V. (Dan. ix. 25, 26), but the R.V. substitutes ' the anointed one.' In the N.T. the Hebrew word ' Messiah' occurs only twice (John i. 41 ; iv. 25), but in its Greek form ' Christ,' of course, innumerable times. The point to note is that the vague and varying anticipations of the O.T. now become focussed upon one Person. So in the N.T. Peter's ' the Christ,' ' the anointed' of vague Jewish hope, passes into a proper name ' Christ,' ' Jesus Christ,' ' Christ Jesus.'

3

There are therefore, in all, fourteen generations from 17
Abraham to David; fourteen from David to the Removal
to Babylon; and fourteen from the Removal to Babylon
to the Christ.

The Birth of Jesus The circumstances of the birth of Jesus Christ 18
were these. After His mother Mary was be-
trothed to Joseph, before they were united in
marriage, she was found to be with child through the Holy
Spirit. But Joseph her husband, being a just man and un- 19
willing publicly to disgrace her, had determined to release
her privately from the betrothal. But while he was con- 20
templating this step, an angel of the Lord appeared to him
in a dream and said,

'Joseph, son of David, do not be afraid to bring home
your wife Mary, for she is with child through the Holy
Spirit. She will give birth to a Son, and you shall call 21
Him JESUS, for He shall save His People from their sins.'

All this took place in fulfilment of what the Lord had 22
spoken through the Prophet,

'MARK! THE MAIDEN WILL BE WITH CHILD AND WILL 23
GIVE BIRTH TO A SON,

AND THEY WILL GIVE HIM THE NAME IMMANUEL' (Isa.
vii. 14)—a word which signifies 'GOD WITH US' (Isa. viii.
8, 10).

When Joseph awoke, he did as the angel of the Lord had 24
commanded, and brought home his wife, but did not live 25
with her as a husband until she had given birth to a son;
and he called the child JESUS.

The Visit of the Magi Now after the birth of Jesus, which took place 1 **2**
at Bethlehem in Judaea in the reign of King
Herod, there came to Jerusalem certain Magi
from the east, inquiring, 2

'Where is the newly-born king of the Jews? For we

18. *Of Jesus Christ*] v.L. 'of Christ.' Cf. verse 16.
20. *Was contemplating*] Lit. 'had conceived in his mind.'
21. *Jesus*] The Greek form of 'Joshua,' which latter (like 'Joram' 2 Kings ix. 14 for
'Jehoram' 2 Kings ix. 15; 'Joash' 2 Kings xii. 20 for 'Jehoash' 2 Kings xii. 1; and
'Jonathan' most commonly for the 'Jehonathan' which we find in the Hebrew in
1 Sam.) is contracted from 'Jehoshua' or rather 'Yehoshua.' In the Hebrew of
the O.T., only the uncontracted form occurs, and (in 1 and 2 Chron., Ezra, and Neh.)
the contracted but altered 'Jeshua' which already approaches the later 'Jesus.'
The full significance of the name 'Jesus' is seen in the original 'Yeho-shua,'
which means 'Jehovah the Saviour,' and not merely 'Saviour,' as the word is
often explained.
25. *A son*] v.L. 'her firstborn son'; apparently a copyist's insertion from Luke ii. 7.
1. *There came*] Lit. 'lo! there came.' See verse 9, n.; viii. 24, n.
Magi] A priestly caste among the Persians, not idolaters.

saw his Star when it rose, and have come here to do him homage.'

Reports of this soon reached the king, and greatly 3 agitated not only him but all the people of Jerusalem. So 4 he assembled all the High Priests and Scribes of the people, and anxiously asked them where the Christ was to be born.

' At Bethlehem in Judaea,' they replied ; ' for so it stands 5 written in the words of the Prophet,

" AND THOU, BETHLEHEM IN THE LAND OF JUDAH, 6
   BY NO MEANS THE LEAST HONOURABLE ART THOU AMONG
     PRINCELY PLACES IN JUDAH !
   FOR FROM THEE SHALL COME A PRINCE—
   ONE WHO SHALL BE THE SHEPHERD OF MY PEOPLE
     ISRAEL " ' (Mic. v. 2).

Thereupon Herod sent privately for the Magi and ascer- 7 tained from them the exact time of the star's appearing. He then directed them to go to Bethlehem, adding, 8

' Go and make careful inquiry about the child, and when you have found him, bring me word, that I too may come and do him homage.'

After hearing what the king said, they went away, while, 9 strange to say, the star they had seen when it rose led them on until it reached and stood over the place where the babe was. When they saw the star, the sight filled them with 10 intense joy. So they entered the house ; and when they 11 saw the babe with His mother Mary, they prostrated themselves and did Him homage, and opening their treasure-chests offered gifts to Him—gold, frankincense, and myrrh. And 12 then being forbidden by God in a dream to return to Herod, they went back to their own country by a different route.

When they were gone, an angel of the Lord appeared to 13 Joseph in a dream and said,

      ' Rise : take the babe and His mother and
The Escape escape to Egypt, and remain there till I bring
into Egypt you word. For Herod is about to make search
for the child in order to destroy Him.'

---

4. *High Priests*] In both the A.V. and the R.V., the Greek word used here is rendered either ' High Priest ' or ' Chief Priest.'

Scribes] The official teachers of the Law, generally associated with the Pharisees as having degraded their high calling into a lifeless formalism. See especially Matt. xxiii.

6. *Princely places in*] Lit. ' the princes of.'

7. *Of the star's appearing*] Lit. ' of the appearing star.'

8. *Do him homage*] Or perhaps ' worship.'

9. *Strange to say*] Lit. ' lo ! ' See v. 1, n.

And Joseph awoke and took the babe and His mother 14
by night and departed into Egypt. There he remained 15
till Herod's death, that what the Lord had said through
the Prophet might be fulfilled,

' OUT OF EGYPT I CALLED MY SON ' (Hos. xi. 1).

The Massacre of the Children Then Herod, finding that the Magi had trifled 16
with him, was furious, and sent and massacred
all the boys under two years of age in Bethlehem
and all its neighbourhood, having in view the date he had
so carefully ascertained from the Magi. Then were these 17
words, spoken by the Prophet Jeremiah, fulfilled,

' A CRY WAS HEARD IN RAMAH, 18
WAILING AND BITTER LAMENTATION :
IT WAS RACHEL BEWAILING HER CHILDREN,
AND SHE REFUSED TO BE COMFORTED, BECAUSE THEY WERE
NO MORE ' (Jer. xxxi. 15).

The Return from Egypt But after Herod's death an angel of the Lord 19
appeared in a dream to Joseph in Egypt, and
said to him,

' Rise, and take the child and His mother, and go to the land 20
of Israel, for those who were seeking the child's life are dead.'

And he awoke and took the child and His mother and 21
came to the land of Israel. But hearing that Archelaus 22
had succeeded his father Herod on the throne of Judaea, he
was afraid to go there ; and being instructed by God in a
dream he withdrew into Galilee, and settled in a town 23
called Nazareth, in order that these words spoken through
the Prophets might be fulfilled,

' HE SHALL BE CALLED A NAZARENE.'

John the Baptist preaches Judgement and Repentance About this time John the Baptist made his 1 **3**
appearance, preaching in the Desert of Judaea.
' Repent,' he said, ' for the Kingdom of heaven 2
is now close at hand.'

He it is who was spoken of through the 3
Prophet Isaiah when he said,

23. *Nazarene*] No such prophecy can be traced.
(vv. 1–10) Cf. Mark i. 1–6 ; Luke iii. 1–14.
1. *The Baptist*] Lit. ' the baptizer.'
2. *Kingdom of heaven*] Lit. ' the Kingdom of the heavens ' ; an expression peculiar
to Matthew (thirty-three times), who also uses the equivalent phrase ' the Kingdom of
God.' xii. 28 ; xix. 24 ; xxi. 31, 43.
3. *In the Desert prepare*] The Greek text (following LXX) joins ' in the Desert '
to ' crying aloud.' This helps the identification of John the Baptist, who came
' preaching in the Desert,' with the nameless voice of the prophecy ; but misses the
poetical parallelism of the Hebrew. See R.V. of Isa. xl. 3.

' THE VOICE OF ONE CRYING ALOUD :
  " IN THE DESERT PREPARE A ROAD FOR THE LORD :
    MAKE HIS HIGHWAYS STRAIGHT " ' (Isa. xl. 3).

This man John wore clothing of camel's hair, and a 4 leather girdle ; and he lived upon locusts and wild honey.

Large numbers of people at that time went out to him— 5 people from Jerusalem and from all Judaea, and from the whole of the Jordan valley—and were baptized by him in 6 the Jordan, making open confession of their sins.

But when he saw many of the Pharisees and Sadducees 7 coming for his baptism, he exclaimed,

' O brood of vipers, who has warned you to flee from the coming wrath ? Let your lives then prove your change 8 of heart ; and do not imagine that you can say to your- 9 selves, " We have Abraham as our forefather," for I tell you that God can raise up descendants for Abraham from these stones. And already the axe is lying at the root of 10 the trees, so that every tree which does not yield good fruit is hewn down and thrown into the fire. I indeed am bap- 11 tizing you in water for repentance ; but He who **He predicts** is coming after me is mightier than I : His **Christ's** **Appearing** sandals I am not worthy to carry ; He will bap- **and Work** tize you in the Holy Spirit and in fire. His 12 winnowing-shovel is in His hand, and He will make a thorough clearance of His threshing-floor, gathering His wheat into the barn, but burning up the chaff in unquenchable fire.'

Just at that time Jesus, coming from Galilee 13 **The Baptism** to the Jordan, presents Himself to John to be **of Jesus** baptized by him. John protested. 14

' It is I,' he said, ' who have need to be baptized by you, and do you come to me ? '

' Let it be so on this occasion,' Jesus replied ; ' for so we 15 ought to fulfil every religious duty.'

Then he consented ; and Jesus was baptized, and imme- 16 diately went up from the water. At that moment the heavens opened, and He saw the Spirit of God descending like a dove and alighting upon Him, while a voice came 17 from heaven, saying,

---

4. *This man*] Lit. ' And John himself.' The dress and fare of the wandering prophet are described. Cf. Elijah, 2 Kings i. 8, R.V. mg.
(vv. 11, 12.) Cf. Mark i. 7–8 ; Luke iii. 15–18.
11. *In water*] Or possibly, ' with water.' Cf. Acts i. 5 ; xi. 16.
(vv. 13–17.) Cf. Mark i. 9–11 ; Luke iii. 21, 22.

' This is My Son, the Beloved, in whom is My delight.'

Jesus is tempted in the Desert At that time Jesus was led up by the Spirit 1 **4** into the Desert in order to be tempted by the Devil. And He fasted for forty days and 2 nights ; and after that He suffered from hunger.

So the Tempter came and said to Him : 3

' If you are the Son of God, command these stones to turn into loaves.'

' It is written,' replied Jesus, ' " IT IS NOT ON BREAD 4 ALONE THAT A MAN SHALL LIVE, BUT ON EVERY WORD THAT PROCEEDS FROM THE MOUTH OF GOD " ' (Deut. viii. 3).

Then the Devil took Him to the holy city and caused 5 Him to stand on the summit of the Temple, and said, 6

' If you are God's Son, throw yourself down ; for it is written,

" TO HIS ANGELS HE WILL GIVE ORDERS CONCERNING THEE,
AND ON THEIR HANDS THEY SHALL BEAR THEE UP,
LEST AT ANY MOMENT THOU SHOULDST STRIKE THY FOOT
AGAINST A STONE " ' (Ps. xci. 11, 12).

' Again it is written,' replied Jesus, ' " THOU SHALT NOT 7 CHALLENGE THE LORD THY GOD " ' (Deut. vi. 16).

Then the Devil took Him to the top of an exceedingly 8 lofty mountain, from which he caused Him to see all the kingdoms of the world and their splendour, and said to Him, 9

' All this I will give you, if you will kneel down and do me homage.'

' Begone, Satan ! ' Jesus replied ; ' for it is written, " To 10 THE LORD THY GOD THOU SHALT DO HOMAGE, AND TO HIM ALONE SHALT THOU RENDER WORSHIP " ' (Deut. vi. 13).

Thereupon the Devil left Him, and angels came and 11 ministered to Him.

Jesus goes into Galilee Now when Jesus heard that John was thrown 12 into prison, He withdrew to Galilee, and 13 leaving Nazareth He went and settled in

---

(vv. 1–11.) Cf. Mark i. 12, 13 ; Luke iv. 1–13.
1. *Led up*] From the valley of the Jordan.
6. *If*] *i.e.* ' since,' ' assuming that.'
7. *Thou shalt not . . God*] Not signifying, as some strangely misapprehend our Lord's meaning, that asserting His divinity He forbade Satan to tempt Him any irther, but that He Himself would have been tempting—that is trying an experiment upon—God, if He had flung Himself down to see whether God would protect Him or not. See Deut. vi. 16 ; Exod. xvii. 1–7.
(vv. 12–25.) Cf. Mark i. 14, 15 ; Luke iv. 14, 15.
12. *Thrown into prison*] Lit. ' delivered up ' (to the gaoler).
13. *Lake*] *i.e.* ' Sea of Galilee.'

Capernaum, a town by the Lake on the frontiers of Zebulun and Naphtali, in order that these words, spoken through the 14 Prophet Isaiah, might be fulfilled,

' ZEBULUN'S LAND AND NAPHTALI'S LAND, 15
THE ROAD OF THE LAKE, THE COUNTRY BEYOND THE JORDAN ;
GALILEE OF THE NATIONS !
THE PEOPLE WHO WERE DWELLING IN DARKNESS HAVE 16 SEEN A BRILLIANT LIGHT ;
AND ON THOSE WHO WERE DWELLING IN THE REGION OF THE SHADOW OF DEATH
LIGHT HAS DAWNED ' (Isa. ix. 1, 2).

He begins to preach. Four Disciples called From that time Jesus began to preach. 17 ' Repent,' He said, ' for the Kingdom of heaven is close at hand.'

And walking along the shore of the Lake 18 of Galilee He saw two brothers—Simon called Peter and his brother Andrew—throwing a drag-net into the Lake ; for they were fishers. And He said to 19 them,

' Come and follow me, and I will make you fishers of men.'

So they immediately left their nets and followed Him. 20 As He went further on, He saw two other brothers, James 21 the son of Zebedee and his brother John, in their boat with their father Zebedee mending their nets ; and He called them. And they at once left the boat and their father, and 22 followed Him.

His Preaching and Cures throughout Galilee Then Jesus travelled through all Galilee, 23 teaching in their synagogues and proclaiming the gospel of the Kingdom, and curing every kind of disease and infirmity among the people. So His fame spread through all Syria ; and 24 they brought all sick persons to Him, who were suffering from various diseases and pains—demoniacs, epileptics, paralytics ; and He cured them. And great 25 crowds followed Him, coming from Galilee, from the Ten Towns, from Jerusalem, and from beyond the Jordan.

16. *Region of the shadow*] Lit. ' region and shadow.'
23. *The gospel of the Kingdom*] *i.e.* the good news that the Kingdom of heaven was close at hand (verse 17).

The Sermon on the Mount: Blessedness

Seeing the multitude of people, Jesus went up 1 the Hill. There He seated Himself, and when His disciples came to Him, He proceeded to 2 teach them, and said :

' Blessed are the poor in spirit, for to them belongs the 3 Kingdom of heaven.

' Blessed are the mourners, for they shall be comforted. 4

' Blessed are the meek, for they shall inherit the 5 earth.

' Blessed are those who hunger and thirst for righteous- 6 ness, for they shall be completely satisfied.

' Blessed are the compassionate, for they shall receive 7 compassion.

' Blessed are the pure in heart, for they shall see God. 8

' Blessed are the peacemakers, for they shall be acknow- 9 ledged as sons of God.

' Blessed are those who have borne persecution in the 10 cause of righteousness, for to them belongs the Kingdom of heaven.

' Blessed are you when they have insulted and per- 11 secuted you, and have said every cruel thing about you falsely for my sake. Be joyful and triumphant, because 12 your reward is great in heaven ; for so were the Prophets before you persecuted.

Salt and Light

' You are the salt of the earth ; but if salt 13 has become tasteless, in what way can it regain its saltness ? It is no longer good for anything but to be thrown away and trodden on by the passers by. You are the light of the world ; a town cannot be hid if built 14 on a hill-top. Nor is a lamp lighted to be put under the 15 bushel-measure, but on the lampstand ; and then it gives light to all in the house. Just so let your light shine before 16 all men, in order that they may see your good deeds and may give glory to your Father who is in heaven.

---

1. *The Hill*] Or ' mountain.' Probably well known to the first readers of the Gospels.

The kernel of the Sermon on the Mount is to be found in Luke vi. With this Matthew groups kindred matter, much of it peculiar to him, much recorded in various contexts by Luke. See the Introduction and the Commentaries.

(vv. 3–12.) Cf. Luke vi. 20–26.

(vv. 3–11.) *Blessed*] or ' Happy.' An adjective in the original, not the past participle of the verb ' bless ' as in xxi. 9. ' Blessedness ' is, of course, an infinitely higher and better thing than mere ' happiness.' People who are blessed may outwardly be much to be pitied, but from the higher and truer standpoint they are to be admired, envied, congratulated, and imitated.

16. *Your good deeds*] ' Not yourselves ; the shining, not the candle' (Bengel).

'Do not for a moment suppose that I have 17
The Law not repealed come to annul the Law or the Prophets: I have not come to annul them but to give them their completion. In truth I tell you that until heaven and 18 earth pass away, not the smallest letter, not a particle shall pass away from the Law until all has taken place. Whoever 19 therefore breaks one of the smallest of these commandments and teaches others to do so, will be called the least in the Kingdom of heaven; but whoever practises them and teaches them, will be acknowledged as great in the Kingdom of heaven. For I assure you that unless your 20 righteousness greatly surpasses that of the Scribes and the Pharisees, you will certainly not find entrance into the Kingdom of heaven.

'You have heard that it was said to the 21
Anger and Murder ancients, "THOU SHALT NOT COMMIT MURDER" (Exod. xx. 13), and whoever commits murder shall be answerable to the magistrate. But I say to you 22 that every one who gets angry with his brother shall be answerable to the magistrate; that whoever says to his brother "Raca," shall be answerable to the Sanhedrin; and that whoever says, "You fool!" shall be liable to the Gehenna of Fire. If therefore when you are offering your 23 gift upon the altar, you remember that your brother has a grievance against you, leave your gift there before the 24 altar, and go and make friends with your brother first, and then return and proceed to offer your gift. Come to 25 terms without delay with your opponent while you are yet

---

17. *The Law*] *i.e.* the moral and ceremonial Law of Moses, which remained binding upon all Jewish Christians until the Mosaic dispensation passed away at the time of the destruction of Jerusalem in 70 A.D. Even St. Paul, who so zealously contended for the exemption of Gentile Christians from this Law, seems never to have claimed a similar freedom for the Jewish believers of his day. See especially Acts xxi. **21**, where the charge brought against him was, of course, a false one.

18. Cf. Luke xvi. 17. *In truth*] Greek 'Amen.' This is a Hebrew word, a verbal adjective, meaning 'firm,' 'solid,' 'immovable,' and so 'faithful,' 'true.' John alone has the double Amen, amen; Verily, verily.

Not the smallest letter, not a particle] The Greek terms signify the smallest letter in the Greek alphabet, and the tiny projecting 'horn' which distinguishes certain Hebrew letters one from another. As we might say in English 'not the dot of an *i* nor the cross of a *t*.'

22. *Angry with his brother*] v.L. adds 'without just cause.'

Raca] 'You empty-headed fellow.'

Sanhedrin] The Supreme Court in Jerusalem.

Gehenna of Fire] Gehenna is the Greek form of the Hebrew for Valley of Hinnom (Gay-Hinnom), a ravine on the west and south of Jerusalem, the site of the fire worship of Molech, defiled by Josiah (2 Kings xvi. 3, xxiii. 10), afterwards the burning-place of the refuse of the city; hence the symbol of the place of future punishment.

(vv. 25, 26.) Cf. Luke xii. 58, 59.

25. *Come to terms*] Or ' be reasonable and accommodating.'

with him on the way to the court ; for fear he should hand you over to the magistrate, and the magistrate should give you in custody to the officer and you be thrown into prison. I solemnly tell you that you will certainly not be released till you have paid the very last farthing. 26

Adultery and impure Thoughts 'You have heard that it was said, "THOU SHALT NOT COMMIT ADULTERY " (Exod. xx. 14). 27 But I tell you that whoever looks at a woman 28 and cherishes lustful thoughts has already in his heart committed adultery with her. If therefore your right eye 29 causes you to fall, tear it out and away with it ; it is better for you that one member should be destroyed rather than that your whole body should be thrown into Gehenna. And if 30 your right hand causes you to fall, cut it off and away with it ; it is better for you that one member should be destroyed rather than that your whole body should go into Gehenna.

The Sacredness of Marriage 'It was also said, "IF ANY MAN PUTS AWAY 31 HIS WIFE, LET HIM GIVE HER A WRITTEN NOTICE OF DIVORCE " (Deut. xxiv. 1). But I tell you 32 that every man who puts away his wife, except on the ground of unchastity, causes her to commit adultery, and whoever marries her when so divorced commits adultery.

Simple Truthfulness of Speech 'Again, you have heard that it was said 33 to the ancients, "THOU SHALT NOT SWEAR FALSELY (Exod. xx. 7), BUT SHALT PERFORM THY VOWS TO THE LORD " (Num. xxx. 2 ; Deut. xxiii. 21). But 34 I tell you not to swear at all ; either by heaven, for it is God's throne ; or by the earth, for it is the footstool under 35 His feet ; or by Jerusalem, for it is the City of the Great King. And do not swear by your head, for you cannot make 36 one hair white or black. But let your language be, " Yes, 37 yes," or " No, no." Anything in excess of this comes from the Evil one.

29. *Causes you to fall*] Lit. ' is tripping you up,' *i.e.* causing you to stumble into sin. The same verb occurs thirty times in the N.T. ; fourteen times in this Gospel. In every case it is translated in the A.V. by ' offend,' which is probably to be often understood in the sense of the Latin verb ' offendere,' to stumble, or cause to stumble.
32. *Unchastity*] In Mark x. 11, Luke xvi. 18, the prohibition of divorce is without any qualification.
34. On the abuse of oaths compare chapter xxiii. 16–22.
35. *By Jerusalem*] Lit. 'into,' implying the turning of the thoughts, and perhaps the face also, towards the City and the Temple.
37. *The Evil one*] Or ' evil.'

All Revenge forbidden

'You have heard that it was said, "EYE FOR 38 EYE, TOOTH FOR TOOTH" (Exod. xxi. 24). But 39 I tell you not to resist a wicked man : if any one strikes you on the right cheek, turn the other to him as well. If any one wishes to go to law with you and to deprive you 40 of your under garment, let him take your outer one also. And if any one compels you to convey his goods one 41 mile, go with him two. To him who asks, give : from him 42 who would borrow, turn not away.

'Love your Enemies'

'You have heard that it was said, "THOU 43 SHALT LOVE THY NEIGHBOUR (Lev. xix. 18) and hate thine enemy." But I tell you to love your 44 enemies, and pray for your persecutors ; that so you may 45 become sons of your Father in heaven ; for He causes His sun to rise on the wicked as well as the good, and sends rain upon those who do right and those who do wrong. For if 46 you love only those who love you, what reward have you earned ? Do not even the tax-gatherers do that ? And if 47 you salute only your brethren, are you doing anything remarkable ? Do not even the heathen do the same ? You 48 however are to be perfect, as your Heavenly Father is perfect.

'Do not parade your Good Deeds'

'Beware of doing your good actions in the 1 **6** sight of men, to attract their gaze ; if you do, there is no reward for you with your Father who is in heaven.

'Avoid Display in Charity'

'When you give in charity, do not blow a 2 trumpet before you as the hypocrites do in the synagogues and streets in order that their praises may be sung by men. I solemnly tell you that they have received in full their reward. But when you are giving in 3 charity, let not your left hand perceive what your right hand is doing, that your charities may be in secret ; and 4 your Father—He who sees in secret—will recompense you.

39. *A wicked man*] Or 'evil.'
(vv. 39–42.) Cf. Luke vi. 27–30.
43. But there is no command in the Law to hate one's enemy.
(vv. 44–48.) Cf. Luke vi. 32–36.
1. *Good actions*] Lit. 'righteousness.' This consisted, according to the teaching of the Scribes, in almsgiving (see verse 2), prayer (verse 5), and fasting (verse 16).
2. *They have received in full their reward*] So too in verses 5, 16 ; Luke vi. 24 ; Phil. iv. 18 ; Philem. 15. Recent discoveries of Papyri in the sands of Egypt show that the Greek word stands for 'received in full' at the foot of a bill. Here a certain grim irony : the account is closed once for all.

'Avoid Display in Prayer' 'And when praying, you must not be like 5 the hypocrites. They are fond of standing and praying in the synagogues or at the corners of the wider streets, in order that men may see them. I solemnly tell you that they have received in full their reward. But you, whenever you pray, go into your own 6 room and shut the door : then pray to your Father who is in secret, and your Father—He who sees in secret—will recompense you.

'Do not use needless Repetitions' 'And when praying, do not use needless 7 repetitions as the heathen do, for they expect to be listened to because of their multitude of words. Do not, then, imitate them ; for your Father 8 knows what things you need before ever you ask Him.

'The Lord's Prayer' 'In this manner therefore pray : " Our 9 Father in heaven, may Thy name be kept holy ; let Thy Kingdom come ; let Thy will be done, as 10 in heaven so on earth ; give us to-day our bread for the day ; 11 and forgive us our shortcomings, as we also have forgiven 12 those who have failed in their duty towards us ; and bring 13 us not into temptation, but rescue us from the Evil one."

'For if you forgive others their offences, your Heavenly 14 Father will forgive you also ; but if you do not forgive 15 others their offences, neither will your Father forgive yours.

'Avoid Display in Fasting' 'When you fast, do not assume gloomy 16 looks as the hypocrites do ; for they disfigure their faces that it may be evident to men that they are fasting. I tell you in truth that they have received in full their reward. But, whenever you fast, pour 17 perfume on your hair and wash your face, that it may not be 18 apparent to men that you are fasting, but to your Father who is in secret ; and your Father—He who sees in secret— will recompense you.

(vv. 9, 10.) Cf. Luke xi. 2.

(vv. 11-13.) Cf. Luke xi. 3, 4.

11. *For the day*] A Greek word of uncertain meaning, found only here and Luke xi. 3. Probably it signifies for the oncoming day, either referring, if the petition is offered in the morning, to the day already begun, or to the morrow. To pray for food one day in advance is not in conflict with the spirit of Matthew vi. 34.

13. *From the Evil one*] Or possibly 'from evil' ; but in that case ' out of,' as used with the same verb in 2 Pet. ii. 9, might have been expected rather than ' from.' The doxology is to be omitted on overwhelming textual authority. There is no evidence for it at Luke xi. 4.

'Lay up Wealth in Heaven' ' Do not lay up stores of wealth for your- 19 selves on earth, where the moth and wear-and-tear destroy, and where thieves break in and steal. But lay up wealth for yourselves in heaven, where 20 neither the moth nor wear-and-tear destroys, and where thieves do not break in and steal. For where your wealth is, 21 there also will your heart be.

The Inner Light ' The eye is the lamp of the body. If then 22 your eye is sound, your whole body will be lighted up ; but if your eye is diseased, your 23 whole body will be dark. If then the very light within you is darkness, how dense must the darkness be !

' No man can serve two masters ; for either he will hate 24 one and love the other, or he will attach himself to one and think lightly of the other. You cannot be servants both of

Anxiety is Faithlessness God and of money. For this reason I say to you 25 do not be anxious about your lives, as to what you are to eat or what to drink, nor about your bodies, as to what clothes you are to put on. Is not life more precious than food, and the body than clothing ? Look at 26 the birds which fly in the air : they do not sow or reap or store up in barns, but your Heavenly Father feeds them : are not you of much greater value than they ? Which of 27 you is able by anxious thought to add a single foot to his height ? And why be anxious about clothing ? Learn a 28 lesson from the wild lilies. Watch their growth. They neither toil nor spin, and yet I tell you that not even 29 Solomon in all his magnificence was arrayed like one of these. And if God so clothes the vegetation in the fields 30 that blooms to-day and to-morrow is feeding the oven, will He not much more clothe you, you men of little faith ? Do 31 not be anxious, therefore, asking " What shall we eat ? "

(vv. 19–21.) Cf. Luke xii. 33, 34.
19. *Wear-and-tear*] Lit. ' rust.'
24. *Money*] Lit. ' Mammon.' A word of uncertain origin but meaning ' wealth.' It occurs also in Luke xvi. 9, 11, 13.
(vv. 25–33.) Cf. Luke xii. 22–31.
27. *A single foot*] Lit. ' one cubit.' The cubit, eighteen inches, need not be taken too literally. It is in Hebrew the recognised measure of estimating a man's height. He may belong to the three-cubit class, or to the four-cubit, or even beyond. He cannot change his class for the next higher by worrying about it. Possibly, however, the true sense is ' can add a single moment to his appointed span of life.' Not one person in ten thousand wishes to add eighteen inches to his stature, but many would gladly prolong their lives.
31. *Anxious*] The form of the verb in verses 31, 34, bears a meaning that differs by a shade from that in verse 25. In verse 25 the sense is ' not to cherish solicitude ' ; in these verses, ' Admit no solicitude,' that is ' Do not even begin to be anxious.'

or " What shall we drink ? " or " What shall we wear ? "
For the Gentiles seek all these things ; your Heavenly 32
Father knows that you need them all. But seek first His 33
Kingdom and righteousness, and these things shall all be
given you in addition. Do not be anxious, therefore, about 34
to-morrow, for to-morrow will bring its own anxieties.
Enough for each day is its own trouble.

The censorious Temper Condemned ' Judge not, that you may not be judged ; 1 **7**
for your own judgement will be dealt—and your 2
own measure accorded—to yourselves. And 3
why look at the splinter in your brother's eye,
and not notice the beam of timber which is in your own eye ?
Or how say to your brother, " Allow me to take the splinter 4
out of your eye," while the beam is in your own eye ?
Hypocrite, first take the beam out of your own eye, and 5
then you will see clearly how to remove the splinter from
your brother's eye.

' Give not that which is holy to the dogs, nor throw 6
your pearls to the swine ; otherwise they will trample them
under their feet and then turn and mangle you.

Prayer : A threefold Promise ' Ask, and it shall be given to you ; seek, and 7
you shall find ; knock, and the door shall be
opened to you. For every one who asks 8
receives, he who seeks finds, and he who knocks has the
door opened to him. What man is there among you, who 9
if his son shall ask him for bread will offer him a stone ?
Or if he shall ask him for a fish will offer him a snake ? If 10
you then, imperfect as you are, know how to give good 11
gifts to your children, how much more will your Father
in heaven give good things to those who ask Him ! What- 12
ever, therefore, you would have men do to you, do you
also to them ; for in this the Law and the Prophets are
summed up.

The Need for Earnestness ' Enter by the narrow gate ; for wide is the 13
gate and broad the road which leads to ruin,
and many there are who enter by it ; because 14

(vv. 1, 2.) Cf. Mark iv. 24 ; Luke vi. 37.
(vv. 3–5.) Cf. Luke vi. 39–42.
3. *Splinter . . beam*] A striking instance of Oriental hyperbole.
(vv. 7–11.) Cf. Luke xi. 9–13. *Ask . . seek . . knock*] Or ' Keep asking . . seeking . . knocking.'
12. Cf. Luke vi. 31.
13. Cf. Luke xiii. 24.
The gate] v.l. omits these words.
14. *Because narrow*] Or ' how narrow . . Life ! '

narrow is the gate and contracted the road which leads to Life, and few are those who find it.

Teachers are to be judged by their Lives ' Beware of the false teachers—men who come to you in sheep's fleeces, but beneath that disguise they are ravenous wolves. By their fruits you will recognize them. Are grapes gathered from thorns or figs from thistles ? Every good tree produces good fruit, but a worthless tree produces bad fruit. A good tree cannot bear bad fruit, nor a worthless tree good fruit. Every tree which does not yield good fruit is hewn down and thrown into the fire. So by their fruits you will recognize them.

Obedience the only Path to the Kingdom ' Not every one who says to me, " Lord, Lord," will enter the Kingdom of heaven, but only those who are obedient to my Father who is in heaven. Many will say to me on that day, ' " Lord, Lord, have we not prophesied in Thy name, and in Thy name expelled demons, and in Thy name performed many mighty works ? "

' And then I will tell them plainly,

' " I never knew you : begone from me, you doers of wickedness."

' Builders upon Rock and Builders upon Sand ' ' Every one who hears these my teachings and acts upon them shall be likened to a wise man who built his house upon rock ; and the rain fell, the swollen torrents came, and the winds blew and beat against the house ; yet it did not fall, for its foundation was on rock. And every one who hears these my teachings and does not act upon them shall be likened to a fool who built his house upon sand. The rain fell, the swollen torrents came, and the winds blew and beat against the house, and it fell ; and disastrous was the fall.'

When Jesus had concluded this discourse, the crowds were filled with amazement at His teaching, for He had been teaching them as one who had authority, and not as their Scribes taught.

15
16
17
18
19
20

21

22

23

24
25

26
27

28
29

14. *To Life*] Or ' to the Life.' See xix. 16, n.
15. *Teachers*] Lit. ' prophets.'
(vv. 16–21.) Cf. Luke vi. 43–46.
(vv. 22, 23.) Cf. Luke xiii. 25–27.
23. *Wickedness*] Lit. ' lawlessness.'
(vv. 24–27.) Cf. Luke vi. 47–49. In Matthew there are *two* foundations, the choice of the one, wise, of the other, foolish. Luke speaks of *one* foundation : the difference is in the care bestowed upon it, digging down to the rock or building upon the surface soil.

Upon descending from the hill country He 1 **8**

A Leper cleansed was followed by immense crowds. And a leper 2 came to Him, and throwing himself at His feet, said,

' Master, if only you are willing, you are able to cleanse me.'

So Jesus put out His hand and touched him, and said, 3 ' I am willing : be cleansed.'

Instantly he was cleansed from his leprosy ; and Jesus 4 said to him,

' Be careful to tell no one, but go and show yourself to the priest, and offer the gift which Moses appointed as evidence for them ' (Lev. xiv. 4).

A Roman Officer's After His entry into Capernaum a captain 5 came to Him, and entreated Him.

Slave restored ' Sir,' he said, ' my servant at home is lying 6 ill with paralysis, and is suffering great pain.'

' I will come and cure him,' said Jesus. 7

' Sir,' replied the captain, ' I am not a fit person to 8 receive you under my roof : merely say the word, and my servant will be cured. For I myself am also under 9 authority, and have soldiers under me. To one I say " Go," and he goes, to another " Come," and he comes, and to my slave " Do this or that," and he does it.'

Jesus listened to this reply, and was astonished, and 10 said to the people following Him,

' I solemnly tell you that in no Israelite have I found faith as great as this. And I tell you that many will come 11 from the east and from the west and will take their seats with Abraham, Isaac, and Jacob in the Kingdom of heaven, while the natural heirs of the Kingdom will be 12 driven out into the darkness outside : there will be the weeping and the gnashing of teeth.'

And Jesus said to the captain, 13

' Go, and just as you have believed, so be it for you.' And the servant recovered precisely at that time.

(vv. 1-4.) Cf. Mark i. 40-45 ; Luke v. 12-16.
(vv. 5-13.) Cf. Luke vii. 1-10. The differences in the two stories leave it at least possible that John iv. 46-53 is yet a third variant of the same incident.
    5. *Captain*] Namely of the Roman army. Cf. Mark xv. 39, n.
    6. *Servant*] Lit. ' boy.' So in verses 8 and 13. Cf. Luke vii. 7.
    8. *A fit person, &c.*] Or ' of sufficient importance.'
    9. v.L. inserts ' ranging myself ' between ' am ' and ' under,' as in Luke vii. 8.
    10. *In no Israelite*] Lit. ' with no one in Israel.' v.L. ' not even in Israel.'
    11. *Take their seats*] Lit. ' recline.' Cf. Luke vii. 38 ; John xiii. 23.

Peter's Mother-in-Law cured After this Jesus went to the house of Peter, 14 whose mother-in-law he found ill in bed with fever. He touched her hand and the fever left 15 her : and then she rose and waited upon Him.

Many other Cures In the evening many demoniacs were brought 16 to Him, and with a word He expelled the demons ; and He cured all persons who were ill, that this prediction of the Prophet Isaiah might be ful- 17 filled,

'He took on Him our weaknesses, and bore the burden of our diseases' (Isa. liii. 4).

Some would follow Him conditionally Seeing great crowds about Him Jesus had 18 given directions to cross to the other side of the Lake, when a Scribe came and said to Him, 19

' Teacher, I will follow you wherever you go.'

' Foxes have holes,' replied Jesus, ' and birds have 20 nests ; but the Son of Man has nowhere to lay His head.'

Another of the disciples said to Him, 21

' Master, allow me first to go and bury my father.'

' Follow me,' said Jesus, ' and leave the dead to bury 22 their own dead.'

A Storm subdued Then He went on board a fishing-boat, and 23 His disciples followed Him. But suddenly 24 there arose a great storm on the Lake, so that the waves threatened to engulf the boat ; but He was asleep. So they came and woke Him, crying, 25

' Master, save us ; we are drowning ! '

He replied, ' Why are you so easily frightened, you men 26 of little faith ? '

Then He rose and reproved the winds and the waves, and there was a perfect calm ; and the men, filled with amaze- 27 ment, exclaimed,

' What kind of man is this ? why, the very winds and waves obey him ! '

(vv. 14, 15.) Cf. Mark i. 29-31 ; Luke iv. 38, 39.
(vv. 16, 17.) Cf. Mark i. 32-34 ; Luke iv. 40, 41.
16. *In the evening*] It was the Sabbath (Mark i. 21, 29, 32) until sunset ; but after sunset people might bring their sick to be cured without violating either the Law or even the traditions of the Elders.
18. Cf. Mark iv. 35 ; Luke viii. 22.
(vv. 19-22.) Cf. Luke ix. 57-62.
20. *Nests*] Or ' roosting-places.'
22. *Dead . . dead*] Spiritually dead . . naturally dead.
(vv. 23-27.) Cf. Mark iv. 35-41 ; Luke viii. 22-25.
24. *Suddenly*] Lit. ' see ' or ' behold.'

On His arrival at the other side, the country 28
of the Gadarenes, there met Him two men
possessed by demons, coming from among the
tombs : they were so dangerously fierce that
no one was able to pass that way. They cried aloud, 29
' What hast Thou to do with us, Thou Son of God ?
Hast Thou come here to torment us before the time ? '

Now at some distance from them a vast herd of swine 30
were feeding. So the demons entreated Him. 31

' If thou drivest us out,' they said, ' send us into the
herd of swine.'

' Go,' He replied. 32

Then they came out from the men and went into the
swine, whereupon the entire herd instantly rushed down
the steep into the Lake and perished in the water. The 33
swineherds fled, and went and told the whole story in the
town, including what had happened to the demoniacs. So 34
at once the whole population came out to meet Jesus ; and
when they saw Him, they besought Him to leave their
district. Accordingly He went on board, and crossing over 1 **9**
came to His own town.

The Cure of a paralysed Man Here they brought to Him a paralysed man, 2
lying on a bed. Seeing their faith Jesus said
to the paralytic,

' Take courage, my child ; your sins are pardoned.'

' Such language is impious,' said some of the Scribes 3
to themselves.

Knowing their thoughts Jesus said, 4

' Why are you cherishing evil thoughts in your hearts ?
Why, which is easier ?—to say, " Your sins are pardoned," 5
or to say " Rise up and walk " ? But, to prove to you that 6
the Son of Man has authority on earth to pardon sins '—

He then says to the paralytic,

' Rise, and take up your bed and go home.'

And he got up, and went home. And the crowd were 7, 8
awe-struck when they saw it, and ascribed the glory to God
for entrusting such power to men.

Side notes:
Two Gadarene Demoniacs cured

(vv. 28-34.) Cf. Mark v. 1-20 ; Luke viii. 26-39.
32. *Instantly*] Lit. ' behold.' Cf. verse 24, n.
(vv. 1-8.) Cf. Mark ii. 1-12 ; Luke v. 17-26.
1. *His own town*] Capernaum. See iv. 13 ; Mark ii. 1.
2. *Bed*] A mere mattress or thick rug. Cf. Mark ii. 4.
4. *Knowing*] v.L. ' seeing.'

The Call of Matthew

Passing on thence Jesus saw a man called 9 Matthew sitting at the Toll Office, and said to him,

' Follow me.'

And he arose and followed Him.

When Jesus was reclining at table, a large number of 10 tax-gatherers and sinners were of the party with Him and His disciples. The Pharisees noticed this, and they in- 11 quired of His disciples,

' Why does your Teacher eat with the tax-gatherers and sinners ? '

He heard the question and replied, 12

' It is not men in good health who require a doctor, but those who are ill. But go and learn what this means, " IT 13 IS MERCY THAT I DESIRE, NOT SACRIFICE " (Hos. vi. 6) ; for I did not come to call the righteous, but sinners.'

The Disciples' Neglect of Fasting

At that time John's disciples came and asked 14 Jesus,

' Why do we and the Pharisees fast, but your disciples do not ? '

' Can the bridegroom's party mourn,' He replied, ' as long 15 as the bridegroom is with them ? Other days will come when the bridegroom has been taken from them, and then they will fast. No one ever mends an old cloak with a 16 patch of unshrunk cloth. Otherwise, the added patch tears away some of the garment, and a worse hole is made. Nor 17 do people pour new wine into old wineskins. Otherwise, the skins split, the wine escapes, and the skins perish. But they put new wine into fresh skins, and both are saved.'

Jairus's Daughter

While He was thus speaking, a Ruler came 18 up and profoundly bowing said,

' My daughter is just dead ; but come and put your hand upon her and she will return to life.'

(vv. 9–13.) Cf. Mark ii. 13–17 ; Luke v. 27–32.
10. *At table*] In Matthew's house, as we learn from Luke v. 29.
Tax-gatherers] They collected tolls, as well as taxes on houses, lands, and persons.
(vv. 14–17.) Cf. Mark ii. 18–22 ; Luke v. 33–39.
14. *Fast*] v.l. adds ' often.' Mark ii. 18 has ' were (then) keeping a fast.'
17. *Wineskins*] Or ' leather bottles,' which were commonly made, as now in Spain and many parts of the world, of goats' skins, but sometimes of the skins of asses or camels.
Escapes . . perish] Lit. ' escapes . . are destroyed.'
(vv. 18–26.) Cf. Mark v. 21–43 ; Luke viii. 40–56.
18. *Ruler*] Of the synagogue (Mark v. 22). *A Ruler*] Lit. ' one Ruler.' Instead of ' one Ruler came up,' v.l. (omitting ' one ') reads ' a Ruler entered.' Mark and Luke give his name, Jairus.
Profoundly bowing] The verb is the same as in ii. 2, 8, 11 ; xv. 25 ; John ix. 38.

And Jesus rose and followed him, as did also His disciples. 19

A Woman cured

Now a woman who for twelve years had been 20
afflicted with hæmorrhage came behind Him
and touched the tassel of His cloak ; for she 21
said to herself,

' If I but touch His cloak, I shall be cured.'

And Jesus turned and saw her, and said, 22

' Take courage, daughter ; your faith has cured you.'

And the woman was restored to health from that moment.

Jairus's Daughter

Entering the Ruler's house, Jesus saw the 23
flute-players and the crowd loudly wailing, and 24
He said,

' Go out of the room ; the little girl is not dead, but
asleep.'

And they laughed at Him.   When however the place was 25
cleared of the crowd, Jesus went in, and on His taking the
little girl by the hand, she rose up.   And the report of 26
this spread throughout all that district.

Two blind Men receive Sight

As Jesus passed on, two blind men followed 27
Him, shouting and saying,
' Pity us, Son of David.'

And when He had gone indoors, they came to Him. 28

' Do you believe that I can do this ? ' He asked them.

' Yes, Master,' they replied.

So He touched their eyes and said, 29

' According to your faith let it be to you.'

Then their eyes were opened.   And assuming a stern 30
tone Jesus said to them,

' Be careful to let no one know.'

But they went out and spread His fame in all that 31
district.

And as they were leaving His presence a dumb demoniac 32
was brought to Him.   When the demon was expelled, 33

A dumb Madman cured

the dumb man could speak.   And the crowds
exclaimed in astonishment,
' Never was such a thing seen in Israel.'

But the Pharisees maintained, 34

20. *Touched*] See Lev. xv. 19.
Tassel] Or ' fringe.'   See Num. xv. 38.
21. *Cured*] The verb here employed is the same as is often rendered by ' save.'   It
signifies to deliver either (1) as here, from present evil of any kind, or (2) from impending or future evil.   The former is the sense twice as frequently as the latter.
(vv. 32–34.) Cf. Luke xi. 14, 15.
34. *By the power of*] Lit. ' in.'

' It is by the power of the Prince of the demons that he drives out the demons.'

The Compassion of Jesus for the Crowd
And Jesus went round all the towns and 35 villages, teaching in their synagogues and proclaiming the gospel of the Kingdom, and curing every kind of disease and infirmity. And 36 when He saw the crowds, He was touched with pity for them, because they were distressed and prostrate like sheep which have no shepherd.

Then He said to His disciples, 37

' The harvest is abundant, but the reapers are few ; therefore entreat the Owner of the Harvest to send out 38 reapers into His fields.'

Twelve Apostles chosen
Then He called to Him His twelve disciples 1 **10** and gave them authority to drive out foul spirits, and to cure every kind of disease and infirmity.

Now the names of the twelve Apostles were these : first, 2 Simon called Peter, and his brother Andrew ; James the son of Zebedee, and his brother John ; Philip and Bartholomew, 3 Thomas and Matthew the tax-gatherer, James the son of Alphaeus, and Thaddaeus ; Simon the Cananaean, and 4 Judas Iscariot, who also betrayed Him.

Their Mission to the People
These twelve Jesus sent on a mission, after 5 giving them their instructions :
' Go not,' He said, ' among the Gentiles, and enter no Samaritan town ; but, instead of that, go to 6 the lost sheep of Israel's race. And as you go, preach and 7 say, " The Kingdom of heaven is close at hand." Cure 8 the sick, raise the dead to life, cleanse lepers, drive out demons : you have received without payment, give without payment.

' Provide no gold, nor silver nor copper to carry in 9 your girdles ; no bag for your journey, nor extra inner 10

(vv. 35–38.) Cf. Mark vi. 6.
38. *Fields*] Lit. ' harvest.'
1. Cf. Mark vi. 7 ; Luke ix. 1.
2. *Apostles*] Cf. Mark iii. 13–18 ; Luke vi. 12–16 ; Acts i. 13.
4. *Cananaean*] Not Canaanite (A.V.), an inhabitant of Canaan. It is an Aramaic word meaning ' zealous,' translated by Luke ' Zelotes' (Luke vi. 16 ; Acts i. 13). Whether the title means that he was formerly a member of the sect of ' Zealots ' or simply describes a fiery enthusiastic nature is uncertain.
Iscariot] *i.e.* ' man of Kerioth ' (Josh. xv. 25).
(vv. 5–15.) Cf. Mark vi. 7–13 ; Luke i. 1–6.
5. *Sent*] Probably two and two, like the Seventy at a later time (Luke x. 1).
6. *Lost sheep*] Or, as we should say, ' lapsed masses.'

garment, nor shoes, nor stick ; for the labourer deserves his food.

' Whatever town or village you enter, inquire who is a 11 deserving man ; and make his house your home till you leave the place. When you enter the house, salute it ; and 12, 13 if the house deserves it, let your peace come upon it ; if not, let your peace return to you. And whoever refuses to 14 receive you or even to listen to your Message, as you leave that house or town, shake off the very dust that is on your feet. I solemnly tell you that it will be more endurable 15 for the land of Sodom and Gomorrah on the day of Judgement than for that town.

Persecution foretold ' Remember it is I who am sending you out, 16 as sheep into the midst of wolves ; prove yourselves therefore as sagacious as serpents, and as innocent as doves. But beware of men ; for they will 17 deliver you up to appear before Sanhedrins, and will flog you in their synagogues ; and you will even be put on trial 18 before governors and kings for my sake, to bear witness to them and to the Gentiles. But when they have delivered 19 you up, have no anxiety as to how you shall speak or what you shall say ; for at that very time it shall be given you what to say ; for it is not you who will speak : it will be the 20 Spirit of your Father speaking through you. Brother will 21 betray brother to death, and father betray child ; and children will rise against their own parents and will put them to death. And you will be objects of univer- 22 sal hatred because you are called by my name ; but he who stands firm to the end shall be saved. Whenever 23 they persecute you in one town, escape to the next ; for I tell you in truth that you will not have gone the round of all the towns of Israel before the Son of Man comes.

' The learner is not superior to his teacher, nor the ser- 24 vant to his master. Enough for the learner to be on a 25 level with his teacher, and for the servant to be on a level with his master. If they have called the master of the

---

12. *Salute it*] When the two Apostles entered the building, they were to salute the household, doubtless in the words prescribed in Luke x. 5, ' Peace be to this house.'
14. *Shake off, &c.*] Cf. xviii. 17 ; Acts xiii. 51.
16. Cf. Luke x. 3.
(vv. 17–22.) Cf. Mark xiii. 9–13 ; Luke xxi. 12–17.
20. *Through you*] Lit. ' in you.'
(vv. 23–25.) Cf. Luke vi. 40.

house Beelzebul, how much more will they slander his servants? Fear them not, however; there is nothing veiled 26 which will not be uncovered, nor secret which will not become known. What I tell you in the dark, speak in day- 27 light; and what is whispered into your ear, proclaim upon the roofs of the houses.

'And do not fear those who kill the body, but cannot 28 kill the soul; rather fear Him who is able to destroy both soul and body in Gehenna. Do not two sparrows sell for 29 a halfpenny? Yet not one of them falls to the ground without your Father's leave. But as for you, the very hairs 30 on your heads are all numbered. Away then with fear; 31 you are more precious than a multitude of sparrows.

'Every man who acknowledges me before men I also 32 will acknowledge before my Father who is in heaven. But 33 whoever disowns me before men I also will disown before my Father who is in heaven.

Conflict must precede Peace 'Do not suppose that I came to bring peace 34 to the earth: I did not come to bring peace but a sword. For I came to set a man against 35 his father, A DAUGHTER AGAINST HER MOTHER, AND A DAUGHTER-IN-LAW AGAINST HER MOTHER-IN-LAW; AND A 36 MAN'S OWN FAMILY WILL BE HIS FOES (Mic. vii. 6). Any one 37 who loves father or mother more than me is not worthy of me, and any one who loves son or daughter more than me is not worthy of me; and any one who does not take up his 38 cross and follow where I lead is not worthy of me. He who 39 finds his life shall lose it, and he who loses his life for my sake shall find it.

He gives the Apostles Authority 'Whoever receives you receives me, and 40 whoever receives me receives Him who sent me. Every one who receives a prophet because he 41 is a prophet will receive a prophet's reward, and every one

---

25. *Beelzebul*] See 2 Kings i. 3, 6.
(vv. 26-33.) Cf. Luke xii. 2-9.
28. *Soul*] Or 'life.' Cf. verse 39.
Fear Him] i.e. God.
Halfpenny] The coin named (the 'assarion') was probably worth about a farthing and four-fifths. Contrast Luke xii. 6: 'Are not five sparrows sold for a penny?' The birds were reckoned as being of such little value, that upon double the number being bought, an extra one was given gratis.
32. *Acknowledges me*] Or 'avows his loyalty to me.' Lit. 'confesses (confidence) in.' The expression occurs only in this verse and in Luke xii. 8.
(vv. 34-36.) Cf. Luke xii. 51-53.
(vv. 37, 38.) Cf. Luke xiv. 26, 27.
38. Cf. xvi. 24; Mark viii. 34; Luke ix. 23; and xvii. 33.
(vv. 40-41.) Cf. Luke x. 16.

who receives a righteous man because he is a righteous man will receive a righteous man's reward. And whoever 42 gives one of these little ones even a cup of cold water to drink because he is a disciple, I solemnly tell you that he will not lose his reward.'

When Jesus had concluded His instructions to His twelve 1 **11** disciples, He left in order to teach and to proclaim His Message in the neighbouring towns.

John the   Now John had heard in prison about the 2
Baptist's Christ's deeds, and he sent by his disciples and
Perplexity inquired of him : 3

'Are you the Coming One, or is it some one else that we are to expect ?'

'Go and report to John what you see and hear,' replied 4 Jesus ; 'blind men receive sight, and cripples walk ; lepers 5 are cleansed, and the deaf hear ; the dead are raised to life, and the poor have the gospel proclaimed to them ; and blessed is every one who does not take offence at my 6 claims.'

The Testi-   When the messengers had taken their leave, 7
mony of Jesus Jesus proceeded to say to the multitude concern-
as to John ing John,

'What did you go out to the Desert to gaze at ? A reed waving in the wind ? But what did you go out 8 to see ? A man finely dressed ? Those who wear fine clothes are to be found in kings' palaces. But why did 9 you go ? To see a prophet ? Yes, I tell you, and far more than a prophet. This is he of whom it is written, 10

'" SEE, I AM SENDING MY MESSENGER BEFORE THY FACE,
AND HE SHALL MAKE THY ROAD READY BEFORE THEE "
(Mal. iii. 1).

'I solemnly tell you that among all of woman born no 11 greater has ever been raised up than John the Baptist ; yet the least in the Kingdom of heaven is greater than he. But 12 from the time of John the Baptist till now, the Kingdom of heaven has been enduring violent assault, and the violent have been seizing it by force. For all the Prophets and the 13

42. Cf. Mark ix. 41.
Even] Lit. ' only.'
(vv. 2–6.) Cf. Luke vii. 18–23.

2. *Some of*] Lit. ' by.' We learn from Luke vii. 18 that the messengers were two in number. In Matthew, according to the four most ancient MSS., the number is not specified.
(vv. 7–19.) Cf. Luke vii. 24–35.
(vv. 12, 13.) Cf. Luke xvi. 16.

Law taught until John. And (if you are willing to receive 14
it) he is the Elijah who was to come. Listen, every one 15
who has ears !

The Per-
versity of
the Jews 'To what shall I compare the present 16
generation ? It is like children sitting in the
open places, who call to their playmates.

' " We have played the flute to you," they say, " and you 17
have not danced : we have sung dirges, and you have not
beaten your breasts."

' For John came neither eating nor drinking, and they 18
say, " He has a demon." The Son of Man came eating 19
and drinking, and they exclaim, " See this man !—given
to gluttony and tippling, a friend of tax-gatherers and
sinners ! " And yet Wisdom is vindicated by her actions.'

Chorazin,
Bethsaïda,
Capernaum Then began He to upbraid the towns where 20
His many mighty works had been done—
because they had not repented.

' Woe to thee, Chorazin ! ' He cried. ' Woe to thee, 21
Bethsaïda ! For had the mighty works been done in Tyre
and Sidon which have been done in both of you, they would
long ere now have repented in sackcloth and ashes. Only 22
I tell you that it will be more endurable for Tyre and
Sidon on the day of Judgement than for you. And thou, 23
Capernaum, shalt thou be exalted even to heaven ? Even
to Hades shalt thou descend. For had the mighty works
been done in Sodom which have been done in thee, that city
would have survived until now. I tell you all, that it will 24
be more endurable for the land of Sodom on the day of
Judgement than for thee.'

About that time Jesus exclaimed, 25

A sublime
Claim ' I praise Thee, Father, Lord of heaven and
of earth, that Thou hast hidden these things
from sages and men of discernment, and hast

16. *To their playmates*] v.L. ' to the other party,' the sense being the same.
19. *Eating and drinking*] Like other men, with no asceticism or austerity of diet.
Actions] v.L. reads ' children,' as in Luke vii. 35.
(vv. 20–24.) Cf. Luke x. 1–16.
23. *Hades*] The unseen World, the abode of departed spirits. In the A.V. both this
word and ' Gehenna ' are rendered ' Hell.' Each occurs twelve times. In this translation the two words are everywhere kept distinct.
Descend] v.L. ' be brought down.'
24. *You all*] Lit. ' you ' in the plural, either as addressed to all three of the towns
named, or parenthetically to the bystanders who heard these denunciations.
25. Cf. Luke x. 21, 22. This saying is unique in the Synoptics and is of supreme
importance because, taken from Q (see Introduction), it contains in germ the whole
Johannine Christology. The saying given in verses 28–30 is peculiar to Matthew. Cf.
the Benediction which follows Luke x. 22.

unveiled them to babes. Yes, Father, for such has been 26 Thy gracious will.

'All things have been handed over to me by my Father, 27 and no one fully knows the Son except the Father, nor does any one fully know the Father except the Son and all to whom the Son chooses to reveal Him.

'Come to me, all you toiling and burdened ones, and I 28 will give you rest. Take my yoke upon you and learn 29 from me; for I am gentle and lowly in heart, and you shall find rest for your souls. For my yoke is easy, and 30 my burden is light.'

A Charge of Sabbath-breaking About that time Jesus passed on the Sabbath 1 **12** through the wheatfields; and His disciples became hungry, and began to gather ears of wheat and eat them. But the Pharisees saw it and said to 2 Him,

'Look! your disciples are doing what the Law forbids them to do on the Sabbath.'

'Have you never read,' He replied, 'what David did 3 when he and his men were hungry? how he entered the 4 House of God and ate the Shewbread, which it was not lawful for him or his men but only for the priests to eat (1 Sam. xxi. 1–6)? And have you not read in the Law 5 how on the Sabbath the priests in the Temple break the Sabbath without incurring guilt? But I tell you that 6 there is here that which is greater than the Temple. And 7 if you knew what this means, "IT IS MERCY I DESIRE, NOT SACRIFICE" (Hos. vi. 6), you would not have condemned those who are without guilt. For the Son of Man is the 8 Lord of the Sabbath.'

A Second Charge of Sabbath-breaking Departing thence He went to their syna- 9 gogue, where there was a man with a shrivelled 10 arm. And they questioned Him, 'Is it right to cure people on the Sabbath?' Their intention was to bring a charge against Him.

'Which of you is there,' He replied, 'who, if he has but 11 a single sheep and it falls into a hole on the Sabbath, will not lay hold of it and lift it out? Is not a man, however, 12

(vv. 1–8.) Cf. Mark ii. 23–28; Luke vi. 1–5.
  1. *Became hungry*] Or ' were hungry,' as in verse 3. **On the ' plucking ' see** Deut. xxiii. 25; Lev. xxiii. 14.
  8. Cf. Mark. ii. 27, 28.
(vv. 9–14.) Cf. Mark iii. 1–6; Luke vi. 6–11.
  10. *Arm*] Rather than ' hand.'

worth far more than a sheep ?   Therefore it is right to do
good on the Sabbath.'

Then He said to the man,   13
' Stretch out your arm.'

And he stretched it out, and it was restored quite sound
like the other.

Then the Pharisees after leaving the syna- 14
A Plot to gogue consulted together against Him, how
kill Jesus they might destroy Him.   Aware of this, Jesus 15
departed elsewhere ; and a great number of people followed
Him, all of whom He cured.   But He gave them strict 16
injunctions not to blaze abroad His doings : that those 17
words of the Prophet Isaiah might be fulfilled,

' THIS IS MY SERVANT WHOM I HAVE CHOSEN,   18
MY BELOVED ONE IN WHOM MY SOUL TAKES
   PLEASURE.
I WILL PUT MY SPIRIT UPON HIM,
AND HE WILL ANNOUNCE JUSTICE TO THE NATIONS.
HE WILL NOT WRANGLE OR CRY ALOUD,   19
NOR WILL HIS VOICE BE HEARD IN THE BROADWAYS.
A CRUSHED REED HE WILL NOT BREAK,   20
NOR WILL HE QUENCH THE SMOULDERING WICK,
UNTIL HE HAS LED ON JUSTICE TO VICTORY.
AND ON HIS NAME SHALL THE NATIONS REST THEIR 21
   HOPES ' (Isa. xli. 8 ; xlii. 1).

He replies At that time a demoniac was brought to 22
to a Him, blind and dumb ; and He cured him, so
Slander that the dumb man could speak and see.   And 23
the crowds of people were all filled with amazement and
said,

' Can this be the Son of David ? '

The Pharisees heard it and said,   24
' This man only expels demons by the power of Beelzebul, the Prince of demons.'

Knowing their thoughts He said to them,   25
' Every kingdom in which civil war rages suffers desolation ; and every city or house in which there is internal
strife will be brought low.   And if Satan expels Satan, he 26

21. *Rest their hopes*] This is one of no fewer than eighteen passages in the A.V. of the
N.T. in which ' trust ' is erroneously used for ' hope.'
(vv. 22–37.) Cf. Mark iii. 20–30 ; Luke vi. 43–45 ; xi. 17–23.
23. *The Son of David*] A Jewish title of the Messiah, specially characteristic of this
Jewish Gospel. i. 1 and 20; ix. 27; xv. 22; xx. 31; xxi. 9, 15.

has begun to make war on himself : how therefore shall
his kingdom last ? And if it is by Beelzebul's power that 27
I expel the demons, by whose power do your disciples
expel them ? They therefore shall be your judges. But if 28
it is by the power of the Spirit of God that I expel the
demons, it is evident that the Kingdom of God has come
upon you. Again, how can any one enter the house of a 29
strong man and carry off his goods, unless first of all he
masters and secures the strong man ? Then will he ransack
his house.

The Guilt of rejecting the Inner Light
' The man who is not with me is against me, 30
and he who is not gathering with me is scattering. This is why I tell you that men will 31
find forgiveness for every other sin and
impious word, but that for impious speaking against the
Holy Spirit they shall find no forgiveness. And whoever 32
shall speak against the Son of Man may obtain forgiveness ;
but whoever speaks against the Holy Spirit shall obtain
forgiveness neither in this nor in the coming age.

As the Heart so the Life
' Either grant the tree to be wholesome and 33
its fruit wholesome, or the tree worthless and its
fruit worthless ; for the tree is known by its
fruit. O brood of vipers, how can you speak what is good 34
when you are evil ? For it is from the fullness of the heart
that the mouth speaks. A good man from his good store 35
produces good things, and a bad man from his bad store
produces bad things. I tell you that for every careless word 36
that men shall speak they will be held accountable on the
day of Judgement. For each of you by his words shall be 37
justified, or by his words shall be condemned.'

The Demand for a Sign
Then He was questioned by certain of the 38
Scribes and of the Pharisees who said,
' Teacher, we wish to see a sign given by you.'

---

27. *Disciples*] Lit. ' sons.' So ' the sons of the prophets ' are repeatedly mentioned in the O.T. The disciples of the Pharisees (verse 24) and of the Scribes had come down from Jerusalem (Mark iii. 22).

28. *Kingdom of God*] Matthew here (as also in vi. 33 ; xix. 24 ; xxi. 31, 43) forsakes his usual expression ' Kingdom of the heavens,' and adopts this other, which alone is found in other parts of the N.T.

Has come upon you] The verb here employed (found nowhere else in the Gospels except in the parallel passage, Luke xi. 20) probably implies ' Before you were ex-pecting its arrival.' Cf. xxiv. 42, 44. This is one of the two outstanding Synoptic utterances (Luke xvii. 21) which seem to imply that the Kingdom is not only future, as generally represented, but actually present.

31. *Men*] v.L. ' you men.'
(vv. 38–42.) Cf. Luke xi. 16, 29–36.

'Wicked and apostate generation!' He replied, 39
'they clamour for a sign, but none shall be given to
them except the sign of the Prophet Jonah. For just as 40
JONAH WAS THREE DAYS AND THREE NIGHTS IN THE SEA-
MONSTER'S BELLY (Jonah i. 17), so will the Son of Man be
three days and three nights in the heart of the earth.
There will stand up men of Nineveh at the Judgement 41
together with the present generation, and will condemn it;
because they repented at the preaching of Jonah; and
mark! there is One greater than Jonah here. The Queen 42
of the South will awake at the Judgement together with the
present generation, and will condemn it; because she
came from the ends of the earth to hear the wisdom of
Solomon; and mark! there is One greater than Solomon
here.

'When the foul spirit has gone out of a man, it roams 43
about in the desert, seeking rest but finding none. Then it 44
says, "I will return to my house that I left"; and it comes
and finds it unoccupied, swept clean, and in good order.
Then it goes and brings back with it seven other spirits 45
more wicked than itself, and they come in and dwell there;
and in the end that man's condition becomes worse than it
was at first. So will it be also with the present wicked
generation.'

The Family of Jesus desire to speak to Him While He was addressing the people, His 46
mother and His brothers were standing on the
edge of the crowd desiring to speak to Him.
So some one told Him, 47

---

40. *Three days and three nights*] The recognition of two main sources for the
Synoptic Gospels, Mark and Q (see Introduction), is of interest. Mark (viii. 11)
records the demand of the Pharisees for a sign from heaven, some portent from the
sky to accredit His divine mission. Cf. John vi. 31. This request Jesus absolutely
refuses, with pained indignation. Matthew (not Luke) adopts this Marcan section
with the unexplained addition 'except the sign of Jonah' (xvi. 4), and he does not
explain because he has already given a section on the sign of Jonah taken from
Q, also given by Luke (Matt. xii. 38-42; Luke xi. 29-32). The meaning of our
Lord's main answer to the demand for an external attesting sign seems clear. Jonah
preached: the Ninevites repented. The Queen of the South was attracted from
the ends of the earth by reports of the wisdom of Solomon. Well, something more
than Jonah or Solomon is here. Himself and His teaching are the only credentials
He will vouchsafe. But Matthew (verse 40), not Luke, prefaces that interpretation of
the sign of Jonah by a different one. Since Matthew and Luke are using a common
source, either Luke must have omitted or Matthew inserted the reference to Jonah's
whale. The parallel in fact hardly holds. Jesus, according to Jewish reckoning,
which counts parts of days as whole days, was three days in the grave—part of the
Friday, all Saturday, and Sunday dawn—but no reckoning, Jewish or other, covers
three nights; Friday night, Saturday night: that is all.

(vv. 43-45.) Cf. Luke xi. 17-26.
(vv. 46-50.) Cf. Mark iii. 31-35; Luke viii. 19-21.
47. v.l. omits the verse.

'Your mother and your brothers are standing outside and desire to speak to you.'

'Who is my mother?' He said to the man; 'and who 48 are my brothers?'

And pointing to His disciples He added, 49

'See here are my mother and my brothers. To obey 50 my Father who is in heaven—that is to be my brother and my sister and my mother.'

A Series of Parables: 'The Sower' That same day Jesus had left the house and 1 13 was sitting on the shore of the Lake, when a vast multitude of people crowded round Him. 2 He therefore went on board a boat and sat there, while all the people stood on the shore. He then spoke many 3 things to them in parables.

'A sower went out,' He said, 'to sow. As he sowed, 4 some of the seed fell by the wayside, and the birds came and pecked it up. Some fell on rocky ground, where it had 5 but scanty soil. It quickly showed itself above ground, because it had no depth of earth; but when the sun was 6 risen, it was scorched by the heat, and through having no root it withered up. Some fell among the thorns; but the thorns 7 sprang up and stifled it. But a portion fell upon good 8 ground, and gave a return, some a hundred for one, some sixty, some thirty. Listen, every one who has ears!' 9

Why Jesus taught in Parables And His disciples came and asked Him, 10 'Why do you speak to them in parables?' 'Because,' He replied, 'while to you it is 11 granted to know the secrets of the Kingdom of heaven, to them it is not. For whoever has, to him more shall be 12 given, and he shall have abundance; but whoever has not, from him even what he has shall be taken away. I speak to 13 them in parables for this reason, that while looking they do not see, and while hearing they neither hear nor understand. And in regard to them the prophecy of Isaiah is being 14 fulfilled:

'"YOU WILL HEAR AND HEAR AND BY NO MEANS UNDER-
  STAND,
AND YOU WILL LOOK AND LOOK AND BY NO MEANS SEE.

(vv. 1–3.) Cf. Mark iv. 1, 2; Luke viii. 4.
(vv. 3–9.) Cf. Mark iv. 3–9; Luke viii. 5–8.
(vv. 10–17.) Cf. Mark iv. 10–12; Luke viii. 9, 10. See note on Mark iv. 10–13.
10. *Came and asked*] Later in the day, as we learn from Mark iv. 10. After verse 23 the series of parables (verse 3) is resumed.

FOR THIS PEOPLE'S MIND IS STUPEFIED, 15
THEIR HEARING HAS BECOME DULL,
AND THEIR EYES THEY HAVE CLOSED ;
LEST THEY SHOULD EVER SEE WITH THEIR EYES,
AND HEAR WITH THEIR EARS,
AND UNDERSTAND WITH THEIR MINDS,
AND TURN BACK,
SO THAT I MIGHT HEAL THEM " (Isa. vi. 9, 10).

' But as for you, blessed are your eyes, for they see, and 16
your ears, for they hear. For I tell you in truth that many 17
Prophets and holy men have longed to see the sights you
see, and have not seen them, and to hear the words you hear,
and have not heard them.

'To you then I will explain the parable of 18
'The Sower' explained the Sower. When a man hears the word 19
concerning the Kingdom and does not under-
stand it, the evil one comes and catches away what has been
sown in his heart. This is he who received the seed by the
roadside. He who received the seed on rocky ground is 20
the man who hears the word and immediately receives it
with joy. It has struck no root, however, within him. He 21
continues for a time, but when suffering comes or persecution because of the word, he at once turns against it. He 22
who received the seed among the thorns is the man who
hears the word, but the cares of the present age and the
delusion of riches quite stifle the word, and it becomes
unfruitful. But he who received the seed on good ground 23
is he who hears and understands. Such hearers give a
return, and yield one a hundred, another sixty, another
thirtyfold.'

'The Wheat and the Darnel' Another parable He put before them. 24
'The Kingdom of heaven,' He said, ' may
be compared to a man who has sown good
seed in his field ; but during the night his enemy comes, and 25
over the first seed he sows darnel among the wheat, and
goes away. When the blade shoots up and the grain is 26
formed, then appears the darnel also.

15. *Mind*] Lit. ' heart,' a common Hebraism.
Is stupefied] Lit. ' has grown thick ' (or ' fat ').
(vv. 18–23.) Cf. Mark iv. 13–20 ; Luke viii. 11–15.
(vv. 24–30.) Matthew alone has the ' Parable of the Tares,' Mark alone the ' Parable of the seed growing of itself ' (Mark iv. 26–29). There are points of similarity between these two, but they differ widely in their moral.
25. *During the night*] Lit. ' while men ' (or ' his men ') ' were sleeping.'

' So the farmer's men come and ask him,   27

' " Master, was it not good seed that you sowed on your land ?   Where then does the darnel come from ? "

' " Some enemy has done this," he said.   28

' " Shall we go and collect it ? " the men inquire.

' " No," he replied, " for fear that while collecting the   29
darnel you should at the same time root up the wheat with it.   Leave both to grow together until the harvest, and at 30
harvest-time I will direct the reapers to collect the darnel first, and make it up into bundles to burn, but to bring all the wheat into my barn." '

'The Mustard Seed' Another parable He put before them.   31
' The Kingdom of heaven,' He said, ' is like a mustard-seed, which a man takes and sows in his ground.   It is the smallest of all seeds, and yet when 32
full-grown it is larger than any herb and forms a tree, so that the birds come and roost in its branches.'

'The Yeast' Another parable He spoke to them.   33
' The Kingdom of heaven,' He said, ' is like yeast which a woman takes and buries in three measures of flour, for it to work there till the whole is leavened.'

All this Jesus spoke to the people in parables, and except 34
in parables He spoke nothing to them, in fulfilment of the 35
saying of the Prophet,

' I WILL OPEN MY MOUTH IN PARABLES :

I WILL UTTER THINGS KEPT HIDDEN SINCE THE CREATION
OF ALL THINGS ' (Ps. lxxviii. 2).

'The Wheat and the Darnel' explained When He had dismissed the people and had 36
returned to the house, His disciples came to Him with the request,
' Explain to us the parable of the darnel sown in the field.'

' The sower of the good seed,' He replied, ' is the Son 37
of Man ; the field is the world ; the good seed—these are 38
the sons of the Kingdom ; the darnel, the sons of the Evil

(vv. 31-33.) Cf. Mark iv. 30-32 ; Luke xiii. 18-21.

33. *Three measures*] *i.e.* ' the usual quantity for a baking,' see Gen. xviii. 6 ;
Judges vi. 19 ; I Sam. i. 24.   This of itself excludes some ancient interpretations of
the *three*—Greeks, Jews, and Samaritans : body, soul, and spirit.   Except in this
parable leaven is a symbol of the pervasive power of evil.   (Cf. chapter xvi. 6,
11 ; I Cor. v. 6-8 ; Gal. v. 9.)

(vv. 34, 35.) Cf. Mark iv. 33, 34.

35. *The Prophet*] Asaph.   See Ps. lxxviii. 2 and heading.

one. The enemy who sowed the darnel is the Devil; the 39
harvest is the close of the age; the reapers are the angels.
As then the darnel is collected together and burnt up with 40
fire, so will it be at the close of the age. The Son of Man 41
will commission His angels, and they will gather out of His
Kingdom all causes of sin and all who violate His laws; and 42
these they will throw into the fiery furnace. There will be
the weeping and the gnashing of teeth. Then will the 43
righteous shine out like the sun in their Father's Kingdom.
Listen, every one who has ears!

'The Treasure' 'The Kingdom of heaven is like treasure 44
buried in the field, which a man finds, but
buries again, and, in his joy about it, goes and
sells all he has and buys that piece of ground.

'The Pearl' 'Again the Kingdom of heaven is like a jewel 45
merchant who is in quest of choice pearls. He 46
finds one most costly pearl; he goes away, and though it
costs all he has, he buys it.

'The Draw-net' 'Again the Kingdom of heaven is like a draw- 47
net let down into the sea, which encloses fish of
all sorts. When it is full, they haul it up on the 48
beach, and sit down and collect the good fish in baskets,
while the worthless they throw away. So will it be at the 49
close of the age. The angels will go forth and separate
the wicked from among the righteous, and will throw them 50
into the fiery furnace. There will be the weeping and the
gnashing of teeth.'

'Have you understood all this?' He asked. 51

'Yes,' they said.

'Then remember,' He said, 'that every Scribe well 52
trained for the Kingdom of heaven is like a householder
who brings out of his storehouse new things and old.'

A Visit to Nazareth Jesus concluded this series of parables and 53
then departed. And He came into His own 54
country and proceeded to teach in their synagogue, so that they were filled with astonishment and
exclaimed,

39. *Close of the age*] Or 'consummation of the age,' *i.e.* the completion of the
transitory course of this present world. (Cf. verse 49; xxiv. 3; xxviii. 20; also
Hebrews ix. 26 'at the consummation of the ages ').
43. *Their Father's Kingdom*] Cf. xxvi. 29; Dan. xii. 3.
49. *Close of the age*] Cf. verse 39, n.
(vv. 54–58.) Cf. Mark vi. 1–6; also Luke iv. 16–30 (an editorial displacement).
54. *Country*] Lit. ' native place.' So in verse 57. Luke more accurately has
where he had been brought up.'

' Where did he obtain such wisdom, and these wondrous powers ? Is not this the carpenter's son ? Is not his 55 mother called Mary ? And are not his brothers, James, Joseph, Simon and Judah ? And his sisters—are they not 56 all living here among us ? Where then did he get all this ? '

So they turned against Him.   57

But Jesus said to them,

' There is no prophet left without honour except in his own country and among his own family.'

And He performed but few mighty deeds there because 58 of their want of faith.

The Murder of John the Baptist   About that time Herod the Tetrarch heard 1 **14** of the fame of Jesus, and he said to his courtiers, 2 ' This is John the Baptist : he has come back to life ; and that is why these miraculous Powers are working in him.'

For Herod had arrested John, and had put him in 3 chains and imprisoned him, for the sake of Herodias (his brother Philip's wife), because John would say to him, 4

' It is not lawful for you to have her.'

And he would have liked to put him to death, but was 5 afraid of the people, because they regarded John as a Prophet. But when Herod's birthday came, the daughter 6 of Herodias danced before all the company, and so pleased Herod that with an oath he promised to give her whatever 7 she asked. So she, instigated by her mother, said, 8

' Give me here on a dish the head of John the Baptist.'

The king was deeply vexed, yet because of his repeated 9 oath and of the guests at his table he ordered it to be given her, and he sent and beheaded John in the prison. The 10, 11 head was brought on a dish and given to the young girl, and she took it to her mother. Then John's disciples went and 12 removed the body and buried it, and came and informed Jesus.

---

55. *This*] Or ' this fellow.'

(vv. 1–12.) Cf. Mark vi. 14–29. This section is a retrospective sequel to the bare mention of the imprisonment of John at chapter iv. 12 ; Mark i. 14. Luke iii. 18–20 briefly expands that bare mention and so avoids the parenthetical explanation here.

12. *And came and informed Jesus*] Cf. Mark vi. 29. Matthew seems to have forgotten that this is past history, and apparently he transfers the report of the disciples on their return from their mission (Mark vi. 30) to a report by John's disciples of their master's death.

Upon receiving these tidings, Jesus went 13
5000 People fed away by boat to an uninhabited and secluded district; but the people heard of it and followed Him in crowds from the towns by land. So Jesus 14 left the boat and saw an immense multitude, and felt compassion for them, and cured those of them who were out of health. But when evening was come, the disciples came to 15 Him and said,

' This is an uninhabited place, and the best of the day is now gone ; send the people away to go into the villages and buy something to eat.'

' They need not go away,' replied Jesus ; ' you your- 16 selves must give them something to eat.'

' We have nothing here,' they said, ' but five loaves and 17 a couple of fish.'

' Bring them here to me,' He said, and He told all the 18, 19 people to sit down on the grass.

Then He took the five loaves and the two fish, and after looking up to heaven and blessing them, He broke up the loaves and gave them to the disciples, and the disciples distributed them to the people. So all ate, and were fully 20 satisfied. The broken portions that remained over they gathered up, filling twelve baskets. Those who had eaten 21 were about five thousand adult men, without reckoning women and children.

Immediately afterwards He made the dis- 22
Jesus prays in Solitude ciples go on board the boat and cross to the opposite shore, leaving Him to dismiss the people. When He had done this, He climbed the hill to 23 pray in solitude. Night came on, and he was there alone. Meanwhile the boat was far out on the Lake, buffeted and 24 tossed by the waves, the wind being adverse.

But towards daybreak He went to them, 25
He walks on the Lake walking over the waves. When the disciples 26 saw Him walking on the waves, they were greatly alarmed.

(vv. 13–21.) Cf. Mark vi. 30–44 ; Luke ix. 10–17 ; John vi. 1–14.
15. *Evening*] Lit. ' a late ' hour.
(vv. 22–33.) Cf. Mark vi. 45–52 ; John vi. 15–21.
23. *Night*] Lit. ' a late ' hour, the same word as in verse 15.
24. *Far out on the Lake*] Lit. ' in the middle of the sea.' v.l. ' was many furlongs from land.'
25. *Towards daybreak*] Lit. ' in the fourth watch of the night,' *i.e.* between 3 and 6 a.m. The four watches—6–9 p.m., 9–12, 12–3, 3–6—are named in Mark xiii. 35.

'It is a ghost,' they exclaimed, and they cried out with terror.

But instantly Jesus spoke to them and said, 27
'There is no danger ; it is I ; do not be afraid.'

'Master,' answered Peter, 'if it is you, bid me come to 28
you upon the water.'

'Come,' said Jesus. 29

Then Peter climbed down from the boat and walked upon the water to go to Him. But when he felt the wind he 30 grew frightened, and beginning to sink he cried out,

'Master, save me.'

Instantly Jesus stretched out His hand and caught hold 31 of him, saying to him,

'Man of little faith, why did you doubt ? '

So they climbed into the boat, and the wind lulled ; and 32 the men on board fell down before him and said, 33

'You are indeed God's Son.'

When they had crossed over, they put 34
Cures in Gennesaret ashore at Gennesaret ; and the men of the place, 35
recognizing Him, sent word to all the country round. So they brought to Him all who were ill, and 36 entreated Him that they might but touch the tassel of His outer garment ; and all who did so were restored to perfect health.

Purity is inward and spiritual Then there came to Jesus some Pharisees and 1 **15** Scribes from Jerusalem, who inquired,

'Why do your disciples transgress the tra- 2 dition of the Elders by not washing their hands before meals?

'Why do you, too,' He retorted, 'transgress God's com- 3 mands for the sake of your tradition ? God said, " HONOUR 4 THY FATHER AND THY MOTHER " (Exod. xx. 12) ; and " LET HIM WHO REVILES FATHER OR MOTHER BE PUT TO DEATH " (Exod. xxi. 17) ; but you say : " If a man says to his father 5 or mother, ' This thing is consecrated, otherwise you should have received it from me,' he shall be absolved from 6

---

29. *To go*] v.l. ' and went.'
30. *Felt*] Lit. ' saw.'
The wind] v.l. ' how strong the wind was.'
(vv. 34–36.) Cf. Mark vi. 53–56.
(vv. 1–20.) Cf. Mark vii. 1–23.
2. *Before meals*] Lit. ' whenever they eat bread.' Cf. Mark vii. 5, n.
4. *Reviles*] Or ' curses.'
5. *Consecrated*] Lit. ' a gift,' *i.e.* to God.

honouring his father"; and so you have rendered futile
God's word for the sake of your tradition. Hypocrites ! 7
Well did Isaiah prophesy of you,

'" THIS PEOPLE HONOURS ME WITH THEIR LIPS,   8
WHILE THEIR HEART IS FAR FROM ME;
IN VAIN DO THEY WORSHIP ME,   9
WHILE GIVING AS DOCTRINES THE MERE PRECEPTS OF
MEN"' (Isa. xxix. 13).

Then, when He had called the people to Him, Jesus said, 10
' Hear and understand. It is not what goes into a man's 11
mouth that makes him unclean, but it is what comes out of
his mouth that makes him unclean.'

Then His disciples came and said to Him,   12
' Do you know that the Pharisees turned against you
when they heard those words ? '

' Every plant,' He replied, ' which my Heavenly Father 13
has not planted will be rooted up. Leave them alone. 14
They are blind guides of the blind ; and if a blind man
leads a blind man, both will fall into some pit.'

' Explain to us this parable,' said Peter.   15
' Are you,' He answered, ' still without intelligence ? 16
Do you not understand that whatever enters the mouth 17
passes into the stomach and is afterwards ejected from the
body ? But the things that come out of the mouth proceed 18
from the heart, and it is these that defile the man. For out 19
of the heart proceed wicked scheming, murder, adultery,
fornication, theft, perjury, slander. These are the things 20
which make a man unclean ; but eating with unwashed
hands does not make unclean.'

Leaving that place, Jesus withdrew into the 21
A Gentile Girl cured neighbourhood of Tyre and Sidon. Here a 22
Canaanitish woman of the district came out and
kept crying—

' Master, Son of David, pity me ; my daughter is cruelly
harassed by a demon.'

---

6. *His father*] v.l. adds ' or his mother.'
Word] v.l. ' law.'
11. *Makes unclean*] Lit. ' makes common.' See Heb. ix. 13, n.
12. *Turned against you*] Cf. v. 29, n. No wonder they were shocked. It was one
thing to question their tradition, quite another to abrogate the Levitical Law as to
meats clean and unclean.
14. *Of the blind*] v.l. omits these words.
Pit] Or ' hole.' Cf. xii. 11, where the same word is used.
19. *Scheming*] Or 'reasonings.'
(vv. 21–28.) Cf. Mark vii. 24–30.
22. *Kept crying*] Or the tense (imperfect) may mean ' began to cry out to Him.'

But He answered her not a word. Then the disciples 23 came up, and begged Him, saying,

' Send her away, because she keeps crying behind us.'

' I have only been sent to the lost sheep of the house of 24 Israel,' He replied.

Then she came and threw herself at His feet and entreated 25 Him.

' Master, help me,' she said.

' It is not right,' He said, ' to take the children's bread 26 and throw it to the dogs.'

' Be it so, Master,' she said, ' for even the dogs eat the 27 scraps which fall from their masters' tables.'

' O woman,' replied Jesus, ' great is your faith : be it done 28 to you as you desire.'

And from that moment her daughter was restored to health.

Many other Cures Moving from that district, Jesus went along 29 by the Lake of Galilee ; and ascending the hill, He sat there. Soon great crowds came to Him, 30 bringing with them those who were crippled, blind, dumb, or maimed, and many besides, and they hastened to lay them at His feet. And He cured them, so that the people 31 were amazed to see the dumb speaking, the maimed with their hands perfect, the lame walking, and the blind seeing ; and they gave the glory to the God of Israel.

4000 People fed Then Jesus called His disciples to Him and 32 said,

' My heart yearns over this mass of people, for it is now the third day that they have been with me and they have nothing to eat. I am unwilling to send them away hungry, lest they should faint on the road.'

24. *Lost sheep*] Or, as we should say, ' lapsed masses.' On account of the limitations divinely imposed upon Him, our Lord doubtless felt a real difficulty in helping this Gentile woman. He did not invent difficulties in order to test and increase her faith.

26. *Dogs*] Lit. ' puppies.' Dogs are not domesticated animals in Palestine. Puppies are often cared for and petted while still young, especially by the children, but when full-grown they are driven away to herd with their savage congeners, which are so serious a nuisance and terror in most Eastern cities.

27. *Be it so*] Namely, that the Gentiles resemble the dogs.

For] The rendering ' yet ' is wholly unauthorised. She means that if we are like the dogs that very fact constitutes our claim.

(vv. 32–38.) Cf. Mark viii. 1–9.

32. *The third day*] Lit. ' three days.' According to English idiom ' two days ' would probably express the true sense, the time indicated being one full day and some fraction of the day preceding and of the day following. Cf. xii. 40, n. and Luke ii. 46, n.

'Where can we,' asked the disciples, 'get bread enough 33 in this remote place to satisfy so vast a multitude?'

'How many loaves have you?' Jesus asked. 34

'Seven,' they said, 'and a few small fish.'

So He bade all the people sit down on the ground, and He 35, 36 took the seven loaves and the fish, and after giving thanks He broke them and then distributed them to the disciples, and they to the people. And they all ate and were satisfied. 37 The broken portions that remained over they took up— seven full baskets. Those who ate were 4000 men, without 38 reckoning women and children.

He then dismissed the people, went on board the boat, 39 and came into the district of Magadan.

Now the Pharisees and Sadducees came to 1 **16** A Sign from Him; and, to make trial of Him, they asked Him Heaven to show them a sign from heaven. He replied, 2 [' In the evening you say, " It will be fine weather, for the sky is red "; and in the mornɪng, " It will be rough weather 3 to-day, for the sky is red and murky." You learn how to distinguish the aspect of the sky, but the signs of the times you cannot.] A wicked and apostate generation are eager 4 for a sign; but none shall be given to them except the sign of Jonah'

And He left them and went away.

When the disciples arrived at the other side 5 The Leaven of the Lake, they found that they had forgotten of the to bring any bread; and when Jesus said to 6 Pharisees them, 'See to it and beware of the leaven of the and Pharisees and Sadducees,' they reasoned with 7 Sadducees one another, and remarked,

'We have not brought any bread.'

Jesus perceived this and said, 8

'What is this discussion among you, you men of little faith, about having no bread? Do you not yet understand? 9 nor even remember the 5000 men and the five loaves, and

---

37. *Baskets*] Or 'store-baskets,' or (Westcott) 'frails.' Except in connection with this miracle, the word is only found in Acts ix. 25. The baskets used in feeding the 5000 were hand-baskets. Yet another word for basket in 2 Cor. xi. 33.

(vv. 39 to xvi. 4.) Cf. Mark viii. 10–12.

1. *From heaven*] Cf. Mark viii. 11, n. See note on xii. 40.

(vv. 2, 3.) Cf. Luke xii. 54.

2. *In the evening . . you cannot*] v.l. omits. The textual authority is decisive for the omission of the bracketed words. An imitation of Luke xii. 54–56.

(vv. 4–12.) Cf. Mark viii. 13–21.

5. *Of the Lake*] Not in the Greek.

6. *Leaven*] or 'yeast,' 'barm.' So in verses 11 and 12.

how many basketfuls you carried away, nor the 4000 and 10 the seven loaves, and how many hampers you carried away? How is it you do not understand that it was not about 11 bread that I spoke to you? But beware of the leaven of the Pharisees and Sadducees.'

Then they perceived that He had not warned them against 12 leaven, but against the teaching of the Pharisees and Sadducees.

Peter con-fesses Jesus to be the Christ   When He arrived in the neighbourhood of 13 Caesarea Philippi, Jesus questioned His disciples.

'Who do people say that the Son of Man is?' He asked.

'Some say John the Baptist,' they replied; 'others 14 Elijah; others Jeremiah or one of the Prophets.'

'But you, who do you say that I am?' He asked 15 again.

'You,' replied Simon Peter, 'are the Christ, the Son of 16 the living God.'

'Blessed are you, Simon Bar-Jonah,' said Jesus; 'for 17 no mortal has revealed this to you, but my Father in heaven. And I declare to you that you are Peter, and that 18 upon this Rock I will build my Church, and the might of Hades shall not triumph over it. I will give you the keys 19 of the Kingdom of heaven; and whatever you bind on earth shall remain bound in heaven, and whatever you loose on earth shall remain loosed in heaven.'

Then He instructed His disciples to tell no one that He 20 was the Christ.

Jesus predicts His own Death and Resur-rection   From this time Jesus began to explain to His 21 disciples that He must go to Jerusalem, and suffer much cruelty from the Elders and the High Priests and the Scribes, and be put to death, and on the third day be raised to life

(vv. 13–28.) Cf. Mark viii. 27–29; Luke ix. 18–27.
13. *Say that the Son of Man is*] v.l. ' say that I the Son of Man am.'
(vv. 17–19.) Matthew only.
17. *No mortal*] Lit. ' flesh and blood has not.'
18. *Peter. Rock*] In the Greek ' petros ' and ' petra.' In Classical Greek these signify ' stone ' and ' rock ' respectively. But the latter being feminine, would be manifestly unsuitable as the name of a man. Cf. John i. 42; Acts xii. 13.
Might] Lit. ' gates.' Cf. the expression ' The Sublime Porte.' The guarded gate was the key to the defence of the city, and hence the symbol of its strength. See Neh. vii. 3, and contrast Isa. lx. 11, Rev. xxi. 25.
19. *You*] Peter. Contrast the plural in chapter xviii. 18, John xx. 23.
21. *Jesus*] v.l. ' Jesus Christ.'

again. Then Peter took Him aside and began to remonstrate 22 with Him.

'Master,' he said, 'God forbid ; this shall not be your lot.'

But He turned and said to Peter. 23

'Get behind me, Satan ; you are a hindrance to me, because your thoughts are not God's thoughts, but men's.'

Self-Renunciation the Way to Life Then Jesus said to His disciples, 24 'If any one wishes to follow me, let him renounce self and take up his cross, and so be my follower. For whoever desires to save his life shall lose it, 25 and whoever loses his life for my sake shall find it. Why, 26 what benefit will it be to a man if he gains the whole world but forfeits his life ? Or what shall a man give to buy back his life ? For the Son of Man is to come in the glory of 27 His Father with His angels, and then will He requite every man according to his actions. I tell you in truth that some 28 of those who are standing here will not taste death till they have seen the Son of Man coming in His Kingdom.'

The Transfiguration Six days later, Jesus took with Him Peter 1 **17** and the brothers James and John, and brought them up a high mountain to a solitary place. There in their presence His form underwent a change ; His 2 face shone like the sun, and His raiment became as white as the light. And suddenly Moses and Elijah appeared to 3 them conversing with Him.

Then Peter said to Jesus, 4 'Master, it is well for us to be here. If you approve, I will put up three tents here, one for you, one for Moses, and one for Elijah.'

22. *God forbid*] Lit. (The Lord be) 'merciful to you ! '
23. *Satan*] A Hebrew word signifying 'Adversary.' Peter, as a Jew, would at once understand the meaning.
Hindrance] Stumbling-block in my way. See v. 29, n.
25. *Life*] Or 'soul.' It is inadmissible to change from 'life' in verse 25 to 'soul' in verse 26 (as A.V.) : the same word is used throughout the passage. If *soul* in verse 26 then verse 25 reads : 'Whosoever desires to save his soul shall lose it.' The primary meaning of 'to save life' is seen in Mark iii. 4, where it is opposed to 'kill'; an unworthy clinging to life at all costs, means that death when it does come involves exclusion from the life of the future Kingdom. But *life* has also an ethical content : it stands for the whole *self* or personality, and so Jesus says that the instinct of self-preservation is interpreted rightly only by self-renunciation (verse 24).
26. *Forfeits*] Cf. Luke ix. 25, n.
To buy back his life] After he has lost it, having paid it as the penalty of his misdeeds. (vv. 1–13.) Cf. Mark ix. 2–13 ; Luke ix. 28–36.
4. *It is well*] A recognition of the privilege accorded them, possibly in an idiomatic sense, 'We are grateful to you that we are here' (cf. Acts x. 33 : Phil. iv. 14). Or, perhaps, as nearer to the Greek, 'It is fortunate for you that we are here, because we can build booths for you and your departing visitors' (Luke ix. 33).

He was still speaking when a luminous cloud spread over 5 them ; and a voice was heard from within the cloud, which said,

' This is My Son the Beloved, in whom is My delight. Listen to Him.'

On hearing this voice, the disciples fell on their faces and 6 were filled with terror. But Jesus came and touched them, 7 and said.

' Rise and have no fear.'

So they looked up, and saw no one but Jesus. 8

As they were descending the mountain, Jesus laid a com- 9 mand upon them.

' Tell no one,' He said, ' of the sight you have seen till the Son of Man has risen from the dead.'

' Why then,' asked the disciples, ' do the 10 **The Coming of Elijah** Scribes say that Elijah must first come ? '

' Elijah was indeed to come,' He replied, 11 ' and would reform everything. But I tell you that he has 12 already come, and they did not recognize him, but dealt with him as they chose. And the Son of Man is about to be treated by them in a similar way.'

Then it dawned upon the disciples that it was John the 13 Baptist about whom He had spoken to them.

When they returned to the people, there 14 **Cure of an Epileptic** came to Him a man who fell on his knees before Him and besought Him.

' Master,' he said, ' have pity on my son, for he is an 15 epileptic and suffers badly. Often he falls into the fire and often into the water. I brought him to your disciples, and 16 they were not able to cure him.'

' O unbelieving and perverse generation ! ' replied Jesus ; 17 ' how long shall I be with you ? how long must I bear with you ? Bring him to me.'

Then Jesus rebuked the demon, and it came out and 18 left him ; and the boy was cured from that moment.

Then the disciples came to Jesus privately 19 **The Power of Faith** and asked Him,

' Why could not we expel the demon ? '

' Because your faith is so small,' He replied ; ' for I 20

---

5. *Spread over*] Lit. ' overshadowed.'
(vv. 14–21.) Cf. Mark ix. 14–29 ; Luke ix. 37–43.
17. *Perverse*] Or ' crooked-minded.'

declare to you in truth that if you have faith like a mustard-seed, you shall say to this mountain, " Remove from this place to that," and it will remove ; and nothing shall be impossible to you. But an evil spirit of this kind is only 21 driven out by prayer and fasting.'

As they were travelling about in Galilee, Jesus said to 22 them,

Jesus again predicts His own Death and Resurrection
' The Son of Man is about to be betrayed into the hands of men ; they will put Him to 23 death, but on the third day He will be raised to life again.'

And they were exceedingly distressed.

He pays the Temple Tax
After their arrival at Capernaum the collec- 24 tors of the half-shekel came and asked Peter, ' Does not your Teacher pay the half-shekel? '

' Yes,' he replied, and then went into the house.   25
But before he spoke a word Jesus said,

' What think you, Simon ?   From whom do this world's kings receive customs or capitation tax ? from their own children, or from others ? '

' From others,' he replied.   26

' Then the children go free,' said Jesus.   ' However, lest 27 we offend them, go and throw a hook into the Lake, and take the first fish that comes up.   When you open its mouth, you will find a shekel in it : bring that coin and give it to them for yourself and me.'

A Lesson in Humility
Just then the disciples came to Jesus and 1 **18** asked,

' Who ranks higher than others in the King-dom of heaven ? '

So He called a young child to Him, and, placing him in 2 the midst of them, said,   3

' In truth I tell you that unless you turn and become like little children, you will in no case be admitted into

---

v.L. omits verse 21.
(vv. 22, 23.) Cf. Mark ix. 30–32 ; Luke ix. 43–45.
22. *Travelling about*] Or ' gathering together.'
(vv. 24–27.) Matthew only.
24. *The half-shekel*] Levied on all Jews for the support of the Temple services, Exod. xxx. 13.
(vv. 1–5.) Cf. Mark ix. 33–41 ; Luke ix. 46–50.
1. *Ranks higher than others*] Lit. ' is greater.'   Or perhaps it may be rendered ' is greatest,' the superlative being almost obsolete in the language of the N.T. (as it is quite obsolete in modern Greek) and the comparative being substituted for it.   So in 1 Cor. xiii. 13.

the Kingdom of heaven. Whoever therefore shall humble 4
himself as this young child, is the one who is greatest
in the Kingdom of heaven. And whoever for my sake 5
receives one young child such as this, receives me. But
whoever shall occasion the fall of one of these little ones 6
who believe in me, it would be better for him to have a
millstone hung round his neck and to be drowned in the
depths of the sea.

'Woe to the world because of causes of 7
Stones of stumbling! They cannot but occur, but woe
Stumbling to the man through whom such cause does occur!
If your hand or your foot is causing you to fall, cut it off and 8
away with it. It is better for you to enter crippled in hand
or foot into Life, than possessing two sound hands or feet to
be thrown into the fire eternal. And if your eye is causing 9
you to fall, tear it out and away with it ; it is better for you
to enter with only one eye into Life, than possessing two
eyes to be thrown into the Gehenna of fire.

'Beware of despising one of these little ones, 10
'Despise no for I tell you that in heaven their angels con-
one': 'The tinually behold the face of my Father who is in
straying heaven. What do you yourselves think? 12
Sheep'
Suppose a man has a hundred sheep and one of them strays
away, will he not leave the ninety-nine on the hills and go
and look for the stray one? And if he succeeds in finding 13
it, in truth I tell you that he rejoices over it more than he does
over the ninety-nine that have not gone astray. Just so it is 14
the will of your Father in heaven that not one of these little
ones should be lost.

How to treat 'If your brother acts wrongly towards you, 15
a sinning go and point out his fault to him when only you
Brother and he are there. If he listens to you, you have
gained your brother. But if he will not listen to you, go 16

(vv. 6–9.) Cf. Mark ix. 42–50 ; Luke xvii. 1, 2.

6. *Millstone*] Lit. ' ass-millstone,' *i.e.* a millstone which an ass turns.

9. *Gehenna of fire*] See v. 22, n., the only other place where this expression occurs.

(vv. 10–14.) Cf. Luke xv. 3–7.

10. *Their angels*] This seems to mean the angels who have special charge over them —guardian angels. Cf. Charlotte Elliott :

'Christian, seek not yet repose,
Hear thy guardian angel say.'

The angels of the little ones are in the innermost circle of the ministering spirits who surround God's throne.

v.L. inserts verse 11, ' For the Son of Man came to save that which is lost,' from Luke xix. 10.

15. *Acts wrongly*] Lit. ' shall have sinned.'

Towards you] v.L. omits these words.

again, and ask one or two to come with you, that every word may be confirmed by two or three witnesses. If he refuses 17 to hear them, appeal to the church ; and if he refuses to hear even the church, regard him just as you regard a heathen or a tax-gatherer. I in truth tell you all that what- 18 ever you bind on earth will in heaven remain bound, and whatever you loose on earth will in heaven remain loosed. I also in truth tell you that if two of you here on earth agree 19 together concerning anything that they shall ask, the prayer shall be granted by my Father who is in heaven. For 20 where there are two or three assembled in my name, there am I in the midst of them.'

How often must we forgive
At this point Peter came to Him with the 21 question,
'Master, how often shall my brother act wrongly towards me and I forgive him ? seven times ? '
' I do not say seven times,' answered Jesus, ' but seventy 22 times seven.

The unmerciful Servant
' For this reason the Kingdom of heaven may 23 be compared to a king who determined to have a settlement of accounts with his servants. But 24 as soon as he began the settlement, one was brought before him who owed 10,000 talents, and was unable to pay. So 25 his master ordered that he and his wife and children and everything that he had should be sold, and payment be made. The servant therefore falling down, prostrated himself at 26 his feet and entreated him.

' " Only give me time," he said, " and I will pay you the whole."

' Whereupon his master, touched with compassion, set 27 him free and forgave him the debt. But no sooner had that 28 servant gone out, than he met with one of his fellow servants who owed him 100 shillings ; and seizing him by the throat and nearly strangling him he exclaimed,

' " Pay me all you owe."

' His fellow servant therefore fell at his feet and entreated 29 him :

17. *The church*] Or ' the assembly.' The second and final occurrence of the word ' church ' in the Gospels. Cf. chapter xvi. 18.
(vv. 21–35.) Cf. Luke xvii. 3, 4.
22. *Seventy times seven*] *i.e.* without limit, and always. Some, however, prefer to render ' seventy-seven times,' comparing this passage with Gen. iv. 24 (where the Greek in the LXX. is the same as here) in contrast with verse 15 of that same chapter. So R.V. there and R.V. mg. here.

' " Only give me time," he said, " and I will pay you."

' He would not, however, but went and threw him into 30 prison until he should pay what was due. His fellow 31 servants, therefore, seeing what had happened, were exceedingly angry ; and they came and told their master all that had happened. At once his master called him 32 and said,

' " Wicked servant, I forgave you all that debt, because you entreated me : ought not you also to have had pity on 33 your fellow servant, just as I had pity on you ? "

' So his master, greatly incensed, handed him over to the 34 gaolers until he should pay all he owed him.

' In the same way my Heavenly Father will deal with 35 you all, if you do not each one forgive his brother from your heart.'

19

When Jesus had finished these sayings, He 1 *Jesus leaves Galilee* removed from Galilee and came into that part of Judaea which lay beyond the Jordan. And a vast multitude followed Him, and He cured 2 them there.

A Question about Divorce Then came some of the Pharisees to Him to 3 put Him to the proof by the question, ' Has a man a right to divorce his wife for any sort of reason ? '

' Have you not read,' He replied, ' that He who made 4 them " MADE THEM " from the beginning " MALE AND FEMALE " (Gen. i. 27), and said, " FOR THIS REASON A MAN 5 SHALL LEAVE HIS FATHER AND MOTHER AND CLING TO HIS WIFE, AND THE TWO SHALL BE ONE ? " (Gen. ii. 24). Thus 6 they are no longer two, but one. What therefore God has joined together, let not man separate.'

' Why then,' said they, ' did Moses command the husband 7 to give her a written notice of divorce, and send her away ? ' (Deut. xxiv. 1).

' Moses,' He replied, ' in consideration of your stubborn 8 hearts, permitted you to put away your wives, but it was not so from the beginning. I tell you that whoever divorces 9

(vv. 1–2.) Cf. Mark x. 1. This journey to Jerusalem occupies a single chapter in Mark (chapter x.), two in Matthew, and nearly ten in Luke (ix. 51 to xix. 29). See Introduction.
(vv. 3–12.) Cf. Mark x. 2–12.
3. *For any sort of reason*] Or ' on any and every ground.'
5. *One*] Lit. ' one flesh.'

his wife for any reason except her unchastity, and marries another woman, commits adultery.'

'If this is a man's position in regard to his wife,' said the disciples to Him, 'it is better not to marry.' 10

'It is not every man,' He replied, 'who can receive this teaching, but only those on whom the grace has been bestowed. There are men who from their birth have been disabled from marriage, others who have been so disabled by men, and others who have disabled themselves for the sake of the Kingdom of heaven. He who is able to receive this, let him receive it.' 11 12

Little Children welcomed and blessed Then young children were brought to Him that He should put His hands on them and pray; but the disciples interfered. Jesus however said, 13 14

'Let the little children come to me, and do not hinder them; for it is to those who are childlike that the Kingdom of heaven belongs.'

So He laid His hands upon them and went away. 15

Eternal Life 'Teacher,' said one man, coming up to Him, 'what good thing shall I do in order to win the Life Eternal?' 16

'Why do you ask me,' He replied, 'about the thing that is good? There is only One who is truly good. But if you desire to enter into Life, keep the Commandments.' 17

'Which Commandments?' he asked. 18

Jesus answered,

'"Thou shalt not kill"; "Thou shalt not commit adultery"; "Thou shalt not steal"; "Thou shalt

---

9. *Unchastity*] See Matthew v. 32, n.
(vv. 13–15.) Cf. Mark x. 13–16 ; Luke xviii. 15–17.
(vv. 16–30.) Cf. Mark x. 17–31 ; Luke xviii. 18–30.
16. *Teacher*] v.L. ' Good Teacher.'
17. *Why do you ask, &c.*] The v.L. (see A.V.) is an assimilation to Mark x. 18, which is adopted in Luke xviii. 19 ; but the true text here seems to shrink from the apparent implication of ' Why callest thou me good ? ' and substitutes for ' Good Teacher . . . . why callest thou me good ? ' ' Teacher, what good thing must I do ? ' with the answer, ' Why askest thou me concerning the (thing) which is good ? One (Person) is good.' The moral is the same. This rich man had, with sincere piety, grafted the externals of religion on to his self-contained life of security and rectitude, and was still haunted by the insistent question, ' What lack I yet ? ' Jesus says to him in effect, ' Give it all up, not to feed the poor (1 Cor. xiii. 3), but to compel yourself to find God.' Entrance to eternal life is gained not by doing some good thing, but by the path of renunciation, sacrifice, and trust, which leads to dependence upon the one Fountain of all goodness. Cf. Browning, *A Grammarian's Funeral* :
' That, has the world here—should he need the next,
Let the world mind him !
This, throws himself on God, and unperplexed
Seeking shall find Him.'

NOT LIE IN GIVING EVIDENCE " ; " HONOUR THY FATHER AND 19
THY MOTHER " (Exod. xx. 12–16 ; Deut. v. 16–20) ; and
" THOU SHALT LOVE THY NEIGHBOUR AS MUCH AS THYSELF " '
(Lev. xix. 18).

' All of these,' said the young man, ' I have carefully 20
obeyed. What do I still lack ? '

' If you desire to be perfect,' replied Jesus, ' go and sell 21
all that you have, and give to the poor, and you shall have
wealth in heaven ; and come and follow me.'

On hearing these words the young man went away sad ; 22
for he had much property.

So Jesus said to His disciples, 23

The Dangers of Wealth ' I tell you in truth that it will be hard for
a rich man to enter the Kingdom of heaven.
Yes, I tell you, it is easier for a camel to go through the eye of 24
a needle than for a rich man to enter the Kingdom of God.'

These words utterly amazed the disciples, and they asked, 25
' Who then can be saved ? '

Jesus looked at them and said, 26
' With men this is impossible, but with God everything
is possible.'

Self-sacrifice for Christ enriches Then Peter said to Jesus, 27
' See, we have given up everything and
followed you ; what then shall be our reward ? '

' I tell you in truth,' replied Jesus, ' that in the New 28
Creation, when the Son of Man has taken His seat on His
glorious throne, all of you who have followed me shall also
sit on twelve thrones and judge the twelve tribes of Israel.
And whoever has forsaken houses, or brothers or sisters, 29
or father or mother, or children or lands, for my sake, shall
receive many times as much and shall have as his inheritance
eternal Life.

' But many who are now first shall be last, and many who 30
are now last shall be first.

' The Vineyard Labourers ' ' For the Kingdom of heaven is like the owner 1 **20**
of an estate who went out early in the morning
to hire men to work in his vineyard, and having 2

20. *Curefully obeyed*] Lit. ' guarded,' a stronger word than in verse 17.
24. *Camel*] A similar extravagance occurs in xxiii. 24.
28. *In the New Creation*] Or ' in the again-birth,' Greek *palingenesia*, in which
there will be a new Genesis either of this earth and all that is in it, or of the individual
man, as in Tit. iii. 5. The word occurs only in these two passages. Cf. 2 Cor. v. 17,
R.V. text and mg.
29. *Many times*] v.L. ' a hundred times.'
(vv. 1–16.) Matthew only.

made an agreement with them for a shilling a day, sent them into his vineyard. Going out about nine o'clock he saw 3 others loitering in the market-place. To these also he said, 4

' " You also, go into the vineyard, and whatever is right I will give you."

' So they went. Again about twelve, and about three 5 o'clock, he went out and did the same. And going out 6 about five o'clock he found others loitering, and he asked them,

' " Why have you been standing here all day long, doing nothing ? "

' " Because no one has hired us," they replied. 7

' " You also, go into the vineyard," he said.

' When evening came, the owner of the vineyard said to 8 his steward,

' " Call the men and pay them their wages. Begin with the last set and finish with the first."

' When those came who had begun at five o'clock, they 9 received a shilling apiece ; and when the first came, they 10 expected to get more, but they also each got the shilling. So when they had received it, they grumbled against the 11 employer, saying, 12

' " These who came last have done only one hour's work, and you have put them on a level with us who have worked the whole day and have borne the scorching heat."

' " My friend," he answered to one of them, " I am doing 13 you no injustice. Did you not agree with me for a shilling ? Take your money and go. I choose to give this last comer 14 just as much as I give you. Have I not a right to do what 15 I choose with my own property ? Or are you envious because I am generous ? "

' So the last shall be first, and the first last.' 16

Jesus a third time predicts His Death and Resurrection
Jesus was now going up to Jerusalem, and 17 He took the twelve disciples aside by themselves, and on the way He said to them,

' We are going up to Jerusalem, and there the 18 Son of Man shall be betrayed to the High Priests and Scribes. They shall condemn Him to death, and hand 19

---

15. *Generous*] The point of the parable is that the Kingdom is of such inestimable worth that it cannot be earned. It is of Grace and all of Grace. ' Tit for tat may do for earth ; it is not good enough for Heaven.'

16. v.l. adds ' For many are called, yet few are chosen,' from xxii. 14.

(vv. 17-19.) Cf. Mark x. 32-34 ; Luke xviii. 31-34.

Him over to the Gentiles to be mocked and scourged and crucified; and on the third day He shall be raised to life.'

Preeminence in the Kingdom
Then the mother of the sons of Zebedee came to Him with her sons, and knelt before Him to make a request of Him. 20

' What is it you desire ? ' He asked. 21

' Command,' she replied, ' that these my two sons may sit one at your right hand and one at your left in your Kingdom.'

' You know not what you are asking,' said Jesus ; ' can you drink out of the cup from which I am about to drink ? ' 22

' We can,' they replied.

' You shall drink out of my cup,' He said, ' but a seat at my right hand or at my left it is not mine to give, but it belongs to those for whom it has been reserved by my Father.' 23

Humble Service is true Greatness
The other ten heard of this, and their indignation was aroused against the two brothers. But Jesus called them to Him, and said, 24 25

' You know that the rulers of the Gentiles lord it over them, and their great men exercise authority over them. Not so shall it be among you ; but whoever desires to be great among you shall be your servant, and whoever desires to be first among you shall be your bond-servant ; just as the Son of Man came not to be served but to serve, and to give His life as the redemption price for many.' 26 27 28

Two blind Men receive Sight
As they were leaving Jericho, with an immense crowd following Him, two blind men sitting by the roadside heard that it was Jesus who was passing by, and cried aloud, 29 30

' Master, Son of David, pity us.'

The people angrily tried to silence them, but they cried all the louder. 31

' Master, Son of David, pity us,' they said.

So Jesus stood still and called to them. 32

(vv. 20-28.) Cf. Mark x. 35-45.
28. *Redemption price*] A saying especially notable, in that, apart from the words of the Last Supper it is the only one which breaks the reticence of the Synoptic Gospels as to the meaning of the ' death of Jesus.' It comes from Mark x. 45. Luke does not record it, but has a partial equivalent at xxii. 27. Of course Jesus does not enunciate any theory of His atonement ; but He has confidence that His death will be to many what the ransom is to the slave whom it sets free. Cf. 2 Macc. vii. 37, 38.

(vv. 29-34.) Cf. Mark x. 46-52 ; Luke xviii. 35-43.

' What shall I do for you ? ' He asked.

' Master, let our eyes be opened,' they replied. 33

Moved with compassion, Jesus touched their eyes, and 34 immediately they regained their sight and followed Him.

An Ass and its Colt are borrowed When they were come near Jerusalem and 1 **21** had arrived at Bethphagé and the Mount of Olives, Jesus sent two of the disciples on in front, saying to them, 2

' Go to the village you see facing you, and at once you will find a she-ass tied up and a colt with it. Untie it and bring them to me. And if any one says anything to you, 3 say, " The Master needs them," and he will at once send them.'

This took place in order that the Prophet's prediction 4 might be fulfilled :

' TELL THE DAUGHTER OF ZION, 5
" SEE, THY KING IS COMING TO THEE,
GENTLE, AND MOUNTED ON AN ASS,
ON A COLT THE FOAL OF A BEAST OF BURDEN " '
. (Isa. lxii. 11 ; Zech. ix. 9).

Jesus rides into Jerusalem So the disciples went and did as Jesus had 6 instructed them : they brought the she-ass and 7 the foal, and threw their outer garments on them. So He sat thereon ; and most of the crowd kept 8 spreading their garments along the road, while others cut branches from the trees and carpeted the road with them, and the multitudes—some of the people preceding Him, 9 and some following—sang aloud,

' HOSANNA TO THE SON OF DAVID !
BLESSED BE HE WHO COMES IN THE LORD'S NAME !
HOSANNA IN THE HIGHEST ! ' (Ps. cxviii. 25, 26).

When He entered Jerusalem, the whole city was thrown 10 into commotion, every one inquiring,

' Who is this ? '

' This is Jesus, the Prophet, from Nazareth in Galilee,' 11 replied the crowds.

(vv. 1-11.) Cf. Mark xi. 1-11 ; Luke xix. 29-44 ; John xii. 12-19.
9. *Hosanna*] Cf. verse 15 ; Mark xi. 9, 10 ; John xii. 13. The word is the trans-literation into Greek of the Hebrew of Psalm cxviii. 25, the last of the Hallel Psalms, which would soon be sung at the Passover. The Hebrew words are a prayer ' Save now,' but the phrase here, ' Hosanna to the Son of David,' as well as the N.T. contexts, show that it had become a shout of praise. So it cannot properly be rendered here, ' God save the Son of David,' or in the following clause, ' God in the highest heavens save Him.' Cf. Luke's paraphrase, xix. 38.

The Dealers driven from the Temple Entering the Temple, Jesus drove out all 12 who were buying and selling there, and overturned the money-changers' tables and the seats of the dove dealers.

' It is written,' He said, ' " My House shall be called 13 the House of Prayer " (Isa. lvi. 7), but you make it a robbers' cave ' (Jer. vii. 11).

And the blind and the lame came to Him in the Temple, 14 and He cured them.

But when the High Priests and the Scribes saw the 15 wonderful things that He had done and the children who were crying aloud in the Temple, ' Hosanna to the Son of David,' they were filled with indignation.

' Do you hear,' they asked Him, ' what these children 16 are saying ? '

' Yes,' He replied ; ' have you never read, " Out of the mouths of infants and of babes at the breast Thou hast perfected praise " ? ' (Ps. viii. 2).

So He left them and went out of the city to Bethany and 17 passed the night there.

A Fig-Tree cursed Early in the morning as He was on His way to 18 return to the city He was hungry, and seeing 19 a fig-tree on the roadside He went up to it, but found nothing on it but leaves.

' On you,' He said, ' no fruit shall ever again grow.'
And immediately the fig-tree withered away.

When the disciples saw it they exclaimed in astonishment, 20 ' How in a moment the fig-tree has withered away ! '

' I tell you in truth,' said Jesus, ' that if you have faith 21 and waver not, you shall not only perform such a miracle as this of the fig-tree, but even if you say to this mountain, " Arise, and hurl yourself into the sea," it shall be done ; and 22

(vv. 12–17.) Cf. Mark xi. 15–19 ; Luke xix. 45–48 ; xxi. 37, 38.

12. *The Temple*] v.l. reads ' God's Temple.'

13. *The House of Prayer*] The quotation from Isaiah in Mark xi. 17 retains the words ' for all the nations.' The non-Jew, debarred on pain of death from the inner courts, had free access to the Court of the Gentiles, and could at least offer ' towards His holy Temple ' the sacrifice of prayer. It was this court, in some sense the holiest of all, as symbol of the universality, and therefore of the spirituality of the Jewish religion, which had been degraded by the Temple guardians into a noisy cattle-market.

(vv. 18, 19.) Cf. Mark xi. 12–14.

(vv. 20–22.) Cf. Mark xi. 20–35.

22. The moral drawn as to the boundless possibilities of faith to work physical marvels is unexpected. If the cursing of the fig-tree is an acted parable, we should have looked for some comment on ' nothing but leaves,' the fair show and utter fruitlessness of the religion of His day. Moreover Jesus uses His miraculous powers with

everything, whatever it be, that you ask for in your prayers, if you have faith, you shall obtain.'

The Leaders of the People silenced He entered the Temple; and while He was 23 teaching, the High Priests and the Elders of the people came to Him and asked Him, ' By what authority are you doing these things ? and who gave you this authority ? '

' I also will put a question to you,' replied Jesus, ' and if 24 you answer me, I in turn will tell you by what authority I do these things. John's baptism, whence was it ?—was it 25 from heaven or from men ? '

So they debated the matter among themselves.

' If we say " from heaven," ' they argued, ' He will say, " Why then did you not believe him ? " and if we say " from 26 men " we have the people to fear, for they all hold John to have been a Prophet.'

So they answered Jesus, 27

' We do not know.'

' Nor do I tell you,' He replied, ' by what authority I do these things.'

Disobedience, apparent and real ' But give me your judgement. There was a 28 man who had two sons. He came to the first of them, and said,

' " My son, go and work in the vineyard to-day."

' " I will not," he replied. 29

' But afterwards he was sorry, and went. He came to the 30 second and spoke in the same manner. His answer was,

' " I will go, Sir."

' But he did not go. Which of the two did as his father 31 desired ? '

' The first,' they said.

a certain reserve, which its exercise to wither up an unoffending tree seems to break. The differences between the narrative of verses 18–22 and that of Mark xi. 12–14, 20–23, will be noted. Luke does not record this *incident*, but has (chapter xiii. 6–9) a *parable* drawn from an unfruitful fig-tree, and illustrating in a very Christ-like way the divine patience and hopefulness. It is not surprising in view of its intrinsic difficulties and the varying records that many find in the ' acted parable ' of Mark and Matthew a traditional distortion of the parable of Luke.

(vv. 23–27.) Cf. Mark xi. 27–33 ; Luke xx. 1–8.

25. *John's baptism*] John's ' baptism ' sums up the whole of his ministry. The religious leaders were within their rights in asking Jesus for His authority or licence to teach or to act as He had acted in the cleansing of the Temple. Of what nature was it, and who bestowed it ? Jesus does not evade their questions, but answers them. What have they to say about the authority of John's ministry ? Was it conferred by men or direct from heaven ? Their refusal to answer is a confessed incompetence to sit in judgement upon this unauthorised teacher.

31. *The first*] v.l. ' the latter,' inverting also the order of the two parts of the parable. The sense remains the same. Others read ' the latter,' without inverting the

' I tell you,' replied Jesus, ' that the tax-gatherers and the harlots are entering the Kingdom of God in front of you. For John came to you and kept to the path of righteousness, 32 and you put no faith in him : the tax-gatherers and the harlots did put faith in him, and you, though you saw this, did not even repent afterwards so as to believe him.

'The wicked Vine-dressers' ' Listen to another parable. There was a 33 householder who planted a vineyard, made a fence round it, dug a wine-tank in it, and built a watchtower ; then let the place to vine-dressers, and went abroad. When vintage-time approached, he sent his 34 servants to the vine-dressers to receive his share of the grapes ; but the vine-dressers seized the servants, and one 35 they cruelly beat, one they killed, one they pelted with stones. Again he sent another party of servants more 36 numerous than the first ; and these they treated in the same manner. Later still he sent to them his son, saying, 37

' " They will respect my son."

' But the vine-dressers, when they saw the son, said to 38 one another,

' " Here is the heir : come, let us kill him and get his inheritance."

' So they seized him, flung him out of the vineyard, and 39 killed him. When then the owner of the vineyard comes, 40 what will he do to those vine-dressers ? '

' He will put the wretches to a wretched death,' was the 41 reply, ' and will entrust the vineyard to other vine-dressers who will render the produce to him at the vintage season.'

' Have you never read in the Scriptures,' said Jesus, 42

' " THE STONE WHICH THE BUILDERS REJECTED

HAS BECOME THE CORNERSTONE :

THIS CAME FROM THE LORD,

AND IT IS WONDERFUL IN OUR EYES " ? (Ps. cxviii. 22, 23).

' That, I tell you, is the reason why the Kingdom of God 43 will be taken away from you, and given to a nation producing the fruits of it. He who falls on this stone will 44 be severely hurt ; but he on whom it falls will be utterly crushed.'

order of the two parts of the parable, explaining it to mean ' he who afterwards (repented and went).' But this seems an impossible translation.

(vv. 33–46.) Cf. Mark xii. 1–12 ; Luke xx. 9–19.

34. *Grapes*] Or perhaps the price obtained by the sale of them. The rent appears to have been a share of the produce, whether paid in kind or in money.

44. *Falls*] v.l. omits this verse.

After listening to His parables the High Priests and the 45
Pharisees perceived that He was speaking about them ; but 46
though they were eager to lay hands upon Him, they
were afraid of the people, for by them He was regarded
as a Prophet.

'The King's Wedding Feast'   Again Jesus spoke to them in parables. 1 **22**
'The Kingdom of heaven,' He said, 'may be 2
compared to a king who celebrated the marriage
of his son, and sent his servants to call the invited 3
guests to the wedding feast, but they were unwilling to
come.

' Again he sent other servants with a message to those 4
who were invited.

' " My banquet is now ready," he said, " my bullocks
and fat cattle are killed, and every preparation is made :
come to the wedding."

' They however gave no heed, but went, one to his home 5
in the country, another to his business ; and the rest seized 6
the king's servants, maltreated them, and murdered them.
So the king's anger was stirred, and he sent his troops and 7
destroyed those murderers and burnt their city. Then he 8
said to his servants,

' " The wedding banquet is ready, but those who
were invited were unworthy of it. Go out therefore 9
to the byways, and invite everybody you meet to the
wedding."

' So they went out into the roads and gathered together all 10
they could find, both bad and good, and the banqueting-
hall was filled with guests.

' Now the king came in to see the guests ; and among 11
them he noticed one who was not wearing a wedding
robe.

' " My friend," he said, " how is it that you came in here 12
without a wedding robe ? "

' The man was speechless. Then the king said to the 13
servants,

' " Bind him hand and foot and fling him into the darkness
outside : there will be the weeping and the gnashing of
teeth."

' For there are many called, but few chosen. 14

(vv. 1–13.) Cf. Luke's more natural and consistent parable of the Great Supper
(Luke xiv. 16–24).

A Question about Tribute Then the Pharisees went and consulted 15 together how they might entrap Him in His talk. So they sent to Him their disciples 16 together with the Herodians ; who said,

' Rabbi, we know that you are truthful and that you truly teach God's Way ; and you pay no special regard to any one, since you do not consider men's outward appearance. Give us your judgement therefore : is it allowable for us to 17 pay a poll-tax to Caesar, or not ? '

Perceiving their wickedness, Jesus replied, 18

' Why are you hypocrites trying to ensnare me ? Show 19 me the tribute coin.'

So they brought Him a shilling.

' Whose likeness and inscription,' He asked, ' is this ? ' 20

' Caesar's,' they replied. 21

' Pay therefore,' He rejoined, ' what· is Caesar's to Caesar ; and what is God's to God.'

They heard this, and were astonished ; then left Him, 22 and went their way.

A Question about the Resurrection On the same day a party of Sadducees came 23 to Him, contending that there is no resurrection. And they put this case to Him.

' Rabbi,' they said, ' Moses enjoined, "IF A MAN DIE 24 CHILDLESS, HIS BROTHER SHALL MARRY HIS WIDOW, AND RAISE UP A FAMILY FOR HIM " (Deut. xxv. 5). Now we had 25 among us seven brothers. The eldest of them married, but died childless, leaving his wife to his brother. So also did 26 the second and the third, down to the seventh. The 27 woman also died, after surviving them all. At the Resur- 28 rection, therefore, whose wife of the seven will she be ? for they all married her.'

The reply of Jesus was, 29

' You are in error through ignorance of the Scriptures and of the power of God. In the Resurrection, neither do men 30 marry nor are women given in marriage, but they are like angels in heaven. But as to the Resurrection of the dead, 31 have you never read what was spoken to you by God, " I 32 AM THE GOD OF ABRAHAM, AND THE GOD OF ISAAC, AND THE

(vv. 15–22.) Cf. Mark xii. 13–17 ; Luke xx. 20–26.
16. *Do not consider men's outward appearance*] Lit. ' do not look at men's faces.' Various similar expressions for the divine impartiality occur in both O.T. and N.T. Cf. Luke xx. 20, 21 ; Acts x. 34 ; Rom. ii. 11 ; Eph. vi. 9 ; James ii. 1, 9.
(vv. 23–33.) Cf. Mark xii. 18–27 ; Luke xx. 27–39.
30. *Angels*] v.L. ' God's angels.'

GOD OF JACOB " ? (Exod. iii. 6). He is not the God of the dead, but of the living.'

All the crowd heard this, and were filled with amazement 33 at His teaching.

Love, the supreme Law Now the Pharisees came up when they heard 34 that He had silenced the Sadducees, and one of 35 them, an expounder of the Law, asked Him as a test question,

' Rabbi, which is the greatest Commandment in the Law ? ' 36

He answered, ' " THOU SHALT LOVE THE LORD THY 37 GOD WITH THY WHOLE HEART, THY WHOLE SOUL, AND THY WHOLE MIND " (Deut. vi. 5). This is the greatest and fore- 38 most Commandment. And the second is similar to it : 39 " THOU SHALT LOVE THY NEIGHBOUR AS MUCH AS THYSELF " (Lev. xix. 18). The whole of the Law and the Prophets is 40 summed up in these two Commandments.'

'David's Son' and 'David's Lord' While the Pharisees were still assembled 41 there, Jesus put a question to them.

' What think you about the Christ,' He said, 42 ' whose son is He ? '

' David's,' they replied.

' How then,' He asked, ' does David, in the Spirit, call 43 Him Lord, when he says,

' " THE LORD SAID TO MY LORD, 44
SIT AT MY RIGHT HAND
UNTIL I HAVE PUT THY FOES BENEATH THY FEET " ?
(Ps. cx. 1).

(vv. 34–40.) Cf. Mark xii. 28–34. Matthew rather spoils Mark's beautiful version of this incident by inserting ' tempting Him ' (verse 35), and by omitting the Scribe's glad welcome to the answer of Jesus, and our Lord's rejoinder, ' Thou art not far from the Kingdom of God.' The eminent Jewish scholar, Mr. C. G. Montefiore, at the close of his Jowett Lectures on the Teaching of Jesus, thus comments on Mark's version :

' If, leaving other things for the moment aside, some one would say, " Here is true Christianity," then, I too, leaving other things for the moment aside, would fain also say, " Here is true Judaism." Thus, like the Scribe and Jesus, we too, the Christian and the Jew, can meet together, and so, perhaps—while each of us will still prefer the accents of his own home—we may yet, with Jesus, say of the other, " Thou art not far from the Kingdom of God." '

39. *As much as thyself*] This, of course, implies that there is a legitimate love of ' self.' ' Selfishness ' is sinful not because it includes care for one's own welfare, but because it excludes (or subordinates to this) care for the welfare of others. There is sin rather than virtue in mere self-neglect.

(vv. 41–46.) Cf. Mark xii. 35–37 ; Luke xx. 41–44. It was not the purpose of Jesus to pronounce on the authorship of the Psalm from which He quotes : questions raised by modern Biblical scholarship hardly came within the horizon of His thought ; but His opponents regarded the Psalm as written by David, and pointing forward to the Messiah. With what consistency, then, could they cling to their notion of Messiah as a purely human monarch, lineal descendant of David ? On their own assumptions as to the character of the Psalm, David speaks not of his son, but of his Lord, not of a natural, but of a supernatural being.

'If therefore David calls Him Lord, how can He be his 45 son?' No one could say a word in reply; nor from that 46 day did any one venture again to put a question to Him.

Scribes and Pharisees denounced

Then Jesus addressed the crowds and His 1 **23** disciples.

'The Scribes,' He said, 'and the Pharisees 2 sit in the chair of Moses. Therefore do and observe every- 3 thing that they command you; but do not imitate their lives, for though they tell others what to do, they do not do it themselves. Heavy and cumbrous burdens they bind 4 together and load men's shoulders with them, while as for themselves, not with one finger do they choose to move them. And everything they do is with a view to being 5 observed by men; for they widen their phylacteries, and make their tassels large, and love the best places at dinner 6 parties or in the synagogues, and like to be bowed to in places 7 of public resort, and to be addressed by men as " Rabbi."

'As for you, do not accept the title of " Rabbi," for one 8 alone is your Teacher, and you are all brothers. And call 9 no one on earth " Father," for One alone is your Father— the Heavenly Father. And do not accept the name of 10 " leaders," for your Leader is one alone—the Christ. He 11 who is the greatest among you shall be your servant; and 12 one who uplifts himself shall be humbled, while one who humbles himself shall be uplifted.

'But woe to you, Scribes and Pharisees, hypocrites, for 13 you lock the door of the Kingdom of heaven against men; you yourselves do not enter, nor do you allow those to enter who are seeking to do so.

'Woe to you, Scribes and Pharisees, hypocrites, for 15 you scour sea and land in order to make one proselyte; and when he is gained, you make him twice as much a son of Gehenna as yourselves.

'Woe to you, you blind guides, who say, 16
' " Whoever swears by the Sanctuary, it is nothing; but

(vv. 1–39.) For the most part Matthew only, but compare Luke xi. and xiii. 34, 35.

4. *And cumbrous*] v.L. omits these words.

5. *Phylacteries*] See Exod. xiii. 9; Deut. vi. 4–9, 11, 13–21. Originally a re- minder of the Law, the phylactery (Lit. ' safe-guard ') had become an amulet or ' mascot,' broadened in size to suggest superior piety.

13. v.L. adds, either here or after verse 12, ' Alas for you, Scribes and Pharisees, hypocrites ! for you devour widows' houses, even while for a pretence you make long prayers; therefore you will receive a far severer sentence !' (from Mark xii. 40).

whoever swears by the gold of the Sanctuary is bound by the oath."

' Blind fools ! Why, which is greater—the gold, or the Sanctuary which has made the gold holy ? And you say, 17 18

' " Whoever swears by the altar, it is nothing ; but whoever swears by the offering lying on it is bound by the oath."

' You are blind ! Why, which is greater — the offering, or the altar which makes the offering holy ? He who swears by the altar swears both by it and by everything on it ; he who swears by the Sanctuary swears both by it and by Him who dwells in it ; and he who swears by heaven swears both by the throne of God and by Him who sits upon it. 19 20 21 22

' Woe to you, Scribes and Pharisees, hypocrites, for you pay the tithe on mint, dill, and cummin, while you have neglected the weightier requirements of the Law—justice, mercy, and faithful dealing. These things you ought to have done, yet without leaving the others undone. You blind guides, straining out the gnat while you gulp down the camel ! 23 24

' Woe to you, Scribes and Pharisees, hypocrites, for you wash clean the outside of the cup and dish, while within they are full of greed and self-indulgence. Blind Pharisee, first wash clean the inside of the cup and dish, that the outside may be clean also. 25 26

' Woe to you, Scribes and Pharisees, hypocrites, for you are just like whitewashed sepulchres, the outside of which pleases the eye, though inside they are full of dead men's bones and of all that is unclean. The same is true of you : outwardly you seem to the human eye to be good and honest men, but, within, you are full of insincerity and lawlessness. 27 28

' Woe to you, Scribes and Pharisees, hypocrites, for you build the sepulchres of the Prophets and keep in order the tombs of the righteous ; and your boast is, 29 30

' " If we had lived in the time of our forefathers, we should not have shared with them in the murder of the Prophets."

23. Cf. Luke xi. 42.
25. Cf. Luke xi. 39.
26. *And dish*] v.l. omits these words.
29. *Keep in order*] Or ' decorate.' Cf. xii. 44, n.

'So you bear witness against yourselves that you are 31 descendants of those who murdered the Prophets. Fill 32 up the measure of your forefathers. O serpents, O brood of 33 vipers, how are you to escape condemnation to Gehenna?

'For this reason I am sending to you prophets and wise 34 men and scribes. Some of them you will put to death— nay, crucify; some of them you will flog in your syna- gogues and chase from town to town; that all the innocent 35 blood shed upon earth may come on you, from the blood of righteous Abel to the blood of Zechariah the son of Bara- chiah whom you murdered between the Sanctuary and the altar. I tell you in solemn truth that all these things 36 will come upon the present generation.

Jesus grieves over Jerusalem 'O Jerusalem, Jerusalem! that murders 37 the Prophets and stones those who have been sent to her! how often have I desired to gather your children to me, just as a hen gathers her chickens under her wings, and you would not come! See, your 38 house will now be left to you desolate! For I tell you that 39 you will never see me again until you say, "BLESSED BE HE WHO COMES IN THE NAME OF THE LORD"' (Ps. cxviii. 26).

Jesus pre- dicts the Destruction of the Temple Jesus had left the Temple and was going on 1 **24** His way, when His disciples came and called His attention to the Temple buildings.

'You see all these?' He replied; 'in 2 solemn truth I tell you that there will not be left here one stone upon another that shall not be pulled down.'

Christ's Return at the End of the Age Now when He was seated on the Mount of 3 Olives, away from the crowd, the disciples came to Him, and said,

'Tell us when this will be; and what will be the sign of your coming and of the close of the age?'

'Take care that no one misleads you,' answered Jesus; 4 'for many will come assuming my name and saying "I am 5

---

33. *Gehenna*] See chapter v. 12, n.
(vv. 34–36.) Cf. Luke xi. 49–51.
35. *Barachiah*] See 2 Chron. xxiv. 21. Barachiah appears to be a slip for Jehoiada, perhaps from a reminiscence of Zech. i. 1. Luke omits the name.
(vv. 37–39.) Cf. Luke xiii. 34, also Luke xix. 40–44.
Cf. Mark xiii; Luke xxi. The clearest outline of this eschatological discourse is in Mark. See notes there.
38. *Desolate*] v.L. omits this word. Cf. Luke xiii. 35.
3. *When this will be*] *i.e.* the destruction of the Temple. The second question is in Matthew only.

the Christ " ; and they will mislead many. And you shall 6
hear of wars and rumours of wars. See that you be not
alarmed, for such things must be ; but the end is not yet.
FOR NATION WILL RISE IN ARMS AGAINST NATION, KINGDOM 7
AGAINST KINGDOM (Isa. xix. 2), and there will be famines and
earthquakes in various places ; but all these are but like 8
the earliest pains of childbirth.

Persecution, Apostasy, and world- wide Preaching ' At that time they will deliver you up to 9
punishment and will put you to death ; and you
will be objects of hatred to all the nations on
account of my name. Then will many turn 10
against me, and they will betray one another
and hate one another. Many false prophets will rise up and 11
mislead many ; and because of the spread of lawlessness 12
the love of the great majority will grow cold ; but he who 13
stands firm to the end shall be saved. And this gospel of 14
the Kingdom shall be proclaimed throughout the whole
world to set the evidence before all the Gentiles ; and then
the end will come.

'The Abom- ination of Desolation' ' When, then, you see (to use the language 15
of the Prophet Daniel) the " ABOMINATION OF
DESOLATION " (Dan. ix. 27) standing in the
Holy Place '—let the reader observe those words—' then 16
let those who are in Judaea escape to the hills ; any one on 17
the roof should not go down to fetch his things in the
house ; nor any one in the fields go home to fetch his 18
cloak. Alas for the women who at that time are with 19
child or have infants at the breast !

Unparalleled Distress ' But pray that your flight may not be in 20
winter, nor on the Sabbath ; for it WILL BE a 21
time of great SUFFERING, SUCH AS NEVER HAS
BEEN FROM THE BEGINNING OF THE WORLD TILL NOW (Dan.

---

10. *Turn against me*] See v. 29, n. Changing the figure, we might render
' make shipwreck of faith.'

14. *The whole world*] Lit. ' all the inhabited ' (earth). The words appear to be
used in Luke ii. 1 ; Acts xi. 28 ; Rom. x. 18 ; Rev. iii. 10, of the Roman Empire
—' the world ' as known to the ancients. For the diffusion of the gospel within
these limits, even in N.T. times, see [Mark xvi. 20] ; Acts i. 8 ; Rom. xvi. 26 ;
Col. i. 6, 23.

15. ' *Abomination of Desolation* '] The reference is to an idol altar which Antiochus
Epiphanes erected in the Temple upon the altar of God. See 1 Macc. i. 54, 59 ; vi. 7 ;
2 Macc. vi. 1-5. Mark has simply the cryptic ' Abomination of Desolation stand-
ing where he ought not.' Matthew adds the reference to Daniel, and to the Holy
Place, *i.e.* either Jerusalem, or the Temple. Luke substitutes plain language,
' When you see Jerusalem being compassed by armies.'

20. *The Sabbath*] *i.e.* the Jewish Sabbath, on which the Law forbade long journeys.
Matthew only.

xii. 1), and assuredly never will be again. And if 22
those days had not been cut short, no one would
escape; but for the sake of the elect those days will
be cut short.

The Coming of the Son of Man ' If at that time any one should say to you, 23
" See, here is the Christ ! " or " Here ! " give
no credence to it. For there will rise up false 24
Christs and false prophets, displaying wonderful signs and
prodigies, so as to deceive, if possible, even the elect.
Remember, I have forewarned you. If therefore they 25, 26
should say to you, " See, He is in the Desert ! " do not go
out there : or " See, He is indoors in the room ! " do not
believe it. For just as the lightning flashes in the east 27
and shoots to the west, so will be the coming of the Son
of Man. Wherever the dead body is, there will the 28
vultures flock together.

' But immediately after those times of distress THE SUN 29
WILL BE DARKENED, THE MOON WILL NOT SHED HER LIGHT,
THE STARS WILL FALL FROM HEAVEN, AND THE FORCES WHICH
CONTROL THE HEAVENS WILL BE DISORDERED (Isa. xiii. 10 ;
xxxiv. 4). Then shall appear the Sign of the Son of Man 30
in the sky ; and THEN SHALL ALL THE NATIONS OF THE
EARTH LAMENT (Zech. xii. 12), when they see THE SON OF
MAN COMING ON THE CLOUDS OF HEAVEN (Dan. vii. 13)
with great power and glory. And He will send out His 31
angels WITH A LOUD TRUMPET-BLAST (Isa. xxvii. 13), and
THEY WILL BRING together the elect to Him FROM NORTH,
SOUTH, EAST AND WEST—FROM ONE EXTREMITY OF THE
WORLD TO THE OTHER (Deut. xxviii. 64 ; xxx. 4).

' Now learn from the fig-tree the lesson it teaches. As 32
soon as its branches have become soft and it is bursting into
leaf, you all know that summer is near. So also, when you 33
see all these signs, you may be sure that it is near, at
your very door. I tell you in solemn truth that the present 34
generation will certainly not pass away until all this has
taken place. Sky and earth will pass away, but my words 35
shall not pass away.

' But as to that day and hour no one knows—not even 36

---

22. *Been cut short*] In God's decrees.
(vv. 23–28.) Cf. Luke xvii. 21–24, 37. See notes there.
31. *With a loud trumpet-blast*] v.L. ' with the great trumpet.' Cf. ' with the trumpet of God,' 1 Thess. iv. 16.
33. *It*] *i.e.* His Coming : Cf. Luke xxi. 31 ; or 'He' : cf. James v. 9.

the angels of heaven, nor the Son, but the Father alone. For as it was in the time of Noah (Gen. vii.), so it will 37 be at the Coming of the Son of Man. At that time, before 38 the Deluge, men were busy eating and drinking, taking wives or giving them, up to the very day when Noah entered the Ark, nor did they realise any danger till the 39 Deluge came and swept them all away ; so will it be at the Coming of the Son of Man. Then will two men be in 40 the field : one will be taken away, and one left behind. Two women will be grinding at the millstone : one will 41 be taken away, and one left behind. Keep watch therefore, 42 for you do not know the day on which your Lord is coming. But of this be assured, that if the master of the house had 43 known the hour at which the robber was coming, he would have kept awake, and not have allowed his house to be broken into. Therefore you also must be ready ; for it is 44 at a time when you do not expect Him that the Son of Man will come.

Faithful and unfaithful Servants ' Who therefore is the faithful and prudent 45 servant whom his master has put in charge of his household to give them their rations at the appointed time ? Blessed is that servant whom his 46 master when he comes shall find so doing ! In solemn 47 truth I tell you that he will give him the management of all his property. But if the man, being a bad servant, 48 should say in his heart, " My master is a long time in coming," and should begin to beat his fellow servants, 49 while he eats and drinks with drunkards ; the master of that 50 servant will arrive on a day when he is not expecting him and at an hour of which he is unaware. He will cut him 51 asunder, and will assign him a place among the hypocrites : there will be the weeping and the gnashing of teeth.

The wise and foolish Bridesmaids ' Then will the Kingdom of heaven be found 1 **25** to be like ten bridesmaids who took their torches and went out to meet the bridegroom. Five 2 of them were foolish and five were wise. For the foolish, 3 when they took their torches, did not provide themselves with oil ; but the wise, besides their torches, took oil in 4

36. *Nor the Son*] v.l. omits these words. In Mark xiii. 32 their genuineness is not questioned. Luke omits the whole verse.
(vv. 37-41.) Cf. Luke xvii. 26-37. See notes there.
(vv. 43-51.) Cf. Luke xii. 39-46.
xxv. 1-12. Matthew only.

their flasks. The bridegroom was a long time in coming, 5 so that meanwhile they all became drowsy and fell asleep. But at midnight there was a loud cry, 6

' " The bridegroom ! Go out and meet him ! "

' Then all those bridesmaids roused themselves and 7 trimmed their torches.

' " Give us some of your oil," said the foolish ones to the 8 wise, " for our torches are going out."

' " But perhaps," replied the wise, " there will not be 9 enough for all of us. Go to the shops rather, and buy some for yourselves."

' So they went to buy. But meanwhile the bridegroom 10 came ; those bridesmaids who were ready went in with him to the wedding banquet ; and the door was shut.

' Afterwards the other bridesmaids came and cried, 11

' " Sir, Sir, open the door to us."

' " In truth I tell you," he replied, " I do not know you." 12

' Keep watch therefore ; for you know neither the day 13 nor the hour.

Privilege and Responsibility ' Why, it is like a man who, when going on 14 his travels, called his servants and entrusted his property to their care. To one he gave 15 five talents, to another two, to another one—to each according to his capacity ; and then started from home. Without delay the one who had received the five talents went 16 and employed them in business, and gained five more. In 17 the same way he who had the two gained two more. But 18 the man who had received the one went and dug a hole and buried his master's money.

' After a long lapse of time the master of those servants 19 returned, and had a reckoning with them. The one who 20 had received the five talents came and brought five more, and said,

' " Sir, it was five talents that you entrusted to me : see, I have gained five more."

' " You have done well, good and trustworthy servant," 21 replied his master ; " you have been trustworthy in the management of a little, I will put you in charge of much. Enter into the joy of your master."

12. Cf. Matt. vii. 23 ; Luke xiii. 25–27.
(vv. 14–30.) Cf. Luke xix. 11–27. See notes there.
21. *Enter into*] The joy is the bliss of the coming Kingdom of God.

' The second, who had received the two talents, came and 22 said,

' " Sir, it was two talents you entrusted to me : see, I have gained two more."

' " Good and trustworthy servant, you have done well," 23 his master replied ; " you have been trustworthy in the management of a little, I will put you in charge of much. Enter into the joy of your master."

' Next, the man who had the one talent in his keeping 24 came and said,

' " Sir, I knew you to be a severe man, reaping where you had not sown and garnering what you had not winnowed. So being afraid I went and buried your talent 25 in the ground : there you have what belongs to you."

' " You bad and slothful servant," replied his master, 26 " did you know that I reap where I have not sown, and garner what I have not winnowed ? Your duty then was 27 to deposit my money in some bank, and so when I came I should have got back my money with interest. So take 28 away the talent from him, and give it to the man who has the ten." (For to every one who has, more shall be given, 29 and he shall have abundance ; but from him who has nothing, even what he has shall be taken away.) " But as 30 for this worthless servant, put him out into the darkness outside : there will be the weeping and the gnashing of teeth."

' When the Son of Man comes in His glory, 31
The Great Assize and all the angels with Him, then will He sit upon His glorious throne, and all the nations 32 will be gathered into His presence. And He will separate them from one another, just as a shepherd separates the sheep from the goats ; and will make the sheep stand at 33 His right hand, and the goats at His left.

' Then the King will say to those at His right, 34

' " Come, my Father's blessed ones, inherit the Kingdom prepared for you ever since the creation of the world. For 35

---

24. *I knew you to be*] Lit. ' I had observed you, that you were.'
What] Lit. ' from (a threshing-floor) where.'
29. *Who has nothing*] *i.e.* ' who acts as though he had nothing and were responsible for nothing.' Cf. 1 Cor. ii. 14, n.
32. *Them*] The individuals composing the nations. The pronoun in the Greek here is masculine, but ' nations ' is neuter. Similarly in Acts xxvi. 17 ' whom ' (after nations) is masculine : the Gospel message is sent to the individual who hears it.
34. *Prepared*] Or ' made sure.' So verse 41. See Hosea vi. 3, comparing the A.V. with the R.V.

I was hungry, and you gave me food ; I was thirsty, and you gave me drink ; I was a stranger, and you gave me a welcome ; I was ill-clad, and you clothed me ; I was ill, and 36 you visited me ; I was in prison, and you came to see me."

' " When, Lord," the righteous will reply, " did we see 37 Thee hungry, and feed Thee ; or thirsty, and give Thee drink ? When did we see Thee a stranger, and give Thee 38 a welcome ? or ill-clad, and clothe Thee ? When did we 39 see Thee ill or in prison, and come to see Thee ? "

' And the King will answer them, 40

' " In truth I tell you that in so far as you rendered such services to one of the humblest of these my brethren, you rendered them to myself."

' Then will He say to those at His left, 41

' " Begone from me, with the curse resting upon you, into the eternal fire, which has been prepared for the Devil and his angels. For I was hungry, and you gave 42 me nothing to eat ; thirsty, and you gave me nothing to drink ; a stranger, and you gave me no welcome ; ill-clad, 43 and you clothed me not ; ill or in prison, and you visited me not."

' Then will they also answer, 44

' " Lord, when did we see Thee hungry or thirsty or a stranger or ill-clad or ill or in prison, and not come to serve Thee ? "

' Then He will reply, 45

' " In truth I tell you that in so far as you withheld such services from one of the humblest of these, you withheld them from me."

' And these shall go away into eternal punishment, but 46 the righteous into eternal life.'

When Jesus had ended all these sayings, He said to 1 **26** His disciples,

' You know that in two days' time the Passover comes. 2 And the Son of Man will be delivered up to be crucified.'

The Plot to murder Jesus Then the High Priests and Elders of the 3 people assembled in the court of the palace of the High Priest Caiaphas, and consulted how to 4 get Jesus into their power by stratagem and to put Him to death. But they said, 5

37. *Thee*] Emphatic. So throughout verses 37, 38, 39.
(vv. 1—5.) Cf. Mark xiv. 1, 2 ; Luke xxii. 1, 2.

' Not during the Festival, lest there be a riot among the people.'

Affection's costly Gift Now when Jesus was come to Bethany and 6 was at the house of Simon the Leper, a woman 7 came to Him with an alabaster jar of very costly ointment, which she poured over His head as He reclined at table.

' Why such waste ? ' indignantly exclaimed the disciples ; 8 ' this might have been sold for a considerable sum, and the 9 money given to the poor.'

Jesus heard it, and said to them, 10

' Why are you vexing her ? It is a gracious thing that she has done to me. The poor you always have 11 with you, but me you have not always. In pouring 12 this ointment over me, her object was to prepare me for burial. In truth I tell you that wherever 13 in the whole world this gospel shall be proclaimed, this deed of hers shall be spoken of in memory of her.'

The Treachery of Judas At that time one of the twelve, called Judas 14 Iscariot, went to the High Priests and said, 15 ' What are you willing to give me if I betray Him to you ? '

So they weighed out to him thirty shekels (Zech. xi. 12), and from that moment he was on the watch for an oppor- 16 tunity to betray Him.

The Disciples prepare the Passover On the first day of the Unleavened Bread 17 the disciples came to Jesus with the question, ' Where shall we make preparations for you to eat the Passover ? '

' Go into the city,' He replied, ' to a certain man, and tell 18 him, " The Teacher says, My time is close at hand. It is at your house that I shall keep the Passover with my disciples." '

The disciples did as Jesus directed them, and got the 19 Passover ready.

(vv. 6–13.) Cf. Mark xiv. 3–9 ; John xii. 1–11 ; also Luke vii. 36–50.
7. *A woman*] In John the woman is named, Mary, sister of Martha and Lazarus. See Luke viii. 2, n.
(vv. 14–16.) Cf. Mark xiv. 10, 11 ; Luke xxii. 3–6. Only Matthew represents Judas as bargaining for the price of betrayal.
(vv. 17–19.) Compare the more detailed descriptions of Mark xiv. 12–16 ; Luke xxii. 7–13. No miraculous foresight is necessary. Jesus may have made a pre-arrangement with a secret disciple.

'The Last Supper': The Traitor indicated When evening came, He was at table with the twelve disciples, and the meal was proceeding, when Jesus said, 20 21

' In solemn truth I tell you that one of you will betray me.'

Intensely grieved they began one after another to ask Him, 22 ' Can it be I, Master ? '

' One who has dipped his fingers in the bowl with me ' 23 He answered, ' is the man who will betray me. The Son 24 of Man goes His way as is written concerning Him ; but alas for that man by whom the Son of Man is betrayed ! It were better for that man if he had never been born.'

Then Judas, the disciple who was betraying Him, asked, 25 ' Can it be I, Rabbi ? '

' It is you,' He replied.

The memorial Meal instituted During the meal Jesus took a Passover loaf, 26 blessed it and broke it. He then gave it to the disciples, saying,

' Take this and eat it : it is my body.'

And He took a cup, and after a thanksgiving gave it to 27 them, saying,

' Drink from it, all of you ; for this is my blood, poured 28 out for many for the forgiveness of sins—the blood of the Covenant. I tell you that I will never again drink the 29 juice of the vine till the day when I drink the new wine with you in my Father's Kingdom.'

So they sang a hymn and went out to the Mount of Olives. 30

Peter's Denial foretold Then said Jesus, 31 ' This night all of you will turn against me ; for it is written, " I WILL STRIKE THE SHEPHERD, AND THE SHEEP OF THE FLOCK WILL BE SCATTERED IN ALL DIRECTIONS " (Zech. xiii. 7). But after 32 I have risen to life again I will go before you into Galilee.

(vv. 20-30.) Cf. Mark xiv. 17-26 ; Luke xxii. 14-38. It will be observed that Luke's version of the Last Supper and the talk with the disciples varies considerably from that of Matthew and Mark. See notes on Luke xxii.

25. *It is you*] Lit. ' you have said ' ; a formula of assent. So verse 64, and xxvii. 11.

28. *The Covenant*] v.L. ' the New Covenant,' as in Luke xxii. 20.

30. *A hymn*] Probably part of the Hallel Psalms (cxiii.–cxviii.) chanted at intervals during the Passover meal. In this hour of troubled foreboding Jesus and the disciples united in the repeated, ' Praise ye the Lord ' of the Psalms, and passed out into the night with the echo in their ears of the last words of their hymn, ' O give thanks unto the Lord ; for He is good : for His mercy endureth for ever.'

32. So Mark. A prediction strange in itself, and as breaking the connection between verse 31 and 33. Luke, who records appearances only in Jerusalem, alters it (xxiv. 6).

' All may turn against you,' said Peter, ' but I will 33
never do so.'

' In truth I tell you,' replied Jesus, ' that this very 34
night, before the cock crows, you will three times disown
me.'

' Even if I must die with you,' declared Peter, ' I will 35
never disown you.'

In like manner protested all the disciples.

The Agony in Gethsemane Then Jesus came with them to a place 36
called Gethsemane. And He said to the
disciples,

' Sit down here, whilst I go yonder and there
pray.'

And He took with Him Peter and the two sons of 37
Zebedee. Then He began to be full of anguish and
distress, and He said to them, 38

' My soul is crushed with anguish to the point of death ;
wait here, and watch with me.'

Going forward a short distance He fell on His face and 39
prayed. ' My Father,' He said, ' if it is possible, let this
cup pass away from me ; nevertheless, not as I will, but as
Thou willest.'

Then He came to the disciples and found them asleep, 40
and He said to Peter,

' So none of you could keep awake with me for a single
hour ! Keep awake, and pray that you may not enter into 41
temptation : the spirit is right willing, but the body is
frail.'

Again a second time He went away and prayed, 42

' My Father, if it is impossible for this cup to pass without my drinking it, Thy will be done.'

He came and again found them asleep, for they were 43
very weary. So He left them, and went away once more 44
and prayed a third time, again using the same words.
Then He came to the disciples and said, 45

' Sleep on and rest. See, the moment is close at hand
when the Son of Man is to be betrayed into the hands of

34. *Before the cock crows*] *i.e.* ' before daybreak.'
(vv. 36–46.) Cf. Mark xiv. 32–42 ; Luke xxii. 40–46.
41. *Temptation*] The temptation is the coming trial of His arrest. ' Keep awake, and pray, lest it surprise you unprepared.'
Body] Or ' human nature.' Lit. ' flesh.'
43. *They were very weary*] Lit. ' their eyes were heavy.'

sinful men. Rouse yourselves. Let us be going. My 46
betrayer is close at hand.'

Judas brings armed Men While He was still speaking, Judas, one of 47
the twelve, came up, accompanied by a great
crowd of men armed with swords and blud-
geons, sent by the High Priests and Elders of the people.
Now the betrayer had agreed upon a signal with them, 48
saying,

' The one whom I kiss is the man : lay hold of Him.'

So he went straight to Jesus and said, 49

' Peace to you, Rabbi ! '

And he kissed Him affectionately.

' Friend,' said Jesus, ' carry out your intention.' 50

Then they came and laid their hands on Jesus and
seized Him. But one of those with Jesus drew his 51
sword and struck the High Priest's servant, cutting off
his ear.

' Put back your sword again,' said Jesus, ' for all who 52
draw the sword shall perish by the sword. Or do you 53
suppose I cannot entreat my Father and He would instantly
send to my help more than twelve legions of angels ? In 54
that case how are the Scriptures to be fulfilled which
declare that thus it must be ? '

Then said Jesus to the crowds, 55

Jesus expostulates. The Apostles flee ' Have you come out as if to fight with a
robber, with swords and bludgeons to take me ?
Day after day I have been sitting teaching in
the Temple, and you did not arrest me. But 56
all this has taken place in order that the writings of the
Prophets may be fulfilled.'

Then the disciples all left Him and fled.

(vv. 47–56.) Cf. Mark xiv. 43–52 ; Luke xxii. 47–53 ; John xviii. 2–11.

49. *Affectionately*] Or ' effusively,' that is with a great pretence of affection. Cf.
' Faithful are the wounds of a friend, but the kisses of an enemy are profuse ' (Prov.
xxvii. 6, R.V.). The same word is used in Mark xiv. 45 ; Luke vii. 38, 45 ; xv. 20 ;
Acts xx. 37. The simple and less emphatic word is employed in verse 48 ; Mark xiv.
44 ; Luke xxii. 47. John does not mention the kiss. Luke xxii. 47, 48 seems to
suggest that Jesus prevented it.

50. *Carry out your intention*] The Greek is elliptical, ' That for which you are come,'
and will hardly bear the A.V. ' Wherefore art thou come ? ' Probably, ' Do that
for which you are come '; *i.e.* ' get it over '; an exclamation from a heart over-
strained. Cf. John xiii. 27, ' That thou doest, do quickly.'

53. *Or do you suppose . . angels*] Matthew only. Compare the absolute mastery
of the situation ascribed to Jesus in John xviii. 6.

56. *But . . fulfilled*] Mark xiv. 49 assigns to our Lord the elliptical ' But that
the Scriptures might be fulfilled.' Matthew expands this saying in verse 54, and here
adds his own familiar comment.

Jesus arrested and taken to Caiaphas But the officers who had laid hold of Jesus 57 led Him away to Caiaphas the High Priest, at whose house the Scribes and the Elders had assembled. And Peter kept following at a 58 distance, till he came to the court of the High Priest's palace, where he entered and sat down among the officers to see the issue.

False Testimony and gross Insults Meanwhile the High Priests and the whole 59 Sanhedrin were seeking false testimony against Jesus in order to put Him to death; but they 60 could find none, although many false witnesses came forward. At length there came two who testified, 61

'This man said, "I am able to pull down the Sanctuary of God and three days afterwards to build a new one."'

Then the High Priest stood up and asked Him, 62

'Have you no answer to make? What is this evidence they are bringing against you?'

Jesus however remained silent. Again the High Priest 63 addressed Him.

'In the name of the living God,' he said, 'I now put you on your oath Tell us whether you are the Christ, the Son of God.'

'I am He,' replied Jesus. 'And I tell you all that, 64 hereafter you shall see THE SON OF MAN SITTING AT THE RIGHT HAND OF THE DIVINE POWER, AND COMING ON THE CLOUDS OF HEAVEN' (Ps. cx. 1; Dan. vii. 13).

Then the High Priest tore his robes, and exclaimed, 65

'Impious words! What further need have we of witnesses! See, you have now heard His impiety. What is 66 your verdict?'

'He deserves to die,' they replied.

Then they spat in His face, and struck Him—some with 67 the fist, some with the open hand, saying, 68

'Christ, prove yourself a Prophet by telling us who it was that struck you.'

(vv. 57, 58 and 69–75.) Cf. Mark xiv. 53, 54, and 66–72; Luke xxii. 54–62; John xviii. 12–18.

63. *I now put you on your oath*] Cf. Exod. xxii. 11; Num. v. 19–22; 1 Kings viii. 31. Jesus by replying, instead of remaining silent, accepted the oath which the High Priest administered to Him. This clearly proves that the prohibition of v. 34 was not meant to apply to judicial oaths.

64. *I am He*] Lit. (it is as) 'you have said.' Cf. verse 25; xxvii. 11; John vi. 36. *Hereafter*] Or 'before long,' 'in the near future.' Lit 'from now.' Cf. the Scotch and north of England use of 'just now' referring to the future in cases where a Londoner says 'directly,' 'immediately.' Cf. Luke xxii. 69.

68. *Prove yourself . . struck you*] Lit. 'prophesy to us. Who is it that struck you?' In Mark and Luke, Jesus is blindfolded.

Peter disowns his Master Peter meanwhile was sitting outside in the 69 court of the palace, when one of the maid-servants came over to him and said,

'You too were with Jesus the Galilaean.'

He denied it before them all, saying, 70

'I do not know what you mean.'

Soon afterwards he went out and stood in the gateway, 71 when another girl saw him, and said, addressing the people there,

'This man was with Jesus the Nazarene.'

Again he denied it with an oath. 72

'I do not know the man,' he said.

A short time afterwards the people standing there came 73 and said to Peter,

'Certainly you too are one of them, for your accent shows it.'

Then with curses and oaths he declared, 74

'I do not know the man.'

Immediately a cock crowed, and Peter recollected the 75 words of Jesus, how He had said,

'Before the cock crows you will three times disown me.'

And he went out and wept aloud, bitterly.

Jesus taken before the Roman Governor When morning came all the High Priests 1 **27** and the Elders of the people consulted together against Jesus to put Him to death ; and binding 2 Him they led Him away and handed Him over to Pilate the Governor.

The Remorse of Judas Then when Judas, who had betrayed Him, 3 saw that He was condemned, smitten with remorse he brought back the thirty shekels to the High Priests and Elders and said, 4

'I have sinned in betraying to death one who is innocent.'

'What does that matter to us ? ' they replied ; 'it is your business.'

Flinging the shekels into the Sanctuary, he left the place, 5 and went and hanged himself. When the High Priests had 6 gathered up the money, they said,

---

75. *Aloud bitterly*] Or ' with bitter sobs and cries.' The verb here used for ' wept ' does not signify the silent shedding of tears, although another verb does in John xi. 35.

(vv. 1, 2.) Cf. Mark xv. 1 ; Luke xxiii. 1 ; John xviii. 28.

(vv. 3–10.) Cf. Acts i. 18, 19. The differences are apparent.

'It is illegal to put it into the Treasury, because it is the price of blood.'

So after consulting together they spent the money in 7 the purchase of the Potter's Field as a burial place for people not belonging to the city; for which reason that 8 piece of ground received the name, which it still bears, of 'the Field of Blood.'

Then were fulfilled the words spoken by the Prophet 9 Jeremiah, 'AND I TOOK THE THIRTY SHEKELS, THE PRICE OF THE ONE WHO WAS PRICED, ON WHOM SOME OF THE ISRAELITES HAD SET A PRICE, AND GAVE THEM FOR THE 10 POTTER'S FIELD, AS THE LORD DIRECTED ME' (Zech. xi. 13).

Pilate questions Jesus Meanwhile Jesus was brought before the 11 Governor, and the latter put the question, 'Are you the King of the Jews?'

'I am,' He answered.

When, however, the High Priests and the Elders 12 brought their charges against Him, He said not a word in reply.

'Do you not hear,' asked Pilate, 'what a mass of 13 evidence they are bringing against you?'

But He made no reply to a single accusation, so that 14 the Governor was greatly astonished.

Jesus sentenced to Death Now it was the Governor's custom at the 15 Festival to release some one prisoner, whom-soever the populace desired; and at this time 16 they had a notorious prisoner called Barabbas. So 17 when they were now assembled Pilate appealed to them.

'Whom shall I release to you,' he said, 'Barabbas, or Jesus the so-called Christ?'

For he knew that it was from envious hatred that Jesus 18 had been brought before him.

While he was sitting on the tribunal a message came to 19 him from his wife.

'Have nothing to do with that innocent man,' she said,

(vv. 11-14.) Cf. Mark xv. 2-5; Luke xxiii. 3-5; John xviii. 33-38.
11. *I am*] Cf. xxvi. 25, 64.
(vv. 15-23.) Cf. Mark xv. 6-14; Luke xxiii. 18-23; John xviii. 39, 40.
17. *Barabbas*] A very interesting v.l. known to Origen and having some support from manuscripts and versions is 'Jesus Barabbas.' The omission of the name 'Jesus' from motives of reverence is more likely than its insertion. 'Jesus Barabbas' is quite probably genuine.
19. Pilate's wife's dream and the hand-washing of verse 24; Matthew only.

' for during the night I have suffered terribly in a dream through him.'

The High Priests, however, and the Elders persuaded 20 the crowd to ask for Barabbas and to demand the death of Jesus. So when the Governor a second time asked them, 21 ' Which of the two shall I release to you ? '—they cried,

' Barabbas ! '

' What then,' said Pilate, ' shall I do with Jesus, the 22 so-called Christ ? '

With one voice they shouted,

' Let him be crucified ! '

' But what crime has he committed ? ' asked Pilate. 23 They however kept on furiously shouting,

' Let him be crucified ! '

So when he saw that he could gain nothing, but that 24 on the contrary there was a riot threatening, he called for water and washed his hands in sight of them all, saying,

' I am not responsible for this murder : you must answer for it.'

' His blood,' replied all the people, ' be on us and on 25 our children ! '

Then he released Barabbas to them ; but he had Jesus 26 scourged, and gave Him up to be crucified.

Then the Governor's soldiers took Jesus into 27 **Jesus made Sport of** the Praetorium, and called together the whole battalion to make sport of Him. Stripping 28 off His garments, they put on Him a scarlet cloak. They 29 twisted a wreath of thorny twigs and put it on His head, and as a sceptre they put a cane in His right hand, and kneeling to Him they shouted in mockery,

' Long live the King of the Jews ! '

Then they spat upon Him, and taking the cane they 30 repeatedly struck Him on the head with it. At last, having 31 finished their sport, they took off the cloak, clothed Him again in His own garments, and led Him away for crucifixion.

Going out they met a Cyrenean named Simon ; whom 32

(vv. 24–30.) Cf. Mark xv. 15–19 ; Luke xxiii. 24, 25 ; John xix. 1–16.
24. *Not responsible for this murder*] Lit. ' guiltless of this blood.' v.l. ' guiltless of the blood of this innocent man.'
(vv. 31–34.) Cf. Mark xv. 20–23 ; Luke xxiii. 26–33 ; John xix. 16, 17.

Jesus taken to Golgotha and crucified they compelled to carry His cross, and so 33 they came to a place called Golgotha, which means 'Skull-ground.' Here they gave Him 34 a mixture of wine and gall to drink, but having tasted it He refused to drink it. After crucifying Him, they divided 35 His garments among them by lot, and sat down there on 36 guard. Over His head they placed a written statement of 37 the charge against Him :

THIS IS JESUS THE KING OF THE JEWS.

At the same time two robbers were crucified with Him, 38 one at His right hand and the other at His left.

The Crowd reviles Him And the passers-by reviled Him. They 39 shook their heads at Him and said, 40 'You who would pull down the Sanctuary and build a new one within three days, save yourself. If you are God's Son, come down from the cross.'

In like manner the High Priests also, together with the 41 Scribes and the Elders, taunted Him.

'He saved others,' they said, 'himself he cannot save ! 42 He is the King of Israel ! Let him now come down from the cross, and we will believe in him. His trust is in God : 43 let God deliver him now, if He will have him ; for he said, " I am God's Son." '

Insults of the same kind were heaped on Him even by 44 the robbers who were crucified with Him.

Jesus dies Now from noon until three o'clock in the 45 afternoon there was darkness over the whole land ; and about three o'clock Jesus cried out in a loud voice, 46 'ELI, ELI, LEMA SABACHTHANI ? ' that is to say, 'MY GOD, MY GOD, WHY HAST THOU FORSAKEN ME ? ' (Ps. xxii. 1).

'The man is calling for Elijah,' said some of the by- 47 standers.

---

34. *Wine and gall*] Mark xv. 23 has ' Wine mingled with myrrh ' ; a narcotic, said to have been provided by the women of Jerusalem to deaden the pains of crucifixion. Matthew seems to have changed this act of mercy into one of derision, under the influence of Psalm lxix. 21.

(vv. 35-38.) Cf. Mark xv. 24-27 ; Luke xxiii. 33, 34, 38 ; John xix. 18-24.

(vv. 39-44.) Cf. Mark xv. 29-32 ; Luke xxiii. 35-37 and 39-43 ; John xix. 25-27.

42. *Himself he cannot save*] Or ' Can he not save himself ? '

(vv. 45-50.) Cf. Mark xv. 33-37 ; Luke xxiii. 44-46 ; John xix. 28-30.

45. *Land*] Or ' earth.'

46. *Eli, Eli, Lema Sabachthani ?*] The first words of Psalm xxii. ; and it is at least possible that the second part of the Psalm, vv.22-31, with its notes of praise and victory, was also in our Lord's thought, if not even upon His lips.

47. *The man*] Or, more contemptuously still, ' The fellow.'

One of them ran forthwith, and filling a sponge with 48
sour wine put it on the end of a cane and offered it Him to
drink ; while the rest said, 49

' Stay ! Let us see whether Elijah is coming to deliver
him.'

Then Jesus uttered another loud cry, and yielded up 50
His spirit.

Marvels follow Immediately the curtain of the Sanctuary 51
was torn in two from top to bottom : the earth
quaked ; the rocks split ; the tombs opened ; 52
and many of the saints who were asleep in death awoke.
And coming out of their tombs after Christ's resurrec- 53
tion they entered the holy city and showed themselves
to many.

The Soldiers are terrified As for the Captain and his soldiers who were 54
with him keeping guard over Jesus, when they
witnessed the earthquake and the other occur-
rences, they were filled with terror, and exclaimed,

' Assuredly He was God's Son.'

And there were there, looking on from a distance, a 55
number of women who had followed Jesus from Galilee in
attendance upon Him ; among them being Mary of Magdaia, 56
Mary the mother of James and Joses, and the mother of
the sons of Zebedee.

Joseph of Arimathaea buries the Body of Jesus Towards sunset there came a wealthy in- 57
habitant of Arimathaea, named Joseph, who
had himself become a disciple of Jesus. He 58
went to Pilate and begged to have the body of
Jesus, and Pilate ordered it to be given to him. So Joseph 59

---

48. *Sour wine*] Probably the posca, a thin sour wine, the ordinary drink of the Roman
soldiers. The act of kindness is met by a jeering protest. In Mark xv. 36 it appears
as an attempt to keep life in Him a little longer ' in case Elijah may really come.'
(vv. 51-56.) Cf. Mark xv. 38-41 ; Luke xxiii. 45, 47-49.

51. *Curtain of the Sanctuary*] There were two curtains or veils, one at the entrance
into the Holy Place, the other separating this from the Holy of Holies. Only the rending of the former could be seen by all ; perhaps, however, the latter is meant, seen
and reported by the priests who at the moment were in the Holy Place. Cf. Heb. ix.
8 ; x. 19, 20.

From top to bottom] And therefore not by human hands.

The earth quaked ; the rocks split ; the tombs opened] Matthew only. Perhaps a traditional heightening of the wonders of the darkness and the rent veil. Such portents
attending a notable death seem to belong rather to the atmosphere of pagan supersti-
tion than of Christian faith. See Shakespeare's *Julius Caesar*, Act 1, Sc. 3 ; Act 2,
Sc. 2. The portents are closely connected with the death : the ' after His
Resurrection ' of verse 53 looks like a later insertion due to 1 Cor. xv. 20.
(vv. 57-61.) Cf. Mark xv. 42-47 ; Luke xxiii. 50-56 ; John xix. 38-42.

57. *Towards sunset*] Lit. ' when evening was come,' *i.e.* just before the Sabbath
began ; but by ' evening ' is meant the interval between three o'clock and sunset. See
Exod. xii. 6 and margin ; Deut. xxi. 23.

took the body and wrapped it in clean linen. He then 60
laid it in his own new tomb which he had hewn in the
solid rock, and after rolling a great stone against the door
of the tomb he went home. Mary of Magdala and the 61
other Mary were both present there, sitting opposite to
the sepulchre.

The High Priests take Precautions On the next day, the day after the Prepara- 62
tion, the High Priests and the Pharisees came in
a body to Pilate.

' Sir,' they said, ' we recollect that during his lifetime 63
that impostor pretended that after three days he was to rise
to life again. So give orders for the sepulchre to be 64
securely guarded till the third day, for fear his disciples
should go and steal the body, and then tell the people
that he has come back to life ; and so the last imposture will
be more serious than the first.'

' You can have a guard,' said Pilate : ' go and make all 65
safe, as best you can.'

So they went there and made the sepulchre secure, 66
sealing the stone, besides setting the guard.

The Women find the Tomb empty After the Sabbath, in the early dawn of the 1 **28**
first day of the week, Mary of Magdala and the
other Mary came to see the sepulchre. But to 2
their surprise there had been a great earthquake ; for
an angel of the Lord had descended from heaven, and had
come and rolled back the stone, and was sitting upon it.
His appearance was like lightning, and his raiment white 3
as snow. For fear of him the guards trembled violently, 4
and became like dead men. But the angel said to the 5
women,

' Dismiss your fears. I know that it is Jesus that you
are looking for—the crucified One. He is not here : 6
He has come back to life, as He foretold. Come and
see the place where He lay. And go quickly and tell 7
His disciples that He has risen from the dead and is going
before you into Galilee : there you shall see Him. Remember, I have told you.'

60. *New tomb*] There was a felt appropriateness in no one having been buried there
before. Cf. John xix. 41 ; Luke xxiii. 53 ; Mark xv. 46.
(vv. 1-4.) Cf. Mark xvi. 1-4 ; Luke xxiv. 1-3 ; John xx. 1.
(vv. 5-7.) Cf. Mark xvi. 5-7 ; Luke xxiv. 4-8.
6. *Where He lay*] v.L. ' where the Lord lay.'
Cf. Mark xvi. 8 ; Luke xxiv. 9-11 ; John xx. 2.

Jesus Himself meets them They quickly left the tomb and ran, still 8 terrified but full of unspeakable joy, to carry the news to His disciples. And then suddenly they 9 saw Jesus coming to meet them.

' Peace be to you,' He said.

And they came and clasped His feet, bowing to the ground before Him. Then He said, 10

' Dismiss all fear ! Go and take word to my brethren to go into Galilee, and there they shall see me.'

The High Priests bribe the Sentries While they went on this errand, some of the 11 guards came into the city and reported to the High Priests all that had happened. So the 12 latter held a conference with the Elders, and after consultation with them they heavily bribed the soldiers, telling 13 them to say,

' His disciples came during the night and stole his body while we were asleep.'

' And if this,' they added, ' is reported to the Governor, 14 we will satisfy him and screen you from punishment.'

So they took the money and did as they were instructed ; 15 and this story was spread about among the Jews, and is current to this day.

The World-wide Mission of the Apostles As for the eleven disciples, they proceeded 16 to Galilee, to the hill where Jesus had arranged to meet them. There they saw Him and 17 prostrated themselves before Him. Yet some doubted.

Jesus however came near and said to them, 18

' All authority in heaven and on earth has been given to me. Go therefore and make disciples of all the nations ; 19 baptize them into the name of the Father, and of the Son, and of the Holy Spirit ; and teach them to obey every 20 command which I have given you. And remember, I am with you always, day by day, until the close of the age.'

(vv. 9–10.) Cf. Mark xvi. 9–11 ; John xx. 11–18.

14. *Is reported, &c.*] Lit. ' shall have been heard before the Governor ' (as sitting judicially).

19. *Therefore*] v.L. omits this word.

Into] Or ' unto.' Baptism into the threefold name is unique in the N.T. Elsewhere Christian baptism is into, or upon the one name of Jesus Christ.

THE GOSPEL ACCORDING TO ST. MARK

CHARACTERISTICS OF ST. MARK

In *substance* a noteworthy feature is the small space given to the teaching of Jesus. Perhaps the Roman Church already possessed a copy of Q (see p. xvi), but needed more information about the historical facts, a tale told and retold in every bazaar of Palestine. Yet, though we miss from *St. Mark* the Sermon on the Mount, the Lord's Prayer, all the parables except four, and find in chapter xiii. the only extended discourse, even the first section of the ministry (i. 21–iii. 6) shows plainly the stress laid upon teaching as the chosen work of Christ, and a misgiving lest the Teacher should be submerged in the Healer. It is to Mark also that we owe the clearest outline of our Lord's ministry as it actually happened, up to the confession of Caesarea Philippi and thenceforward along the way of the Cross. More than one-third of the Gospel is devoted to the last week in Jerusalem : the fragmentary narrative becomes a diary.

In *form* the story is marked by a vividness of narration, both as a whole and in its parts. This shortest of the Gospels yet finds room for lifelike touches—a look, movement, emotion, or pregnant word—which are absent from Matthew and Luke. Compare, for example, the three records of the cure of the Gerasene demoniac and of the epileptic boy (Mark v. and ix.). Surely Mark received his graphic tale from the lips of an eye-witness ?

For the problem of the last twelve verses see note at xvi. 9.

THE GOSPEL ACCORDING TO ST. MARK

The beginning of the gospel of Jesus Christ, 1 **1**
the Son of God.

John the Baptist preaches Repentance

As it is written in Isaiah the Prophet, 2

' SEE, I AM SENDING MY MESSENGER BEFORE
THY FACE,

WHO WILL PREPARE THY WAY ' (Mal. iii. 1) ;

' THE VOICE OF ONE CRYING ALOUD : 3

" IN THE DESERT PREPARE A ROAD FOR THE LORD :

MAKE HIS HIGHWAYS STRAIGHT " ' (Isa. xl. 3).

So John the Baptizer came, and was in the Desert, pro- 4
claiming a baptism of the penitent for forgiveness of sins.
There went out to him people of all classes from Judaea, 5
and from the inhabitants of Jerusalem, and were baptized
by him in the river Jordan, making open confession
of their sins.

He predicts Christ's Appearing and Work

John's clothing was of camel's hair, and 6
he wore a leather girdle ; and his food was
locusts and wild honey. His proclamation 7
was,

' There is One coming after me mightier than I—One
whose sandal-strap I am unworthy to stoop down and
unfasten. I have baptized you with water, but He will 8
baptize you with the Holy Spirit.'

The Baptism of Jesus

At that time Jesus came from Nazareth in 9
Galilee and was baptized by John in the Jordan ;
and immediately on His coming up out of the 10
water He saw the sky parting asunder, and the Spirit like a

(vv. 1–6.) Cf. Matt. iii. 1–10 ; Luke iii. 1–14.
1. *The Son of God*] V.L. omits these words.
3. *Crying aloud in the Desert*] See Matt. iii. 3, n.
4. *The Baptizer*] Lit. ' the baptizing ' (man).
(vv. 7, 8.) Cf. Matt. iii. 11, 12 ; Luke iii. 15–18.
(vv. 9–11.) Cf. Matt. iii. 13–17 ; Luke iii. 21, 22.
10. *Immediately*] The Greek word here used (which may also be rendered by
' forthwith,' ' straightway,' ' directly,' ' at once ') occurs very frequently in this
Gospel. It is found in Matthew 15 times, in Luke 7 times, in John 4 times, but in
Mark 37 times.

dove coming down upon Him ; and a voice came from the 11 sky, saying,

' Thou art My Son, the Beloved : in Thee is My delight ' (Ps. ii. 7 ; Isa. xlii. 1).

Jesus is tempted in the Desert At once the Spirit impelled Him to go out 12 into the Desert, where He remained for forty 13 days, tempted by Satan ; and He was among the wild beasts, but the angels waited upon Him.

Jesus begins to preach Then, after John had been thrown into 14 prison, Jesus came into Galilee proclaiming the gospel of God.

' The time has fully come,' He said, ' and the Kingdom of 15 God is close at hand : repent, and believe this Good News.'

Four Disciples called One day, passing along the shore of the Lake 16 of Galilee, He saw Simon and Andrew, Simon's brother, throwing their nets in the Lake ; for they were fishermen.

' Come and follow me,' said Jesus, ' and I will make 17 you fishers for men.'

At once they left their nets and followed Him. Going 18, 19 on a little further He saw James the son of Zebedee and his brother John : they also were in their boat mending the nets, and He immediately called them. They therefore 20 left their father Zebedee in the boat with the hired men, and followed Him.

Jesus cures a Demoniac So they came to Capernaum. And on the 21 next Sabbath He went to the synagogue and began to teach. The people listened with 22 amazement to His teaching ; for there was authority about it : it was very different from that of the Scribes. All at 23 once, a man with a foul spirit in their synagogue screamed out :

' What have you to do with us, Jesus the Nazarene ? 24 Have you come to destroy us ? I know who you are— God's Holy One.'

(vv. 12, 13.) Cf. Matt. iv. 1-11 ; Luke iv. 1-13.
(vv. 14-20.) Cf. Matt. iv. 12-22 ; Luke iv. 14.
14. *Thrown into prison*] See Matt. iv. 12, n.
(vv. 21-28.) Cf. Luke iv. 31-37.
It is significant that this Gospel which records so little of the teaching of Jesus opens with a vivid picture of Him as Teacher, etched in in two strokes. There is no hint of what He taught : simply, He taught, and men were amazed ; but the ' spreading fame ' of verse 28 was not the fame of the Teacher, but of one who could cast out demons. The sequel plainly shows how the desire to preach had constantly to contend with the importunity of sick folk wanting to be healed.

But Jesus rebuked the spirit, saying, 25
' Silence ! come out of him.'

So the foul spirit, after throwing the man into con- 26
vulsions, came out of him with a loud cry. And all were 27
awe-struck, so that they began to ask one another,
' What does this mean ? Here is a new sort of teaching
—and a tone of authority ! Even to foul spirits he issues
orders and they obey him ! '

And His fame spread at once everywhere through all the 28
surrounding country of Galilee.

Peter's Mother-in-Law cured Then on leaving the synagogue they came 29
at once, with James and John, to the house of
Simon and Andrew. Now Simon's mother-in- 30
law was ill in bed with a fever, and without delay they told
Him about her. So He went to her, and taking her hand 31
He raised her to her feet : the fever left her, and she began
to wait upon them.

Many other Cures When it was evening, after sunset, people 32
came bringing Him all who were ill and the
demoniacs ; and the whole town was assembled 33
at the door. And He cured numbers of people who were ill 34
with various diseases, and He drove out many demons ; not
allowing the demons to speak, because they knew Him.

Jesus preaches throughout Galilee In the morning He rose early, while it was 35
still quite dark, and leaving the house He
went away to a solitary place and there prayed.
And Simon and the others searched everywhere 36
for Him. When they found Him they said, 37
' Every one is looking for you.'

He replied, ' Let us go elsewhere, to the neighbouring 38
country towns, in order that I may preach there also ;
because for that purpose I came forth.'

And He went through all Galilee, preaching in the syna- 39
gogues and expelling the demons.

A Leper cleansed One day there came a leper to Jesus en- 40
treating Him, and pleading on his knees.
' If you are willing,' he said, ' you are
able to cleanse me.'

(vv. 29–31.) Cf. Matt. viii. 14, 15 ; Luke iv. 38, 39.
(vv. 35–39.) Cf. Luke iv. 42–44. Not in Matthew, except iv. 23.
38. *I came forth*] *i.e.* from Capernaum. The same verb as in verse 35. Luke alters
to ' was sent,' *i.e.* from God.

Moved with pity Jesus reached out His hand and touched 41
him.

'I am willing,' He said ; 'be cleansed.'

The leprosy at once left him, and he was cleansed.   Jesus 42, 43
at once sent him away, sternly charging him, and saying, 44
'Be careful not to tell any one, but go and show yourself
to the Priest, and for your purification present the offerings
that Moses appointed as evidence to them.'

But the man went out and began to tell every one and to 45
spread the news in all directions, so that it was no longer
possible for Jesus to go openly into any town ; but He had to
remain outside in unfrequented places, and people came to
Him from all parts.

After some days He entered Capernaum 1 **2**

A paralysed again, and it soon became known that He was
Man cured at home ; and such numbers of people came 2
together that there was no longer room for them even round
the door.   He was speaking the word to them, when 3
there came a party of people bringing a paralysed man—
four men carrying him.   Finding themselves unable, how- 4
ever, to bring him to Jesus because of the crowd, they un-
tiled the roof just over His head, and after clearing an
opening they lowered the mat on which the paralytic was
lying.

Seeing their faith, Jesus said to the paralytic, 5
'My son, your sins are pardoned.'

Now there were some of the Scribes sitting there, who 6
reasoned in their hearts,

'Why does this man use such words ? he is blasphem- 7
ing.   Who can pardon sins but One—that is, God ? '

At once becoming aware that they were thus reasoning 8
in their minds, Jesus asked them,

'Why do you thus argue in your minds ?   Which is 9
easier ?—to say to this paralytic, " Your sins are pardoned,"
or to say, " Rise, take up your mat, and walk " ? But 10
that you may know that the Son of Man has authority on
earth to pardon sins '—

43. *Sent him away*] Lit. ' In indignation against him, He forthwith drove him
away.'   The impulse of compassion and the ready act of healing are followed by
apprehension of that hindrance to His chosen work of teaching, from which His
withdrawal from Capernaum was an escape ; and verse 45 shows that the misgiving
was well founded.

(vv. 1–12.) Cf. Matt. ix. 1–8 ; Luke v. 17–26.

10. *Son of Man*] See ii. 28, n.

He turned to the paralytic, and said,

' To you I say, " Rise, take up your mat and go home." ' 11

The man rose, and immediately under the eyes of all 12 took up his mat and went out, so that they were all filled with astonishment, gave the glory to God, and said,

' We never saw anything like this.'

The Call of Levi Again He went out to the shore of the Lake, 13 and the whole multitude kept coming to Him, and He taught them. And as He passed by, He 14 saw Levi the son of Alphaeus sitting at the Toll Office, and said to him,

' Follow me.'

So he rose and followed Him.

When He was sitting at table in Levi's house, a large 15 number of tax-gatherers and sinners were at table with Jesus and His disciples ; for there were many such who followed Him. But when the Scribes of the Pharisee sect 16 saw Him eating with the sinners and the tax-gatherers, they said to His disciples,

' He is eating and drinking with the tax-gatherers and sinners ! '

Jesus heard the words, and He said, 17

' It is not the healthy who require a doctor, but the sick : I did not come to call the righteous, but sinners.'

The Disciples' Neglect of Fasting Now John's disciples and those of the 18 Pharisees were keeping a fast. And they came and asked Him,

' How is it that John's disciples and those of the Pharisees are fasting, and yours are not ? '

' Can a wedding party fast while the bridegroom is among 19 them ? ' replied Jesus. ' As long as they have the bridegroom with them, fasting is impossible. But a time will 20 come when the bridegroom will be taken away from them ; then they will fast. No one mends an old garment with a 21 patch of unshrunk cloth. Otherwise the added patch tears away from it—the new from the old—and a worse hole is made. And no one pours new wine into old wineskins. 22 Otherwise the wine would burst the skins, and both wine and skins would be lost. New wine needs fresh skins ! '

(vv. 13–17.) Cf. Matt. ix. 9–13 ; Luke v. 27–32 ; xv. 1.
16. *And drinking*] v.L. omits.
(vv. 18–22.) Cf. Matt. ix. 14–17 ; Luke v. 33–39.

A Charge of Sabbath-breaking One Sabbath He was walking through the 23 wheatfields, when His disciples began to pluck the ears of wheat as they went. So the 24 Pharisees said to Him,

' Look ! why are they doing what on the Sabbath is unlawful ? '

' Have you never read,' Jesus replied, ' what David did 25 when he had need and he and his men were hungry : how 26 he entered the house of God in the High-priesthood of Abiathar, and ate the Presented Loaves—which none but the priests are allowed to eat—and gave some to his men also ? ' (1 Sam. xxi. 6).

And Jesus said to them : 27

' The Sabbath was made for man, not man for the Sabbath ; so that the Son of Man is Lord even of the 28 Sabbath.'

A Second Charge of Sabbath-breaking At another time, when He went to the 1 **3** synagogue, there was a man there with one arm shrivelled up. They closely watched Him to 2 see whether He would cure him on the Sabbath, so as to have a charge to bring against Him.

' Come forward,' said He to the man with the shrivelled 3 arm.

Then He asked them, 4

' Are we allowed to do good on the Sabbath, or to do evil ? to save a life, or to destroy one ? '

They remained silent. Grieved and indignant at the 5 hardening of their hearts, He looked round on them with anger, and said to the man,

' Stretch out your arm.'

He stretched it out, and the arm was completely restored. But the Pharisees left the synagogue and at once held a 6 consultation with the Herodians against Jesus, to devise some means of destroying Him.

(vv. 23–28.) Cf. Matt. xii. 1–8 ; Luke vi. 1–5.

27. *The Sabbath was made for man*] An emancipating saying, preserved in Mark alone.

28. *Son of Man*] The logic of the situation would rather require ' man ' ; so at ii. 10. Cf. Matt. xii. 8. The Messianic title ' Son of Man ' occurs only in these two places in Mark before its decisive adoption at viii. 31 ; and it is possible that in these it should rather be interpreted as the Hebrew or Aramaic equivalent for ' man.' Cf. Ezek. ii. 1, &c.

(vv. 1–6.) Cf. Matt. xii. 9–14 ; Luke vi. 6–11.

6. *Herodians*] Matt. xxii. 16 · Mark xii. 13. Cf. Mark viii. 15. The adherents of Herod Antipas, who looked for a restoration of the monarchy under the dynasty of the Herods. This unnatural alliance between religious strictness and worldly policy made Galilee unsafe for Jesus. Hence, perhaps, the subsequent wanderings.

Other Cures So Jesus withdrew with His disciples to the 7
Lake, and a vast crowd of people from Galilee
followed Him. And from Judaea and Jerusalem and 8
Idumaea and from beyond the Jordan and from the district
of Tyre and Sidon there came to Him a vast crowd, hearing
of all that He was doing. Therefore He gave directions 9
to His disciples to keep a small boat always ready because
of the throng, to prevent their crushing Him. For He 10
had cured many of the people, so that all who had any
ailments pressed upon Him, to touch Him. And the foul 11
spirits, whenever they saw Him, threw themselves down
at His feet, screaming out :

' You are the Son of God.'

But He absolutely forbade them to say who He was. 12

Twelve Disciples chosen Then He went up the hill, and called those 13
whom He Himself chose, and they came to
Him. And He appointed twelve of them, that 14
they might be with Him, and that He might send them
forth to preach, with authority to expel the demons. 15
These twelve were Simon (to whom He gave the surname 16
of Peter), James the son of Zebedee, and John the 17
brother of James (these two He surnamed Boanerges, that
is ' Sons of Thunder '), Andrew, Philip, Bartholomew, 18
Matthew, Thomas, James the son of Alphaeus, Thaddaeus,
Simon the Cananaean, and Judas Iscariot, the man who 19
also betrayed Him.

The Family of Jesus try to restrain Him And He went into a house. But again the 20
crowd assembled, so that there was no oppor-
tunity for them even to snatch a meal. Hear- 21
ing of this, His relatives came to seize Him by force, for
they said,

' He is out of His mind.'

The Scribes, too, who had come down from Jerusalem said, 22

He replies to a Slander ' He has Beelzebul in him ; and it is by
the power of the Prince of the demons that he
expels the demons.'

(vv. 7–12 and 16–19.) Cf. Matt. x. 2–4 ; IV. 24, 25 ; Luke vi. 14–19.
(vv. 13–15.) Cf. Luke vi. 12, 13.
14. *Twelve of them*] v.L. adds ' whom also He named Apostles.'
18. *Cananaean*] See Matt. x. 4, n.
20. *To snatch a meal*] Lit. ' to eat bread.'
21. See the sequel in verses 31–35.
22. *Beelzebul*] See Matt. x. 25, n.
(vv. 22–30.) Cf. Matt. xii. 22–37 ; Luke vi. 43–45 ; xi. 17–23.

So He called them to Him, and with a parable He 23 appealed to them, saying,

' How is it possible for Satan to expel Satan ? For if 24 civil war breaks out in a kingdom, nothing can make that kingdom last ; and if a family splits into parties, that family 25 cannot continue. So if Satan has risen in arms and has 26 made war upon himself, stand he cannot, but meets his end. Indeed, no one can go into a strong man's house and carry 27 off his property, unless he first binds the strong man, and then he will plunder his house. In truth I tell you that 28 all their sins may be pardoned to the sons of men, and all their blasphemies, however they may have blasphemed ; but whoever blasphemes against the Holy Spirit remains 29 for ever unpardoned : he is guilty of an eternal sin.'

This was because they said, 30

' He is possessed by a foul spirit.'

The true Kinsfolk of Jesus By this time His mother and His brothers 31 arrive, and standing outside they send a mes- sage to Him to call Him. Now a crowd was 32 sitting round Him ; so they tell Him,

' Your mother and your brothers and sisters are outside, inquiring for you.'

' Who are my mother and my brothers ? ' He replied. 33

And, fixing His eyes on the people who were sitting round 34 Him in a circle, He said,

' Here are my mother and my brothers. For wherever 35 there is one who has been obedient to God, there is my brother, my sister, and my mother.'

A Series of Parables : ' The Sower ' Once more He began to teach by the side of 1 **4** the Lake, and a vast multitude of people came together to listen to Him. He therefore went on board the boat and sat there, a little way from the land ; and all the people were on the shore close to the water. Then He taught them much by means of parables ; and 2 in His teaching He said,

' Listen ! A sower went out to sow. As he sowed, some 3, 4

29. To attribute His deeds of mercy to the power of Satan is to put the critics beyond the reach of further appeal. No moral discernment is left. They say with Milton's Satan :

> ' All good to me is lost ;
> Evil be thou my good.' Cf. Heb. vi. 4–6 ; x. 26–31.

(vv. 31–35.) Cf. Matt. xii. 46–50 ; Luke viii. 19–21.
(vv. 1–25.) Cf. Matt. xiii. 1–23 ; Luke viii. 4–18.

of the seed fell by the way-side, and the birds came and
pecked it up. Some fell on the rocky ground where it found 5
but little earth, and it shot up quickly because it had no
depth of soil ; but when the sun was risen, it was scorched, 6
and through having no root it withered away. Some, again, 7
fell among the thorns ; and the thorns sprang up and stifled
it, so that it yielded no crop. But some of the seed fell 8
into good ground, and gave a return : it came up and
increased, and yielded thirty, sixty, or a hundred-fold.'

'Listen,' He added, 'every one who has ears to hear ! ' 9

When He was alone, the Twelve and the others who were 10
about Him asked Him to explain His parables.

'To you,' He replied, 'has been entrusted the secret 11
truth concerning the Kingdom of God ; but to those others
outside your number all this is spoken in parables ; that 12

'" THEY MAY LOOK AND LOOK BUT NOT SEE,

AND LISTEN AND LISTEN BUT NOT UNDERSTAND,

LEST PERCHANCE THEY SHOULD TURN AND BE PAR-
DONED "' (Isa. vi. 10).

'Do you all miss the meaning of this parable ? ' He 13
added ; 'how then will you understand the rest of my
parables ? '

'What the sower sows is the word. Those 14
'The Sower' explained who receive the seed by the way-side are 15
those in whom the word is sown, but, when
they have heard it, Satan comes at once and carries away
the word sown in them. In the same way those who 16
receive the seed on the rocky places are those who, when
they have heard the word, at once accept it joyfully, but 17
they have no root within them. They last for a time ; then,
when suffering or persecution comes because of the word,
they stumble and fall. Others there are who receive the 18
seed among the thorns : these are they who have heard
the word, but worldly cares and the deceitfulness of 19
wealth and absorption in other attractions come in and
stifle the word, and it becomes unfruitful. Those, on 20
the other hand, who have received the seed on the good
ground, are all who hear the word and welcome it, and
yield a return of thirty, sixty, or a hundred-fold.'

(vv. 10–13.) These verses and verses 33, 34, raise well-known difficulties as to our
Lord's purpose in teaching by parables. See the Commentaries.
11. *The secret truth*] *i.e.* ' the truth hitherto unrevealed.' Cf. Rom. xvi. 25–27.

He went on to say, 21

Lamps are for giving Light

' Is the lamp brought in to be put under the bushel measure or under the bed ? Is it not that it may be placed on the lampstand ? Why, there 22 is nothing hidden except to be disclosed, nor has anything been made a secret but that it may come to light. Listen, 23 every one who has ears to hear ! '

He also said to them, 24

' Take care what you hear. With what measure you measure, it will be measured to you, and that with interest. For he who has will have more given him ; and from him 25 who has not, even what he has will be taken away.'

'The Seed growing of itself'

Another saying of His was this : 26

' The Kingdom of God is as if a man scattered seed over the ground : he spends 27 days and nights, now awake, now asleep, while the seed sprouts and grows tall, he knows not how. Of itself the 28 land produces the crop—first the blade, then the ear ; afterwards the perfect grain in the ear. But no sooner is the crop 29 ripe, than he sends the reapers, because the time of harvest has come.'

'The Mustard Seed'

Another saying of His was this : 30

' How are we to picture the Kingdom of God ? or by what parable shall we represent it ? It is like a mustard-seed, which, when sown in the 31 earth, is the smallest of all the seeds in the world ; yet 32 when sown it springs up and becomes larger than all the herbs, and throws out great branches, so that the birds roost under its shadow.'

With many such parables He would speak the word 33 to them according to their capacity for receiving it. But 34 except in parables He spoke nothing to them ; while to His own disciples He explained everything, in private.

The same day, in the evening, He said to 35

A Storm subdued

them,

' Let us cross to the other side.'

So they got away from the crowd, and took Him, as 36 He was, in the boat ; and other boats accompanied Him. But a heavy squall came on, and the waves were now 37

---

29. *Reapers*] Lit. ' sickle.'
(vv. 30-32.) Cf. Matt. xiii. 31-33 ; Luke xiii. 18-21.
(vv. 35-41.) Cf. Matt. viii. 18, 23-27 ; Luke viii. 22-25.

dashing into the boat, so that it was fast filling. But He 38
Himself was in the stern asleep, with His head on the
cushion : so they woke Him.

' Rabbi,' they cried, ' is it nothing to you that we are
drowning ? '

So He roused Himself, and rebuked the wind, and said to 39
the waves,

' Silence ! Be still ! '

The wind sank, and there was perfect calm.

' Why are you so timid ? ' He asked ; ' have you still no 40
faith ? '

Then they were filled with terror, and began to say to one 41
another,

' Who then is this ? For even wind and sea obey Him.'

A Gerasene   So they arrived at the opposite shore of the 1 **5**
Demoniac Lake, in the country of the Gerasenes. At 2
cured once, on His landing, there came from the
tombs to meet Him a man possessed by a foul spirit. This 3
man lived among the tombs, nor could any one now secure
him even with a chain ; for many a time he had been left 4
securely bound in fetters and chains, but afterwards the
chains lay torn link from link, and the fetters in fragments,
and there was no one strong enough to master him. And 5
constantly, day and night, he remained among the tombs
or on the hills, shrieking, and mangling himself with sharp
stones. When he saw Jesus in the distance, he ran and 6
threw himself at His feet, crying out in a loud voice, 7

' What hast Thou to do with me, Jesus, Son of God
Most High ? In God's name I implore Thee not to
torment me.'

For He had said to him, 8

' Foul spirit, come out of the man.'

Jesus also questioned him. 9

' What is your name ? ' He said.

' Legion,' he replied, ' for there are a host of us.'

And he earnestly entreated Him not to send them away 10
out of the country.

---

38. *Rabbi*] Lit. ' Teacher.'
(vv. 1–20.) Cf. Matt. viii. 28–34 ; Luke viii. 26–39.
1. *Gerasenes*] So Luke viii. 26. Matthew has Gadarenes. Gadara and Gerasa were
cities of Decapolis (verse 20), but distant respectively from the Lake six and thirty
miles. The spot is now generally identified with another Gerasa, the ruined Kersa
on the east of the Lake, which may have been included in the territory of Gadara.

Feeding there, on the mountain slope, was a great herd of 11
swine. So they besought Jesus. 12

'Send us to the swine,' they said, 'that we may enter
them.'

He gave them leave; and the foul spirits came out and 13
entered the swine; and the herd—about 2000 in number
—rushed headlong down the steep into the Lake and were
drowned in the Lake. The swineherds fled, and spread the 14
news in town and country. So the people went to see what
had happened. And when they came to Jesus, they beheld 15
the demoniac quietly seated, clothed and of sane mind—
the man who had had the legion; and they were awe-
stricken. And those who had seen it told them what had 16
happened to the demoniac, and all about the swine. Then 17
they began to entreat Him to depart from their district.

As He was embarking, the man who had been possessed 18
asked permission to accompany Him. But He would not 19
allow it.

'Go home to your family,' He said, 'and report to
them all that the Lord has done for you, and the mercy He
has shown you.'

The man departed, and proclaimed everywhere in 20
Decapolis all that Jesus had done for him; and all were
astonished.

When Jesus had re-crossed in the boat to the 21
Jairus's Daughter other side, a vast multitude collected round
Him; and He was on the shore of the Lake,
when there came one of the rulers of the synagogue (he 22
was called Jairus) who, on beholding Him, threw himself
at His feet, and besought Him with many entreaties. 23

'My little daughter,' he said, 'is at the point of death:
I pray you come and lay your hands upon her, that she may
recover and live.'

19. 'Legion' could not so quickly be changed into an Apostle.
20. The man obeys, with a difference. His commission was to tell his friends;
he proceeds to publish (lit. 'herald,' 'preach') the matter throughout the whole
of Decapolis. He was to see in his cure the power and mercy of God; but
he thinks only of what Jesus had done for him. A difference of the Greek tense
in the 'has done' of verse 19, and the 'had done' of verse 20, suggests that,
bidden to lay stress on the abiding change in himself, rather than on the story of
what befell on the hillside, he chose to tell and re-tell the details of that story
till men were agape with wonder. His message was lacking in reserve and in truth;
and in both because it lacked obedience.

Decapolis] The 'Ten-city' land; originally a league of ten Greek cities in eastern
Palestine.

(vv. 21–43.) Cf. Matt. ix. 18–26; Luke viii. 40–56.

And Jesus went with him. And a dense 24
A Woman cured crowd followed Him, and thronged Him on all sides.

Now a woman who for twelve years had been troubled 25
with hæmorrhage, and had suffered much from a number 26
of doctors and had spent all she had without receiving
benefit but rather growing worse, heard of Jesus. And 27
she came in the crowd behind Him and touched His cloak ;
for she said, 28

' If I but touch His clothes, I shall be cured.'

In a moment the flow of her blood ceased, and she felt 29
in herself that her complaint was cured. Immediately 30
Jesus, well knowing that healing power had gone from
Him, turned round in the crowd and asked,

' Who touched my clothes ? '

' You see the multitude pressing you on all sides,' His 31
disciples exclaimed, ' and yet you ask, " Who touched
me ? " '

But He continued looking about to see the person who 32
had done this, until the woman, frightened and trembling, 33
knowing what had happened to her, came and threw herself
at His feet, and told Him all the truth.

' Daughter,' He said, ' your faith has cured you : go in 34
peace, and be free from your complaint.'

While He is yet speaking, men come from 35
Jairus's Daughter the house to the ruler, and say,
' Your daughter is dead : why trouble the
Rabbi further ? '

But Jesus, disregarding their words, said to the ruler, 36
' Do not be afraid ; only have faith.'

And He allowed no one to accompany Him except Peter 37
and the brothers James and John. So they come to the 38
ruler's house. Here He gazes on a scene of uproar,
with people weeping aloud and wailing. He goes in. 39

' Why all this outcry and loud weeping ? ' He asks ;
' the child is asleep, not dead.'

And they jeered at Him. But He puts them all out, 40
takes the child's father and mother and those He has brought
with Him, and enters the room where the child lies. Then, 41
taking her by the hand, He says to her,

(vv. 25, 26.) Matthew (ix. 20) and Luke (viii. 43) tone down this description.
36. *Disregarding*] Or ' overhearing.'

'Talithà, koum'; that is to say, 'Little girl, I bid you to wake!'

Instantly the little girl rises to her feet and begins to walk (for she was twelve years old). They were at once beside themselves with utter astonishment; but He gave strict injunctions that the matter should not be made known, and directed them to give her something to eat. 42 43

A Visit to Nazareth Leaving that place He came into His own country, accompanied by His disciples. On the Sabbath He began to teach in the synagogue; and many, as they heard Him, were astonished. 1 **6** 2

'Where did He acquire all this?' they asked. 'What is this wisdom that has been given to Him? And what are these miracles which His hands perform? Is not this the carpenter, Mary's son, the brother of James and Joses, Jude and Simon? And do not His sisters live here among us?' 3

So they took offence at Him. But Jesus said to them, 'There is no Prophet without honour except in his own country, and among his own relatives, and in his own home.' 4

And He could not do any miracle there, except that He laid His hands on a few sick folk and cured them; and He wondered at their unbelief. So He went round the adjacent villages, teaching. 5 6

Then summoning the twelve to Him, He proceeded to send them out by twos, and gave them authority over the foul spirits. He charged them to take nothing for the journey except a stick; no bread, no bag, and not a penny in their pockets, but to go wearing sandals. 7 8 9

'And do not,' He said, 'put on an extra inner garment. Wherever you enter a house, make it your home till you leave that place. But wherever they will not receive you or 10 11

(vv. 1–6.) Cf. Matt. xiii. 54–58.
1. *Own country*] Cf. Matt. xiii. 54, n.
2. *Many*] v.L. 'the many.' Cf. Matt. xxiv. 12.
These] Lit. 'such.'
6. Cf. Matt. ix. 35–38.
(vv. 7–13.) Cf. Matt. x. 1, 5–15; Luke ix. 1–6.
8. *Stick*] Matthew and Luke prohibit even this useful help in a journey.
Not a penny] Lit. 'bronze.'
Pockets] Lit. 'waist-scarf' or 'girdle.'
9. *Sandals*] *i.e.* stout soles (or shoes without uppers) fastened on with leather straps passing round the ankles. In the N.T. the word is only found elsewhere in Acts xii. 8.

listen to you, when you leave shake off the very dust from under your feet as a protest against them.'

So they set out, and preached, in order that men might 12 repent. Many demons they expelled, and many invalids 13 they anointed with oil and cured.

The Murder of John the Baptist King Herod heard of all this (for the name 14 of Jesus had become widely known), and he said,

'John the Baptizer has come back to life, and that is why these miraculous Powers are working in him.'

Others asserted that he was Elijah. 15

Others again said,

'He is a Prophet, like one of the great Prophets.'

But when Herod heard of him, he said, 16

'That John, whom I beheaded, has come back to life.'

For Herod himself had sent and arrested John and had 17 kept him in prison in chains, for the sake of Herodias, his brother Philip's wife; because he had married her. For 18 John told Herod,

'You have no right to be living with your brother's wife.'

Therefore Herodias bore a grudge against him and 19 wished to take his life, but could not; for Herod stood in 20 awe of John, knowing him to be an upright and holy man, and he protected him. After listening to him he was in great perplexity, and yet he found a pleasure in listening. At 21 length Herodias found her opportunity. Herod on his birthday gave a banquet to the nobles of his court and to the tribunes and the principal people in Galilee, at which 22 Herodias's own daughter came in and danced, and so charmed Herod and his guests that he said to her,

'Ask me for anything you please, and I will give it to you.'

He even swore to her, 23

(vv. 14–16.) Cf. Matt. xiv. 1, 2 ; Luke ix. 7–9.
14. *He used to declare*] v.l. 'people were saying.'
(vv. 17–20.) Cf. Matt. xiv. 3–5 ; Luke iii. 19, 20.
20. *Was in great perplexity*] v.l. 'did many things'; *i.e.* in many things he obeyed his instructions.
(vv. 21–29.) Cf. Matt. xiv. 6–12.
21. *Tribunes*] No one English word— 'major,' 'colonel,' 'brigadier,' or any other —represents the Latin 'tribunus' for which the Greek word here used stands. In John xviii. 12 and Acts xxi. 31, we find a tribune commanding a whole battalion. See Matt. xxvii. 27, n.
22. *Herodias's own daughter*] The best authorities have the impossible reading 'his daughter Herodias,' giving to Salome her mother's name, and making her the daughter instead of the niece of Herod Antipas.

' Whatever you ask me for I will give you, up to half my kingdom.'

She at once went out and said to her mother : 24
' What shall I ask for ? '

' The head of John the Baptizer,' she replied.

The girl immediately came in, in haste, to the king and 25 made her request.

' My desire is,' she said, ' that you will give me, here and now, on a dish, the head of John the Baptist.'

Then the king, though intensely sorry, yet for the sake of 26 his oaths, and of his guests, would not break faith with her. He at once sent a soldier of his guard with orders to bring 27 John's head. So he went and beheaded him in the prison, and brought his head on a dish and gave it to the young girl, 28 who gave it to her mother. When John's disciples heard 29 of it, they came and took away his body and laid it in a tomb.

The Apostles return from their Mission When the apostles re-assembled round Jesus, 30 they reported to Him all they had done and all they had taught. Then He said to them, 31
' Come away, all of you, to a quiet place, and rest awhile.'

For there were many coming and going, so that they had no time even for meals. Accordingly they went away in the 32 boat to a solitary place. But the people saw them going, 33 and many recognized them ; so they hastened there on foot from all the neighbouring towns, and arrived before them. So when Jesus landed, He saw a vast multitude ; 34 and His heart was moved with pity for them, because they were like sheep which have no shepherd, and He proceeded to teach them many things.

5000 People fed By this time it was late ; so His disciples 35 came to Him, and said,
' This is a lonely place, and the hour is now late : send them away that they may go to the farms and 36 villages near and buy themselves something to eat.'

' Give them food yourselves,' He replied. 37

' Are we,' they asked, ' to go and buy two hundred shillings' worth of bread and give them food ? '

' How many loaves have you ? ' He inquired ; ' go and 38 see.'

So they found out, and said,

' Five ; and a couple of fish.'

So He directed them to make all recline in companies on 39
the green grass. And they settled down in groups of 40
hundreds and of fifties. Then He took the five loaves and 41
the two fish, and lifting His eyes to Heaven He blessed
the food. Then He broke the loaves into portions, which
He handed to the disciples to distribute ; giving pieces
also of the two fish to them all. All ate and were fully 42
satisfied. And they took up broken portions enough to 43
fill twelve baskets, besides pieces of the fish. Those who 44
ate the bread were five thousand men.

Immediately afterwards He made His dis- 45
Jesus prays ciples go on board the boat and cross over to
in Solitude Bethsaïda, leaving Him behind to dismiss the
crowd. He then bade the people farewell, and went away 46
up the hill to pray.

When evening was come, the boat was half 47
He walks on way across the Lake, while He Himself was on
the Lake shore alone. But seeing them distressed with 48
rowing (for the wind was against them), about the fourth
watch of the night He came towards them walking on the
Lake, as if intending to pass them by. They saw Him 49
walking on the water, and thinking that it was a ghost they
cried out ; for they all saw Him and were terrified. He, 50
however, immediately spoke to them.

' There is no danger,' He said ; ' it is I ; do not be
alarmed.'

Then He went up to them and entered the boat, and 51
the wind lulled ; and they were beside themselves with
amazement ; for they had not learned the lesson taught by 52
the loaves, but their minds were dull.

Having crossed over they drew to land at 53
Cures in Gennesaret and made fast to the shore. But no 54
Gennesaret sooner had they left the boat than the people
immediately recognized Him. And they scoured the whole 55
district, and began to bring to Him on their mats those who
were ill, wherever they heard He was. And enter wherever 56
He might—village or town or hamlet—they laid their sick in
the open places, and entreated Him to let them touch were

40. *Groups*] Lit. ' garden beds.' A picturesque description of the brightly dressed
groups upon the green grass.
(vv. 45–52.) Cf. Matt. xiv. 22–33 ; John vi. 15–21.
(vv. 53–56.) Cf. Matt. xiv. 34–36.

it but the tassel of His robe ; and all, whoever touched Him, were restored to health.

Purity, inward and spiritual Then the Pharisees, with certain Scribes who 1 had come from Jerusalem, came to Him in a body. They had noticed that some of His dis- 2 ciples were eating their food with ' unclean ' (that is to say, unwashed) hands. (For the Pharisees and all the 3 Jews—being, as they are, zealous for the traditions of the Elders—never eat without first carefully washing their hands, and when they come from market they will not eat 4 without bathing first ; and they have a good many other customs which they have received traditionally and cling to, such as the washing of cups and pots and of bronze vessels, and of beds). So the Pharisees and Scribes put the question 5 to Him :

' Why do your disciples transgress the traditions of the Elders, and eat their food with unclean hands ? '

' Rightly did Isaiah prophesy of you hypocrites,' He 6 replied ; ' as it is written,

' " This People honours Me with their lips,
While their heart is far from Me :
In vain do they worship Me 7
While giving as doctrines the mere precepts of men " (Isa. xxix. 13).

' You neglect God's Commandment : you hold fast to 8 men's traditions.'

' Praiseworthy indeed ! ' He added, ' to set at nought 9 God's Commandment in order to observe your own traditions ! For Moses said, " Honour thy father and 10 thy mother " (Exod. xx. 12), and again, " He who reviles father or mother, let him be put to death " (Exod. xxi. 17). But you say, " If a man says to his father or mother, 11 This thing is Korban (that is, consecrated to God) ; otherwise you should have received it from me— " you no 12

(vv. 1–23.) Cf. Matt. xv. 1–20.

3. *Carefully washing their hands*] Or ' up to the wrist,' which, however, is a doubtful rendering of the literal ' with the fist,' perhaps rubbed vigorously into the palm of the other hand—a bit of the prescribed ritual.

4. *Bathing*] v.l. ' sprinkling themselves.'

Of beds] v.l. omits these words. Of course they do not mean what we English call ' beds.' They were mere mattresses or thick rugs. Travellers in Eastern countries often witness the complete submersion of ' beds,' which are then dried in the sun.

5. *Food*] Lit. ' bread,' as often in Hebrew. See *e.g.* Num. xxviii. 2, 24, R.V. and margin.

11. *Consecrated to God*] Lit. ' a gift ' (*i.e.* to God).

longer allow him to do anything for his father or mother, thus nullifying God's precept by your tradition which you 13 have handed down. And many things of that kind you do.'

Then Jesus called the people to Him again. 14

'Listen to me, all of you,' He said, 'and understand. There is nothing outside a man which entering into him can 15 make him unclean ; but it is the things which come out of a man that make him unclean.'

After He had left the crowd and gone indoors, His dis- 17 ciples began to ask Him about this parable.

'Is it so that you also are without understanding ? ' He 18 replied ; ' do you not see that anything whatever that enters a man from outside cannot make him unclean, because it 19 does not go into his heart, but into his stomach, and passes away ? '

By these words Jesus pronounced all kinds of food clean.

'It is what comes out of a man,' He added, ' that makes 20 him unclean. For from within, out of men's hearts, their 21 evil purposes proceed—fornication, theft, murder, adultery, 22 covetousness, wickedness, deceit, licentiousness, envy, slander, pride, reckless folly : all these wicked things come 23 out from within and make a man unclean.'

Then He rose and left that place and went into the 24 neighbourhood of Tyre and Sidon.

Here He entered a house and wished no one

A Gentile Girl cured to know it, but He could not escape observation. Forthwith a woman whose little daughter was 25 possessed by a foul spirit heard of Him, and came and flung herself at His feet. She was a Gentile woman, a Syro- 26 phoenician by nation : and she begged Him to expel the demon from her daughter.

'Let the children first eat all they want,' He said ; ' it 27 is not right to take the children's bread and throw it to the dogs.'

'True, Sir,' she replied, ' but even the dogs under the 28 table eat the children's scraps.'

---

17. See Matt. xv. 12, n.
v.L. adds verse 16, ' Listen, every one who has ears to hear ! '
(vv. 24–30.) Cf. Matt. xv. 21–28.
24. *And Sidon*] v.L. omits these words.
26. *Gentile*] Lit. ' Greek.'
27. *Dogs*] Lit. ' puppies.' Cf. Matt. xv. 26, n.

' For those words of yours, go home,' He replied ; ' the 29
demon has gone out of your daughter.'

So she went home, and found the child lying on the bed, 30
and the demon gone.

A deaf Stammerer cured Returning from the neighbourhood of 31
Tyre, He came by way of Sidon to the Lake
of Galilee, passing through the district of
Decapolis. Here they brought to Him a deaf man who 32
stammered, on whom they begged Him to lay His hands.
So Jesus taking him aside, apart from the crowd, put His 33
fingers into his ears, and spat, and moistened his tongue ;
and looking up to heaven He sighed, and said to him, 34
' Ephphatha ! ' (that is, ' Open ! ').

And the man's ears were opened, and his tongue became 35
untied, and he began to speak clearly. Then Jesus charged 36
them to tell no one ; but the more He charged them, all
the more did they spread the news far and wide. The 37
amazement was extreme.

' How well He has done everything,' they exclaimed ;
' He even makes deaf men hear and dumb men speak ! '

4000 People fed About that time there was again an immense 1 **8**
crowd, and they found themselves with
nothing to eat. So He called His disciples to
Him. ' My heart aches for the people,' He said ; ' for this 2
is now the third day they have remained with me, and they
have nothing to eat. If I were to send them home hungry, 3
they would faint on the way, some of them having come a
great distance.'

' Where can we possibly get bread here in this remote 4
place to satisfy such a crowd ? ' answered His disciples.

' How many loaves have you ? ' He asked. 5

' Seven,' they said.

So He passed the word to the people to sit down on the 6
ground. Then taking the seven loaves He blessed them,
and broke them into portions and proceeded to give them to
His disciples for them to distribute, and they distributed
them to the people. They had also a few small fish. He 7
blessed them, and He told His disciples to distribute these

(vv. 31–37.) Mark only.
(vv. 1–9.) Cf. Matt. xv. 32–38.
2. *The third day . . with me*] *i.e.* ' they have been with me ever since the day
before yesterday,' not ' for three days ' in the English sense of the phrase. Cf.
Luke ii. 46, n, and Acts xxviii. 12, n.

also. So the people ate an abundant meal ; and what 8
remained over they took up—seven large baskets of broken
pieces. The number fed was about 4000. Then He sent 9
them away, and at once going on board with His disciples 10
He came into the district of Dalmanutha.

'A Sign from Heaven' The Pharisees followed Him and began to 11
dispute with Him, asking Him for a sign from
heaven, to make trial of Him. But with a deep 12
and troubled sigh, He said,

' Why do the men of to-day ask for a sign ? In truth I
tell you that no sign shall be given to the men of to-day.'

So He left them, went on board again, and crossed to the 13
other side of the Lake.

The Leaven of the Pharisees and of Herod Now they had forgotten to take bread, nor 14
had they more than a single loaf with them in
the boat ; and when He admonished them, 15
' See that you are on your guard against the
leaven of the Pharisees and the leaven of 16
Herod,' they reasoned with one another and remarked,

' We have no bread ! '

He perceived what they were saying, and He said to them, 17
' What is this discussion about having no bread ? Do
you not yet see and understand ? Are you so dull of mind ?
YOU HAVE EYES ! CAN YOU NOT SEE ? YOU HAVE EARS ! CAN 18
YOU NOT HEAR ? (Jer. v. 21) and have you no memory ?
When I broke up the five loaves for the 5000 men, how many 19
baskets did you take up full of broken portions ? '

' Twelve,' they said.

' And when the seven for the 4000, how many hampers 20
full of portions did you take away ? '

' Seven,' they answered.

' Do you not yet understand ? ' He said. 21

A blind Man at Bethsaida receives Sight And they came to Bethsaida. And a blind 22
man was brought to Jesus and they entreated
Him to touch him. So He took the blind man 23
by the arm and brought him out of the village,
and spitting into his eyes He put His hands on him and
asked him,

' Can you see anything ? '

(vv. 10–12.) Cf. Matt. xv. 39–xvi. 4.
(vv. 11, 12.) Cf. Matt. xii. 40, n.
(vv. 13–21.) Cf. Matt. xvi. 4–12.
(vv. 22–26.) Mark only.

He looked up and said, 24
' I can see people : I see them like trees—only walking.'

Then for the second time He put His hands on the man's 25
eyes, and the man, looking steadily, recovered his sight and
saw everything distinctly. So He sent him home, and added, 26
' Do not even go into the village.'

Peter ac-   From that place Jesus and His disciples went 27
knowledges to the villages belonging to Caesarea Philippi.
Jesus as the On the way He began to ask His disciples,
Christ   ' Who do people say that I am ? '

' John the Baptist,' they replied, ' but others say Elijah, 28
and others, that you are one of the Prophets.'

Then He asked them, 29
' But you yourselves, who do you say that I am ? '
' You are the Christ,' answered Peter.

And He strictly forbade them to tell this about Him 30
to any one.

    And now for the first time He told them, 31
Jesus pre- ' The Son of Man must suffer much cruelty,
dicts His
own Death and be rejected by the Elders and the High
and Resur- Priests and the Scribes, and be put to death,
rection and on the third day rise to life.'

This He told them plainly ; whereupon Peter took Him 32
and began to remonstrate with Him. But turning round 33
and seeing His disciples, He rebuked Peter.

' Get behind me, Satan,' He said, ' for your thoughts are
not God's thoughts, but men's.'

Self-renun-   Then calling to Him the crowd and also His 34
ciation the disciples, He said to them,
Way to Life ' If any one wishes to follow me, let him
renounce self and take up his cross, and so be my follower.
For whoever desires to save his life shall lose it, but he who 35
loses his life for my sake, and for the sake of the gospel,
shall save it. Why, what does it benefit a man to gain 36
the whole world and forfeit his life ? For what could a 37
man give to buy back his life ? Every one who has been 38
ashamed of me and of my teachings in this apostate and
sinful age, of him the Son of Man also will be ashamed
when He comes in His Father's glory with the holy angels.'

(viii. 27–ix. 1.) Cf. Matt. xvi. 13–28 ; Luke ix. 18–27 ; John vi. 66–71.
35. *Life*] See Matt. xvi. 25, n.
36. *Forfeit*] Cf. Luke ix. 25, n.

He went on to say,   1 **9**

'I tell you in truth that some of those who are standing
here will not taste death till they have seen the Kingdom
of God already come in power.'

Six days later, Jesus took with Him Peter, 2
The Trans- James, and John, and brought them alone, apart
figuration from the rest, up a high mountain; and in
their presence His appearance underwent a change. His 3
garments also became dazzling with brilliant whiteness—
such whiteness as no bleaching on earth could give. More- 4
over there appeared to them Elijah, with Moses; and the
two were conversing with Jesus, when Peter said to Jesus, 5

'Rabbi, it is well that we are here. Let us put up
three tents—one for you, one for Moses, and one for
Elijah.'

For he knew not what to say: they were filled with such 6
awe. Then there came a cloud spreading over them, and 7
a voice issued from the cloud,

'This is my Son, the Beloved: listen to Him.'

Instantly they looked round, and now they could no longer 8
see any one, but only Jesus with them.

As they were coming down from the moun- 9
The Coming tain, He very strictly forbade them to tell any one
of Elijah what they had seen 'until after the Son of Man
has risen from among the dead.' So they kept the matter 10
to themselves, although discussing one with another what
was meant by this rising from the dead. They also asked 11
Him,

'How is it that the Scribes say that Elijah must first come?'

'Elijah,' He replied, 'does indeed come first and reforms 12
everything; but how is it that it is written of the Son of Man
that He will endure much suffering and be held in contempt? Yet I tell you that not only has Elijah come, but 13
they have also done to him whatever they chose, as the
Scriptures say about him.'

Cure of an   As they came to rejoin the disciples, they 14
Epileptic   saw an immense crowd surrounding them
and a party of Scribes disputing with them.
Immediately the whole multitude on beholding Him 15

(vv. 2–13.) Cf. Matt. xvii. 1–13.
5. *It is well*] See Matt. xvii. 4, n.
Tents] Or ' booths.'
(vv. 14–29.) Cf. Matt. xvii. 14–21; Luke ix. 37–43.

were awestruck, and they ran forward and greeted Him.

'What are you discussing?' He asked them.   16

'Rabbi,' answered one of the crowd, 'I have brought 17 you my son. He has a dumb spirit in him; and wherever 18 it comes upon him, it dashes him to the ground, and he foams at the mouth and grinds his teeth, and he is pining away. I begged your disciples to expel it, but they were unable.'

'O unbelieving generation!' replied Jesus; 'how long 19 must I be with you? how long must I bear with you? Bring him to me.'

So they brought him to Jesus. And the spirit, when he 20 saw Jesus, immediately threw the youth into convulsions, so that he fell on the ground and rolled about, foaming at the mouth. Then Jesus asked the father,   21

'How long has he been like this?'

'From early childhood,' he said; 'and often it has 22 thrown him into the fire or into pools of water to destroy him. But, if you can, have pity on us and help us.'

'"If I can!"' replied Jesus. 'Why, everything is 23 possible to him who believes.'

Immediately the father cried out,   24

'I do believe: aid my weak faith.'

Then Jesus, seeing that a crowd was rapidly gathering, 25 rebuked the foul spirit, and said to it,

'Dumb and deaf spirit, I command you, come out of him and never enter into him again.'

So with a loud cry it threw the boy into fit after 26 fit, and came out. The boy looked as if he were dead, so that most of them said he was dead; but Jesus 27 took his hand and raised him up, and he stood on his feet.

After the return of Jesus to the house His disciples asked 28 Him privately,

'How is it that we could not expel the spirit?'

'An evil spirit of this kind,' He answered, 'can only be 29 driven out by prayer.'

18. *Dashes him to the ground*] Or ' tears him with spasms.'
24. *Cried out*] v.l. adds ' with tears.'
29. *By prayer*] v.l. adds ' and fasting '; as in Matt. xvii. 21.

Jesus again predicts His own Death and Resurrection

Departing thence they passed through Gali- 30 lee, and He was unwilling that any one should know it ; for He was teaching His disciples, 31 and telling them,

' The Son of Man is to be betrayed into the hands of men, and they will put Him to death ; and after being put to death, in three days He will rise to life again.'

They, however, did not understand what He meant, and 32 were afraid to question Him.

A Lesson in Humility

So they came to Capernaum ; and when in 33 the house He asked them,

' What were you arguing about on the way ? '

But they remained silent ; for on the way they had 34 debated with one another who was the chief of them. Then sitting down He called the twelve, and said to 35 them,

' If any one wishes to be first, he must be last of all and servant of all.'

And taking a young child He set him in their midst, 36 threw His arms round him, and said,

' Whoever for my sake receives one such young child as 37 this receives me ; and whoever receives me, receives not so much me as Him who sent me.'

Intolerance Rebuked

' Rabbi,' said John to Him, ' we saw a man 38 making use of your name to expel demons, and we tried to hinder him, because he did not follow us.'

' Hinder him not,' replied Jesus, ' for there is no one 39 who will perform a miracle in my name and be able the next minute to speak evil of me. He who is not against us is for 40 us ; and whoever gives you a cup of water to drink because 41 you belong to Christ, I tell you that he will certainly not lose his reward.

(vv. 30–32.) Cf. Matt. xvii. 22, 23 ; Luke ix. 43–45.
(vv. 33–37.) Cf. Matt. xviii. 1–5 ; Luke ix. 46–48.
37. *For my sake*] Or ' as being mine,' ' in my name.'   Cf. verse 39 ; Matt. xviii. 5 ; xxiv. 5.
(vv. 38–40.) Cf. Luke ix. 49, 50 ; not in Matthew.
40. In another connection, Matthew (xii. 30) and Luke (xi. 23) give a saying which, if applied to the same circumstances, would contradict the declaration that neutrality is not necessarily hostility, ' He that is not with me is against me ' ; but that was addressed to a situation of avowed and virulent hostility to Jesus, in which indifference meant alliance with His foes. Interpretation must always pay heed to context. Cf. iii. 29, n.

'Whoever shall occasion the fall of one of 42
Stones of Stumbling these little ones who believe, it would be better
for him if with a millstone hanging round his
neck he had been thrown into the sea. If your hand 43
should cause you to fall, cut it off : it would be better for
you to enter into Life maimed, than possessing both your
hands to go into Gehenna, into the fire which cannot be
put out. Or if your foot should cause you to fall, cut it 45
off : it would be better for you to enter into Life crippled,
than possessing both your feet to be thrown into Gehenna.
Or if your eye should cause you to fall, tear it out. It would 47
be better for you to enter into the Kingdom of God with
one eye, than possessing two eyes to be thrown into
Gehenna, where THEIR WORM DOES NOT DIE AND THE FIRE 48
IS NOT PUT OUT (Isa. lxvi. 24). Every one shall be salted 49
with fire. Salt is a good thing, but if the salt should become 50
tasteless, with what will you restore the saltness ? Have
salt within you and live at peace with one another.'

A Question about Divorce Setting out from that place, He enters the 1 **1**
district of Judaea and crosses the Jordan : again
the people flock to Him, and again, as usual,
He taught them. Presently a party of Pharisees come to 2
Him with the question—seeking to entrap Him,

'May a man divorce his wife ?'

'What rule did Moses lay down for you ?' He answered. 3

'Moses,' they said, 'permitted a man to draw up a 4
written notice of divorce, and to send his wife away'
(Deut. xxiv. 1).

'It was in consideration of your stubborn hearts,' said 5
Jesus, 'that Moses made this law for you ; but at the 6
creation, "MALE AND FEMALE DID GOD MAKE THEM (Gen.
i. 27). FOR THIS REASON A MAN SHALL LEAVE HIS FATHER 7

(vv. 42–50.) Cf. Matt. xviii. 6–9 ; Luke xvii. 1, 2.
42. *Believe*] v.l. adds ' in me.'
Millstone] Lit. ' ass-millstone.'
43. *Gehenna*] Cf. Matt. v. 22, n.
v.l. adds as in verse 48, ' Where their worm does not die and the fire is not put out.'
49. *With fire*] *i.e.* with some kind of discipline or (it may be) self-chastisement.
Cf. Mal. iii. 2, 3 ; 1 Pet. i. 7 ; iv. 12. v.l. adds ' and every sacrifice shall be salted with salt.' In the moral making of a man he must suffer pain, self-inflicted or inflicted upon him, sharp and fierce as the pain of fire ; but the fire acts as the purifying and preserving salt of God.
1. Cf. Matt. xix. 1, 2 ; Luke xvii. 11.
(vv. 2–12.) Cf. Matt. xix. 3–12.
7. *Shall*] Or ' will.'

AND HIS MOTHER, AND SHALL CLING TO HIS WIFE, AND THE 8
TWO SHALL BE ONE " (Gen. ii. 24) ; so that they are two
no longer, but one. What, therefore, God has joined 9
together let not man separate.'

Indoors the disciples began questioning Jesus again on 10
the same subject. He replied, 11
' Whoever divorces his wife and marries another woman,
commits adultery against the first wife ; and if a woman 12
divorces her husband and marries another man, she
commits adultery.'

Children welcomed and blessed One day people were bringing young children 13
to Jesus for Him to touch them, but the dis-
ciples interfered. Jesus, however, on seeing 14
this, was moved to indignation, and said to them,
' Let the little children come to me : do not hinder them ;
for to those who are childlike the Kingdom of God belongs.
In truth I tell you that whoever does not receive the 15
Kingdom of God like a little child will certainly not
enter it.'

Then He took them in His arms and blessed them 16
lovingly, laying His hands upon them.

Eternal Life As He went out on the road, there came a 17
man running up to Him, who knelt at His feet
and asked,
' Good Rabbi, what am I to do in order to inherit eternal
life ? '

' Why do you call me good ? ' asked Jesus in reply ; 18
' there is no one good except One—that is, God. You 19
know the Commandments—" DO NOT MURDER "; " DO
NOT COMMIT ADULTERY "; " DO NOT STEAL "; " DO
NOT LIE IN GIVING EVIDENCE "; " DO NOT DEFRAUD ";
" HONOUR THY FATHER AND THY MOTHER "' (Deut. v.
16–20).

' Rabbi,' he replied, ' all these Commandments I have 20
carefully obeyed from my youth.'

Then Jesus looked at him and loved him, and said, 21
' One thing is lacking in you : go, sell all you possess

---

7. *And shall cling to his wife*] v.L. omits these words.
8. *One*] Lit. ' one flesh.'
(vv. 13–16.) Cf. Matt. xix. 13–15 ; Luke xviii. 15–17.
16. *Took them in His arms*] Or ' threw His arms round them.' The same word is
used in ix. 36.
(vv. 17–31.) See notes on Matt. xix. 16–30.
17. *A man*] Or ' one man.' Cf. Matt. vi. 27, n.

and give the proceeds to the poor, and you shall have riches in heaven ; and come and follow me.'

At these words his brow darkened, and he went away 22 sad ; for he possessed great wealth.

Then looking round on His disciples Jesus 23 said,

The Dangers of Wealth

' How hard will it be for the possessors of riches to enter the Kingdom of God ! '

The disciples were amazed at His words. Jesus, how- 24 ever, said again,

' Children, how hard it is for those who trust in riches to enter the Kingdom of God ! It is easier for a camel to 25 go through the eye of a needle than for a rich man to enter the Kingdom of God.'

They were astonished beyond measure, and said to one 26 another,

' Who then can be saved ? '

Jesus, looking on them, said, 27

' With men it is impossible, but not with God ; for everything is possible with God.'

Self-sacrifice for Christ enriches

Peter said to Him, ' See, we gave up every- 28 thing and have followed you.'

' In truth I tell you,' replied Jesus, ' that there 29 is no one who has forsaken house, or brothers or sisters, or mother or father, or children or lands, for my sake and for the sake of the gospel, but will receive a hundred 30 times as much now in this present life—houses, brothers, sisters, mothers, children, lands—and persecution with them—and in the coming age eternal life. But many who 31 are now first will be last, and the last, first.'

Jesus a third time predicts His Death and Resurrection

They were on the road going up to Jerusalem, 32 and Jesus was walking ahead of them ; they were awe-struck, and those who followed did so in fear. Then, once more calling to Him the twelve, He began to tell them what was about to happen to Him.

' See,' He said, ' we are going up to Jerusalem, where 33

---

24. *For those who trust in riches*] v.l. omits these words.
(vv. 32–34.) Again one of the vivid pictures which we owe to Mark alone. For 'And as they followed,' R.V. has 'And they that followed': Jesus a little in front, absorbed and unapproachable ; then the disciples, awe-stricken at the tension of a new purpose they could not understand ; then a larger company, their eagerness to follow Jesus now chilled by vague foreboding of coming disaster.

the Son of Man will be betrayed to the High Priests and the Scribes. They will condemn Him to death, and will hand Him over to the Gentiles ; they will mock Him, 34 spit on Him, scourge Him, and put Him to death ; but on the third day He will rise to life again.'

Preeminence in the Kingdom Then James and John, the sons of Zebedee, 35 came up to Him and said,

' Rabbi, we wish you would grant us what we may ask of you.'

' What would you have me do for you ? ' He asked. 36

' Allow us,' they replied, ' to sit one at your right hand 37 and the other at your left hand, in your glory.'

' You know not,' said He, ' what you are asking. Are 38 you able to drink out of the cup from which I am to drink, or to be baptized with the baptism with which I am to be baptized ? '

' We are able,' they replied. 39

' Out of the cup,' said Jesus, ' from which I am to drink you shall drink, and with the baptism with which I am to be baptized you shall be baptized ; but as to sitting at my 40 right hand or at my left, that is not mine to give : it will be for those for whom it has been reserved.'

Humble Service true Greatness The other ten, hearing of it, were at first 41 highly indignant with James and John. Jesus, 42 however, called them to Him and said to them,

' You are aware how those who are deemed rulers among the Gentiles lord it over them, and their great men make them feel their authority ; but it is not so among you. No, 43 whoever desires to be great among you must be your servant ; and whoever desires to be first among you must 44 be the bondservant of all. For indeed the Son of Man did 45 not come to be served, but to serve others, and to give His life as the redemption-price for many.'

A blind Man receives Sight They came to Jericho ; and as He was 46 leaving that town—Himself and His disciples and a great crowd—Bartimaeus (the son of Timaeus), a blind beggar, was sitting by the way-side. Hearing that it was Jesus the Nazarene, he began to cry out, 47

' Son of David, Jesus, have pity on me.'

(vv. 35–45.) Cf. Matt. xx. 20–28.
45. See Matt. xx. 28, n.
(vv. 46–52.) Cf. Matt. xx. 29–34 ; Luke xviii. 35–43.

Many angrily told him to leave off shouting ; but he only 48
cried out all the louder,

' Son of David, have pity on me.'

Then Jesus stood still. 49

' Call him,' He said.

So they called the blind man.

' Cheer up,' they said ; ' rise, he is calling you.'

The man flung away his cloak, sprang to his feet, and 50
came to Jesus.

' What shall I do for you ? ' said Jesus. 51

' Rabboni,' replied the blind man, ' let me recover my
sight.'

' Go,' said Jesus, ' your faith has cured you.' 52

Instantly he regained his sight, and followed Him along
the road.

An Ass's Colt is borrowed   When they were getting near Jerusalem and 1 **11**
had arrived at Bethphagé and Bethany, at the
Mount of Olives, Jesus sent two of His disciples
on in front, with these instructions. 2

' Go to the village facing you, and immediately on
entering it you will find an ass's colt tied up which no one
has ever yet ridden : untie it and bring it here. And if any 3
one asks you, " Why are you doing that ? " say, " The
Master needs it, and will send it back here without
delay." '

So they went and found a young ass tied up at the front 4
door of a house. They were untying it, when some of the 5
bystanders called out,

' What are you doing, untying the colt ? '

And they told them what Jesus had said, and they let 6
them take it.

Jesus rides into Jerusalem   So they brought the colt to Jesus, and threw 7
their garments over it ; and He mounted.
Then many spread their garments to carpet the 8
road, and others leafy branches which they had cut down in
the fields ; while those who led the way and those who 9
followed kept shouting,

' HOSANNA !

BLESSED BE HE WHO COMES IN THE LORD'S NAME

(Ps. cxviii. 25, 26).

51. *Rabboni*] Cf. John xx. 16.
(vv. 1–11.) Cf. Matt. xxi. 1–11 ; Luke xix. 29–44 ; John xii. 12–19.

Blessings on the coming Kingdom of our forefather 10
David !
HOSANNA IN THE HIGHEST ! ' (Ps. cxlviii. 1).

So He came into Jerusalem and entered the Temple ; and 11 after looking round upon everything there, the hour being now late, He went out to Bethany with the twelve.

A Fig-tree cursed The next day, after they had left Bethany, 12 He was hungry. In the distance He saw a 13 fig-tree in full leaf, and went to see whether perhaps He could find some figs on it. When, however, He came to it, He found nothing but leaves (for it was not fig-time) ; and He said to the tree, 14

' Let no one ever again eat fruit from thee ! '

And His disciples heard this.

The Dealers driven from the Temple They came to Jerusalem, and entering the 15 Temple He began to drive out the buyers and sellers, and upset the money-changers' tables and the stools of the dealers in doves, and would not allow 16 any one to carry any vessel through the Temple. And 17 He remonstrated with them.

' Is it not written,' He said,

' " MY HOUSE SHALL BE CALLED A HOUSE OF PRAYER FOR ALL THE NATIONS " (Isa. lvi. 7) ? But you have made it what it now is—A ROBBERS' CAVE ' (Jer. vii. 11).

This the High Priests and Scribes heard, and they 18 sought means to destroy Him. For they were afraid of Him, because all the people were amazed at His teaching. When evening came on, Jesus and His disciples used to 19 leave the city.

The Fig-tree withers. In the early morning, as they passed by, 20 they saw the fig-tree withered to the roots ;

The Power of Faith and Peter, recollecting, said to Him, 21 ' Look, Rabbi, the fig-tree which you cursed is withered up.'

Jesus said to them, 22

' Have faith in God. I tell you **in** truth that if any 23 one shall say to this mountain, " Arise, and hurl yourself into the sea," and has no doubt about it in his heart, but stedfastly believes that what he says will happen, it shall

(vv. 12–14.) Cf. Matt. xxi. 18, 19, 22, n.
(vv. 15–19.) Cf. Matt. xxi. 12–17 ; Luke xix. 45–48 ; xxi. 37, 38.
(vv. 20–25.) Cf. Matt. vi. 14, 15 ; xxi. 20–22.

be granted him. That is why I tell you, whatever you pray 24
and ask for, if you believe that you have received it, it shall
be yours. And whenever you stand praying, if you have a 25
grievance against any one, forgive it, so that your Father in
heaven may also forgive you your offences.'

The Leaders of the People silenced They came again to Jerusalem ; and as He 27
was walking in the Temple, the High Priests, and
the Scribes and Elders came and asked Him, 28
' By what authority are you doing these
things ? and who gave you authority to do them ? '

' And I will put a question to you,' replied Jesus ; 29
' answer me, and then I will tell you by what authority I
do these things. John's Baptism—was it from heaven or 30
from men ? Answer me.'

So they debated the matter with one another. 31

' Suppose we say, " from heaven," ' they argued, ' he will
ask, " Why then did you not believe him ? " Or should 32
we say, " from men " '—they were afraid of the people ; for
all agreed in holding John to have been really a Prophet.
So they answered Jesus, 33

' We do not know.'

' Nor do I tell you,' said Jesus, ' by what authority I do
these things.'

'The wicked Vine-dressers' Then He began to speak to them in parable. 1 **12**
' There was once a man,' He said, ' who
planted a vineyard, fenced it round, dug a pit
for the wine-vat, and built a watch-tower. Then he let the
place to vine-dressers and went abroad. At vintage-time 2
he sent one of his servants to receive from the vine-dressers
a share of the vintage. But they seized him, beat him 3
cruelly, and sent him away empty-handed. Again he sent 4
to them another servant ; and him they wounded in the head
and treated shamefully. Yet a third he sent, and him they 5
killed. And he sent many besides, and them also they ill-
treated, beating some and killing others. He had still one 6
left whom he could send, a dearly-loved son : he sent him
last of all, saying,

' " They will treat my son with respect."

' But those men—the vine-dressers—said to one another, 7

---

25. v.l. inserts verse 26 here : ' But if you do not forgive, neither will your Father
in heaven forgive your offences,' from Matt. vi. 15.
(vv. 28–33.) See Matt. xxi. 25, n.
(vv. 1–12.) Cf. Matt. xxi. 33–46 ; Luke xx. 9–19.

' " Here is the heir : come, let us kill him, and then the inheritance shall be ours."

' So they seized him and killed him, and flung his body 8 outside the vineyard. What, therefore, will the owner of 9 the vineyard do ? '

' He will come and put the vine-dressers to death, and will give the vineyard to others.'

' Have you not read even this passage,' He added, 10

' " THE STONE WHICH THE BUILDERS REJECTED

HAS BECOME THE CORNERSTONE :

THIS CAME FROM THE LORD, 11

AND IT IS WONDERFUL IN OUR EYES " ? '

(Ps. cxviii. 22, 23).

Now they were looking out for an opportunity to seize 12 Him, but were afraid of the people ; for they saw that in this parable He had referred to themselves. So they left Him and went away.

A Question about Tribute Their next step was to send to Him some of 13 the Pharisees and of Herod's partisans to entrap Him in conversation. So they came to Him. 14

' Rabbi,' they said, ' we know that you are a truthful man and you pay no special regard to any one, since you do not consider men's outward appearance, but teach God's way truly. Is it allowable to pay poll-tax to Caesar, or not ? Shall we pay, or shall we refuse to pay ? ' 15

But He, knowing their hypocrisy, replied,

' Why try to ensnare me ?   Bring me a shilling for me to look at.'

They brought one ; and He asked them, 16

' Whose is this likeness and this inscription ? '

' Caesar's,' they replied.

' What is Caesar's,' replied Jesus, ' pay to Caesar—and 17 what is God's, pay to God.'

And they wondered exceedingly at Him.

A Question about the Resurrection Then came to Him a party of Sadducees, a 18 sect which denies that there is any resurrection, and they proceeded to question Him.

' Rabbi,' they said, ' Moses made it a law for us : " IF A 19 MAN'S BROTHER SHOULD DIE AND LEAVE A WIFE, BUT NO CHILD, THE MAN SHALL MARRY THE WIDOW AND RAISE UP A

(vv. 13–17.) Cf. Matt. xxii. 15–22 ; Luke xx. 20–26.
(vv. 18–27.) Cf. Matt. xxii. 23–33 ; Luke xx. 27–39.

FAMILY FOR HIS BROTHER " (Deut. xxv. 5, 6). There were 20 once seven brothers, the eldest of whom took a wife, but at his death left no family. The second married the widow, 21 and died, leaving no family ; and the third did the same. And so did the rest of the seven, all dying childless. 22 Finally the woman also died. At the Resurrection whose 23 wife will she be ? For they all seven married her.'

' Is not this the cause of your error,' replied Jesus— 24 ' your ignorance alike of the Scriptures and of the power of God ? For when they have risen from the dead, men do 25 not marry and women are not given in marriage, but they are as angels are in heaven. But as to the dead rising to life, 26 have you never read in the Book of Moses, in the passage about the Bush, how God said to him, " I AM THE GOD OF ABRAHAM, AND THE GOD OF ISAAC, AND THE GOD OF JACOB " (Exod. iii. 2–6) ? He is not the God of dead, but of living 27 men. You are in grave error.'

Love, the supreme Law Then one of the Scribes, who had heard them 28 disputing and well knew that Jesus had given them an answer to the point, came forward and asked Him,

' Which is the chief of all the Commandments ? '

' The chief Commandment,' replied Jesus, ' is this : 29 " HEAR, O ISRAEL ! THE LORD OUR GOD IS ONE LORD ; AND THOU SHALT LOVE THE LORD THY GOD WITH THY 30 WHOLE HEART, THY WHOLE SOUL, THY WHOLE MIND, AND THY WHOLE STRENGTH " (Deut. vi. 4, 5).

' The second is this : " THOU SHALT LOVE THY NEIGHBOUR 31 AS THYSELF " (Lev. xix. 18).

' There is no other Commandment greater than these.' And the Scribe said to Him, 32

' Rightly, in very truth, Rabbi, have you said that He stands alone, and there is no other than He ; and to love 33 Him with all one's heart, with all one's understanding, and with all one's strength, and to love one's neighbour no less than oneself is far better than all our whole burnt-offerings and sacrifices ' (1 Sam. xv. 22).

Perceiving that the Scribe had answered wisely, Jesus 34 said to him,

' You are not far from the Kingdom of God.'

No one from that time forward ventured to put any question to Him.

David's Son and David's Lord Now, while teaching in the Temple Jesus asked, 35

'How is it the Scribes say that the Christ is a son of David? David himself, taught by the Holy Spirit, said, 36

'"THE LORD SAID TO MY LORD,
SIT AT MY RIGHT HAND,
UNTIL I HAVE MADE THY FOES A FOOTSTOOL UNDER THY FEET" (Ps. cx. 1).

'David himself calls Him "Lord": how then can He be his son?' 37

And the mass of the people heard Jesus gladly.

And in the course of His teaching He said, 38

The Scribes denounced 'Be on your guard against the Scribes, who like to walk about in long robes and to be bowed to in places of public resort, and to occupy the best places in the synagogues and at dinner-parties, and who swallow up the property of widows and then mask their wickedness by making long prayers: the heavier the punishment these men shall receive.' 39 40

The Widow's Gift Having taken a seat opposite the Treasury, He observed how the people were dropping money into the Treasury, and that many of the wealthy threw in large sums. But there came one poor widow and dropped in two mites, equal in value to a farthing. So He called His disciples to Him and said, 41 42 43

'I tell you in truth that this widow, poor as she is, has thrown in more than all the other contributors to the Treasury; for they have all contributed what they could well spare, but she out of her need has thrown in all she possessed—all she had to live on.' 44

Jesus predicts the Destruction of the Temple As He was leaving the Temple, one of His disciples exclaimed, 1 **13**

'Look, Rabbi, what wonderful stones! what wonderful buildings!'

'You see all these great buildings?' Jesus 2

(vv. 35–37.) Cf. Matt. xxii. 41–46 ; Luke xx. 41–44.
(vv. 38–40.) Cf. Matt. xxiii. 1–39 ; Luke xx. 45–47.
38. *Be on your guard against*] Lit. ' look away from.'
(vv. 41–44.) Cf. Luke xxi. 1–4.
(vv. 1–37.) Cf. Matt. xxiv ; Luke xxi. For detailed exposition see the Commentaries.

replied ; 'not one stone will be left here resting upon another, and not thrown down.'

Things which would happen first He was sitting on the Mount of Olives 3 opposite to the Temple, when Peter, James, John, and Andrew, apart from the others, asked Him,

'Tell us, when will these things be ? and what will be 4 the sign when all these predictions are about to be fulfilled ? '

So Jesus began to tell them : 5

'Take care that no one misleads you. Many will come 6 in my name, and say, " I am He " ; and they will mislead many. But when you hear of wars and rumours of wars, 7 do not be alarmed : come they must, but the end is not yet. For NATION WILL RISE IN ARMS AGAINST NATION, 8 AND KINGDOM AGAINST KINGDOM (Isa. xix. 2). There will be earthquakes in various places ; there will be famines. These miseries are but like the early pains of childbirth.

Persecution and world-wide Preaching 'You yourselves must be on your guard. 9 They will deliver you up to Sanhedrins : you will be brought into synagogues and cruelly beaten ; and you will stand before governors and kings for my sake, to be witnesses to them for me. But 10 the proclamation of the gospel must be carried to all nations before the end comes. And when they are march- 11 ing you along under arrest, do not be anxious beforehand about what you are to say, but speak what is given you

---

Certain features of the discourse stand out most clearly in Mark's record of it.

(1) The prediction is of the destruction of the Temple ; and the question of the disciples refers to this one event—when ? and heralded by what signs ? The addition in Matthew (Thy Coming, and the end of the world) and the discourse itself seem to link the three events into one.

(2) The prophecy does not allow of a double reference. It is not possible to pick out some parts as describing the destruction of Jerusalem (A.D. 70), and others the end of the world, still to come.

(3) In its form the prophecy has many of the characteristics of Jewish Apocalyptic literature, e.g. the successive stages of the beginning of travail (verse 8), tribulation (verse 19), and the final ushering in of the crisis (verses 24–26). Cf. the three Woes of Rev. ix. 12 ; xi. 14.

(4) The one event of which Jesus spoke was the Coming of the Son of Man (verse 26), and at the close of the continuous prophecy comes the clear statement, ' This generation shall not pass away until all these things be accomplished.' It may be said that the catastrophe of A.D. 70 was indeed a ' Coming of the Son of Man in power.' For it made a new world and set free the spiritual forces of the gospel of the Kingdom of God.

(vv. 9–13.) Cf. Matt. x. 17–22.

Matthew adds explicitly ' And then shall the end come.' This description of the universal preaching of the gospel does not necessarily look beyond that generation. Cf. Col. i. 6, 23.

when the time comes ; for it will not be you who speak, but
the Holy Spirit.

Stedfastness would be rewarded ' Brother will betray brother to death, and 12
fathers will betray children ; and CHILDREN
WILL RISE AGAINST THEIR PARENTS (Mic. vii. 6)
and have them put to death. You will be objects of uni- 13
versal hatred because you are called by my name, but
those who stand firm to the end shall be saved.

' The Abomination of Desolation' ' But when you see the ABOMINATION OF 14
DESOLATION (Dan. ix. 27) standing where he
ought not '—let the reader observe these words
—' then let those in Judaea escape to the hills ; let him 15
who is on the roof not come down and enter the house to
fetch anything out of it ; and let not him who is in the 16
field turn back to pick up his outer garment. And alas for 17
the women who at that time are with child or have infants
at the breast !

Unparalleled Distress ' But pray that it may not come in the winter. 18
For those will be times of SUFFERING THE LIKE 19
OF WHICH HAS NEVER BEEN FROM THE FIRST
CREATION OF GOD'S WORLD UNTIL NOW (Dan. xii. 1), and
assuredly never will be again ; and but for the fact that the 20
Lord has cut short those days, no one would escape ; but
for the sake of His elect whom He has chosen for Himself
He has cut short the days.

False Messiahs and false Teachers ' At that time if any one says to you, " See, 21
here is the Christ ! " or " See, He is there ! "
do not believe it. For there will rise up false 22
Christs and false prophets, displaying signs
and prodigies with a view to lead astray, if possible, even
the elect. Do you, however, be on your guard : I have 23
forewarned you of everything.

The Coming of the Son of Man ' But at that time, after that distress, THE 24
SUN WILL BE DARKENED AND THE MOON WILL
NOT SHED HER LIGHT ; THE STARS WILL BE SEEN 25

(vv. 14–37.) Cf. Matt. xxiv. 15–42 ; Luke xxi. 20–36.
Escape to the hills] At the outbreak of the Jewish war (67–70 A.D.) the Christians
in Jerusalem carried out these instructions, availing themselves of an unexpected
opportunity to flee across the mountains to the desert of Perea beyond the Jordan.
(Josephus, *Wars*, ii. 20, iii. 33).
(vv. 21–23.) Cf. Luke xvii. 20–37.
(vv. 24–27.) The details of this description are, of course, not to be taken
literally. They are the attempt of poetic imagery to realise what it means that
God should intervene in human history. Cf. Ps. xviii. 6–17 ; Isa. xiii. 9, 10, 13 ;
xxxiv. 4, 5.

FALLING FROM HEAVEN (Isa. xiii. 10), AND THE FORCES
WHICH ARE IN THE HEAVENS WILL BE DISORDERED (Isa. xxxiv.
4). And then will they see THE SON OF MAN COMING IN 26
CLOUDS (Dan. vii. 13) with great power and glory. Then He 27
will send forth the angels and gather together His elect
from north, south, east, and west — from the furthest
bounds of earth and heaven.

' Learn from the fig-tree the lesson it teaches. As soon 28
as its branch has become soft and it is bursting into leaf,
you know that summer is near. So also do you, when you 29
see these things happening, be sure that He is near, at
your very door. I tell you in truth that the present 30
generation will not pass away until all these things have
happened. Sky and earth will pass away, but my words 31
shall not pass away.

' But as to that day or the hour no one knows—not even 32
the angels in heaven, not even the Son, but the Father alone.
Take care, be on the alert, and pray ; for you do not know 33
when it will happen. It is like a man gone abroad, who has 34
left his house, and given the management to his servants—
to each one his special duty—and has ordered the porter to
keep awake. Keep watch therefore, for you know not 35
when the master of the house is coming—in the evening,
at midnight, at cock-crow, or at dawn. Beware lest He 36
should arrive unexpectedly and find you asleep. And 37
what I say to you I say to all—Keep watch ! '

The Plot to murder Jesus   It was now two days before the Passover and 1 **14**
the feast of Unleavened Bread, and the High
Priests and Scribes were bent on finding how to
seize Him by craft and put Him to death. But they 2
said,

' Not during the Festival, for fear there should be a riot
among the people.'

Affection's costly Gift   Now when He was at Bethany, in the house 3
of Simon the leper, while He was at table, there
came a woman with an alabaster jar of pure
spikenard, very costly : she broke the jar and poured the
ointment over His head. But there were some who said 4
to one another with indignation,

29. *He*] Or ' it.'
32. *Not even the Son*] Cf. Matt. xxiv. 36, n.
(vv. 3–9.) Cf. Matt. xxvi. 6–13 ; John xii. 1–8. Compare also Luke vii. 36–50.
3. *Pure*] Or ' liquid.'

'Why has the ointment been thus wasted? For it 5
might have been sold for fifteen pounds or more, and the
money given to the poor.'

And they were very angry with her. But Jesus said, 6
'Leave her alone: why are you troubling her? She
has done me a most gracious service. You always have 7
the poor among you, and whenever you choose you can do
acts of kindness to them; but me you have not always.
What she could she did: she has perfumed my body in 8
preparation for my burial. And I solemnly tell you that 9
wherever in the whole world the gospel shall be proclaimed, this which she has done shall also be told in
remembrance of her.'

The Treachery of Judas But Judas Iscariot, one of the Twelve, went 10
to the High Priests to betray Jesus to them.
They gladly listened to his proposal, and pro- 11
mised to give him a sum of money. So he looked out for
an opportunity to betray Him.

The Passover prepared On the first day of the feast of Unleavened 12
Bread—the day for killing the Passover lamb—
His disciples asked Him,
'Where shall we go and prepare for you to eat the Pass-
over?'

So He sent two of His disciples with instructions, saying, 13
'Go into the city, and you will meet a man carrying a
pitcher of water: follow him, and whatever house he enters, 14
tell the master of the house, "The Rabbi asks, Where is my
room where I can eat the Passover with my disciples?"
Then he will himself show you a large room upstairs, ready 15
furnished: there make preparation for us.'

So the disciples went out and came to the city, and found 16
everything just as He had told them; and they got the
Passover ready.

'The Last Supper.' The Traitor indicated When it was evening, He came with the 17
twelve. And while they were at table Jesus said, 18
'I tell you in truth that one of you will
betray me—one who is eating with me.'

They were filled with sorrow, and began asking Him, one 19
by one,

---

5. *Fifteen pounds or more*] Lit. 'over 300 denarii.'
(vv. 12–16.) Cf. Matt. xxvi. 17–19; Luke xxii. 7–13.
(vv. 18–21.) Cf. Matt. xxvi. 21–25; Luke xxii. 21–23; John xiii. 21–26.

' Not I, is it ? '

' It is one of the twelve,' He replied ; ' he who is dipping 20 his fingers in the dish with me. For the Son of Man is 21 going His way as it is written about Him ; but woe to the man by whom the Son of Man is betrayed ! It were a happy thing for that man had he never been born.'

The memorial Meal instituted   Also during the meal He took a loaf, blessed 22 it, and broke it. He then gave it to them, saying,

' Take this, it is my body.'

Then He took a cup, gave thanks, and handed it to them, 23 and they all of them drank from it.

' This is my blood,' He said, 'which is to be poured out 24 on behalf of many—the blood that ratifies the Covenant. I tell you that never again shall I drink the produce of the 25 vine till I drink the new wine in the Kingdom of God.'

After singing the hymn, they went out to the Mount 26 of Olives.

Peter's Denial foretold   Then said Jesus to them, 27
' All of you are about to turn against me, for it is written, " I WILL STRIKE DOWN THE SHEP-HERD, AND THE SHEEP WILL BE SCATTERED IN ALL DIRECTIONS " (Zech. xiii. 7). But after I have risen to life again I will go 28 before you into Galilee.'

' All may turn against you,' said Peter, ' yet I will never 29 do so.'

' I tell you in truth,' replied Jesus, ' that to-day—this 30 night—before the cock crows twice, you yourself will three times disown me.'

' Even if I must die with you,' declared Peter again and 31 again, ' I will never disown you.'

In like manner protested also all the disciples.

The Agony in Gethsemane   So they came to a place called Gethsemane. 32 There He said to His disciples,
' Sit down here till I have prayed.'

Then He took with Him Peter and James and John, and 33 began to be full of terror and distress, and He said to them, 34

(vv. 22–25.) Cf. Matt. xxvi. 26–29 ; Luke xxii. 19, 20 ; 1 Cor. xi. 23–25.
24. *The Covenant*] v.L. ' the New Covenant,' as in Luke xxii. 20.
26. *The hymn*] See Matt. xxvi. 30, n.
Cf. Matt. xxvi. 30 ; Luke xxii. 39 ; John xviii. 1.
(vv. 27–31.) Cf. Matt. xxvi. 31–35 ; Luke xxii. 31–38 ; John xiii. 36–38.
(vv. 32–42.) Cf. Matt. xxvi. 36–46 ; Luke xxii. 40–46.

' My heart is crushed with anguish to the point of death : wait here and keep awake.'

Going forward a short distance He threw Himself upon 35 His face, and prayed that, if it were possible, He might be spared that time of agony ; and He said, 36

' Abba ! Father ! all things are possible for Thee : take this cup away from me : and yet not what I will, but what Thou willest.'

Then He came and found them asleep, and He said to 37 Peter,

' Simon, are you asleep ? Were you not able to keep awake a single hour ? Keep awake, all of you, and pray, 38 that you may not come into temptation : the spirit is right willing, but the flesh is frail.'

He again went away and prayed, using the very same 39 words. When He returned He again found them asleep, 40 for they were very weary ; and they knew not how to answer Him. A third time He came, and then He 41 said,

' Sleep on and rest.—Enough ! the hour has come. Even now they are betraying the Son of Man into the hands of sinful men. Rouse yourselves, let us be going : my be- 42 trayer is close at hand.'

Immediately, while He was still speaking, 43 **Judas brings** Judas, one of the Twelve, came and with him **armed Men** a crowd of men armed with swords and cudgels, sent by the High Priests and Scribes and Elders. Now the 44 betrayer had arranged a signal with them.

' The one I kiss,' he said, ' is the man : lay hold of him, and take him safely away.'

So he came, and going straight to Jesus he said, ' Rabbi ! ' 45 and kissed Him affectionately ; whereupon they laid hands 46 on Him and held Him firmly. But one of those who stood 47 by drew his sword and struck a blow at the High Priest's servant, cutting off his ear.

' Have you come out,' said Jesus, ' with 48 **Jesus** **expostulates.** swords and cudgels to arrest me, as if you **The Apostles** had to fight with a robber ? Day after day I 49 **forsake Him** used to be among you in the Temple teaching,

35. *He might be spared that time of agony*] Lit. ' the hour might pass by from Him.'

(vv. 43–52.) Cf. Matt. xxvi. 47–56 ; Luke xxii. 47–53 ; John xviii. 2–11.

and you never seized me. But this is happening in order that the Scriptures may be fulfilled.'

Then they all forsook Him and fled. One youth indeed 50, 51 did follow Him, wearing only a linen cloth round his bare body. Of him they laid hold, but he left the linen cloth 52 in their hands and ran away naked.

Jesus is taken to the High Priest So they led Jesus away to the High Priest, 53 and with him there assembled all the High Priests, Elders, and Scribes. Peter followed 54 Jesus at a distance, as far as the court of the High Priest's palace, where he remained, sitting among the officers, and warming himself by the fire.

False Testimony and gross Insults Meanwhile the High Priests and the entire 55 Sanhedrin were endeavouring to get evidence against Jesus in order to put Him to death, but could find none ; for though many gave false testimony 56 against Him, their statements did not tally. Then some 57 came forward as witnesses and falsely declared,

' We have heard Him say, " I will pull down this Sanctuary 58 built by human hands, and three days afterwards I will erect another built without hands." '

But not even in this was their testimony consistent. 59

At last the High Priest stood up, and, advancing into the 60 midst of them all, asked Jesus,

' Have you no answer to make ? What is this that these witnesses allege against you ? '

But He remained silent, and gave no reply. A second 61 time the High Priest questioned Him.

' Are you the Christ, the Son of the Blessed One ? ' he said.

' I am,' replied Jesus, ' and you all shall see the Son of Man 62 sitting at the right hand of the divine Power, and coming amid the clouds of heaven ' (Ps. cx. 1 ; Dan. vii. 13).

Rending his garments the High Priest exclaimed, 63

' What need have we of witnesses after that ? You all 64 heard His impious words. What is your judgement ? '

Then with one voice they condemned Him as deserving of death. Thereupon some began to spit on Him, and 65 to blindfold Him, while striking Him with their fists and crying,

---

(vv. 53, 54 and 66–72.) Cf. Matt. xxvi. 57, 58, 69–75 ; Luke xxii. 54–62 ; John xviii. 12–18 and 25–27.
(vv. 55–65.) Cf. Matt. xxvi. 59–68 ; Luke xxii. 63–71 ; John xviii. 19–24.

' Prove that you are a prophet.'

The officers too struck Him with open hands.

Peter disowns his Master Now while Peter was below in the court, 66 one of the High Priest's maidservants came, and seeing Peter warming himself she looked 67 at him and said,

' You also were with Jesus, the Nazarene.'

But he denied it, and said, 68

' I don't know, I don't understand—What do you mean ? '

And then he went out into the forecourt. Just then a cock crowed. Again the maidservant saw him, and again 69 began to say to the people standing by,

' He is one of them.'

A second time he repeatedly denied it. Soon afterwards 70 the bystanders again accused Peter, saying,

' You are surely one of them, for indeed you are a Galilaean.'

But he broke out into curses and oaths, declaring, 71

' I know nothing of the man you are talking about.'

No sooner had he spoken than a cock crowed for the 72 second time, and Peter recollected the words of Jesus,

' Before the cock crows twice, you will three times disown me.'

And as he thought of it, he wept aloud.

Jesus is taken before the Roman Governor At earliest dawn, after the High Priests had 1 **15** held a consultation with the Elders and Scribes, they and the entire Sanhedrin bound Jesus and took Him away and handed Him over to Pilate.

So Pilate questioned Him. 2

' Are you the King of the Jews ? ' he asked.

' I am,' replied Jesus.

Then, as the High Priests went on heaping accusations on 3 Him, Pilate again asked Him, 4

---

65. *Struck Him . . hands*] Lit. (in all the best MSS.) ' received Him with blows.'
68. *Just then a cock crowed*] V.L. omits.
72. *He wept aloud*] Matthew and Luke agree in writing ' wept bitterly.' Mark's Greek phrase is different from theirs, *epibalōn eklaie*, Lit. ' throwing (or ' falling ') upon, he wept,' and is of very doubtful interpretation. A.V. and R.V. have ' When he thought thereon he wept,' *i.e.* ' throwing his mind upon it '; A.V. mg. and R.V. mg. ' He began to weep,' *i.e.* ' He threw himself on weeping.' Another suggestion is ' He covered his head and wept '; but a papyrus of B.C. 112 has the same participle ' epibalōn ' joined with a verb, apparently in the sense ' He *set to*, and dammed up the water course '; so perhaps Mark means ' He *fell a-weeping*,' ' burst into tears,' ' broke out into loud lamentations.'
(vv. 2–5.) Cf. Matt. xxvii. 11–14 ; Luke xxiii. 3–5 ; John xviii. 33–38.

' Do you make no reply ? Listen to the many charges they are bringing against you.'

But Jesus made no further answer : so that Pilate wondered. 5

Pilate hesitates, but condemns Him Now at the Festival it was customary for Pilate to release to the Jews any one prisoner whom they might beg for ; and at this time a man named Barabbas was in prison among the insurgents—persons who in the insurrection had committed murder. So the people came crowding up, asking Pilate to grant them the usual favour. 6 7 8

' Shall I release for you the King of the Jews ? ' answered Pilate. 9

For he could see that it was out of sheer spite that the High Priests had handed Him over. But the High Priests urged on the crowd to get him to release Barabbas instead. And Pilate again asked them, ' What then shall I do to the man you call the King of the Jews ? ' They once more shouted out, 10 11 12 13

' Crucify him ! '

' But, what crime has he committed ? ' asked Pilate. But all the more they shouted, 14

' Crucify him ! '

So Pilate, wishing to satisfy the mob, released Barabbas to them, and then scourged Jesus and handed Him over for crucifixion. 15

Jesus is grossly insulted and ill-treated Then the soldiers led Him away into the court of the Palace (the Praetorium), and calling together the whole battalion they arrayed Him in purple, placed on His head a wreath of thorny twigs which they had twisted, and went on to salute Him with shouts of ' Long live the King of the Jews ' ! Then they began to beat Him on the head with a cane, to spit on Him, and to do Him homage on bended knees. At last, having finished their sport, they took the robe off Him, put His own clothes on Him, and led Him out to crucify Him. 16 17 18 19 20

Golgotha One Simon, a Cyrenean, the father of Alexander and Rufus, was passing along, coming from the country : him they compelled to carry His cross. 21

(vv. 6–15.) Cf. Matt. xxvii. 15–26 ; Luke xxiii. 18–25 ; John xviii. 39 ; xix. 1.
(vv. 16–20.) Cf. Matt. xxvii. 27–31 ; John xix. 1–16.
(vv. 21–24.) Cf. Matt. xxvii. 31–34 ; Luke xxiii. 26–33 ; John xix. 17, 18.

So they brought Him to the place called Golgotha, which, 22
being translated, means ' Skull - ground.' Here they 23
offered Him wine mixed with myrrh ; but He refused it.
Then they crucified Him, and they divided His garments 24
among them, drawing lots to decide what each should take.
It was nine o'clock in the morning when they crucified 25
Him. And the written inscription of the charge against 26
Him was,

THE KING OF THE JEWS.

The People and their Rulers revile Him

And together with Jesus they crucified two 27
robbers, one at His right hand and one at His
left. And all the passers-by reviled Him. 29
They shook their heads at Him and said,

' Ah ! you who were for destroying the Sanctuary and
building a new one in three days, come down from the 30
cross and save yourself.'

In the same way the High Priests also, as well as the 31
Scribes, kept on scoffing at Him, saying to one another,

' He has saved others : himself he cannot save ! This 32
Christ, the King of Israel, let him come down now from
the cross, that we may see and believe.'

Even the men crucified with Him heaped insults on
Him.

Jesus dies

At noon there came a darkness over the whole 33
land, lasting till three o'clock in the afternoon.
And at three o'clock Jesus cried out with a 34
loud voice,

' ELÔI, ELÔI, LEMA SABACHTHANI ? ' which means, ' MY
GOD, MY GOD, WHY HAST THOU FORSAKEN ME ? '
(Ps. xxii. 1).

Some of the bystanders, hearing Him, said, 35

' Listen, He is calling for Elijah ! '

Then a man ran to fill a sponge with sour wine, and 36
he put it on the end of a cane and placed it to His lips,
saying at the same time,

23. Cf. Matt. xxvii. 34, n.
(vv. 24-26.) Cf. Matt. xxvii. 35-38 ; Luke xxiii. 33, 34, 38 ; John xix. 18-24.
27. V.L. adds verse 28, ' And the Scripture was fulfilled which says, And He was
reckoned among the lawless ' (Isa. liii. 12).
(vv. 29-32.) Cf. Matt. xxvii. 39-44 ; Luke xxiii. 35-37 and 39-43 ; John xix.
25-27.
32. *Saved . . save*] Or ' cured . . cure.'
Himself he cannot save !] Or ' can he not save himself ? '
(vv. 33-37.) Cf. Matt. xxvii. 45-50 ; Luke xxiii. 44-46 ; John xix. 28-30.
36. *Sour wine*] Cf. Matt. xxvii. 48, n.

' Wait ! let us see whether Elijah will come and take Him down.'

But Jesus uttered a loud cry and yielded up His 37 spirit.

And the curtain of the Sanctuary was torn in two, from 38 top to bottom.

When the Centurion who stood in front of the cross saw 39 that He was dead, he exclaimed,

' This man was indeed the Son of God.'

There were also women looking on from a distance; among 40 them being both Mary of Magdala and Mary the mother of James the little and of Joses, and Salome—all of whom 41 in the Galilaean days had habitually been with Him and attended upon Him, as well as many other women who had come up to Jerusalem with Him.

Joseph of Arimathaea buries the Body of Jesus Towards sunset, as it was the Preparation— 42 that is, the day preceding the Sabbath—Joseph 43 of Arimathaea came, a highly respected member of the Council, who himself was living in expectation of the Kingdom of God. He summoned up courage to go in to see Pilate and beg for the body of Jesus. But Pilate could hardly believe that He was already dead. 44 And he called for the Centurion and inquired whether He had been long dead ; having ascertained the fact, he granted 45 the body to Joseph. Then Joseph bought a sheet of linen, 46 took Him down, wrapped Him in the sheet and laid Him in a tomb hewn in the rock ; after which he rolled a stone against the entrance to the tomb. Mary of Magdala and 47 Mary the mother of Joses were looking on to see where He was put.

The empty Tomb When the Sabbath was over, Mary of Mag- 1 **16** dala, Mary the mother of James, and Salome, bought spices, in order to come and anoint His body. So, very soon after sunrise on the first day of 2 the week, they came to the tomb ; and they said to one 3 another,

(vv. 38–41.) Cf. Matt. xxvii. 51–56 ; Luke xxiii. 45 and 47–49.
38. *Was torn*] Cf. Matt. xxvii. 51, n.
39. *Centurion*] Or ' captain.' But Mark uses the Latin name here and in verses 44, 45. It occurs nowhere else in the N.T.
(vv. 42–47.) Cf. Matt. xxvii. 57–61 ; Luke xxiii. 50–56 ; John xix. 38–42.
42. *Towards sunset*] Lit. ' and when evening was now come.' See Matt. xxvii. 57, n.
43. *Council*] *i.e.* ' Sanhedrin.'
(vv. 1–4.) Cf. Matt. xxviii. 1–4 ; Luke xxiv. 1–3 ; John xx. 1.

' Who will roll away the stone for us from the entrance
to the tomb ? '

But then, looking up, they saw that the stone was already 4
rolled back : it was of immense size. Upon entering the 5
tomb, they saw a young man sitting at their right hand,
clothed in a long white robe. They were terrified. But 6
he said to them,

' Do not be terrified. It is Jesus you are looking for—
the Nazarene, the crucified one. He has come back to life :
He is not here : this is the place where they laid Him.
But go and tell His disciples and Peter that He is going 7
before you into Galilee : and that there you will see Him,
as He told you.'

So they came out, and fled from the tomb, for they were 8
trembling and amazed ; and they said not a word to any
one, for they were afraid.

Jesus is seen [Now when He rose to life early on the first 9
by Mary of day of the week, He appeared first to Mary
Magdala of Magdala, from whom He had expelled
seven demons. She brought the tidings to those who 10
had been with Him, who were now mourning and
weeping. But they, when they were told that He 11
was alive and that He had been seen by her, could not
believe it.

And on the Afterwards He showed Himself in another 12
Road to form to two of them as they were walking, on
Emmaus their way into the country. These, again, went 13
and told the news to the rest ; but they did not believe
them either.

Later still He showed Himself to the eleven themselves 14
whilst they were at table, and He upbraided them with their
unbelief and obstinacy in not believing those who had seen
Him alive. Then He said to them, 15

(vv. 5–7.) Cf. Matt. xxviii. 5–7 ; Luke xxiv. 4–8.

8. Cf. Matt. xviii. 8 ; Luke xxiv. 9–11 ; John xx. 2.

9. v.L. omits verses 9–20. It may now be regarded as an assured finding of criticism
that these verses are not part of Mark's Gospel. The internal evidence, in itself
really decisive for their rejection, is confirmed by the external testimony. (See
R.V. mg.). Mark, master of vivid and effective narrative, can hardly have intended to finish his story with the inartistic and impotent ending of verse 8.
Possibly all copies of the Gospel descended from a single manuscript which had
lost its last leaf.

(vv. 9–11.) Cf. Matt. xxviii. 9, 10 ; John xx. 11–18.

(vv. 12, 13.) Cf. Luke xxiv. 13–35.

14. Cf. Luke xxiv. 36–43 ; John xx. 19–25.

(vv. 15–18.) Cf. Matt. xxviii. 16–20.

The Mission of the Apostles to the World ' Go the whole world over, and proclaim the gospel to all mankind. He who believes and 16 is baptized shall be saved, but he who disbelieves will be condemned. And signs shall 17 attend those who believe, even such as these : by my name they shall expel demons ; they shall speak new languages ; they shall take up venomous snakes ; and 18 even if they drink any deadly poison, it shall do them no harm whatever ; they shall lay their hands on the sick, and they shall recover.'

Jesus is taken up into Heaven So the Lord Jesus after having thus spoken 19 to them was taken up into heaven, and He sat down at the right hand of God. And they 20 went out and preached everywhere, the Lord working with them and confirming the word by the signs which accompanied it.]

15. *Mankind*] Lit. ' the creation.'
17. *New languages*] Lit. ' with new tongues.' v.l. omits ' new.'
(vv. 19, 20.) Cf. Luke xxiv. 44–53 ; Acts i. 3–12.
19. *Jesus*] v.l. omits.

THE GOSPEL ACCORDING TO ST. LUKE

CHARACTERISTICS OF ST. LUKE

This ' most beautiful book that ever was written ' has already been characterized as the Gospel of *grace*. The reader is prepared for this indefinable quality by the incomparable stories of chapters i. and ii., with their embedded hymns : he finds it in prevailing features, which have often been summarized but may better be discovered than catalogued—gladness, kindliness, sympathy, emphasis on prayer and praise, prominence of women and domestic scenes. Wherever the writer has free play, there penetrates the story, like some sweet subtle essence, the same note of tender, gracious humanity. The later tradition which described Luke as a painter is at least justified by many an immortal picture from his pen.

The Preface (i. 1–4) is of unique interest. It shows us the scholarly historian, claiming only the merit of diligent investigation and orderly arrangement of the sources available to him.

The ' Great Interpolation ' (ix. 51 to xviii. 14) has already been noted. Reason for this is partly found in Luke's omission of St. Mark vi. 45 to viii. 26 (St. Luke ix. 17 is parallel to St. Mark vi. 44 : St. Luke ix. 18 carries us forward to St. Mark viii. 27). The added material of our first and third Gospels had to respect the recognized limits of the length of a papyrus roll. The three longest books of the New Testament—St. Matthew, St. Luke, Acts—are nearly identical in extent.

THE GOSPEL ACCORDING TO ST. LUKE

Seeing that many have attempted to draw up a narrative 1 **1**
of the events that are received with full assurance among
us on the authority of those who were from the begin- 2
ning eye-witnesses and became devoted to the service of
the word, it has seemed right to me also, after careful 3
investigation of the facts from their commencement, to
write for you, most noble Theophilus, a connected account,
that you may fully know the truth of what you have been 4
taught.

The Parents of John the Baptist There was in the time of Herod, king of 5
Judaea, a priest of the name of Zechariah,
belonging to the order of Abijah. He had a
wife who was a descendant of Aaron, and her name was
Elizabeth. They were both of them upright before God, 6
blamelessly obeying all the Lord's precepts and ordinances.
But they had no child, because Elizabeth was barren ; and 7
both of them were far advanced in life.

John's Birth predicted Now while he was doing priestly duty before 8
God in the prescribed course of his order, it fell 9
to his lot—according to the custom of the
priesthood—to go into the Sanctuary of the Lord and burn
the incense ; and the whole multitude of the people were 10
outside praying at the hour of incense. Then there 11
appeared to him an angel of the Lord standing on the
right side of the altar of incense ; and Zechariah on 12
seeing him was startled and terrified. But the angel 13
said to him,

' Do not be frightened, Zechariah, for your petition has
been heard : your wife Elizabeth will bear you a son, and
you shall call his name John. You shall have gladness and 14
exultant joy, and many will rejoice over his birth. For he 15
will be great in the sight of the Lord ; no wine or fermented

---

1. *Are received with full assurance*] Or ' have been fulfilled ' (R.V.).
5. *Abijah*] See 1 Chron. xxiv. 10.

drink shall he ever drink ; but he will be filled with the
Holy Spirit from the very hour of his birth. Many of the 16
sons of Israel will he turn to the Lord their God ; and he 17
will go before Him in the spirit and power of Elijah, to
turn fathers' hearts to the children, and cause the rebellious
to walk in the wisdom of the upright, to make a people
perfectly ready for the Lord.'

' How am I to know this ? ' asked Zechariah. ' For I am 18
an old man, and my wife is far advanced in years.'

' I am Gabriel, who stand in the presence of God,' 19
answered the angel, ' and I have been sent to speak with you
and tell you this good news. And now you shall be dumb 20
and unable to speak until the day when this takes place ;
because you have not believed my words—words which will
be fulfilled at their appointed time.'

Meanwhile the people were waiting for Zechariah, and 21
were surprised that he stayed so long in the Sanctuary.
And when he came out, he was unable to speak to them ; 22
and they knew that he must have seen a vision in the
Sanctuary ; but he made signs to them and continued
dumb.

When his days of service were at an end, he went to his 23
home ; and in course of time his wife Elizabeth conceived, 24
and kept herself secluded five months.

' Thus has the Lord dealt with me at this time,' she said ; 25
' He has graciously taken away my reproach among men.'

The Birth of Jesus predicted Now in the sixth month the angel Gabriel 26
was sent from God to a town in Galilee called
Nazareth, to a maiden betrothed to a man of 27
the name of Joseph, a descendant of David. The maiden's
name was Mary.

So Gabriel went in and said to her, 28

' Hail, favoured one ! the Lord be with you.'

She was greatly startled at his words, and wondered 29
what such a greeting meant. But the angel said, 30

' Do not be frightened, Mary, for you have found favour
with God. You will conceive in your womb and bear a 31
son ; and you are to call His name JESUS. He will be 32
great, and He will be called " Son of the Most High." And

25. *Graciously taken away*] Lit. ' looked on me to take away.'
28. *With you*] v.l. adds ' Blest are you among women,' as in verse 42.
31. *Jesus*] Cf. Matt. i. 21,' n.

the Lord God will give Him the throne of His forefather David ; and He will be King over the House of Jacob for ever, and of His reign there will be no end.' 33

'How can this be,' Mary replied, 'seeing that I have no husband ?' 34

The angel answered, 35

'The Holy Spirit will come upon you, and the power of the Most High will overshadow you ; and for this reason your offspring will be called holy, "the Son of God." And see, your relative Elizabeth—she also has conceived 36 a son in her old age ; and this is the sixth month with her who was called barren. For no promise from God will be 37 impossible of fulfilment.'

'I am the Lord's maidservant,' Mary replied ; 'may it 38 be with me in accordance with your words !'

And then the angel left her.

Mary and Elizabeth Not long after this, Mary made herself ready 39 and went in haste into the hill country to a town in Judah. Here she came to the house of 40 Zechariah and greeted Elizabeth ; and as soon as Elizabeth 41 heard Mary's greeting, the babe leapt within her. And Elizabeth was filled with the Holy Spirit, and uttered a loud 42 cry of joy.

'Blest among women are you,' she said, 'and blest is the fruit of your womb ! But why is this honour done me, 43 that the mother of my Lord should come to me ? For, 44 the moment your greeting reached my ears, the babe within me leapt for joy. And blessed is she who believed, for the 45 word spoken to her from the Lord shall be fulfilled.'

Then Mary said : 46

The Magnificat 'My soul extols the Lord,
And my spirit triumphs in God my Saviour ; 47
Because He has not turned from His maidservant in her 48
    lowly position,
For from this time forward all generations will account
    me happy,
Because the mighty One has done great things for me— 49
Holy is His name !—
And His compassion is, generation after generation, 50

35. *Offspring*] Or 'thing that is to be born,' or 'that which is born will be called holy, Son of God.'
46. The first of three hymns (cf. verse 68 ; ii. 29), known from the opening words of the Latin version as the Magnificat, the Benedictus, and the Nunc Dimittis.

Upon those who fear Him.

He has displayed His might with His arm. 51

He has scattered those who were haughty in the thoughts of their hearts.

He has cast monarchs down from their thrones, 52
And exalted men of low estate.

The hungry He has satisfied with choice gifts, 53
But the rich He has sent empty-handed away.

His servant Israel He has helped, 54
Remembering His compassion—

As He promised our forefathers— 55
To Abraham and his posterity for ever.'

So Mary stayed with Elizabeth about three months, and 56
then returned home.

The Birth of John the Baptist Now when Elizabeth's full time was come, 57
she gave birth to a son; and her neighbours 58
and relatives heard how the Lord had shown
great compassion to her; and they rejoiced with her. And 59
on the eighth day they came to circumcise the child, and
were going to call him Zechariah, after his father.

His mother, however, said, 60

' No, he is to be called John.'

' There is not one of your family,' they said, ' who has 61
that name.'

They asked his father by signs what he wished him to be 62
called. So he asked for a writing-tablet, and wrote, 63

' His name is John.'

And they all wondered. Instantly his mouth and his 64
tongue were set free, and he began to speak and bless God.
And all who lived round about them were filled with awe, 65
and throughout the hill country of Judaea reports of all
these things were spread abroad. All who heard the story 66
treasured it in their memories.

' What then will this child be ? ' they said.

For the Lord's hand was indeed with him.

And Zechariah his father was filled with the Holy Spirit, 67
and he prophesied, saying,

' Blessed be the Lord, the God of Israel, 68

The Benedictus Because He has not forgotten His people
but has effected redemption for them,

And has raised up a mighty Deliverer for us 69
In the house of David His servant—

As He has spoken from of old by the lips of His holy 70
Prophets——

To deliver us from our foes and from the power of all 71
who hate us,

To deal pitifully with our forefathers, 72
And to remember His holy covenant,

The oath which He swore to Abraham our forefather, 73
To grant us to be rescued from the power of our foes 74
And so render worship to Him free from fear,

In holiness and uprightness before Him all our days. 75
And you, O child, shall be called Prophet of the Most 76
High ;

For you shall go on in front before the Lord to prepare
the way for Him,

To give to His people a knowledge of salvation 77
In the forgiveness of their sins,

Through the tender compassion of our God, 78
Through which the daybreak from on high will come to us,

Dawning on those who now dwell in the darkness and 79
shadow of death—

To direct our feet into the path of peace.'

And the child grew and became strong in character, and 80
lived in the Desert till the time came for him to appear
publicly to Israel.

The Birth of Jesus at Bethlehem In these days an edict was issued by Caesar 1 **2**
Augustus for a census of the whole Empire.
It was the first census made during the governor- 2
ship of Quirinius in Syria ; and all went to be registered— 3
every one to the town to which he belonged. So Joseph 4
went up from Galilee, from the town of Nazareth, to Judaea,
to David's town of Bethlehem, because he was of the house
and lineage of David, to have himself registered together 5
with Mary, who was betrothed to him and was with child.
While they were there, her full time came, and she gave birth 6, 7
to her first-born son, and wrapped Him round, and laid Him
in a manger, because there was no room for them in the inn.

The Shepherds and the Angels Now there were shepherds in the same part 8
of the country keeping watch over their sheep
by night in the open fields, when suddenly an 9

---

78. *Will come to*] v.l. ' has come to.'
1. *The whole Empire*] Which comprised ' the world ' as then known. Lit. ' all
the inhabited ' (earth). Cf. Matt. xxiv. 14 ; Acts xi. 28 ; Rom. x. 18 ; Rev. iii. 10.

angel of the Lord stood by them, and the glory of the Lord shone round them ; and they were filled with terror. But 10 the angel said to them,

' Put away all fear ; for I am bringing you good news of great joy—joy for all the people. For a Saviour who 11 is the Christ is born to you to-day, in the town of David. And this is the token for you : you will find a babe wrapped 12 in swaddling clothes and lying in a manger.'

And immediately there was with the angel a multitude 13 of the host of heaven praising God and saying,

' Glory be to God in the highest heavens, 14
     And on earth peace among men in whom He is well
        pleased ! '

Then, as soon as the angels had left them and returned 15 to heaven, the shepherds said to one another,

' Let us now go as far as Bethlehem and see this event that the Lord has made known to us.'

So they came in haste and found Mary and Joseph, with 16 the babe lying in the manger. And when they saw the 17 child, they told what had been said to them about Him ; and 18 all who listened were astonished at what the shepherds told them. But Mary treasured up all their story, often 19 dwelling on it in her mind. And the shepherds returned, 20 glorifying and praising God for all that they had heard and seen, agreeing as it did with what had been told to them.

The Naming of the Child When eight days had passed and the time for 21 circumcising Him had come, He was called JESUS, the name given Him by the angel before His conception in the womb.

He is taken to Jerusalem And when the days for their purification 22 appointed by the Law of Moses had passed, they took Him up to Jerusalem to present Him to the Lord, as it is written in the Law of the Lord : 23

' EVERY FIRST-BORN MALE SHALL BE CALLED HOLY TO THE
     LORD ' (Exod. xiii. 2) ;

and also to offer a sacrifice, as commanded in the Law of 24 the Lord,

---

14. *Men in whom He is well pleased*] The Greek text followed by the A.V. and R.V. mg. differs from that adopted here and in R.V. text by a single letter only. The former reads as the last word in the Greek ' eudokia ' (nominative), the latter ' eudokias ' (genitive). The genitive is almost overwhelmingly attested. The expression ' men of good pleasure ' is difficult, but seems to mean ' men to whom God shows favour,' viz. by the birth of a Saviour. Thus the hymn has two members only, instead of the familiar three of the A.V.

'A PAIR OF TURTLE DOVES OR TWO YOUNG PIGEONS'
(Lev. xii. 8).

The Nunc Now there was a man in Jerusalem of the 25
Dimittis name of Symeon, an upright and God-fearing
man, who was waiting for the consolation of Israel;
and the Holy Spirit was upon him. To him it had been 26
revealed by the Holy Spirit that he should not see death
until he had seen the Lord's Anointed One. Led by 27
the Spirit he came to the Temple; and when the parents
brought in the babe Jesus to carry out with regard to Him
the custom of the Law, he took Him up in his arms and 28
blessed God and said,

'Now, O Sovereign Lord, Thou dost release Thy 29
  servant in peace, in fulfilment of Thy word,
Because mine eyes have seen Thy salvation, 30
Which Thou hast made ready in the sight of all 31
  nations—
A light to shine upon the Gentiles, 32
And the glory of Thy people Israel.'

And while the child's father and mother were wondering 33
at the words of Symeon concerning Him, Symeon blessed 34
them and said to Mary the mother,

'This child is appointed for the falling and for the uprising
of many in Israel and for a sign to be spoken against; and 35
a sword will pierce through your own soul also; that the
reasonings in many hearts may be revealed.'

Anna There was also Anna, a prophetess, the 36
daughter of Phanuel, belonging to the tribe of
Asher. She was of a very great age, having had after her
maidenhood seven years of married life, and then being a 37
widow of eighty-four years. She was never absent from the
Temple, but worshipped, by day and by night, with fasting
and prayer. And coming up just at that moment, she gave 38
thanks to God, and spoke about the child to all who were
expecting the redemption of Jerusalem.

The Return Then, as soon as they had accomplished all 39
to that the Law required, they returned to Galilee
Nazareth to their own town of Nazareth. And the child 40

26. *Not see death*] Cf. Matt. xvi. 28; Mark ix. 1; Luke ix. 27.
27. *Led by*] Lit. ' in.'
32. *To shine upon*] Lit. ' for the unveiling of.' Cf. Isa. xxv. 7; 2 Cor. iii. 14.
34. *Uprising*] Or, as in the A.V., ' rising again.' Cf. Eph. iv. 8, n.
35. *In*] Lit. ' out of.' Cf. xi. 13; Acts xvii. 13.
Revealed] Or ' unveiled.'

grew and became strong and full of wisdom, and the grace of God rested upon Him.

The Boy Jesus in the Temple Now His parents used to go up year by year 41 to Jerusalem at the Feast of the Passover. And 42 when He was twelve years old they went up as was customary at the time of the Feast, and, after staying 43 the full number of days, they started back home ; but the boy Jesus remained behind in Jerusalem. His parents did not discover this, but, supposing Him to be in the caravan, 44 they proceeded a day's journey. Then they searched up and down for Him among their relatives and acquaintances ; but 45 being unable to find Him they returned to Jerusalem, making anxious inquiry for Him.

On the third day they found Him in the Temple sitting 46 among the Rabbis, both listening to them and asking them questions, while all who heard Him were astonished at His 47 intelligence and at the answers He gave. When they saw 48 Him, they were amazed, and His mother said to Him,

' My child, why have you behaved thus to us ? Your father and I have been searching for you in sore anxiety.'

' Why is it that you have been searching for me ? ' He 49 replied ; ' did you not know that I must be in my Father's house ? '

But they did not understand the meaning of these words. 50

His Obedience and Growth Then He went down with them and came to 51 Nazareth, and was obedient to them ; but His mother carefully treasured up all these incidents in her heart. And Jesus increased both in wisdom 52 and in stature, and in favour with God and man.

Now in the fifteenth year of the reign of Tiberius 1 **3** Caesar, Pontius Pilate being Governor of Judaea, Herod

46. *On the third day*] Lit. ' After three days.' One day was occupied by the journey from Jerusalem, the second by the return journey, and on the third He was found.

Rabbis] Lit. ' Teachers.'

Questions] Which He doubtless put as a child for the sake of gaining information for Himself, and not for the purpose of instructing the Rabbis.

49. *In my Father's house*] Lit. ' in the things of my Father.' The Greek phrase ' the things of someone,' ' his belongings,' is especially applied to his possession of house and home, though it might mean ' the concerns of ' ; but the boy of twelve would hardly rebuke His parents for not understanding that their claims must come second to the claims of His Father's business. He rather expresses wonder that they had to search when they might have guessed where He was to be found. For the notable title given to the Temple ' My Father's house,' cf. John ii. 16.

(vv. 1, 2.) This placing of the ministry of John in its chronological setting is peculiar to Luke, and shows the careful historian of his Prologue (i. 1-4).

(vv. 1-14.) Cf. Matt. iii. 1-12 ; Mark i. 1-8.

John the
Baptist
preaches
Judgement
and
Repentance Tetrarch of Galilee, his brother Philip Tetrarch of Ituraea and Trachonitis, and Lysanias Tetrarch of Abilene, during the High-priest- 2 hood of Annas and Caiaphas, a message from God came to John, the son of Zechariah, in the Desert. So John went into all the district of the Jordan 3 proclaiming a baptism of repentance for the forgiveness of sins ; as it is written in the book of the Prophet Isaiah, 4

'THE VOICE OF ONE CRYING ALOUD :
"IN THE DESERT PREPARE A ROAD FOR THE LORD :
MAKE HIS HIGHWAYS STRAIGHT.
EVERY RAVINE SHALL BE FILLED UP, 5
AND EVERY MOUNTAIN AND HILL LEVELLED DOWN,
THE CROOKED PLACES SHALL BE TURNED INTO STRAIGHT
ROADS,
AND THE RUGGED WAYS INTO SMOOTH ;
AND THEN SHALL ALL MANKIND SEE GOD'S SALVATION "' 6
(Isa. xl. 3–5).

So John said to the crowds who came out to be baptized 7 by him,

' O brood of vipers, who has warned you to flee from the coming Wrath ? Let your lives then prove your change of 8 heart ; and do not begin to say to yourselves, " We have Abraham as our forefather," for I tell you that God can raise up children for Abraham from these stones. And even 9 now the axe is lying at the root of the trees, so that every tree which does not produce good fruit will be hewn down and thrown into the fire.'

The crowds asked him, 10
' What then are we to do ? '
' Let the man who has two coats,' he answered, ' give 11 one to the man who has none ; and let the man who has food share it with others.'

There came also a party of tax-gatherers to be baptized, 12 and they asked him,
' Rabbi, what are we to do ? '
' Do not exact more than the legal amount,' he replied. 13
Soldiers also inquired of him, 14
' And we, what are we to do ? '
His answer was,

4. See Matt. iii. 3, n.
7. *Warned . . to flee*] Or ' taught . . how to escape.'

' Neither intimidate any one nor lay false charges ; and be content with your pay.'

He predicts the Appearing and Work of Christ And while the people were in suspense, and 15 all were debating in their minds whether John might possibly be the Christ, he answered by 16 saying to them all,

' I am baptizing you with water, but One mightier than I is coming, whose very sandal-strap I am not worthy to unfasten : He will baptize you in the Holy Spirit and in fire. His winnowing-shovel is in His hand to clear 17 out His threshing-floor, and to gather the wheat into His storehouse ; but the chaff He will burn up in fire unquenchable.'

John thrown into Prison With many exhortations besides these he 18 declared the gospel to the people. (But Herod 19 the Tetrarch, being rebuked by him about Herodias, his brother's wife, and about all the wicked deeds that he had done, now added this to crown all, that he threw 20 John into prison.)

The Baptism of Jesus Now when all the people had been baptized, 21 and Jesus also had been baptized and was praying, the sky opened, and the Holy Spirit 22 came down in bodily shape, like a dove, upon Him, and a voice came from heaven,

' Thou art My Son, the Beloved : in Thee is My delight.'

The Ancestry of Jesus And Jesus, when He began His ministry, was 23 about thirty years old. He was the son (it was supposed) of Joseph, son of Heli, son of Matthat, 24 son of Levi, son of Melchi, son of Jannai, son of Joseph, son of Mattathias, son of Amos, son of Nahum, son of Esli, 25 son of Naggai, son of Mahath, son of Mattathias, son of 26 Semein, son of Josech, son of Joda, son of Johanan, son of 27 Resa, son of Zerubbabel, son of Shealtiel, son of Neri, son 28 of Melchi, son of Addi, son of Cosam, son of Elmadam, son of Er, son of Joshua, son of Eliezar, son of Jorim, son of 29 Maththat, son of Levi, son of Symeon, son of Judah, son of 30

(vv. 15-18.) Cf. Matt. iii. 11, 12 ; Mark i. 7, 8.
(vv. 19-20.) Cf. Matt. xiv. 1-12, n.
(vv. 21, 22.) Cf. Matt. iii. 13-17 ; Mark i. 9-11.
22. *In Thee is My delight*] v.l. ' To-day have I begotten Thee' (Ps. ii. 7).
(vv. 23-38.) Many attempts have been made to reconcile this genealogy with the quite different one of Matt. i. 1-16. The problem must be left unsolved. The Jewish Matthew traces the line *down* from Abraham, the universalistic Luke *up* to God.

Joseph, son of Jonam, son of Eliakim, son of Melea, son of 31
Menna, son of Mattatha, son of Nathan, son of David, son of 32
Jesse, son of Obed, son of Boaz, son of Salmon, son of
Nahshon, son of Amminadab, son of Admin, son of Arni, 33
son of Hezron, son of Perez, son of Judah, son of Jacob, son 34
of Isaac, son of Abraham, son of Terah, son of Nahor, son of 35
Serug, son of Reu, son of Peleg, son of Eber, son of Shelah,
son of Cainan, son of Arpachshad, son of Shem, son of Noah, 36
son of Lamech, son of Methuselah, son of Enoch, son of 37
Jared, son of Mahalalel, son of Kenan, son of Enosh, son of 38
Seth, son of Adam, son of God.

His Tempta-
tions in the
Desert Then Jesus, full of the Holy Spirit, returned 1 **4** from the Jordan, and was led about by the Spirit in the Desert for forty days, tempted all 2 the while by the Devil. During those days He ate nothing, and at the close of them He suffered from hunger.

Then the Devil said to Him, 3
' If you are God's Son, tell this stone to become bread.'
' It is written,' replied Jesus, ' " IT IS NOT ON BREAD 4
ALONE THAT A MAN SHALL LIVE " ' (Deut. viii. 3).

The Devil next led Him up and caused Him to see at a 5
glance all the kingdoms of the world. And the Devil said 6
to Him,
' To you will I give all this power and this splendour ; for
it has been handed over to me, and on whomsoever I will
I bestow it. If therefore you do homage to me, it shall all 7
be yours.'

Jesus answered him, 8
' It is written, " To THE LORD THY GOD THOU SHALT DO
HOMAGE, AND TO HIM ALONE SHALT THOU RENDER WORSHIP " '
(Deut. vi. 13).

Then he brought Him to Jerusalem and set Him on the 9
summit of the Temple, and said to Him,
' If you are God's Son, throw yourself down from here ;
for it is written, 10

" HE WILL GIVE ORDERS TO HIS ANGELS CONCERNING THEE,
    TO GUARD THEE " ;
and 11

" ON THEIR HANDS THEY SHALL BEAR THEE UP,
    LEST EVER THOU SHOULDST STRIKE THY FOOT AGAINST A
    STONE " ' (Ps. xci. 11, 12).

(vv. 1–13.) Cf. Matt. iv. 1–11 ; Mark i. 12, 13.

The reply of Jesus was,   12

'It is said, "Thou shalt not put the Lord thy God to the proof "' (Deut. vi. 16).

So the Devil, having fully tried every kind of temptation 13 on Him, left Him for a time.

He returns to Galilee, and begins to preach   Then Jesus returned in the Spirit's power to 14 Galilee ; and His fame spread through all the adjacent districts. And He proceeded to teach 15 in their synagogues, winning praise from all.

His Visit to Nazareth He came to Nazareth also, where He had been brought 16 up ; and, as was His custom, He went to the synagogue on the Sabbath, and stood up to read. And there was handed to Him the book 17 of the Prophet Isaiah. Opening the book, He found the place where it was written,

'The Spirit of the Lord is upon me,   18
  Because He has anointed me to proclaim Good News
    to the poor ;
  He has sent me to announce release to the prisoners
  And recovery of sight to the blind :
  To free those whom tyranny has crushed,
  To proclaim the year of acceptance with the Lord ' 19
                  (Isa. lxi. 1, 2).

And rolling up the book, He returned it to the attendant, 20 and sat down. And the eyes of all in the synagogue were fixed on Him.

Then He proceeded to say to them,   21

'To-day is this Scripture fulfilled in your hearing.'

And they all spoke well of Him, wondering at the words 22 of grace which fell from His lips, while they asked one another,

'Is not this Joseph's son ? '

'Doubtless,' said He, 'you will quote to me the 23 proverb, "Physician, cure yourself : all that we hear that you have done at Capernaum, do here also in your own country. "'

'I tell you in truth,' He added, 'that no Prophet is 24

---

12. Cf. Matt. iv. 7, n.
13. *For a time*] Or ' till another convenient opportunity presented itself.'
(vv. 16–30.) Cf. Matt. xiii. 54–58, n.
20. *Sat down*] Such is the custom of Jewish teachers when teaching. Cf. Matt.
v. 1 ; xxiii. 2.
22. *Spoke well of Him*] Or ' bore witness to Him that this was true.'

welcomed among his own people. And I tell you that there 25
was many a widow in Israel in the time of Elijah, when
there was no rain for three years and six months and there
came a severe famine over all the land ; and yet to not one of 26
them was Elijah sent, but only to a widow of Zarephath
of Sidon (1 Kings xvii.). And there was also many a leper 27
in Israel in the time of the Prophet Elisha, and yet not
one of them was cleansed, but only Naaman the Syrian' (2
Kings v.).

His Fellow Townsmen try to murder Him Then all in the synagogue, while listening to 28
these words, were filled with fury They rose, 29
hurried Him outside the town, and brought
Him to the brow of the hill on which their town
was built, to hurl Him down ; but He passed through the 30
midst of them and went His way.

Jesus cures a Demoniac at Capernaum So He came down to Capernaum, a town 31
in Galilee. There He taught the people on
the Sabbath ; and they were exceedingly 32
struck by His teaching, because He spoke with the
language of authority. Now in the synagogue there was a 33
man possessed by the spirit of a foul demon. In a loud
voice he cried out,

' Ha ! Jesus the Nazarene, what have you to do with us ? 34
I know who you are—God's Holy One ! '

But Jesus rebuked the demon. 35

' Silence ! ' He exclaimed ; ' come out of him.'

Upon this, the demon hurled the man into the midst of
them, and came out of him without doing him any harm.
All were awe-struck ; and they asked one another, 36

' What sort of language is this ? For with authority and
power He gives orders to the foul spirits and they come
out.'

And the talk about Him spread into every part of the 37
neighbouring country.

Peter's Mother-in-Law restored to Health Now when He rose and left the synagogue 38
He went to Simon's house. Simon's mother-
in-law was suffering from an acute attack of
fever ; and they consulted Him about her.

25. *There was no rain*] Lit. ' The heaven was shut ' ; a Hebrew figure of speech,
as in Gen. viii. 2.
(vv. 31-37.) Cf. Matt. iv. 13-16 ; Mark i. 21-28.
31. *So He came down to Capernaum*] Evidently the first coming to Capernaum. Yet,
see verse 23—an indication of the editorial displacement noted at Matt. xiii. 54, n.

Then standing over her He rebuked the fever, and it left 39
her ; and she at once rose and waited on them.

Many other Miracles At sunset all who had persons suffering from 40
any illness brought them to Him, and He laid
His hands on them all, one by one, and cured
them. Demons also came out of many, loudly calling out, 41
' You are the Son of God.'

But He rebuked them and forbade them to speak, because
they knew Him to be the Christ.

Jesus preaches throughout Galilee Next morning, at daybreak, He left the town 42
and went away to a solitary place ; but the people
flocked out to find Him, and, coming to the
place where He was, they tried to detain Him
that He might not leave them. But He said to them, 43

' I have to tell the gospel of the Kingdom of God to the
other towns also, because for this purpose I was sent.'

So for some time He preached in the synagogues in 44
Galilee.

Three Disciples called On one occasion the crowd was pressing on 1 **5**
Him and listening to God's Message, while He
was standing by the Lake of Gennesaret. And 2
He saw two fishing-boats drawn up on the beach (for
the men had gone out of them and were washing the nets),
and going on board one of them, which was Simon's, He 3
asked him to push out a little from the land. Then He sat
down and taught the crowd of people from the boat.

When He had finished speaking, He said to Simon, 4
' Push out into deep water, and let down your nets for
a haul.'

' Rabbi,' replied Peter, ' all night long we have worked 5
hard and caught nothing ; but at your command I will
let down the nets.'

This they did, and enclosed a vast number of fish ; and 6
their nets began to break. So they signalled to their 7
partners in the other boat to come and help them ; they
came, and they filled both the boats so that they almost sank.

---

39. *Rebuked*] Or ' reprimanded ' ; the fever being regarded as a servant under
His orders. Cf. Matt. viii. 9.
(vv. 42–44.) Cf. Mark. i. 35–39.
43. Cf. Mark i. 38, n.
44. *Galilee*] So in Mark ; v.l. ' Judaea.' Even if Judaea is original, Luke probably means it to cover Palestine in general. (Cf. xxiii. 5 ; Acts ii. 9 ; x. 37.) The
inference that Judaea here points to a ministry in Jerusalem, prominent in John,
but otherwise absent from the Synoptics, is thus quite unwarranted.

When Simon Peter saw this, he fell down at the knees of 8
Jesus, and exclaimed,

' Master, leave me, for I am a sinful man.'

For he was awe-struck—he and all his companions— 9
at the haul of fish which they had taken ; and so were 10
Simon's partners James and John, the sons of Zebedee.

But Jesus replied to Simon,

' Fear not : from this time you shall be a catcher of men.'

Then, after bringing their boats to land, they left every- 11
thing and followed Him.

On another occasion when He was in one of 12
A Leper the towns, there was a man there covered with
cured leprosy, who, seeing Jesus, threw himself at
His feet and implored Him, saying,

' Sir, if only you are willing, you are able to make me
clean.'

Reaching out His hand and touching him, Jesus said, 13

' I am willing ; be cleansed ! '

And instantly the leprosy left him. He ordered him 14
to tell no one.

' But go,' He said, ' show yourself to the Priest, and make
the offering for your cleansing which Moses appointed, as
evidence to them.'

All the more, however, the report about Him spread 15
abroad, and great multitudes crowded to hear Him and to
be cured of their diseases ; but Jesus Himself constantly 16
withdrew into the Desert and there prayed.

The Cure of One day He was teaching, and there were 17
a paralysed Pharisees and teachers of the Law sitting there
Man who had come from every village in Galilee and
Judaea and from Jerusalem. And the power of the Lord
was present that He might heal. And a party of men 18
came carrying a paralysed man on a bed, and they endeavoured to bring him in and lay him before Jesus. But 19
when they could find no way of doing so because of the
crowd, they went up on the roof and let him down through
the tiling—bed and all—into the midst, in front of Jesus.
He saw their faith and said to him, 20

' Friend, your sins are pardoned.'

Then the Scribes and Pharisees began to cavil, asking, 21

(vv. 12-16.) Cf. Matt. viii. 1-4 ; Mark i. 40-45.
(vv. 17-26.) Cf. Matt. ix. 1-8 ; Mark ii. 1-12.

147

'Who is this, uttering blasphemies? Who but God alone can pardon sins?'

Well aware of their reasonings, Jesus answered their 22 questions by asking,

'What is this that you are debating in your hearts? Which is easier?—to say, "Your sins are pardoned," or to 23 say, "Rise and walk"? But to prove to you that the Son 24 of Man has authority on earth to pardon sins'—

Turning to the paralytic He said,

'I bid you, arise, take up your bed, and go home.'

Instantly he stood up in their presence, took up the 25 mat on which he had been lying, and went home, giving glory to God. All were seized with amazement, and they 26 began to glorify God. Awe-struck, they said,

'We have seen strange things to-day.'

The Call of Levi

After this He went out and noticed a tax-gatherer, Levi by name, sitting at the Toll office; and He said to him, 27

'Follow me.'

He rose, left everything, and followed Him. Now Levi 28, 29 gave a great entertainment at his house in honour of Jesus, and there was a large party of tax-gatherers and others at table with them. This led the Pharisees and Scribes of 30 their party to expostulate with His disciples and ask,

'Why are you eating and drinking with these tax-gatherers and sinners?'

Jesus replied to them, 31

'It is not men in good health who require a physician, but those who are ill. I have not come to call the righteous 32 to repentance, but sinners.'

The Disciples' Neglect of Fasting

Again they said to Him, 33

'John's disciples fast often and pray, as do also those of the Pharisees; but yours eat and drink.'

'Can you compel the bridal party to fast,' replied Jesus, 34 'so long as they have the bridegroom among them? But 35 a time will come when the bridegroom is taken from them: then at that time they will fast.'

He also spoke in a parable to them. 36

'No one,' He said, 'tears a piece from a new garment to

(vv. 27–32.) Cf. Matt. ix. 9–13 ; Mark ii. 13–17.
(vv. 33–39.) Cf. Matt. ix. 14–17 ; Mark ii. 18–22.

mend an old one. If he does, he will not only spoil the new, but the patch from the new will not match the old. Nor 37 does any one pour new wine into old wine-skins. If he does, the new wine will burst the skins, the wine itself will escape, and the skins will perish. But new wine must be put 38 into fresh wine-skins. Nor does any one after drinking old 39 wine wish for new ; for he says, " The old is good." '

A Charge of Sabbath-breaking Now on the Sabbath, while He was passing 1 **6** through the wheatfields, His disciples plucked the ears and rubbed them with their hands to eat the grain. And some of the Pharisees asked, 2 ' Why are you doing what is unlawful on the Sabbath ? '

Jesus answered, ' Have you never even read what David 3 did when he and his followers were hungry ; how he 4 entered the house of God and took and ate the Shewbread and gave some to his followers—loaves which none but the Priests are allowed to eat ? ' (1 Sam. xxi. 1–6).

' The Son of Man,' He added, ' is Lord of the Sabbath.' 5

A second Charge of Sabbath-breaking On another Sabbath He had gone to the 6 synagogue and was teaching there ; and in the congregation was a man whose right arm was withered. The Scribes and the Pharisees were 7 on the watch to see whether He would cure him on the Sabbath, that they might be able to bring an accusation against Him. He knew their thoughts, and said to the man 8 with the withered arm,

' Rise, and stand there in the midst.'

And he rose and stood there. Then Jesus said to 9 them,

' I put it to you all whether we are allowed to do good on the Sabbath, or to do evil ; to save a life, or to destroy it.'

And looking round upon them all He said to the man, 10 ' Stretch out your arm.'

He did so, and the arm was restored. But they were 11 filled with madness, and began to discuss what they should do to Jesus.

(vv. 1–5.) Cf. Matt. xii. 1–8 ; Mark ii. 23–28.
5. See Mark ii. 28, n. One ancient manuscript, Codex Bezae, transposes verse 5 to follow verse 10, and after verse 4 inserts another remarkable Sabbath incident : ' On the same day, perceiving someone at work on the Sabbath, He said to him, " Man, if indeed you know what you are doing, then you are blessed; but if you do not know, you are accursed and a transgressor of the Law." ' The tradition may well be authentic. (Cf. Rom. xiv. 5 and 23.)
(vv. 6–11.) Cf. Matt. xii. 9–14 ; Mark iii. 1–6.

Twelve Apostles chosen

It was at about that time that He went 12 into the hill country to pray ; and He remained all night in prayer to God. When it was day, 13 He called His disciples ; and He selected from among them twelve, whom He also named Apostles. These 14 were Simon, to whom He also gave the name of Peter, Andrew his brother, James, John, Philip, Bartholomew, Matthew, Thomas, James the son of Alphaeus, Simon 15 called the Zealot, James's son Judas, and Judas Iscariot 16 (who proved to be a traitor).

With these He came down and took His stand on a level 17 place, where there was a great crowd of His disciples, and a multitude of people from every part of Judaea, from Jerusalem, and from the sea-side district of Tyre and Sidon, who came to hear Him and to be cured of their diseases ; and those who were tormented by foul spirits were cured. 18 The whole crowd were eager to touch Him, because power 19 went forth from Him and cured every one.

The Sermon on the Plain: Blessings and Woes

Then fixing His eyes upon His disciples, 20 Jesus said to them,

' Blessed are you poor, because the Kingdom of God is yours.

' Blessed are you who hunger now, because 21 your hunger shall be satisfied.

' Blessed are you who now weep aloud, because you shall laugh.

' Blessed are you when men shall hate you and 22 exclude you from their society and insult you, and spurn your very name as an evil thing, for the Son of Man's sake.

' Be glad at such a time, and leap for joy ; for your 23 reward is great in heaven ; for just so their forefathers behaved to the Prophets.

' But woe to you rich men, because you already have 24 your consolation.

' Woe to you who now have plenty to eat, because you 25 will be hungry.

' Woe to you who laugh now, because you will mourn and weep aloud.

(vv. 12–16.) Cf. Matt. x. 2–4 ; Mark iii. 13–19.
(vv. 17–19.) Cf. Matt. iv. 24, 25 ; Mark iii. 7–12.
(vv. 20–49.) Cf. Matt. v. to vii.

'Woe to you when men speak well of you; for just so 26 their forefathers behaved to the false prophets.

'But to you who are listening to me I say, 27 **'Love your Enemies'** Love your enemies; seek the welfare of those who hate you; bless those who curse you; pray 28 for those who revile you. To him who gives you a blow on 29 one side of the face offer the other side also; and to him who is robbing you of your outer garment refuse not the under one also. To every one who asks, give; and from 30 him who takes away your property, do not demand it back. And act towards your fellow-men just as you would have 31 them act towards you.

'If you love those who love you, what credit is it to you? 32 Why, even bad men love those who love them. And if you 33 are kind to those who are kind to you, what credit is it to you? Even bad men act thus. And if you lend to those 34 from whom you hope to receive, what credit is it to you? Even bad men lend to their fellows so as to receive back an equal amount. But love your enemies, be good to them, 35 and lend without hoping for any repayment. Then your recompense shall be great, and you will be sons of the Most High; for He is kind to the ungrateful and wicked. Be 36 compassionate, just as your Father is compassionate.

The censorious Temper condemned 'Judge not, and you shall not be judged; 37 condemn not, and you shall not be condemned; pardon, and you shall be pardoned; give, and 38 gifts shall be bestowed on you. Full measure, pressed, shaken down, and running over, shall they pour into your laps; for with the same measure that you use they shall measure to you in return.'

He also spoke to them in a parable. 39

'Can a blind man lead a blind man?' He asked; 'would not both fall into the ditch? There is no learner 40 superior to his teacher; but he whose instruction is complete will be like his teacher.

'And why look at the splinter in your brother's eye and 41 not notice the beam of timber in your own? How say to 42 your brother, "Brother, let me take that splinter out of

---

35. *Without hoping for any repayment*] So A.V., but the only known meaning of the compound Greek verb *ap-elpizo* is not ' to hope for (something) back,' but ' to lose hope,' ' despair '; so R.V. (cf. v.l., R.V. mg.) and most Commentaries. Possibly, however, Luke gives the verb a unique sense under the influence of verse 34, where the verb, compounded by the same preposition, *apo-lambano*, does mean ' to receive back.'

your eye," when all the while you do not see the beam in your own eye? Hypocrite! take the beam out of your own eye first, and then you will see clearly to take the splinter out of your brother's eye.

'There is no good tree that yields worthless fruit, nor 43 again any worthless tree that yields good fruit. Every tree 44 is known by its fruit. It is not from thorns that men gather figs, nor from the bramble that they can get a bunch of grapes. A good man from the good stored up in his heart 45 brings out what is good; and an evil man from the evil stored up brings out what is evil; from the fulness of his heart his mouth speaks.

'And why call me "Master, Master," and yet not do 46 what I tell you? If any one comes to me, listens to 47 my words and puts them in practice, I will show you whom he is like. He is like a man who built a house, 48 dug deep and laid the foundation on the rock; and when a flood came, the torrent burst upon that house, but was unable to shake it, because it was securely built. But he 49 who has heard and not obeyed is like a man who built a house upon soft soil without a foundation. Against it the torrent burst, and immediately it collapsed, and terrible was the wreck and ruin of that house.'

An Officer's Slave restored
After He had ended all these words in the 1 **7** hearing of the people, He went to Capernaum. Here an army captain's servant, a man dear 2 to his master, was ill and at the point of death; and the captain, hearing about Jesus, sent to 3 Him some of the Jewish Elders, begging Him to come and restore his servant to health. And they, 4 when they came to Jesus, earnestly entreated Him, pleading,

'He deserves to have this favour granted him, for he 5 loves our nation, and at his own expense he built our synagogue for us.'

Then Jesus went with them. But when He was not 6 far from the house, the captain sent friends to Him with the message:

'Sir, do not trouble to come. I am not worthy of having

(vv. 46–49.) Cf. Matt. vii. 24–27, n.
(vv. 1–10.) Cf. Matt. viii. 5–13, n.
2. *Servant*] Or ' slave.' So in verses 3, 10.

you come under my roof ; and therefore I did not deem 7
myself worthy to come to you. Only speak the word, and
let my young man be cured. For I too am a man obedient 8
to authority, and have soldiers under me ; and I say to
one, " Go," and he goes ; to another, " Come," and he
comes ; and to my slave, " Do this or that," and he does it.'

Jesus listened to the captain's message and was astonished 9
at him, and He turned and said to the crowd that followed
Him,

' I tell you that not even in Israel have I found faith like
this.'

And the friends who had been sent, on returning to the 10
house, found the servant in perfect health.

The Widow's Son at Nain Shortly afterwards He went to a town called 11
Nain, attended by His disciples and a great
crowd of people. And just as He reached the 12
gate of the town, they happened to be bringing out for
burial a dead man who was his mother's only son ; and
she was a widow ; and a great number of the townspeople
were with her. The Lord saw her, was moved with pity for 13
her, and said to her,

' Do not weep.'

Then He went close and touched the bier, and the 14
bearers halted.

' Young man,' He said, ' I command you, awake ! '

The dead man sat up and began to speak ; and Jesus 15
restored him to his mother. All were awe-struck, and they 16
gave glory to God, saying,

' A Prophet, a great Prophet, has risen up among us.'

And again,

' God has not forgotten His people.'

And the report of what Jesus had done spread through 17
the whole of Judaea and all the surrounding district.

John the Baptist's Perplexity John's disciples brought to John an account 18
of all these things ; so he called two of his 19
disciples and sent them to the Lord.

7. *Young man*] Or ' boy.' So the English in India speak of their native menservants as ' boys.'
11. *Shortly afterwards*] v.l. ' The next day.'
(vv. 11–16.) Luke only. John alone records the raising of Lazarus (xi.) ; the
raising of the little daughter of Jairus is common to the three Synoptic Gospels.
It is interesting to note the growing wonder of our Lord's power over death—the
little girl who had just breathed her last, the young man being carried to burial,
Lazarus dead four days.
(vv. 18–23.) Cf. Matt. xi. 2–6.

' Are you the Coming One ? ' he asked, ' or is there another whom we are to expect ? '

The men came to Jesus and said, 20

' John the Baptist has sent us to you with this question : " Are you the Coming One, or is there another whom we are to expect ? " '

So then and there He cured many of diseases, severe pain, 21 and evil spirits, and to many who were blind He gave sight. Then He answered the messengers, 22

' Go and report to John what you have seen and heard. Blind men receive sight, the lame walk, lepers are cleansed, deaf persons hear, the dead are raised to life, the poor have the gospel preached to them. And blessed is every one 23 who does not take offence at my claims.'

The Testimony of Jesus to John
When John's messengers were gone, He 24 proceeded to say to the multitude concerning John,

' What did you go out into the Desert to gaze at ? A reed waving in the wind ? But what did 25 you go out to see ? A man wearing fine clothes ? People who are gorgeously dressed and live in luxury are found in palaces. But what did you go out to see ? A Prophet ? 26 Aye, I tell you, and far more than a Prophet. John is the 27 man about whom it is written,

' " SEE, I AM SENDING MY MESSENGER BEFORE THY FACE, AND HE SHALL MAKE READY THY WAY BEFORE THEE "

(Mal. iii. 1).

' I tell you that among all of women born there is not 28 one greater than John. Yet one who is of least rank in the Kingdom of God is greater than he.'

And all the people, including the tax-gatherers, when 29 they listened to him justified God, being baptized with John's baptism. But the Pharisees and expounders of the 30 Law frustrated God's purpose for them, by refusing to be baptized.

' To what then,' said Jesus, ' shall I compare the men of the 31 present generation, and what are they like ? They are like 32 children sitting in the public square and calling out to one another, " We have played the flute to you, and you have

(vv. 24–35.) Cf. Matt. xi. 7–19.
(vv. 29, 30.) It is doubtful whether this is a parenthetical comment of the Evangelist, or part of the discourse of Jesus.

not danced : we have sung dirges, and you have not shown sorrow." For John the Baptist has come eating no bread 33 and drinking no wine, and you say, " He has a demon ! " The Son of Man has come eating and drinking, and you 34 say, " See this man ! given to gluttony and tippling, a friend of tax-gatherers and sinners ! " But wisdom is 35 justified by all her children.'

The Woman who was a Sinner Now one of the Pharisees invited Him to a 36 meal at his house ; so He entered the house and reclined at the table. And there was a 37 woman in the town who was a sinner. Having learnt that Jesus was at table in the Pharisee's house she brought an alabaster jar of perfume, and, standing behind close to His 38 feet, weeping, began to wet His feet with her tears ; and with her hair she wiped the tears away again, while she lovingly kissed His feet and poured the perfume over them. Noticing this, the Pharisee, His host, said to 39 himself,

' This man, if he were really a Prophet, would know who and what sort of person this woman is who is touching Him, that she is an immoral woman.'

In answer to his thoughts Jesus said to him, 40
' Simon, I have a word to say to you.'
' Rabbi, say on,' he replied.
' There were once two men in debt to one money-lender,' 41 said Jesus ; ' one owed him five hundred shillings and the other fifty. But neither of them could pay anything ; so 42 he freely forgave them both. Tell me, then, which of them will love him most ? '

' I suppose,' replied Simon, ' the one to whom he forgave 43 most.'

And Jesus said, ' You have judged rightly.'

Then turning towards the woman He said to Simon, 44
' Do you see this woman ? I came into your house : you gave me no water for my feet ; but she has made my feet wet with her tears, and then wiped the tears away with her hair. No kiss did you give me ; but she from the 45 moment I came in has not left off tenderly kissing my feet. No oil did you pour even on my head ; but she has poured 46 perfume upon my feet. This is the reason why I tell you 47

35. *Her children*] See Matt. xi. 19, n.
(vv. 36–50.) Luke only, who omits the later anointing at Bethany.

that her sins, her many sins, are forgiven—because she has loved much ; but he who is forgiven little, loves little.'

And He said to her,   48

' Your sins are forgiven.'

Then the other guests began to say to themselves,   49

' Who can this man be who even forgives sins ? '

But He said to the woman,   50

' Your faith has saved you : go, and be at peace.'

8   Shortly after this He visited town after town, 1 and village after village, proclaiming His Message and telling the Good News of the Kingdom of God. The twelve were with Him, and certain 2 women whom He had delivered from evil spirits and various diseases—Mary of Magdala, out of whom seven demons had gone, and Joanna the wife of Chuza, Herod's steward, 3 and Susanna, and many other women, who ministered to Jesus and His Apostles.

A preaching Tour

Now when a great crowd was assembling, 4 and was receiving additions from one town after another, He spoke a parable to them.

The Parable of the Sower

' A sower,' He said, ' went out to sow his seed ; and as 5 he sowed, some of the seed fell by the way-side, and was trodden upon, or the birds pecked it up. Another part 6 dropped upon the rock, and after growing up it withered away for want of moisture. Another part fell among the 7 thorns, and the thorns grew up with it and stifled it. But 8 some of the seed fell into good ground, and grew up and yielded a return of a hundred for one.'

While thus speaking, He cried aloud and said,

' Listen, every one who has ears to hear ! '

The disciples asked Him what this parable 9 meant.

' The Sower ' explained

' To you,' He replied, ' it is granted to know 10 the secrets of the Kingdom of God ; but all others are taught by parables, in order that they may see and yet not see, and may hear and yet not understand. The meaning 11 of the parable is this. The seed is the word. Those 12

---

47. The ' loved much ' is *proof* of the lavish forgiveness. The *reason* for the forgiveness is the woman's faith (verse 50).

2. *Mary of Magdala*] This Mary of Magdala has been identified with the sinful woman of ch. vii., the seven demons being supposed to be the demons of unchastity ; hence, the modern connotation of Magdalen—Magdalen Hospital. This has no support whatever from Luke.

(vv. 4–18.) Cf. Matt. xiii. 1–23 ; Mark iv. 1–25.

by the way-side are those who have heard, and then the Devil comes and carries away the word from their hearts, lest they should believe and be saved. Those on 13 the rock are the people who on hearing the word receive it joyfully ; but they have no root : for a time they believe, but when trial comes they fall away. That which fell 14 among the thorns means those who have heard, but, as they go on their way, the word is stifled by the anxieties, the wealth, and the pleasures of life, and they bring nothing to perfection. But that in the good ground means those 15 who, having listened to the word with open minds and in a right spirit, hold it fast, and patiently yield a return.

Lamps are for giving Light ‘ When any one lights a lamp, he does not 16 cover it with a vessel or hide it under a couch ; he puts it on a lampstand, that people who enter the room may see the light. There is nothing hidden, 17 which shall not be openly seen ; nor anything secret, which shall not be known and come to light. Be careful, there- 18 fore, how you hear ; for whoever has anything, to him more shall be given, and whoever has nothing, even what he thinks he has shall be taken away from him.’

The Family of Jesus try to speak to Him Then came to Him His mother and His 19 brothers, but could not get near Him for the crowd. He was told, 20

‘ Your mother and brothers are standing on the edge of the crowd, and want to see you.’

‘ My mother and my brothers,’ He replied, ‘ are those 21 who hear God's word and obey it.’

One day He went on board a boat—both He and His 22 disciples ; and He said to them,

A Storm subdued ‘ Let us cross over to the other side of the Lake.’

So they set sail. During the passage He fell asleep, and 23 there came down a squall of wind on the Lake, so that the boat began to fill and they were in deadly peril. So they 24 came and woke Him, crying,

‘ Rabbi, Rabbi, we are drowning.’

Then He roused Himself and rebuked the wind and the surging of the water, and they ceased and there was a calm.

(vv. 19–21.) Cf. Matt. xii. 46–50 ; Mark iii. 31–35.
21. *Those who*] ‘ Pointing to His disciples,’ says Matthew (xii. 49).
(vv. 22–25.) Cf. Matt. viii. 18 and 23–27 ; Mark iv. 35–41.

'Where is your faith?' He asked them. 25

They were filled with terror and amazement, and said to one another,

'Who then is this? for he gives orders both to wind and waves, and they obey him.'

A Gerasene Then they put in to shore in the country of 26
Demoniac the Gerasenes, which lies opposite to Galilee.
cured Here, on landing, He was met by one of the 27
townsmen who was possessed by demons : for a long time he had not put on any garment, nor did he live in a house, but among the tombs. When he saw Jesus, he called out 28 and fell down before Him, and cried aloud,

'What hast Thou to do with me, Jesus, Son of God Most High? Do not torture me, I beseech Thee.'

For already He had commanded the foul spirit to come 29 out of the man. Many a time it had seized and held the man ; and they had repeatedly put him in chains and fetters and kept guard over him, but he would break the chains to pieces, and, impelled by the demon, escape into the desert.

'What is your name?' Jesus asked him. 30

'Legion,' he replied—because a great number of demons had entered into him ; and they besought Him not to 31 command them to be gone to the Abyss.

Now there was a great herd of swine there feeding on 32 the hill-side ; and the demons begged Him to give them leave to go into them ; and He gave them leave. The 33 demons came out of the man and left him, and entered into the swine ; and the herd rushed violently down the steep into the Lake and were drowned.

The The swineherds, seeing what had happened, 34
Effects of fled and reported it both in town and country ;
the Cure whereupon the people came out to see what had 35
happened. They came to Jesus, and they found the man from whom the demons had gone out sitting at the feet of Jesus, clothed, and in his right mind ; and they were awe-stricken. Those who had seen it told them how the 36 demoniac had been cured. Then the whole population of 37 the Gerasenes and of the adjacent districts begged Him to

(vv. 26–39.) Cf. Matt. viii. 28–34 ; Mark v. 1–20.
26. *Gerasenes*] Some authorities read ' Gadarenes,' and yet others ' Gergesenes.'
32. *A great herd of swine*] Lit. ' a herd of many swine '; 2000 according to Mark v. 13.

depart from them ; for their terror was extreme. So He went on board and returned.

The man from whom the demons had gone out had 38 begged to go with Him ; but He sent him away.

'Return home,' He said, 'and tell there all that God 39 has done for you.'

So he went away, and published through the whole town all that Jesus had done for him.

Now when Jesus returned, the people gave 40 **Jairus's Daughter** Him a warm welcome ; for they had all been looking out for Him. Just then there came a 41 man named Jairus, a ruler of the Synagogue, who threw himself at the feet of Jesus, and entreated Him to come to his house ; for he had an only daughter, about twelve years 42 old, and she was dying. So He went, and the dense throng crowded on Him.

Now a woman, who for twelve years had been 43 **A Woman cured** afflicted with hæmorrhage, and had spent on doctors all she had, none of them being able to cure her, came close behind Him and touched the 44 tassel of His robe ; and instantly her flow of blood stopped.

'Who is it that touched me ?' Jesus asked. 45

And when all denied having done so, Peter and the rest said,

'Rabbi, the crowds are hemming you in and pressing on you.'

'Some one has touched me,' Jesus replied, 'for I feel 46 that power has gone out from me.'

Then the woman, perceiving that she had not escaped 47 notice, came trembling, and throwing herself down at His feet she stated before all the people the reason why she had touched Him, and how she was instantly cured.

'Daughter,' said He, 'your faith has cured you ; go, 48 and be at peace.'

While He was still speaking, some one came 49 **Jairus's Daughter** to the ruler of the Synagogue from his house and said,

---

37. *Their terror was extreme*] Lit. 'they were in the grip of (or 'holden with,' R.V.) great terror.' The verb here used occurs nine times in Luke's writings, and three times in the rest of the N.T. Cf. Luke iv. 38.

(vv. 40–56.) Cf. Matt. ix. 18–26 ; Mark v. 21–43.

43. *None of them being able to cure her*] Or 'she had not sufficient strength of constitution to be cured by any of them.' Cf. Mark v. 25, 26, n.

' Your daughter is dead ; trouble the Rabbi no further.'
Jesus heard the words and said to him,　　　　50
' Have no fear. Only believe, and she shall recover.'

So He came to the house, but allowed no one to go in with 51
Him but Peter and John and James and the girl's father and
mother. The people were all weeping aloud and beating 52
their breasts for her ; but He said,

' Leave off wailing ; for she is not dead, but asleep.'

And they jeered at Him, knowing that she was dead. 53
He, however, took her by the hand and called aloud,　　54
' Child, awake ! '

And her spirit returned, and instantly she stood up ; and 55
He directed them to give her some food. Her parents were 56
astounded ; but He forbade them to mention the matter to
any one.

Then calling the twelve together He conferred on them 1 **9**
power and authority over all the demons and to cure
diseases ; and sent them out to proclaim the Kingdom 2
of God and to cure the sick. And He commanded them, 3

' Take nothing for your journey—neither stick nor bag
nor bread nor money ; and do not have an extra under-
garment. Whatever house you enter, make that your home, 4
and from it start afresh. Wherever they refuse to receive 5
you, as you leave that town shake off the very dust from
your feet as a protest against them.'

So they departed and visited village after village, spread- 6
ing the gospel and performing cures everywhere

Now Herod the Tetrarch heard of all that was going on ; 7
and he was bewildered, because it was said by some that
John had come back to life, by others that Elijah had 8
appeared, and by others that one of the ancient Prophets
had risen again. And Herod said,　　　　9
' John I beheaded ; but who is this, of whom I hear
such reports ? '

And he sought to see Him.

　　　　The apostles, on their return, related to 10
**5000
People fed** Jesus all they had done. Then He took them
　　　　and withdrew to a quiet retreat, to a town
called Bethsaida. But the immense crowd, aware of this, 11

(vv. 1–6.) Cf. Matt. x. 1 and 5–15 ; Mark vi. 7–13.
　2. *The sick*] v.L. omits these words.
(vv. 7–9.) Cf. Matt. xiv. 1, 2 ; Mark vi. 14–16.
(vv. 10–17.) Cf. Matt. xiv. 13–21 ; Mark vi. 30–44 ; John vi. 1–14.

followed Him ; and receiving them kindly He talked to them about the Kingdom of God, and those who needed healing, He cured.

Now when the day began to decline, the twelve came to 12 Him and said,

' Send the people away, that they may go to the villages and farms round about and find lodging and a supply of food ; because here we are in an uninhabited district.'

' You yourselves,' He said, ' must give them food.' 13

' We have nothing,' they replied, ' but five loaves and a couple of fish, unless indeed we were to go and buy provisions for all this host of people.'

(For there were about 5000 men.) But He said to His 14 disciples,

' Make them sit down in parties of about fifty each.'

They did so, making them all sit down. Then He took 15, 16 the five loaves and the two fish, and looking up to heaven He blessed them and broke them into portions which He gave to the disciples to distribute to the people. So they ate 17 and were fully satisfied, all of them ; and what they had remaining over was gathered up, twelve baskets of fragments.

Peter acknowledges Jesus as the Christ One day when He was praying by Himself 18 the disciples were near at hand ; and He asked them,

' Who do the people say that I am ? '

' John the Baptist,' they replied ; ' but others say 19 Elijah ; and others that some one of the ancient Prophets has come back to life.'

' But you,' He asked, ' who do you say that I am ? ' 20

' The Christ of God,' replied Peter.

Jesus predicts His own Death and Resurrection And Jesus strictly forbade them to tell this 21 to any one ; and He said, 22

' The Son of Man must suffer much cruelty, be rejected by the Elders and High Priests and Scribes, and be put to death, and on the third day be raised to life.'

Self-Renunciation the Way to Life And He said to all, 23

' If any one wishes to follow me, let him renounce self and take up his cross day by

(vv. 18-27.) Cf. Matt. xvi. 13-28 ; Mark viii. 27 to ix. 1.
23. *Renounce self*] Let him disown the usurped authority of his own lower nature, and say ' no ' to its dictates.

day, and so be my follower. For whoever desires to 24
save his life shall lose it, and whoever loses his life for
my sake shall save it. Why, what benefit is it to a 25
man to have gained the whole world, but to have lost or
forfeited his own self ? For whoever is ashamed of me 26
and my teachings, of him the Son of Man will be ashamed
when He comes in His own glory and in that of the Father
and of the holy angels. I tell you truly that there are some 27
of those who stand here who will certainly not taste death
till they have seen the Kingdom of God.'

The Trans-figuration It was about eight days after saying this that 28
Jesus, taking with Him Peter, John, and James,
went up the mountain to pray. And while 29
He was praying the appearance of His face underwent
a change, and His clothing became white and radiant.
And suddenly there were two men conversing with Him, 30
who were Moses and Elijah. They appeared in glory, 31
and were speaking about His departure, which He was to
effect in Jerusalem. Now Peter and the others were 32
weighed down with sleep ; but, when they were fully awake,
they saw His glory, and the two men standing beside Him.
And when they were preparing to depart from Jesus, Peter 33
said to Him,

' Rabbi, it is well that we are here. Let us put
up three tents—one for you, one for Moses, and one for
Elijah.'

He did not know what he was saying. But while he 34
was thus speaking, there came a cloud which spread over
them ; and they were awe-struck as they entered the
cloud. Then there came a voice from within the cloud : 35

' This is My Son, My Chosen One : listen to Him.'

After this voice was heard, Jesus was found alone. 36

They kept it to themselves, and said not a word to any
one at that time about what they had seen.

25. *Forfeited*] Or ' had to pay his own self—his own existence—as a fine.' Cf.
Heb. x. 34, n.
(vv. 28–36.) Cf. Matt. xvii. 1–13 ; Mark ix. 2–13. The vision of the Cross is
succeeded by a vision of the heavenly glory which lies beyond the Cross. ' The
Transfiguration corrects the perspective of the sufferings, and preludes the triumph '
(Loisy).
29. *Radiant*] Or ' like the flashing lightning.'
31. *Departure*] Lit. ' His exodus which He was about to accomplish.' Mark and
Matthew have simply ' conversing with Him.' For a similar theological touch in
Luke, cf. iv. 43, n. Cf. Matt. xvii. 4, n.
33. *It is well*] Cf. Matt. xvii. 4, n.
35. *My Chosen One*] v.L. ' My Beloved,' from Matthew and Mark.

On the following day, when they came down 37
The epileptic Boy cured from the mountain, a great crowd came to meet Him ; and a man in the crowd called out, 38 ' Rabbi, I beg you to pity my son, for he is my only child. At times a spirit seizes him and he suddenly cries 39 out. It convulses him, and makes him foam at the mouth, and does not leave him till it has well-nigh covered him with bruises. I entreated your disciples to drive out the 40 spirit, but they could not.'

' O unbelieving and perverse generation ! ' replied Jesus ; 41 ' how long shall I be with you and bear with you ? Bring your son here to me.'

Now while the youth was coming, the spirit dashed him 42 to the ground and cruelly convulsed him. But Jesus rebuked the demon, cured the youth, and gave him back to his father. And all were awe-struck at the mighty 43 power of God.

Jesus again predicts His Betrayal and Death And while every one was expressing wonder at all that He was doing, He said to His disciples,

' Store these my sayings in your memory ; 44 for the Son of Man must be betrayed into the hands of men.'

But they did not grasp His meaning : it was veiled from 45 them, so that they might not perceive it, and they were afraid to ask Him about it.

Lessons in Humility and brotherly Love Now there arose a dispute among them, as 46 to which of them was the greatest. And Jesus, 47 knowing the reasoning in their hearts, took a young child and made him stand by His side and He said to them, 48

' Whoever for my sake receives this little child, receives me ; and whoever receives me, receives Him who sent me. For the lowliest among you all—he is great.'

' Rabbi,' replied John, ' we saw a man making use of 49

(vv. 37–43.) Cf. Matt. xvii. 14–21 ; Mark ix. 14–29.
42. *Dashed him to the ground*] Or ' tore him with spasms.'
(vv. 43–45.) Cf. Matt. xvii. 22, 23 ; Mark ix. 30–32.
43. *Mighty power*] Lit. ' majesty.' The same word occurs in Acts xix. 27 ; 2 Pet. i. 16.
(vv. 46–50.) Cf. Matt. xviii. 1–5 ; Mark ix. 33–41.
46. *Greatest*] Cf. Matt. xviii. 1, n.
47. *Knowing*] v.L. ' seeing.'
48. *For my sake*] Or ' as being mine.' Lit. ' in my name.' Cf. Matt. xviii. 5 ; Mark ix. 37, n.

your name to expel demons ; and we forbade him, because
he does not follow with us.'

'Do not forbid him,' said Jesus, 'for he who is not 50
against you is on your side.'

Now when the time drew near for Him to 51
Unfriendly be taken up into heaven, He proceeded with
Samaritans fixed purpose towards Jerusalem. And He 52
sent messengers in advance, who entered a village of the
Samaritans to make ready for Him. But the people there 53
would not receive Him, because He was evidently going to
Jerusalem. When the disciples James and John saw this, 54
they said,

'Master, do you wish us to order fire to come down
from heaven and consume them ? ' (2 Kings i. 10).

But He turned and rebuked them. And they went to 55,
another village.

Some would As they proceeded on their way, a man came 57
follow Him to Him, and said,
conditionally 'I will follow you wherever you go.'

'Foxes have holes,' said Jesus, 'and birds have nests ; 58
but the Son of Man has nowhere to lay His head.'

'Follow me,' He said to another. 59

'Master,' the man replied, 'allow me first to go and
bury my father.'

'Leave the dead,' said Jesus, 'to bury their own dead ; 60
but do you go and announce far and wide the Kingdom of
God.'

'Master,' said yet another, ' I will follow you ; but allow 61
me first to go and say good-bye to my friends at home.'

Jesus answered him, 62

'No one who has put his hand to the plough, and then
looks behind him, is of use for the Kingdom of God.'

The After this the Lord appointed seventy others, 1
Seventy and sent them before Him, by twos, to go to
Evangelists every town or place which He Himself in-
tended to visit. And He addressed them thus : 2

51. Luke now leaves Mark, to rejoin him again at xviii. 15. See Introduction.
54. *Consume them*] v.l. adds ' as Elijah also did.' Cf. 2 Kings i. 10.
55. *Them*] v.l. adds ' and said, You do not know the kind of Spirit of which you
are the servants ; for the Son of Man did not come to destroy men's lives, but to
save them.'
(vv. 57–62.) Cf. Matt. viii. 19–22.
58. *Nests*] Or ' roosting-places.'
1. *Seventy*] v.l. ' seventy-two.' So in verse 17.

'The harvest is abundant, but the reapers are few : therefore entreat the Owner of the harvest to send out more reapers into His fields. And now go. Remember that I am sending 3 you out as lambs into the midst of wolves. Carry no purse, 4 bag, nor change of shoes ; and salute no one on your way.'

'Whatever house you enter, first say, " Peace be to this 5 house ! " And if there is a lover of peace there, your peace 6 shall rest upon it ; otherwise it shall come back upon you. And in that same house stay, eating and drinking at their 7 table ; for the labourer deserves his wages. Do not move from one house to another.

'And whatever town you come to and they receive you, 8 eat what they put before you. Cure those who are ill in 9 that town, and tell them,

'" The Kingdom of God is at your door."

'But whenever you come to a town and they will not 10 receive you, go out into the streets and say,

'" The very dust of your town that clings to our feet 11 we wipe off as a protest. Only be sure of this—the Kingdom of God is close at hand."

'I tell you that it will be more endurable for Sodom on 12 the Great Day than for that town.

Chorazin, Bethsaida, Capernaum

'Woe to thee, Chorazin ! Woe to thee, 13 Bethsaida ! For had the miracles been performed in Tyre and Sidon which have been performed in you, long ere now they would have repented, sitting in sackcloth and ashes. However, for Tyre and 14 Sidon it will be more endurable at the Judgement than for you. And thou, Capernaum, shalt thou be lifted as high 15 as heaven ? Thou shalt be brought down as low as Hades.

'He who listens to you listens to me ; and he who 16 disregards you disregards me, and he who disregards me disregards Him who sent me.'

Return of the Seventy

When the seventy returned, they exclaimed 17 joyfully,

'Master, even the demons submit to us when we utter your name.'

2. *Fields*] Lit. ' harvest.'
4. *Salute no one*] Eastern salutations are complicated and tedious. Cf. 2 Kings iv. 29.
6. *Lover*] Lit. ' son,' a Hebraism.
Upon it] Or ' upon him.'
16. *Disregards*] Or ' sets at nought.'
(vv. 17-24.) Cf. Matt. xi. 25-30.
17. *When we utter your name*] Lit. simply ' in your name.'

And He said to them, ' I saw Satan fall like a lightning- 18
flash out of heaven. I have given you power to tread 19
serpents and scorpions underfoot, and to trample on all
the power of the enemy ; and in no case shall anything do
you harm. Nevertheless rejoice not at this, that the spirits 20
submit to you ; but rejoice that your names are enrolled
in heaven.'

A sublime Claim At that hour Jesus was filled by the Holy 21
Spirit with rapturous joy.

' I praise Thee,' He exclaimed, ' O Father,
Lord of heaven and earth, that Thou hast hidden these
things from sages and men of understanding, and hast
revealed them to babes. Yes, Father, for such has been
Thy gracious will. All things are delivered to me by my 22
Father ; and no one knows who the Son is but the Father,
nor who the Father is but the Son and he to whom the Son
may choose to reveal Him.'

And He turned towards His disciples and said to them 23
apart,

' Blessed are the eyes which see what you see ! For I tell 24
you that many prophets and kings have desired to see the
things you see, and have not seen them, and to hear the
things you hear, and have not heard them.'

How to win Eternal Life Then an expounder of the Law stood up to 25
test Him with a question.

' Rabbi,' he asked, ' what shall I do to
inherit eternal Life ? '

' What is written in the Law ? ' said Jesus ; ' how does 26
it read ? '

' " THOU SHALT LOVE THE LORD THY GOD," ' he replied, 27
' " WITH THY WHOLE HEART, THY WHOLE SOUL, THY WHOLE

---

18. The thought is not that of Milton's rebel angel (' hurled headlong flaming from
the ethereal sky '), banished for ever from the abode of bliss, but, rather, brought
down low from the place of his pride and power. Cf. verse 15. Jesus was watching
the while the modest successes of His disciples, and saw in them the prophecy of the
final defeat of the powers of evil.

Fall] It is the fact of falling—the act as a whole—not in progress—that the tense
(the aorist) here signifies. Not ' falling ' (pres. part. Cf. xii. 54) nor ' fallen ' (perf.
part. Cf. Rev. ix. 1, n.). A.V. rightly ' fall ' ; R.V. wrongly changes to ' fallen.'
20. *Rejoice not at this*] *i.e.* ' but rather in the thought of the forces behind you.'
Your names are enrolled in heaven, and just as the might of Imperial Rome is at the
disposal of her meanest citizen all the world over, so the power of heaven is for you
to wield. Omnipotence is on your side.
(vv. 21, 22.) Cf. Matt. xi. 25–27, n.
22. *Him*] Or ' it.'
27. *With*] Lit. ' out of,' the heart standing for the centre of the whole mental life
in all its varied range ; then the preposition changes to a thrice repeated ' in.' The
love flows out from its central source into three channels, manifesting itself in the

STRENGTH, AND THY WHOLE MIND ; AND THY NEIGHBOUR AS MUCH AS THYSELF " ' (Deut. vi. 5 ; Lev. xix. 18).

'A right answer,' said Jesus ; 'do that, and you shall live.' 28

But he, desiring to justify himself, said to Jesus, 29

'But what is meant by my "neighbour"?'

Jesus replied, 30

'The good Samaritan' 'A man was once on his way down from Jerusalem to Jericho when he fell among robbers, who after both stripping and beating him went away, leaving him half dead. Now a priest happened to 31 be going along that road, and on seeing him passed by on the other side. In like manner a Levite also came to the 32 place, and seeing him, passed by on the other side. But a 33 certain Samaritan, being on a journey, came where he lay, and seeing him was moved with pity. He went to him, 34 and dressed his wounds with oil and wine and bound them up. Then placing him on his own mule he brought him to an inn, and took care of him. The next day he took out 35 two shillings and gave them to the innkeeper.

' "Take care of him," he said, "and whatever further expense you are put to, I will repay you at my next visit."

'Which of those three seems to you to have acted like 36 a neighbour to him who fell among the robbers?'

'The one who showed him pity,' he replied. 37

'Go,' said Jesus, 'and act in the same way.'

As they pursued their journey He came to 38 **Martha and Mary** a certain village, where a woman named Martha welcomed Him to her house. She had a sister 39 called Mary, who also seated herself at the Lord's feet, and listened to His teaching. Martha meanwhile was busy 40 and distracted in attending to her guest, and she came up to Him and said,

'Master, do you not care that my sister is leaving me to do all the serving? Tell her to assist me.'

several spheres of feeling, will, and intellect. The obligation upon the *intellect* of whole-hearted love of God is sometimes forgotten.

34. *Mule*] Or ' ass.'

Inn] Not the same word as in ii. 7. This word is not found elsewhere in the N.T. The story makes the lawyer answer his own question from a changed point of view. He asked, ' Who is my neighbour ? ' Jesus says in effect, ' You will never get at your duty that way.' The point of the story is not, who stood in the legal relation of neighbour to Priest, Levite, and Samaritan, but which of these three showed himself possessed of the neighbourly spirit ?

40. *Busy and distracted*] Lit. ' pulled this way and that.'

Came] Lit. ' stood over (or, by) Him.' Our Lord was probably reclining at table.

Is leaving] Lit. ' has been leaving,' the imperfect tense. But v.L. gives the aorist, ' has left me.'

'Martha, Martha,' replied Jesus, 'you are anxious and 41
worried about a multitude of things; and yet only one 42
thing is needful. Mary has chosen the good portion and
she shall not be deprived of it.'

At one place He was praying, and when 1 **11**
'The Lord's He ceased, one of His disciples said to Him,
Prayer'
'Master, teach us to pray, just as John taught
his disciples.'

So He said to them, 2

'When you pray, say, "Father, may Thy name be kept
holy; let Thy Kingdom come; give us day after day our 3
bread for the day; and forgive us our sins, for we ourselves 4
also forgive every one who is indebted to us; and bring
us not into temptation."'

And He said to them, 5
Persistent 'Which of you shall have a friend and shall
Prayer go to him in the middle of the night and say,
'"Friend, lend me three loaves of bread; for a friend of 6
mine has just come to my house from a distance, and I
have nothing for him to eat"?

'And he from indoors shall answer, 7

'"Do not pester me. The door is now barred, and I
am here in bed with my children. I cannot get up and
give you bread."

'I tell you that even if he will not rise and give him 8
the loaves because he is his friend, at any rate because
of his persistency he will rouse himself and give him
whatever he wants.

'So I say to you, "Ask, and it shall be given 9
A threefold to you; seek, and you shall find; knock, and
Promise the door shall be opened to you." For every 10
one who asks, receives; and he who seeks, finds; and he
who knocks shall have the door opened to him. What 11
father is there among you, who, if his son shall ask for
bread, will offer him a stone? or if he asks for a fish, will
instead of a fish offer him a snake? or if he asks for an egg, 12

(vv. 41, 42.) There is a bewildering variety of various readings, on which see R.V.
mg. and the Commentaries. The primary reference of the variant 'few things or
one' seems to be to the simplicity of the meal He needed.

(vv. 1–13.) Cf. Matt. vi. 9–13; vii. 7–11.

(vv. 1–4.) This historical setting of the Lord's Prayer and its shorter form are
peculiar to Luke.

3. *Give us*] The tense (present) makes this a petition for constant giving, unlike
Matt. vi. 11.

will offer him a scorpion ? If you then, imperfect as you 13
are, know how to give your children gifts that are good for
them, how much more will your Father who is in heaven
give the Holy Spirit to those who ask Him ! '

He replies to a Slander On one occasion He was expelling a dumb 14
demon ; and when the demon was gone out
the dumb man could speak, and the people
were astonished. But some among them said, 15
' It is by the power of Beelzebul, the Prince of the
demons, that he expels the demons.'

Others, to put Him to the test, asked Him for a sign from 16
heaven. And, knowing their thoughts, He said to them, 17
' Every kingdom in which civil war rages goes to ruin :
family attacks family and is overthrown. And if Satan 18
has engaged in conflict with himself, how shall his kingdom
stand ?—because you say that I expel demons by the power
of Beelzebul. And if it is by the power of Beelzebul 19
that I expel the demons, by whom do your disciples expel
them ? They therefore shall be your judges. But if it is 20
by the power of God that I drive out the demons, it is
evident that the Kingdom of God has come upon you.

The Devil's Power overcome ' Whenever a strong man, fully armed and 21
equipped, is guarding his own house, he enjoys
peaceful possession of his property ; but as soon 22
as another stronger than he attacks him and overcomes
him, he takes away that armour of his in which he trusted,
and distributes the plunder. Whoever is not with me is 23
against me, and whoever is not gathering with me is
scattering abroad.

Moral Reformation may not last ' When a foul spirit has left a man, it roams 24
about in the desert, seeking rest ; but unable
to find any, it says, " I will return to the
house I have left " ; and when it comes, it finds the house 25
swept clean and in good order. Then it goes and fetches 26
seven other spirits more malignant than itself, and they
enter and dwell there ; and in the end that man's condition
becomes worse than at first.'

16. *From heaven*] Cf. Matt. xii. 38–42 ; Mark viii. 11 and note.
(vv. 17–26.) Cf. Matt. xii. 43–45.
17. *In which civil war rages*] Lit. ' which has been divided against itself.'
Family attacks family and is overthrown] Lit. ' house falls upon (or, against) house.'
19. *Your disciples*] Cf. Matt. xii. 27, n.
20. *Power*] Lit. ' finger.' Cf. Exod. viii. 19.
Has come upon you] Cf. Matt. xii. 28, n.

Only the Obedient are to be envied

As He thus spoke a woman in the crowd 27 called out in a loud voice,

'Blessed is the mother who carried you, and the breasts that you have sucked.'

'Nay rather,' He replied, 'they are blessed who hear 28 the word of God and carefully keep it.'

The Jews more guilty than the ancient Heathen

Now when the crowds came thronging upon 29 Him, He proceeded to say,

'The present generation is a wicked one: it requires some sign, but no sign shall be given to it except that of Jonah. For just as 30 Jonah became a sign to the men of Nineveh, so the Son of Man will be a sign to the present generation. The 31 Queen of the South will arise at the Judgement together with the men of the present generation, and will condemn them ; because she came from the ends of the earth to hear the wisdom of Solomon ; and mark ! One greater than Solomon is here. There will arise men of Nineveh at the 32 Judgement together with the present generation, and will condemn it ; because they repented at the preaching of Jonah ; and mark ! something more than Jonah is here.

Lamps are for giving Light

'When any one lights a lamp, he never puts 33 it in the cellar or under the bushel-measure, but on the lampstand, that people who come in may see the light. The lamp of the body is the eye. When 34 your eye is sound, your whole body is lighted up ; but when it is diseased, your body is dark. Consider therefore 35 whether the light that is in you is anything but mere darkness. If, however, your whole body is full of light, and 36 has no part dark, it will be lighted, all of it, as when the lamp with its bright shining gives you light.'

A Meal at a Pharisee's House

When He had thus spoken, a Pharisee invited 37 Him to a meal at his house ; so He entered and took His place at table. Now the Pharisee 38 saw to his surprise that He did not wash before eating. The Master, however, said to him, 39

'Here we see how you Pharisees clean the outside of the cup and plate, while the inside, your heart, is full of greed and wickedness. Foolish men ! Did not He who 40

---

28. *Carefully keep it*] The same verb is rendered ' guard ' in verse 21.
(vv. 29–32.) Cf. Matt. xii. 40, n.
(vv. 29–36.) Cf. Matt. xii. 38–42.
38. *Wash*] Lit. ' bathe.'

made the outside make the inside also ? But what is within, 41 give in charity, and behold all is clean for you.

'But woe to you Pharisees ! for you pay tithes on your 42 mint and rue and every kind of garden vegetable, and are indifferent to justice and the love of God. These things you ought to have done, yet without neglecting the others. Woe to you Pharisees ! for you love the best seats in 43 the synagogues, and you like to be bowed to in places of public resort. Woe to you ! for you are like tombs 44 which lie hidden, and the people who walk over them are not aware of them.'

Hereupon one of the expounders of the Law exclaimed, 45 'Rabbi, in saying such things you reproach us also.'

'Woe also to you expounders of the Law !' replied Jesus, 46 'for you load men with cumbrous burdens which you your-selves will not touch with one of your fingers. Woe to you ! 47 for you build the tombs of the Prophets, whom your fore-fathers killed. It follows that you are witnesses to and 48 approve of your fathers' actions. They slew, you build.

'For this reason also the Wisdom of God has said, " I 49 will send Prophets and Apostles to them, of whom they will kill some and persecute others"; so that the blood 50 of all the Prophets that is shed from the creation of the world may be required from the present generation. Yes, I tell you that, from the blood of Abel down to 51 the blood of Zechariah who perished between the altar and the House, it shall all be required from the present generation.

'Woe to you expounders of the Law ! for you have 52 taken away the key of knowledge : you yourselves have not entered in, and those who wanted to enter in you have hindered.'

After He had left the house, the Scribes and Pharisees 53 began a vehement attempt to entangle Him and make Him give off-hand answers on numerous points, lying in 54 wait to catch some unguarded expression from His lips.

---

49. *The Wisdom of God*] Probably 'God in His Wisdom.' Matthew has 'I am sending' (Matt. xxiii. 34). Jesus is interpreting the Divine counsels and messages of the O.T. record.

51. *Required*] Cf. 2 Chron. xxiv. 22. This reference is to all the murders of righteous men recorded in the O.T. Scriptures, 2 Chron. being the last book of the Hebrew Bible.

A Warning against Hypocrisy Meanwhile the people had come streaming 1 towards Him by thousands, so that they were trampling one another underfoot. And now He proceeded to say to His disciples first,

'Beware of the leaven of the Pharisees, that is to say, beware of hypocrisy. There is nothing that is covered up 2 which will not be uncovered, nor hidden which will not become known. Whatever therefore you have said in the 3 dark, will be heard in the light; and what you have whispered within closed doors, will be proclaimed from the house-tops.

'But to you who are my friends I say, 4

A Warning against the Fear of Men ' " Be not afraid of those who kill the body and after that can do nothing further. I will 5 show you whom to fear : fear Him who after killing has power to throw into Gehenna : yes, I say to you, fear Him. Are not five sparrows sold for a penny ? 6 and yet not one of them is a thing forgotten in God's sight. But the very hairs on your head are all counted. Away 7 with fear : you are more precious than many sparrows."

The Importance of not disowning Christ ' And I tell you that every man who acknow- 8 ledges me before men, the Son of Man will also acknowledge before the angels of God. But whoever disowns me before men will be 9 disowned before the angels of God.

The Guilt of rejecting the inner Light ' Moreover every one who shall speak against 10 the Son of Man may obtain forgiveness ; but he who blasphemes the Holy Spirit will never obtain forgiveness. And when they are bringing you before 11 synagogues and magistrates and governors, do not anxiously ponder the manner or matter of your defence, nor what you are to say ; for the Holy Spirit shall teach you at that very 12 moment what you must say.'

Jesus refuses to be an Arbitrator Just then a man in the crowd appealed to 13 Him. ' Rabbi,' he said, ' tell my brother to give me a share of the inheritance.'

' Man,' He replied, ' who made me a judge 14 or arbitrator over you ? '

And to the people He said, 15

6. *A penny*] Lit. ' two assaria.' Cf. Matt. x. 29, n.
8. *Acknowledges*] Cf. Matt. x. 32, n.
10. Cf. Mark iii. 29, n.

'Take care, be on your guard against all covetousness, for no one's life consists in the superabundance of his possessions.'

Worldly Greed

And He spoke a parable to them. 16 'A certain rich man's lands,' He said, 'yielded abundant crops, and he debated within 17 himself, saying,

'"What am I to do? for I have no place in which to store my crops."

'And he said to himself, 18

'"This is what I will do : I will pull down my barns and build larger ones, and in them I will store up all my harvest and my goods ; and I will say to my soul, 19

'"Soul, you have ample possessions laid up for many years to come : take your ease, eat, drink, enjoy yourself."

'But God said to him, 20

'"Foolish man, this night they are demanding your soul from you ; and these preparations—for whom shall they be ?"

'So is it with him who amasses treasure for himself, but 21 has no riches in God.'

Anxiety is Faithlessness

Then turning to His disciples He said, 22 'For this reason I say to you, "Do not be anxious for your lives, what you are to eat, and for your persons, what you are to put on." For 23 a man's life is more than his food, and his person than his clothing. Look at the ravens. They do not sow or 24 reap, and they have neither store-chamber nor barn. And yet God feeds them. How far more precious are you than the birds ! And which of you is able by anxious thought 25 to add a foot to his height ? If then you are unable to do 26 even a very little thing, why be anxious about other matters ? Look at the lilies, how they grow. They 27 neither toil nor spin. And yet I tell you that not even Solomon in all his magnificence was arrayed like one of these. But if God so clothes the grass of the fields, 28 that blooms to-day and to-morrow is feeding the oven, how much more will He clothe you, you men of little faith !

21. *In God*] Or perhaps the sense is ' in relation to God.' (vv. 24–31.) Cf. Matt. vi. 26–33.

27. *Was arrayed*] In Palestine the lilies are not all white. They resemble the rainbow in the brilliancy and variety of their colours.

'Therefore, do not be asking what you are to eat or 29
what you are to drink ; and do not waver between hope and
fear. For the nations of the world seek all these things ; 30
your Father knows that you need them. But seek His 31
Kingdom, and these things shall be given you in addition.

'Lay up Wealth in Heaven' 'Dismiss your fears, little flock : your Father 32
finds pleasure in giving you the Kingdom.
Sell your possessions and give alms. Provide 33
yourselves with purses that will never wear out, wealth
inexhaustible in heaven, where no thief can come nor
moth consume. For where your wealth is, there also will 34
your heart be.

'Be on the alert for your Master's Return' 'Have your girdles on, and let your lamps 35
be alight ; and be like men waiting for their 36
master—on the look-out till he shall return
from the wedding feast—that, when he comes
and knocks, they may open the door instantly. Blessed are 37
those servants, whom their Master when He comes shall
find on the watch. I tell you, in solemn truth, that He
will tie an apron round Him, and will bid them recline at
table while He comes and waits on them. And whether 38
it be in the second watch or in the third that He comes and
finds them so, blessed are they. Of this be sure, that if 39
the master of the house had known at what time the robber
was coming, he would have kept awake and not have
allowed his house to be broken into. Be you also ready, 40
for at an hour when you are not expecting Him the Son of
Man will come.'

'Master,' said Peter, 'are you addressing this parable 41
to us, or to all alike ? '

'Who, then,' replied the Lord, ' is the faithful and 42
prudent steward whom his master will put in charge of
his household to serve out their rations at the proper times ?
Blessed is that servant whom his master when he comes 43
shall find so doing. I tell you truly that he will put him 44
in authority over all his possessions. But if that servant 45
should say in his heart, " My master is a long time in
coming," and should begin to beat the menservants and
maidservants, and to eat and drink, drinking even to excess ;
that servant's master will come on a day when he is not 46

36. *Return*] This sense seems required, but elsewhere the verb means ' to depart.'
See Phil. i. 23 ; and the cognate noun in 2 Tim. iv. 6.

expecting him and at an hour that he knows not of, and
cut him asunder, and make him share the lot of the unfaithful. And that servant who has been told his master's 47
will and yet made no preparation and did not obey his
will, will receive many lashes. But he who had not been 48
told it and yet did what deserved the scourge, will receive
but few lashes. To whomsoever much has been given, from
him much will be required ; and to whom much has been
entrusted, of him the more will be demanded.

**Conflict
predicted** ' I came to throw fire upon the earth, and 49
what is my desire ? Oh that it were even now
kindled ! But I have a baptism to undergo ; and 50
how am I pent up till it is accomplished ! Do you suppose 51
that I came to bring peace to the earth ? No, I tell you 52
that I came to bring dissension. For from this time there
will be in one house five persons split into parties. Three
will form a party against two and two against three ; father 53
against son and son against father ; mother attacking
daughter and daughter her mother, mother-in-law her
daughter-in-law and daughter-in-law her mother-in-law '
(Micah vii. 6).

Then He said to the people also, 54
' When you see a cloud rising in the west, you immediately say, " There is to be a shower " ; and it comes to
pass. And when you see a south wind blowing, you 55
say, " It will be burning hot " ; and it comes to pass. 56
Hypocrites ! You know how to read the aspect of earth
and sky. How is it you cannot read this present
time ?

' Why, too, do you not of yourselves judge what is 57
right ? For when, with your opponent, you are going 58
before the magistrate, on the way take pains to be quit of
him ; for fear that he should drag you before the judge, and
the judge hand you over to the officer of the court, and the
officer lodge you in prison. Never, I tell you, will you get 59
free till you have paid the last farthing.'

(vv. 49, 50.) Luke only. The Greek of verse 49 is of doubtful interpretation.
A.V. and R.V. have ' What will I if it be (or is) already kindled ? ' *i.e.* ' What have I
to complain of ? ' But the translation here given better accords with the emotional
strain of verse 50. Cf. ix. 41. Better still, perhaps, the American R.V. mg. : ' upon
the earth. How I would that it were already kindled ! '
(vv. 51–53.) Cf. Matt. x. 34–36.
(vv. 54–56.) Cf. Matt. xvi. 2, 3, n.
(v.v 57–59.) Cf. Matt. v. 23–26.

A Foretaste of national Judgement Just at that time people came to tell Him 1 **13** about the Galilaeans whose blood Pilate had mingled with their sacrifices.

'Do you suppose,' He asked in reply, 'that those Gali- 2 laeans were worse sinners than the mass of the Galilaeans, because this happened to them? I assure you it was not so. 3 Nay, if you are not penitent, you will all lose your lives just as they lost theirs. Or those eighteen persons whom the 4 tower in Siloam fell on and killed, do you suppose they were offenders more than any one else in Jerusalem? I 5 assure you it was not so. Nay, I tell you, if you do not repent, you will all lose your lives just as they lost theirs.'

And He told them this parable. 6

The unfruitful Fig-tree 'A man,' He said, 'who had a fig-tree growing in his garden came to look for fruit on it and could find none. So he said to the gardener, 7

' " See, this is the third year I have come to look for fruit on this fig-tree and cannot find any. Cut it down. Why should so much ground be actually wasted?"

'But the gardener pleaded, 8

' " Leave it, Sir, this year also, till I have dug round it and manured it. If next year it bears fruit, well and good; 9 if not, then you shall cut it down." '

A Sabbath Cure Once He was teaching on the Sabbath in 10 one of the synagogues where a woman was 11 present who for eighteen years had had a spirit of weakness: she was bent double and was quite unable to raise herself. But Jesus saw her, and calling to her, He 12 said to her,

'Woman, you are free from your weakness.'

And He put His hands on her, and she immediately stood 13 upright and began to give glory to God.

Then the ruler of the Synagogue, indignant that Jesus 14 had cured her on a Sabbath, said to the crowd,

'There are six days in the week on which people ought to work. On those days therefore come and get yourselves cured, and not on the Sabbath day.'

But the Lord's reply to him was, 15

'Hypocrites, does not each of you on the Sabbath untie his bullock or his ass from the stall and lead him to water? And this woman, daughter of Abraham as she is, whom 16

(vv. 6–9.) Cf. Matt. xxi. 21, n.

Satan had bound for no less than eighteen years, was she not to be loosed from this chain because it is the Sabbath day?'

When He said this, all His opponents were ashamed, 17 while the whole multitude was delighted at the many glorious things continually done by Him.

'The Mustard Seed,' and 'Yeast'   This prompted Him to say, 18 'What is the Kingdom of God like? and to what shall I compare it? It is like a mustard- 19 seed which a man drops into the soil in his garden, and it grows and becomes a tree in whose branches the birds roost.'

And again He said, 20

'To what shall I compare the Kingdom of God? It is like 21 leaven which a woman takes and buries in three measures of flour, to work there till the whole is leavened.'

Earnestness demanded   He was passing through town after town and 22 village after village, teaching and steadily pro- ceeding towards Jerusalem, when some one 23 asked Him,

'Sir, are there but few who are to be saved?'

'Strive your hardest to enter by the narrow gate,' He 24 answered; 'for many, I tell you, will try to find a way in and will not succeed. As soon as the Master of the house 25 has risen and shut the door, and you have begun to stand outside and knock at the door and say,

'"Sir, open the door for us,"

'He will answer, "I do not know where you come from."

'Then you will plead, 26

'"We have eaten and drunk in your company, and you have taught in our streets."

'But He will reply, 27

'"I tell you that I do not know where you come from. Begone from me, all of you, wrongdoers!"

'There will be the weeping and gnashing of teeth, when 28 you see Abraham and Isaac and Jacob and all the Prophets inside the Kingdom of God, and yourselves thrown out. They will come from east and west, from north and 29

(vv. 18-21.) Cf. Matt. xiii. 31-33; Mark iv. 31, 32.
24. Some put no stop at the end of verse 24, and translate 'will not succeed when once the Master.'
25. *Where you come from*] Or, ' whence (*i.e.* of what family) you are.'

south, and will sit down at the banquet in the Kingdom of God. And mark! some now last will be first, and some 30 now first will be last.'

Just at that time there came some Pharisees, 31 **Herod Antipas** who warned Him, saying,

' Leave this place and continue your journey; Herod means to kill you.'

' Go,' He replied, ' and take this message to that fox: 32 ' " See, to-day and to-morrow I am driving out demons and effecting cures, and on the third day I finish."

Jesus grieves over Jerusalem ' Yet I must continue my journey to-day and 33 to-morrow and the day following; for it is not conceivable that a Prophet should perish outside of Jerusalem.

34

' O Jerusalem, Jerusalem, that murders the Prophets and stones those who have been sent to her! How often have I desired to gather your children as a hen gathers her brood under her wings, and you would not come! See, 35 your house is abandoned to you. I tell you that you will never see me again until you say, " BLESSED IS HE WHO COMES IN THE NAME OF THE LORD! " ' (Ps. cxviii. 26).

A Sabbath Cure of Dropsy One day—it was a Sabbath—He entered 1 the house of one of the Rulers of the Pharisee party to take a meal, while they were closely watching Him. In front of Him was a man suffering from 2 dropsy. This led Jesus to ask the lawyers and Pharisees, 3 ' Is it allowable to cure people on the Sabbath? '

They gave Him no answer; so He took hold of the 4 man, cured him, and sent him away. Then He turned 5 to them and said,

' Which of you shall have a child or an ox fall into a well on the Sabbath day, and will not immediately lift him out? '

To this they could make no reply. 6

A Lesson in Humility Then, when He noticed how the invited 7 guests chose the best places, He spoke this parable, and said to them,

' When any one invites you to a wedding banquet, do 8 not take the best place, lest perhaps some more honoured

(vv. 34, 35.) Cf. Matt. xxiii. 1–39.
35. *Is left*] Cf. Matt. xxiii. 38, n.
5. *A child or an ox*] Lit. ' son.' Various readings are; sheep or ox, ox or ass, son or ox or ass.

guest than you may have been asked, and the man who 9
invited you both will come and say to you, " Make room
for him," and then you, ashamed, will move to the lowest
place.   But, when invited, take the lowest place, that when 10
your host comes he may say to you, " Friend, come up
higher."   This will be doing you honour in the presence of
all the other guests.   For whoever uplifts himself shall be 11
humbled, and he who humbles himself shall be uplifted.'

Also to His host, who had invited Him, He 12

**True
Charity** said,

'When you give a breakfast or a dinner, do
not invite your friends or brothers or relatives or rich
neighbours, lest perhaps they should in turn invite you, and
so repay your hospitality.   But when you entertain, invite 13
the poor, the crippled, the lame, and the blind ; and you 14
will be blessed, because they have no means of repaying you,
but you will be repaid at the Resurrection of the righteous.'

On hearing this, one of His fellow guests said 15

**The great
Supper** to Him,

'Blessed is he who shall feast in God's
Kingdom.'

' A man once gave a great feast,' replied Jesus, ' to 16
which he invited a large number of guests.   At dinner-time 17
he sent his servant with a message to those invited,

' " Come, for things are now ready,"

' But they all without exception began to excuse them- 18
selves.   The first told him,

' " I have just purchased a piece of land, and must of
necessity go and look at it.   Pray hold me excused."

' A second pleaded, 19

' " I have just bought five yoke of oxen, and am on my way
to try them.   Pray hold me excused."

' Another said, 20

' " I am just married.   It is impossible for me to come."

' So the servant came and brought these answers to his 21
master ; and it stirred his anger.

' " Go out quickly," he said, " into the streets of the city
—the wide ones and the narrow, and fetch in poor men,
the crippled, blind, and lame : fetch them all in here."

' Soon the servant reported, 22

' " Sir, what you ordered is done, and there is room still."

(vv. 16–24.) Cf. Matt. xxii. 1–14, n.

' " Go out," replied the master, " to the high roads and 23
hedge-rows, and compel the people to come in, so that my
house may be filled. For I tell you that not one of those 24
who were invited shall taste my feast." '

Christ's Claim is supreme On His journey vast crowds attended Him, 25
towards whom He turned and said,

' If any one comes to me who does not hate 26
his father and mother, wife and children, brothers and
sisters, yes and his own life also, he cannot be a disciple of
mine. No one who does not carry his own cross and come 27
after me can be a disciple of mine.

Counting the Cost ' Which of you, desiring to build a tower, 28
does not sit down first and calculate the cost,
asking if he has the means to finish it ?—lest 29
perhaps, when he has laid the foundation, and is unable to
finish, all who see it shall begin to jeer at him, saying, 30
" This man began to build, but could not finish." Or what 31
king, marching to encounter another king in war, does not
first sit down and deliberate whether he is able with ten
thousand men to meet the one who is advancing against
him with twenty thousand ? If not, while the other is still 32
a long way off, he sends envoys and sues for peace. Just 33
so no one of you who does not bid farewell to all that
belongs to him can be a disciple of mine.

' Salt is good : but if even the salt has become tasteless, 34
how will you restore its flavour ? Neither for land nor 35
for dunghill is it of any use ; they throw it away. Listen,
every one who has ears to hear ! '

'The lost Sheep' Now the tax-gatherers and the sinners were 1
everywhere in the habit of coming close to
Him to listen to Him ; and this led the Phari- 2
sees and the Scribes to complain,

' He gives a welcome to sinners, and joins them at
their meals ! '

So in a parable He asked them, 3

(vv. 26, 27.) Cf. Matt. x. 37.
26. *Hate*] This word must be interpreted in the light of a sanctified commonsense.
Taken literally it is as impossible to Jesus as to ourselves. Matthew. (x. 37) has a
parallel saying : ' He that loves father or mother more than me is not worthy
of me.' Possibly this is a softened version of the more original utterance recorded
faithfully by Luke. In the matter of discipleship our Lord insists that no earthly
affection, however dear or sacred, must be allowed to hinder the urgency of His
call (cf. Luke ix. 62).
(vv. 34, 35.) Cf. Matt. v. 13 ; Mark ix. 50, n.
3. *A parable*] Of the three parables of ' lost and found,' the first is given in another
context and in less graphic form by Matthew (xviii. 10-14). The parable of the

' Which of you men, if he has a hundred sheep and has 4
lost one of them, does not leave the ninety-nine in their
desert pasture and go in search of the lost one till he finds
it ?   And when he has found it, he lifts it on his shoulders, 5
glad at heart.   Then coming home he calls his friends and 6
neighbours together, and says, " Rejoice with me, for I
have found my sheep—the one I had lost." I tell 7
you that in the same way there will be rejoicing in
heaven over one repentant sinner—more rejoicing than
over ninety-nine blameless persons who have no need
of repentance.

'The lost   ' Or what woman who has ten silver coins, if 8
Coin'   she loses one of them, does not light a lamp and
            sweep the house and search carefully till she
finds it ?   And when she has found it, she calls together 9
her friends and neighbours, and says,

' " Congratulate me, for I have found the coin which I
had lost."

' I tell you that in the same way there is rejoicing in the 10
presence of the angels of God over one repentant sinner.'

'The lost   He went on to say,   11
Son'   ' There was a man who had two sons.   The 12
            younger of them said to his father,

' " Father, give me the share of the property that comes
to me."

' So he divided his property between them.   No long 13
time afterwards the younger son got all together and
travelled to a distant country, where he wasted his money
in debauchery and excess.   At last, when he had spent 14
everything, there came a terrible famine throughout that
country, and he began to feel the pinch of want.   So he 15
hired himself to one of the inhabitants of that country, who
sent him on to his farm to tend swine; and he longed to 16
make a meal of the pods the swine were eating, but no one
gave him any.

' On coming to his senses he said,   17

' " How many of my father's hired men have more bread

' Prodigal Son ' gives opportunity for stressing the human side of sin and repentance ;
but the real emphasis is still on the Divine seeking and forgiving grace.   He was
the lost son, and God was the loser.

   7. Blameless persons] This was not spoken in irony.

   9. Friends] Lit. ' woman friends.'

   14. To feel . . want] The middle voice of the Greek verb used here marks not the
want merely, but the sense of want.   Cf. Rom. iii. 24, ' consciously fall short.'

than they want, while I here am dying of hunger ! I will 18
rise and go to my father, and will say to him, Father, I
have sinned against heaven and before you : I no longer 19
deserve to be called a son of yours : treat me as one of your
hired men."

'So he rose and came to his father. But while he was 20
still a long way off, his father saw him and pitied him, and
ran and threw his arms round his neck and kissed him.

'"Father," cried the son, "I have sinned against heaven 21
and before you : no longer do I deserve to be called a son
of yours."

'But the father said to his servants, 22

'"Fetch the best coat quickly and put it on him ; and
bring a ring for his finger and shoes for his feet. Fetch 23
the fat calf and kill it, and let us feast and enjoy ourselves ;
for my son here was dead and has come to life again : he 24
was lost and has been found."

'And they began to be merry.

'Now his elder son was out on the farm ; and when 25
he came near the house, he heard music and dancing.
Then he called one of the lads to him and asked what all 26
this meant.

'"Your brother has come," he replied ; "and your 27
father has had the fat calf killed, because he has got him
home safe and sound."

'Then he was angry and would not go in. But his 28
father came out and entreated him.

'"All these years," replied the son, "I have served you, 29
and I have never at any time disobeyed any of your orders,
and yet you have never given me so much as a kid, for me
to enjoy myself with my friends ; but now that this son of 30
yours is come who has squandered your property among
harlots, you have killed the fat calf for him."

'"You, my dear son," said the father, "are always 31
with me, and all that is mine is also yours. We are bound 32

21. A group of manuscripts (including the two oldest) adds, 'Treat me as one of
your hired men' as in verse 19 ; but the omission (attested by the majority of
witnesses) is a fine touch. The father interrupts his son before he can get out the
humiliating request.

30. *This son*] 'This precious son of yours' is his meaning. But that there was
something to be said for his complaint is made clear by the tenderness of his father's
rejoinder to his reproaches, 'Son,' 'this brother of yours' ; and it must not be forgotten that this gentle rebuke is our Lord's answer to the murmuring of the Scribes
and Pharisees. On occasion Jesus could adopt a very different tone (Matt. xxiii.).

31. *My dear son*] Lit. 'child.'

to make merry and rejoice, for this brother of yours was dead and has come back to life, he was lost and has been found." '

'The dishonest Bailiff' He said also to His disciples : 1 **16** ' There was a rich man who had a steward about whom a report was brought to him, that he was wasting his property. He called him and said, 2 ' " What is this I hear about you ? Render an account of your stewardship, for I cannot let you hold it any longer."

' Then the steward said to himself, 3

' " What am I to do ? My master is taking away the stewardship from me. I am not strong enough for field labour : to beg, I should be ashamed. Ah ! I see 4 what to do, in order that when I am discharged from the stewardship people may give me a home in their houses."

' So he called all his master's debtors, one by one, and 5 asked the first, " How much are you in debt to my master ? "

' " A hundred measures of oil," he replied. 6

' " Here is your account," said the steward : " sit down quickly and alter it to fifty measures."

' To a second he said, 7

' " And how much do you owe ? "

' " A hundred quarters of wheat," was the answer.

' " Here is your account," said he : " alter it to eighty."

' And the master praised the dishonest steward for his 8 shrewdness ; for, in dealing with their fellows, the men of this world are shrewder than the sons of Light.

The right Use of Wealth ' And I charge you, so to use wealth tainted 9 with dishonesty as to win friends who, when it fails, shall welcome you to the tents that never perish. The man who is honest in a very small 10 matter is honest in a great one also ; and he who is dishonest in a very small matter is dishonest in a great one also. If therefore you have not proved yourselves honest 11 in dealing with wealth tainted with dishonesty, who will

6, 7. *Measures. Quarters*] These are not intended as exact translations.
6. *Alter it to*] Lit. ' write.'
9. *Wealth tainted with dishonesty*] Lit. ' the Mammon of dishonesty.'
It fails] v.L. ' we fail,' *i.e.* ' die.'
11. *Wealth*] Lit. ' Mammon.'

entrust to you the true good ? And if you have not been 12
honest with what belongs to another, who will give you
what is your own ?

Divided
Service
impossible 'No servant can serve two masters. For 13
either he will hate one and love the other, or
else he will attach himself to one and think
lightly of the other. You cannot be servants both of God
and of money.'

The
Pharisees
rebuked To all this the Pharisees listened, bitterly 14
jeering at Him ; for they were lovers of money.
'You are persons,' He said to them, ' who 15
boast of their own goodness before men, but God sees your
hearts ; for what is exalted by men may be an abomination
in God's sight. The Law and the Prophets continued until 16
John came : from that time the gospel of the Kingdom of
God has been spreading, and every one presses into it.
And it is easier for sky and earth to pass away than for the 17
smallest detail of the Law to fall through. Any man who 18
divorces his wife and marries another commits adultery ;
and he who marries a woman so divorced from her husband
commits adultery.

'The rich
Man and
the Beggar' ' There was once a rich man who used to 19
array himself in purple and fine linen, and
enjoyed a splendid banquet every day, while 20
at his outer door there lay a beggar, Lazarus by name,
covered with sores and longing to make a meal off 21
the scraps falling on the floor from the rich man's
table. Nay, the dogs, too, used to come and lick his
sores.

' In course of time the beggar died ; and he was carried 22
by the angels to Abraham's bosom. The rich man also
died, and was buried. And in Hades, being in torment, 23

---

13. *Servant*] Or ' house-slave.' Cf. Acts x. 7, n. (The noun is not expressed in the parallel passage, Matt. vi. 24.)
14. *Bitterly jeering*] Perhaps more exactly ' turning up their noses,' ' disdainfully sneering.' The same compound verb occurs in xxiii. 35, and the simple verb in Gal. vi. 7.
17. Cf. Matt. v. 18.
18. Cf. Matt. v. 32. The connection here is not obvious.
(vv. 19-31.) The story is to warn the rich and comfort the poor. Its main moral is the future reversal of earthly circumstances, a comment on the sayings of Christ (vi. 20-26). The Jewish imagery is of course not to be taken literally, as if it was a revelation by Jesus of the actual conditions of the ' after-life.'
23. *Hades*] The Greek equivalent of the Hebrew Sheol—the dim underworld to which all the dead go—with no idea of torment. Here Luke uses the word in the sense of ' Gehenna,' as distinguished from the other part of Sheol—' Paradise ' in later Jewish thought—where the blessed await their resurrection.

he looked and saw Abraham in the far distance, and Lazarus
resting in his arms.   So he cried aloud, and said,   24

' " Father Abraham, take pity on me and send Lazarus
to dip the tip of his finger in water and cool my tongue,
for I am in agony in this flame."

' " Remember, my son," said Abraham, " that you had 25
good fortune during your life, and that Lazarus in like
manner had bad fortune.   But he is comforted here now,
while you are in agony.   Besides all this there is set a vast 26
chasm between us and you, in order that those who desire
to cross from this side to you, or from your side to us, may
not be able to do so."

' " I entreat you then, father," said he, " to send him to my 27
father's house.   For I have five brothers.   Let him earnestly 28
warn them, lest they also come to this place of torment."

' " They have Moses and the Prophets," replied 29
Abraham ; " let them hear them."

' " No, father Abraham," he pleaded ; " but if some one 30
goes to them from the dead, they will repent."

' " If they are deaf to Moses and the Prophets," replied 31
Abraham, " they would not be led to believe even if some
one should rise from the dead." '

                   Jesus said to His disciples,   1 **17**

**Stones of
Stumbling**   ' It is inevitable that causes of stumbling
should occur ; but woe to him through whom
they occur !   Better for him if with a millstone hanging 2
round his neck he had been hurled into the sea, rather than
that he should cause a single one of these little ones to
fall.   Be on your guard.   3

           ' If your brother acts wrongly, reprove him ;
**The Duty of
Forgiveness** and if he is sorry, forgive him ; and if seven 4
times in a day he acts wrongly towards you,
and seven times turns again to you and says, " I am sorry,"
you must forgive him.'

And the Apostles said to the Lord,   5

          ' Increase our faith.'
**The immense
Power of
Faith**   ' If your faith,' replied the Lord, ' were 6
merely like a mustard-seed, you might say to

---

   23. *In his arms*] *i.e.* ' Reclining at table on Abraham's right hand.' Cf. John
xiii. 23, n.
   (vv. 1, 2.) Cf. Matt. xviii. 6, 9 ; Mark ix. 42–50.
   2. *Millstone*] Cf. Matt. xviii. 6 ; Mark ix. 42, n.
   (vv. 3, 4.) Cf. Matt. xviii. 21–35.

this black-mulberry tree, " Tear up your roots and plant yourself in the sea," and instantly it would obey you.

Fidelity to Duty ' Which of you who has a servant ploughing, 7 or tending sheep, will say to him when he comes in from the farm, " Come at once and take your place at table," and will not rather say to him, " Get 8 my dinner ready, gird yourself, and wait upon me till I have finished my dinner, and then you shall have yours " ? Does 9 he thank the servant for obeying his orders ? So you also, 10 when you have obeyed all the orders given you, must say,

' " There is no merit in our service : we have merely done our duty." '

Cure of ten Lepers As they pursued their journey to Jerusalem, 11 He passed between Samaria and Galilee. And 12 as He entered a certain village, ten men met Him who were lepers and stood at a distance. In loud 13 voices they cried out,

' Jesus, Rabbi, take pity on us.'

Perceiving this, He said to them, 14

' Go and show yourselves to the Priests.'

And while on their way to do this they were made clean.

One of them, seeing that he was cured, came back, glori- 15 fying God in a loud voice, and he threw himself at the feet 16 of Jesus, thanking Him. He was a Samaritan.

' Were not all ten made clean ? ' Jesus asked ; ' but 17 where are the nine ? Have none been found to come 18 back and give glory to God except this foreigner ? '

And He said to him, 19

' Rise and go : your faith has cured you.'

The Coming of the Kingdom Being asked by the Pharisees when the 20 Kingdom of God was coming, He answered, ' The Kingdom of God does not so come that you can watch closely for it. Nor shall they say, " See 21 here ! " or " See there ! "—for the Kingdom of God is within you.'

Then, turning to His disciples, He said, 22

(vv. 7–10.) Compare the lavish and condescending reward of duty faithfully discharged in xii. 33–38.

10. *There is no merit, &c.*] Lit. ' We are unprofitable servants.' The early Syriac version omits ' unprofitable,' reading ' We are but slaves.'

11. *They pursued their*] Or ' He pursued His.' Cf. Matt. xix. 1–2 ; Mark x. 1.

21. *Within you*] *i.e.* requires subjective, spiritual qualifications for its apprehension. Or ' among you,' *i.e.* has already come into your midst, although as yet you do not recognize its existence. (See Matt. xii. 28, n.) Or possibly referring to the *future* ;

' There will come a time when you will wish you could see but a single one of the days of the Son of Man, but will not see one. And they will say to you, " See there ! " 23 " See here ! " Do not go in pursuit. For just as the 24 lightning, when it flashes, shoots across the sky, so will the Son of Man be on His day. But first He must endure 25 much suffering, and be rejected by the present generation.

Compared to the Days of Noah and Lot ' And as it was in the time of Noah, so will 26 it also be in the time of the Son of Man. Men were eating and drinking, taking wives 27 and giving wives, up to the very day Noah entered the Ark, and the Deluge came and destroyed them all. As it was also in the time of Lot ; they were eating 28 and drinking, buying and selling, planting and building ; but on the day that Lot left Sodom, it rained fire and brim- 29 stone from the sky and destroyed them all. Exactly so will 30 it be on the day that the veil is lifted from the Son of Man.

' On that day, if a man is on the roof and his goods 31 indoors, let him not go down to fetch them ; and, in the same way, he who is in the field, let him not turn back. Remember Lot's wife. Any man who seeks to save his life 32,33 shall lose it ; but whoever loses his life shall retain it. On 34 that night, I tell you, there will be two men in one bed : one will be taken away and the other left. There will be 35 two women turning the mill together : one will be taken away and the other left.'

' Where, Master ? ' they inquired. 37

' Where the dead body is,' He replied, ' there also will the vultures flock together.'

He also taught them by a parable that they 1 **18** must always pray and never lose heart.

The unjust Judge ' In a certain town,' He said, ' there was a 2 judge who had no fear of God and no respect for man. And in the same town was a widow who repeatedly came 3 and entreated him, saying,

' " Give me justice and stop my adversary."

' For a time he would not, but afterwards he said to 4 himself,

all waiting for signs is futile : ' like a lightning flash it will be among you before you are aware.' But if Luke had meant ' in the midst of you,' he would probably have used another phrase, as in ii. 46 ; xxiv. 36, etc. On the whole ' within you ' is to be preferred.

v.L. inserts verse 36, ' There will be two men in the field : one will be taken away and the other left behind.' From Matt. xxiv. 40.

' " Though I have neither fear of God nor respect for man, yet because she annoys me I will give her justice, to 5 prevent her from constantly coming to pester me." '

And the Lord said, 6

' Hear those words of the unjust judge. And will not 7 God avenge the wrongs of His own people who cry aloud to Him day and night, although He delays vengeance on their behalf ? Yes, He will soon avenge their wrongs. Yet, 8 when the Son of Man comes, will He find faith on earth ? '

' The Pharisee and the Tax-Gatherer ' And to some who relied on themselves as 9 being righteous men, and looked down upon all others, He addressed this parable.

' Two men went up to the Temple to pray, 10 one a Pharisee and the other a tax-gatherer. The Pharisee, 11 standing erect, prayed as follows by himself :

' " O God, I thank Thee that I am not like other people —I am not a thief nor a cheat nor an adulterer, nor even like this tax-gatherer. I fast twice a week. I pay the 12 tithe on all my gains."

' But the tax-gatherer, standing far back, would not so 13 much as lift his eyes to heaven, but kept beating his breast and saying,

' " O God, have mercy on me, sinner that I am."

' I tell you that this man went home set right with 14 God rather than the other ; for every one who uplifts himself shall be humbled, but he who humbles himself shall be uplifted.'

Little Children blessed On one occasion people brought with them 15 their infants, for Him to touch them ; but the disciples, noticing this, found fault with them. 16 Jesus, however, called for the infants.

' Let the little children come to me,' He said ; ' do not hinder them ; for it is to those who are childlike that the Kingdom of God belongs. I tell you in truth that, 17

5. *Pester*] Cf. the rendering of the same verb in 1 Cor. ix. 27. ' Hit hard and straight ' ; Lit. ' Give a black eye.'

7. *On their behalf*] Or ' against their foes.'

8. *Faith*] Or ' this belief.' The sense may be, ' Will their trials be so severe and protracted that the faith of one and all will succumb ? ' Cf. Matt. xxiv. 12, 22.

11. *By himself*] v.l. places these words before ' prayed.'

13. *Have mercy*] Or ' be propitiated '—the human view of God's infinite mercy. Cf. John iii. 16 ; Tim. ii. 4.

(vv. 15-17.) Cf. Matt. xix. 13-15 ; Mark x. 13-16. Here Luke rejoins Mark ; see Introduction.

15. *People*] Not the mothers only, for the ' them ' at the end of the verse is masculine—although it no doubt includes the mothers.

whoever does not receive the Kingdom of God like a little child will certainly not enter it.'

The question was put to Him by a ruler: 18

Eternal Life ' Good Rabbi, what shall I do to inherit eternal Life ? '

' Why do you call me good ? ' replied Jesus ; ' there is 19 no one good but One, namely God. You know the Com- 20 mandments : " DO NOT COMMIT ADULTERY " ; " DO NOT MURDER " ; " DO NOT STEAL " ; " DO NOT LIE IN GIVING EVIDENCE " ; " HONOUR THY FATHER AND THY MOTHER." '

' All these,' he replied, ' I have carefully obeyed from 21 my youth.'

On receiving this answer Jesus said to him, 22 ' There is still one thing wanting in you. Sell everything you possess and give the money to the poor, and you shall have wealth in heaven ; and come and follow me.'

But on hearing these words he was very sorrowful, for 23 he was exceedingly rich.

Jesus looked at him, and said, 24

The Dangers of Wealth ' How hard it will be for the possessors of riches to enter the Kingdom of God ! Why, 25 it is easier for a camel to go through a needle's eye than for a rich man to enter the Kingdom of God.'

' Who then can be saved ? ' exclaimed the hearers. 26

' Things impossible to man,' He replied, ' are possible 27 to God.'

Self-sacrifice for Christ enriches Then Peter said, 28 ' See, we have given up our homes and have followed you.'

' I tell you in truth,' replied Jesus, ' that there is no 29 one who has left house or wife, or brothers or parents or children, for the sake of God's Kingdom, who shall not 30 receive many times as much in this life, and in the age that is coming eternal Life.'

Jesus a third time predicts His Death and Resurrection Then He drew the twelve to Him and said, 31 ' See, we are going up to Jerusalem, and everything written in the Prophets about the Son of Man will be fulfilled. For He will be 32 handed over to the Gentiles, and be mocked, outraged, and spat upon. They will scourge Him and put 33

(vv. 18-30.) Cf. Matt. xix. 16-30 : Mark x. 17-31.
25. *Needle's*] Different words are used both for ' needle ' and ' eye ' in Matt. xix.
24 ; Mark x. 25. Therefore it is hardly a Greek proverb.

Him to death, and on the third day He will rise to life again.'

Nothing of this did they understand. The words were 34 a mystery to them, nor could they see what He meant.

A blind Man receives Sight As Jesus came near to Jericho, there was a 35 blind man sitting by the way-side begging. He heard a crowd of people going past, and 36 inquired what it all meant.

'Jesus the Nazarene is passing by,' they told him. 37

Then, at the top of his voice, he cried out, 38

'Jesus, Son of David, take pity on me.'

Those in front reproved him and tried to silence him ; but 39 he continued shouting, louder than ever.

'Son of David, take pity on me.'

So Jesus stopped and bade them bring the man to 40 Him ; and when he had come close to Him He asked him,

'What shall I do for you ?' 41

'Sir,' he replied, 'let me recover my sight.'

'Recover your sight,' said Jesus : 'your faith has cured 42 you.'

No sooner were the words spoken than the man regained 43 his sight and followed Jesus, giving glory to God ; and all the people, seeing it, gave praise to God.

Zacchaeus So He entered Jericho and proceeded through 1 **19** the town. There was a man there called 2 Zacchaeus, who was the chief collector of taxes, and was wealthy. He was anxious to see what sort of man Jesus 3 was ; but he could not because of the crowd, for he was short in stature. So he ran on in front and climbed up a 4 mulberry tree to see Him ; for He was about to pass that way.

As soon as Jesus came to the place, He looked up and 5 said to him,

'Zacchaeus, come down quickly, for I must stay at your house to-day.'

So he came down in haste, and welcomed Him joyfully. 6 When they all saw this, they began to complain with 7 indignation.

---

34. Or 'It was divinely concealed from them.' An answer to the perplexed question 'Why did their Lord's death, thrice explicitly predicted, take them all by surprise ?'

(vv. 35-43.) Cf. Matt. xx. 29-34 ; Mark x. 46-52.

' He has gone in to be the guest of a sinner ! ' they said.

Zacchaeus, however, stood up, and addressing the Lord 8 said,

' Here and now, Master, I give half my property to the poor, and if I have unjustly exacted money from any man, I pledge myself to repay to him four times the amount.'

Jesus said to him,   9

' To-day salvation has come to this house, seeing that he too is a son of Abraham. For the Son of Man has come 10 to seek and to save what is lost.'

Privilege and Responsibility As they were listening to His words, He 11 went on to teach them by a parable, because He was near to Jerusalem and they supposed that the Kingdom of God was going to appear immediately. So 12 He said to them,

' A man of noble family travelled to a distant country to obtain the rank of king, and to return. And he called ten of 13 his servants and gave each of them a pound, instructing them to trade with the money during his absence.

' Now his countrymen hated him, and sent a deputation 14 after him to say, " We are not willing that he should become our king." And upon his return, after he had obtained the 15 sovereignty, he ordered those servants to whom he had given the money to be summoned before him, that he might learn their success in trading.

' So the first came, and said,   16

' " Sir, your pound has produced ten pounds more."

' " Well done, good servant," he replied ; " because you 17 have been faithful in a very small matter, be in authority over ten towns."

' The second came, and said,   18

' " Your pound, Sir, has produced five pounds."

8. *I pledge myself to repay*] Lit. ' I repay.'

(vv. 11–28.) Cf. Matt. xxv. 14–30. The main point of difference between Matthew's parable of the talents and Luke's of the pounds is of course between unequal gifts used with equal fidelity, and equal gifts used with varying success. But the structure of the two parables is on very similar lines.

13. *Servants*] Or ' slaves.' So in verses 15, 17, 22.

During his absence] Lit. ' while I am coming.'

14. An indication of the rejection of Christ by the Jews, as verse 27 is of their punishment when He shall return from the ' distant country.' There seems to be a reference to actual history. Some thirty years before, Archelaus (Matt. ii. 22) had gone to Rome to receive his kingdom, and was followed by a protesting deputation of fifty Jews.

' So he said to this one also, 19
' " And you, be the governor of five towns."
' The next came. 20
' " Sir," he said, " here is your pound, which I have kept wrapt up in a cloth. For I was afraid of you, because you 21 are a severe man : you take up what you did not lay down, and you reap what you did not sow."
' " By your own words," he replied, " I will judge you, 22 you bad servant. You knew me to be a severe man, taking up what I did not lay down, and reaping what I did not sow ! Why then did you not put my money into a bank, that 23 when I came I might have received it back with interest ? "
' And he said to those who stood by, 24
' " Take the pound from him and give it to him who has the ten pounds."
' They said to him, 25
' " Sir, he already has ten pounds."
' " I tell you that to every one who has anything, more 26 shall be given ; and from him who has not anything, even what he has shall be taken away. But as for those enemies 27 of mine who were unwilling that I should become their king, bring them here, and slay them in my presence." '

An Ass's Colt is borrowed After thus speaking, He journeyed onward, 28 proceeding to Jerusalem. And when He was 29 come near Bethphagé and Bethany, at the Mount called the Oliveyard, He despatched two of the disciples, saying to them, 30
' Go into the village facing you. On entering it you will find an ass's colt tied up which no one has ever yet ridden : untie it, and bring it here. And if any one asks you, " Why 31 are you untying the colt ? " simply say, " The Lord needs it." '

So those who were sent went and found things as He had 32 told them. And while they were untying the colt the 33 owners called out, ' Why are you untying the colt ? ' and 34 they replied, ' The Lord needs it.'

Jesus rides into Jerusalem Then they brought it to Jesus, and after 35 throwing their outer garments on the colt they placed Jesus on it. So He rode on, while they 36 carpeted the road with their garments. And when He was 37 now getting near Jerusalem, and descending the Mount of

(vv. 29–44.) Cf. Matt. xi. 1–11 ; Mark xi. 1–11 ; John xii. 12–19.

192

Olives, the whole multitude of the disciples began in their joy to praise God in loud voices for all the mighty deeds they had witnessed, saying, 38

' BLESSED IS the King,' they cried, ' WHO COMES IN THE NAME OF THE LORD (Ps. cxviii. 26): in heaven peace, and glory in the highest realms.'

Thereupon some of the Pharisees in the crowd appealed 39 to Him, saying,

' Rabbi, reprove your disciples.'

' I tell you,' He replied, ' that if they became silent, the 40 very stones would cry out.'

He weeps over the City When He came into full view of the city, He 41 wept aloud over it, and exclaimed, 42

' O that at this time thou only knewest what makes for peace ! But now it is hid from thine eyes. For 43 the time is coming upon thee when thy foes will throw up around thee earthworks and a wall, investing thee and hemming thee in on every side. And they will dash thee 44 to the ground and thy children within thee, and will not leave one stone upon another within thee ; because thou didst not recognize the time of thy visitation.'

The Dealers driven from the Temple Then Jesus entered the Temple and pro- 45 ceeded to drive out the dealers.

' It is written,' He said, ' " AND MY HOUSE 46 SHALL BE THE HOUSE OF PRAYER " (Isa. lvi. 7), but you have made it A ROBBERS' CAVE ' (Jer. vii. 11).

And day after day He taught in the Temple, while the 47 High Priests and the Scribes were devising some means of destroying Him, as were also the leading men of the people. But they could not find any way of doing it, for the people 48 all hung upon His lips.

The Leaders of the People silenced On one of those days while He was teaching 1 **20** the people in the Temple and preaching the gospel, the High Priests came upon Him, and the Scribes, together with the Elders, and they asked 2 Him,

' Tell us, by what authority are you doing these things ? And who is it that gave you this authority ? '

41. Cf. xiii. 34, 35.
43. *Earthworks and a wall*] Lit. simply ' a rampart,' or ' a palisade.'
(vv. 45–48.) Cf. Matt. xxi. 12–17 ; Mark xi. 15–19.
46. Cf. Matt. xxi. 13, n.
(vv. 1–8.) Cf. Matt. xxi. 23–27 ; Mark xi. 27–33.

'I also will put a question to you,' He said; 'was 3, 4 John's baptism from heaven or from men?'

So they debated the matter with one another. 5

'If we say "from heaven,"' they argued, 'He will say, "Why did you not believe him?" And if we say "from 6 men," the people will all stone us; for they are convinced that John was a Prophet.'

And they answered that they did not know the origin of it. 7

'Nor do I tell you,' said Jesus, 'by what authority I do 8 these things.'

'The wicked Vine-dressers' Then He proceeded to speak a parable to the 9 people.

'There was a man,' He said, 'who planted a vineyard, let it out to vine-dressers, and went abroad for a considerable time. At vintage-time he sent a servant to 10 the vine-dressers, for them to give him a share of the crop; but the vine-dressers beat him cruelly and sent him away empty-handed. Then he sent a second servant; and him 11 too they beat and ill-treated and sent away empty-handed. Then again he sent a third; and this one also they wounded 12 and drove away. Then the owner of the vineyard said, 13

'"What am I to do? I will send my son—my dearly-loved son: they will probably respect him."

'But when the vine-dressers saw him, they discussed the 14 matter with one another, and said,

'"This is the heir: let us kill him, that the inheritance may be ours."

'So they flung him out of the vineyard and killed him. 15 What then will the owner of the vineyard do to them? He will come and put these vine-dressers to death, and give 16 the vineyard to others.'

'God forbid!' exclaimed the hearers.

He looked at them and said, 17

'What then does that mean which is written,

'"THE STONE WHICH THE BUILDERS REJECTED
HAS BECOME THE CORNERSTONE" (Ps. cxviii. 22)?
Every one who falls on that stone will be severely hurt, but 18 he on whom it falls will be utterly crushed.'

At this the Scribes and the High Priests wanted to lay 19

16. *God forbid*] Lit. 'May it not happen.' Manifestly a prayer to God, and in some cases best rendered as such. The expression occurs here and fourteen times in the Epistles of Paul. Cf. Rom. iii. 4, n.

18. *Will be utterly crushed*] Rather 'it will scatter him as dust.'

hands on Him, then and there ; only they were afraid of the people. For they saw that in this parable He had referred to them.

A Question about Tribute So watching their opportunity, they sent 20 spies who were to act the part of honest men, that they might fasten on some expression of His, so as to hand Him over to the ruling power and the Governor's authority. So they put a question to Him. 21

'Rabbi,' they said, 'we know that you say and teach what is right and that you make no distinctions between one man and another, but teach God's way truly. May 22 one pay a tax to Caesar, or not ? '

But He saw through their knavery and replied, 23

' Show me a shilling. Whose likeness and inscription 24 does it bear ? '

' Caesar's,' they said.

' Pay therefore,' He replied, ' what is Caesar's to Caesar 25 —and what is God's to God.'

There was nothing here that they could lay hold of before 26 the people, and marvelling at His answer they said no more.

A Question about the Resurrection Some of the Sadducees (who deny that there 27 is a resurrection) next came forward and asked Him,

' Rabbi, Moses made this a law for us, IF A MAN'S 28 BROTHER DIE, LEAVING A WIFE BUT NO CHILDREN, THE MAN SHALL MARRY THE WIDOW AND RAISE UP A FAMILY FOR HIS BROTHER (Deut. xxv. 5). Now there were seven brothers. 29 The first of them took a wife and died childless. The 30 second and the third also took her ; and all seven, having 31 done the same, left no children when they died. Finally the 32 woman also died. Whose wife, then, at the Resurrection 33 shall the woman be ? for they all seven married her.'

' People in this world,' replied Jesus, ' marry, and are 34 given in marriage. But as for those who are deemed worthy 35 to find a place in that other age and in the Resurrection from the dead, the men do not marry and the women are not given in marriage. For indeed they cannot die again ; they 36 are like angels, and are sons of God through being sons of the Resurrection. But that the dead rise to life even 37

19. *Then and there*] Lit. ' that same hour.'
(vv. 20–26.) Cf. Matt. xxii. 15–22 ; Mark xii. 13–17.
21. Cf. Matt. xxii. 16, n.
(vv. 27–39.) Cf. Matt. xxii. 23–33 ; Mark xii. 18–27.

Moses clearly implies in the passage about the Bush, where he calls the Lord "THE GOD OF ABRAHAM, AND THE GOD OF ISAAC, AND THE GOD OF JACOB" (Exod. iii. 2–6). He is not 38 a God of the dead, but of the living, for to Him all are living.'

Then some of the Scribes replied, 39
' Rabbi, you have spoken well.'

From that time no one ventured to put a single question 40 to Him.

But He asked them, 41
' How is it they say that the Christ is son of David ? Why, David himself says in the Book of Psalms, 42

' " THE LORD SAID TO MY LORD,
 SIT AT MY RIGHT HAND
 UNTIL I HAVE MADE THY FOES A FOOTSTOOL UNDER THY 43
 FEET " (Ps. cx. 1).

' David himself therefore calls Him Lord, and how can 44 He be his son ? '

Then, in the hearing of all the people, He 45
The Scribes said to the disciples,
denounced
  ' Beware of the Scribes, who like to walk 46 about in long robes, and love to be bowed to in places of public resort and to occupy the best places in the synagogues or at dinner-parties ; who swallow up the property 47 of widows and by way of excuse make long prayers. The heavier the punishment these men will receive.'

Looking up He saw the people putting their 1 **21**
The Widow's gifts into the Treasury—the rich people. He 2
Gift
  also saw a poor widow dropping in two mites, and He said, 3
' In truth I tell you that this widow, so poor, has thrown in more than any of them. For from what they could well 4 spare they have all of them contributed to the offerings, but she in her neediness has thrown in all she had to live on.'

When some were remarking about the 5
Jesus pre- Temple, how it was embellished with beautiful
dicts the
Destruction stones and dedicated gifts, He said,
of the
Temple ' As to these things which you now admire, the 6
  time is coming when there will not be one stone left here upon another which will not be pulled down.'

(vv. 41–44.) Cf. Matt. xxii. 41–46 ; Mark xii. 35–37.
(vv. 45–47.) Cf. Mark xii. 38–40.
(vv. 1–4.) Cf. Mark xii. 41–44.
(vv. 5–19.) Cf. Matt. xxiv. 1–14 ; Mark xiii. 1–13.

Things which would precede it 'Rabbi, when will this be?' they asked 7 Him, 'and what will be the sign when these things are about to take place?'

'See to it,' He replied, 'that you are not misled; for 8 many will come in my name professing, " I am He," or saying, " The time is close at hand." Do not go and follow them. But when you hear of wars and turmoils, 9 be not afraid; for these things must happen first, but the end does not come immediately.'

Then He said to them, 10

Wars and Earthquakes ' NATION WILL RISE IN ARMS AGAINST NATION, AND KINGDOM AGAINST KINGDOM (Isa. xix. 2). And there will be great earthquakes, and in places famines 11 and pestilence; and there will be terrors and wonderful signs from heaven.

Persecution ' But before all these things happen they 12 will lay hands on you and persecute you. They will deliver you up to synagogues and to prison, and you will be brought before kings and governors for my sake. In the end all this will be evidence of 13 your fidelity.

Promises of Deliverance ' Make up your minds, however, not to pre- 14 pare a defence beforehand, for I will give you 15 utterance and wisdom which none of your opponents will be able to withstand or reply to. You will 16 be betrayed even by parents, brothers, relatives, and friends; and some of you they will put to death. You will be hated 17 by all men because you are called by my name; and yet 18 not a hair of your heads shall perish. By your endurance 19 you shall win your souls.

Jerusalem surrounded by Armies ' But when you see Jerusalem with armies 20 encamping round her on every side, then be certain that her desolation is close at hand. Then let those in Judaea escape to the hills; let 21 those who are in the city leave it, and those in the country not enter therein. For those are THE DAYS OF 22 VENGEANCE (Hos. ix. 7) in order to fulfil all that is written.

The City trampled underfoot ' Alas for women who at that time are with 23 child or have infants at breast; for there will be great distress in the land, and anger towards this people. They will fall by the edge of the sword, or be 24 carried off into captivity among all the Gentiles. And Jerusalem will be trampled underfoot by the Gentiles, till the times of the Gentiles have expired.

The Coming of the Son of Man 'There will be signs in sun, moon, and 25 stars; and on earth anguish among the nations in their bewilderment at the roaring of the sea and its billows; men's hearts fainting for fear, and for 26 apprehension of what is coming on the world. For THE FORCES WHICH CONTROL THE HEAVENS WILL BE DISORDERED (Isa. xxxiv. 4). And then shall they see the SON OF MAN 27 COMING IN A CLOUD (Dan. vii. 13) with great power and glory. But when all this is beginning to take place, look 28 up. Lift up your heads, because your deliverance is drawing near.'

And He spoke a parable to them. 29

'See,' He said, 'the fig-tree and all the trees. As soon 30 as they have shot out their leaves, you know at a glance that summer is now near. So also, when you see these 31 things happening, you may be sure that the Kingdom of God is near. I tell you in truth that the present genera- 32 tion will not pass away without all these things first taking place. Heaven and earth will pass away, but my words 33 will not pass away.

Warnings 'But take heed to yourselves, lest your souls 34 be weighed down with self-indulgence and drunkenness or the anxieties of this life, and that day come upon you, suddenly, like a falling trap; for it will come on 35 all the dwellers on the face of the whole earth (Isa. xxiv. 17). Beware of slumbering; at all times pray that you may 36 be fully strengthened to escape from all these coming evils, and to take your stand in the presence of the Son of Man.'

At this time He would teach in the Temple by day, but 37 go out and spend the night on the Mount called the Olive-yard. And all the people came to Him in the Temple, 38 early in the morning, to listen to Him.

The Treachery of Judas Meanwhile the Festival of the Unleavened 1 **22** Bread, called the Passover, was approaching, and the High Priests and the Scribes were 2 contriving how to destroy Him. For they feared the people. But Satan entered into Judas (the one called 3

(vv. 1, 2.) Cf. Matt. xxvi. 1-5; Mark xiv. 1, 2.
(vv. 3-6.) Cf. Matt. xxvi. 14-16; Mark xiv. 10, 11.

Iscariot—one of the twelve); who went away and con- 4
ferred with the High Priests and Commanders as to how
he should deliver Him up to them. They were glad 5
and they agreed to pay him. He accepted their offer, and 6
then looked out for an opportunity to betray Him when
the people were not there.

Peter and John prepare the Passover When the day of the Unleavened Bread came 7
—the day for the Passover lamb to be sacrificed
—Jesus sent Peter and John with instructions. 8
' Go,' He said, ' and prepare the Passover for
us, that we may eat it.'

' Where shall we prepare it ? ' they asked. 9

' You will no sooner have entered the city,' He replied, 10
' than you will meet a man carrying a pitcher of water.
Follow him into the house to which he goes, and say to 11
the master of the house.

' " The Rabbi asks you, Where is the room where I can
eat the Passover with my disciples ? "

' And he will show you a large furnished room upstairs. 12
There make your preparations.'

So they went and found all as He had told them ; and 13
they got the Passover ready.

' The last Supper ' When the time was come, and He had taken 14
His place at table, and the apostles with Him,
He said to them, 15

' Earnestly have I longed to eat this Passover with you before
I suffer ; for I tell you that I certainly shall not eat one again 16
till its full meaning is brought out in the Kingdom of God.'

Then, having received a cup and given thanks, He said, 17

' Take this and share it among you ; for I tell you that 18
from this time I will never drink the produce of the vine
till the Kingdom of God has come.'

The memorial Meal instituted. The Traitor indicated Then, taking a loaf, He gave thanks and broke 19
it, and handed it to them, saying,
' This is my body which is being given on
your behalf : this do in remembrance of me.'
He handed them the cup in like manner, 20
when the meal was over.

(vv. 7–13.) Cf. Matt. xxvi. 17–19 ; Mark xiv. 12–16.
(vv. 14–23.) Cf. Matt. xxvi. 20–29 ; Mark xiv. 17–25 ; 1 Cor. xi. 23–25 (the earliest
account). It will be noted that Luke records two cups. The various readings in
verses 16–20 raise a difficult textual problem, which cannot here be discussed. (See
the Commentaries.)

'This cup,' He said, 'is the new Covenant ratified by my blood which is to be poured out on your behalf. Yet 21 the hand of my betrayer is at the table with me. For 22 indeed the Son of Man goes on His pre-destined way; but woe to the man who is betraying Him!'

Thereupon they began to discuss with one another 23 which of them it could possibly be who was about to do this.

Ambition rebuked

There arose also a dispute among them as 24 to which of them should be regarded as greatest. But He said to them, 25

'The kings of the Gentiles are their masters, and those who exercise authority over them are called "Benefactors." With you it is not so; but let the greatest among you be 26 as the younger, and the leader be like him who serves. For which is the greater—he who sits at table, or he who 27 waits on him? Is it not he who sits at table? But I am among you as he who waits. You, however, have remained 28 with me amid my trials; and I assign to you, as my 29 Father has assigned to me, a Kingdom—so that you may 30 eat and drink at my table in my Kingdom, and sit on thrones as judges over the twelve tribes of Israel.

Peter's Denial foretold

'Simon, Simon, I tell you that Satan has 31 obtained permission to have all of you to sift as wheat is sifted. But I have prayed for yourself 32 that your faith may not fail, and you, as soon as you have repented, must strengthen your brethren.'

'Master,' replied Peter, 'with you I am ready to go 33 both to prison and to death.'

'I tell you, Peter,' said Jesus, 'that the cock will not 34 crow to-day till you have three times denied that you know me.'

The coming Danger. A veiled Warning

Then He asked them, 35 'When I sent you out without purse or bag or shoes, was there anything you needed?' 'No, nothing,' they replied.

'But now,' said He, 'let the one who has a purse take 36 it, and he who has a bag must do the same. And let any

---

20. *Is to be poured*] Lit. 'is being poured.'
(vv. 21–23.) Cf. Matt. xxvi. 21–25; Mark xiv. 18–21; John xiii. 21–35.
(vv. 24–26.) Cf. ix. 46; Matt. xx. 25–27; Mark x. 42–44.
27. Cf. Matt. xx. 28, n.
(vv. 28–38.) Most of this is peculiar to Luke.
31. *Obtained permission*] Or 'earnestly begged.'

one who has no sword sell his coat and buy one. For I tell 37
you that those words of Scripture must be fulfilled in my
case : " AND HE WAS RECKONED AMONG THE LAWLESS "
(Isa. liii. 12) ; for indeed that saying about me has now its
accomplishment.'

' Master, here are two swords,' they exclaimed. 38

' Enough,' He replied.

The Agony in Gethsemane On going out, He proceeded as usual to the 39
Mount of Olives, and His disciples followed
Him. When He arrived at the place, He 40
said to them,

' Pray that you may not come into temptation.'

He Himself withdrew from them about a stone's throw, 41
and knelt down and prayed, saying, 42

' Father, if it be Thy will, take this cup away from me ;
yet not my will but Thine be done ! '

And there appeared to Him an angel from heaven, 43
strengthening Him ; while He—an agony of distress having 44
come upon Him—prayed all the more with intense earnestness, and His sweat became like clots of blood dropping
on the ground.

When He rose from His prayer and came to His disciples, 45
He found them sleeping for sorrow.

' Why are you sleeping ? ' He said ; ' rise up ; and pray 46
that you may not come into temptation.'

Judas brings armed Men While He was still speaking there came a 47
crowd, with the man called Judas, one of the
twelve, at their head. And he went up to Jesus
to kiss Him.

' Judas,' said Jesus, ' are you betraying the Son of Man 48
with a kiss ? '

Those who were about Him, seeing what was likely to 49
happen, asked Him,

' Master, shall we strike with the sword ? '

And one of them struck a blow at the High Priest's 50
servant and cut off his right ear.

39. Cf. Matt. xxvi. 30 ; Mark xiv. 26 ; John xviii. 1.
(vv. 40–46.) Cf. Matt. xxvi. 36–46 ; Mark xiv. 32–42.
42. *Take . . away*] Cf. Mark xiv. 36, and note.
(vv. 43, 44.) Luke only. See R.V. mg.—'Many ancient authorities omit verses
43 and 44.'
46. *Pray*] Not merely 'Offer the prayer once for all'; but rather 'Keep on
praying,' though this would be a little too emphatic. Cf. verse 46 and Matt. xxvi.
41, n.

'Permit me thus far,' said Jesus. 51
And He touched the ear and healed it.

Jesus
expostulates

Then Jesus said to the High Priests and 52
Commanders of the Temple and Elders, who
had come to arrest Him,

'Have you come out as if to fight with a robber, with
swords and cudgels? While day after day I was with you 53
in the Temple, you did not lay hands upon me, but to you
belongs this hour and the power of darkness.'

Peter's
Denial

And they arrested Him and led Him away, 54
and brought Him into the High Priest's house,
while Peter followed a good way behind. And 55
when they had lighted a fire in the middle of the court and
had seated themselves in a group round it, Peter was sitting
among them, when a maidservant saw him sitting by the 56
fire, and, looking fixedly at him, she said,

'This man also was with Him.'

But he denied it, and declared, 57
'Woman, I do not know Him.'

Shortly afterwards a man saw him and said, 58
'You, too, are one of them.'

'No, man, I am not,' said Peter.

After an interval of about an hour some one else stoutly 59
maintained:

'Certainly this man also was with Him, for he is a
Galilaean.'

'I don't know what you mean, man,' replied Peter. 60

No sooner had he spoken than a cock crowed. The 61
Master turned and looked on Peter; and Peter recollected
the Master's words, how He had said to him,

'This very day, before the cock crows, you will disown
me three times.'

And he went out and wept bitterly. 62

Jesus
insulted

Meanwhile the men who held Jesus in custody 63
beat Him in cruel sport, blindfolded Him, and 64
then challenged Him.

51. *Permit me thus far*] An appeal for a moment's freedom to enable Him to perform the act of healing; or 'suffer thus far,' addressed either to His captors in
excuse for the one rash moment of resistance, or to His disciples to remain passive.
The restoration of the severed ear is recorded by Luke only.

(vv. 54–62.) Cf. Matt. xxvi. 57, 58, and 69–75; Mark xiv. 53, 54, and 66–72;
John xviii. 12–18, and 25–27.

56. *By the fire*] Lit. ' towards the light.' The same expression occurs in Mark xiv.
54. No doubt the light falling on his face led to his being recognized, although it was
only the dull light given by a charcoal fire. Cf. John xviii. 18.

(vv. 63–71.) Cf. Matt. xxvi. 59–68; Mark xiv. 55–65; John xviii. 19–24.

'Prove to us,' they said, 'that you are a prophet, by telling us who it was that struck you.'

And they said many other insulting things to Him. 65

Jesus questioned by the Sanhedrin As soon as it was day, the whole body of the 66 Elders, both High Priests and Scribes, assembled. Then He was brought into their Sanhedrin, and they asked Him,

'Are you the Christ ? Tell us.' 67

'If I tell you,' He replied, 'you will not believe ; and 68 if I ask you questions, you will not answer. But from this 69 time forward the Son of Man will be seated at the right hand of the Divine Power' (Dan. vii. 13 ; Ps. cx. 1).

Thereupon they cried out with one voice, 70

'You, then, are the Son of God ?'

'It is as you say,' He answered ; 'I am.'

'What need have we of further evidence ?' they said ; 71 'for we ourselves have heard it from his own lips.'

Jesus is taken to Pilate Then the whole assembly rose and brought 1 **23** Him to Pilate, and began to accuse Him. 2 'We have found this man,' they said, 'an agitator among our nation, forbidding the payment of tribute to Caesar, and claiming to be himself King Messiah.'

Then Pilate asked Him, 3

'You, then, are the King of the Jews ?'

'It is as you say,' He replied.

Pilate said to the High Priests and to the crowd, 4

'I can find no crime in this man.'

But they violently insisted. 5

'He stirs up the people,' they said, 'throughout all Judaea with his teaching—even from Galilee (where he first started) to this city.'

On hearing this, Pilate inquired, 6

'Is the man a Galilaean ?'

Jesus is sent to Herod And learning that He belonged to Herod's 7 jurisdiction he sent Him to Herod, for he too was in Jerusalem at that time.

To Herod the sight of Jesus was a great gratification, 8 for, for a long time, he had been wanting to see Him,

---

68. *Answer*] v.l. adds 'nor release me.'
70. *I am*] Or 'because I am,' or 'you say that I am.' Cf. John xviii. 37.
1. Cf. Matt. xxvii. 1, 2 ; Mark xv. 1 ; John xviii. 28.
(vv. 3–5.) Cf. Matt. xxvii. 11–14 ; Mark xv. 2–5 ; John xviii. 33–38.
(vv. 7–12.) Luke only.

because he had heard so much about Him. He hoped also
to see some miracle performed by Him. So he put a 9
number of questions to Him, but Jesus gave him no reply.
Meanwhile the High Priests and the Scribes were standing 10
there and vehemently accusing Him. Laughing to scorn the 11
claims of Jesus, Herod (and his soldiers with him) made
sport of Him, dressed Him in a gorgeous costume, and
sent Him back to Pilate. And on that very day Herod and 12
Pilate became friends again, for they had been for some
time at enmity.

Pilate declares Jesus innocent   Then calling together the High Priests and 13
the Rulers and the people, Pilate said, 14
' You have brought this man to me on a
charge of corrupting the loyalty of the people. But, you see,
I have examined him in your presence and have discovered
in the man no ground for the accusations which you bring
against him. No, nor does Herod; for he has sent him 15
back to us; and, you see, there is nothing he has done that
deserves death. I will therefore chastise him and release 16
him.'

Then the whole multitude burst out into a shout. 18

' Away with this man,' they said, ' and release Barabbas
to us '—Barabbas ! who had been lodged in gaol for some 19
time in connection with a riot which had occurred in the
city, and for murder.

He passes Sentence of Death   But Pilate once more addressed them, wish- 20
ing to set Jesus free. They, however, per- 21
sistently shouted,

' Crucify, crucify him ! '

A third time he appealed to them : 22

' But what crime has the man committed ? I have
discovered in him nothing that deserves death. I will
therefore chastise him and release him.'

But they urgently insisted, demanding with frantic out- 23
cries that He should be crucified ; and their clamour pre-
vailed. So Pilate gave judgement, yielding to their 24
demand. The man who was lying in prison charged 25

8. *Miracle*] Lit. ' token or ' sign.'
15. *He has sent him back to us*] v.L. ' I remitted your case to him.'
v.L. inserts verse 17, ' Now he was obliged to release one prisoner to them at
every Festival.'
(vv. 18–23.) Cf. Matt. xxvii. 15–23 ; Mark xv. 6–14 ; John xviii. 39, 40.
(vv. 24, 25.) Cf. Matt. xxvii. 24–30 ; Mark xv. 15–19 ; John xix. 1–16.

with riot and murder and for whom they clamoured he set free, but Jesus he gave up to be dealt with as they desired.

The Women of Jerusalem As soon as they led Him away, they laid 26 hold on one Simon, a Cyrenean, who was coming in from the country, and on his shoulders they put the cross, for him to carry it behind Jesus. A vast crowd of the people also followed Him, 27 and of women who were beating their breasts and wailing for Him. But Jesus turned towards them and 28 said,

' Daughters of Jerusalem, weep not for me, but weep for yourselves and for your children. For a time is coming 29 when they will say, " Blessed are the women who never bore children, and the breasts which have never given milk." Then will they begin to say to the mountains, 30 " Fall on us " ; and to the hills, " Cover us " (Hos. x. 8). For if they are doing these things with the green wood, 31 what will be done with the dry ? '

They brought also two others, criminals, to put them to 32 death with Him.

Golgotha When they reached the place called ' The 33 Skull,' there they nailed Him to the cross, and the criminals also, one at His right hand and one at His left. Jesus prayed,   34

' Father, forgive them, for they know not what they are doing.'

And they divided His garments among them, drawing lots for them (Ps. xxii. 18) ; and the people stood looking on. 35

Jesus is reviled The Rulers, too, repeatedly uttered their bitter taunts.

' This fellow,' they said, ' saved others : let him save himself, if he is God's Anointed, the Chosen One.'

And the soldiers also made sport of Him, coming and 36 offering Him sour wine and saying,   37

' You the King of the Jews ! Save yourself, then ! '

(vv. 26–33.) Cf. Matt. xxvii. 31–34 ; Mark xv. 20–23 ; John xix. 16, 17.
30. Cf. Rev. vi. 16.
(vv. 33, 34, 38.) Cf. Matt. xxvii. 35–38 ; Mark xv. 24–27 ; John xix. 18–24.
33. *The Skull*] In Latin ' Calvary.'
34. R.V. margin. Some ancient authorities omit this verse. Cf. Acts vii. 60.
(vv. 35–37 and 39–43.) Cf. Matt. xxvii. 39–44 ; Mark xv. 29–32 ; John xix. 25–27.
36. *Sour wine*] See Matt. xxvii. 48, n.

There was moreover a writing over His head :   38
THIS IS THE KING OF THE JEWS.

The penitent Robber   Now one of the criminals who had been 39
crucified insulted Him, saying,
   ' Are not you the Christ ? Save yourself
and us.'

But the other replied, reproving him.   40
' Do you not even fear God when you are suffering the
same punishment ? And we indeed are suffering justly, 41
for we are getting our deserts for what we have done. But
He has done nothing amiss.'

And he said,   42
' Jesus, remember me when you come in your
Kingdom.'

' I tell you in truth,' replied Jesus, ' that this very day 43
you shall be with me in Paradise.'

Jesus dies   It was now about noon, and a darkness 44
came over the whole land till three o'clock in
the afternoon. The sun was darkened, and the curtain 45
of the Sanctuary was torn down the middle. Then Jesus 46
cried out in a loud voice, and said,
  ' Father, to Thy hands I entrust my spirit' (Ps. xxxi. 5).
And after uttering these words He yielded up His spirit.

The People were greatly moved   The captain, seeing what had happened, 47
gave glory to God, saying,
   ' Beyond question this man was innocent.'

And all the crowds that had come together to this sight, 48
after seeing all that had occurred, returned to the city
beating their breasts. But all His acquaintances, and the 49
women who had been His followers after leaving Galilee,
continued standing at a distance and looking on.

Joseph of Arimathaea buries the Body of Jesus   There was a member of the Council of the 50
name of Joseph, a good and upright man, who 51
came from the Jewish town of Arimathaea and
was awaiting the coming of the Kingdom of
God. He had not concurred in the design or action of
the Council, and now he went to Pilate and asked for the 52

(vv. 40–43.) Luke only.
42. *In*] v.l. ' into.'
44. *Afternoon. The sun was darkened*] v.l. ' afternoon, the sun failing (or, having failed).'
(vv. 44–49.) Cf. Matt. xxvii. 45–55 ; Mark xv. 33–41.
(vv. 50–56.) Cf. Matt. xxvii. 57–61 ; Mark xv. 42–47 ; John xix. 38–42.

body of Jesus. Then, taking it down, he wrapped it in a 53
linen sheet and laid it in a tomb in the rock, where no one
else had yet been put. It was the Preparation Day, and 54
the Sabbath was near at hand. The women—those who 55
had come with Jesus from Galilee—followed close behind,
and saw the tomb and how His body was placed. Then 56
they returned, and prepared spices and perfumes.

On the Sabbath they rested in obedience to
The empty the Commandment. And, on the first day 1 **24**
Tomb of the week, at early dawn, they came to the
tomb, bringing the spices they had prepared. But they 2
found the stone rolled back from the tomb, and on 3
entering they found that the body of the Lord Jesus
was not there.

At this they were in great perplexity, when 4
A Vision of suddenly there stood by them two men whose
Angels raiment flashed like lightning. The women 5
were terrified ; but, as they stood with their faces bowed
to the ground, the men said to them,
' Why do you search among the dead for Him who is
living ? He is not here. He has come back to life. 6
Remember how He spoke to you while He was still in
Galilee, when He told you that the Son of Man must be 7
betrayed into the hands of sinful men, and be crucified,
and on the third day rise again.'
Then they remembered His words, and returning from the 8, 9
tomb they reported all this to the eleven and to all the rest.

The women were Mary of Magdala, Joanna, 10
The Women and Mary the mother of James ; and they and
bring the the rest of the women related all this to the
News to the apostles. But the whole story seemed to them 11
Apostles an idle tale ; they could not believe the women. Peter, 12
however, rose and ran to the tomb. Stooping and looking
in, he saw nothing but the linen wrappings : so he went
away home, wondering what had happened.

53. *Linen*] Cf. Mark xiv. 51.
(vv. 1–3.) Cf. Matt. xxviii. 1–4 ; Mark xvi. 1–4 ; John xx. 1.
3. *Of the Lord Jesus*] v.L. omits.
(vv. 4–8.) Cf. Matt. xxviii. 5–7 ; Mark xvi. 5–7.
4. *Suddenly*] Cf. Matt. viii. 24, n.
Flashed like lightning] One word in the Greek, found also in xvii. 24, and nowhere
else in the N.T.
(vv. 5–35.) Luke only.
(vv. 9–11.) Cf. Matt. xxviii. 8 ; Mark xvi. 8 ; John xx. 2.
12. v.L. omits this verse.

On that same day two of the disciples were 13
The Walk to Emmaus walking to Emmaus, a village seven or eight miles from Jerusalem, and were conversing 14 about all these events; and, in the midst of their con- 15 versation and discussion, Jesus Himself came and joined them, though they were prevented from recognizing Him, 16 and He asked them, 17

'What is it you are talking so earnestly about, as you walk?'

And they stood still, looking sad. Then one of them, 18 named Cleopas, answered,

'Are you a stranger lodging alone in Jerusalem, that you have known nothing of what has lately happened in the city?'

'What may that be?' He asked. 19

'All about Jesus the Nazarene,' they said, 'who was a Prophet powerful in work and word before God and all the people; and how our High Priests and Rulers delivered 20 Him up to be sentenced to death, and crucified Him? We 21 were hoping that it was He who was about to ransom Israel. Yes, it was but the day before yesterday that this happened. Besides, some of the women of our company 22 have amazed us. They went to the tomb at daybreak, and, 23 finding that His body was not there, they came and declared to us that they had even seen a vision of angels who asserted that He was alive. Thereupon some of our 24 party went to the tomb and found things just as the women had said; but Jesus Himself they did not see.'

'O dull-witted men,' He replied, 'with minds so slow 25 to believe all that the Prophets have spoken! Was there 26 not a necessity for the Christ thus to suffer, and then enter into His glory?'

And beginning with Moses and all the Prophets, He 27 explained to them the passages in Scripture which referred to Himself.

When they had come near the village to which they were 28 going, He appeared to be going further. But they pressed 29 Him to remain with them.

(vv. 13-35.) Cf. Mark xvi. 12, 13.
17. *Walk? And they, &c.*] v.l. has ' walk and are looking so full of sorrow? '
18. *Are you . . known*] Or ' Surely you must be the only person of all living (or, lodging) in Jerusalem who has known.'
21. *The day before yesterday*] Lit. in accordance with the Hebrew reckoning, ' it is the third day since.' Cf. ii. 46, n.

'Because,' said they, 'it is getting towards evening, and the day is nearly over.'

So He went in to stay with them. But as soon as He 30 had sat down with them, and had taken the bread and had blessed and broken it, and was handing it to them, their 31 eyes were opened and they recognized Him. But He vanished from them.

'Were not our hearts,' they said one to the other, 32 'burning within us while He talked to us on the way and explained the Scriptures to us?'

The two Disciples return to Jerusalem So they rose and without an hour's delay 33 returned to Jerusalem, and found the eleven and the rest met together, who said to them, 34

'Yes, it is true : the Master has come back to life. He has been seen by Simon.'

Then they related what had happened on the way, and 35 how He had been recognized by them in the breaking of the bread.

Jesus appears to the Apostles While they were thus talking, He Himself 36 stood in their midst and said, 'Peace be to you!'

Startled, and in the utmost alarm, they thought they were 37 looking at a ghost ; but He said to them, 38

'Why such alarm? And why are there such questionings in your minds? See my hands and my feet—it is my 39 very self. Feel me and see, for a ghost has not flesh and bones as you see I have.'

And then He showed them His hands and His feet. 40

He eats in their Presence But, while they still could not believe it for joy 41 and were full of astonishment, He asked them, 'Have you any food here?'

And they gave Him a piece of broiled fish, and He took 42, 43 it and ate it in their presence.

He again explains the Scriptures And He said to them, 44 'This is what I told you while I was still with you—that everything must be fulfilled that is written in the Law of Moses and in the Prophets and the Psalms concerning me.'

(vv. 36–43.) Cf. Mark xvi. 14 ; John xx. 19–25.
36. *And said, 'Peace be to you!'*] v.l. omits these words.
40. v.l. omits this verse.
42. *Fish*] v.l. adds 'and some honeycomb.'
(vv. 44–53.) Cf. Mark xvi. 19, 20 ; Acts i. 3–12.

Then He opened their minds to understand the Scrip- 45
tures, and He said, 46

' Thus it is written that the Christ would suffer and on
the third day rise from the dead ; and that proclamation 47
would be made, in His name, of repentance and forgiveness
of sins to all nations, beginning from Jerusalem. You are 48
witnesses as to this. And remember that I am about to 49
send out upon you the promise of my Father. But do you
wait patiently in the city until you are endued with power
from on high.'

He is taken   And He brought them out as far as Bethany, 50
up into   and then lifted up His hands and blessed
Heaven   them. And while He was blessing them, He 51
parted from them and was carried up into heaven. They 52
worshipped Him, and returned to Jerusalem with great
joy. Afterwards they were continually in the Temple, 53
blessing God.

(vv. 51, 52.) v.l. omits ' and was carried up into heaven ' and ' worshipped Him.'
See R.V. margin and Commentaries.   Cf. Luke's completed story in Acts i. 9-11.
53. *Blessing*] Some authorities read ' praising '; others, ' praising and blessing.'

THE GOSPEL ACCORDING TO ST. JOHN

CHARACTERISTICS OF ST. JOHN

The contrast between this Gospel and the Synoptics has already been noted. The Prologue relates the author's theme to Greek and Jewish (Philo's) philosophy of the Logos, the Word, Reason and Purpose of God in Creation, Revelation and Redemption, personified as a *Being* intermediate between Him and His world. (Cf. the personification of Wisdom in Proverbs viii.) But the faith of the evangelist bridges the gulf which philosophy could not cross. ' The Logos became flesh and dwelt among us.'

> ' And so the Word had breath and wrought
> With human hands the creed of creeds,
> In loveliness of perfect deeds
> More strong than all poetic thought.'

We hear no more of the Logos after i. 14 : the cold philosophical abstraction is exchanged for the glowing story of the earthly ministry of Jesus Christ, the Incarnate Son of God, ' full of grace and truth.'

> ' For in Him was hid the secret
> That through all the ages ran.'

At the heart of the universe, the secret of its unfolding process and its sure goal, is nothing else than, and nothing short of, the Love of God in the Ministry and Cross of His beloved Son.

The author himself explains the purpose and plan of his work at its close (xx. 30, 31 : chapter xxi. is an appendix) : *signs*, *believe*, *life*—these are the significant terms. For *sign* see note on ii. 11. The verb *to believe* pervades the whole book : in its first section, chapters i.-iv., the reader is introduced to every type of faith, half-faith, unfaith. Thereafter the shadow of rejection deepens, until in chapter xii. the sad sentence is passed. The *life* is expounded to the believing disciples in chapters xiii. to xvii.

THE GOSPEL ACCORDING TO ST. JOHN

1 In the beginning was the Word, and the **1** Word was with God, and the Word was God. **2, 3** He was in the beginning with God. All things came into being through Him, and apart from Him nothing that now exists came into being. In Him **4** was Life, and that Life was the Light of men. The Light **5** shines on in the darkness, and the darkness has never overpowered it.

The Divine 'Word'

There was a man sent from God, whose name was John. **6** He came as a witness, in order that he might give testimony **7** concerning the Light, so that all might believe through Him. He was not the Light, but he came that he might **8** give testimony concerning the Light. There was the true **9** Light, which lightens every man, coming into the world. He was in the world, and the world came into existence **10** through Him, and the world did not recognize Him. He **11** came to His own home, and His own people gave Him no welcome. But to all who have received Him—that is, to **12** those who trust in His name—He has given the privilege of becoming children of God ; who were begotten **13** not by human descent, nor through an impulse of the flesh, nor through the will of a human father, but from God.

And the Word became flesh, and lived awhile in our **14**

(vv. 1–18.) See the prefatory note to the Gospel.
   1. *In the beginning*] Or ' Before all time.' Cf. Gen. i. 1.
   (vv. 2–4.) Some prefer an alternative punctuation. See R.V. mg.
   2. *Through Him*] *i.e.* ' through His agency,' as Matt. i. 22 ; or ' by,' with no intermediate agency, as in Gal. iv. 7.
   5. *Overpowered*] A.V. ' comprehended.' The verb means ' to seize,' either physically or mentally. But the latter sense is expressed in N.T. by the middle voice : Acts iv. 13 ; x. 34 ; xxv. 25 ; Eph. iii. 18. Here the verb is active, and the decisive passage for its interpretation is John xii. 35.
   9. *Coming*] The participle is ambiguous in gender and case ; it may be neuter nominative, agreeing with ' Light,' either ' lightens by its coming,' or ' was coming ' ; or it may be masculine accusative, agreeing with ' man,' ' lightens every man on his coming.' The A.V. ' every man that cometh ' would require the Greek article before the participle.
   11. *His own home*] Lit. ' His own things.' Cf. Luke ii. 49, n.
   14. *Lived awhile*] Lit. ' had His tent.'

midst, so that we saw His glory, glory such as a father bestows on his only son, full of grace and truth.

John bears Witness to Jesus John gave testimony concerning Him and cried aloud, saying, 15

'This is He of whom I said, "He who is coming after me has taken precedence of me," for He was before me.'

For it is from His fulness we have all received, and grace 16 upon grace. The Law was given through Moses ; grace 17 and truth came through Jesus Christ. No human eye 18 has ever seen God : the only Son, who is in the Father's bosom—He has made Him known.

This also is John's testimony, when the Jews sent to 19 him a deputation of Priests and Levites from Jerusalem to ask him who he was. He avowed—he did not conceal 20 the truth, but avowed,

' I am not the Christ.'

' What then ? ' they inquired ; ' are you Elijah ? ' 21

' I am not,' he said.

' Are you the Prophet ? '

' No,' he answered.

So they pressed the question. 22

' Who are you ? ' they said—' that we may take an answer to those who sent us. What account do you give of yourself ? '

' I am THE VOICE,' he replied, ' OF ONE CRYING ALOUD, 23 " MAKE STRAIGHT THE LORD'S WAY IN THE DESERT," fulfilling the words of the Prophet Isaiah ' (Isa. xl. 3).

Some of those who had been sent were Pharisees. And 24, 25 they questioned him.

' Why then do you baptize,' they said, ' if you are neither the Christ nor Elijah nor the Prophet ? '

' I baptize in water only,' John answered, ' but in your 26 midst stands One whom you do not know—He who is to 27 come after me, and whose sandal-strap I am not worthy to unfasten.'

This conversation took place at Bethany beyond the 28 Jordan, where John was baptizing.

14. *Only*] Lit. ' only born.' Cf. Luke vii. 12 ; viii. 42 ; ix. 38. The word is also found in Heb. xi. 17 and in five passages in John's writings.

18. *The only Son*] Or ! the only-born Son,' as in verse 14. v.l. ' the only-born God.'

Bosom] *i.e.* In closest and most intimate fellowship. Cf. xiii. 23 ; Luke xvi. 22.

23. *In the Desert*] Cf. Matt. iii. 3, n.

He points to the Lamb of God The next day John saw Jesus coming towards 29 him and exclaimed,

' Look, there is the Lamb of God who is to take away the sin of the world ! This is He about whom I 30 said, " After me is to come One who has taken precedence of me, because He was before me." I did not know Him ; 31 but that He may be openly shown to Israel is the reason why I have come baptizing in water.'

John also gave testimony by stating : 32

' I have seen the Spirit coming down like a dove out of heaven ; and it rested on Him. I did not know Him, 33 but He who sent me to baptize in water said to me,

' " He on whom you see the Spirit coming down and resting is the One who baptizes in the Holy Spirit."

' This I have seen, and I am become a witness that He 34 is the Son of God.'

Two of John's Disciples become Disciples of Jesus Again the next day John was standing with 35 two of his disciples, when he saw Jesus passing 36 by, and said,

' Look ! that is the Lamb of God ! '

The two disciples heard his exclamation, and 37 they followed Jesus. Then Jesus turned round, and seeing 38 them following He asked them,

' What is your wish ? '

' Rabbi,' they replied (' Rabbi ' means ' Teacher ') ' where are you staying ? '

' Come and you shall see,' He said. 39

So they went and saw where He was staying, and they remained and spent that day with Him. It was then about four o'clock in the afternoon.

Andrew, Simon Peter's brother, was one of the two who 40

39. *About four o'clock in the afternoon*] Lit. ' about the tenth hour.' This is the first of four notes of time in the Gospel : (iv. 6) ' about the sixth hour ' ; (iv. 52) ' yesterday at the seventh hour ' ; (xix. 14) ' about the sixth hour.' In the earlier editions of this work the translator followed Westcott in supposing that this Evangelist forsook the usual Jewish reckoning of the hours of the day, from 6 a.m. to 6 p.m., for the Roman reckoning from midnight to noon, and noon to midnight. We should naturally assume that, like the other Evangelists, John adopts the Jewish mode ; in which case it follows that the two disciples (i. 39) found Jesus at 4 p.m. and stayed with him for two hours : that the Samaritan woman (iv. 6) went for her water at the unusual hour of noon : that the nobleman (iv. 52) learnt in the evening that at 1 p.m. of ' yesterday ' (which would be to-day of our reckoning) the fever had left his son : that the close of the Trial of Jesus (xix. 14) was at noon. The alternative probabilities in these several cases of 10 a.m., 6 p.m., 7 p.m. (on the previous evening), 6 a.m. may be weighed separately and collectively ; but opinion is strongly in favour of the Jewish reckoning, now adopted in this translation.

heard John's exclamation and followed Jesus. He first 41 found his own brother Simon, and said to him,

'We have found the Messiah!' (which means the Christ).

He brought him to Jesus. Jesus looked at him and said, 42 'You are Simon, son of John: you shall be called Cephas' (which means 'Peter,' that is, 'Rock').

Philip and Nathanael also follow Christ The next day, having decided to leave for 43 Galilee, Jesus found Philip, and said to him: 44 'Follow me.' (Now Philip came from Bethsaida, the same town as Andrew and Peter.) Then Philip found Nathanael, and said to him, 45

'We have found Him about whom Moses in the Law wrote, as well as the Prophets—Jesus, the son of Joseph, a man of Nazareth.'

'Can anything good come out of Nazareth?' replied 46 Nathanael.

'Come and see,' said Philip.

Jesus saw Nathanael approaching, and said of him, 47 'Look! Here is a true Israelite, in whom there is no guile!'

'How do you know me?' Nathanael asked. 48

'Before Philip called you,' said Jesus, 'when you were under the fig-tree I saw you.'

'Rabbi,' cried Nathanael, 'you are the Son of God, you 49 are Israel's King!'

'Because I said to you, "I saw you under the fig-tree," ' 50 replied Jesus, 'do you believe? You shall see greater things than that.'

'I tell you all in very truth,' He added, 'that you shall 51 see heaven opened wide, and God's angels going up, and coming down upon the Son of Man.'

Christ's first Miracle Two days later there was a wedding at Cana 1 **2** in Galilee, which the mother of Jesus attended, and to which Jesus also was invited and His 2 disciples. Now the wine ran short; whereupon the mother 3 of Jesus said to Him,

'They have no wine.'

'Leave it to me,' He replied; 'my hour has not yet 4 come.'

---

51. The figure, taken from Gen. xxviii. 12, probably describes the connection between heaven and earth which marks the whole ministry of the Son of Man.

4. Lit. 'What to me and to thee, woman!' For the term 'woman' addressed to His mother, cf. xix. 26. Cf. also xx. 13, 15, and Matt. xv. 28. There is no tone of disrespect in the term in these passages.

Hour] Cf. vii. 8; viii. 20; xii. 23; xiii. 1; xvii. 1.

His mother said to the attendants, 5
' Whatever He tells you to do, do it.'

Now there were six stone jars standing there (in accord- 6
ance with the Jewish regulations for purification), each large
enough to hold twenty gallons or more. Jesus said to the 7
attendants,

' Fill the jars with water.'

And they filled them to the brim. Then He 8
said,

' Now, take some out, and carry it to the president of the
feast.'

So they carried some to him. And no sooner had the 9
president tasted the water now turned into wine, than—not
knowing where it came from, though the attendants who
had drawn the water knew—he called to the bridegroom
and said to him, 10

' Every one puts on the good wine first, and when people
have drunk freely, then that which is inferior. But you have
kept the good wine till now.'

This, the first of His signs, Jesus performed at Cana 11
in Galilee, and thus displayed His glory ; and His disciples
believed in Him.

Afterwards He went down to Capernaum— 12
He, and His mother, and His brothers, and His
disciples ; and they made a short stay there.
But the Jewish Passover was approaching, and for this Jesus 13
went up to Jerusalem. Now He found in the Temple 14
dealers in cattle and sheep and doves, and
money-changers sitting there. So He plaited a 15
whip of rushes, and drove all—both sheep and
bullocks—out of the Temple. The small coin
of the brokers He poured on the ground and
overturned their tables. And to the dove-dealers He 16
said,

Capernaum and Jerusalem

Jesus drives the Dealers from the Temple Courts

' Take these things away. Do not turn my Father's
house into a market.'

This recalled to His disciples the words of Scripture, 17
' MY ZEAL FOR THY HOUSE WILL CONSUME ME '

(Ps. lxix. 9).

---

11. *Signs*] Lit. ' tokens ' or ' indications ' (of who and what He was). Our Lord's
miracles are called by this name throughout the Fourth Gospel. Contrast Mark
viii. 12.
17. v.l. ' hath consumed,' as in the Psalm.

His Right to do this is challenged So the Jews asked Him, 18 'What authority can you show us for doing this?'

'Demolish this Sanctuary,' said Jesus, 'and in three 19 days I will rebuild it.'

'It has taken forty-six years,' replied the Jews, 'to build 20 this Sanctuary, and will you rebuild it in three days?'

But He was speaking of the Sanctuary of His body. 21 When, however, He had risen from the dead, His disciples 22 recollected that He had said this; and they believed the Scripture and the words which Jesus had spoken to them.

He gains many new Adherents Now when He was in Jerusalem, at the 23 Festival of the Passover, many became believers in His name, beholding the signs which He wrought. But for His part, Jesus did not trust Himself 24 to them, because He knew them all, and did not need any 25 one's evidence concerning a man, for He of Himself knew what was in the man.

Nicodemus Now there was one of the Pharisees whose 1 **3** name was Nicodemus, a ruler among the Jews. He came to Jesus by night and said, 2

'Rabbi, we know that you are a teacher come from God; for no one can do these signs which you are doing, unless God is with him.'

'In very truth I tell you,' answered Jesus, 'that unless 3 a man is born anew he cannot see the Kingdom of God.'

'How is it possible,' Nicodemus asked, 'for a man to 4 be born when he is old? Can he a second time enter his mother's womb and be born?'

'In very truth I tell you,' replied Jesus, 'that unless a 5 man is born of water and the Spirit, he cannot enter the Kingdom of God. Whatever is born of the flesh is flesh, 6 and whatever is born of the Spirit is spirit. Do not be 7 astonished at my telling you, "You must all be born anew." The wind blows where it chooses, and you hear its sound, 8 but you do not know where it comes from or where it is going. So is it with every one who is born of the Spirit.'

'How is all this possible?' asked Nicodemus. 9

'Are you,' replied Jesus, '"the Teacher of Israel," and 10

18. *Authority*] Lit. 'sign.' Cf. Mark xi. 28.
20. The restoration of the Temple was begun by Herod the Great in B.C. 20.
3. *Anew*] Or 'from above,' as in verse 31.
8. *The wind . . the Spirit*] One and the same word in the Greek.

yet do you not understand these things? In very truth 11
I tell you that we speak what we know, and give evidence
concerning what we have witnessed, and yet you all reject
our evidence. If I have told you of things on earth and 12
none of you believe me, how will you believe me if I
tell you of things in heaven? There is no one who has 13
gone up to heaven, except One who has come down
from heaven, namely the Son of Man whose home is
in heaven. And just as Moses lifted high the serpent 14
in the desert, so must the Son of Man be lifted up, in 15
order that every one who trusts in Him may have eternal
Life.'

For so greatly did God love the world that He gave His 16
only Son, that every one who trusts in Him may not perish
but may have eternal Life. God did not send His Son 17
into the world to judge the world, but that the world might
be saved through Him. He who trusts in Him does not 18
come up for judgement. He who does not trust has
already received sentence, because he has not his trust
resting on the name of God's only Son. And this is the 19
test by which men are judged—the Light has come into
the world, and men have loved the darkness rather than
the Light, because their deeds have been wicked. For 20
every wrongdoer hates the light, and does not come into it,
for fear his actions should be exposed. But he whose 21
actions are true comes into the light, that his actions may
be plainly shown to have been done in God.

John's renewed Testimony After this Jesus and His disciples went to 22
Judaea; and there He stayed in company with
them and baptized. And John too was bap- 23
tizing at Aenon, near Salim, because there were many pools
and streams there; and people came and received baptism.
(For John was not yet thrown into prison.) So, a discus- 24,25
sion having arisen on the part of John's disciples with a
Jew about purification, they came to John and reported 26
to him,

' Rabbi, He who was with you on the other side of the

---

11. *We*] Cf. ix. 4, n.
(vv. 16–21.) That this section is a commentary on the nature of the mission of the
Son, and that it contains the reflections of the Evangelist, and is not a continuation
of the words of the Lord seems to be conclusively proved by Westcott (so probably
vv. 31–36). Cf. xii. 37–50.
16. *Only*] Or ' only-born.' Cf. i. 14, n. The word is also used of the Lord Jesus
in 1 John iv. 9.
23. *Pools and streams*] Lit. ' waters.'

Jordan and to whom you bore testimony is now baptizing, and great numbers of people are resorting to Him.'

'A man cannot obtain anything,' replied John, 'unless 27 it has been granted to him from heaven. You yourselves 28 can bear witness to my having said, "I am not the Christ," but "I am His appointed forerunner." He who has the 29 bride is the bridegroom ; and the bridegroom's friend who stands by his side and listens to him, rejoices heartily on account of the bridegroom's voice. This is my joy now complete. He must grow greater, but I must grow less. 30 He who comes from above is above all. He who springs 31 from the earth not only springs from the earth, but speaks of the earth. He who comes from heaven is above all. What He has seen and heard, to that He bears wit- 32 ness ; but His evidence no one accepts. Any man who 33 has accepted His evidence has solemnly declared that God is true. For He whom God has sent speaks God's words ; 34 God does not give the Spirit in sparing measure.'

The Father loves the Son and has entrusted everything 35 to His hands. He who believes in the Son has eternal 36 Life ; he who disobeys the Son will not see Life, but God's anger remains upon him.

Now as soon as the Lord was aware that the 1 **4**
Christ goes Pharisees had heard it said, ' Jesus is gaining and
into Galilee baptizing more disciples than John '—though 2
Jesus Himself did not baptize them, but His disciples did—
He left Judaea and returned to Galilee. His road lay through 3, 4
Samaria, and so He came to Sychar, a town in Samaria 5
near the piece of land that Jacob gave to his son Joseph. 6
Jacob's Well was there : so Jesus, tired out with His journey, sat down by the well to rest. It was about noon.

The Presently there came a woman of Samaria to 7
Samaritan draw water. Jesus asked her to give Him
Woman some water ; for His disciples were gone to the 8
town to buy provisions.

' How is it,' replied the woman, ' that a Jew like you 9 asks me, who am a Samaritan woman, for water ? '
(For Jews have no dealings with Samaritans.)

---

26. *Great numbers of people*] Lit. ' all.'
28. *I am His appointed forerunner*] Lit. ' I have been sent before Him.'
33. *Solemnly declared*] Lit. ' put his seal to it.'
6. *Noon*] Cf. i. 39, n.
9. *For Jews, &c.*] v.l. omits this clause.

'If you had known God's free gift,' replied Jesus, 'and 10 who it is that said to you " Give me some water," you would have asked Him, and He would have given you living water.'

'Sir,' she said, 'you have nothing to draw with, and the 11 well is deep ; so where can you get the living water from ? Are you greater than our forefather Jacob, who gave us 12 the well, and himself drank from it, as did also his sons and his cattle ? '

'Every one,' replied Jesus, 'who drinks this water will 13 be thirsty again ; but whoever drinks the water that I shall 14 give him will never, never thirst. The water that I shall give him will become a fountain within him of water springing up for eternal Life.'

'Sir,' said the woman, 'give me that water, that I may 15 never be thirsty, nor continually be coming all the way here to draw water.'

'Go and call your husband,' said Jesus ; 'and come 16 back.'

'I have no husband,' she replied. 17

'You rightly say that you have no husband,' said Jesus ; 'for you have had five husbands, and the man you have 18 at present is not your husband. You have spoken the truth in saying that.'

'Sir,' replied the woman, 'I see that you are a prophet. 19 Our forefathers worshiped on this mountain, but you 20 Jews say that the place where people must worship is in Jerusalem.'

'Believe me,' said Jesus, 'the time is coming when you 21 will worship the Father neither on this mountain nor in Jerusalem. You worship that of which you know nothing. 22 We worship that which we know ; for salvation comes from the Jews. But a time is coming—indeed, has already 23 come—when true worshippers will worship the Father in spirit and truth ; for indeed the Father desires such worshippers. God is Spirit ; and those who worship Him 24 must worship in spirit and truth.'

'I know,' replied the woman, 'that Messiah is coming 25 —" the Christ," as He is called. When He has come, He will tell us everything.'

11. *Well*] Or 'pit.'
21. *Believe me*] Lit. 'Believe me, woman.' Cf. ii. 4, n.
25. *Christ*] In verse 29 she uses this Greek name.

' I am He,' said Jesus—' I who am now talking to you.' 26

Just then His disciples came, and were surprised to find Him talking with a woman. Yet not one of them asked Him, ' What are you seeking ? ' or ' Why are you talking with her ? ' 27

So the woman, leaving her pitcher, went away to the town, and called the people. 28

' Come,' she said, ' and see a man who has told me everything I have ever done. Can this be the Christ, do you think?' 29

They left the town and made their way to see Him. 30

Meanwhile the disciples were urging Jesus, ' Rabbi,' they said, ' eat something.' 31

' I have food to eat,' He replied, ' of which you do not know.' 32

So the disciples began questioning one another. 33

' Can it be,' they said, ' that some one has brought Him something to eat ? '

' My food,' said Jesus, ' is to do the will of Him who sent me, and to accomplish His work. Are you not saying, 34 35 " It wants four months yet to the harvest " ? But look round, I tell you, and observe these plains, how they are ripe for the harvest. Already the reaper is getting pay 36 and gathering in a crop in preparation for eternal Life, so that sower and reaper may rejoice together. In this you 37 see the real meaning of the saying, " One sows, but another reaps." I have sent you to reap a harvest which is not 38 the result of your own labours. Others have laboured, and you are getting the benefit of their labour.'

Of the Samaritan population of that town a good many believed in Him because of the woman's statement, 39

' He told me all that I have ever done.'

When the Samaritans came to Him, they asked Him to 40 stay with them ; and He stayed there two days. Then a 41 far larger number of people believed because of His own words, and they said to the woman, 42

' We no longer believe in Him simply because of your statement ; we have now heard for ourselves, and we know that this really is the Saviour of the world.'

After the two days He departed, and went 43 into Galilee ; for Jesus Himself declared that 44 a prophet has no honour in his own country.

So when He reached Galilee, the Galilaeans welcomed 45
Him eagerly, having been eye-witnesses of all that He had
done in Jerusalem at the Festival ; for they also had been
to the Festival.

So He came once more to Cana in Galilee, where He had 46
made the water wine.

The Officer's dying Son cured Now there was a certain official of the King's
court whose son was ill at Capernaum. Having 47
heard that Jesus had come from Judaea to
Galilee, he came to Him and begged Him to go down and
cure his son ; for he was at the point of death.

' Unless you and others see signs and marvels,' said 48
Jesus, ' nothing will induce you to believe.'

' Sir,' pleaded the official, ' come down before my child dies.' 49

' You may return,' replied Jesus ; ' your son is alive.' 50

He believed the words of Jesus, and started back home ;
and he was already on his way down when his servants met 51
him and told him that his son was alive. So he inquired 52
of them at what hour he had shown improvement.

' Yesterday, about one o'clock,' they replied, ' the fever
left him.'

Then the father recollected that that was the time at 53
which Jesus had said to him, ' Your son is alive,' and he
and his whole household became believers.

This is the second sign that Jesus wrought after coming 54
from Judaea into Galilee.

Jesus cures a Cripple at Bethesda After this there was a Festival of the Jews, 1 **5**
and Jesus went up to Jerusalem. Now there 2
is in Jerusalem near the Sheep Gate a pool,
called in Hebrew ' Bethesda.' It has five alcoves. In these 3
there used to lie a great number of invalids, and of people
who were blind or lame or with withered limbs. And 5
there was one man there who had been an invalid for thirty-
eight years. Jesus saw him lying there, and knowing that 6
he had been a long time in that condition, He asked him,

48. Addressed rather to the Galilaeans generally than to the simple and genuine
faith of the distressed father. Cf. verse 50.

50. *You may return*] Lit. ' Go.' But the English monosyllable has an abrupt and
brusque tone which does not belong to the Greek word.

52. *One o'clock*] Cf. i. 39, n.

54. *The second*] Lit. ' again the second.' *Again* has reference to Cana : *second* to
the sign. Cf. ii. 1–11.

3. *Withered limbs*] v.L. adds to verse 3, ' on the look-out for the moving of the
water.' (4) For at times an angel went down into the pool and disturbed the water.
Whoever then stepped in first, after the disturbance of the water, was cured, whatever the ailment might be from which he was suffering.

'Do you wish to be made strong again?'

'Sir,' replied the sufferer, 'I have no one to put me into 7 the pool when the water is disturbed; but while I am coming some one else steps down before me.'

'Rise,' said Jesus, 'take up your mat and walk.' 8

Instantly the man was restored to perfect health, and he 9 took up his mat and began to walk.

His Right to do this is challenged That day was a Sabbath. So the Jews said 10 to the man who had been cured,

'It is the Sabbath: you must not carry your mat.'

'He who cured me,' he replied, 'said to me, "Take up 11 your mat and walk."'

'Who is it,' they asked, 'that said to you, "Take up 12 your mat and walk"?'

But the man who had been cured did not know who it 13 was; for Jesus had passed out unnoticed, there being a crowd in the place.

Afterwards Jesus found him in the Temple and said to 14 him,

'You are now restored to health. Do not sin any more, or a worse thing may befall you.'

The man went away and told the Jews that it was Jesus 15 who had restored him to health; and on this account the 16 Jews began to persecute Jesus—because He did these things on the Sabbath.

His reply was, 17

'My Father works unceasingly, and so do I.'

The Jews therefore were all the more eager to put Him 18 to death, because He not only broke the Sabbath, but also spoke of God as being in a special sense His Father, thus putting Himself on a level with God.

Jesus justifies Himself 'In very truth I tell you,' replied Jesus, 19 'the Son can do nothing of Himself—He can only do what He sees the Father doing; for whatever He does, the Son does in like manner. The 20 Father loves the Son and reveals to Him all that He Himself is doing. And greater deeds than these will He reveal to Him, in order that you may wonder. For just as 21 the Father awakens the dead and gives them life, so the Son also gives life to whom He wills. The Father indeed 22

17. *Works unceasingly*] Even on the Sabbath. Lit. 'works until now.'

does not judge any one, but He has entrusted the passing of judgement wholly to the Son, that all may honour the 23 Son even as they honour the Father. The man who honours not the Son honours not the Father who sent Him.

Obedience leads to Life ' In very truth I tell you that he who listens 24 to my teaching and believes Him who sent me has eternal Life, and does not come under judgement, but has passed over out of death into Life.

Resurrection and Judgement ' In very truth I tell you that a time is 25 coming—indeed, has already come—when the dead will hear the voice of the Son of God, and those who hear it will live. For just as the Father has life 26 in Himself, so He has also given to the Son to have life in Himself. And He has conferred on Him authority to act 27 as Judge, because He is the Son of Man. Wonder not at 28 this. For a time is coming when all who are in the graves will hear His voice and will come forth—those who have 29 done right to the resurrection to Life, and those whose actions have been evil to the resurrection to judgement.

' I can of my own self do nothing. As I hear, so I 30 judge ; and mine is a just judgement, because my own will I seek not to do, but the will of Him who sent me.

The Witness borne to Jesus ' If I give evidence concerning myself, 31 my evidence cannot be accepted. There is 32 Another who gives evidence concerning me, and I know that the evidence is true which He offers concerning me.

John the Baptist ' You sent to John, and he has been a wit- 33 ness to the truth. But the evidence on my 34 behalf which I accept is not from man ; though I say all this that you may be saved. He was the 35 lamp that burned and shone, and for a time you were willing to be gladdened by his light.

The Testimony of God Himself ' But the evidence which I have is weightier 36 than that of John ; for the work the Father has appointed me to complete—the very work which I am doing—affords evidence about me that the Father has sent me. And the Father who sent me has 37

30. *Hear*] *i.e.* from the Father.
31. *Cannot be accepted*] Lit. ' is not true.'
36. *Work*] Lit. ' works,' the whole series of operations which in the aggregate we speak of as ' the work of Christ.' ' The works ' would suggest to the English reader the miracles only, which can hardly be the true sense.

Himself supplied evidence about me. Never have any of you ever either heard His voice or seen what He is like. Nor have you His word abiding within you, for you refuse 38 to believe Him whom He has sent.

The Testimony of the Old Testament ' You search the Scriptures, because you 39 suppose that in them you will find eternal Life ; it is those Scriptures that yield evidence about me ; yet you are unwilling to come to me that you may 40 have Life.

Two Sorts of Glory ' I do not accept glory from man, but I know 41, 42 that in your hearts you do not really love God. I am come in my Father's name, and you do 43 not receive me. If some one else comes in his own name, you will receive him. How is it possible for you to believe, 44 while you receive glory from one another and have no desire for the glory that comes from the only God ?

The Jews unfaithful to Moses ' Do not suppose that I will accuse you to 45 the Father. There is one who accuses you, namely Moses, on whom your hope rests. For 46 if you believed Moses, you would believe me ; for he wrote about me. But if you disbelieve his writings, how are you 47 to believe my words ? '

5000 People fed After this Jesus went away across the Sea 1 **6** of Galilee (that is, the Sea of Tiberias). A 2 vast multitude followed Him, because they witnessed the signs He performed on persons who were ill.

Then Jesus went up the hill, and sat there with His 3 disciples. The Jewish Festival, the Passover, was at hand. 4 And when He looked round and saw an immense crowd 5 coming towards Him, He said to Philip,

' Where shall we buy bread for all these people to eat ? '

He said this to put Philip to the test, for He Himself 6 knew what He was going to do.

' Seven pounds' worth of bread,' replied Philip, ' is not 7 enough for them all to get even a scanty meal.'

One of His disciples, Andrew, Simon Peter's brother, 8 said to Him,

39. *You search*] Or ' Search.'
You will find] Lit. ' you have.'
45. *Do not suppose*] The Greek implies, ' as some of you are supposing.'
(vv. 1–14.) Cf. Matt. xiv. 13–21 ; Mark vi. 30–44 ; Luke ix. 10–17.

'There is a boy here with five barley loaves and a couple 9 of fish ; but what is that among so many ?'

'Make the people sit down,' said Jesus. 10

The ground was covered with thick grass ; so they sat down, the men numbering about 5000. Then Jesus took 11 the loaves, and after giving thanks He distributed them to those who were resting on the ground ; and also the fish in like manner—as much as they desired.

When all were fully satisfied, He said to His disciples, 12 'Gather up the broken portions that remain over, so that nothing be lost.'

Accordingly they gathered them up ; and with the 13 fragments of the five barley loaves—the broken portions that remained over after they had done eating—they filled twelve baskets. Thereupon the people, having seen the 14 sign He had performed, said,

'This is indeed the Prophet who was to come into the world.'

Jesus withdraws into Solitude But perceiving that they were about to come 15 and carry Him off by force to make Him a king, Jesus withdrew again up the hill alone by Himself. When evening came on, His disciples went 16 down to the Lake. There they got on board a boat, and 17 pushed off to cross the Lake to Capernaum. By this time it had become dark, and Jesus had not yet **He walks on the Lake** joined them. The Lake also was getting rough, 18 because a strong wind was blowing. When, 19 however, they had rowed three or four miles, they saw Jesus walking on the water and coming near the boat. They were terrified ; but He called to them. 20

'It is I,' He said ; 'do not be afraid.'

Then they were willing to take Him on board ; and in 21 a moment the boat reached the shore at the point to which they were going.

Next morning the crowd who were still standing about 22 on the other side of the Lake found that there had been but one small boat there, and they had seen that Jesus did not go on board with His disciples, but that they went away without Him. Yet a number of small boats came from 23 Tiberias to the neighbourhood of the place where they had eaten the bread after the Lord had given thanks. So 24

(vv. 15-21.) Cf. Matt. xiv. 22-33 ; Mark vi. 45-52.

when the crowd saw that neither Jesus was there nor His disciples, they themselves got into the boats and came to Capernaum to look for Him.

So when they had crossed the Lake and found Him, 25 they asked Him,

' Rabbi, when did you come here ? '

' In very truth I tell you,' replied Jesus, ' that you are 26 searching for me not because you have seen signs, but because you ate the loaves and were satisfied. Work not 27 for the food that perishes, but for the food that lasts to eternal Life—that food which will be the Son of Man's gift to you ; for on Him the Father, God, has set His seal.'

' What are we to do,' they asked, ' to carry 28 **God's great Demand** out what God requires ? '

' This,' replied Jesus, ' is above all what 29 God requires—that you should be believers in Him whom He has sent.'

' What sign then,' they asked, ' do you per- 30 **The Bread from Heaven** form for us to see and become believers in you ? What can you do ? Our forefathers 31 ate the manna in the Desert, as it is written, " HE GAVE THEM BREAD OUT OF HEAVEN TO EAT "' (Exod. xvi. 15 ; Ps. lxxviii. 24).

' In very truth I tell you,' replied Jesus, ' that Moses did 32 not give you the bread out of heaven, but my Father is giving you the bread—the true bread—out of heaven. For 33 God's bread is that which comes down from heaven and gives Life to the world.'

' Sir,' they said, ' give us that bread for ever.' 34

' I am the bread of Life,' replied Jesus ; ' he who comes 35 to me shall never hunger, and he who believes in me shall never thirst. But it is as I have said to you : you have 36 seen me and yet you do not believe. Every one whom 37 the Father gives me will come to me, and him who comes to me I will never drive away. For I have left heaven 38 and have come down to earth not to seek my own pleasure, but to do the will of Him who sent me. And this is the will of Him who sent me, that of all that 39 He has given me I should lose nothing, but should raise it to life on the last day. This is my Father's will, that 40

37. *Every one whom*] Lit. ' all that ' or ' everything that.'
39. *All that*] Or ' all whom.' The same expression as in verse 37.

every one who beholds the Son of God and believes in Him should have eternal Life, and I will raise him to life on the last day.'

The Jews find Fault Now the Jews began to murmur about Him 41 because He said, 'I am the bread which came down from heaven.' And they said, 42 'Is not this man Joseph's son? Is he not Jesus, whose father and mother we know? What does he mean by now saying, " I am come down from heaven " ? '

'Do not murmur to one another,' replied Jesus; 'no 43, 44 one can come to me unless the Father who sent me draws him; then I will raise him to life on the last day. It stands 45 written in the Prophets, " AND THEY SHALL ALL OF THEM BE TAUGHT BY GOD " (Isa. liv. 13). Every one who listens to the Father and learns from Him comes to me. No 46 one has ever seen the Father—except that He alone who is from God has seen the Father.

Jesus is the Bread of Life 'In very truth I tell you that he who believes 47 has eternal Life. I am the bread of Life. 48 Your forefathers ate the manna in the Desert, 49 and they died. Here is the bread that comes down from 50 heaven, that a man may eat it and not die. I am the living 51 bread come down from heaven. If a man eats this bread, he shall live for ever. Moreover the bread which I will give is my flesh given for the life of the world.'

The growing Anger of the Jews This led to an angry debate among the Jews. 52 ' How can this man,' they argued, ' give us his flesh to eat ? '

'In very truth I tell you,' said Jesus, 'that unless you 53 eat the flesh of the Son of Man and drink His blood, you have no Life in you. He who eats my flesh and drinks my 54 blood has eternal Life, and I will raise him up on the last day. For my flesh is true food, and my blood is true 55 drink. He who eats my flesh and drinks my blood abides 56 in me and I in him. As the living Father has sent me, 57 and I live because of the Father, so also he who eats me will live because of me. This is the bread which came 58 down out of heaven; it is unlike that which your forefathers ate—for they ate and yet died. He who eats this bread shall live for ever.'

---

51. *Given*] Not expressed in the Greek, although v.l. adds ' which I will give.'
53. *In you*] Lit. ' in yourselves.'

Jesus said all this in the synagogue while teaching at 59
Capernaum.

Disciples whose Faith failed

Many therefore of His disciples, when they 60
heard it, said,

'This is hard to accept. Who can listen to
such teaching?'

But, knowing in His heart that His disciples were mur- 61
muring about it, Jesus asked them,

'Is this a stumbling-block to you? What then if you 62
were to see the Son of Man ascending again where He was
before? It is the Spirit which gives life. The flesh con- 63
fers no benefit whatever. The words I have spoken to
you are Spirit and are Life. But there are some of you who 64
do not believe.'

For Jesus knew from the beginning who those were that
did not believe, and who it was that would betray Him.
So He added, 65

'That is why I told you that no one can come to me
unless it be granted him by the Father.'

Thereupon many of His disciples left Him, and no 66
longer associated with Him.

Peter acknowledges Jesus as the Messiah

Jesus therefore appealed to the twelve. 67

'Will you go also?' He asked.

'Master,' replied Simon Peter, 'to whom 68
shall we go? Your teachings tell us of eternal
Life. And we have come to believe and know that you 69
are indeed the Holy One of God.'

'Did not I choose you—the twelve?' said Jesus, 'and 70
even of you one is a devil.'

He meant Judas, the son of Simon Iscariot. For he it 71
was who, though one of the twelve, was about to betray
Him.

Christ's Brothers unsympathetic

After this Jesus moved from place to place 1 7
in Galilee. He would not go about in Judaea,
because the Jews were seeking to kill Him.
But the Jewish Festival of Tabernacles was approaching. 2
So His brothers said to Him, 3

'Leave these parts and go to Judaea, that your disciples

60. *To such teaching*] Or ' to Him.'
68. *Your teachings tell us*] Lit. ' You have words.'
70. *A devil*] Or ' a malicious accuser.' The word (*diabŏlos*) is used as the name of
Satan in xiii. 2 ; Matt. iv. 1 ; and elsewhere. It is a different word from that which
in this translation is everywhere rendered ' demon.'

also may witness the works you perform. For no one 4
acts in secret while desiring to be known publicly. Since
you are doing these deeds, show yourself openly to the
world.'

For even His brothers were not believers in Him. 5

' My time,' replied Jesus, ' has not yet come, but for you 6
any time is suitable. The world cannot hate you ; but it 7
does hate me, because I give testimony that its works are
evil. As for you, go up to the Festival. I am not going 8
up to this Festival, because my time is not yet come.'

Such was His answer, and He remained in Galilee. 9
When, however, His brothers had gone up to the Festival, 10
then He also went up, not openly, but as it were privately.

Diversity of Opinion Meanwhile the Jews at the Festival were 11
looking for Him and were inquiring,
' Where is he ? '

Among the mass of the people there was much muttered 12
debate about Him.

Some said,

' He is a good man.'

Others said,

' Not so : he is imposing on the people.'

Yet for fear of the Jews no one spoke out boldly about 13
Him.

Jesus claims to have come from God But when the Festival was already half 14
over, Jesus went up to the Temple and was
teaching. The Jews were astonished. 15
' How does this man know anything of books,'
they said, ' although he has never been taught ? '

Jesus answered their question by saying, 16

' My teaching is not mine, but comes from Him who
sent me. If any one is willing to do His will, he shall 17
know about the teaching, whether it is from God or
originates with me. The man whose teaching originates 18
with himself aims at his own glory. He who aims at the
glory of Him who sent him teaches the truth, and there is

8. *I am not going up*] That is, perhaps, not as they had expected, coming
with the twelve and an imposing body of followers to join the long caravan of
intending worshippers who were starting for the Festival, and certainly not for the
purpose which they had urged upon Him. There is a v.L. ' not yet.' But this looks
like a correction to escape the apparent inconsistency of verses 8 and 10.

(vv. 15–24.) This paragraph gives a better connection if, as by many commentators, it be transposed to follow v. 47. The *writings* of v. 47 and the *books* of
vii. 15 are the same word in the Greek ; and the *one deed* of vii. 21 would naturally
refer to the *recent* cure of the cripple of Bethesda, v. 2–18. Cf. v. 18 and vii. 19.

no deception in him. Did not Moses give you the Law? 19
And yet not a man of you obeys the Law. Why do you
want to kill me?'

'You are possessed by a demon,' replied the crowd; 20
' no one wants to kill you.'

'One deed I have done,' replied Jesus, ' and you are all 21
full of wonder. Well then, Moses gave you the rite of 22
circumcision (not that it began with Moses, but with your
earlier forefathers), and even on a Sabbath day you circumcise a child. If to save the Law of Moses from being 23
broken a child is circumcised even on a Sabbath day, are
you bitter against me because I have restored a whole man
to health on a Sabbath day? Do not judge hastily, but 24
form a just judgement.'

The People Some, however, of the people of Jerusalem 25
and their said,
Rulers 'Is not this the man they are wanting to
kill? But here he is, speaking out boldly, and they say 26
nothing to him! Can the Rulers really have discovered
that this man is the Christ? And yet we know this man, 27
and where he comes from; but as for the Christ, when He
comes, no one will know where He comes from.'

Jesus therefore, while teaching in the Temple, cried 28
aloud, and said,

'Yes, you know me, and you know where I am from.
And yet I have not come of my own accord; but there is
One who has really sent me, of whom you have no knowledge. I know Him, because I came from Him, and He 29
sent me.'

On hearing this they wanted to arrest Him; yet not a 30
hand was laid on Him, because His time had not yet come.
But among the crowd a large number believed in Him. 31

'When the Christ comes,' they said, ' will He perform
more signs than this teacher has performed?'

Jesus was The Pharisees heard the people thus ex- 32
going back pressing their various doubts about Him, and
to God the High Priests and the Pharisees sent some
officers to apprehend Him. So Jesus said, 33

'Still for a short time I shall be with you, and then I go
my way to Him who sent me. You will look for me and will 34
not find me, and where I am you cannot come.'

27. Cf. the divergent tradition of verse 42.

The Jews therefore said to one another, 35
' Where is he about to betake himself, so that we shall not find him ? Will he betake himself to the Dispersion among the Greeks, and teach the Greeks ? What do those 36 words of his mean, " You will look for me, but will not find me, and where I am you cannot come " ? '

A Promise of living Water   On the last day of the Festival—the great 37 day—Jesus stood up and cried aloud.
' Whoever is thirsty,' He said, ' let him come to me and drink. He who believes in me, from within 38 him—as the Scripture has said—rivers of living water shall flow.'

He referred to the Spirit which those who believed in 39 Him were to receive ; for the Spirit was not yet, because Jesus had not yet been glorified.

The People divided in Opinion   After listening to His words, some of the 40 crowd began to say,
' This is beyond doubt the Prophet.'

Others said, 41
' He is the Christ.'
But others again,
' Not so : is the Christ to come from Galilee ? Has 42 not the Scripture declared that the Christ is to come of the family of David (Ps. lxxxix. 3, 4) and from Bethlehem, David's village ' (Mic. v. 2) ?

So there was a dissension among the people on His 43 account. Some of them wanted to arrest Him, but no 44 one laid hands upon Him.

The Attempt to arrest Him quite fails   Meanwhile the officers returned to the High 45 Priests and Pharisees, who asked them,
' Why have you not brought him ? '
' No mere man has ever spoken as this man 46 speaks,' said the officers.

' Are you deluded too ? ' replied the Pharisees ; ' has 47, 48 any one of the Rulers or of the Pharisees believed in him ? But this rabble who understand nothing about the Law 49 are accursed ! '

---

35. An unconscious prophecy of the Christian mission of the Gentile world. A touch of irony on the part of the Evangelist. Cf. xii. 20-23.
(vv. 37, 38.) The words may be punctuated (after ' come to me ')—' And let him who believes in me drink.' Then the ' from within Him ' would refer not to the believer as a secondary source (a thought hardly exampled in the Gospel) ; but to Jesus Himself as the one fountain of life. Cf. iv. 13, 14. The ' Scripture ' cannot be identified.

Nicodemus interposed—he who had formerly gone to 50
Jesus, being himself one of them.

'Does our Law,' he asked, 'judge a man without first 51
hearing what he has to say and ascertaining what he is
doing?'

'Do you also come from Galilee?' they asked in 52
reply. 'Search and see for yourself that no prophet is of
Galilaean origin.'

The Sin of a betrothed Woman [So they went away to their several homes; 53
but Jesus went to the Mount of Olives. At 1, 2 **8**
break of day, however, He returned to the
Temple, and there the people came to Him in crowds. He
seated Himself, and was teaching them, when the Scribes 3
and the Pharisees brought to Him a woman who had been
found committing adultery. They made her stand in the
centre of the court, and they put the case to Him. 4

'Rabbi,' they said, 'this woman has been found in the
very act of committing adultery. Now, in the Law, Moses 5
has ordered us to stone such women to death. But what
do you say?'

They asked this in order to put Him to the test, so that 6
they might have some charge to bring against Him. But
Jesus leant forward and began to write with His finger on
the ground. When, however, they persisted with their 7
question, He raised His head and said to them,

'Let the sinless man among you be the first to throw a
stone at her.'

Then He leant forward again, and began to write on 8
the ground. They listened to Him, and then, beginning 9
with the eldest, took their departure, one by one, till all were
gone. And Jesus was left behind alone—and the woman in
the centre of the court. Then, raising His head, Jesus said 10
to her,

'Where are they? Has no one condemned you?'

'No one, Sir,' she replied. 11

'And I do not condemn you either,' said Jesus; 'go,
and from this time do not sin any more.']

(vv. 53–viii. 11.) The evidence, external and internal (un-Johannine words and
phrases and numerous various readings), seems decisive against regarding this section
as part of the Gospel of John, which of course is not to say that it may not be a
fragment of genuine evangelical tradition. Cf. xxi. 25. While many authorities
omit it altogether, others place it at the end of the Gospel, others after Luke xxi. 38.
Cf. the similar setting of vii. 53; viii. 1, 2; and of Luke xxi. 37, 38.

6. *Leant forward*] As a teacher, He was sitting on the ground. See verse 2.

The Testimony of the Father and of the Son Once more Jesus addressed them. ' I am the Light of the world,' He said; ' the man who follows me shall not walk in the dark, but shall have the light of Life.' 12

' You are giving evidence about yourself,' said the Pharisees ; ' your evidence is not valid.' 13

' Even if I am giving evidence about myself,' replied Jesus, ' my evidence is true ; for I know where I came from and where I am going, but you know neither the one nor the other. You judge according to appearances : I am judging no one. And even if I do judge, my judgement is just ; for I am not alone, but the Father who sent me is with me. In your own Law, too, it is written that THE TESTIMONY OF TWO MEN IS TRUE (Deut. xix. 15). I am one giving testimony about myself, and the Father who sent me gives testimony about me.' 14 15 16 17 18

' Where is your Father ? ' they asked. 19

' You know my Father as little as you know me,' He replied ; ' if you knew me, you would know my Father also.'

These sayings He uttered in the Treasury, while teaching in the Temple ; yet no one arrested Him, because His time had not yet come. 20

Christ's Departure near at hand Again He said to them, ' I am going away. Then you will try to find me, but you will die in your sins. Where I am going, it is impossible for you to come.' 21

The Jews began to ask one another, ' Is he going to kill himself, since he says, " Where I am going, it is impossible for you to come " ? ' 22

' You,' He continued, ' are from below, I am from above : you are of this present world, I am not of this present world. That is why I told you that you will die in your sins ; for, unless you believe that I am He, you will die in your sins.' 23 24

' You—who are you ? ' they asked. 25

' How is it that I even speak to you at all ? ' replied

24. *I am He*] Some would render, ' I am ' (as in verse 58). The Greek in these passages and in xiii. 19 is the same as that of the LXX in Deut. xxxii. 39 ; Isa. xliii. 10 ; but is not the same as that of Exod. iii. 14, last clause. So also in verses 28 and 58.

25. *How is it, &c.*] The meaning of the Greek is very uncertain. The rendering adopted here is that of R.V. mg. A.V. and R.V. text have (virtually), ' That which I have spoken to you from the beginning.' Amer. R.V. mg. ' Altogether that which I also speak unto you.'

Jesus. 'Many things I have to speak and to judge con- 26
cerning you. But He who sent me is true, and what I have
heard from Him I tell forth to the world.'

They did not perceive that He was speaking to them of 27
the Father. So Jesus added, 28

'When you have lifted up the Son of Man, then you will
know that I am He. Of myself I do nothing ; but as the
Father has taught me, so I speak. And He who sent me is 29
with me. He has not left me alone : for I do always what
is pleasing to Him.'

As He thus spoke, many became believers in Him. 30

Jesus therefore said to those of the Jews who 31
The Jews had now believed in Him,
boast of
Descent 'As for you, if you hold fast to my teach-
from ing, then you are truly my disciples ; and 32
Abraham you shall know the truth, and the truth will
make you free.'

'We are descendants of Abraham,' they answered, 'and 33
have never at any time been in slavery to any one. What
do those words of yours mean, "You shall become
free"?'

'In very truth I tell you,' replied Jesus, 'that every one 34
who commits sin is the slave of sin. Now a slave 'oes not 35
remain always in his master's house, but a son does. If 36
then, the Son shall make you free, you will be free indeed.
You are descendants of Abraham, I know ; but you want 37
to kill me, because my teaching gains no ground within
you. I speak of what I have seen with the Father. You, 38
then, also are doing what you have heard from your father.'

'Our father is Abraham,' they said. 39

'If you were Abraham's children,' replied Jesus, 'it is
Abraham's deeds that you would be doing. But, in fact, 40
you are longing to kill me, a man who has spoken to you
the truth which I have heard from God. Abraham did not
do that. You are doing the deeds of your father.' 41

'We,' they replied, 'are not illegitimate children. We
have one Father, namely God.'

'If God were your Father,' said Jesus, 'you would love 42
me ; for it is from God that I came and I am now here. I
have not come of myself, but He sent me. How is it you 43
do not understand me when I speak ? It is because you

39. *It is Abraham's deeds, &c.*] v.l. 'do Abraham's deeds.'

are unable to listen to my words. The father whose sons 44
you are is the devil ; and you desire to do what gives him
pleasure. He was a murderer from the beginning, and
does not stand firm in the truth—for there is no truth in
him. Whenever he utters his lie, he speaks what is his
own ; for he is a liar, and the father of lies. But because 45
I speak the truth, you do not believe me. Which of you 46
convicts me of sin ? If I speak the truth, why do you not
believe me ? Only he who is a child of God listens to 47
God's words. You do not listen to them : and why ? It
is because you are not God's children.'

Jesus accused of being a Demoniac   ' Are we not right,' answered the Jews, ' in 48
saying that you are a Samaritan and are
possessed by a demon ? '

' I am not possessed by a demon,' replied 49
Jesus. ' But I honour my Father, and you dishonour me.
I, however, am not aiming at glory for myself : there is 50
One who aims at glory for me—and who judges. In very 51
truth I tell you that if any one obeys my word he shall never
see death.'

' Now,' exclaimed the Jews, ' we know that you are 52
possessed by a demon. Abraham died, and so did the
prophets, and yet you say, " If any one obeys my teaching,
he shall never taste death." Are you really greater than 53
our forefather Abraham ? For he died. And the prophets
died. Whom do you make yourself out to be ? '

' Were I to glorify myself,' answered Jesus, ' I should 54
have no real glory. There is One who glorifies me—namely
my Father, who you say is your God. You do not know 55
Him, but I know Him ; and were I to deny my knowledge
of Him, I should be like you, a liar. But I do know Him,
and I obey His commands. Abraham your forefather 56
rejoiced in the hope of seeing my day : and he saw it, and
was glad.'

' You are not yet fifty years old,' cried the Jews, ' and 57
have you seen Abraham ? '

' In very truth,' answered Jesus, ' I tell you that before 58
Abraham came into existence, I am.'

Thereupon they took up stones to throw at Him, but He 59
hid Himself and went away out of the Temple.

---

44. *Does not stand*] v.l. ' did not stand.'
57. *Have you seen Abraham ?*] v.l. ' Has Abraham seen you ? '

A blind Man receives Sight   As He passed by, He saw a man who had been blind from his birth. So His disciples asked Him, 1 9
2

' Rabbi, who sinned—this man or his parents—that he was born blind ? '

' Neither he nor his parents sinned,' answered Jesus, 3 ' but he was born blind in order that God's work might be openly shown in him. We must do the works of Him 4 who sent me while there is daylight. Night is coming on, when no one can work. When I am in the world, I am 5 the Light of the world.'

After thus speaking, He spat on the ground, and then, 6 kneading the dust and spittle into clay, He smeared the clay over the man's eyes and said to him, 7

' Go and wash in the pool of Siloam '—the name means ' Sent.'

So he went and washed his eyes, and returned seeing.

His Acquaintances question him   His neighbours, therefore, and the other people to whom he had been a familiar sight as a beggar, began asking, 8

' Is not this the man who used to sit and beg ? '

' Yes, it is,' replied some of them. 9

' No, it is not,' said others, ' but he is like him.'

But he said,

' I am the man.'

' How then were your eyes opened ? ' they asked. 10

' He whose name is Jesus,' he answered, ' made clay 11 and smeared my eyes with it, and then told me to go to Siloam and wash. So I went and washed and obtained sight.'

' Where is he ? ' they inquired. 12

' I do not know,' he said.

The Pharisees question him   They brought him to the Pharisees—this man 13 who had been blind. Now the day on which 14 Jesus made the clay and opened the man's eyes was the Sabbath. So the Pharisees in their 15 turn asked him how he had obtained his sight.

2. *This man*] The belief in the possibility of a soul's prenatal innocence or sin appears in Wisdom viii. 19, 20. ' A good soul fell to my lot : nay rather, being good, I came into a body undefiled.'

4. *We*] The Lord associates His disciples with Himself, as in iii. 11. v.l. has ' I ' for ' we.'

11. *Obtained*] Cf. Mark x. 52, n. So in verses 15, 18. Lit. ' recovered sight,' as frequently in the cure of the blind. Cf. Mark x. 52. The man *born blind* regained his normal heritage of vision.

' He put clay on my eyes,' he replied, ' and I washed, and now I can see.'

This led some of the Pharisees to say, 16

' That man has not come from God, for he does not keep the Sabbath.'

' How is it possible for a bad man to do such signs ? ' argued others.

And there was a division among them. So again they 17 asked the once blind man,

' What do you say about his opening your eyes.'

' He is a prophet,' he replied.

The Jews, however, did not believe the state- 18
The Pharisees appeal to his Parents
ment concerning him—that he had been blind and had obtained his sight—until they called his parents and asked them, 19

' Is this your son, who you say was born blind ?   How is it then that he can now see ? '

' We know,' replied the parents, ' that this is our son 20 and that he was born blind ; but how it is that he can now 21 see or who has opened his eyes we do not know.   Ask him himself ; he is of full age ; he himself will give his own account of it.'

This was their answer, because they were afraid of the 22 Jews ; for the Jews had already settled among themselves that if any one should acknowledge Jesus as the Christ, he should be excluded from the synagogue.   That was why his 23 parents said,

' He is of full age : ask him himself.'

A second time therefore they called the man 24
The Pharisees drive the Man away
who had been blind, and said,

' Give God the praise : we know that that man is a sinner.'

' Whether he is a sinner or not, I do not know,' he 25 replied ; ' one thing I know—that I was once blind and that now I can see.'

' What did he do to you ? ' they asked ; ' how did he 26 open your eyes ? '

' I have told you already,' he replied, ' and you did not 27 listen to me.   Why do you want to hear it again ?   Do you also mean to be disciples of his ? '

24. *Give God the praise*] That is, perhaps, ' Do not praise the man Jesus who is a sinner.'   But the primary meaning of the phrase seems rather to be ' Confess your error,' and its just condemnation by the authorities. Cf. Joshua vii. 19.

Then they railed at him, and said, 28
'You are that man's disciple, but we are disciples of
Moses. We know that God spoke to Moses; but as for 29
this fellow we do not know where he comes from.'

'Why, this is marvellous!' the man replied; 'you do 30
not know where he comes from, and yet he has opened my
eyes! We know that God does not listen to bad people, 31
but that if any one is a God-fearing man and does His will,
He listens to him. From the beginning of the world such 32
a thing was never heard of as that any one should open the
eyes of a man blind from his birth. Had that man not 33
come from God, he could have done nothing.'

'You,' they replied, 'were wholly begotten and born in 34
sin, and do you teach us?'

And they put him out of the synagogue.

Jesus finds him Jesus heard that they had done this. So 35
having found him, He asked him,
'Do you believe in the Son of God?'

'Who is He, Master?' replied the man. 'Tell me, so 36
that I may believe in Him.'

'You have seen Him,' said Jesus; 'and not only so: 37
He is now speaking to you.'

'I believe, Master,' he said. 38

And he threw himself at His feet.

The Blindness of the Pharisees 'I came into this world,' said Jesus, 'to 39
judge men, that those who do not see may see,
and that those who do see may become blind.'

These words were heard by those of the Pharisees who 40
were present, and they asked Him,
'Are we also blind?'

'If you were blind,' answered Jesus, 'you would have 41
no sin; but as a matter of fact you boast that you see. So
your sin remains!'

'The Sheepfold' 'In very truth I tell you that the man 1 **10**
who does not enter the sheepfold by the door,
but climbs over some other way, is a thief
and a robber. He who enters by the door is the shepherd 2
of the sheep. To him the porter opens the door, and the 3
sheep hear his voice; and he calls his own sheep by their
names and leads them out. When he has brought his own 4

35. *Son of God*] v.l. 'Son of Man.'
41. *If you were . . you would have*] Or ' If you had been . . you would have had.'

sheep all out, he walks at the head of them ; and the sheep
follow him, because they know his voice. But a stranger
they will by no means follow, but will run away from 5
him, because they do not know the voice of strangers.'

Jesus spoke to them in this allegorical language, but they 6
did not understand what He meant.

The Door Again therefore Jesus said to them, 7
of the ' In very truth I tell you that I am the Door
Sheepfold of the sheep. All who have come before me 8
are thieves and robbers ; but the sheep would not listen
to them. I am the Door. If any one enters by me, he will 9
find safety, and will go in and out and find pasture. The 10
thief comes only to steal and kill and destroy : I have come
that they may have Life, and may have it in abundance.

' I am the Good Shepherd. The good 11
'The Good shepherd lays down his very life for the sheep.
Shepherd' The hired servant, who is not the shepherd 12
and does not own the sheep, no sooner sees the wolf coming
than he leaves the sheep and runs away ; and the wolf
worries and scatters them. For he is only a hired servant 13
and cares nothing for the sheep.

' I am the Good Shepherd. And I know my sheep and 14
my sheep know me, just as the Father knows me and I 15
know the Father ; and I lay down my life for the sheep.
I have also other sheep—which do not belong to this fold. 16
Those also I must bring, and they will listen to my voice ;
and they shall become one flock under one Shepherd. For 17
this reason my Father loves me, because I am laying down
my life to receive it back again. No one is taking it away 18
from me, but I myself am laying it down. I am authorized
to lay it down, and I am authorized to receive it back again.
This is the command I received from my Father.'

Again there arose a division among the Jews because of 19
these words. Many of them said, 20
' He is possessed by a demon and is mad. Why do you
listen to him ? '

16. *This fold . . one flock*] The A.V., following the Latin Vulgate, reads ' this
fold . . one fold.' But the two Greek words are quite distinct, and the change
from ' fold ' to ' flock ' is most significant. The textual evidence for ' flock,' whether
of Greek MSS. or Versions, is unanimous. Even the old Latin, on which Jerome
based his revised Vulgate, translates correctly ovile (sheep-fold) . . grex (flock).
The falsification—for it is nothing less—to ' ovile . . ovile,' is convenient for the
inclusive claims of the Roman See, but our Lord's conception of Christian unity
allows for many folds, diverse one from another, yet gathered into one flock under
the One Shepherd of the sheep.

Others argued, 21
' That is not the language of a demoniac : can a demon open blind men's eyes ? '

Jesus appeals to His Miracles The Dedication Festival came on in Jeru- 22 salem. It was winter, and Jesus was walking 23 in the Temple in Solomon's Portico, when the 24 Jews gathered round Him and asked Him,

' How long do you mean to keep us in suspense ? If you are the Christ, tell us so plainly.'

' I have told you,' answered Jesus, ' and you do not 25 believe. The deeds that I do in my Father's name—they bear witness about me. But you do not believe, because 26 you are not my sheep. My sheep listen to my voice, and 27 I know them, and they follow me. I give them eternal 28 Life, and they shall never perish, nor shall any one wrest them from my hand. What my Father has given me is 29 greater than all, and no one is able to wrest anything from my Father's hand. I and the Father are one.' 30

The Jews talk of killing Him Again the Jews brought stones to throw at 31 Him. Jesus remonstrated with them. 32 ' Many good deeds from the Father have I shown you ; for which of them will you stone me ? '

' For no good deed,' the Jews replied, ' are we going to 33 stone you, but for blasphemy, and because you, who are only a man, are making yourself out to be God.'

' Does it not stand written in your Law,' replied Jesus, 34 ' " I SAID, YOU ARE GODS " (Ps. lxxxii. 6) ? If those to 35 whom God's word was addressed are called gods (and the Scripture cannot be annulled), how is it that you say to one 36 whom the Father consecrated and sent into the world, " You are blaspheming," because I said, " I am God's Son " ? If 37 the deeds I do are not my Father's deeds, do not believe me. But if they are, then even if you do not believe me, at least 38 believe the deeds, that you may recognize and see clearly that the Father is in me, and that I am in the Father.'

This made them once more try to arrest Him, but He 39 withdrew out of their power.

He crosses the Jordan Then He went away again to the other side 40 of the Jordan, to the place where John had been baptizing at first ; and there He stayed. And 41 many people came to Him. Their report was,

22. *Came on*] v.l. adds ' at that time.'

' John did not work any sign, but all that John said about this man was true.'

And many became believers in Him there. 42

The Illness of Lazarus Now a certain man was lying ill, named 1 **11** Lazarus, of Bethany, the village of Mary and her sister Martha. This Mary, whose brother 2 Lazarus was ill, was the one who poured the perfume over the Lord and wiped His feet with her hair. So the 3 sisters sent to Him to say,

' Master, he whom you hold dear is ill.'

Jesus received the message and said, 4

' This illness is not to end in death, but is to promote the glory of God, in order that the Son of God may be glorified by it.'

Jesus goes to Bethany Now Jesus loved Martha, and her sister, and 5 Lazarus. When, therefore, He heard that 6 Lazarus was ill, He still remained two days in that same place. Then, after that, He said to the disciples, 7

' Let us return to Judaea.'

' Rabbi,' exclaimed the disciples, ' the Jews have just 8 been trying to stone you, and do you think of going back there again ? '

' Are there not twelve hours in the day ? ' replied Jesus. 9 ' If any one walks in the daytime, he does not stumble— because he sees the light of this world. But if a man walks 10 by night, he does stumble, because he has no light in him.'

He said this, and afterwards He added, 11

' Our friend Lazarus is sleeping, but I will go and wake him.'

' Master,' said the disciples, ' if he is asleep he will recover.' 12

Now Jesus had spoken of his death, but they thought He 13 referred to the rest of natural sleep. So then He told 14 them plainly,

' Lazarus is dead ; and for your sakes I am glad I was not 15 there, in order that you may believe. But let us go to him.'

' Let us go also,' Thomas (called the Twin) said to his 16 fellow disciples, ' that we may die with him.'

Lazarus was now dead and buried On His arrival Jesus found that Lazarus had 17 already been four days in the tomb. Bethany 18 was near Jerusalem, the distance being a little less than two miles ; and a considerable number of the 19

4. Cf. ix. 3.

Jews were with Martha and Mary, having come to express
sympathy with them on the death of their brother.   Martha, 20
then, as soon as she heard the tidings, ' Jesus is coming,'
went to meet Him ; but Mary remained sitting in the house.
So Martha said to Jesus, 21

' Master, if you had been here, my brother would not
have died.   And even now I know that whatever you ask 22
from God, He will give it.'

' Your brother shall rise again,' replied Jesus. 23

'The Resur-   ' I know,' said Martha, ' that he will rise 24
rection and   again at the resurrection, on the last day.'
the Life'   ' I am the Resurrection and the Life,' said 25
Jesus ; ' he who believes in me, even if he has died, shall
live ; and every one who is living and is a believer in me 26
shall never die.   Do you believe this ? '

' Yes, Master,' she replied ; ' I believe that you are 27
the Christ, the Son of God, who was to come into the
world.'

After saying this, she went and called her sister Mary 28
privately, telling her,

' The Rabbi is here and is asking for you.'

So she, on hearing that, rose up quickly to go to Him. 29
Now Jesus was not yet come into the village, but was still 30
at the place where Martha had met Him.   So the Jews 31
who were with Mary in the house sympathizing with her,
when they saw that she had risen hastily and had gone out,
followed her, supposing that she was going to the tomb
to wail there.

Lazarus   Mary then, when she came to Jesus and saw 32
brought   Him, fell at His feet and exclaimed,
back to Life   ' Master, if you had been here, my brother
would not have died.'

Seeing her wailing, and the Jews in like manner wailing 33
who had come with her, Jesus, in indignation and deeply
troubled, asked them, 34

' Where have you laid him ? '

' Master, come and see,' was their reply.

Jesus burst into tears. 35
' See how dear he held him,' said the Jews. 36
But others asked, 37

35. *Burst into tears*] But not aloud as in verses 31, 33.   This verb, signifying the
silent shedding of tears, occurs nowhere else in the N.T.

'Was not he who opened the blind man's eyes even able to prevent this man from dying?'

Jesus, however, again in indignation, came to the tomb. 38 It was a cave, and a stone had been laid against the mouth of it.

'Take away the stone,' said Jesus. 39

Martha, the sister of the dead man, exclaimed, 'Master, by this time there is a foul smell; for it is the fourth day since he died.'

'Did I not promise you,' replied Jesus, 'that if you 40 believe, you shall see the glory of God?'

So they removed the stone. Then Jesus lifted up His 41 eyes and said,

'Father, I thank Thee that Thou hast heard me. I 42 know that Thou always hearest me; but for the sake of the crowd standing round I have said this—that they may believe that Thou didst send me.'

After speaking thus, He cried out in a loud voice, 43 'Lazarus, come forth.'

The dead man came out, his hands and feet wrapped in 44 cloths, and his face wrapped round with a towel.

'Untie him,' said Jesus, 'and let him go.'

Sympathy and Opposition Thereupon a number of the Jews who had 45 come to Mary and had witnessed His deeds became believers in Him; though some of them 46 went off to the Pharisees and told them what He had done.

Christ's Death for others predicted The High Priests and the Pharisees there- 47 fore held a meeting of the Sanhedrin.

'What steps are we taking?' they asked one another; 'for this man is performing a great number of signs. If we leave him alone in this way, 48 everybody will believe in him, and the Romans will come and blot out both our holy place and our nation.'

But one of them, named Caiaphas, being High Priest that 49 year, said,

'You know nothing about it. You do not reflect that 50 it is to your interest that one man should die for the people rather than the whole nation perish.'

It was not of his own impulse that he thus spoke. But 51 being High Priest that year he was inspired to declare that Jesus was to die for the nation, and not for the nation only, 52 but in order to unite into one body all the far-scattered

children of God. So from that day forward they schemed 53
to put Him to death.

Jesus with- Therefore Jesus no longer went about openly 54
draws to among the Jews, but He left that neighbourhood
Ephraim and went into the district near the desert, to a
town called Ephraim, and remained there with the disciples.
The Jewish Passover was coming near, and many from the 55
country went up to Jerusalem before the Passover, to purify
themselves. They therefore looked out for Jesus, and 56
asked one another as they stood in the Temple,

' What do you think ?—will he come to the Festival at
all ? '

Now the High Priests and the Pharisees had issued orders 57
that if any one knew where He was, he should give information, so that they might arrest Him.

Jesus, however, six days before the Passover, 1 **12**
Mary's came to Bethany, where Lazarus was whom
costly Gift He had raised from the dead. So they gave a 2
dinner there in honour of Jesus, at which Martha waited
at table, but Lazarus was one of those who were at table
with Him. Mary then took a pound weight of pure 3
spikenard, very costly, and poured it over His feet, and
wiped His feet with her hair, so that the house was filled
with the fragrance of the perfume. Then said Judas Iscariot, 4
one of the twelve, the one who was to betray Jesus,

' Why was not that perfume sold for 300 shillings and 5
the money given to the poor ? '

The reason he said this was not that he cared for the poor, 6
but that he was a thief, and that, being in charge of the
money-box, he used to steal what was put into it. But 7
Jesus interposed.

' Do not blame her,' He said, ' it was that she might keep
it for the time of my preparation for burial. For the poor 8
you always have with you, but you have not me always.'

Now it became widely known among the Jews that Jesus 9
was there ; and they came not only on His account, but also
in order to see Lazarus whom He had brought back to life.
The High Priests, however, consulted together to put 10
Lazarus also to death, for because of him many of the Jews 11
left them and became believers in Jesus.

(vv. 1-11.) Cf. Matt. xxvi. 6-13 ; Mark xiv. 3-9 ; Luke vii. 36-50.
3. *Pure*] Or ' liquid.'

Jesus rides into Jerusalem — The next day a great crowd of those who 12 had come to the Festival, hearing that Jesus was coming to Jerusalem, took branches of 13 palm trees and went out to meet Him, shouting as they went,

' HOSANNA ! BLESSINGS ON HIM WHO COMES IN THE NAME OF THE LORD (Ps. cxviii. 26), on the King of Israel ! '

And Jesus, having procured a young ass, sat upon it, just 14 as the Scripture says,

' FEAR NOT, DAUGHTER OF ZION ! SEE, THY KING IS 15 COMING RIDING ON AN ASS'S COLT ' (Zech. ix. 9).

The meaning of this His disciples did not understand at 16 the time ; but after Jesus was glorified they recollected that this was written about Him, and that they had done this to Him. The crowd therefore that had been present when 17 He called Lazarus out of the tomb and brought him back to life, related what they had witnessed. This was why the 18 crowd came to meet Him, because they had heard of His having performed that sign. The Pharisees therefore said 19 to one another,

' See how futile your efforts are ! The world is gone after him ! '

A higher Life the Result of Death — Now some of those who were coming up to 20 worship at the Festival were Greeks. They 21 came to Philip, of Bethsaida in Galilee, with the request,

' Sir, we wish to see Jesus.'

Philip came and told Andrew : Andrew and Philip told 22 Jesus. His answer was, 23

' The time has come for the Son of Man to be glorified. In very truth I tell you that unless a grain of wheat falls 24 into the ground and dies, it remains what it was—a single grain ; but if it dies, it makes a rich yield. He who 25 holds his life dear, destroys it ; and he who makes his life of no account in this world shall keep it to eternal Life. If a man serves me, let him follow me ; and where I am, 26

(vv. 12–19.) Cf. Matt. xxi. 1–11 ; Mark xi. 1–11 ; Luke xix. 29–44.
21. The coming of these Greeks seems to symbolise the seeking of the Gentile world after Christ, which is a signal to Him that His earthly mission was accomplished and His hour was come. Cf. vii. 35, n.
23. *Glorified*] Not only after death, but in and through death. Cf. vii. 39 ; xiii. 31, &c. It is rather the thought of the writer of Hebrews (ii. 9), ' With a view to the suffering of death crowned with glory and honour,' than of Paul (Phil. ii. 8, 9), ' Obedient unto death. Wherefore God also highly exalted him.'

there too shall my servant be. If a man serves me, the
Father will honour him.

'Now is my soul full of trouble; and what shall I say? 27
Father, save me from this hour? No, but for this purpose
I have come to this hour. Father, glorify Thy name.' 28

A Voice from Heaven Then there came a voice from the sky,
'I have glorified it and will glorify it again.'
The crowd that stood by and heard it, said 29
it had thundered. Others said,

'An angel spoke to him.'

'It is not for my sake,' said Jesus, 'that this voice came, 30
but for your sakes. Now comes judgement upon this world: 31
now will the Prince of this world be driven out. And I—if 32
I am lifted up from the earth—will draw all men to me.'

He said this to indicate the kind of death He would die. 33
The crowd answered Him, 34

'We have heard out of the Law that the Christ remains
for ever. Why do you say that the Son of Man must be
lifted up? Who is that Son of Man?'

'A little while longer,' He replied, 'the light will be 35
among you. Live and act according to the light that you
have, for fear darkness overtake you; for a man who walks
in the dark does not know where he is going. Inasmuch as 36
you have the light, believe in the light, so that you may
become sons of light.'

Much Unbelief, yet many secret Disciples Jesus said this, and went away and hid Himself from them. Though He had performed 37
so many signs in their presence, they did not
believe in Him—in order that the words of 38
Isaiah the Prophet might be fulfilled,

'LORD, WHO HAS BELIEVED OUR PREACHING?

AND THE ARM OF THE LORD—TO WHOM HAS IT BEEN
REVEALED?' (Isa. liii. 1).

For this reason they were unable to believe—because 39
Isaiah said again,

'HE HAS BLINDED THEIR EYES AND MADE THEIR MINDS 40
CALLOUS,

---

27. *Save me from this hour*] Cf. Matt. xxvi. 39; Mark xiv. 36; Luke xxii. 42.
Or we may understand the clause to mean, 'Shall I pray, "Father . . hour"?'
The Evangelist seems to rewrite the Gethsemane agony of the Synoptics. In Mark
there is a real cry for deliverance: here rather 'Shall I say? "Father, save me
from this hour!"' No! because for this very purpose I have come to this hour.'
Jesus is now feeling the nearness of the arrest and trial: He is absolutely master of
His fate. The Johannine Christ must not be pressed into the Synoptic mould.

Lest they should see with their eyes and perceive
with their minds,
And should turn,
And I should heal them ' (Isa. vi. 9, 10).

Isaiah uttered these words because he saw His glory ; 41
and he spoke of Him.

Nevertheless even from among the Rulers many 42
believed in Him. But because of the Pharisees they did
not avow their belief, for fear they should be excom-
municated. They loved honour from men rather than 43
honour from God.

Jesus and His heavenly Father

But Jesus cried aloud, 44
' He who believes in me, believes not in me,
but in Him who sent me ; and he who sees me 45
sees Him who sent me. I have come like light 46
into the world, in order that no one who believes in me
may remain in the dark. If any one hears my teachings 47
and regards them not, I do not judge him ; for I did not
come to judge the world, but to save the world. He who 48
sets me at naught and does not receive my teachings is
not left without a judge : the words I have spoken will
judge him on the last day ; because I have not spoken on 49
my own authority ; but the Father who sent me, Himself
gave me a command what to say and in what words to
speak. And I know that His command is eternal Life. 50
What therefore I speak, I speak just as the Father has
bidden me.'

13

A Lesson in Humility

Now before the Feast of the Passover, Jesus 1
knew that the time had come for Him to
leave this world and go to the Father. Having
loved His own who were in the world, He loved them to
the end. While supper was proceeding, the devil having 2
already suggested to Judas Iscariot, the son of Simon, the
thought of betraying Him, Jesus, knowing that the Father 3
had put everything into His hands, and that He had come
forth from God and was now going to God, rose from table, 4
threw off His upper garments, and took a towel and tied
it round Him. Then He poured water into a basin, and 5
proceeded to wash the feet of the disciples and to wipe
them with the towel which He had put round Him. When 6
He came to Simon Peter, Peter objected.

' Master,' he said, ' are you going to wash my feet ? '

'What I am doing,' answered Jesus, 'for the present 7 you do not know, but afterwards you shall know.'

'Never, so long as I live,' said Peter, 'shall you wash 8 my feet.'

'If I do not wash you,' replied Jesus, 'you have no share with me.'

'Master,' said Peter, 'wash not only my feet, but also 9 my hands and my head.'

'Any one who has lately bathed,' said Jesus, 'does not 10 need to wash more than his feet, but is clean all over. And you my disciples are clean, and yet this is not true of all of you.'

For He knew who was betraying Him, and that was 11 why He said,

'You are not all of you clean.'

So after He had washed their feet, put on His garments 12 again, and returned to the table, He said to them,

'Do you understand what I have done to you? You 13 call me "The Rabbi" and "The Master," and rightly so, for such I am. If I then, your Master and Rabbi, have 14 washed your feet, it is also your duty to wash one another's feet. For I have set you an example in order that you 15 may do what I have done to you. In very truth I tell you 16 that a servant is not superior to his master, nor is a messenger superior to him who sent him. If you know all this, blessed 17 are you if you act accordingly. I am not speaking of all of 18 you. I know whom I have chosen, but it is that the Scripture may be fulfilled, which says, " HE WHO EATS MY BREAD HAS LIFTED UP HIS HEEL AGAINST ME " (Ps. xli. 9). From this time forward I tell you things before they happen, 19 in order that when they do happen you may believe that I am He. In very truth I tell you that he who receives 20 any one I send receives me, and that he who receives me receives Him who sent me.'

The Traitor indicated After speaking thus Jesus was troubled in 21 spirit and said with deep earnestness,

'In very truth I tell you that one of you will betray me.'

The disciples began looking at one another, at a loss to 22 know to which of them He was referring. There was at 23

10. *More than his feet*] v.l. omits these words.
13. *Master*] Or 'Lord.'
18. *My bread*] v.l. ' bread with me.'

table one of His disciples—one whom Jesus loved—reclin- 24
ing with his head on Jesus' bosom. Making a sign therefore to him, Simon Peter said,

'Tell us whom He means.'

So he, having his head on Jesus' bosom, leaned back 25
and asked,

'Master, who is it?'

'It is the one,' answered Jesus, 'to whom I shall give 26
this piece of bread when I have dipped it.'

Accordingly He dipped the piece of bread, and took it
and gave it to Judas, the son of Simon Iscariot. Then, 27
after Judas had received the piece of bread, Satan entered
into him.

'What you are doing, do quickly,' said Jesus to
him.

But why He said this to him no one at the table under- 28
stood. Some supposed that because Judas had the money- 29
box Jesus meant, 'Buy what we require for the Festival,'
or that he should give something to the poor. So Judas 30
took the piece of bread and immediately went out. And
it was night.

The new Law—the Law of Love When he was gone out, Jesus said, 31
'Now is the Son of Man glorified, and God
is glorified in Him. Moreover God will glorify 32
Him in Himself, and will glorify Him without delay. Dear 33
children, I am still with you a little longer. You will seek
me, but, as I said to the Jews, "Where I am going you
cannot come," so for the present I say to you. A new 34
commandment I give you, to love one another ; that as I
have loved you, you also may love one another. It is by 35
this that every one will know that you are my disciples—
if you love one another.'

Peter's Denial foretold 'Master,' inquired Simon Peter, 'where are 36
you going?'
'Where I am going,' replied Jesus, 'you
cannot follow now, but you shall follow later.'

'Master,' asked Peter again, 'why cannot I follow you 37
now? I will lay down my life on your behalf.'

'You say you will lay down your life on my behalf!' 38
said Jesus ; 'in very truth I tell you that the cock will not
crow before you have three times disowned me.'

33. *Dear children*] Lit. ' Little children.'

14

Christ's Departure and Return

'Let not your hearts be troubled. Trust in God: trust in me also. In my Father's house there are many resting-places. Were it otherwise, I would have told you; for I am going to make ready a place for you. And if I go and make ready a place for you, I will return and take you to be with me, that where I am you also may be. And where I am going, you all know the way.'

'Master,' said Thomas, 'we do not know where you are going. How should we know the way?'

'I am the Way, the Truth, and the Life,' replied Jesus. 'No one comes to the Father except through me. If you had known me, you would have known my Father also. From this time forward you know Him and have seen Him.'

His Union with the Father

'Master,' said Philip, 'show us the Father: that is all we need.'

'Have I been so long among you,' Jesus answered, 'and yet you, Philip, do not know me? He who has seen me has seen the Father. How can you say to me, "Show us the Father"? Do you not believe that I am in the Father and that the Father is in me? The things that I tell you all I do not speak on my own authority: but the Father dwelling within me carries on His own work. Believe me, all of you, that I am in the Father and that the Father is in me; or at any rate, believe me because of what I do. In very truth I tell you that he who trusts in me shall do the deeds I do; and he shall do greater deeds than these, because I am going to the Father. And whatever any of you ask in my name, I will do, in order that the Father may be glorified in the Son. If you make any request of me in my name, I will do it.

The Holy Spirit promised to the Obedient

'If you love me, you will obey my commandments. And I will ask the Father, and He will give you another Advocate to be for ever with you—the Spirit of truth. That Spirit the

1 2 3 4 5 6 7 8 9 10 11 12 13 14 15 16 17

---

1. *Trust* (twice)] The repeated Greek word is ambiguous, as between the indicative 'you trust' and the imperative 'trust'—A.V. and R.V., 'Ye believe'—'believe.' Amer. R.V. transposes R.V. text and margin.

14. *Of me*] v.l. omits.

16. *Advocate*] Or 'Helper' or 'Champion.' According to etymology 'one called to one's side to help.' Although one meaning of the cognate verb is 'to comfort,' this verbal adjective, *paraclete*, is passive in form, and cannot directly mean 'one who comforts,' though this may be one function of the Helper. Probably the 'Comforter' of A.V. meant 'Strengthener,' rather than 'Consoler.' The word occurs again in verse 26; xv. 26; xvi. 7; 1 John ii. 1.

world cannot receive, because it does not see Him or know Him. You know Him, because He remains by your side and is in you. I will not leave you bereaved : I am coming 18 to you. Yet a little while and the world will see me no more, 19 but you will see me : because I live, you also shall live. At 20 that time you will know that I am in my Father, and that you are in me, and that I am in you. He who has my com- 21 mandments and obeys them is the one who loves me. And he who loves me will be loved by my Father, and I will love him and will reveal myself to him.'

Obedience and Love find God

Judas (not Judas Iscariot) asked, 22 ' Master, how is it that you will reveal your-self to us and not to the world ? '

' If any one loves me,' replied Jesus, ' he will keep my 23 words ; and my Father will love him, and we will come to him and make our home with him. He who has no love for 24 me does not obey my teaching ; and yet the teaching to which you are listening is not mine, but is that of the Father who sent me.

The Holy Spirit the great Teacher

' All this I have spoken to you while still with 25 you. But the Advocate, the Holy Spirit whom 26 the Father will send in my name, will teach you everything, and will bring to your memories all that I have said to you. Peace I leave with you : my 27 own peace I give to you. Not as the world gives do I give to you. Let not your hearts be troubled or dismayed.

Christ's Departure to the Father

' You heard me say to you, " I am going 28 away, and I am coming back to you." If you loved me, you would have rejoiced because I am going to the Father ; for the Father is greater than I am. I have now told you before it comes to pass, that when 29 it has come to pass you may believe. In future I shall not 30 talk much with you, for the Prince of this world is coming. And yet in me he has nothing ; but in order that the 31 world may know that I love the Father, I thus act in accordance with the command which the Father gave me. Rise, let us be going.'

18. *Bereaved*] Or ' orphans.'
19. *Will see*] Lit. ' sees.'
22. *How is it*] Lit. ' What has happened.'
31. *Rise, let us be going*] Westcott supposes that chapters xv. to xvii. were spoken on the way to Gethsemane, before the crossing of the Kidron (xviii. 1). Others suggest some displacement, and rearrangement, *e.g.* xiii. 31, ' Jesus said,' followed by chapters xv., xvi., then xiii. 31-38, xiv., xvii.

The true Vine and its Branches ' I am the true Vine, and my Father is the 1 **15** vine-dresser. Every branch in me that bears 2 no fruit He takes away; and every branch that bears fruit He cleans, that it may bear more fruit. Already 3 you are cleaned—through the teaching which I have given you. Continue in me, and let me continue in you. 4 As the branch cannot bear fruit of itself if it does not continue in the vine, so you cannot if you do not continue in me. I am the Vine, you are the branches. He who continues in 5 me and I in him bears abundant fruit, for apart from me you can do nothing. If any one does not continue in me, he is 6 thrown away like the unfruitful branch, and then withers. Such branches they gather up and throw into the fire and they are burned.

A close Union with Christ through Obedience ' If you continue in me and my sayings con- 7 tinue in you, ask what you will and it shall be done for you. By this is God glorified—by 8 your bearing abundant fruit and being my disciples. As the Father has loved me, I have 9 also loved you: continue in my love. If you obey my 10 commands, you will continue in my love, as I have obeyed my Father's commands and continue in His love.

The Joy which will result ' These things I have spoken to you that 11 I may have joy in you, and that your joy may become perfect. This is my commandment 12 to you, to love one another as I have loved you. No one 13 has greater love than this—that a man lay down his life for his friends. You are my friends, if you do what I command 14 you. No longer do I call you servants, because a servant 15 does not know what his master is doing; but I have called you friends, because all that I have heard from the Father I have made known to you. It is not you who chose me, 16 but it is I who chose you and appointed you that you might go and be fruitful and that your fruit might be lasting; so that whatever petition you present to the Father in my name He may give you.

The World will hate and persecute ' This I command you, to love one another. 17 If the world hates you, you know that it has 18 first hated me. If you belonged to the world, 19 the world would love its own. But because you do not belong to the world, and I have chosen you out

18. *You know*] Or ' know.'

of the world—for that reason the world hates you. Bear in 20 mind what I said to you, " A servant is not superior to his master." If they have persecuted me, they will also persecute you : if they have obeyed my teaching, they will obey yours also. But they will inflict all this suffering upon you 21 on account of your bearing my name—because they do not know Him who sent me.

The Guilt of sinning against Light ' If I had not come and spoken to them, they 22 would have had no sin ; but as it is they are without excuse for their sin. He who hates me 23 hates my Father also. If I had not done among 24 them such deeds as no one else ever did, they would have had no sin ; but now they have seen and also hated both me and my Father. But this has been so that the words 25 written in their Law might be fulfilled, " THEY HAVE HATED ME WITHOUT REASON " (Ps. xxxv. 19 ; lxix. 4).

Inward Light and external Testimony ' When the Advocate is come whom I will 26 send to you from the Father—the Spirit of truth who comes forth from the Father—He will be a witness concerning me. And you also 27 are witnesses, because you have been with me from the first.

Excommuni- cation and Martyrdom foretold ' These things I have spoken to you in order 1 **16** to clear stumbling-blocks out of your path. You 2 will be excluded from the synagogues ; nay more, the time is coming when any one who has murdered you will suppose he is offering service to God. And they will do these things because they have not known 3 the Father or myself. But I have spoken this to you that 4 when the time for their accomplishment comes you may recollect that I told you. I did not, however, tell you all this at first, because I was still with you. But now I am 5 returning to Him who sent me ; and not one of you asks me where I am going. But grief has filled your hearts because 6 I have said all this to you.

The Holy Spirit to come when Jesus goes away ' Yet it is the truth that I am telling you—it is 7 to your advantage that I go away. For unless I go away, the Advocate will not come to you ; but if I go, I will send Him to you. And He, 8 when He comes, will convict the world in respect of sin, of righteousness, and of judgement ;—of sin, because 9 they do not believe in me ; of righteousness, because I am 10 going to the Father, and you will no longer see me ; of 11 judgement, because the Prince of this world is under sentence.

Truth, and our Capacity for receiving it 'I have much more to say to you, but you 12 are unable just now to bear it. But when He has 13 come—the Spirit of truth—He will guide you into all the truth. For He will not speak of His own accord, but all that He hears He will speak, and He will make known what is coming to you. He will glorify me, because He will take of what is mine and 14 will make it known to you. Everything that the Father 15 has is mine; that is why I said that the Spirit of truth takes of what is mine and will make it known to you.

Eternal Joy would follow brief Sorrow 'A little while and you see me no more, and 16 again a little while and you shall see me.' Some of His disciples therefore said to 17 one another,

'What does this mean which He is telling us, "A little while and you do not see me, and again a little while and you shall see me," and "Because I am going to the Father"?'

So they asked one another, 18

'What can that "little while" mean which He speaks of? We do not understand His words.'

Jesus perceived that they wanted to ask Him, and He 19 said,

'Is this what you are questioning one another about— my saying, "A little while and you do not see me, and again a little while and you shall see me"? In very truth 20 I tell you that you will weep aloud and lament, but the world will be glad. You will mourn, but your grief will be turned into gladness. A woman, when she is in labour, has 21 sorrow, because her time has come. But when she has given birth to the babe, she no longer remembers the pain, because of her joy at a child being born into the world. So you also now have sorrow; but I shall see 22 you again, and your hearts will be glad, and your gladness no one will take away from you. You will put no 23 questions to me then.

Prayer in Christ's Name 'In very truth I tell you that whatever you ask the Father for in my name He will give you. As yet you have not asked for any- 24 thing in my name: ask, and you shall receive, that your hearts may be filled with gladness.

Later on He would speak more plainly 'All this I have spoken to you in veiled 25 language. The time is coming when I shall no longer speak to you in veiled language, but will tell you about the Father in plain words. At that time 26 you will make your requests in my name ; and I do not promise to ask the Father on your behalf, for the Father 27 Himself holds you dear, because you have loved me and have believed that I came from the Father. I came out 28 from the Father and have come into the world. Again I am leaving the world and am going to the Father.'

'Ah, now you are using plain language,' said His disciples, 29 'and are uttering no figure of speech ! Now we know that 30 you have all knowledge, and do not need to be pressed with questions. Through this we believe that you came from God.'

'Do you at last believe ? ' replied Jesus. 'Remember 31, 32 that the time is coming—indeed, has already come—for you all to be dispersed each to his own home and to leave me alone. And yet I am not alone, for the Father is with me.

Concluding Words of Encouragement 'I have spoken all this to you in order that 33 in me you may have peace. In the world you have affliction. But keep up your courage : I have won the victory over the world.'

Christ prays for Himself When Jesus had thus spoken, He raised His 1 **17** eyes towards heaven and said,

'Father, the hour has come. Glorify Thy Son that the Son may glorify Thee ; even as Thou hast 2 given Him authority over all mankind, so that on all whom Thou hast given Him He may bestow eternal Life. And 3 this is eternal Life, to know Thee the only true God and Jesus Christ whom Thou hast sent. I have glorified Thee 4 on earth, having done perfectly the work which Thou hast given me to do. And now, Father, do Thou glorify me in 5 Thine own presence, with the glory that I had in Thy presence before the world existed.

Christ prays for His Apostles 'I have revealed Thy perfections to the men 6 whom Thou gavest me out of the world. Thine they were, and Thou gavest them to me, and they have obeyed Thy word. Now they know that 7 whatever Thou hast given me is from Thee. For the 8 truths which Thou didst teach me I have taught them. And they have received them, and have known for certain that I came out from Thee, and have believed that Thou didst send me.

' I am making request for them : for the world I do 9 not make any request, but for those whom Thou hast given me. Because they are Thine, and everything that is mine 10 is Thine, and everything Thine is mine ; and I am crowned with glory in them. I am now no longer in the world, but 11 they are in the world and I am coming to Thee.

' Holy Father, keep them in Thy name, which Thou hast given me, that they may be one, even as we are. While I 12 was with them, I kept them true to Thy name—the name Thou hast given me to bear—and I kept watch over them, and none of them is lost but the one doomed to destruction —that the Scripture may be fulfilled.

' But now I am coming to Thee, and I speak these words 13 while I am in the world, in order that they may have my gladness within them filling their hearts. I have given them 14 Thy word, and the world has hated them, because they do not belong to the world, just as I do not. I do not ask 15 that Thou wilt remove them out of the world, but that Thou wilt protect them from the evil one. They do not belong 16 to the world, just as I do not. Sanctify them by the truth : 17 Thy word is truth. As Thou didst send me into the 18 world, I also have sent them into the world ; and on their 19 behalf I consecrate myself, that they also may be consecrated by the truth.

Christ prays for His future Followers ' Nor is it for them alone that I make request, 20 but also for those who trust in me through their teaching ; that they may all be one, even as 21 Thou art in me, O Father, and I am in Thee ; that they also may be in us ; that the world may believe that Thou didst send me. And the glory which Thou hast 22 given me I have given them, that they may be one, just as we are one : I in them and Thou in me ; that they may 23 stand perfected in union ; that the world may come to understand that Thou didst send me and hast loved them even as Thou hast loved me.

' Father, I desire that those whom Thou hast given me 24 may be with me where I am, that they may see my glory— my gift from Thee, which Thou hast given me because Thou didst love me before the creation of the world. And, 25 righteous Father, though the world has failed to recognize

Thee, I have known Thee, and these have perceived that
Thou didst send me. And I have made known Thy 26
name to them and will make it known, that the love with
which Thou hast loved me may be in them, and I in them.'

Judas brings armed Men After offering this prayer Jesus went out with 1 **18**
His disciples to a place on the further side of
the Ravine of the Cedars, where there was a
garden, which He entered—Himself and His disciples.
Now Judas also, who was betraying Him, knew the place, 2
for Jesus had often resorted there with His disciples. So 3
Judas, taking the battalion and a detachment of the Temple
police sent by the High Priests and Pharisees, came there with
torches and lamps and weapons. Jesus therefore, knowing 4
all that was about to befall Him, went out to meet them.

' Whom are you looking for ? ' He asked them.

' For Jesus the Nazarene,' was the answer. 5

' I am he,' He replied.

(Now Judas who was betraying Him was also standing
with them.) As soon then as He said to them, ' I am he,' 6
they went backwards and fell to the ground. Again there- 7
fore He asked them,

' Whom are you looking for ? '

' For Jesus the Nazarene,' they said.

' I have told you,' replied Jesus, ' that I am he. If 8
therefore you are looking for me, let these my disciples go
their way.'

It was that the Scripture might be fulfilled which said, 9

' Of those whom Thou hast given me, I have not lost one.'

Peter's rash Act Now Simon Peter having a sword drew it, 10
and, aiming at the High Priest's servant, cut
off his right ear. The servant's name was
Malchus. Jesus therefore said to Peter, 11

' Put back your sword. Shall I refuse to drink the cup of
sorrow which the Father has given me to drink ? '

Jesus arrested and taken to Annas So the battalion and their tribune and the 12
Jewish police closed in, and took Jesus and
bound Him. They then brought Him to 13
Annas first ; for Annas was the father-in-law
of Caiaphas who was High Priest that year. (It was this 14
Caiaphas who had advised the Jews, saying,

---

1. *Ravine of the Cedars*] Or ' the Ravine Kidron.' The connection with the
Greek word for Cedar is doubtful.

' It is to your interest that one man should die for the people.')

Peter disowns his Master Simon Peter was following Jesus, and so also 15 was another disciple. The latter was known to the High Priest, and went in with Jesus into the court of the High Priest's palace. But Peter remained 16 standing without at the door, till the disciple who was acquainted with the High Priest came out and induced the portress to let Peter in. This led the girl, the portress, to 17 ask Peter,

' Are you also one of this man's disciples ? '

' No, I am not,' he replied.

Now because it was cold the servants and the police had 18 lighted a charcoal fire, and were standing and warming themselves ; and Peter too remained with them, standing and warming himself.

The High Priest questions Jesus So the High Priest questioned Jesus about 19 His disciples and His teaching.

' I,' replied Jesus, ' have spoken openly to the 20 world. I have continually taught in some synagogue or in the Temple where all the Jews are wont to assemble, and I have said nothing in secret. Why do you question me ? 21 Question those who heard what it was I said to them : these witnesses here know what I said.'

Upon His saying this, one of the officers standing by 22 struck Him with his open hand, asking Him as he did so,

' Is that the way you answer the High Priest ? '

' If I have spoken wrongly,' replied Jesus, ' bear witness 23 to the wrong ; but if rightly, why that blow ? '

So Annas sent Him bound to Caiaphas the High Priest. 24

Peter again disowns his Master But Simon Peter remained standing and 25 warming himself. So they said to him,

' Are you also one of his disciples ? '

He denied it, and said,

' No, I am not.'

One of the High Priest's servants, a relative of the man 26 whose ear Peter had cut off, said,

' Did I not see you in the garden with him ? '

19. *The High Priest*] It is difficult, in view of the designation of Caiaphas as High Priest in verses 13–24, to attribute this examination to Annas. The difficulty is emphasized by the A.V. incorrect translation of verse 24—' had sent.'

25. *Warming himself*] The fire was apparently in the court-yard of Annas's palace (verse 15) ; but possibly this court was common to both palaces, as our Lord was able (Luke xxii. 61) while in the palace of Caiaphas to turn round and look at Peter.

Once more Peter denied it, and immediately a cock crowed. 27

Christ taken before the Roman Governor
So they brought Jesus from Caiaphas's house 28 to the Praetorium. It was the early morning, and they would not enter the Praetorium themselves for fear of defilement, that they might be able to eat the Passover. Accordingly Pilate came out to 29 them and inquired,

' What accusation have you to bring against this man ? '

' If the man were not a criminal,' they replied, ' we would 30 not have handed him over to you.'

' Take him yourselves,' said Pilate, ' and judge him by 31 your Law.'

' We have no power,' replied the Jews, ' to put any man to death.'

They said this that the words might be fulfilled in which 32 Jesus predicted the kind of death He was to die.

Pilate questions Him
Re-entering the Praetorium, therefore, Pilate 33 called Jesus and asked Him, ' Are you the King of the Jews ? '

' Do you say this of yourself, or have others told it you 34 about me ? ' replied Jesus.

' Am I a Jew ? ' exclaimed Pilate ; ' it is your own nation 35 and the High Priests who have handed you over to me. What have you done ? '

' My Kingdom,' replied Jesus, ' does not belong to this 36 world. If my Kingdom did belong to this world, my subjects would have fought to save me from being delivered up to the Jews. But, in fact, my Kingdom has not this origin.'

' So then you are a king ! ' rejoined Pilate. 37

' Yes,' said Jesus, ' you say truly that I am a king. For this purpose I was born, and for this purpose I have come into the world—to give testimony to the truth. Every one who is a friend of the truth listens to my voice.'

Pilate willing to release Him
' What is truth ? ' said Pilate. 38 So saying, he went out again to the Jews and told them,

' I find no crime in him. But you have a custom that I 39

28. But according to the Synoptics the Passover had already been eaten on the previous evening. See the Commentaries.
Praetorium] Or ' Governor's Palace.'
The dramatic setting of the trial before Pilate is noteworthy ; a succession of scenes alternately within and without the palace.

should release one prisoner to you at the Passover. So shall I release to you the King of the Jews?'

With a roar of voices they again cried out, saying,   40
' Not this man, but Barabbas!'

Now Barabbas was a robber.

Jesus scourged and mocked   Then Pilate took Jesus and scourged Him. 1 19 And the soldiers, twisting twigs of thorn into a 2 wreath, put it on His head, and threw round Him a purple cloak.   Then they came up to Him and 3 said,

' Hail, King of the Jews!'

And they struck Him with the palms of their hands.

Pilate pronounces Him innocent   Once more Pilate came out and said to the 4 Jews,

' See, I am bringing him out to you to let you clearly understand that I find no crime in him.'

So Jesus came out, wearing the wreath of thorns and the 5 purple cloak.   And Pilate said to them,

' See, there is the man.'

As soon then as the High Priests and the officers saw Him, 6 they shouted,

' To the cross!   To the cross!'

' Take him yourselves and crucify him,' said Pilate; ' for I, at any rate, find no crime in him.'

' We,' replied the Jews, ' have a Law, and in accordance 7 with that Law he ought to die, for having claimed to be the Son of God.'

He again questions Him   More alarmed than ever, Pilate no sooner 8 heard these words than he re-entered the 9 Praetorium and began to question Jesus.

' What is your origin?' he asked.

But Jesus gave him no answer.

' Do you refuse to speak even to me?' asked Pilate; 10 ' do you not know that I have it in my power either to release you or to crucify you?'

' You would have had no power whatever over me,' 11 replied Jesus, ' had it not been granted you from above.   On that account he who has delivered me up to you is more guilty than you are.'

He passes sentence of Death   Upon receiving this answer, Pilate was for 12 releasing Him.   But the Jews kept shouting,

' If you release this man, you are no friend of

Caesar's. Every one who sets himself up as king declares himself a rebel against Caesar.'

On hearing this, Pilate brought Jesus out, and sat down 13 on the judge's seat in a place called the Pavement—or, in Hebrew, Gabbatha. It was the day of Preparation for the 14 Passover, about mid-day. Then he said to the Jews,

' There is your king ! '

This caused a storm of outcries, 15

' Away with him ! Away with him ! Crucify him ! '

' Am I to crucify your king ? ' Pilate asked.

' We have no king, except Caesar,' answered the High Priests.

Then Pilate gave Him up to them to be crucified. 16

Jesus is taken to Golgotha and crucified Accordingly they took Jesus ; and He went 17 out carrying His own cross, to the place called Skull-place—or, in Hebrew, Golgotha—where 18 they nailed Him to a cross, and two others at the same time, one on each side and Jesus in the middle. And Pilate wrote a notice and had it fastened to 19 the top of the cross. It ran thus :

JESUS THE NAZARENE, THE KING OF THE JEWS.

Many of the Jews read this notice, for the place where 20 Jesus was crucified was near the city, and the notice was in three languages—Hebrew, Latin, and Greek. The 21 Jewish High Priests therefore remonstrated with Pilate.

' You should not write " The King of the Jews," ' they said, ' but that he claimed to be King of the Jews.'

' What I have written I have written,' was Pilate's 22 answer.

The Soldiers take His Clothes So the soldiers, as soon as they had crucified 23 Jesus, took His garments, including His tunic, and divided them into four parts—one part for each soldier. The tunic was without seam, woven from the top in one piece. So they said to one another, 24

' Do not let us tear it. Let us draw lots for it.'

This happened that the Scripture might be fulfilled which says,

13. *Sat down*] Or ' made Him sit ' ; in mockery. And said (verse 14), ' There is your king ! ' The verb may be either transitive or intransitive. But in the fragment of the Petrine Gospel, discovered 1886-87, we read, ' They clothed Him in purple, and made Him sit on the judge's seat.'

14. *Mid-day*] Cf. i. 39, n.

' THEY SHARED MY GARMENTS AMONG THEM, AND DREW
LOTS FOR MY CLOTHING ' (Ps. xxii. 18).

That was what the soldiers did.

Mary and John Now standing close to the cross of Jesus were 25
His mother and His mother's sister, Mary the
wife of Clopas, and Mary of Magdala. So 26
Jesus, seeing His mother, and seeing the disciple whom He
loved standing near, said to His mother,

' Look, your son ! '

Then He said to the disciple, 27

' Look, your mother ! '

And from that time the disciple received her into
his own home.

Jesus dies After this, Jesus, knowing that everything 28
was now brought to an end, said—that the
Scripture might be fulfilled (Ps. lxix. 21),

' I am thirsty.'

There was a jar of wine standing there. With this wine 29
they filled a sponge, put it on the end of a stalk of hyssop,
and lifted it to His mouth. As soon as Jesus had taken the 30
wine, He said,

' It is finished.'

And then, bowing His head, He yielded up His spirit.

His Body pierced Meanwhile the Jews, because it was the day 31
of Preparation for the Passover, and in order
that the bodies might not remain on the crosses
during the Sabbath (for that Sabbath was one of special
solemnity), requested Pilate to have the legs of the dying
men broken, and the bodies removed. Accordingly the 32
soldiers came and broke the legs of the first man, and also
of the other who had been crucified with Jesus. Then 33
they came to Jesus: but when they saw that He was
already dead, they refrained from breaking His legs. One 34
of the soldiers, however, made a thrust at His side with a
lance, and immediately blood and water flowed out. This 35
statement is the testimony of an eye-witness, and it is true.
He knows that he is telling the truth—in order that you

---

25. *Mary the wife of Clopas*] This seems the most probable sense ; lit. ' Clopas's
Mary.' There is nothing in the Greek to settle the question whether she was the
sister of Mary, the mother of Jesus.
26. *Look, your son*] Lit. ' Woman, behold your son ! ' Cf. ii. 4, n. ; viii. 10 ; xx.
13, n.
29. *Wine* (twice)] Lit. ' vinegar ' or ' sour wine.' So in verse 30. Cf. Matt.
xxvii. 48, n.

also may believe. For all this took place that the Scripture 36
might be fulfilled which declares,

' NOT ONE OF HIS BONES SHALL BE BROKEN ' (Exod. xii. 46 ;
Ps. xxxiv. 20).

And again another Scripture says, 37

' THEY SHALL LOOK ON HIM WHOM THEY HAVE PIERCED '
(Zech. xii. 10).

Joseph and Nicodemus bury it After this, Joseph of Arimathaea, who was 38
a disciple of Jesus, but for fear of the Jews a
secret disciple, asked Pilate's permission to carry
away the body of Jesus ; and Pilate gave him leave. So
he came and removed the body. Nicodemus too—he who 39
at first had visited Jesus by night—came bringing a mixture
of myrrh and aloes, in weight about seventy or eighty
pounds. Taking down the body they wrapped it in linen 40
cloths along with the spices, in accordance with the Jewish
mode of preparing for burial. There was a garden at the 41
place where Jesus had been crucified, and in the garden
a new tomb, in which no one had yet been buried.
Therefore, because it was the day of Preparation for 42
the Jewish Passover, and the tomb was close at hand, they
put Jesus there.

The Tomb found empty On the first day of the week, very early, 1 **20**
while it was still dark, Mary of Magdala came
to the tomb and saw that the stone had been
removed from it. So she ran off and found Simon Peter 2
and the other disciple—the one who was dear to Jesus—and
said to them,

' They have taken the Lord out of the tomb, and we do not
know where they have put Him.'

Peter and the other disciple started at once to go to the 3
tomb, both of them running, but the other disciple ran 4
faster than Peter and reached it before him. Stooping 5
and looking in, he saw the linen cloths lying there on the
floor, but he did not go in. Simon Peter, however, also 6
came, following him, and entered the tomb. There on the
floor he saw the cloths ; and the towel, which had been 7
placed over the face of Jesus, not lying with the cloths, but
folded up and put by itself. Then the other disciple, who 8

39. *Mixture*] v.L. ' roll.'
Seventy or eighty pounds] Lit. ' 100 (Roman) pounds.'
5. *Stooping and looking in*] One word in the Greek. Cf. verse 11 and 1 Pet. i.
12.   The tombs were cut horizontally into the face of the solid rock.

had been the first to come to the tomb, also went in and saw and was convinced. For until now they had not understood 9 the Scripture, that He must rise again from the dead (Ps. xvi. 10). Then the disciples returned home. 10

But Mary remained standing near the tomb, 11
Mary sees two Angels weeping aloud. She did not enter the tomb, but as she wept she stooped and looked in, and 12 saw two angels clothed in white raiment, sitting one at the head and one at the feet where the body of Jesus had been. They spoke to her. 13

' Why are you weeping ? ' they asked.

' Because,' she replied, ' they have taken away my Lord, and I do not know where they have put Him.'

While she was speaking, she turned round 14
Mary talks with Jesus and saw Jesus standing there, but did not recognize Him.

' Why are you weeping ? ' He asked ; ' whom are you 15 looking for ? '

She, supposing that He was the gardener, replied,

' Sir, if you have carried him away, tell me where you have put him and I will remove him.'

' Mary ! ' said Jesus. 16

She turned to Him.

' Rabboni ! ' she cried in Hebrew : the word means ' Teacher ! '

' Do not cling to me,' said Jesus, ' for I have not yet 17 ascended to the Father. But take this message to my brethren : " I am ascending to my Father and your Father, to my God and your God." '

Mary of Magdala came and brought word to the disciples. 18

' I have seen the Lord,' she said.

And she told them that He had said these things to her.

Jesus appears to His Disciples On that same first day of the week, when it 19 was evening and, for fear of the Jews, the doors of the house where the disciples were had been locked, Jesus came and stood in their midst, and said to them,

13. *Why*] Lit. ' Woman, why '; but in modern English we seldom use the simple vocative in the language of sympathy and condolence. Cf. ii. 4, n. ; viii. 10 ; xix. 26, n.

16. *Rabboni*] The word occurs also in Mark x. 51.

17. *Do not cling to me*] Contrast Matt. xxviii. 9, and see John xx. 27. Apparently the Evangelist conceives of the Ascension as taking place immediately after the appearance to Mary, followed a little later by a brief renewal of the old human fellowship with the disciples.

'Peace be to you!'

Having said this He showed them His hands and His 20
side; and the disciples were filled with joy at seeing the
Lord. A second time, therefore, He said to them, 21
'Peace be to you! As the Father sent me, I also now
send you.'

Having said this He breathed upon them and said, 22
'Receive the Holy Spirit. If you remit the sins of any 23
persons, they remain remitted to them. If you bind fast the
sins of any, they remain bound.'

Thomas, who was absent, sceptical Thomas, one of the twelve—called 'the 24
Twin'—was not among them when Jesus came.
So the rest of the disciples told him, 25
'We have seen the Lord!'

His reply was,

'Unless I see in His hands the wound made by the nails
and put my finger into the wound, and put my hand into
His side, I will never believe it.'

Jesus appears again. Thomas worships Him A week later the disciples were again in the 26
house, and Thomas was with them, when Jesus
came—though the doors were locked—and
stood in their midst, and said,

'Peace be to you.'

Then He said to Thomas, 27
'Bring your finger here and see my hands; bring your
hand and put it into my side; and be not incredulous but
believe.'

'My Lord and my God!' replied Thomas. 28
'Because you have seen me,' replied Jesus, 'you have 29
believed? Blessed are those who have not seen and yet
have believed.'

The Object of the Fourth Gospel There were also many other signs which Jesus 30
performed in the presence of the disciples, which
are not recorded in this book. But these have 31
been recorded in order that you may believe that He is the
Christ, the Son of God, and that, believing, you may have
Life through His name.

Jesus at the Sea of Galilee After this, Jesus again showed Himself to the 1 **21**
disciples. It was at the Lake of Tiberias. The
circumstances were as follows.

Simon Peter was with Thomas (called 'the Twin'), 2

31. See Introduction.

The Draught of Fish Nathanael from Cana in Galilee, the sons of Zebedee, and two others of His disciples. And Simon Peter said to them, 3

' I am going fishing.'

' We will go too,' said they.

So they went on board their boat ; but they caught nothing that night. Now when day was dawning, Jesus 4 stood on the beach, though the disciples did not know that it was Jesus. He called to them. 5

' Boys,' He said, ' have you any food there ? '

' No,' they answered.

' Throw the net in on the right of the boat,' He said, 6 ' and you will find fish.'

So they threw the net in, and now they could scarcely drag it along for the quantity of fish. This made the disciple 7 whom Jesus loved say to Peter,

' It is the Lord.'

Simon Peter therefore, when he heard the words, ' It is the Lord,' drew on his fisherman's shirt—for he had not been wearing it—put on his girdle, and sprang into the water. But the rest of the disciples came in the small 8 boat (for they were not far from land—only about a hundred yards), dragging the net full of fish.

A Meal of Bread and Fish As soon as they landed, they saw a charcoal 9 fire burning there, with fish broiling on it, and bread close by. Jesus told them to 10 fetch some of the fish which they had just caught. So 11 Simon Peter went on board the boat and drew the net ashore full of large fish, one hundred and fifty-three in number ; yet, although there were so many, the net had not broken.

' Come to breakfast,' said Jesus. 12

Now not one of the disciples ventured to ask Him who He was, for they felt sure that it was the Lord. Then Jesus 13 came and took the bread and gave them some, and the fish likewise. This was now the third occasion on which 14 Jesus showed Himself to the disciples after He had risen from the dead.

Jesus tests Peter's Love for Him When they had finished breakfast, Jesus asked 15 Simon Peter,

' Simon, son of John, do you love me more than these others do ? '

268

' Yes, Lord,' was his answer ; ' you know that you are dear to me.'

' Then feed my lambs,' replied Jesus.

Again a second time He asked him, 16

' Simon, son of John, do you love me ? '

' Yes, Lord,' he said, ' you know that you are dear to me.'

' Then be a shepherd to my sheep,' He said.

A third time Jesus put the question : 17

' Simon, son of John, am I dear to you ? '

It grieved Peter that Jesus asked him the third time,

' Am I dear to you ? '

' Lord,' he replied, ' you know everything, you can see that you are dear to me.'

' Then feed my sheep,' said Jesus. ' In very truth 18 I tell you that whereas, when you were young, you used to put on your girdle and walk wherever you chose, when you have grown old you will stretch out your arms and some one else will put a girdle round you and carry you where you have no wish to go.'

This He said to indicate by what kind of death that 19 disciple would bring glory to God. After speaking thus, He said to him,

' Follow me.'

John and the Return of Jesus Peter turned round and noticed the disciple 20 whom Jesus loved following—the one who at the supper had leaned back on His breast and had asked,

' Lord, who is it that is betraying you ? '

On seeing him, Peter asked Jesus, 21

' And, Lord, what about him ? '

' If I desire him to remain till I come,' replied Jesus, 22 ' what concern is that of yours ? Follow me yourself.'

Hence the report spread among the brethren that that 23 disciple would never die. Yet Jesus did not say, ' He is not to die,' but, ' If I desire him to remain till I come, what concern is that of yours ? '

The Testimony of an Eye-witness This is the disciple who gives his testi- 24 mony as to these facts, and has written this history ; and we know that his testi-

---

17. In this third question Jesus adopts Peter's warmer word of affection ; but the two terms for love seem almost interchangeable throughout this Gospel.

mony is true. But there are many other things 25
that Jesus did—so vast a number indeed that if they
were all described in detail, I suppose the world
itself could not contain the books that would be
written.

THE ACTS OF THE APOSTLES

The *importance* of the Book for modern investigation into the origins of Christianity (see Introduction to *St. Luke*) may be gathered from the fact that the mere ' Prolegomena ' of the editors of ' *The Beginnings of Christianity* ' devote to *Acts* three large volumes. They write in their Preface to vol. i. : ' *Acts* takes its natural place as the opening contribution to the beginnings of Christianity. Whatever be the historian's judgement as to its value as a record, without it he would be compelled to wander without a guide in the trackless forest of conjecture as to the way in which the Church organized itself, and began its work.'

The *scope* of the Book is indicated at i. 8—Jerusalem, all Judaea, Samaria, the end of the earth. This outward expansion of the primitive Jerusalem community was prepared for by the gradual inward emancipation of Christianity from its Jewish origin and environment. The first great factor in this was the martyrdom of Stephen, and the consequent scattering of the Church. Two lines of concurrent Evangelism are traced (viii. 4 ; xi. 19). The writer evidently attaches great importance to the admission into the Church of the Gentile Cornelius (x. 1–xi. 18). At xiii. 1 we are introduced to the Antiochene Mission. Thenceforward Paul dominates the scene : ' so we turn to the Gentiles ' (xiii. 46).

The *authorship* has been touched on in the Introduction to *St. Luke*.

The *date* is still undetermined, between wide limits. Professor Harnack argues (' *The Date of the Acts and the Synoptic Gospels* ') that the only reasonable interpretation of the abrupt ending (xxviii. 30, 31) is that Luke ends because he has no more to tell ; which means that he writes before the trial was finished and before Paul's martyrdom in A.D. 64. This, of course, would involve a very early date for the Gospel of St. Luke, which Harnack does not think it necessary to place after the destruction of Jerusalem in A.D. 70. (See note on xxviii. 30, 31.)

THE ACTS OF THE APOSTLES

Introduction

The risen Jesus seen for six Weeks My former narrative, Theophilus, dealt with 1 **1** all that Jesus did and taught as a beginning, down to the day when, after giving instructions 2 through the Holy Spirit to the Apostles whom He had chosen, He was taken up to heaven. He had also, 3 after His Passion, shown Himself alive to them with many sure proofs, appearing to them at intervals during forty days, and speaking of the Kingdom of God. And while in their 4 company He charged them not to leave Jerusalem, but to wait for the Father's promised gift.

' This you have heard of,' He said, ' from me. For John 5 indeed baptized with water, but before many days have passed you shall be baptized with the Holy Spirit.'

Now when they were with Him, they asked Him, 6 ' Lord, is it the time for you to restore the Kingdom to Israel ? '

' It is not for you,' He replied, ' to know times or occasions 7 which the Father has reserved within His own authority ; but you shall receive power when the Holy Spirit has come 8 upon you, and you shall be my witnesses in Jerusalem and in all Judaea and Samaria and to the remotest parts of the earth.'

Christ taken up into Heaven When He had said this, and while they were 9 looking at Him, He was carried up, and a cloud closing beneath Him hid Him from their sight. And while they stood intently gazing into the sky as He 10 went, suddenly there were two men in white garments standing by them, who said, 11

' Galilaeans, why stand looking into the sky ?   This same

---

1. *As a beginning*] So laying the first foundation of the Christian Church. Or ' from the beginning.' Lit. ' began both to do and to teach.'
3. *Proofs*] Of the reality of His resurrection.
4. *While in their company*] Or ' while eating with them.'
8. This verse outlines the whole purpose and plan of the book of Acts.

Jesus who has been taken up from you into heaven will come in just the same way as you have seen Him departing into heaven.'

The Church in Jerusalem

The Apostles meet in Jerusalem for Prayer Then they returned to Jerusalem from the 12 mountain called the Oliveyard, which is near Jerusalem, about a mile off. They entered 13 the city, and then went to the upper room which was now their fixed place for meeting. Their names were Peter, John, James and Andrew, Philip and Thomas, Bartholomew and Matthew, James the son of Alphaeus, Simon the Zealot, and Judas the brother of James. All of these with one mind continued earnest in prayer, together 14 with some women, and Mary the mother of Jesus, and His brothers.

Peter's Speech It was on one of these days that Peter stood 15 up in the midst of the brethren—the entire number of persons present being about one hundred and twenty—and said,

'Brethren, it was necessary that the Scripture should 16 be fulfilled—the prediction which the Holy Spirit uttered by the lips of David, about Judas, who acted as guide to those who arrested Jesus. For Judas was reckoned as one 17 of our number, and a share in this ministry was allotted to him.'

(Now Judas, having bought a piece of ground with the 18 money paid him for his wickedness, fell there with his face downwards, and, his body bursting open, he became disembowelled. This fact became widely known to the 19 people of Jerusalem, so that the place received the name, in their language, of Akel-damach, which means 'The Field of Blood.')

'For it is written in the Book of Psalms, 20

'" LET HIS HABITATION BE DESOLATE :

11. *In just the same way*] The language must not be unduly pressed. The astronomical conceptions of the first century are not identical with those of the twentieth.
12. *About a mile*] Lit. ' a Sabbath's journey.'
16. *Brethren*] Preceded in the Greek by 'Men' (approaching in sense our ' Gentlemen ' or ' Sirs ').
(vv. 18-20.) Cf. Matt. xxvii. 1-10.
Some are of opinion that these verses are not (as here printed) a parenthetical statement by Luke, but a part of Peter's address, as if the 120 believers needed to be informed of a fact which was ' widely known to the people of Jerusalem.'

Let there be no one to dwell there " (Ps. lxix. 25) ; and

' " His work let another take up " (Ps. cix. 8).

' It is necessary, therefore, that of the men who have been 21 with us all the time that the Lord Jesus went in and out among us—beginning from His baptism by John down to 22 the day on which He was taken up from us into heaven— one should be appointed to become a witness with us as to His resurrection.'

Matthias selected in Place of Judas So they proposed two names, Joseph called 23 Bar - Sabbas — and surnamed Justus — and Matthias. And the brethren prayed, saying, 24 ' Thou, Lord, who knowest the hearts of all, show clearly which of these two Thou hast chosen to occupy 25 the place in this ministry and apostleship, from which Judas through transgression fell, in order to go to his own place.' Then they drew lots between them. The lot fell on 26 Matthias, and a place with the eleven Apostles was voted to him.

The Out-pouring of the Holy Spirit Now, in the course of the day of Pentecost, 1 **2** they had all met in one place ; when suddenly 2 there came from the sky a sound as of a strong rushing blast of wind, filling the whole house where they were sitting. And there appeared to them 3 tongues of what looked like fire, distributing themselves over the assembly ; and on the head of each person a tongue alighted. They were all filled with the Holy Spirit, and 4 began to speak in other tongues according as the Spirit gave them words to utter.

'The Gift of Tongues' Now there were Jews residing in Jerusalem, 5 devout men from every part of the world. So 6 when this noise was heard, they came crowding together, and were amazed because every one heard his own language spoken. They were beside themselves with 7 wonder, and exclaimed,

' Are not all these speakers Galilaeans ? How then does 8

20. *Work*] Lit. ' overseership.' The same word, sometimes rendered ' visitation ' or ' bishopric,' is found in Luke xix. 44 ; 1 Tim. iii. 1 ; 1 Pet. ii. 12.

4. *Speak in other tongues*] There can be little doubt that Luke means to record a supernatural endowment of speaking in unlearnt languages. Such a psychological miracle, however, seems unparalleled and unnecessary. There is no trace of it in the after record, and the Apostles, speaking Greek and their native Aramaic, could carry the gospel throughout the whole Roman world. If we may trust to the earliest record, 1 Cor. xiv., the gift of ' tongues ' would appear to have been some form of ecstatic utterance under stress of strong emotion. Cf. verse 15 ; x. 46 ; xix. 6.

each of us hear his own native language spoken by them ? Parthians, Medes, Elamites, inhabitants of Mesopotamia, of 9 Judaea and Cappadocia, of Pontus and the Asian Province, of Phrygia and Pamphylia, of Egypt and of the parts of 10 Africa towards Cyrene, visitors from Rome, both Jews and converts, Cretans and Arabians, we all alike hear these 11 Galilaeans speaking in our own language about the majesty of God.'

They were all astounded and bewildered, and asked one 12 another,

'What can this mean ? '

But others, scornfully jeering, said, 13

'They are brimful of sweet wine.'

Peter's Speech Peter, however, together with the eleven, 14 stood up and addressed them in a loud voice. 'Men of Judaea, and all you inhabitants of Jerusalem,' he said, 'let this be known to you, and attend

These Marvels the Fulfilment of Prophecy to what I say. These men are not drunken, as 15 you suppose, it being only nine o'clock in the morning. But that which was predicted through 16 the Prophet Joel has happened :

'"AND IT SHALL COME TO PASS IN THE LAST DAYS, says 17 God,

THAT I WILL POUR OUT MY SPIRIT UPON ALL MANKIND ;

AND YOUR SONS AND YOUR DAUGHTERS SHALL PROPHESY,

AND YOUR YOUNG MEN SHALL SEE VISIONS,

AND YOUR OLD MEN SHALL DREAM DREAMS ;

AND EVEN UPON MY SERVANTS, BOTH MEN AND 18 WOMEN,

AT THAT TIME I WILL POUR OUT MY SPIRIT, AND THEY SHALL PROPHESY.

I WILL DISPLAY MARVELS IN THE SKY ABOVE, 19

AND SIGNS ON THE EARTH BELOW,

BLOOD AND FIRE, AND CLOUD OF SMOKE.

THE SUN SHALL BE TURNED INTO DARKNESS 20

AND THE MOON INTO BLOOD,

TO USHER IN THE DAY OF THE LORD—

THAT GREAT AND ILLUSTRIOUS DAY ;

AND EVERY ONE WHO CALLS ON THE NAME OF THE LORD 21 SHALL BE SAVED " (Joel ii. 28–32).

9. *Parthians, &c.*] *i.e.* Parthian Jews, &c.

The Resurrection of Jesus of Nazareth

'Listen, Israelites, to what I say. Jesus, the 22 Nazarene, a man accredited to you from God by mighty works and marvels and signs which God did among you through Him, as you yourselves know, this man—delivered up through God's settled purpose 23 and foreknowledge—you by the hands of wicked men have nailed to a cross and have put to death. But God has raised 24 Him to life, ending the pangs of death. It was not possible for Him to be held fast by death ; for David says in reference 25 to Him,

'" I HAVE EVER FIXED MY EYES UPON THE LORD,
BECAUSE HE IS AT MY RIGHT HAND THAT I MAY ABIDE
UNSHAKEN.
FOR THIS CAUSE MY HEART IS GLAD AND MY TONGUE 26
EXULTS.
MY BODY ALSO SHALL REST IN HOPE.
FOR THOU WILT NOT LEAVE ME IN THE GRAVE FORSAKEN, 27
NOR GIVE UP THY HOLY ONE TO UNDERGO DECAY.
THOU HAST MADE KNOWN TO ME THE WAYS OF LIFE : 28
THOU WILT FILL ME WITH GLADNESS IN THY PRESENCE "
(Ps. xvi. 8-11).

'As to the patriarch David, I need hardly remind you, 29 brethren, that he died and was buried, and that we still have his tomb among us. Being a prophet, however, and 30 knowing that God had solemnly sworn to him to seat a descendant of his upon his throne (Ps. cxxxii. 11), with 31 prophetic foresight he spoke of the resurrection of the Christ, to the effect that He was not left forsaken in the grave, nor did His body undergo decay (Ps. xvi. 10). This 32 Jesus God has raised to life—a fact to which all of us testify.

The promised Holy Spirit

'Being therefore lifted high by the right hand 33 of God, He has received from the Father the promised Holy Spirit and has poured forth what you see and hear. For it was not David that ascended into 34 heaven, but he says himself,

'" THE LORD SAID TO MY LORD,
SIT AT MY RIGHT HAND
UNTIL I MAKE THY FOES A FOOTSTOOL UNDER THY 35
FEET " (Ps. cx. 1).

---

30. *To seat*] Or ' that . . should take his seat.' Cf. John xix. 13, n.
32. *A fact to which all of us testify*] Or the relative may be masculine, and refer to Jesus : ' whose witnesses we all are.' Cf. i. 8 ; xiii. 31.

' Therefore let the whole House of Israel know beyond 36
all doubt that God has made Him both LORD and CHRIST
—this Jesus whom you crucified.'

3000 new Adherents gained Struck to the heart by these words, they said 37
to Peter and the rest of the Apostles,
' Brethren, what are we to do ? '

' Repent,' replied Peter, ' and be baptized, every one of 38
you, in the name of Jesus Christ, for the remission of your
sins, and you shall receive the gift of the Holy Spirit. For 39
to you belongs the promise, and to your children, and to all
who are far off, as many as the Lord our God may call.'

And with many more appeals he solemnly warned and 40
entreated them, saying,

' Escape from this perverse generation.'

Those, therefore, who joyfully welcomed his word were 41
baptized ; and on that one day about three thousand
persons were added to them ; and they were constant in 42
attendance on the teaching of the Apostles, and in the
fellowship, the breaking of the bread, and at the prayers.

The daily Life of the Church Awe came upon every one, and many marvels 43
and signs were wrought by the Apostles. And 44
all the believers kept together, and had everything in common. They sold their lands and other pro- 45
perty, and distributed the proceeds among all, according to
every one's necessities. And, day by day, attending con- 46
stantly in the Temple with one accord, and breaking bread
at home, they took their meals with great happiness and
single-heartedness, praising God and being regarded with 47
favour by all the people. Also day by day the Lord added
to their number those whom He was saving.

A lame Beggar cured One day Peter and John were going up to the 1 **3**
Temple for the hour of prayer—three o'clock—
and, just then, some men were carrying there 2
one who had been lame from his birth, whom they were wont
to place every day close to the Gate of the Temple called

---

37. *Struck*] Lit. ' pierced ' or ' stabbed deep,' as with the thrust of a spear. A less
emphatic word occurs in John xix. 34.
42. *Fellowship*] Probably the term here rendered ' fellowship ' (lit. ' communion ')
is to be taken in a wider sense than in 1 Cor. x, 16, where the reference is to individual or joint participation in the blood and body of Christ at the Lord's Supper.
The root idea is expressed by the cognate adjective ' in common ' (cf. verse 44 ; iv. 32).
The fact of unity in Christ, so vital to the existence and growth of the first Christian
Church, found expression in, and was nurtured by the frequent observance of the
Eucharist, the meetings for prayer, and, for a time, actual community of goods.
46. *At home*] Or ' from house to house.'

the Beautiful Gate, to beg from the people as they went in.
Seeing Peter and John about to go into the Temple, he asked 3
them for alms. Peter fixing his eyes on him, as John did 4
also, said,

'Look at us.'

So he looked and waited, expecting to receive something 5
from them.

'I have no silver or gold,' Peter said, ' but what I have, 6
I give you. In the name of Jesus Christ, the Nazarene—
walk!'

Then taking his hand Peter lifted him up, and immedi- 7
ately his feet and ankles were strengthened. Leaping up, 8
he stood upright and began to walk, and went into the
Temple with them, walking, leaping, and praising God.
All the people saw him walking and praising God ; and 9, 10
recognizing him as the man who used to sit at the Beautiful
Gate of the Temple asking for alms, they were filled with
awe and amazement at what had happened to him.

Peter's Speech. This Miracle the Work of Christ While he still clung to Peter and John, the 11
people, awe-struck, ran up and crowded round
them in what was known as Solomon's Portico.
Peter, seeing this, spoke to the people, 12

'Israelites,' he said, ' why do you wonder at
this ? Or why gaze at us, as though by any power or piety of
our own we had enabled him to walk ? The God of Abraham, 13
Isaac, and Jacob, the God of our forefathers, has glorified
His Servant Jesus, whom you delivered up and disowned in
the presence of Pilate, when he had decided to let Him go.
Yes, you disowned the holy and righteous One, and asked 14
as a favour the release of a murderer. The Prince of Life 15
you put to death ; but God has raised Him from the dead,
of which we are witnesses. In virtue of faith in His name, 16
His name has strengthened this man whom you behold and
know ; and the faith which He has bestowed has entirely
restored this man, as you can all see.

An Appeal for Faith and Obedience 'And now, brethren, I know that it was in 17
ignorance that you did it, as was the case with
your rulers also. But in this way God has 18
fulfilled the declarations He made through all the Prophets,
that His Christ would suffer. Repent, therefore, and 19
reform your lives, so that the record of your sins may be
cancelled, and that there may come seasons of refreshment

from the Lord, and that He may send the Christ appointed 20
beforehand for you—even Jesus. Heaven must receive 21
Him until those times of which God has spoken from the
earliest ages through the lips of His holy Prophets—the
times of the reconstitution of all things. Moses declared, 22
'"THE LORD YOUR GOD WILL RAISE UP A PROPHET FOR YOU
FROM AMONG YOUR BRETHREN AS HE HAS RAISED ME. IN ALL
THAT HE SAYS TO YOU, YOU MUST LISTEN TO HIM. AND 23
EVERY ONE WHO REFUSES TO LISTEN TO THAT PROPHET SHALL
BE UTTERLY DESTROYED FROM AMONG THE PEOPLE" (Deut.
xviii. 15-19). Yes, and all the Prophets from Samuel 24
onwards who have spoken have also predicted these days.

'You are the heirs of the Prophets, and of the Covenant 25
which God made with your forefathers when He said to
Abraham, "AND THROUGH YOUR POSTERITY ALL THE FAMILIES
OF THE WORLD SHALL BE BLESSED" (Gen. xii. 3 ; xxii. 18). It 26
is to you first that God, after raising His Servant from the
grave, has sent Him to bless you, by causing every one of
you to turn from your wickedness.'

Arrest of Peter and John While they were saying this to the people, the 1 **4**
Priests, the Commander of the Temple Guard,
and the Sadducees came upon them, highly 2
incensed at their teaching the people and proclaiming in
the case of Jesus the Resurrection from the dead. They 3
arrested the two Apostles and lodged them in custody till
the next day ; for it was already evening. But many of 4
those who had listened to their preaching believed ; the
number of the men now grew to about five thousand.

Their Trial and Defence The next day a meeting was held in Jerusalem 5
of their Rulers, Elders, and Scribes, with Annas 6
the High Priest, Caiaphas, John, Alexander, and
the other members of the High Priest's family. So they 7
made the Apostles stand forward, and demanded of them,

'By what power or in what name have you done this ?'
Then Peter, filled with the Holy Spirit, replied, 8

'Rulers and Elders of the people, if we to-day are under 9
examination concerning the benefit conferred on a man
helplessly lame, as to how this man has been cured, be it 10
known to you all, and to all the people of Israel, that through
the name of Jesus Christ, the Nazarene, whom you crucified,
but whom God has raised from the dead—through that
name this man stands here before you in perfect health.

This Jesus is THE STONE TREATED WITH CONTEMPT BY you 11
THE BUILDERS, BUT IT HAS BEEN MADE THE CORNERSTONE
(Ps. cxviii. 22). And in no other is salvation to be found ; 12
for, indeed, there is no second name under heaven that has
been given to men through which we are to be saved.'

The two As they looked on Peter and John so fear- 13
Apostles lessly outspoken—and also discovered that they
released were illiterate persons, untrained in the schools
—they were surprised ; and now they recognized them as
having been with Jesus. But seeing the man who had been 14
cured standing with them, they had no reply to make. So 15
they ordered them to withdraw from the Sanhedrin while
they conferred among themselves.

'What are we to do with these men ? ' they asked one 16
another ; ' for the fact that a notable miracle has been performed by them is well known to every one in Jerusalem, and
we cannot deny it. But to prevent the matter spreading 17
any further among the people, let us stop them by threats
from speaking in future in this name to any man.'

So they recalled the Apostles, and ordered them altogether 18
to give up speaking or teaching in the name of Jesus. But 19
Peter and John replied,

' Whether it is right in God's sight to listen to you instead
of listening to God, do you judge. As for us, what we have 20
seen and heard we cannot help speaking about.'

The Court added further threats and then let them go, 21
being quite unable on account of the people to find any way
of punishing them, because all men gave God the glory
for what had happened. For the man was over forty 22
years of age on whom this miracle of healing had been
performed.

The Church After their release the two Apostles went to 23
prays for their friends, and told them all that the High
Courage Priests and Elders had said. And they, upon 24
hearing the story, one and all lifted up their voices to God
and said,

' O Sovereign Lord, Thou didst make heaven and earth
and sea, and all that is in them, and didst say through the 25
Holy Spirit by the lips of our forefather David, Thy servant,

' " WHY HAVE THE NATIONS RAGED,

25. *Through the Holy Spirit by the lips of our forefather David*] v.l. ' through the
lips of David.' The Greek text here on which most modern critics are agreed is
untranslatable.

AND THE PEOPLES IMAGINED VAIN THINGS ?
THE KINGS OF THE EARTH STOOD BY,   26
AND THE RULERS ASSEMBLED TOGETHER
AGAINST THE LORD AND AGAINST HIS ANOINTED "
(Ps. ii. 1, 2).

'They did indeed assemble in this city in hostility to 27
Thy holy Servant Jesus whom Thou hadst anointed—Herod
and Pontius Pilate with the Gentiles and also the tribes of
Israel—to do all that Thy power and Thy will had pre- 28
determined should be done. And now, Lord, listen to their 29
threats, and enable Thy servants to proclaim Thy word
with fearless courage, whilst Thou stretchest out Thy 30
hand to cure men, and to give signs and marvels through
the name of Thy holy Servant Jesus.'

The Request granted When they had prayed, the place in which 31
they were assembled shook, and they were, one
and all, filled with the Holy Spirit, and spoke
God's word with boldness.

The brotherly Love of the Church Among all those who had embraced the faith 32
there was but one heart and soul, so that none of
them claimed any of his possessions as his own,
but everything they had was common property ;
while the Apostles with great effect delivered their testimony 33
as to the resurrection of the Lord Jesus ; and great grace
was upon them all. And, in fact, there was not a needy 34
man among them, for all who were possessors of lands or
houses sold them, and brought the money which they
realized, and gave it to the Apostles, and distribution was 35
made to every one according to his wants. In this way 36
Joseph, to whom the Apostles gave the name of Barnabas—
signifying ' Son of Encouragement '—a Levite, a native
of Cyprus, sold a farm which he had, and brought the money 37
and gave it to the Apostles.

Falsehood punished There was a man of the name of Ananias who, 1 **5**
with his wife Sapphira, sold some property,
but, with her full knowledge and consent, dis- 2
honestly kept back part of the price which he received for it,
though he brought the rest and gave it to the Apostles.

'Ananias,' said Peter, ' why has Satan taken possession 3
of your heart, that you should try to deceive the Holy Spirit

34. *Gave it to the Apostles*] Lit. ' laid it at the feet of the Apostles.'
36. *A farm*] Or ' an estate.' A ' field ' erroneously suggests a few acres of ground
surrounded by a hedge.

and dishonestly keep back part of the price paid you for this land ? While it remained unsold, was not the land your 4 own ? And when sold, was it not at your own disposal ? How is it that you have cherished this design in your heart ? It is not to men you have told this lie, but to God.'

Upon hearing these words Ananias fell down dead, and all 5 who heard the words were awe-struck. The younger men, 6 however, rose, and wrapping the body up, carried it out and buried it.

About three hours had passed, when his wife came in, 7 knowing nothing of what had happened. Peter at once 8 questioned her.

' Tell me,' he said, ' whether you sold the land for so much.'

' Yes,' she replied, ' for so much.'

' How was it,' replied Peter, ' that you two agreed to 9 put the Spirit of the Lord to the test ? The men who have buried your husband are already at the door, and they will carry you out.'

Instantly she fell down dead at his feet, and the young 10 men came in and found her dead. So they carried her out and buried her by her husband's side. The whole Church 11 was awe-struck, and so were all who heard of this incident.

Many signs and marvels continued to be done 12 **Many other Miracles** among the people by the Apostles ; and by common consent they all met in Solomon's Portico. But none of the others dared to attach themselves to 13 them. Yet the people held them in high honour—and more 14 and more believers in the Lord joined them, including great numbers both of men and women—so that they would even 15 bring out their sick friends into the streets and lay them on light couches or mats, in order that when Peter came by, at least his shadow might fall on one or other of them. The 16 inhabitants, too, of the towns in the neighbourhood of Jerusalem came in crowds, bringing sick persons and some who were harassed by foul spirits, and they were cured, one and all.

4. *It is not to men, &c.*] *i.e.* 'Your attempt to deceive us men is nothing in comparison with your idle attempt to deceive God.'

9. *To put . . to the test*] 'To test the omniscience of the Spirit, then visibly dwelling in the Apostles and the Church, was in the highest sense to tempt the Spirit of God' (Alford). See Matt. iv. 7, n.

The men] Lit. ' the feet of those.'

The Apostles miraculously released from Prison This roused the High Priest. He and all his 17 party—the sect of the Sadducees—were filled with angry jealousy, and they laid hands upon 18 the Apostles, and put them into the public gaol. But during the night an angel of the Lord opened 19 the prison doors and brought them out, and said,

' Go and stand in the Temple, and continue proclaiming 20 to the people all this Message of Life.'

On hearing this, they went into the Temple just before 21 daybreak, and began to teach.

They openly teach in the Temple Courts So when the High Priest and his party came, and had called together the Sanhedrin as well as all the Elders of the sons of Israel, they sent to the gaol to fetch the Apostles. But the officers 22 went and could not find them in the prison. So they came back and brought word, saying, 23

' The gaol we found quite safely locked, and the warders were on guard at the doors, but upon going in we found no one there.'

When the Commander of the Temple Guards and the 24 High Priests heard this statement, they were utterly at a loss with regard to it, wondering what would happen next. And 25 some one came and brought them word, saying,

' The men you put in prison are standing in the Temple, and teaching the people.'

Peter again testifies to the Resurrection Upon this the Commander went with the 26 officers, and brought the Apostles ; but without using violence ; for they were afraid of being stoned by the people. So they brought them 27 and set them before the Sanhedrin. And the High Priest questioned them.

' We strictly forbade you to teach in that name—did we 28 not ? ' he said. ' And see, you have filled Jerusalem with your teaching, and are trying to make us responsible for that man's death ! '

Peter and the other Apostles replied, 29

' We must obey God rather than man. The God of our 30 forefathers has raised Jesus to life, whom you crucified and put to death. God has exalted Him to His right hand as 31

---

21. *Elders*] Lit. ' Eldership ' or ' Senate.' The word here employed occurs nowhere else in the N.T., though it is found more than twenty times in the LXX.
31. *To His right hand*] Or ' with His right hand.' Cf. ii. 33.

Prince and Saviour, to give Israel repentance and forgive- 32
ness of sins. And we—and the Holy Spirit whom God
has given to those who obey Him—are witnesses as to
these things.'

Gamaliel urges the Sanhedrin to be cautious Infuriated at getting this answer, they were 33
disposed to kill the Apostles. But a Pharisee 34
of the name of Gamaliel, a teacher of the
Law, held in honour by all the people, rose
and requested that they should be sent out for a few
minutes.

' Israelites,' he said, ' be careful what you are about to do 35
in dealing with these men. Years ago Theudas appeared, 36
professing to be a person of importance, and a body of men,
some four hundred in number, joined him. He was killed,
and all his followers were dispersed and annihilated. After 37
him, at the time of the Census, came Judas, the Galilaean,
and was the leader in a revolt. He too perished, and all his
followers were scattered. And now I tell you to hold aloof 38
from these men and leave them alone—for if this scheme or
work is of human origin, it will come to nothing. But if 39
it is really from God, you will be powerless to put them
down—lest perhaps you find yourselves to be actually fighting against God.'

The Apostles discharged His advice carried conviction. So they called 40
the Apostles in, and—after flogging them—
ordered them not to speak in the name of Jesus,
and then let them go. They, therefore, left the Sanhedrin 41
and went their way, rejoicing that they had been deemed
worthy to suffer disgrace on behalf of the Name. But 42
they did not desist from teaching every day, in the Temple
or at home, and telling the gospel about Jesus, the
Christ.

33. *Infuriated*] Lit. ' sawn asunder.' The word occurs here and in vii. 54.
34. *Gamaliel*] Cf. xxii. 3.
(vv. 36, 37.) *Theudas . . After him . . Judas the Galilaean*] A well-known chronological difficulty. The attempt of Judas was in A.D. 6-7, and *prior* to him Gamaliel
places Theudas ; but the only revolt under a Theudas mentioned by Josephus
occurred about 44 or 45 A.D., some ten years after Gamaliel's speech. For discussion
see the Commentaries. This is the passage most relied upon by those who make
Luke guilty of a glaring mistake, due to his reading and misunderstanding of consecutive passages in Josephus (whose *Jewish Antiquities* was published about 94
A.D.), with the consequence that the book of Acts is relegated to the close of the
century.
40. *Flogging*] This would be the Jewish ' forty stripes save one,' not the Roman
scourging (with the *horrible flagellum*) which our Lord suffered. See Deut. xxv. 2, 3 ;
2 Cor. xi. 24.
41. *Rejoicing*] Cf. the Lord's beatitudes (Matt. v. 10-12).
The Name] Of Jesus. Cf. Lev. xxiv. 11, 16 ; 3 John 7, in the Greek.

Seven Church Officers appointed About this time, as the number of the disciples 1 **6** was increasing, complaints were made by the Greek-speaking Jews against the Hebrews because their widows were habitually overlooked in the daily ministration. So the twelve called 2 together the general body of the disciples and said,

' It does not seem fitting that we Apostles should neglect the word of God and attend to the tables. Therefore, 3 brethren, pick out from among yourselves seven men of good repute, full of the Spirit and of wisdom, and we will appoint them to undertake this duty. But, as for us, we will 4 devote ourselves to prayer and to the ministry of the word.'

The suggestion met with general approval, and they 5 selected Stephen, a man full of faith and of the Holy Spirit, Philip, Prochorus, Nicanor, Timon, Parmenas, and Nicolas, a proselyte of Antioch. These men they brought to the 6 Apostles, and, after prayer, they laid their hands upon them.

Rapid Growth of the Church Meanwhile God's word continued to spread, 7 and the number of the disciples in Jerusalem very greatly increased, and very many priests became obedient to the faith. And Stephen, full of grace 8 and power, performed great marvels and signs among the people.

Stephen is arrested But some members of the synagogue called 9 that of the Libertines, and some Cyreneans, Alexandrians, and men of Cilicia and Asia, were roused to encounter Stephen in debate. They 10 were quite unable, however, to resist the wisdom and the Spirit with which he spoke. Then they privately put 11 forward men who declared,

1. *The Greek-speaking Jews*] Lit. ' the Hellenists.'
Hebrews] When used, as here, in opposition to Hellenists this word denotes the Jews of Palestine, who spoke Aramaic.
The two words ' ministration ' and ' minister ' are derivatives of the one which we have anglicized into ' deacon,' and hence the officials named below are commonly called ' the seven deacons.' The term ' deacon ' itself had not yet acquired its distinctive sense ; but in Rom. xvi. 1, Phoebe is called a ' deaconess.' Cf., later, Phil. i. 1.
2. *Fitting*] Lit. ' pleasing.'
We Apostles] Lit. simply ' we.'
All the seven bear Greek names, and were very likely Hellenists ; perhaps an advisory committee, to help the Jewish Apostles, who retained the responsibility, to see fair play between the complaining Hellenists and the Hebrews. Nothing is known of any of them except Stephen and Philip, and nothing of these two as ' serving tables.' The one assumes immediate prominence as emancipator and martyr of the faith, the other as Philip the Evangelist, viii. ; xxi. 8.
9. *Libertines*] Lit. ' freed men.' An interesting conjecture, involving little change in the Greek word, is ' Libyans,' linking on to the other African Jews of Cyrene and Alexandria.

' We have heard him speak blasphemous words against Moses and against God.'

In this way they excited the people, the Elders, and the 12 Scribes. At length they came upon him, seized him with violence, and took him before the Sanhedrin. Here they 13 brought forward false witnesses who declared,

' This fellow is incessantly speaking against the Holy Place and the Law. For we have heard him say that Jesus, 14 the Nazarene, will pull this place down to the ground and will change the customs which Moses handed down to us.'

The High Priest questions him At once the eyes of all who were sitting in 15 the Sanhedrin were fastened on him, and they saw his face like the face of an angel. Then the 1 7 High Priest asked him,

' Are these statements true ? '

The reply of Stephen was, 2

Stephen's Defence. A Review of the Nation's History ' Sirs—brethren and fathers—listen to me. The God of Glory appeared to our forefather Abraham when he was living in Mesopotamia, before he settled in Haran, and said to him, 3

' " Leave your country and your kindred, and go into whatever land I point out to you " (Gen. xii. 1).

' Thereupon he left Chaldaea and settled in Haran till after 4 the death of his father, when God caused him to remove into this country where you now live. But He gave him no 5 inheritance in it, no, not a single square yard of ground (Deut. ii. 5). And yet He promised to bestow the land as a permanent possession on him and his posterity after him— and promised this at a time when Abraham was childless (Gen. xvii. 8). And God declared that Abraham's posterity 6 should for four hundred years make their home in a country not their own, and be reduced to slavery and be oppressed.

' " And the nation, whichever it is, that enslaves them, I 7 will judge," said God ; " and afterwards they shall come out " (Gen. xv. 13, 14), " and they shall worship Me in this place " (Exod. iii. 12).

' Then He gave him the Covenant of circumcision (Gen. 8 xvii. 10), and under this Covenant he became the father of

---

14. *This place*] The Temple with its courts. ' The Sanhedrin, usually assembled under the presidency of the High Priest, sat in the chamber called *Gazith*, on the south side of the Temple.'

(vv. 2, 3.) This and other historical difficulties raised by comparison of Stephen's speech with the O.T. record cannot here be discussed.

Isaac—whom he circumcised on the eighth day (Gen. xxi. 4). Isaac became the father of Jacob, and Jacob became the father of the twelve Patriarchs.

' The Patriarchs were jealous of Joseph and sold him into 9 slavery in Egypt (Gen. xxxvii. 11, 28). But God was with him (Gen. xxxix. 2, 21) and delivered him from all his 10 afflictions, and gave him favour and wisdom when he stood before Pharaoh, king of Egypt, who appointed him governor over Egypt and all the royal household (Gen. xli. 37, 40, 43, 55 ; Ps. cv. 21). But there came a famine throughout the 11 whole of Egypt and Canaan—and great distress—so that our forefathers could find no food (Gen. xli. 54). When, how- 12 ever, Jacob heard that there was wheat to be had, he sent our forefathers into Egypt (Gen. xlii. 1) ; that was the first time. On their second visit Joseph made himself known to 13 his brothers (Gen. xlv. 4), and Pharaoh was informed of Joseph's parentage. Then Joseph sent and invited his 14 father Jacob and all his family, numbering seventy-five persons (Gen. xlv. 9 ; xlvi. 27), to come to him, and Jacob 15 went down into Egypt (Gen. xlvi. 5). There he died, and so did our forefathers (Gen. xlix. 33 ; Exod. i. 6), and they 16 were taken to Shechem and were laid in the tomb which Abraham had bought from the sons of Hamor at Shechem for a sum of money paid in silver (Gen. l. 13 ; Josh. xxiv. 32).

' But as the time drew near for the fulfilment of the 17 promise which God had made to Abraham, the people be- came many times more numerous in Egypt, until there 18 arose a foreign king over Egypt who knew nothing of Joseph (Exod. i. 7, 8). He adopted a crafty policy towards our 19 race, and oppressed our forefathers, making them cast out their infants so that they might not be permitted to live (Exod. i. 10, 22). At this time Moses was born—a wonder- 20 fully beautiful child (Exod. ii. 2) ; and for three months he was cared for in his father's house. At length he was cast 21 out, but Pharaoh's daughter adopted him, and brought him up as her own son (Exod. ii. 5, 10). So Moses was educated 22 in all the learning of the Egyptians, and possessed great influence through his eloquence and his achievements.

' And when he was just forty years old, it occurred to him 23

19. *Be permitted to live*] The same verb is used in Exod. i. 17, LXX.
20. *Wonderfully beautiful*] Lit. ' beautiful to God,' a Hebraism. So in Jonah iii. 3, Nineveh is described as (literally) ' a city great to God.'

to visit his brethren the descendants of Israel. Seeing one 24 of them wrongfully treated he took his part, and secured justice for the ill-treated man by striking down the Egyptian. He supposed his brethren to be aware that by him God was 25 sending them deliverance ; this, however, they did not understand. The next day, also, he came and found two of them 26 fighting, and he endeavoured to make peace between them.

' " Sirs," he said, " you are brothers. Why are you wronging one another ? "

' But the man who was doing the wrong resented his 27 interference, and asked,

' " Who appointed you ruler and judge over us ? Do you 28 mean to kill me as you killed the Egyptian yesterday ? "

' Alarmed at this question, Moses fled from the country 29 and went to live in the land of Midian (Exod. ii. 11–15). There he became the father of two sons.

' But at the end of forty years there appeared to him in the 30 Desert of Mount Sinai an angel in a flame of fire in a bush. When Moses saw this he wondered at the sight ; but on his 31 going up to look further, the voice of the Lord was heard, saying, 32

' " I am the God of your forefathers, the God of Abraham, of Isaac, and of Jacob."

' Quaking with fear Moses did not dare gaze.

' " Take off your shoes," said the Lord, " for the spot on 33 which you are standing is holy ground. I have seen, yes, 34 I have seen the oppression of My people who are in Egypt and have heard their groans, and I have come down to deliver them. And now come, let me send you to Egypt " (Exod. iii. 10).

' The Moses whom they rejected, asking him, " Who 35 appointed you ruler and judge ? "—that same Moses we find God sending as a ruler and a deliverer by the help of the angel who appeared to him in the bush. This was he who 36 brought them out, after performing marvels and signs in Egypt and at the Red Sea, and in the Desert for forty years. This is the Moses who said to the descendants of Israel, 37

' " GOD WILL RAISE UP A PROPHET FOR YOU FROM AMONG

---

27. *Resented his interference*] Or ' pushed him away.'
37. Already quoted at iii. 22. The original promise refers to a succession of prophets as distinct from all the tribe of heathen fortune-tellers prohibited in Deut. xviii. 9–14. It is not surprising that the N.T. writers should find the supreme fulfilment of the promise in Jesus Christ. (Cf. also John i. 21, 25 ; vi. 14 ; vii. 40).

YOUR BRETHREN, JUST AS HE RAISED ME UP" (Deut. xviii.
15, 18).

'This is he who was among the Congregation in the 38
Desert, together with the angel who spoke to him on Mount
Sinai and with our forefathers, who received ever-living
utterances to hand on to us.

'Our forefathers, however, would not submit to him, but 39
spurned his authority and in their hearts turned back to
Egypt. They said to Aaron, 40

'"Make gods for us, to march in front of us; for as for
this Moses who brought us out of the land of Egypt, we do
not know what has become of him" (Exod. xxxii. 1–8).

'Moreover they made a calf at that time, and offered a 41
sacrifice to the idol, and kept rejoicing in the gods which
their own hands had made. So God turned from them and 42
gave them up to the worship of the Host of heaven, as it is
written in the Book of the Prophets,

'"DID YOU OFFER ME VICTIMS AND SACRIFICES
FORTY YEARS IN THE DESERT, O HOUSE OF ISRAEL?
NAY, YOU LIFTED UP MOLOCH'S TENT 43
AND THE STAR OF THE GOD REPHAN—
THE IMAGES WHICH YOU MADE IN ORDER TO WORSHIP
THEM;
AND I WILL REMOVE YOU BEYOND BABYLON"
(Amos v. 25–27).

'Our forefathers had the Tent of Witness in the Desert, 44
built as He who spoke to Moses had instructed him to make
it in imitation of the model which he had seen. That Tent 45
was bequeathed to the next generation of our forefathers.
Under Joshua they brought it with them when they were
taking possession of the land of the Gentile nations, whom
God drove out before them. So it continued till David's
time. David obtained favour with God, and asked leave to 46
provide a dwelling-place for the God of Jacob. But it was 47
Solomon who built a house for Him. Yet the Most High 48

38. *Congregation*] The word here used by Luke ('ecclesia') means in the LXX. the
congregation or assembly of all Israel, as in Deut. xviii. 16. There are as many as
seventy passages in all. Elsewhere in the N.T. it is translated 'Church.'

(vv. 42, 43.) The discussion of this difficult passage belongs rather to a commentary
on Amos.

44. *The Tent of Witness*] *i.e.* the Tent which contained 'the Ark of the Testimony'
(Exod. xl. 21)—the Law of the Ten Commandments—which, so long as they preserved it and obeyed it, bore witness to the presence of God and to His gracious
promises; also called 'the Tent of Meeting,' not, as A.V., 'the Tabernacle of the
Congregation.' The proper significance of 'meeting house' is not a place where men
meet with one another, but where man meets with God.

does not dwell in buildings erected by men's hands.   But, as the Prophet declares,

> ' " THE SKY IS MY THRONE,   49
>   AND EARTH IS THE FOOTSTOOL FOR MY FEET.
>   WHAT KIND OF HOUSE WILL YOU BUILD FOR ME, SAYS
>   THE LORD,
>   OR WHAT RESTING PLACE SHALL I HAVE ?
>   DID NOT MY HAND FORM THIS UNIVERSE " (Isa. lxvi. 1, 2).   50

These Jews resembled their Forefathers   ' O stiff-necked men, uncircumcised in heart 51 and ears, you are continually at strife with the Holy Spirit—just as your forefathers were. Which of the Prophets did not your forefathers 52 persecute ?   Yes, they killed those who foretold the advent of the righteous One, whose betrayers and murderers you have now become—you who received the Law given through 53 angels, and yet have not obeyed it.'

Stephen is stoned to Death   As they listened to these words, they became 54 infuriated and gnashed their teeth at him.   But, 55 full of the Holy Spirit and looking up to heaven, Stephen saw the glory of God, and Jesus standing at God's right hand.

' I can see heaven wide open,' he said, ' and the Son of 56 Man standing at God's right hand.'

Upon this, with a loud outcry they stopped their ears, 57 rushed upon Stephen in a body, dragged him out of the city, 58 and stoned him, the witnesses throwing off their outer garments and giving them into the care of a young man called Saul.   So they stoned Stephen, while he prayed, 59

' Lord Jesus, receive my spirit.'

Then, rising on his knees, he cried aloud, 60

' Lord, do not reckon this sin against them.'

And with these words he fell asleep.   And Saul fully 1 **8** approved of his murder.

Believers persecuted and scattered   That day a great persecution broke out against the Church in Jerusalem, and all except the Apostles were scattered throughout Judaea and Samaria.   A party of devout men buried 2

---

53. *Given through*] Lit. ' as ordinances of.' Cf. Gal. iii. 19.
55. *Stephen*] Lit. ' he.'
56. *I can see*] Lit. ' I see.'
59. *While he prayed*] Lit. ' calling on ' (the Lord).
Lord Jesus, receive my spirit] Cf. ' Father, into Thy hands I entrust my spirit ' (Luke xxiii. 46).
60. *Lord, do not reckon, &c.*] Cf. ' Father, forgive them ' (Luke xxiii. 34) ; and contrast ' Lord, look on it, and require it ' (2 Chron. xxiv. 22).

Stephen, and made loud lamentation over him. But Saul 3
cruelly harassed the Church. He went into house after
house, and, dragging off both men and women, threw them
into prison.

The Church in Judaea and Samaria

Philip's Preaching and Miracles So those who were scattered abroad went 4
from place to place spreading the gospel of
God's word; while Philip went down to the 5
city of Samaria and proclaimed Christ there.
Crowds of people with one accord gave attention to what 6
they heard from him, listening, and witnessing the signs
which he wrought. For with a loud cry foul spirits came out 7
of many possessed by them, and many paralytics and lame
persons were restored to health. And there was great joy 8
in that city.

Simon the Magian Now for some time past there had been a man 9
named Simon living there, who had been prac-
tising magic and astonishing the Samaritans,
pretending that he was more than human. To him people 10
of all classes paid attention, declaring,

'This man is the Power of God, known as the Great
Power.'

His influence over them arose because he had, for a long 11
time, bewildered them by his sorceries. But when Philip 12
began to tell the gospel about the Kingdom of God
and the Name of Jesus Christ, and they embraced the
faith, they were baptized, men and women alike. Simon 13
himself also believed, and after being baptized remained in
close attendance on Philip, and was full of amazement at
seeing such signs and such great miracles performed.

Peter and John visit Samaria When the Apostles in Jerusalem heard that 14
the Samaritans had accepted God's word, they
sent Peter and John to visit them. They, 15
when they came down, prayed for them that they might
receive the Holy Spirit. For He had not as yet fallen upon 16
any of them: they had only been baptized into the name of
the Lord Jesus. Then the Apostles laid their hands upon 17
them, and they received the Holy Spirit.

14. *John*] Not hereafter mentioned in this book.

The Magian is sternly rebuked When, however, Simon saw that it was 18 through the laying on of the Apostles' hands that the Spirit was bestowed, he offered them money.

' Give me too,' he said, ' that power, so that every one 19 on whom I place my hands will receive the Holy Spirit.'

' Perish your money and yourself,' replied Peter, ' because 20 you have imagined that you can obtain God's free gift with money ! No part or lot have you in this matter, for your 21 heart is not right in God's sight. Repent, therefore, of this 22 wickedness of yours, and pray to the Lord, in the hope that the purpose which is in your heart may perhaps be forgiven you. For I perceive that you have fallen into the gall of 23 bitterness and the bondage of iniquity.'

' Pray, both of you, to the Lord for me,' answered 24 Simon, ' that nothing of what you have said may come upon me.'

Philip and the pious Abyssinian So the Apostles, after giving a solemn charge 25 and delivering the Lord's word, travelled back to Jerusalem, making known the gospel also in many of the Samaritan villages. And an angel 26 of the Lord said to Philip,

' Rise and proceed south to the road that runs down from Jerusalem to Gaza, crossing the desert.'

Upon this he rose and went. Now, as it happened, an 27 Ethiopian eunuch who was in a position of high authority with Candace, queen of the Ethiopians, as her treasurer, had visited Jerusalem to worship there, and was now on his way 28 home ; and as he sat in his chariot he was reading the Prophet Isaiah. Then the Spirit said to Philip, 29

' Go and join that chariot.'

So Philip ran up, and heard the eunuch reading the 30 Prophet Isaiah.

' Do you understand what you are reading ? ' he asked.

' Why, how can I,' replied the eunuch, ' unless some 31 one explains it to me ? '

And he earnestly invited Philip to come up and sit with

26. *South*] Or, possibly, ' towards noon.'
Crossing the Desert] Or ' a town which is desert '; the reference in that case being to the more ancient of the two towns which bore the name of Gaza.
27. *As it happened*] Lit. ' behold.'

him. The passage of Scripture which he was reading was 32
this :

' LIKE A SHEEP HE WAS LED TO SLAUGHTER,
AND AS A LAMB BEFORE ITS SHEARER IS DUMB,
SO HE OPENED NOT HIS MOUTH.
IN HIS HUMILIATION JUSTICE WAS DENIED HIM. 33
WHO WILL MAKE KNOWN HIS POSTERITY ?
FOR HE IS DESTROYED FROM AMONG MEN '

(Isa. liii. 7, 8).

' Pray, of whom is the Prophet speaking ? ' inquired the 34
eunuch ; ' of himself or of some one else ? '

Then Philip began to speak, and, commencing with that 35
same portion of Scripture, told him the gospel about Jesus.

Philip baptizes him So they proceeded on their way till they came 36
to some water ; and the eunuch exclaimed,
' See, here is water ; what is there to prevent
my being baptized ? '

So he stopped the chariot ; and both of them—Philip and 38
the eunuch—went down into the water, and Philip baptized
him. But no sooner had they come up out of the water 39
than the Spirit of the Lord caught Philip away, and the
eunuch did not see him again. With a glad heart he
resumed his journey ; but Philip found himself at Azotus. 40
Then visiting town after town he everywhere made known
the gospel until he reached Caesarea.

Saul of Tarsus is suddenly converted Now Saul, whose every breath was a threat 1 **9**
of destruction for the disciples of the Lord,
went to the High Priest and begged from him 2
letters addressed to the synagogues in Damascus,
in order that if he found any who were of the Way there,
either men or women, he might bring them in chains to
Jerusalem. But on the journey, as he was getting near 3
Damascus, suddenly there flashed round him a light from
heaven ; and falling to the ground he heard a voice which 4
said to him,

' Saul, Saul, why are you persecuting Me ? '

33. *In His humiliation justice was denied Him*] Or ' By His humiliation His sentence
was removed.' The LXX. of the passage differs considerably from the Hebrew. Cf.
1 Pet. ii. 21-25.

35. *Began, &c.*] Lit. ' opened his mouth.'

36. v.L. adds verse 37 here. ' You may,' said Philip, ' if you believe with all
your heart.' ' I believe,' he replied, ' that Jesus Christ is the Son of God.' The
evidence is decisive for the omission.

4. *Saul, Saul*] Notice the impressiveness gained, as so often in Hebrew, by the
repetition of the word. Cf. ' Abraham, Abraham ' (Gen. xxii. 11) ; ' Babylon has

'Who art thou, Lord?' he asked. 5

'I am Jesus, whom you are persecuting,' was the reply. 'But rise and go to the city, and you will be told what you 6 are to do.'

Meanwhile the men who travelled with Saul were standing 7 dumb with amazement, hearing a sound, but seeing no one. Then he rose from the ground, but when he had opened his 8 eyes, he could not see, and they led him by the arm and brought him to Damascus. And till the third day he 9 remained without sight, and did not eat or drink anything.

Now in Damascus there was a disciple of the name of 10 Ananias. The Lord spoke to him in a vision, saying,

'Ananias!'

'I am here, Lord,' he answered.

'Rise,' said the Lord, 'and go to Straight Street, and 11 inquire at the house of Judas for a man called Saul, from Tarsus, for see, he is praying. He has seen a man called 12 Ananias come and lay his hands upon him so that he may recover his sight.'

'Lord,' answered Ananias, 'I have heard about that man 13 from many, and about the great mischief he has done to Thy saints in Jerusalem; and here he is authorized by the 14 High Priests to arrest all who call upon Thy name.'

'Go,' replied the Lord; 'he is a chosen instrument of 15 Mine to carry My name to the Gentiles and to kings and to the sons of Israel. For I will let him know the great 16 sufferings which he must pass through for My sake.'

So Ananias went and entered the house; and, laying his 17 hands upon Saul, said,

'Saul, brother, the Lord—even Jesus who appeared to you on your journey—has sent me, that you may recover your sight and be filled with the Holy Spirit.'

Instantly there dropped from his eyes what seemed to be 18 scales, and he could see once more. Upon this he rose and received baptism; after which he took food and regained 19 his strength.

fallen, has fallen' (Rev. xiv. 8; xviii. 2); 'Crucify, crucify him' (Luke xxiii. 21): 'O Jerusalem, Jerusalem' (Luke xiii. 34); 'Sir, Sir' (Matt. xxv. 11); 'Martha, Martha' (Luke x. 41); 'Rabbi, Rabbi' (Luke viii. 24); 'Moses, Moses' (Exod. iii. 4); 'My God, my God' (Matt. xxvii. 46); 'Samuel, Samuel' (1 Sam. iii. 10); 'Simon, Simon' (Luke xxii. 31).

6. *But rise*] v.L. 'You are finding it painful to kick against the ox-goad. And he, trembling and amazed, said, Lord, what dost thou wish me to do? And the Lord said to him, Rise'; an addition from xxvi. 14.

Then he remained some little time with the
He preaches at Damascus disciples in Damascus. And in the synagogues 20
he began at once to proclaim Jesus as the Son
of God ; and his hearers were all amazed, and began to ask 21
one another,

' Is not this the man who in Jerusalem made havoc of
those who called upon that Name, and came here on purpose
to carry them off in chains to the High Priests ? '

Saul, however, gained power more and more, and as for 22
the Jews living in Damascus, he confounded them with his
proofs that Jesus is the Christ.

At length the Jews plotted to kill Saul ; but 23, 24
A Plot to kill Saul information of their intention was given to him.
They even watched the gates, day and night, in
order to murder him ; but his disciples took him by 25
night and let him down through the wall, lowering him
in a basket.

So he came to Jerusalem and made several 26
He goes to Jerusalem, Caesarea, and Tarsus attempts to associate with the disciples, but they
were all afraid of him, being in doubt as to
whether he was a disciple. Barnabas, however, 27
came to his assistance. He brought Saul to the Apostles,
and related to them how, on his journey, he had seen the
Lord, and that the Lord had spoken to him, and how in
Damascus he had fearlessly taught in the name of Jesus.
Henceforth Saul was one of them, going in and out of the 28
city, and speaking fearlessly in the name of the Lord. 29
And he often talked with the Hellenists and had discussions
with them. But they tried to take his life. On learning 30
this, the brethren brought him down to Caesarea, and then
sent him by sea to Tarsus.

The Church greatly prospers The Church, however, throughout the whole 31
of Judaea, Galilee, and Samaria, had peace and
was built up ; and grew in numbers, living
in the fear of the Lord and in the encouragement of the
Holy Spirit.

Peter cures Aeneas at Lydda Now Peter, as he went to town after town, 32
came down also to the saints at Lydda. There 33
he found a man of the name of Aeneas, who

25. *Through the wall*] *i.e.* ' through an opening in the wall.' Cf. 2 Cor. xi. 33.
30. *Sent him by sea*] Lit. ' sent him out.' He would disembark at Seleuceia, go up
to Antioch, and then proceed by land to Tarsus.
31. *Living*] Lit. ' walking.'

for eight years had kept his bed, being paralysed. Peter 34
said to him,

'Aeneas, Jesus Christ cures you. Rise and make your
own bed.'

He at once rose to his feet. And all the people of Lydda 35
and Sharon saw him ; and they turned to the Lord.

At Joppa he Among the disciples at Joppa was a woman 36
brings back called Tabitha, or, as the name may be trans-
Dorcas to lated, ' Dorcas.' Her life was full of the good
Life and charitable actions which she was constantly
doing. But it happened, just at that time, that she was 37
taken ill and died. After washing her body they laid it out
in a room upstairs. Lydda, however, being near Joppa, the 38
disciples, who had heard that Peter was at Lydda, sent two
men to him with an urgent request that he would come over
to them without delay. So Peter rose and went with them. 39
On his arrival they took him upstairs, and the widows all
stood by his side, weeping and showing him all the clothing
and cloaks that Dorcas used to make while she was still with
them. Peter, however, putting every one out of the room, 40
knelt down and prayed, and then turning to the body, he said,

' Tabitha, rise.'

Dorcas opened her eyes, and, seeing Peter, sat up. Then, 41
giving her his hand, he raised her to her feet and, calling to
him the saints and the widows, he gave her back to them
alive. This became known throughout Joppa, and many 42
believed in the Lord ; and Peter remained for a consider- 43
able time at Joppa, staying at the house of a man called
Simon, a tanner.

An Angel Now a Captain of the Italian regiment, 1 **10**
brings a named Cornelius, was quartered at Caesarea.
Message to He was religious and God-fearing—and so was 2
Cornelius every member of his household. He was also
liberal in his charities to the people, and continually offered
prayer to God. About three o'clock one afternoon he had a 3
vision, and distinctly saw an angel of God enter his house,
who called him by name, saying,

' Cornelius ! '

Looking steadily at him, and being much alarmed, he said, 4

---

1. The space devoted by Luke (x. 1–xi. 18) to the ' Cornelius episode ' clearly shows
the importance it had for him in the freeing of the new faith from the shackles of
Judaism. The prominence of Peter, not Paul, in this new departure is reflected
in xv. 7–11.

' What is it, Lord ? '

' Your prayers and charities,' he replied, ' have gone up 5
as a memorial before God. And now send to Joppa and
fetch Simon, surnamed Peter. He is lodging with one, 6
Simon, a tanner, who has a house close to the sea.'

So when the angel who had been speaking to him was 7
gone, Cornelius called two of his servants and a God-fearing
soldier who was in constant attendance on him, and, after 8
telling them everything, he sent them to Joppa.

Peter's Vision 'The next day, while they were still on their 9
journey and were getting near the town, about
noon Peter went up on the house-top to pray.
He had got very hungry and wished for some food ; but, 10
while they were preparing it, he fell into a trance. The sky 11
had opened to his view, and what seemed to be an enormous
sheet was descending, being let down to the earth by ropes at
the four corners. In it were all kinds of quadrupeds, 12
reptiles, and birds, and a voice came to him which said, 13

' Rise, Peter, kill and eat.'

' On no account, Lord,' he replied ; ' for I have never yet 14
eaten anything common and unclean.'

Again a second time a voice was heard which said, 15
' What God has cleansed, you must not regard as
common.'

This was said three times, and immediately the sheet was 16
drawn up out of sight.

Arrival of the Servants of Cornelius Now just while Peter was wondering as to 17
the meaning of the vision he had seen, the
men sent by Cornelius, having by inquiry found
out Simon's house, came to the door and called the servant, 18
and asked,

' Is Simon, surnamed Peter, staying here ? '

And Peter was still pondering over the vision, when the 19
Spirit said to him,

' Three men are now inquiring for you. Rise, go down, 20
and go with them without any misgivings ; for it is I who
have sent them to you.'

So Peter went down and said to the men, 21
' I am the man you are inquiring for. What is the
reason of your coming ? '

16. *Was said*] Lit. ' took place.'
Out of sight] Lit. ' into the sky.'

They said, 22

' Cornelius, a captain, an upright and God-fearing man, of whom the whole Jewish nation speaks well, has been divinely instructed by a holy angel to send for you to his house and listen to what you have to say.'

On hearing this, Peter invited them in, and gave them 23 a lodging.

Peter with Cornelius in Caesarea The next day he set out with them, some of the brethren from Joppa going with him, and 24 the day after that they reached Caesarea. There Cornelius was awaiting their arrival, and had invited all his kinsmen and intimate friends to be present. When Peter entered the house, Cornelius met him, and, 25 falling at his feet, did him homage. But Peter lifted 26 him up.

' Stand up,' he said ; ' I myself also am but a man.'

So Peter went in and conversed with him, and found a 27 large company assembled. He said to them, 28

' You are aware that a Jew is strictly forbidden to associate with a Gentile or visit him ; but God has taught me to call no one common or unclean. Hence, when sent 29 for, I came without raising any objection. I therefore ask why you sent for me.'

' Just at this hour, three days ago,' replied Cornelius, 30 ' I was offering afternoon prayer in my house, when suddenly a man in shining raiment stood in front of me, who 31 said,

' " Cornelius, your prayer has been heard, and your charities have been put on record before God. Send there- 32 fore to Joppa, and invite Simon, surnamed Peter, to come here. He is staying in the house of Simon, a tanner, close to the sea."

' Immediately, therefore, I sent to you, and I thank you 33 heartily for having come. That is why all of us are now assembled here in God's presence, to listen to what the Lord has commanded you to say.'

Peter's Speech Then Peter began to speak. 34 ' I clearly see,' he said, ' that God makes no distinctions between one man and another ; but 35 that in every nation those who fear Him and live good lives

33. *I thank you heartily*] Lit. ' you have done well.' Cf. Matt. xvii. 4, n. ; Phil. iv. 14.

34. *God makes no distinctions*] See Luke xx. 21, n.

are acceptable to Him. The word which He sent to the 36
sons of Israel, when He announced the gospel of peace
through Jesus Christ—He is Lord of all—that word you 37
cannot but know ; the story, I mean, which has spread
through the length and breadth of Judaea, beginning in
Galilee after the baptism which John proclaimed. It tells 38
how God anointed Jesus of Nazareth with the Holy Spirit and
with power, so that He went about doing good, and curing
all who were oppressed by the devil—for God was with Him.

' And we are witnesses to all that He did both in the 39
country of the Jews and in Jerusalem. But they even put
Him to death, by crucifixion. That same Jesus, God raised 40
to life on the third day, and permitted Him to appear, not 41
to all the people, but to witnesses—men previously chosen
by God—namely, to us, who ate and drank with Him after
He rose from the dead. And He has commanded us to 42
preach to the people and solemnly declare that this is He
who has been appointed by God to be the Judge of the living
and the dead. To Him all the Prophets bear witness that 43
through His name all who believe in Him receive the
forgiveness of their sins.'

Gentiles receive the Holy Spirit and Baptism While Peter was speaking these words, the 44
Holy Spirit fell on all who were listening to
the word. And all the Jewish believers who 45
had come with Peter were astonished that on
the Gentiles also the gift of the Holy Spirit was poured out.
For they heard them speaking in tongues and extolling the 46
majesty of God. Then Peter said,

' Can any one forbid the use of water for the baptism of 47
these people—men who have received the Holy Spirit just
as we did ? '

And he directed that they should be baptized in the 48
name of Jesus Christ. Then they begged him to remain
with them for a time.

Peter is censured. His Defence Now the Apostles, and the brethren in various 1 **1**
parts of Judaea, heard that the Gentiles also
had received God's word ; and, when Peter 2

(vv. 36, 37.) The Greek is difficult, and the translation can only be approximate.
In verse 36, v.l. omits 'which' ; then, 'He is Lord of all,' instead of being
parenthetical, becomes the central affirmation, and 'You know' introduces a fresh
sentence.
37. *You cannot but*] Not 'you yourselves.' Lit. an emphatic ' you ' ; you, *i.e.* as
men religiously disposed, living in Judaea, and at the headquarters of the Roman
provincial government ; you, perhaps, best of all men.
38. *Anointed*] Thus making Him the Anointed One, the Christ, the Messiah.

returned to Jerusalem, the party of circumcision found fault with him.

'You went into the houses of men who are not Jews,' 3 they said, ' and you ate with them.'

Peter, however, explained the whole matter to them from 4 the beginning.

' While I was in the town of Joppa, offering prayer,' he 5 said, ' in a trance I saw a vision. There descended what seemed to be an enormous sheet, being let down from the sky by ropes at the four corners, and it came close to me. Fixing my eyes on it, I examined it closely, and saw various 6 kinds of quadrupeds, wild beasts, reptiles, and birds. I also 7 heard a voice saying to me,

' " Rise, Peter, kill and eat."

' " On no account, Lord," I replied, " for nothing 8 common or unclean has ever gone into my mouth."

' But a voice answered, speaking a second time from the 9 sky,

' " What God has cleansed, you must not regard as common."

' This was said three times, and then everything was 10 drawn up again out of sight.

' Now at that very moment three men came to the house 11 where we were, having been sent from Caesarea to find me. And the Spirit told me to accompany them without any 12 misgivings. There also went with me these six brethren who are now present, and we entered the Centurion's house. Then he described to us how he had seen the angel standing 13 in his house and saying,

' " Send to Joppa and fetch Simon, surnamed Peter. He 14 will teach you truths by which you and all your household will be saved."

' And,' said Peter, ' no sooner had I begun to speak than 15 the Holy Spirit fell upon them, just as He fell upon us at the first. Then I remembered the Lord's words, how He 16 said,

' " John baptized with water, but you shall be baptized in the Holy Spirit."

' If therefore God gave them the same gift as He gave 17

---

12. *Without any misgivings*] Or possibly, ' making no distinction.' The verb is the same as in x. 20, and it is difficult to believe that a totally different sense can have been intended, in spite of the difference of voice (active instead of middle). It is more likely that (as in other instances) Peter's Greek was faulty.

us when we first believed in the Lord Jesus Christ, why, who was I to be able to thwart God ? '

On hearing this they were silenced, and they extolled the 18 goodness of God, and said,

' So then, to the Gentiles also God has given the repentance which leads to Life.'

The Church in Antioch

The first Gentile Church Those, however, who had been driven in 19 various directions by the persecution which broke out on account of Stephen, made their way to Phoenicia, Cyprus, and Antioch, delivering the word to none but Jews. But some of them were Cyprians 20 and Cyreneans, who, on coming to Antioch, spoke to the Greeks also and told them the gospel concerning the Lord Jesus. The power of the Lord was with them, and there 21 were a vast number who believed and turned to the Lord.

Barnabas sent to Antioch When tidings of this reached the ears of the 22 Church in Jerusalem, they sent Barnabas as far as Antioch. On arriving he was delighted to 23 see the grace of God ; and he encouraged them all to remain, with fixed resolve, faithful to the Lord. For he was 24 a good man, and was full of the Holy Spirit and of faith ; and the number of believers in the Lord greatly increased.

He brings Saul from Tarsus Then Barnabas paid a visit to Tarsus to try to 25 find Saul. He succeeded, and brought him to 26 Antioch ; and for a whole year they were the guests of the Church, and taught a large number of people. And it was in Antioch that the disciples first received the name of ' Christians.'

Relief for the poor Christians in Judaea At that time certain Prophets came down 27 from Jerusalem to Antioch, one of whom, named 28 Agabus, publicly predicted by the Spirit the speedy coming of a great famine throughout the

19. The story now returns on viii. 4 to trace a second line of missionary activity, consequent on Stephen's martyrdom.

20. *Greeks*] *i.e.* ' Gentiles ' ; a notable extension of the Christian mission, already foreshadowed by the conversion of the Ethiopian eunuch and of Cornelius, and culminating in the resolve of xiii. 46-48. The v.l. ' Hellenists,' *i.e.* Greek-speaking Jews, is strongly supported, but probably comes from ix. 29. These bolder spirits from Cyprus and Cyrene evidently take a revolutionary step, but there would be no novelty in preaching the gospel to Hellenists (cf. vi. 1 ; ix. 29) ; and the ' Jews ' of verse 19 would, of course, include Hellenistic Jews. The context requires as the only valid antithesis, Jews—Greeks. It is one of those various readings in which a reasonable probability must outweigh the textual evidence.

26. *Christians*] The word only occurs here and in xxvi. 28 and in 1 Pet. iv. 16.

world. (It came in the reign of Claudius.) So the disciples 29
put aside money, every one in proportion to his means, 30
for the relief of the brethren living in Judaea. This they
did, forwarding their contributions to the Elders by
Barnabas and Saul.

James beheaded. Now, about that time, King Herod laid 1 **12**
hands on certain members of the Church, to do
Peter imprisoned them violence ; and James, John's brother, he 2
beheaded. Finding that this gratified the Jews, 3
he proceeded to seize Peter also : these were the days of
Unleavened Bread. He had him arrested and lodged in 4
gaol, handing him over to the care of sixteen soldiers ; he
intended after the Passover to bring him out again to the
people. So Peter was kept in gaol ; but long and fervent 5
prayer was offered to God by the Church on his behalf.

An Angel rescues Peter Now when Herod was on the point of taking 6
him out of prison, that very night Peter was
asleep between two soldiers, bound with two
chains, and guards were on duty outside the door. Suddenly 7
an angel of the Lord stood by him, and a light shone in the
cell ; and, striking Peter on the side, he woke him and said,

' Rise quickly.'

And the chains dropped off his wrists.

' Fasten your girdle,' said the angel, ' and tie on your 8
sandals.'

He did so. Then the angel said,

' Throw your cloak round you, and follow me.'

So Peter went out, following him, yet could not believe 9
that what the angel was doing was real, but supposed that
he saw a vision. And passing the first guard and the 10
second, they came to the iron gate leading into the city.
This opened to them of itself ; and, going out, they passed
on through one street, and then suddenly the angel left him.
Peter coming to himself said, 11

' Now I know for certain that the Lord has sent His
angel and has rescued me from the power of Herod and
from all that the Jewish people were anticipating.'

The Surprise and Joy of the Church So, on reflection, he went to the house of Mary, 12
the mother of John surnamed Mark, where a
large number of people were assembled,

4. *Sixteen*] Lit. ' four parties of four each.'
10. *The first guard and the second*] Between ' going out ' and ' they passed ' Codex
Bezae inserts ' and going down the seven steps.'

praying. When he knocked at the door in the gate, a 13
maidservant named Rhoda came to answer the knock; and 14
recognizing Peter's voice, for very joy she did not open the
door, but ran in and told them that Peter was standing there.

'You are mad,' they said. 15

But she stoutly maintained that it was true.

'It is his guardian angel,' they said.

Meanwhile Peter went on knocking, until at last they 16
opened the door and saw that it was really he, and were filled
with amazement. But he motioned with his hand for 17
silence, and then described to them how the Lord had
brought him out of the prison.

'Tell all this to James and the brethren,' he added.

Then he left them, and went to another place.

The two Sentries executed When morning came, there was no little com- 18
motion among the soldiers as to what could
possibly have become of Peter. And when 19
Herod had had him searched for and could not find him,
after questioning the guards he ordered them away to
execution. He then went down from Judaea to Caesarea
and remained there.

Herod's dreadful Death Now the people of Tyre and Sidon had 20
incurred Herod's violent displeasure. So they
sent a large deputation to wait on him; and
having secured the good will of Blastus, his treasurer, they
begged the king to be friendly with them again, because
their country was dependent on his for its food supply. So, 21
on an appointed day, Herod, having arrayed himself in royal
robes, took his seat on the tribunal, and was haranguing
them; and the assembled people raised a shout, 22

'It is the voice of a god, and not of a man!'

Instantly an angel of the Lord struck him, because he 23
had not given the glory to God; and being eaten up by
worms, he died.

Barnabas and Saul return to Antioch But God's word prospered and multiplied. 24
And Barnabas and Saul returned from Jeru- 25
salem, having discharged their mission, and
they brought with them John, surnamed Mark.

13. *Rhoda*] Or 'Rose'; a feminine form (as alone suitable for a woman's name) of the neuter noun *rhodon*, a rose. Cf. Matt. xvi. 18, n.
15. *Guardian angel*] Or 'spirit.' Lit. 'angel.'
20. *To be friendly with them again*] He was hostile in commercial matters.
23. Josephus states that Herod died after five days of agony (*Antiquities*, xix. 8, 2).
25. *From Jerusalem*] *i.e.* 'to Antioch'; a curious various reading, strongly

They are ordained as Missionaries Now there were in Antioch, in the Church there — as Prophets and teachers — Barnabas, Symeon surnamed 'Niger,' Lucius the Cyrenean, Manaen (who was Herod the Tetrarch's foster-brother), and Saul. While they were worshipping the Lord and fasting, the Holy Spirit said, 1 2

' Set me apart Barnabas and Saul, for the work to which I have called them.'

So, after fasting and prayer and the laying on of hands, they let them go. 3

First Missionary Tour of Barnabas and Saul

Cyprus They therefore, being thus sent out by the Holy Spirit, went down to Seleuceia, and from there sailed to Cyprus. Having reached Salamis, they began to announce the word of God in the synagogues of the Jews. And they had John as their assistant. 4 5

Sergius Paulus and Elymas When they had gone through the whole length of the island as far as Paphos, they there met with a Jewish magician and false prophet, Bar-Jesus by name, who was a friend of the Proconsul Sergius Paulus. The Proconsul was a man of keen intelligence. He sent for Barnabas and Saul, and asked to be told the word of God. But Elymas (or ' the Magician,' for such is the meaning of the name) opposed them, and tried to prevent the Proconsul from accepting the faith. Then Saul, who is also called Paul, was filled with the Holy Spirit, and, fixing his eyes on Elymas, said, 6 7 8 9 10

' You who are full of every kind of craftiness and unscrupulous cunning—you son of the devil and foe to all that is right—will you never cease to misrepresent the straight paths of the Lord ? The Lord's hand is now upon you, 11

supported, is ' to Jerusalem,' a reading which may possibly mean, ' returned (to Antioch) having discharged their mission to Jerusalem.'

1. *In the Church*] Lit. ' throughout the Church ' (cf. xi. 1), an easily intelligible expression if we suppose the ' Church ' to signify the entire body of believers in the city, and that they were wont to meet for worship in private houses (xviii. 7) in distinct and scattered congregations, each probably with its own leader.

Who was Herod the Tetrarch's foster-brother] Or ' who had been Herod the Tetrarch's companion in his boyhood.'

6. *Bar-Jesus*] i.e. ' son of Joshua.'

8. *Elymas*] Either an Aramaic word meaning ' the wise man,' or an Aramaic word meaning ' the mighty man.'

9. *Saul, who is also called Paul*] Probably he had the two names from the first— Hebrew and Roman. Now, on his entrance on his world-wide mission to the Roman Empire, the Roman name fitly becomes prominent.

and you will be blind for a time and unable to see the light of day.'

Instantly there fell upon him a mist and a darkness, and, as he walked about, he begged people to lead him by the hand. Then the Proconsul, seeing what had happened, 12 believed, being struck with amazement at the teaching of the Lord.

Perga and the Pisidian Antioch From Paphos, Paul and his party put out to 13 sea and sailed to Perga in Pamphylia. John, however, left them and returned to Jerusalem. But they themselves, passing through from Perga, came to 14 Antioch in Pisidia.

Paul's great Speech to the Jews in Antioch Here, on the Sabbath day, they went into the synagogue and sat down. After the reading of 15 the Law and the Prophets, the Wardens of the synagogue sent word to them.

' Brethren,' they said, ' if you have anything encouraging to say to the people, speak.'

So Paul rose, and motioning with his hand for silence, 16 said,

' Israelites, and you others who fear God, pay attention to me. The God of this people of Israel chose our fore- 17 fathers, and made the people great during their stay in Egypt, until with wondrous power He brought them out from that land. For about forty years He fed them like a 18 nurse in the desert. Then, after overthrowing seven 19 nations in the land of Canaan, He divided that country among them as their inheritance for about four hundred and fifty years ; and afterwards He gave them judges down 20 to the time of the Prophet Samuel. Next they asked for a 21 king, and God gave them Saul the son of Kish, a Benjamite, who reigned forty years. After removing him, He raised up 22 David to be their king, to whom He also bore witness when He said,

' " I have found David the son of Jesse, a man I love, who will obey all My commands."

' It is from among David's descendants that God, in 23 fulfilment of His promise, has raised up a Saviour for Israel, even Jesus. Before the coming of Jesus, John had 24

17. *Wondrous power*] Lit. ' uplifted arm.'
18. *Fed them like a nurse*] v.l. ' bore with their manners.' The two Greek words differ only in a single letter.

proclaimed to all the people of Israel a baptism of repentance. But John, towards the end of his career, repeatedly asked 25 the people,

' " What do you suppose me to be ? I am not the Christ. But there is One coming after me whose sandal I am not worthy to unfasten."

' Brethren, descendants of the family of Abraham, and all 26 among you who fear God, to us has the word of this salva- tion been sent. For the people of Jerusalem and their 27 rulers, by the judgement they pronounced on Jesus, have actually fulfilled the predictions of the Prophets which are read Sabbath after Sabbath, through ignorance of those predictions and of Him. Without having found Him 28 guilty of any capital offence they urged Pilate to have Him put to death ; and when they had carried out everything 29 which had been written about Him, they took Him down from the cross and laid Him in a tomb.

' But God raised Him from the dead.   And, after a few 30, 31 days, He appeared to the people who had gone up with Him from Galilee to Jerusalem and are now witnesses con- cerning Him to the Jews.   And we bring you the Good 32 News about the promise made to our forefathers, that God 33 has amply fulfilled it to our children in raising up Jesus ; as it is also written in the second Psalm, " THOU ART MY SON : TO-DAY I HAVE BECOME THY FATHER " (Ps. ii. 7).   And as to 34 His having raised Him from among the dead, never again to be in the position of one soon to return to decay, He speaks thus : " I WILL GIVE YOU THE HOLY AND TRUST- WORTHY PROMISES MADE TO DAVID " (Isa. lv. 3).   Because in 35 another Psalm also He says, " THOU WILT NOT GIVE UP THY HOLY ONE TO UNDERGO DECAY " (Ps. xvi. 10).   For David, 36 after having been useful to his own generation in accordance with God's purpose, did fall asleep, was gathered to his forefathers, and did undergo decay.   But He whom God 37 raised to life underwent no decay.

' Understand therefore, brethren, that through this Jesus 38 forgiveness of sins is announced to you ; and in Him every 39 believer is absolved from all offences, from which you could

---

27. The Greek is difficult, and the translation tentative.
34. *I will give . . to David*] Lit. ' the trustworthy holy things of David.'   The Hebrew has ' the sure mercies of David.'
36. *After having been useful, &c.*] Or ' after having in his own lifetime served God's purpose.'

not be absolved under the Law of Moses.   Beware, then, 40
lest what is spoken in the Prophets should come true of
you : " BEHOLD, YOU DESPISERS, BE ASTONISHED AND PERISH, 41
BECAUSE I AM CARRYING ON A WORK IN YOUR TIME—A WORK
WHICH YOU WILL UTTERLY REFUSE TO BELIEVE, THOUGH IT
BE FULLY DECLARED TO YOU " ' (Hab. i. 5).

The People are deeply impressed   As Paul and Barnabas were leaving the syna- 42
gogue, the people earnestly begged to have all
this repeated to them on the following Sabbath.
And, when the congregation had broken up, many of the 43
Jews and of the devout converts from heathenism continued
with Paul and Barnabas, who talked to them and urged them
to hold fast to the grace of God.

But, being opposed, the Apostles turn to the Gentiles   On the next Sabbath almost the whole popu- 44
lation of the city came together to hear the word
of the Lord.   Seeing the crowds, the Jews, 45
filled with angry jealousy, opposed Paul's statements and abused him.   Then, throwing off all 46
reserve, Paul and Barnabas said,

' We were bound to proclaim the word of God to you first.
But since you spurn it and judge yourselves to be unworthy
of eternal Life—well, we turn to the Gentiles.   For such is 47
the Lord's command to us.

' " I HAVE PLACED THEE AS A LIGHT TO THE GENTILES, IN
ORDER THAT THOU MAYEST BE A SAVIOUR TO THE ENDS OF THE
EARTH " ' (Isa. xlix. 6).

The Gentiles listened with delight and extolled the Lord's 48
word ; and all who were predestined to eternal Life believed.

Persecution drives them to Iconium   So the word of the Lord spread through the 49
whole district.   But the Jews influenced the 50
gentlewomen of rank who worshipped with them,
and also the leading men in the city, and stirred up persecution against Paul and Barnabas and drove them out of the
district.   The Apostles shook off the dust from their feet as 51
a protest against them and came to Iconium ; and as for the 52
disciples, they were more and more filled with joy and with
the Holy Spirit.

There they escape from the Jews into Lycaonia   At Iconium the Apostles went together to the 1 **1**
Jewish synagogue and preached, with the result
that a great number both of Jews and Greeks
believed.   But the Jews who had refused 2

42. *Paul and Barnabas were*] Or ' the congregation was.'   v.L. ' the Jews were.'

obedience stirred up the Gentiles and embittered their minds against the brethren. For a considerable time, 3 however, Paul and Barnabas remained there, speaking freely and relying on the Lord, while He bore witness to the word of His grace by permitting signs and marvels to be done by them. At length the people of the city split into parties, 4 some siding with the Jews and some with the Apostles. And when a hostile movement was made by both Gentiles 5 and Jews, with the sanction of their magistrates, to maltreat and stone them, the Apostles, having become aware of it, 6 made their escape into the Lycaonian towns of Lystra and Derbe, and the neighbouring country. And there they 7 continued to preach the gospel.

Now a man who had no power in his feet used 8
A lame Man to sit in the streets of Lystra : he had been
cured at
Lystra. The lame from his birth and had never walked.
Result This man heard Paul speaking. And the 9 Apostle, looking steadily at him and perceiving that he had faith to be cured, said in a loud voice, 10

'Stand upright upon your feet !'

So he sprang up and began to walk about. Then the 11 crowds, seeing what Paul had done, rent the air with their shouts in the Lycaonian language, saying,

'The gods have come down to us in the form of men.'

They called Barnabas 'Zeus,' and Paul, as being the 12 principal speaker, 'Hermes.' And the priest of Zeus—the 13 temple of Zeus being at the entrance to the city—brought bullocks and garlands to the gates, and in company with the crowd was intending to offer sacrifices to them. But 14 the Apostles, Barnabas and Paul, heard of it ; and tearing their clothes they rushed out into the middle of the crowd, exclaiming,

'Sirs, why are you doing all this ? We also are but 15 men, with natures kindred to your own ; and we bring you the good news that you are to turn from these unreal things, to worship the living God, the Creator of earth and sky and sea and of everything that is in them. In times gone by He 16 allowed all the nations to go their own ways ; and yet by His 17 beneficence He has not left His existence unattested, in that

---

3. Possibly this verse should follow verse 1, . . 'believed. So Paul and Barnabas,' &c.

He sends you rain from heaven and fruitful seasons, satis-
fying your hearts with food and gladness.'

Even with words like these they had difficulty in prevent- 18
ing the thronging crowd from offering sacrifices to them.

Paul stoned. The Apostles retrace their Steps But now a party of Jews came from Antioch 19
and Iconium, and, having won over the crowd,
they stoned Paul, and dragged him out of the
town, believing him to be dead. When, how- 20
ever, the disciples had collected round him, he rose and
went back into the town. The next day he went with
Barnabas to Derbe; and, after proclaiming the gospel to the 21
people there and gaining a large number of converts, they
retraced their steps to Lystra, Iconium, and Antioch.
Everywhere they strengthened the disciples by encouraging 22
them to hold fast to the faith, and warned them saying,

' It is through many afflictions that we must make our
way into the Kingdom of God.'

And in every Church, after prayer and fasting, they 23
selected Elders by show of hands, and commended them
to the Lord on whom their faith rested.

They make a Stay in Antioch Then passing through Pisidia they came into 24
Pamphylia; and after telling the word at 25
Perga they came down to Attaleia. Thence 26
they sailed to Antioch, where they had previously been
commended to the grace of God in connexion with the
work which they had now completed. Upon their arrival 27
they called the Church together and proceeded to report
in detail all that God, working with them, had done, and
how He had opened for the Gentiles the door of faith.
And they remained a considerable time in Antioch with 28
the disciples.

Gentile Christians and the Law of Moses But certain persons who had come down 1 **15**
from Judaea tried to convince the brethren,
saying,
' Unless you are circumcised in accordance
with the Mosaic custom, you cannot be saved.'

Between these new-comers and Paul and Barnabas there 2
was no little disagreement and controversy, until at last it
was decided that Paul and Barnabas and some other
brethren should go up to consult the Apostles and Elders
in Jerusalem on this matter. So they set out, being accom- 3
panied for a short distance by the Church; and as they

passed through Phoenicia and Samaria, they told the whole story of the conversion of the Gentiles and inspired all the brethren with great joy.

Upon their arrival in Jerusalem they were cordially 4 received by the Church, the Apostles, and the Elders ; and they reported all that God, working with them, had done. But certain men who belonged to the sect of the Pharisees 5 and were now believers stood up in the assembly and said,

' Gentile believers ought to be circumcised and be ordered to keep the Law of Moses.'

A Council in Jerusalem. Peter's Speech Then the Apostles and Elders met to consider 6 the matter ; and after there had been a long 7 discussion Peter rose.

' It is within your own knowledge,' he said, ' that God originally made choice among you that from my lips the Gentiles were to hear the word of the gospel, and believe. And God, who knows all hearts, gave His testi- 8 mony in their favour by bestowing the Holy Spirit on them just as He did on us ; and He made no difference between 9 us and them, in that He cleansed their hearts by their faith. Now, therefore, why provoke God, by laying on the necks of 10 these disciples a yoke which neither our fathers nor we have been able to bear ? On the contrary, we believe that it is 11 by the grace of the Lord Jesus that we, as well as they, shall be saved.'

A Statement by Paul and Barnabas Then the whole assembly remained silent 12 while they listened to the statement made by Paul and Barnabas as to all the signs and marvels that God had done among the Gentiles by means of them.

The Advice of James When they had finished speaking, James said, 13 ' Brethren, listen to me. Symeon has related 14 how God first looked graciously on the nations to take from among them a people to be called by His name. And this is in harmony with the language of the Prophets, 15 which says :

' " ' AFTERWARDS I WILL RETURN, AND WILL REBUILD 16 DAVID'S FALLEN TENT.

ITS RUINS I WILL REBUILD, AND I WILL SET IT UP AGAIN ;

THAT THE REST OF MANKIND MAY SEEK AFTER THE 17 LORD—

EVEN ALL THE NATIONS WHICH ARE CALLED BY MY NAME,'

SAYS THE LORD, WHO HAS BEEN MAKING THESE THINGS 18
KNOWN FROM AGES LONG PAST " (Amos ix. 11, 12).

' My judgement, therefore, is against inflicting un- 19
expected vexation on those of the Gentiles who are turning
to God. Yet let us send them written instructions to 20
abstain from things polluted by connexion with idolatry,
from fornication, from flesh of strangled animals, and from
blood. For Moses from the earliest times has had his 21
preachers in every town, being read, as he is, Sabbath after
Sabbath, in the various synagogues.'

A Letter to   Thereupon it was decided by the Apostles and 22
the Gentile   Elders, with the approval of the whole Church,
Churches   to choose persons from among themselves and
send them to Antioch, with Paul and Barnabas. Judas,
called Barsabbas, and Silas, leading men among the brethren,
were selected, and they took with them the following 23
letter :

' The Apostles and the Elders of the brotherhood send
greeting to the Gentile brethren throughout Antioch, Syria,
and Cilicia. As we have been informed that certain persons 24
who have gone from our midst have disturbed you by their
teaching and have unsettled your minds, without having
received any such instructions from us, we have unani- 25
mously decided to select certain men and send them to you
in company with our beloved friends Barnabas and Paul,
who have endangered their lives for the sake of our Lord 26
Jesus Christ. We have therefore sent Judas and Silas, who 27
are themselves bringing you the same message by word of
mouth. For it has seemed good to the Holy Spirit and to 28
us to lay upon you no burden heavier than these necessary
requirements : you must abstain from things sacrificed to 29
idols, from blood, from flesh of strangled animals, and from

20. By comparing with verse 29, the Apostolic Decree appears to be a triple food
regulation, joined with a moral injunction against impurity. The enforcement of
Jewish food restrictions upon Gentile converts creates an obvious difficulty. Perhaps
it is a compromise rather than a Decree, rejecting the rigour of the demand of verse
5, but advising certain concessions to Jewish custom in the interests of peace. The
law as to abstinence from blood is found in Lev. xvii. 10–14, where there is no
express reference to animals slain by strangulation. The avoidance of meat from
an animal which had been offered in sacrifice to heathen gods was a very practical
problem for a Christian in a heathen city. It was raised by the Christians in Corinth,
and dealt with by Paul with a noble blend of freedom and consideration in 1 Cor.
viii.–x, with no reference to any Apostolic Decree. There is some evidence, both in
verses 20 and 29, for the omission of ' things strangled,' as well as for the addition of
a negative form of the Golden Rule, ' Do not to others what you would not have
done to yourselves.' Some interpreters, accepting the shortened text, regard
the Decree as a three-fold *moral* prohibition, of idolatry, bloodshed (murder), and
fornication.

fornication. Keep yourselves clear of these things, and it
will be well with you. Farewell.'

They, therefore, having been formally sent, came down 30
to Antioch, where they called together the whole assembly
and delivered the letter. The people read it, and were 31
delighted with the comfort it brought them. And Judas 32
and Silas, being themselves also prophets, gave them a long
and encouraging talk, and strengthened them in the faith.
After spending some time there they received an affectionate 33
farewell from the brethren to return to those who had sent
them. But Paul and Barnabas remained in Antioch, 35
teaching and, in company with many others, telling the
gospel of the word of the Lord.

St. Paul's Second Missionary Tour

Silas takes
the Place of
Barnabas

After a while Paul said to Barnabas, 36
' Come, let us return and visit the brethren in
the various towns in which we have made known
the Lord's word—to see how they fare.'

Now Barnabas was bent on taking with them John, 37
whose other name was Mark, while Paul deemed it undesir- 38
able to have as their companion one who had deserted
them in Pamphylia and had not gone on with them to
the work. So there arose a sharp altercation between them, 39
which resulted in their parting from one another, Barnabas
taking Mark and setting sail for Cyprus. But Paul chose 40
Silas, and set out, commended by the brethren to the grace
of the Lord ; and he passed through Syria and Cilicia, 41
strengthening the Churches.

Timothy
joins them
at Lystra

He also came to Derbe and to Lystra. At 1 **16**
Lystra he found a disciple, Timothy by name—
the son of a Christian Jewess, but of a Greek
father. Timothy was well spoken of by the brethren at 2
Lystra and Iconium, and Paul, desiring that he should 3
accompany him on his journey, had him circumcised on
account of the Jews in those parts, for they all knew that his
father was a Greek.

31. *Read*] No doubt, as was the custom in the assemblies of the people in Athens,
some authorised individual read the document aloud, while the rest of the people
present listened. Cf. Col. iv. 16 ; 1 Thess. v. 27. The public reading and interchange of Paul's letters are the first steps towards the Canon of his Epistles.

33. v.L. inserts verse 34, ' But Silas thought proper to remain there still.' (Probably an insertion due to verse 40.)

As they journeyed on from town to town, they handed 4
to the brethren for their observance the decisions which had
been arrived at by the Apostles and Elders in Jerusalem.
So the Churches were strengthened in faith, and grew in 5
numbers from day to day.

Phrygia,   Then Paul and his companions passed 6
Galatia,   through Phrygia and Galatia, having been
Troas   forbidden by the Holy Spirit to tell the word in
the province of Asia. When they reached the frontier of 7
Mysia, they were about to enter Bithynia, but the Spirit of
Jesus would not permit this. So, passing along Mysia, 8
they came to Troas.

An Appeal   And here, one night, Paul saw a vision. 9
from   There stood a Macedonian entreating him and
Macedonia   saying,

' Come over to Macedonia and help us.'

So when he had seen the vision, we immediately sought 10
to pass to Macedonia, confidently inferring that God had
called us to preach the gospel to the people there.

          Accordingly we put out to sea from Troas, 11
Arrival in   and ran a straight course to Samothrace. The
Philippi   next day we came to Neapolis; and thence to 12
Philippi, which is a city in Macedonia, the first in its district,
and a Roman colony. And there we stayed some little time.

          On the Sabbath we went beyond the city gate 13
Conversion   to the riverside, where we had reason to believe
of Lydia   that there was a place for prayer ; and sitting
down we talked with the women who had come together.
Among our hearers was one named Lydia, a dealer in purple. 14
She belonged to the city of Thyatira, and was a worshipper
of God. The Lord opened her heart, so that she gave
attention to what Paul was saying. When she and her 15
household had been baptized, she urged us, saying,

---

6. *Phrygia and Galatia*] Lit. ' the Phrygian and Galatian land.' Apparently *one*
district, which might be styled both Phrygian and Galatian. The only other reference
to Galatia in Acts is at xviii. 23, where the phrase is varied, and *two* districts are
clearly indicated. The question where the churches of Galatia (Gal. i. 3) were
situated, in ethnological Galatia in the North, or in the Southern part of the political
Roman Province of Galatia, including Antioch, Iconium, Lystra, Derbe, is a matter
of still unsettled controversy.

8. *Passing along*] Or ' passing by,' ' neglecting ' so far as their work of preaching
was concerned.

10. *We*] The author now joins Paul (see Introduction).

12. *The first*] In what sense, whether in geographical position or in importance, is
uncertain.

13. *Where, &c.*] v.l. ' where prayer was accustomed to be offered.' So A.V.

' If in your judgement I am a believer in the Lord, come and stay at my house.'

And she made us go there.

One day, as we were on our way to the place 16 **Cure of a Slave Girl** of prayer, a slave girl met us who had a spirit of divination and was accustomed to bring her owners large profits by telling fortunes. She kept following 17 close behind Paul and the rest of us, crying aloud,

' These men are the servants of the Most High God, and are proclaiming to you the way of salvation.'

This she persisted in for a considerable time, until Paul 18 in vexation turned round and said to the spirit,

' I command you in the name of Jesus Christ to depart from her.'

And it departed immediately.

Paul and Silas arrested But when her owners saw that their hope of 19 gain had also departed, they seized Paul and Silas and dragged them off to the magistrates in the Forum. Bringing them before the praetors, they said, 20 ' These men are creating a great disturbance in our city. They are Jews, and are teaching customs which we, as 21 Romans, are not permitted to adopt or practise.'

The crowd, too, joined in the outcry against them : and 22 the praetors ordered them to be stripped and beaten with rods ; and, after severely flogging them, they threw them 23 into gaol and bade the gaoler keep them safely. Having 24 received an order like that, he lodged them in the inner prison, and secured their feet in the stocks.

Conversion of their Gaoler About midnight Paul and Silas were praying 25 and singing hymns to God, and the prisoners were listening to them, when suddenly there 26 was such a violent shock of earthquake that the prison shook to its foundations. Instantly the doors all flew open, and the chains fell off every prisoner. Starting up from 27 sleep and seeing the doors of the gaol wide open, the gaoler drew his sword and was on the point of killing himself, supposing that the prisoners had escaped. But Paul shouted 28 loudly to him, saying,

' Do yourself no injury : we are all here.'

16. *Divination*] Lit. ' ventriloquism.'

19. *Magistrates*] Their proper title was ' duumviri,' but they often assumed the higher rank of praetors, to which they had no right, although Luke concedes it to them five times in this chapter.

Then, calling for lights, he sprang in and fell trembling 29
at the feet of Paul and Silas ; and, bringing them out of the 30
prison, he exclaimed,

' O sirs, what must I do to be saved ? '

' Believe on the Lord Jesus,' they replied, ' and both you 31
and your household will be saved.'

And they told the Lord's word to him as well as to 32
all who were in his house. Then he took them, even at 33
that time of night, washed their wounds, and he and all
his household were immediately baptized ; and bringing 34
the Apostles up into his house, he spread a meal for them,
and was filled with gladness, with his whole household, his
faith resting on God.

The two Apostles released In the morning the praetors sent their lictors 35
with the order,

' Release those men.'

So the gaoler brought Paul word, saying, 36

' The praetors have sent orders for you to be released.
Now therefore you can go, and proceed on your way in
peace.'

But Paul said to them, 37

' After cruelly beating us in public, without trial, Roman
citizens though we are, they have thrown us into prison,
and are they now going to send us away privately ? No,
indeed ! Let them come in person and fetch us out.'

This answer the lictors took back to the praetors, who 38
were alarmed when they were told that Paul and Silas were
Roman citizens. Accordingly they came and apologized 39
to them ; and, bringing them out, asked them to leave the
city. Then Paul and Silas, having come out of the prison, 40
went to Lydia's house ; and, after seeing the brethren and
encouraging them, they left Philippi.

Paul preaches to the Jews in Thessalonica Then, passing through Amphipolis and Apol- 1 17
lonia, they went to Thessalonica. Here there
was a synagogue of the Jews. Paul—following 2
his usual custom—betook himself to it, and for
three successive Sabbaths reasoned with them from the
Scriptures, which he clearly explained, pointing out that it 3

32. *The Lord's*] v.l. ' God's.'
37. *No, indeed !*] Or ' Why, no ! '
39. *Apologized to*] Lit. ' entreated.'
2. *Three successive Sabbaths*] 1 Thess. seems to indicate that these three weeks'
preaching to the Jews were followed by a longer and highly successful ministry to the
Greek population of the city.

had been necessary for the Christ to suffer and rise again from the dead, and insisting,

'The Jesus whom I am proclaiming to you is the Christ.'

Some of the people were won over, and attached them- 4 selves to Paul and Silas, including a great number of God-fearing Greeks and not a few prominent gentlewomen.

A serious Riot follows But the jealousy of the Jews was aroused, and, 5 calling to their aid some ill-conditioned and idle fellows, they got together a riotous mob and filled the city with uproar. They then attacked the house of Jason and searched for Paul and Silas, to bring them out before the assembly of the people. But, failing to find them, 6 they dragged Jason and some of the other brethren before the magistrates of the city, loudly accusing them.

'These men,' they said, 'who have raised a tumult throughout the Empire, have come here also. Jason has 7 received them into his house; and they all set Caesar's authority at defiance, declaring that there is another King—one called Jesus.'

Great was the excitement among the crowd, and among 8 the magistrates of the city, when they heard these charges. They required Jason and the rest to find substantial bail, 9 and after that they let them go.

Beroea The brethren at once sent Paul and Silas 10 away by night to Beroea, and they, on their arrival, went to the synagogue of the Jews. The Jews at 11 Beroea were of a nobler disposition than those in Thessalonica, for they very readily received the word, and day after day searched the Scriptures to see whether it was as Paul stated. Many of them therefore became believers, and 12 so did not a few of the Greeks—gentlewomen of good position, and men.

Athens As soon, however, as the Jews of Thessalonica 13 learnt that God's word had been proclaimed by Paul at Beroea, they came there also, and incited the mob to a riot. Then the brethren promptly sent Paul down to 14 the sea-coast, but Silas and Timothy remained behind.

---

6. *Magistrates*] Lit. 'politarchs.' It was only in Thessalonica that the magistrates of the town were so called. The word is found in an inscription on an arch from Thessalonica, now in the British Museum.

7. *One called Jesus*] Lit. simply 'Jesus.'

9. *Bail*] Perhaps Jason and the rest were bound over to prevent any revisit from Paul. An absolute barrier, to which reference may perhaps be found in the 'Satan hindered us' of 1 Thess. ii. 18.

Those who were escorting Paul went with him as far as 15
Athens, and then left him, taking a message from him to
Silas and Timothy to join him as speedily as possible.

Paul argues with Jews and Greeks While Paul was waiting for them in Athens, 16
his spirit was stirred within him when he
noticed that the city was full of idols. So he 17
had discussions in the synagogue with the Jews and the
other worshippers, and in the market place, day after day,
with those whom he happened to meet there. A few of the 18
Epicurean and Stoic philosophers also encountered him.
Some of them asked,

' What has this beggarly babbler to say ? '

' His business,' said others, ' seems to be to cry up some
foreign gods.'

This was because he had been telling the gospel of Jesus
and the Resurrection. Then they took him and brought 19
him up to the Areopagus, asking him,

' May we be told what this new teaching of yours is ?
For the things you are saying sound strange to us. We 20
should therefore like to be told exactly what they mean.'

(For all the Athenians and their foreign visitors used to 21
devote their whole leisure to telling or listening to the latest
new thing.)

Paul's Speech in the Areopagus So Paul, taking his stand in the middle of the 22
Areopagus, spoke as follows :
' Men of Athens, I perceive that you are in
every respect remarkably religious. For as I 23
passed along and observed your objects of worship, I found
also an altar bearing the inscription,

" TO AN UNKNOWN GOD."

' What, therefore, you in your ignorance revere, I now
proclaim to you. The God who made the universe and 24
everything in it—He, being Lord of heaven and earth,
does not dwell in sanctuaries built by men. Nor is He 25

16. Chap. xviii. 5 gives the impression that Silas and Timothy did not rejoin Paul
till he had gone on to Corinth. But from 1 Thess. iii. 2 we learn that Timothy at
least returned from Thessalonica to Athens.

18. *Beggarly babbler*] Lit. ' seed-picker.' Paul is compared by these ' philosophers '
to a little bird picking up seeds. He has gathered a few scraps of knowledge and
parades them as learning. Sir Wm. Ramsay suggests ' bounder.'

Resurrection] Greek ' Anastasis,' a word which some of them may have supposed to
be the name of a new goddess.

19. *The Areopagus*] The hill, or possibly the Court, that bore that name. At
any rate one member of that Court was among Paul's hearers ; verse 34.

ministered to by human hands, as though He needed anything; but He Himself gives to all men life and breath and
all things. He caused to spring from one forefather people 26
of every race, for them to live on the whole surface of the
earth, and marked out for them their appointed periods and
the limits of their settlements; that they might seek God, 27
if perhaps they could grope for Him and find Him. Yes,
though He is not far from any one of us. For it is in Him 28
we live and move and have our being; as in fact some of
your own poets have said, " For we are also His offspring."
Since then we are God's offspring, we ought not to imagine 29
that His nature resembles gold or silver or stone, sculptured
by the art and inventive faculty of man. Those times of 30
ignorance God viewed with indulgence. But now He
commands all men everywhere to repent, seeing that He 31
has appointed a day on which He will judge the world in
righteousness, in the person of a man whom He has destined
for this work, giving assurance of this to all mankind by
raising Him from the dead.'

Opposition
and
Sympathy

When they heard Paul speak of a resurrection 32
of dead men, some began to scoff. But others
said,

' We will hear you again on that subject.'

So Paul went away from them. A few, however, attached 33, 34
themselves to him and believed, among them being Diony-
sius a member of the Council, a woman named Damaris,
and some others.

Corinth.
Aquila and
Priscilla

After this he left Athens and came to Corinth. 1 **18**
Here he found a Jew, a native of Pontus, by 2
name Aquila. He and his wife Priscilla had
recently come from Italy because of Claudius's edict
expelling all the Jews from Rome. So Paul paid them a
visit; and because he was of the same trade—that of tent- 3
maker—he lodged with them and worked with them.
Sabbath after Sabbath, he preached in the synagogue and 4
tried to win over both Jews and Greeks.

Arrival of
Silas and
Timothy

Now at the time when Silas and Timothy 5
arrived from Macedonia, Paul was preaching
fervently, solemnly affirming to the Jews that

---

26. *From one forefather*] Or ' from one origin.' Lit. ' from one ' simply, as in the
R.V. v.L. ' from one blood.'
28. The quotation is from Aratus, a poet of Paul's native Cilicia. Almost the
same expression occurs in the Hymn to Zeus of Cleanthes.

the Christ was Jesus. But upon their opposing him with 6
abusive language, he shook his clothes by way of protest, and
said to them,

'Your blood be upon your own heads! I am not
responsible : in future I will go among the Gentiles.'

Eighteen   So he left the place and went to the house 7
Months' Stay of a person called Titius Justus, a worshipper
in Corinth of God, whose house was next door to the
synagogue. And Crispus, the ruler of the synagogue, 8
believed in the Lord, and so did all his household ; and
from time to time many of the Corinthians who heard Paul
believed and received baptism. And, in a vision by night, 9
the Lord said to Paul,

'Dismiss your fears : go on speaking, and do not be silent.
I am with you, and no one shall attack you to injure you ; 10
for I have very many people in this city.'

So Paul remained in Corinth for a year and six months, 11
teaching among them the word of God.

Paul is   But when Gallio became Proconsul of 12
brought   Greece, the Jews with one accord made a dead
before Gallio set at Paul, and brought him before the court.

'This man,' they said, ' is inducing people to offer wor- 13
ship to God in an unlawful manner.'

Now when Paul was about to begin his defence, Gallio 14
said to the Jews,

'If it had been some wrongful act or piece of cunning
knavery I might reasonably have listened to you Jews. But 15
since these are questions about words and names and
your Law, you yourselves must see to them. I refuse to be
a judge in such matters.'

So he drove them out of court. Then the people all set 16, 17
upon Sosthenes, the ruler of the synagogue, and beat
him severely in front of the court. Gallio did not concern
himself in the least about this.

Ephesus,   After remaining a considerable time longer 18
Caesarea, in Corinth, Paul took leave of the brethren and
Jerusalem, set sail for Syria ; and Priscilla and Aquila were
Antioch with him. He had shaved his head at Cenchreae,
because he was bound by a vow. They put in at Ephesus, 19
and there Paul left his companions behind. As for himself,

---

16. *People*] v.l. ' Greeks.'
18. *He*] Probably Paul, possibly Aquila.

he went to the synagogue and had a discussion with the Jews. When they asked him to remain longer he did not consent, 20 but took leave of them with the promise, 21

' I will return to you, God willing.'

So he set sail from Ephesus.

Landing at Caesarea, he went up to Jerusalem and greeted 22 the Church, and then went down to Antioch.

St. Paul's Third Missionary Tour

Galatia and Phrygia revisited After spending some time in Antioch, Paul 23 set out on a tour, visiting the whole of Galatia and Phrygia in order, and strengthening all the disciples.

Apollos in Ephesus and Corinth Meanwhile a Jew named Apollos came to 24 Ephesus. He was a native of Alexandria, a man of learning and well versed in the Scriptures. He had been instructed in the way of the Lord, and, 25 being full of burning zeal, he used to speak and teach accurately the facts about Jesus, though he knew of no baptism but John's. He began to speak boldly in the 26 synagogue, and Priscilla and Aquila, after hearing him, took him home and explained God's Way to him more accurately. Then, as he had made up his mind to cross over to Greece, 27 the brethren wrote to the disciples in Corinth, begging them to give him a kindly welcome. Upon his arrival he rendered valuable help to those who through grace had believed ; for 28 he powerfully and in public overcame the Jews in argument, proving from the Scriptures that Jesus is the Christ.

Disciples who had not the Holy Spirit During the stay of Apollos in Corinth, Paul, 1 **19** after passing through the inland districts, came to Ephesus, where he found a few disciples.

' Did you receive the Holy Spirit when you 2 first believed ? ' he asked them.

' No,' they replied, ' we have not even heard that there is a Holy Spirit.'

' Into what then were you baptized ? ' he asked. 3

' Into John's baptism,' they replied.

23. *Galatia and Phrygia*] Cf. xvi. 6, n.
24. *A man of learning*] Or ' an eloquent man.'
1. *The inland districts*] Lit. ' the upper parts.' The translation here adopted fits in with the North Galatian theory. In the South Galatian view the phrase may mean the shorter hill route from Antioch to Ephesus, a little north of the main road down the Lycus valley.

'John,' he said, 'administered a baptism of repentance, 4 bidding the people believe on One who was to come after him ; namely, on Jesus.'

On hearing this, they were baptized into the name of the 5 Lord Jesus ; and when Paul laid his hands upon them, the 6 Holy Spirit came on them, and they began to speak in tongues and to prophesy. They numbered in all about 7 twelve men.

Ephesus a Missionary Centre for Paul   Afterwards he went into the synagogue. 8 There for three months he continued to preach fearlessly, reasoning persuasively concerning the Kingdom of God. But some grew 9 obstinate in unbelief and spoke evil of the Way before all the congregation. So Paul left them, and, taking with him those who were disciples, held discussions daily in the lecture-hall of Tyrannus. This went 10 on for two years, so that all the inhabitants of the province of Asia, Jews as well as Greeks, heard the Lord's Message.

Remarkable Miracles   God also brought about extraordinary 11 miracles through Paul. Towels or aprons, for 12 instance, which Paul had handled, would be carried to the sick, and they would recover from their ailments, or the evil spirits would leave them.

The seven Sons of Sceva   But there were also some wandering Jewish 13 exorcists who undertook to invoke the name of Jesus over those who had the evil spirits, saying, 'I command you by that Jesus whom Paul preaches.'

There were seven sons of one Sceva, a Jew of high-priestly 14 family, who were doing this.

'Jesus I acknowledge,' the evil spirit answered, 'and 15 Paul I know, but who are you ? '

And the man in whom the evil spirit was sprang on them, 16 over-mastered them, and treated them with such violence, that they fled from the house stripped of their clothes and wounded. All the people of Ephesus, Jews as well as 17 Greeks, came to know of this. There was widespread awe, and they began to hold the name of the Lord Jesus in high honour.

9. *The lecture-hall of Tyrannus*] An interesting v.l. adds ' from 11 o'clock till 4.' The school, which opened at day-break, would then be free, and the zeal of Paul and his hearers thought little of the heat of the day, when work for the most part was at a standstill.

The Sorcerers' Books are burned

Many also of those who believed came con- 18 fessing without reserve their practices, and not 19 a few of those who had practised magical arts brought their books together and burnt them in the presence of all. The total value was reckoned and found to be fifty thousand silver pieces. Thus mightily 20 did the Lord's word spread and triumph.

Paul's Hopes and Plans

When matters had reached this point, Paul, 21 guided by the Spirit, decided to travel through Macedonia and Greece and go to Jerusalem.

' After that,' he said, ' I must also see Rome.'

But he sent two of his assistants, Timothy and Erastus, 22 to Macedonia, while he himself remained for a while in Roman Asia.

Demetrius creates an Uproar

Now just at that time there arose no small 23 commotion about the Way. For there was a 24 certain Demetrius, a silversmith, who made miniature silver shrines of Artemis, a business which brought great profit to the craftsmen in his employ. He 25 called his men together, and others who were engaged in similar trades, and said to them,

' You men well know that our prosperity depends on this business of ours ; and you see and hear that, not in 26 Ephesus only but throughout almost the whole province of Asia, this fellow Paul has led away a vast number of people by asserting that those are not gods at all that are made by men's hands. There is danger, therefore, not only that this 27 our trade will become of no account, but also that the temple of the great goddess Artemis will fall into utter disrepute, and that before long she will be actually deposed from her majestic rank—she who is now worshipped by the whole province of Asia ; nay, by the whole world.'

After listening to this harangue, they became furiously 28 angry and began shouting,

' Great is Artemis of Ephesus ! '

The riot and uproar spread through the whole city, till 29 at last with one accord they rushed into the Theatre, dragging with them Gaius and Aristarchus, two Macedonians who were fellow travellers with Paul. Then Paul would 30 have liked to go in and address the people, but the disciples

---

19. *Fifty thousand silver pieces*] Possibly worth £2000, or 10,000 dollars.
24. *Artemis*] The Latin name of this goddess was Diana, the Greek name Artemis.

would not let him do so. A few of the public officials, too, 31
who were friendly to him, sent repeated messages entreating
him not to venture into the Theatre. The people, mean- 32
while, kept shouting, some one thing and some another ;
for the assembly was all uproar and confusion, and the
greater part had no idea why they had come together. Then 33
some of the people crowded round Alexander, whom the
Jews had pushed forward ; and Alexander, motioning with
his hand to get silence, was prepared to make a defence to the
people. No sooner, however, did they see that he was a Jew, 34
than there arose from them all one roar of shouting, lasting
about two hours.

' Great is Artemis of Ephesus,' they said.

A Protest   At length the Recorder quieted them down. 35
from the   ' Men of Ephesus,' he said, ' who is there of
Recorder   all mankind that needs to be told that the city
of Ephesus is the guardian of the temple of the great
Artemis and of the image which fell down from heaven ?
These facts, then, being unquestioned, it becomes you to 36
maintain your self-control and not act recklessly. For you 37
have brought these men here, who are neither robbers of
temples nor blasphemers of our goddess. If, however, 38
Demetrius and the mechanics who support his contention
have a grievance against any one, there are Assize-days and
there are Proconsuls : let them bring their charges. But if 39
you desire anything further, it will have to be settled in the
regular assembly. For in connexion with to-day's pro- 40
ceedings there is danger of our being charged with attempted
insurrection, there having been no real reason for this riot ;
nor shall we be able to justify the behaviour of this disorderly mob.'

With these words he dismissed the assembly.   41

Paul in   When the uproar had ceased, Paul sent for 1 20
Macedonia,   the disciples ; and, after speaking words of
Greece, and encouragement to them, he took his leave, and
Troas   started for Macedonia. Passing through those 2
districts he much encouraged the disciples, and then
came into Greece, and spent three months there. The 3
Jews having planned to waylay him whenever he might
be on the point of taking ship for Syria, he decided to travel

31. *Public officials*] Lit. ' Asiarchs.' An accurate designation of the provincial
officers of the province of Asia.
33. *Crowded round*] The text and the meaning are alike uncertain.

back by way of Macedonia. He was accompanied as far 4
as the province of Asia by Sopater of Beroea, the son of
Pyrrhus; by Aristarchus and Secundus of Thessalonica;
by Gaius of Derbe, and Timothy; and by Tychicus and
Trophimus, men of Asia. These brethren had gone on 5
and were waiting for us in Troas. But we ourselves sailed 6
from Philippi after the days of Unleavened Bread, and
five days later joined them in Troas, where we remained
for a week.

He restores
Eutychus to
Life On the first day of the week, when we had 7
met to break bread, Paul, who was going away
the next morning, was preaching to them, and
prolonged his discourse till midnight. Now there were a 8
good many lamps in the room upstairs where we all were,
and a youth of the name of Eutychus was sitting at the 9
window. This lad, gradually sinking into deep sleep while
Paul preached at unusual length, overcome at last by sleep,
fell from the third story and was taken up dead. Paul, 10
however, went down, threw himself upon him, and folding
him in his arms said,

'Cease your wailing; his life is still in him.'

Then he went upstairs again, broke bread, and took some 11
food; and after a long conversation which was continued
till daybreak, at last he parted from them. They had taken 12
the lad home alive, and were greatly comforted.

Paul at the
Port of
Ephesus The rest of us had already embarked, and 13
set sail for Assos, intending to take Paul
on board there; for so he had arranged, he
himself intending to go by land. Accordingly, when he 14
met us at Assos, we took him on board and came to
Mitylene. Sailing from there, we arrived the next day 15
off Chios. On the next we touched at Samos; and on
the day following reached Miletus. For Paul's plan was to 16
sail past Ephesus, so as not to spend much time in the
province of Asia; since he was very desirous of being in
Jerusalem, if possible, on the day of Pentecost.

His Farewell
Address From Miletus he sent to Ephesus for the 17
Elders of the Church to come to him. Upon 18
their arrival he said to them,

'You Elders well know, from the first day of my setting
foot in the province of Asia, the kind of life I lived among
you the whole time, serving the Lord in all humility, and 19

with tears, and amid trials which came upon me through
the plotting of the Jews—and that I never shrank from 20
declaring to you anything that was profitable, or from
teaching you in public and in your homes, bearing witness 21
to both Jews and Greeks of their need of conversion to God
and of belief in Jesus our Lord.

' And now, under the constraint of the Spirit, I am on my 22
way to Jerusalem, not knowing what will happen to me there,
except that the Holy Spirit, at town after town, testifies to 23
me that imprisonment and suffering are awaiting me. But 24
even the sacrifice of my life I count as nothing, if only I
may perfect my earthly course, and be faithful to the duty
which the Lord Jesus has entrusted to me of bearing
witness to the gospel of God's grace.

' And now, I know that none of you among whom I have 25
gone in and out proclaiming the Kingdom will any longer
see my face. Therefore I solemnly affirm to you to-day that 26
I am not responsible for the ruin of any of you. For I have 27
not shrunk from declaring to you God's whole plan.

' Take heed to yourselves and to all the flock among 28
which the Holy Spirit has placed you as overseers and
shepherds to the Church of God, which He has bought
with His own blood. I know that, when I am gone, cruel 29
wolves will come among you and will not spare the flock ;
and that from among your own selves men will rise up 30
who will seek with their perverse talk to draw away the
disciples after them. Therefore be on the alert ; and 31
remember that, night and day, for three years, I never
ceased admonishing every one, even with tears.

' And now I commend you to God and to the word of His 32
grace. He is able to build you up and to give you your
inheritance among the saints. No one's silver or gold or 33
clothing have I coveted. You yourselves know that these 34
hands of mine have provided for my own necessities and for
the people with me. In every way I have shown you how, 35
by working as I do, you ought to help the weak, and
to bear in mind the words of the Lord Jesus, how He
Himself said,

28. *The Church of God*] v.l. ' The Church of the Lord,' a unique phrase, which
may be a correction to avoid the obvious difficulty of ' God purchased with His
own blood.' Possibly ' the blood that was His own,' as being that of His Son. But
if the original text was ' the blood of His own Son,' in the Greek the last two syllables
of ' own ' are all but identical with the following two syllables of ' son,' and these
latter may, by a familiar source of corruption, have been accidentally omitted.

' " It is more blessed to give than to receive." '

Having spoken thus, Paul knelt down and prayed with 36
them all; and with loud lamentation they all threw their 37
arms round his neck, and kissed him lovingly, grieved 38
above all things at his having told them that they were
never to behold his face again. And they went with
him to the ship.

He resumes   When, at last, we had torn ourselves away 1 **21**
his Journey and had set sail, we ran in a straight course to
to Jerusalem Cos ; the next day to Rhodes, and from there
to Patara. Finding a ship bound for Phoenicia, we went 2
on board and put to sea. After sighting Cyprus and 3
leaving it on our left, we continued our voyage to Syria
and put in at Tyre ; for there the ship was to unload her
cargo. Having searched for the disciples and found them, 4
we stayed at Tyre for seven days ; and, taught by the Spirit,
they repeatedly urged Paul not to proceed to Jerusalem.
When, however, our time was up, we went on our way, 5
escorted by all the disciples with their wives and children
till we were out of the city. Then, after kneeling down
on the beach and praying, we took leave of one another ; 6
and we went on board, while they returned home.

Our voyage was over when having sailed 7
With Philip from Tyre we reached Ptolemais. Here we
in Caesarea inquired after the welfare of the brethren, and
remained a day with them. We left on the morrow 8
and went on to Caesarea, where we entered the house
of Philip the Evangelist, who was one of the seven, and
stayed with him. Philip had four unmarried daughters 9
who were prophetesses.

Now during our somewhat lengthy stay a 10
Agabus pre- prophet of the name of Agabus came down
dicts Paul's from Judaea. When he came to us, he took 11
Imprison-   Paul's girdle, and bound his own feet and arms
ment   with it, and he said,

' Thus says the Holy Spirit, " So will the Jews in

---

35. *It is more blessed, &c.*] Perhaps more accurately ' Blessedness is to be found
rather in giving than in receiving.' Other *Agrapha* (sayings of Jesus unrecorded
in the Gospels) are no doubt embedded in other books of the New Testament,
especially in the Epistle of James. This is the only one definitely ascribed to Him.
Compare the sayings of Jesus recovered from the sands of Egypt by Messrs. Grenfell
and Hunt.

4. *The disciples*] They seem to have formed a small church in a great city.

7. *Our voyage, &c.*] Or ' Continuing our voyage from Tyre we reached Ptolemais.'

8. *Seven*] Cf. vi. 5 ; viii. 5.

Jerusalem bind the owner of this girdle, and will hand him over to the Gentiles." '

As soon as we heard these words, both we and the 12 brethren at Caesarea entreated Paul not to go up to Jerusalem. His reply was, 13

' What can you mean by thus unmanning me with your weeping ? Why, I am ready not only to go to Jerusalem, and be put in chains, but even to die there for the sake of the Lord Jesus.'

So when he was not to be dissuaded, we ceased remon- 14 strating with him and said,

' The Lord's will be done ! '

A few days afterwards we packed our baggage 15
Paul reaches Jerusalem and continued our journey to Jerusalem. Some 16 of the disciples from Caesarea also joined our party, and brought with them Mnason, a Cyprian, one of the early disciples, at whose house we were to lodge. We 17 reached Jerusalem, and there the brethren gave us a hearty welcome.

Paul in Jerusalem

An Interview with James and others On the following day we went with Paul to 18 call on James, and all the Elders of the Church came also. After exchanging greetings, Paul 19 told in detail all that God had done among the Gentiles by his ministry. And they, when they had heard 20 his statement, gave glory to God.

Then they said,

Paul tries to conciliate the Jewish Christians ' You see, brother, how many tens of thousands of Jews there are among those who have accepted the faith, and they are all zealous upholders of the Law. Now what they have been told 21 about you is that you teach all the Jews among the Gentiles to abandon Moses, telling them not to circumcise their children or observe old-established customs. What then 22 ought you to do ? They are sure to hear of your arrival ; so do what we now tell you. We have four men here 23 who are under a vow. Associate with these men and 24

16. *Brought . . Mnason . . at whose house we were to lodge*] Or, possibly, ' brought us to the house of Mnason . . to lodge there.' Apparently Mnason had a house half-way between Caesarea and Jerusalem.

20. *How many tens of thousands*] Or perhaps ' what multitudes,' the definite numeral being used for the indefinite. Cf. Luke xii. 1.

purify yourself with them, and pay their expenses so that
they can shave their heads. Then everybody will know
that there is no truth in these stories about you, but that
in your own actions you yourself obey the Law. As for 25
the Gentiles who have accepted the faith, we have communicated to them our decision that they are carefully to
abstain from anything sacrificed to an idol, from blood,
from what is strangled, and from fornication.'

So Paul associated with the men ; and the next day, 26
having purified himself with them, he went into the Temple,
giving notice when the days of their purification would be
finished, and there he remained until the sacrifice for each
of them was offered.

But, when the seven days were nearly over, 27
He is seized the Jews from the province of Asia, seeing
by the Mob Paul in the Temple, stirred up all the people
against him. They laid hands on him, crying out, 28
' Men of Israel, help ! This is the man who goes everywhere preaching to everybody against the Jewish people
and the Law and this place. And besides, he has even
brought Gentiles into the Temple and has desecrated this
holy place.'

For they had previously seen Trophimus the Ephesian 29
with him in the city, and imagined that Paul had brought
him into the Temple. The excitement spread through the 30
whole city, and the people rushed up in a crowd and laid
hold of Paul and proceeded to drag him out of the Temple ;
and the Temple gates were immediately closed.

The Roman   But while they were trying to kill Paul, word 31
Tribune   was taken up to the Tribune in command of the
rescues him battalion that all Jerusalem was in a ferment.
He instantly sent for a few soldiers and their officers, and 32
came down among the people with all speed. At the sight
of the Tribune and the troops they ceased beating Paul.
Then the Tribune, making his way to him, arrested him, 33
and, having ordered him to be secured with two chains,
asked who he was and what he had been doing. Some 34
of the crowd shouted one accusation against Paul and
some another, until, as the uproar made it impossible for
the truth to be ascertained, the Tribune ordered him to be
brought into the barracks. When Paul was at the steps, he 35
had to be carried by the soldiers because of the violence

of the mob ; for the whole mass of the people pressed on 36 in the rear, shouting, ' Away with him ! '

Paul explains who he is When he was about to be taken into the 37 barracks, Paul said to the Tribune, ' May I speak to you ? '

' Do you know Greek ? ' the Tribune asked. ' Are 38 you not the Egyptian who some years ago excited the riot of the 4000 cut-throats, and led them out into the Desert ? '

' I am a Jew,' replied Paul, ' belonging to Tarsus in 39 Cilicia, and am a citizen of no unimportant city. Give me leave, I pray you, to speak to the people.'

So with his permission Paul stood on the steps and 40 motioned to the people to be quiet ; and when there was silence he addressed them in Hebrew.

Paul tells the Crowd the Story of his Conversion ' Brethren and fathers,' he said, ' listen to 1 **22** my defence which I now make before you.'

And on hearing him address them in Hebrew, 2 they kept all the more quiet ; and he said,

' I am a Jew, born at Tarsus in Cilicia, but 3 brought up in this city. I was carefully trained at the feet of Gamaliel in the Law of our forefathers, and, like all of you to-day, was zealous for God. I persecuted to death 4 this Way, continually binding both men and women and throwing them into prison ; as the High Priest also and 5 all the Elders can bear me witness. It was, too, from them that I received letters to the brethren in Damascus, and I was already on my way to Damascus, intending to bring those also who had fled there, in chains to Jerusalem, to be punished.

' But on my way, when I was now not far from Damas- 6 cus, about noon a sudden blaze of light from heaven shone round me. I fell to the ground and heard a voice say to 7 me,

' " Saul, Saul, why are you persecuting me ? "

" Who art thou, Lord ? " I asked. 8

' " I am Jesus, the Nazarene," He replied, " whom you are persecuting."

' Now the men who were with me, though they saw the 9 light, did not hear the words of Him who spoke to me. And I asked, 10

9. *Words*] Lit. ' voice.' Contrast ix. 7 ; xxvi. 14. There the verb ' to hear ' is followed by the genitive case, here by the accusative ; a distinction possibly signi- fying that they heard a sound, but could not distinguish the words.

' " What am I to do, Lord ? "

' And the Lord said to me,

' " Rise, and go into Damascus.   There you shall be told of all that has been appointed for you to do."

' And as I could not see because the light had been so 11 dazzling, those who were with me had to lead me by the arm, and so I came to Damascus.

' And a certain Ananias, a pious man who obeyed the 12 Law and bore a good character with all the Jews of the city, came to me and standing at my side said, 13

' " Brother Saul, recover your sight."

' I instantly regained my sight and looked up at him. Then he said, " The God of our fathers has appointed you 14 to know His will, and to see the righteous One and hear Him speak.   For you shall be a witness for Him, to all 15 men, of what you have seen and heard.   And now why 16 delay ?   Rise, be baptised, and wash away your sins, calling upon His name."

' After my return to Jerusalem, and while praying in the 17 Temple, I fell into a trance.   I saw Him, and He said to me, 18

' " Make haste and leave Jerusalem quickly, because they will not accept your testimony about me."

' " Lord," I replied, " they themselves well know how 19 active I was in imprisoning, and in flogging in synagogue after synagogue those who believe in thee ; and when they 20 were shedding the blood of Stephen, thy witness, I was standing by, fully approving of it, and I held the clothes of those who were killing him."

' " Go," He replied ; " I will send you to nations far 21 away." '

Although a Roman Citizen he is bound Until they heard this last statement the people 22 listened to Paul, but now with a roar of disapproval they cried out,

' Away with such a fellow from the earth ! He ought not to be allowed to live.'

And when they continued their furious shouts, throwing 23 their clothes into the air and flinging dust about, the Tribune 24 ordered him to be brought into the barracks, and be examined by flogging, in order to ascertain the reason why they thus cried out against him.   But, when they had tied 25 him up with the straps, Paul said to the captain who stood by,

25. *With the straps*] Or perhaps ' for the lash.'

'Does the law permit you to flog a Roman citizen, one too who is uncondemned?'

On hearing this question, the captain went to report the 26 matter to the Tribune.

'What are you intending to do?' he said. 'This man is a Roman citizen.'

So the Tribune came to Paul and asked him, 27 'Tell me, are you a Roman citizen?'

'Yes,' he said.

'I paid a large sum for my citizenship,' said the Tribune. 28 'But I was born free,' said Paul.

So the men who had been on the point of putting him 29 under torture immediately left him. And the Tribune, too, was frightened when he learnt that Paul was a Roman citizen, for he had had him bound.

Paul brought before the Sanhedrin The next day, wishing to know exactly what 30 charge was being brought against him by the Jews, the Tribune ordered his chains to be removed; and, having sent word to the High Priests and all the Sanhedrin to assemble, he brought Paul down and made him stand before them.

He protests that he is innocent Then Paul, fixing a steady gaze on the **1 23** Sanhedrin, said,

'Brethren, I have lived with a perfectly clear conscience before God up to this day.'

On hearing this the High Priest Ananias ordered those 2 who were standing near Paul to strike him on the mouth.

'God will strike you, you white-washed wall!' exclaimed 3 Paul. 'Are you sitting there to judge me in accordance with the Law, and you yourself break the Law by ordering me to be struck!'

'Do you rail at God's High Priest?' cried the men who 4 stood by him.

'I did not know, brethren,' replied Paul, 'that he was 5 the High Priest; for it is written, "THOU SHALT NOT SPEAK EVIL OF A RULER OF THY PEOPLE"' (Exod. xxii. 28).

Dissension between Pharisees and Sadducees Noticing, however, that the Sanhedrin con- 6 sisted partly of Sadducees and partly of Pharisees, he called out loudly among them,

'Brethren, I am a Pharisee, the son of Pharisees. It is because of my hope of a resurrection of the dead that I am on my trial.'

These words of his caused an angry dispute between the 7
Pharisees and the Sadducees, and the assembly took different
sides. For the Sadducees maintain that there is no resur- 8
rection, and neither angel nor spirit ; but the Pharisees
acknowledge them all. So there arose a great uproar ; and 9
some of the Scribes belonging to the sect of the Pharisees
sprang to their feet and fiercely contended, saying,

'We find no harm in the man. What if a spirit has
spoken to him, or an angel—— !'

Paul again rescued by the Tribune But when the struggle was becoming violent, 10
the Tribune, fearing that Paul would be torn
to pieces by the people, ordered the troops to go
down and take him from among them by force and bring
him into the barracks.

Jesus comforts Paul. The following night the Lord came and stood 11
at Paul's side, and said,

A Plot to kill the Apostle 'Be of good courage, for as you have borne
faithful witness about me in Jerusalem, so you
must also bear witness in Rome.'

Now, when daylight came, the Jews formed a conspiracy 12
and solemnly swore not to eat or drink till they had killed
Paul. There were more than forty of them who bound 13
themselves by this oath. These went to the High Priests 14
and Elders and said to them,

'We have bound ourselves under a heavy curse to take
no food till we have killed Paul. Now therefore do you 15
and the Sanhedrin make representations to the Tribune
for him to bring him down to you, as if you intended to
inquire more minutely about him ; and we are prepared
to assassinate him before he comes near the place.'

His Nephew informs the Tribune of it But Paul's nephew heard of the intended 16
attack upon him. So he came and entered
the barracks and told Paul about it ; and Paul 17
called one of the captains and said,

'Take this young man to the Tribune, for he has
information to give him.'

So he took him and brought him to the Tribune, and said, 18
'Paul, the prisoner, called me to him and begged me to
bring this youth to you, because he has something to say
to you.'

Then the Tribune, taking him by the arm, withdrew 19
out of the hearing of others and asked him,

' What have you to tell me ? '

' The Jews,' he replied, ' have agreed to request you to 20
bring Paul down to the Sanhedrin to-morrow for the purpose of making yourself more accurately acquainted with
the case. I beg you not to comply ; for more than forty 21
men among them are lying in wait for him, who have
solemnly vowed that they will neither eat nor drink till they
have assassinated him ; and even now they are ready, awaiting that promise from you.'

So the Tribune sent the youth home, cautioning him. 22

' Do not let any one know that you have given me this
information,' he said.

The Tribune Then, calling to him two of the captains, he 23
sends him to gave his orders.
Caesarea ' Get ready two hundred men,' he said, ' to
march to Caesarea, with seventy cavalry and two hundred
light infantry, starting at nine o'clock to-night.'

He further told them to provide horses to mount 24
Paul on, so as to bring him safely to Felix the Governor.
He also wrote a letter of which these were the con- 25
tents :

' Claudius Lysias to his Excellency, Felix the Governor : 26
greetings. This man Paul had been seized by the Jews, 27
and was on the point of being killed by them, when I
came upon them with the troops and rescued him, for I had
been informed that he was a Roman citizen. Wishing to 28
know with certainty the offence of which they were accusing him, I brought him down into their Sanhedrin, and I 29
discovered that the charge had to do with questions of their
Law, but that he was accused of nothing for which he
deserves death or imprisonment. But now that I have 30
received information of a plot against the man, I immediately
send him to you, directing his accusers also to state before
you the case they have against him.'

Paul's So, in obedience to their orders, the soldiers 31
Reception took Paul and brought him by night as far as
by Felix Antipatris. The next day the infantry returned 32
to the barracks, leaving the cavalry to proceed with him ;
and the cavalry, having reached Caesarea, delivered the 33
letter to the Governor, and brought Paul also to him. Felix, 34
after reading the letter, inquired from what province he
was ; and being told ' from Cilicia,' he said, 35

' I will hear all you have to say, when your accusers also have come.'

And he ordered him to be detained in custody in Herod's Palace.

Tertullus impeaches the Apostle Five days after this, Ananias the High Priest 1 **24** came down to Caesarea with a number of Elders and a pleader called Tertullus. They stated to the Governor the case against Paul. So Paul was sent for, 2 and Tertullus began to impeach him as follows :

' Indebted as we are,' he said, ' to you, most noble Felix, for the perfect peace which we enjoy, and for reforms which your wisdom has conferred upon this nation in every way 3 and in every place, we accept them with profound gratitude. But—not to detain you too long—I beg you in your for- 4 bearance to listen to a brief statement from us. We have 5 found this man Paul a source of mischief and a disturber of the peace among all the Jews throughout the Empire, and a ringleader in the sect of the Nazarenes. He even 6 attempted to profane the Temple, but we arrested him. You, however, by examining him, will yourself be able to 8 learn the truth as to all this which we allege against him.'

The Jews also joined in the charge, maintaining that 9 these were facts.

Paul protests that he is innocent Then, at a sign from the Governor, Paul 10 answered,

' Knowing that for many years you have administered justice to this nation, I cheerfully make my defence. For you have it in your power to 11 ascertain that it is not more than twelve days ago that I went up to worship in Jerusalem ; and that neither in the 12 Temple nor in the synagogues, nor anywhere in the city, did they find me disputing with any opponent or collecting a crowd about me. Nor can they prove the charges which 13 they are now bringing against me. But this I confess to 14 you—that in the way which they style a heresy, I worship the God of our fathers, believing everything that is taught in the Law or is written in the Prophets, and having a hope 15 in God, which my accusers themselves also entertain, that there will be a resurrection both of the righteous and the unrighteous. This, too, is my own earnest endeavour— 16

6. *Arrested him*] v.l. adds ' and desired to judge him in accordance with our Law. (7) But Lysias the Tribune came, and carried him off, (8) bidding his accusers come before you.'

always to have a clear conscience in relation to God and man.

'Now after several years' absence I came to bring a sum of 17
money to my countrymen, and to offer sacrifices While I 18
was busy about these, they found me in the Temple purified,
with no crowd around me and no uproar. But there were
certain Jews from the province of Asia, who ought to 19
have been here before you, and to have been my prosecutors,
if they have any charge to bring against me. Or let these 20
men themselves say what misdemeanour they found me
guilty of when I stood before the Sanhedrin, unless it was 21
that one expression which I made use of when I shouted
out as I stood among them,

'" The resurrection of the dead is the thing about which
I am on my trial before you to-day."'

Felix acts considerately towards Paul At this point Felix, who was fairly well 22
informed about the new faith, adjourned the
trial, saying to the Jews,

'When the Tribune Lysias comes down, I will decide
your case.'

And he gave orders to the Captain that Paul was to be 23
kept in custody, but be treated with indulgence, and that
his personal friends were not to be prevented from showing
him kindness.

Felix procrastinates for two Years Not long after this, Felix came with Drusilla 24
his wife, a Jewess, and, sending for Paul,
listened to him as he spoke about faith in
Christ Jesus. But when he reasoned about 25
justice, self-control, and the future judgement, Felix
became alarmed and said,

'For the present leave me, and when I can find an
opportunity I will send for you.'

At the same time he hoped that Paul would give him 26
money ; and for this reason he sent for him the oftener to
converse with him. But after the lapse of two years Felix 27
was succeeded by Porcius Festus ; and, being desirous of
gratifying the Jews, Felix left Paul still in prison.

Festus becomes Governor Festus, having entered on his duties as 1 **2**
governor of the province, three days later went
up from Caesarea to Jerusalem ; whereupon 2
the High Priests and the leading men among the Jews

27. *In prison*] Lit. 'bound.' Perhaps meaning ' in chains.'

immediately made representations to him against Paul, and
begged him—asking it as a favour, to Paul's prejudice—to 3
have him brought to Jerusalem. They were planning an
ambush to kill him on the way. Festus, however, replied 4
that Paul was in custody in Caesarea, and that he was
himself going there very soon.

' Therefore let those of you,' he said, ' who have influence 5
go down with me, and impeach the man, if there is anything amiss in him.'

Paul again After a stay of eight or ten days in Jerusalem 6
pleads ' Not —not more—he went down to Caesarea ; and
Guilty ' the next day, taking his seat on the tribunal,
he ordered Paul to be brought in. Upon Paul's arrival, 7
the Jews who had come down from Jerusalem stood round
him, and brought many grave charges against him which
they were unable to substantiate. In reply, Paul said, 8
' Neither against the Jewish Law, nor against the
Temple, nor against Caesar, have I committed any offence
whatever.'

Paul appeals Then Festus, being anxious to gratify the 9
to the Jews, asked Paul,
Emperor ' Are you willing to go up to Jerusalem, and
there stand your trial before me on these charges ? '

' I am standing before Caesar's tribunal,' replied Paul, 10
' where alone I ought to be tried. The Jews have no real
ground of complaint against me, as indeed you know well
enough. If, however, I have done wrong and have com- 11
mitted any offence for which I deserve to die, I do not ask
to be excused that penalty. But if there is no truth in what
these men allege against me, no one has the right to give me
up to them as a favour. I appeal to Caesar.'

Then, after conferring with the Council, Festus replied, 12
' To Caesar you have appealed : to Caesar you shall go.'

Festus tells A short time after this, Agrippa the king 13
Herod and Bernice came to Caesarea to pay a com-
Agrippa plimentary visit to Festus ; and, during their 14
about Paul rather long stay, Festus laid Paul's case
before the king.

' There is a man here,' he said, ' whom Felix left a
prisoner, about whom, when I went to Jerusalem, the High 15
Priests and the Elders of the Jews made representations to
me, begging that sentence might be pronounced against

him. My reply was that it is not the custom among the 16
Romans to give up any one for punishment before the
accused has had his accusers face to face, and has had an
opportunity of defending himself against the charge which
has been brought against him.

'When, therefore, a number of them came here, the next 17
day I took my seat on the tribunal, without any loss of
time, and ordered the man to be brought in. But, when 18
his accusers stood up, they did not charge him with mis-
demeanours such as I had expected. But they quarrelled 19
with him about certain matters connected with their own
religion, and about a certain Jesus who had died, but—so Paul
maintained—is now alive. I was at a loss how to investi- 20
gate such questions, and asked Paul whether he would care
to go to Jerusalem and there stand his trial on these matters.
But when Paul appealed to have his case kept for the 21
Emperor's decision, I ordered him to be kept in prison until
I could send him up to Caesar.'

'I should like to hear the man myself,' said Agrippa. 22

He brings   'To-morrow,' replied Festus, ' you shall.'
Paul before   Accordingly, on the next day Agrippa and 23
Agrippa   Bernice came in state and took their seats in
the Judgement Hall, attended by the Tribunes and the men
of high rank in the city ; and, at the command of Festus,
Paul was brought in. Then Festus said, 24

' King Agrippa and all who are present with us, you see
here the man about whom the whole nation of the Jews
made suit to me, both in Jerusalem and here, crying out
that he ought not to live any longer. I could not discover 25
that he had done anything for which he deserved to die ;
but as he has himself appealed to the Emperor, I have
decided to send him to Rome. I have nothing very definite, 26
however, to tell our Sovereign about him. So I have
brought the man before you all—and especially before you,
King Agrippa—that after he has been examined I may find
something which I can put into writing. For, when send- 27
ing a prisoner to Rome, it seems to me to be absurd not
to state the charges against him.'

Paul tells   Then Agrippa said to Paul, 1 2
the Story of   ' You have permission to speak for yourself.'
his own Life   So Paul, with outstretched arm, proceeded to
make his defence.

'As regards all the accusations brought against me by 2
the Jews,' he said, 'I think myself fortunate, King Agrippa,
in being about to defend myself to-day before you, who 3
are so familiar with all the customs and questions that pre-
vail among the Jews ; and for this reason, I pray you, give
me a patient hearing.

'The kind of life I have lived from my youth upwards, 4
as exemplified in my early days among my nation and in
Jerusalem, is known to all the Jews. For they all know 5
me of old—if they would but testify to the fact—how, being
an adherent of the strictest sect of our religion, my life was
that of a Pharisee. And now I stand here impeached 6
because of my hope in the promise made by God to
our fathers—the promise which our twelve tribes, wor- 7
shipping day and night with intense devoutness, hope to
have made good to them. It is on the subject of this hope,
O King, that I am accused by the Jews. Why is it deemed 8
with all of you a thing past belief if God raises the dead to
life ?

'I myself, however, thought it a duty to be active in 9
hostility to the name of Jesus, the Nazarene. This is how 10
I acted in Jerusalem : armed with authority received from
the High Priests I shut up many of the saints in various
prisons, and when they were put to death I gave my vote
against them. In all the synagogues also I punished them 11
many a time, and tried to make them blaspheme ; and in
my wild fury I chased them even to foreign towns.

'While thus engaged, I was travelling one day to Damas- 12
cus, armed with authority and a commission from the High
Priests, and on the journey, at noon, O King, I saw a light 13
from heaven—brighter than the brightness of the sun—
shining around me and around those who were travelling
with me. We all fell to the ground ; and I heard a voice 14
which said to me in Hebrew,

'"Saul, Saul, why are you persecuting me ? You are
finding it painful to kick against the ox-goad."

'"Who art thou, Lord ?" I asked. 15

'"I am Jesus whom you are persecuting," the Lord
replied. "But rise, and stand on your feet ; for I have 16
appeared to you for the very purpose of appointing you my
servant and my witness both as to the things you have
already seen and as to those in which I will appear to you.

I will save you from the Jewish people and from the 17
Gentiles, to whom I send you to open their eyes, that they 18
may turn from darkness to light and from Satan's authority
to God, in order to receive forgiveness of sins and an
inheritance among those who are sanctified through faith
in me."

'Therefore, King Agrippa, I was not disobedient to the 19
heavenly vision ; but I proceeded to preach first to the 20
people in Damascus, and then to those in Jerusalem and
in all Judaea, and to the Gentiles, that they must repent and
turn to God, and live lives consistent with such repentance.

'It was on this account that the Jews seized me in the 21
Temple and tried to kill me. Having, however, obtained 22
the help which comes from God, I have stood firm until
now, and have solemnly exhorted rich and poor alike, saying
nothing except what the Prophets and Moses predicted, how 23
that the Christ was to be a suffering Christ, and being the
first to rise from the dead he was to proclaim a message
of light both to the Jewish people and to the Gentiles.'

As Paul thus made his defence, Festus exclaimed in a 24
loud voice,

'You are mad, Paul ; your great learning is turning
your brain.'

'I am not mad, most noble Festus,' replied Paul ; 'I 25
am speaking words of sober truth. The king, to whom I 26
speak freely, knows about these matters. I do not believe
that any detail of them has escaped his notice ; for all
this has not been done in a corner. King Agrippa, do 27
you believe the Prophets ? I know that you believe
them.'

Agrippa answered, 28

'In brief, you are easily persuading yourself that you
can make me a Christian ! '

'My prayer to God, whether briefly or at length,' replied 29
Paul, 'would be that not only you but all who are my hearers
to-day, might become such as I am—except these chains.'

28. The A.V. ' Almost thou persuadest me to be a Christian ' is impossible. For :—
(1) The initial phrase cannot mean ' almost,' but (as in Eph. iii. 3) ' with a few
words,' or ' in a short time.'
(2) The ' to be ' is displaced by the better attested reading ' to make.'
(3) ' Thou persuadest ' should rather be rendered ' thou art trying to persuade ';
R.V. ' With but little persuasion thou wouldest fain make me a Christian ' is a
dubious rendering of all but untranslatable Greek. Probably the use of the nickname
' Christian ' (xi. 26, n.) is decisive against any earnest purpose on the part of Agrippa.
He seems to say, with irony, ' What a hurry you are in to make a Christian of me.'

Paul declared innocent So the king rose, and the Governor, and Bernice, and those who were sitting with them ; and they retired and conversed together and said, 30 31

'This man does nothing for which he deserves death or imprisonment.'

And Agrippa said to Festus, 32

'He might have been set at liberty, if he had not appealed to Caesar.'

Paul's Voyage to Italy

The Ship from Adramyttium takes Paul to Sidon Now when it was decided that we should sail for Italy, they handed over Paul and a few other prisoners into the custody of Julius, an officer of the Augustan battalion ; and going on board a ship of Adramyttium which was about to sail to the ports of the province of Asia, we put to sea ; Aristarchus, the Macedonian, from Thessalonica, being one of our party. The next day we put in at Sidon. There Julius treated Paul with thoughtful kindness and allowed him to visit his friends and enjoy their care. 1 27 2 3

Myra, Cnidus, Salmone, Fair Havens Putting to sea again, we sailed under the lee of Cyprus, because the winds were against us ; and, sailing the whole length of the sea that lies off Cilicia and Pamphylia, we reached Myra in Lycia. There Julius found an Alexandrian ship bound for Italy, and put us on board of her. It took several days of slow and difficult sailing for us to come off Cnidus ; from which point, as the wind did not allow us to get on by the direct course, we ran under the lee of Crete by Salmone. Then, coasting along with difficulty, we reached a place called 'Fair Havens,' near the town of Lasea. 4 5 6 7 8

Paul's Advice to his Companions Our voyage thus far had occupied a long time, and the navigation being now unsafe because the Fast was already over, Paul warned them. 9

'Sirs,' he said, 'I perceive that the voyage will be 10

---

4. *Against us*] A ship attempting to sail in a straight course from Sidon to the province of Asia would have the prevailing N.W. wind dead against her.

9. *The Fast*] This was the Great Day of Atonement (September–October). The dangerous season for sailing was reckoned from September 14 to November 11, when all navigation ceased up to March 5.

attended with danger and heavy loss, not only to the cargo and the ship but to our own lives also.'

But Julius let himself be persuaded by the pilot and by 11 the owner rather than by Paul's arguments ; and as the 12 harbour was inconvenient for wintering in, the majority were in favour of putting out to sea, to try whether they could get to Phoenix—a harbour on the coast of Crete facing north-east and south-east—to winter there. And a 13 light breeze from the south sprang up, so that they supposed they were now sure of their purpose. So weighing anchor they ran along the coast of Crete, keeping close inshore.

The Storm But it was not long before a furious north- 14 east wind, coming down from the mountains, burst upon us and carried the ship out of her course. She 15 was unable to make headway against the gale ; so we gave up and let her drive. Then we ran under the lee of a 16 little island called Cauda, where we managed with great difficulty to secure the boat ; and, after hoisting it on board, 17 they used frapping-cables to undergird the ship, and, as they were afraid of being driven on the Syrtis quicksands, they lowered the gear and lay to. But, as the storm was 18 still violent, the next day they began to lighten the ship ; and, on the third day, with their own hands they threw 19 the ship's spare gear overboard. Then, when for several 20 days neither sun nor stars were seen and the terrific gale still harassed us, the last ray of hope was now vanishing.

Paul, divinely comforted, cheers his Companions When for a long time they had taken but 21 little food, Paul, standing up among them, said, ' Sirs, you ought to have listened to me and not have sailed from Crete. You would then have escaped this suffering and loss. But now take courage, for there 22 will be no loss of life among you, but of the ship only.

12. *Facing north-east and south-east*] Lit. ' looking down the S.W. wind and down the N.W. wind.'

14. *A furious north-east wind*] Lit. ' a typhonic wind (or cyclone), the one called Euraquilo.' v.L. ' Euroclydon,' lit. ' a wind causing broad waves.'

Down from the mountains] Lit. ' down from it,' *i.e.* from Crete. The phrase may possibly mean ' against it ' (the ship), as in A.V.

16. *Cauda*] v.L. ' Clauda.'

17. *To undergird*] By passing these cables under the keel and over the gunwales, and drawing them tight by means of pulleys and levers.

Lowered the gear] The ' gear ' was possibly some form of ' sea anchor,' which, lowered forward and dragging in the water, would cause the drift of the ship, with her head to the wind, to be very slow ; but it is more usually taken to refer to the upper sails and spars lowered to the deck.

Lay to] Or ' drifted.'

For there stood by my side, last night, an angel of the 23
God to whom I belong, and whom also I worship, and 24
he said,

'"Dismiss all fear, Paul, for you must stand before
Caesar; and God has granted you the lives of all who are
sailing with you."

'Therefore, Sirs, take courage; for I believe God, and 25
am convinced that things will happen exactly as I have
been told. But we are to be stranded on a certain island.' 26

The Ship drifts near an unknown Shore It was now the fourteenth night, and we were 27
drifting through the Sea of Adria, when, about
midnight, the sailors suspected that land was
close at hand. So they hove the lead and 28
found twenty fathoms of water; and after a short time
they hove again and found fifteen fathoms. Then for fear 29
of possibly running on rocks, they threw out four anchors
from the stern and longed for daylight. The sailors, how- 30
ever, wanted to make their escape from the ship, and had
lowered the boat into the sea, pretending that they were
going to lay out anchors from the bow. But Paul, address- 31
ing Julius and the soldiers, said,

'Your lives will be sacrificed, unless these men remain
on board.'

Then the soldiers cut the ropes of the ship's boat and 32
let her fall off.

Paul persuades his Companions to take Food And as day was dawning Paul urged all on 33
board to take some food.

'This is the fourteenth day,' he said, 'that
you have been on the strain and have fasted,
eating little or nothing. I therefore strongly advise you to 34
take some food. This is essential for your safety. For
not a hair will perish from the head of any one of you.'

Having said this he took some bread, and, after giving 35
thanks to God for it before them all, he broke it in pieces
and began to eat it. This raised the spirits of all, and they 36
too took food. There were two hundred and seventy-six of 37
us, crew and passengers, all told. After eating a hearty meal 38
they lightened the ship by throwing the wheat overboard.

27. *Drifting through*] Or 'tossed about in.' Not 'driven to and fro' or 'driven
up and down'; for these expressions would imply shifting winds, of which there is
no trace in the narrative.
The Sea of Adria] Which included, besides the Adriatic, the central portion of
the Mediterranean.

When daylight came, they could not recog- 39
nize the coast. But they noticed an inlet with
a sandy beach, and now their object was, if
possible, to run the ship aground in this inlet. So they cut 40
away the anchors and left them in the sea, unloosing at the
same time the bands which secured the paddle-rudders.
Then, hoisting the foresail to the wind, they made for the
beach. But coming to a place where two seas met, they 41
stranded the ship, and her bow sticking fast remained
immovable, while the stern began to go to pieces under the
heavy hammering of the sea.

The Ship is wrecked

Now the soldiers recommended that the 42
prisoners should be killed, for fear some one of
them might swim ashore and effect his escape.
But their captain, bent on securing Paul's safety, kept them 43
from their purpose, and gave orders that those who could
swim should first jump overboard and get to land, and that 44
the rest should follow, some on planks, and others on
various things from the ship. In this way they all got
safely to land.

All on board land safely at Malta

Our lives having been thus preserved, we 1 **28**
discovered that the island was called Malta.
The natives showed us remarkable kindness, 2
for they lit a fire and made us all welcome because of the
pelting rain and the cold. Now, when Paul had gathered 3
a bundle of sticks and had thrown them on the fire, a viper,
driven by the heat, came out and fastened itself on his
hand. When the natives saw the creature hanging to his 4
hand, they said to one another,

Paul and the Viper

' Beyond doubt this man is a murderer, for, though saved
from the sea, Justice does not permit him to live.'

He, however, shook the reptile off into the fire and was 5
unhurt. They expected him soon to swell with inflamma- 6
tion or suddenly fall down dead ; but, after waiting a long
time and seeing no harm come to him, they changed their
minds and said that he was a god.

Now in the same part of the island there were 7
lands belonging to the Governor, whose name
was Publius. He welcomed us to his house,

The Father of Publius cured

40. *Paddle-rudders*] Every ship had two of these—large and strong paddles with
very wide blades, one on each quarter—instead of the single rudder now used.
They had probably been hauled up and lashed while the ship was at anchor.
1. *Malta*] Lit. ' Melita.' v.l. ' Melitene.'

and for three days generously made us his guests. It 8
happened, however, that his father was lying ill of dysentery
and attacks of fever ; so Paul went to see him, and, after
praying, laid his hands on him and cured him. After this, 9
all the other sick people in the island came and were cured.
They also paid us great honour, and when at last we sailed 10
they put supplies on board for us.

Syracuse, Rhegium, Puteoli, Rome Three months passed before we set sail in an 11
Alexandrian vessel, called the ' Twin Brothers,'
which had wintered at the island. At Syracuse 12
we put in and stayed for three days. From 13
there we worked round and reached Rhegium ; and a day
later, a south wind sprang up which brought us the next
day to Puteoli. Here we found brethren, who invited us 14
to remain with them for a week ; and so we reached Rome.
Meanwhile the brethren there, hearing of our movements, 15
came as far as Appii Forum and Tres Tabernae to meet
us ; and when Paul saw them he thanked God and took
courage. Upon our arrival in Rome, Paul received per- 16
mission to live by himself, guarded by a soldier.

Paul in Rome

An Interview with the Jews After three days he invited the leading men 17
among the Jews to meet him ; and, when they
were come together, he said to them,
' Although, brethren, I had done nothing prejudicial to
our people or contrary to the customs of our forefathers, I
was handed over as a prisoner from Jerusalem into the
power of the Romans : who, after they had sharply 18
questioned me, were willing to set me at liberty, because
they found no offence in me for which I deserve to die.
But owing to the opposition of the Jews I was compelled 19
to appeal to Caesar ; not, however, that I had any charge
to bring against my nation. For these reasons, then, I 20
have invited you here, that I might see you and speak to
you ; for it is for the hope of Israel that I wear this chain.'

11. *Called the ' Twin Brothers* '] Lit. ' with the sign Dioscuri,' *i.e.* Sons of Zeus,
Castor, and Pollux.
13. *Worked round*] v.l. ' cast loose.'
16. *In Rome*] v.l. adds here ' the Captain handed the prisoners over to the
Prefect of the Praetorian Camp, but.'
By himself] v.l. adds ' outside the barracks.'
19. *Owing to the opposition*] Or ' the persistent opposition.'

' For our part,' they replied, ' we have not received any 21
letters from Judaea about you, nor have any of our countrymen come here and reported or stated anything to your
disadvantage. But we should be glad to hear from you 22
what it is that you believe ; for as for this sect all we know
is that it is everywhere spoken against.'

Paul begins to preach in Rome So they arranged a day with him and came 23
to him to his lodgings in considerable numbers.
And then he solemnly explained to them the
Kingdom of God, endeavouring from morning till evening
to convince them about Jesus, both from the Law of Moses
and from the Prophets. Some were convinced ; others 24
refused to believe. Unable to agree among themselves, 25
they at last left him, but not before Paul had spoken a
parting word to them, saying,

' Right well did the Holy Spirit say to your fathers
through the Prophet Isaiah :

' " Go to this people and tell them, 26
You will hear and hear, and by no means understand ;
And will look and look, and by no means see.
For this people's mind has grown callous, 27
Their hearing has become dull,
And their eyes they have closed ;
Lest they should see with their eyes,
Or hear with their ears,
Or understand with their minds,
And turn back,
That I might cure them " (Isa. vi. 9, 10).

' Be assured, therefore, that this salvation—God's salva- 28
tion—has been sent to the Gentiles : they, at any rate, will
give heed.'

The two Years that followed After this Paul lived for fully two years in a 30
hired house of his own, receiving all who came to
see him. He preached the Kingdom of God and 31
the gospel of the Lord Jesus Christ without let or hindrance.

---

28. v.l. inserts verse 29, ' And when he had said this, the Jews went away, carrying on a long debate with one another.'
30. *Lived for fully two years*] A similar note of time at xviii. 11 (cf. with xviii. 12)
suggests that at the end of the two years some change took place in Paul's circumstances. Or, possibly, Luke writes at the end of the two years, and has no more to
tell, with the implication of an early date (about 62 A.D. for Acts, and a still earlier
one for the Gospels of Mark and Luke). Otherwise it is strange that the author
should leave his readers in suspense as to the issue of the trial, whether acquittal
or condemnation. The suggestion that he intended to continue his narrative in
another book is hazardous.

THE CORRESPONDENCE OF ST. PAUL

THE CORRESPONDENCE OF ST. PAUL

The New Testament consists of twenty-seven books, of which no fewer than twenty-one are letters (while the book of Revelation is introduced by the letters to seven Churches), a mode of revelation for which even the 'many fragments and various methods' of Hebrews i. 1 hardly prepares us. Probably Paul is the originator of this earliest stratum of the inspired New Testament literature ; but it would be a mistake to think of him as sitting down at his desk to compose theological treatises. He was above all things an ardent missionary, a man of force, a man of action. But he could not be in two places at once ; and so, when he was divided from some field of his labour by long stretches of sea, and just when his heart was moved by yearning for his beloved children, or by anxiety whether they might not suffer themselves to be led astray, he would take up his pen, or (speaking more accurately) would call for an amanuensis and would dictate to him the meditations, the thoughts, the plans which moved his spirit and took form within his soul.

Primarily the Epistles are not dogmatic treatises. They are intended to be read as letters are read, not verse by verse, not in detached portions, not in sentences torn from their context, but in one connected reading. Each Epistle is intended to take effect as a whole.

It may not be denied that there is a wide difference in doctrinal intention between, say, *Philemon* and *Romans*, *Philippians* and *Ephesians*, nor that these writings have lived down the ages for other qualities than those of occasional letters. Yet it should be remembered that they had their origin in the special needs of individual Churches. It is a double misfortune that, as presented to us in the New Testament, they are torn from their historical setting and are artificially broken up into chapter and verse. A modern author of 'The Life and Letters of So-and-so' does not arrange the letters in order of length and importance, but weaves them into a consecutive story of the life.

The thirteen Epistles (for of course *Hebrews* was not

written by Paul) can be placed with only a narrow margin of uncertainty.

Galatians has been commonly assigned to the third missionary journey, partly on account of Gal. iv. 13, interpreted as referring to the former of two previous visits (Acts xvi. 6 ; xviii. 23), partly because of its doctrinal affinity to the Epistles to Corinth and Rome. The latter reason is doubtful : the order of Paul's letters is to be determined not so much by tracing progress in his Christian thinking as by the special circumstances of the Churches addressed ; and the ' South Galatian ' theory leaves it at least possible that if there were two visits prior to the writing of the Epistle, they might be those from Pisidian Antioch to Derbe and back again to Antioch. In this case it would be the earliest Epistle, written immediately after the first missionary journey.

The order of the Epistles of the Imprisonment has also been in question. Lightfoot's great authority placed *Philippians* before the group *Colossians*, *Ephesians*, *Philemon* ; but the trend of critical opinion is to reverse this order. Professor von Soden writes of *Philippians* : ' We are treading upon very sacred ground as we read this Epistle. It is without doubt the last from Paul's hand.' This, of course, is a verdict adverse to the authenticity of the Pastorals (1st and 2nd Timothy, Titus). If genuine, these imply Paul's acquittal and a renewed period of missionary activity, followed by a second imprisonment and condemnation. The historical evidence for this is very scanty, and the peculiarities of diction, as well as the advanced stage of church organisation, lead many scholars to reject the Pauline authorship, while recognizing that genuine Pauline fragments may be embedded.

Reserving the doubt as to *Galatians*, we may arrange Paul's correspondence in the following order :—

Time.	Epistle.	Written from
Second Missionary Journey	1 Thessalonians } 2 Thessalonians }	Corinth.
Third Missionary Journey	1 Corinthians	Ephesus.
	2 Corinthians	Macedonia.
	Romans	Corinth.

THE CORRESPONDENCE OF ST. PAUL

Time.	Epistle.	Written from
Imprisonment in Rome	Colossians Ephesians Philemon	Rome
	Philippians	Rome.
After Release ?	1 Timothy Titus	? ?
Second Imprison- ment ?	2 Timothy	Rome.

The ten Epistles which can be certainly connected with Paul's missionary labours fall approximately within the decade 52 to 62 A.D.

THE EPISTLE OF PAUL TO THE
ROMANS

There is every probability that this Epistle was written during Paul's three months' stay in Corinth on his last missionary journey (Acts xx. 2, 3 ; Romans xv. 25, 26). He had never visited Rome : perhaps the Church there arose from a gradual infiltration from Paul's eastern Churches. ' All roads lead to Rome ' (see also Acts ii. 10). Now he hopes, after taking the collection to Jerusalem, to realize his longing to visit a church of which he had heard so much good (i. 8). But with characteristic delicacy he makes it clear that he comes with no apostolic claim, but simply, for mutual encouragement in the faith, passes through Rome on his way to Spain (i. 10–15 ; xv. 18–29).

It was fitting that this great uncontroversial interpretation of the Gospel he preached should be addressed to the centre of the Empire. The first eight chapters have been called ' The Gospel according to St. Paul,' or ' The Fifth Gospel.' The heart of the Gospel he preaches is, of course, ' Justification by faith,' the vain quest after a legal righteousness replaced by a new and vital relationship to God, ' the one Fountain of all goodness,' carrying with it free forgiveness, mediated by the atoning death and resurrection of Jesus Christ.

In chapters ix. to xi. Paul faces the question which must have perplexed the Gentile world, ' Why have not the Jews accepted this Christ ? ' Chapters xii. 1 to xv. 13 set forth the ethical obligations of the new faith. It is not unlikely that chapter xvi. is a separate letter of commendation of Phoebe addressed to the Church at *Ephesus*.

THE EPISTLE OF PAUL TO THE ROMANS

Introduction

Paul's Message and Apostleship

Paul, a servant of Jesus Christ, called to be an 1 **1** Apostle, set apart to proclaim God's gospel, which He promised through His Prophets in 2 Holy Writ concerning His Son, who, by 3 human descent, belonged to the family of David, but by 4 His Spirit of holiness was miraculously marked out Son of God after Resurrection from the dead, Jesus Christ our Lord, through whom I have received grace and a com- 5 mission for His Name's sake to win men to the obedience that springs from faith among all the Gentiles, among whom 6 you too are called to belong to Jesus Christ; to all of you 7 in Rome who are loved by God, and called to be saints: grace to you and peace from God our Father and the Lord Jesus Christ.

The Christians in Rome and Paul

First of all I thank my God through Jesus 8 Christ for you all, because the report of your faith is spreading through the whole world. I 9 call God to witness—to whom I render priestly and spiritual service by preaching the gospel of His Son— how constantly I make mention of you in my prayers, entreating that now, at length, if such be His will, the way 10 may by some means be made clear for me to come to you. For I am longing to see you in order to impart to you some 11 spiritual help, so that you may be strengthened; in other 12 words, that while I am among you, you and I may be mutually encouraged by one another's faith. And I desire 13 you to know, brethren, that I have many a time intended to come to you—though until now I have been prevented—

1. *Servant of Jesus Christ*] The word thus applied to himself by Paul here and elsewhere is that which has the meaning 'slave.'
Called, &c.] Or, perhaps, 'an apostle by calling set apart,' &c.
5. *Commission*] Lit. 'apostleship.'
The obedience that springs from faith] Or perhaps 'obedience to the faith'; lit. 'unto obedience of faith.'

353

in order that I might gather some fruit from my labours, among you, as well as among the other Gentiles. To 14 Greek and non-Greek, to wise and foolish alike, I have a duty to perform : so for my part I am eager to preach the 15 gospel to you in Rome also.

The main Subject of the Letter

Salvation through Faith For I am not ashamed of the gospel. It is 16 God's power working for salvation for everyone who believes, Jew first, and then Greek. For in the gospel a righteousness which comes from 17 God is revealed, alike depending on faith and leading to faith ; as the Scripture has it,

' THE RIGHTEOUS MAN SHALL LIVE BY FAITH ' (Hab. ii. 4).

God's Anger against Sin For God's anger is revealed from heaven 18 against all the impiety and the wickedness of men who through their wickedness suppress the truth ; because what may be known of God is plain 19 to their minds ; for God has made it plain to them. From the very creation of the world, His invisible per- 20 fections—namely, His eternal power and divine nature— have been perceptible and clearly visible from His works, so that they are without excuse. For though they knew 21 God they have not glorified Him as God, nor rendered Him thanks, but have become absorbed in useless discussions, and their senseless minds darkened. While 22 boasting of their wisdom they are fools ; and they have 23 exchanged the glory of the immortal God for images of mortal man, or of birds, beasts, or reptiles.

The notorious Wickedness of the Gentiles For this reason, through the lust of their 24 hearts, God has given them up to impurity to dishonour themselves, since they have ex- 25 changed God's truth for what is false, and have offered worship and service to the creature rather than to the Creator ever blessed ! Amen.

This is why God has given them up to vile passions. 26 Not only have their women exchanged their natural functions for unnatural ones, but the men also, in the same 27

16. *Greek*] Stands here typically for non-Jew, Gentile ; and so in a number of other passages.
17. *The righteous man, &c.*] Or ' The man who is righteous by faith shall live.'
19. *Because, &c.*] justifies, ' suppress the truth.'

way, neglecting sexual intercourse with women, have burned fiercely in their lust for one another, men practising shameful vice with men, and receiving in themselves the fitting retribution for their misconduct.

And just as they did not think fit to retain knowledge 28 of God, so God left them with the minds of reprobates to do unseemly things ; with hearts filled with all sorts of 29 dishonesty, mischief, greed and malice ; full of envy and bloodthirstiness, quarrelsome, crafty, spiteful, secret back- 30 biters, open slanderers ; hateful to God, insolent, haughty, ostentatious ; inventors of mischief, disobedient to parents, destitute of sense, faithless, without affection, and with- 31 out pity. In short, though knowing well the sentence 32 which God pronounces against such deeds as deserving death, they not only do them, but applaud others who practise them.

All Mankind without exception are Sinners You are therefore without excuse, whoever 1 **2** you are who pass judgement upon others. In passing judgement on your neighbour you condemn yourself ; for you who pass judgement commit the same misdeeds ; and we know that God's 2 judgement falls rightly upon those who commit such sins. And you who judge those who commit such sins and yet 3 do the same yourself—do you imagine that you yourself will escape God's judgement ? Or is it that you think 4 lightly of the wealth of His goodness, forbearance and patience, unaware that the goodness of God is drawing you to repentance ?

Judgement awaits both Jew and Gentile In the stubbornness of your impenitent heart 5 you are treasuring up for yourself wrath on the day of Wrath when God's righteous judgement will stand revealed. To each man He will 6 make an award according to his deeds (Ps. lxii. 12 ; Prov. xxiv. 12) ; to those, who, by lives of persistent right- 7 doing strive for glory, honour and immortality, eternal life ; while on the self-willed who disobey the truth and obey 8 unrighteousness, there will fall wrath and anger, affliction 9 and anguish upon every human soul who does wrong— upon the Jew first, and then upon the Greek ; but glory, 10

---

30. *Hateful to God*] Or perhaps ' haters of God.'
2. *Falls rightly, &c.*] Or ' against those who commit such sins is in accordance with the truth.'

honour and peace for everyone who does what is good—
the Jew first and then the Greek. For God pays no atten- 11
tion to this world's distinctions.

The Im-   All who sin outside the Law will also perish 12
partiality of outside the Law, and all who sin in the sphere
Retribution of Law will be judged by the Law. For it is 13
not those who hear the Law read who are righteous in the
sight of God, but it is those who obey the Law who will be
pronounced righteous. When Gentiles who have no law 14
obey by instinct the commands of the Law, they, without
having a law, are a law to themselves ; since they exhibit 15
engraved on their hearts the action of the Law, while their
conscience at the same time bears witness to the Law,
and their moral judgements alternately accuse or perhaps
defend them—on the day when, according to the gospel 16
I preach, God will judge the secrets of men's lives by
Jesus Christ.

The Jews   Suppose you claim the name of Jew, find 17
expostulated rest in the Law, pride yourself in God, 18
with for   know the Will, are instructed by the Law to
Disobedience
appreciate distinctions, and have persuaded 19
yourself that you are a guide to the blind, a light to those
in darkness, a schoolmaster for the foolish, a teacher of 20
novices, because in the Law you possess the embodiment
of knowledge and of truth : you then who teach your 21
fellow-man, do you teach yourself ? You who cry out
against stealing, are you a thief ? You who forbid 22
adultery, do you commit adultery ? You who loathe idols,
do you plunder temples ? You who pride yourself in the 23
Law, do you violate the Law and so dishonour God ? WHY, 24
THE NAME OF GOD IS BLASPHEMED AMONG THE GENTILES
BECAUSE OF YOU, as Holy Writ declares (Isa. lii. 5).

What makes   Circumcision does indeed profit, if you obey 25
a Man a true the Law ; but if you are a Law-breaker your
Israelite   circumcision counts for nothing. In the same 26
way if an uncircumcised man observes the requirements
of the Law, shall not his uncircumcision be reckoned circumcision, and if he in his natural state of uncircumcision 27
carries out the Law, shall he not judge you who, for all

12, 13. *The Law*] Or ' Law.'
15. *Alternately*] Lit. ' between one another,' ' mutually.'
Verse 16 properly continues verse 13, verses 14, 15 being parenthetic.
18. *Appreciate distinctions*] Or ' approve the better course.'

your written Law and circumcision, are yet a Law-breaker ?
For the true Jew is not the man who is outwardly a Jew, 28
and true circumcision is not that which is outward and
bodily. But the true Jew is one inwardly, and true circum- 29
cision is heart-circumcision—not literal, but spiritual.
Such a man receives praise not from men, but from God.

Paul replies to Objections What special privilege, then, has a Jew ? 1 **3**
Or what is the benefit of circumcision ?
Great in every way. First, the fact that the 2
Jews were entrusted with God's oracles. What if some 3
Jews have proved unfaithful ? Shall their faithlessness
nullify God's faithfulness ? God forbid ! Let God be 4
true, though every man be false. As it stands written,

   ' THAT THOU MAYEST PROVE RIGHT IN THY CONTENTIONS,
     AND SUCCEED IN THY CAUSE ' (Ps. li. 4).

But if our wickedness sets God's righteousness in a 5
clearer light, what shall we say ? (Is God unrighteous—
I use a human analogy—when He inflicts punishment ?
God forbid ! For in that case how shall He judge 6
all mankind ?) But if my falsehood has brought out 7
God's truthfulness, redounding to His glory, why am I
still judged as a sinner ? And why not say—as some 8
people wickedly assert that we do say—' Let us do evil that
good may come ? ' The condemnation of such men is just.

Scripture proves the Guilt of all Men What then ? Are we Jews at a disadvan- 9
tage ? Not in the least ; for we have already
charged all Jews and Gentiles alike with being
in thraldom to sin. Thus it stands written, 10

   ' THERE IS NOT A SINGLE RIGHTEOUS MAN :
   THERE IS NOT ONE INTELLIGENT, NOT ONE A SEEKER 11
     AFTER GOD.

   ALL HAVE TURNED ASIDE ; 12
   THEY HAVE ALIKE BECOME WORTHLESS ;
   THERE IS NO ONE WHO DOES GOOD—NO, NOT ONE '
                        (Ps. xiv. 1–3).

   ' THEIR THROAT IS AN OPENED GRAVE ; 13

3. *Unfaithful*] Or ' unbelieving.'
God forbid !] Lit. ' May it not be !' The expression is found ten times in Romans,
once in 1 Corinthians, and three times in Galatians. These letters were probably all
written about the same time.
   4. *Contentions*] Lit. ' words.'
   5. *When He inflicts, &c.*] Lit. ' who inflicts anger.'
   9. *Are we Jews, &c.*] The meaning is uncertain. Alternative renderings are : (1)
Have we Jews any advantage ? (2) Do we excuse ourselves ? See A.V., R.V., and
Amer. R.V.

'WITH THEIR TONGUE THEY HAVE TALKED DECEITFULLY'
(Ps. v. 9).
'THE VENOM OF VIPERS LIES BEHIND THEIR LIPS'
(Ps. cxl. 3).
'THEIR MOUTH IS FULL OF CURSING AND BITTERNESS' 14
(Ps. x. 7).
'THEIR FEET MOVE SWIFTLY TO SHED BLOOD. 15
RUIN AND MISERY MARK THEIR PATH; 16
AND THE WAY TO PEACE THEY KNOW NOT' (Isa. lix. 7, 8). 17
'THERE IS NO FEAR OF GOD BEFORE THEIR EYES' 18
(Ps. xxxvi. 1).

The Jews are included in the Indictment But we know that all that the Law says is 19 addressed to those who are living subject to the Law, in order that every mouth may be silenced, and that the whole world may await sentence from God. For no man living will be declared 20 righteous before Him on the ground of obedience to Law. Law simply brings a knowledge of sin.

Forgiveness through Faith in Christ But now a righteousness of God has been 21 brought to light apart from any Law, both Law and Prophets bearing witness to it—a 22 righteousness of God conditional on faith in Jesus Christ for all who believe. No distinction is made; for all alike have sinned, and consciously fall short of the 23 glory of God, but are acquitted freely by His grace through 24 the ransom given in Christ Jesus, whom God put forward 25 as a propitiation available to faith in virtue of His blood. It was to demonstrate His justice, in view of the condoning by God's forbearance of sins previously committed—that 26 is, to demonstrate His justice at the present time, that He may be shown to be just Himself, and the justifier of the man who believes in Jesus.

Human Pride is excluded Where then is there room for boasting? It 27 is shut out. On what principle? On that of merit? No, but on the principle of faith.

13. *Behind*] Lit. 'under.'
22. *Conditional on*] Lit. 'through.'
For all] v.L. adds 'and upon all.'
25. *A propitiation*] Or perhaps 'propitiatory.' The Greek word has the meaning 'mercy-seat' in the LXX translation of the Pentateuch, and also in Heb. ix. 5; but this meaning is improbable here. It would make Christ 'at once priest and victim and place of sprinkling' (Sanday and Headlam).
Previously committed] *i.e.* in O.T. times.
26. *May be shown to be*] Lit. 'may be.'
27. *Principle*] Lit. 'law.'
Merit] Lit. 'works.'

For we deem that a man is counted righteous by faith, apart 28
from fulfilment of the Law.

The one God saves all alike through Faith Is God simply the God of Jews, and not of 29
Gentiles also? Yes, He is the God of Gen-
tiles also, if indeed it is one and the same 30
God who will acquit the circumcised on the
ground of faith, and the uncircumcised through
the same faith. Do we then by means of this faith abolish 31
the Law? God forbid! We confirm the Law.

Abraham's Acceptance with God What then shall we say of Abraham, our 1 **4**
natural forefather? For if he was held to 2
be righteous on the ground of his actions,
he has something to boast of. Yes, but not in the
presence of God. For what says the Scripture? 'ABRAHAM 3
BELIEVED GOD, AND THIS WAS CREDITED TO HIM AS RIGHTEOUS-
NESS' (Gen. xv. 6). But in the case of a man who works, 4
pay is not reckoned as a favour but as something due;
whereas in the case of a man who in place of working 5
believes in Him who acquits the ungodly, his faith is
credited to him as righteousness. In this way David also 6
tells of the blessedness of the man whom God credits
with righteousness apart from his actions.

'BLESSED,' he says, 'ARE THOSE WHOSE INIQUITIES ARE 7
  FORGIVEN, AND WHOSE SINS ARE COVERED.

BLESSED IS THE MAN OF WHOSE SIN THE LORD WILL NOT 8
  TAKE ACCOUNT' (Ps. xxxii. 1, 2).

Not dependent on Circumcision Is this declaration of blessedness, then, for 9
the circumcised, or for the uncircumcised as
well? For ABRAHAM'S FAITH—so we affirm—
WAS CREDITED TO HIM AS RIGHTEOUSNESS (Gen. xv. 6). In 10
what circumstances, then? Was it after he had been circumcised, or before? Before, not after. And he received 11
circumcision as a sign, a seal attesting the righteousness which was his by faith while still uncircumcised, that
he might be the father of all those who believe even though
uncircumcised—in order that this righteousness might be
credited to them; and also the father of the circumcised, 12
namely, of those who not merely are circumcised, but

---

31. *The Law*] Or ' Law.'
1. *Of Abraham*] v.l. 'that Abraham has gained.'
2. *In the presence of*] Or ' in relation to.'
5. *Believes in*] Lit. ' believes on.'
11. *Circumcision as a sign*] Lit. ' a sign of circumcision.'

also walk in the steps of the faith which our father Abraham had while he was as yet uncircumcised. Again, the pro- 13
mise that he should inherit the world did not come to Abraham or his posterity through Law, but through righteousness depending on faith. For if it is those who rely on Law who 14 are heirs, then faith is useless and the promise counts for nothing. For the effect of the Law is wrath ; but where 15 no Law exists, there can be no transgression. All depends 16 on faith for this reason—that righteousness may be by grace, so that the promise should be made sure to all his posterity ; not merely to those who rely on the Law, but also to those who rely on a faith like Abraham's. For in the sight of God in whom he believed, who gives life to the dead and speaks of things non-existent as though existing, Abraham is the father of all of us. As it is 17 written,

Not dependent on the Law of Moses

'I HAVE MADE YOU FATHER OF MANY NATIONS'

(Gen. xvii. 5).

He believed, hoping against hope, so that he 18
might become the father of many nations, in accordance with the words 'SO GREAT SHALL YOUR POSTERITY BE' (Gen. xv. 5). And with- 19
out growing weak in faith, he could note his own vital powers now decayed—for he was about a hundred years old—and Sarah's barrenness. Nor did he stagger at God's 20 promise in unbelief, but became mighty in faith, giving glory to God, and being absolutely certain that what- 21 ever He has promised He can also carry out. For this 22 reason also his faith WAS CREDITED TO HIM AS RIGHTEOUS-NESS (Gen. xv. 6).

Abraham the Father of all who have Faith

Nor was the fact of its being credited to 23
him recorded for his sake only, but for our 24
sakes too. Faith is going to be credited to us who believe in Him who raised Jesus, our Lord, from the dead, who was delivered up because 25 of our offences, and was raised to life for our acquittal.

Acceptance with God is still due to Faith

13. *Again*] Or ' Yes, for.' The conclusion (that faith is the one supreme need) is sound, for it is confirmed by another distinct argument.
15. *Wrath*] Or ' punishment.' Cf. v. 9 ; xiii. 4.
16. *Righteousness*] Not in the Greek.
Grace] *i.e.* God's free favour. Cf. iii. 24.

The happy Results which follow Acquitted then as the result of faith, let us 1 **5** enjoy peace with God through our Lord Jesus Christ, through whom we have been brought 2 by our faith into the position of favour in which we stand, and we exult in hope of seeing God's glory. And not only 3 so: we also exult in our afflictions, knowing as we do that affliction produces endurance; endurance, ripeness of 4 character; and ripeness of character, hope; and that 5 this hope never disappoints, because God's love for us floods our hearts through the Holy Spirit who has been given to us.

The Love manifested in Christ's Death For already, while we were still helpless, Christ 6 at the fitting time died for the ungodly. Why, 7 it is scarcely conceivable that anyone would die for a just man, although for a good man perhaps some one might have the courage even to die. But God 8 gives proof of His love to us in Christ's dying for us while we were still sinners.

Union with the now living Christ Much more, then, now that we have been 9 acquitted by His blood, shall we be delivered from God's anger through Him. For if while 10 we were hostile we were reconciled to Him through the death of His Son, the more certainly, after being reconciled, shall we obtain salvation through Christ's life. And 11 not only so, but we also exult in God through our Lord Jesus Christ, through whom we have now obtained our reconciliation.

Through Adam Death has come to all For as through one man sin entered into 12 the world, and through sin death, and so death passed to all mankind, in that all sinned— For prior to the Law sin was already in the 13 world; only sin is not entered in the account when no Law exists. Yet death reigned from Adam to Moses, 14 even over those who had not sinned in the manner of Adam's transgression. In Adam we have a type of him who was to come.

1. *Let us enjoy*] v.l. ' We have peace.'
2. *By our faith*] Or ' by faith.' v.l. omits altogether.
3. *We also exult*] Or ' let us also exult.'
5. *This hope*] Or ' hope.'
Floods] Lit. ' has been poured out in.'
The hope cannot disappoint, because God's Spirit makes us conscious of His love for us.
6. *For already*] v.l. ' If at least.'
9. *Anger*] Or ' punishment.'

Through
Christ
Redemption
has come
to all
But it is not the same with the transgression 15
as with God's free gift. For if through the transgression of one single man the mass of mankind
have died, all the more have God's grace, and the
gift made through the grace of the one man
Jesus Christ, been abundant for the mass of mankind. And 16
the gift is not comparable with the results of one man's
sinning ; for the judgement upon that one man's sin led to
condemnation, whereas the free gift after many transgressions leads to acquittal. For if, through the transgression 17
of one, death entered on his reign by means of one man,
all the more shall those who receive God's overflowing
grace and gift of righteousness reign in life through the
One—Jesus Christ.

Well then, just as the result of a single transgression is 18
condemnation for all mankind, so also the result of a single
deed of righteousness is a life-giving acquittal for all mankind. For as through the disobedience of one individual 19
the mass of mankind were made sinners, so also through the
obedience of One the mass of mankind will be made
righteous. Law crept in later on, so that transgression 20
might increase. But where sin increased, all the more was
grace abundant ; in order that as sin has reigned and 21
brought death, so grace, too, may reign by means of
righteousness leading to eternal life through Jesus Christ
our Lord.

A new Life and Character result from Acceptance with God

Real Union
with Christ
kills Sin
What shall we say then ? Are we to persist 1 **6**
in sinning in order that God's grace may be
the greater ? God forbid ! How can we who 2
have died to sin, live in it any longer ? Or do you not 3
know that all of us who were baptized into Christ Jesus
were baptized into His death ? Well, then, by our bap- 4
tism we were buried with Him in death, in order that, just

---

15. *The mass of mankind*] Lit. ' The many.'
All the more] What we know of the character of God as displayed in Christ makes
us more certain of the good result than of the evil (S.-H.).
20. *That transgression, &c.*] Or ' to increase transgression.'
4. *By our baptism, &c.*] Or ' When we descended into the baptismal water, that
meant that we died with Christ—to sin ' (S.-H.).
In death] Lit. ' into (or unto) death.' Some connect these words with ' baptism,'
and translate ' by our baptism unto death we were buried with Him.'

as Christ was raised from the dead by the Father's glorious power, we also should live an entirely new life. For if we 5 have become one with Him by sharing in His death, we shall also be one with Him by sharing in His resurrection. This we know—that our old self was nailed to the cross 6 with Him, in order that our sinful nature might be neutralized, so that we should no longer be the slaves of sin ; for he who has died is absolved from his sin. 7

But if we have died with Christ, we believe that we shall 8 also live with Him ; because we know that Christ, once 9 raised from the dead, is no longer liable to die. Death has no longer any power over Him. For the death that He 10 died, He died once for all to sin ; but the life that He lives, He lives to God. So too do you regard yourselves as 11 dead to sin, but as alive in Christ Jesus to God.

Let not sin then reign in your mortal bodies, causing you 12 to be subject to their passions ; and no longer offer your 13 faculties as instruments of wickedness for sin to use. But rather offer yourselves to God as living men risen from the dead, and your faculties to God as instruments of righteous- ness. For sin shall not be lord over you, since you are 14 subjects, not of Law, but of grace.

Christians are pledged to live Christlike Lives Are we therefore to sin because we are no 15 longer under the authority of Law, but under grace ? God forbid ! Do you not know that 16 you are the servants of the man at whose disposal you put yourselves, to obey him—it may be servants of sin, which leads to death, or of duty, which leads to righteousness ? But thanks be to God that though you 17 were once in thraldom to sin, you have now yielded a hearty obedience to that kind of teaching to which you were com- mitted. You were set free from the tyranny of sin, and 18 became the servants of righteousness—the infirmity of 19 your natures leads me to employ a metaphor from human affairs—but just as you once put your faculties at the ser- vice of impurity and of ever-increasing disregard of Law, so you must now put them at the service of righteousness, with holiness as your goal. For when you were the ser- 20 vants of sin, you were independent of righteousness.

5. *By sharing in*] Lit. ' by the likeness of.' Possibly the connection should be ' one with the likeness of.'
17. *Committed*] Lit. ' handed over.'

Well, what benefit did you get then from conduct which 21
you now regard with shame ? Why, such things finally
issue in death. But now, emancipated from sin, you have 22
your reward in holiness, and eternal life as the result.
For sin's wages are death ; but God's free gift is eternal 23
life in Christ Jesus our Lord.

Christ frees us from mere outward Rules

Brethren, do you not know—for I am speak- 1 **7**
Death frees ing to people acquainted with law—that it is
us from Law during our lifetime that we are subject to the
Law ? A wife, for instance, while her husband is living 2
is bound to him by law ; but if her husband dies,
she is released from the law regarding the husband.
Consequently, if during her husband's life she unites 3
herself to another man, she will get the name of an
adulteress ; but if her husband is dead she is free from
that law, so that though she marries again, she is not
an adulteress.

Union with So, my brethren, you also became dead to 4
Christ frees the Law through the body of Christ, that you
us from Law might belong to Another, namely to Him who
rose from the dead that we might yield fruit to God. For 5
while we obeyed our lower natures, sinful passions—
evoked by the Law—were always at work in the organs
of our bodies, to fructify and result in death. But we 6
are released by death from the Law by which we were
restrained, so that we render a service which is new and
spiritual, not old and ceremonial.

The Law What follows ? Is the Law itself a sinful 7
a good and thing ? God forbid ! On the contrary,
holy Thing except through the Law I should have known
nothing of sin as sin. For instance, I should not have
known what covetousness is, if the Law did not say, ' THOU
SHALT NOT COVET ' (Exod. xx. 17 ; Deut. v. 21). Sin
took advantage of this, and by means of the command- 8
ment roused within me every kind of coveting ; for apart
from Law sin would be dead. Once I was living apart 9

21. *Get then from conduct, &c.*] Or ' Get then ? Only what you are now
ashamed of.'
4. *Body*] *i.e.* death.

from Law, but when the commandment came, sin sprang into life, and I died. The commandment designed to 10 bring me life, brought me death. For sin seized the advan- 11 tage, and by means of the commandment beguiled me, and also put me to death. So that the Law was holy, and 12 the commandment holy, just, and good. Did then this 13 good thing become death to me ? God forbid ! But sin did ; so that it might be seen in its true light as sin : it utilized what was good to bring about my death, that by means of the commandment the unspeakable sinfulness of sin might be plainly shown.

Man's higher and lower Natures We know, indeed, that the Law is spiritual ; 14 but I am unspiritual, sold to sin. For I do 15 not recognize what I am doing. I do not act as I would, but I do what I loathe. But if I do what I do 16 not desire, I admit the excellence of the Law ; and now it 17 is no longer I that do it, but the sin which has its home within me. For I know that in me, that is, in my lower 18 self, nothing good has its home ; for the wish to do right is there but not the power. What I do is not the good deed 19 I desire, but the evil deed I do not desire. But if I do 20 what I do not desire, it is no longer I who do it, but sin which has its home within me.

I find therefore this rule, that when I desire to do what 21 is right, evil is there with me. In my inmost self all my 22 sympathy is with the law of God ; but I discover in my 23 faculties a different law, at war with the law of my under- standing, and leading me captive to the law which is in my faculties—the law of sin.

Not the Law, but Christ gives Deliverance Unhappy man that I am ! who will rescue 24 me from this body of death ? God ! to whom 25 be thanks through Jesus Christ our Lord ! So then I myself serve with my understanding the law of God, but with my lower nature the law of sin.

---

9. *Sprang*] Or ' returned.'
18. *Lower self*] Lit. ' flesh ' ; a word conveying a much narrower sense than that which Paul often intended. Man has a higher nature which links him to God, and to which we give the names of ' spirit,' ' conscience.' He has also a lower nature which makes him to some extent akin to the beasts which perish, and includes not simply his body, but also his mind in the degree in which that consists of merely earthly thoughts, feelings, affections, appetites, and ambitions. The Apostle gives the name of ' flesh ' to the whole of this earthly nature, especially so long as it remains sinful, *i.e.* continues in rebellion against the higher nature, which is its God-appointed ruler.

Christ frees us from Sin and Death

Forgiveness and spiritual Power There is therefore now no condemnation for 1 those who are in Christ Jesus ; for the Spirit's 2 law—life in Christ Jesus—has set me free from the law of sin and death. For what was impossible 3 to the Law—thwarted as it was by human frailty—God effected. Sending His own Son in the form of sinful humanity to deal with sin, God pronounced sentence upon sin in human nature ; in order that in our case the require- 4 ments of the Law might be fully met. For our lives are ruled not by our lower, but by our spiritual natures.

Our sinful Natures bear deadly Fruit If men comply with their lower nature, their 5 thoughts are shaped by the lower nature ; if with their spiritual nature, by the spiritual. Thoughts shaped by the lower nature mean death ; 6 thoughts shaped by the spiritual mean life and peace. For thoughts shaped by the lower nature mean a state of 7 enmity to God. They do not submit to God's Law, and indeed cannot. Those who obey the lower nature cannot 8 please God.

God gives us His own Spirit of Life You, however, are not absorbed in such 9 things, but in things spiritual, if the Spirit of God is dwelling in you ; whereas if any man has not the Spirit of Christ, he does not belong to Him. But if Christ is in you, though your body is dead because of 10 sin, yet your spirit has life because of righteousness. And if the Spirit of Him who raised up Jesus from the 11 dead is dwelling in you, He who raised up Christ from the dead will give life also to your mortal bodies through His Spirit dwelling in you.

A holy Life is now possible Therefore, brethren, it is not to our lower 12 nature that we are under obligation, to live by its rule. If you so live you are on your way 13 to death ; but if, by the power of the spirit, you put your merely bodily habits to death, you will live.

2. *Me*] v.l. ' you.'
3. *Human frailty*] Lit. ' flesh.'
The form of sinful humanity] Lit. ' likeness of flesh of sin,' *i.e.* the flesh that is prone to sin.
11. *Through*] v.l. ' Because of.'
13. *The spirit*] *i.e.* man's higher nature. Cf. verses 4, 5.
Your merely bodily habits] Lit. ' the practices of the body,' *i.e.* conduct not refined by the spirit.

Through the Spirit we are Sons of God For all who are led by God's Spirit are God's 14 sons. You have not acquired the spirit of 15 slavery again, to inspire terror ; but the spirit of adopted sons—in which spirit we cry ' Abba ! Father ! ' The Spirit Himself bears witness with our own spirits 16 that we are children of God ; and if children, then 17 heirs too—heirs of God and co-heirs with Christ ; if indeed we share Christ's sufferings, in order to share also His glory.

All Creation to be perfected and glorified Why, the sufferings of the present I deem 18 not worth considering compared with the glory soon to be disclosed to us. All creation 19 is yearning, longing to see the manifestation of the sons of God. For the Creation was made subject to 20 futility, not of its own choice, but by the will of Him who so subjected it ; yet with the hope that at last the 21 Creation itself would be set free from the thraldom of decay to enjoy the liberty that comes with the glory of the children of God.

Man's whole Nature will be glorified For we know that the whole of Creation is 22 moaning in the pangs of childbirth until this hour. And more than that, we ourselves, 23 though we possess the Spirit as a foretaste of bliss, yet we ourselves inwardly moan as we wait for full sonship in the redemption of our bodies. It is by hope that we have 24 been saved. But an object of hope is such no longer when it is seen : for why should a man hope for what he already sees ? But if we hope for something we do not see, then 25 we patiently wait for it. In the same way the Spirit 26 also helps us in our weakness ; for we know not how **The Help of the Holy Spirit in Prayer** to pray as we ought. But the Spirit Himself pleads for us in yearnings that can find no words, and the Searcher of hearts knows 27 what the Spirit's meaning is, because His intercessions for the saints are in harmony with God's will.

20. Paul says that the Creation lacks, or seems to man to lack, an ideal perfection, which will only be realised along with the perfecting of man.

23. *The Spirit as a foretaste of bliss*] Lit. ' the firstfruits of the Spirit.' Cf. 2 Cor. i. 22 ; v. 5 ; Eph. i. 14.

24. *Object of hope*] Lit. ' hope.' Cf. Tit. ii. 13.

Why should a man hope] v.L. ' who hopes.'

26. *In the same way*] The Spirit moans with us, and interprets our moaning.

Confidence in the fulfilment of God's purpose respecting His Saints Now we know that all things are working 28 together for good to those who love God, who are called according to the Divine purpose. Those whom He has foreknown He has also 29 predestined to share the likeness of His Son, that He might be the Eldest in a vast family of brothers ; and 30 those whom He has predestined He has also called ; and those whom He has called He has also acquitted ; and those whom He has acquitted He has also glorified.

God's marvellous Love What then shall we say to this ? If God is 31 for us, who can be against us ? He who did 32 not withhold even His own Son, but gave Him up for all of us, will He not also with Him freely give us all things ? Who shall impeach those whom God has 33 chosen ? Will God, who acquits them ? Who is there to 34 condemn them ? Will Christ Jesus, who died, or rather who rose to life again, who is also at the right hand of God, who moreover is interceding for us ? Who shall separate us from 35 Christ's love ? Shall affliction or distress, persecution or hunger, nakedness or danger or the sword ? As it is written, 36

' FOR THY SAKE WE ARE BEING KILLED ALL DAY LONG.
WE ARE COUNTED AS SHEEP FOR SLAUGHTER '

(Ps. xliv. 22).

Yet amid all these things we are more than conquerors 37 through Him who has loved us. For I am convinced that 38 neither death nor life, nor angels nor sovereignties, nor things present or future, nor powers nor height nor depth, 39 nor any other created thing, shall be able to separate us from the love of God which is in Christ Jesus our Lord.

The Unbelief of the Jews

9

Paul's Grief at the Rejection of the Jews I am telling you the truth as a Christian—it 1 is no falsehood, for my inspired conscience bears me out—when I declare that I have deep 2 grief and unceasing anguish of heart. For I 3 could pray to be myself accursed from Christ for the sake of my brethren, my natural kinsfolk, who are 4 Israelites ; to whom belong adoption by God, His glorious Presence, the Covenants, the giving of the Law,

---

28. *All things are working, &c.*] v.l. ' In all things God is working for good with those.'

the Temple service, and the Promises. To them the 5
Patriarchs belong, and from them in respect of His human
lineage came the Christ, who is exalted above all, God
blessed throughout the ages. Amen.

The Promises of God had Limitations Not, however, that God's word has failed ; 6
for not all who have sprung from Israel count
as Israel, nor because they spring from 7
Abraham are they all his. No ! ' THROUGH
ISAAC SHALL YOUR POSTERITY BE RECKONED ' (Gen. xxi. 12).
In other words, it is not the children by natural descent 8
who are God's children, but the children made such by
the promise are regarded as Abraham's posterity. For 9
the words of the promise were ' ABOUT THIS SEASON I WILL
COME, AND SARAH SHALL HAVE A SON ' (Gen. xviii. 10). Nor 10
is that all : there is Rebecca too. When she was with
child by her husband, our father Isaac, even then, though 11
they were not then born and had not done anything either
good or evil, yet in order that God's electing purpose might
stand, based not on their actions but on His calling them,
she was told, ' THE ELDER WILL BE SERVANT TO THE YOUNGER ' 12
(Gen. xxv. 23). This agrees with another passage, ' JACOB 13
I HAVE LOVED, BUT ESAU I HAVE HATED ' (Mal. i. 2, 3).

God's Freedom of Action defended What then are we to say ? That there is 14
injustice in God ? God forbid ! His words 15
to Moses are, ' I WILL BE MERCIFUL TO WHOM
I WILL, AND SHOW COMPASSION ON WHOM I
WILL ' (Exod. xxxiii. 19).

From this we learn that it is not a matter of man's will 16
or endeavour, but of God's mercy. For the Scripture says 17
to Pharaoh,
' IT IS FOR THIS VERY PURPOSE THAT I HAVE LIFTED YOU
SO HIGH—THAT I MAY MAKE MANIFEST IN YOU MY POWER,
AND THAT MY NAME MAY BE PROCLAIMED FAR AND WIDE IN
ALL THE EARTH ' (Exod. ix. 16).

This means that He has mercy on whom He will, and 18
hardens whom He will.

The Potter and the Clay ' Why then does God still find fault ? ' you 19
will ask ; ' for who is resisting His will ? '

5. *The Christ, who, &c.*] Or ' the Christ. He who is God over all be blessed
for ever. Amen.'
6. *Not, however, that, &c.*] *i.e.* Israel's forfeiture of privileges does not involve the
failure of God's word.
16. *Endeavour*] Lit. ' him who runs.'

Nay, but who are you, a mere man, to cavil against 20 God?

SHALL THE THING MOULDED SAY TO HIM WHO MOULDED IT, 'WHY HAVE YOU MADE ME THUS?' (Isa. xxix. 16). Or 21 has not the potter rightful power over the clay, to make out of the same lump one vessel for a noble and another for an ignoble use? And what if God, while having the will 22 to make manifest His anger and to show His power, has yet borne with great patience with the vessels of His anger who stand ready for destruction, in order to make known the 23 wealth of His glory towards the vessels of His mercy whom He has prepared beforehand for glory, even towards us 24 whom He has called not only from the Jews but also from the Gentiles?

So also in Hosea He says, 25

Old Testament Predictions on the Subject

'I WILL CALL THAT NATION MY PEOPLE WHICH WAS NOT MY PEOPLE,

AND HER BELOVED WHO WAS NOT BELOVED.

AND IN THE PLACE WHERE IT WAS SAID TO THEM, 26

" YOU ARE NOT MY PEOPLE,"

THERE SHALL THEY BE CALLED SONS OF THE LIVING GOD '
(Hos. ii. 23).

And Isaiah cries concerning Israel, 27

' THOUGH THE NUMBER OF THE SONS OF ISRAEL BE LIKE THE SANDS OF THE SEA, ONLY A REMNANT SHALL BE SAVED ; FOR THE LORD WILL HOLD A FINAL AND SUMMARY RECKON- 28 ING UPON THE EARTH ' (Isa. x. 22 ; xxviii. 22).

Even as Isaiah says in an earlier place, 29

' WERE IT NOT THAT THE LORD, THE GOD OF HOSTS, HAD LEFT US SOME SURVIVORS, WE SHOULD HAVE BEEN AS SODOM, AND HAVE BECOME LIKE GOMORRAH ' (Isa. i. 9).

Gentiles find Acceptance. The Jews do not

To what conclusion does this bring us? 30 Why, that the Gentiles, who were not in pursuit of righteousness, have grasped it—a righteousness dependent on faith ; while Israel, 31 who was in pursuit of a Law that could give righteous-ness, has not attained to one. And why? Because it 32

20. *A mere man*] Lit. ' O man ! '
23. *In order to, &c.*] v.L. ' and in order,' &c.
Prepared] Or ' destined.'
28. *Hold a . . reckoning*] Or ' execute a . . sentence.'
29. *Says in an earlier place*] Lit. ' has said.' Or perhaps ' has foretold.'
30. *The Gentiles*] Or perhaps ' Gentiles,' without the article.

was not a righteousness based on faith, but on their deeds. They stumbled at the stone of stumbling, as 33 Scripture says,

' SEE, I AM PLACING ON ZION A STONE TO STUMBLE AT, A ROCK TO TRIP OVER, YET HE WHOSE FAITH RESTS UPON IT SHALL NEVER BE MADE ASHAMED ' (Isa. viii. 14 ; xxviii. 16).

10

Brethren, my heart's longing, and my prayer 1 to God is for my countrymen's salvation. I 2 bear witness that they possess an enthusiasm for God, but it is an unenlightened one.

Israel refuses Salvation through Faith

Ignorant of the righteousness provided by God 3 and seeking to establish their own, they have refused submission to God's righteousness. For the consum- 4 mation of Law is Christ, to bring righteousness to every believer.

The Nearness of Christ and His Salvation

Moses writes that he who performs the 5 righteousness required by the Law shall live by that righteousness. But the righteousness 6 based on faith speaks thus :

' Say not in your heart, " Who shall ascend to heaven ? " '—that is, to bring Christ down ; ' nor " Who 7 shall go down into the abyss ? " '—that is, to bring Christ up from the grave. But what does it say ? 8

' The word is close to you, in your mouth and in your heart ' (Deut. xxx. 12–14) ; that is, the word which we · are publishing about the faith—that if with your mouth 9 you confess Jesus as Lord and in your heart believe that God raised Him from the dead, you shall be saved. For with the heart men believe and obtain righteous- 10 ness, and with the mouth they make confession and obtain salvation.

The Promise is for all

The Scripture says, ' NO ONE WHO BELIEVES 11 IN HIM SHALL BE MADE ASHAMED ' (Isa. xxviii. 16). Jew and Greek are on the same footing ; 12 the same Lord is Lord over all, rich in blessing to all who call upon Him. For ' EVERY ONE WHO CALLS ON THE 13 NAME OF THE LORD SHALL BE SAVED ' (Joel ii. 32).

---

1. *Longing*] Lit. ' good pleasure.'
4. *The consummation of Law*] Or ' the end that the Law had in view.'
   The sequence of thought is—they have not submitted to God's righteousness, for God's plan is righteousness through Christ.

Preaching makes known the Saviour's Name But how are they to call on One in 14 whom they have not believed? How are they to believe in One whose voice they have never heard? How are they to hear without a preacher? And how are men to 15 preach unless they are sent? As it is written, ' How BEAUTIFUL ARE THE FEET OF THOSE WHO BRING GOOD TIDINGS ! ' (Isa. lii. 7).

The world-wide Diffusion of the Gospel But, some will say, they have not all 16 hearkened to the gospel. No, for Isaiah asks, ' LORD, WHO HAS BELIEVED OUR MESSAGE ? ' (Isa. liii. 1). Faith then comes from a message 17 heard, and the message from the lips of Christ. But, I 18 ask, have they not heard? Yes, indeed :

' TO THE WHOLE WORLD THEIR VOICE HAS SOUNDED
    FORTH,
AND THEIR WORDS TO THE BOUNDS OF THE EARTH '
                         (Ps. xix. 4).

But again, did Israel fail to understand? Listen to 19 Moses first. He says,

' I WILL FIRE YOU WITH JEALOUSY AGAINST A NATION
    WHICH IS NO NATION,
AND WITH FURY AGAINST A NATION DEVOID OF UNDER-
    STANDING ' (Deut. xxxii. 21).

And Isaiah, with strange boldness, exclaims,   20

' I HAVE BEEN FOUND BY THOSE WHO WERE NOT LOOKING
    FOR ME,
I HAVE REVEALED MYSELF TO THOSE WHO WERE NOT
    INQUIRING OF ME ' (Isa. lxv. 1).

While as to Israel He says,   21

' ALL DAY LONG I HAVE STRETCHED OUT MY HANDS TO A
    SELF-WILLED AND FAULT-FINDING PEOPLE '
                        (Isa. lxv. 2).

Israel will at last be saved I ask then, Has God cast off His People? 1 God forbid ! Why, I myself am an Israelite, of the posterity of Abraham and of the tribe of Benjamin. God has not cast off His People whom He 2 foreknew. Do you not know what Scripture says in the case of Elijah—how he pleads with God against Israel, saying, ' LORD, THEY HAVE PUT THY PROPHETS TO DEATH, 3 AND HAVE OVERTHROWN THINE ALTARS ; AND, NOW THAT I ALONE REMAIN, THEY ARE SEEKING MY LIFE ' (1 Kings

xix. 10) ? But what is the Divine response ? 'I HAVE 4
RESERVED FOR MYSELF 7000 MEN WHO HAVE NOT BENT KNEE
TO BAAL ' (1 Kings xix. 18). So also at the present time 5
there has come to be a remnant—a selection by grace. But 6
if it is by grace, it is no longer on the basis of men's deeds ;
else grace were no longer grace.

Jewish Believers few as yet Well, then : what Israel is pursuing it has 7
not obtained : but the elect have obtained it,
and the rest have become callous. And so 8
Scripture says,

' GOD HAS GIVEN THEM A SPIRIT OF STUPOR—EYES TO
SEE NOTHING and EARS TO HEAR NOTHING—EVEN UNTIL
NOW ' (Isa. xxix. 10 ; Deut. xxix. 4).

And David says, 9
' BE THEIR BANQUETS A SNARE AND A TRAP TO THEM,
A STUMBLING-BLOCK AND A RETRIBUTION.
BE THEIR EYES DARKENED THAT THEY SEE NOT, 10
MAKE THEIR BACKS STOOP FOR EVER ' (Ps. lxix. 22, 23).

I ask next, 11
A glorious Prospect ' Have they stumbled irretrievably ? '
God forbid ! But by their lapse salvation
has come to the Gentiles in order to arouse their
jealousy ; and if their lapse is the enrichment of the 12
world, and their defeat the enrichment of the Gentiles,
what an enrichment will follow their reinstatement !

But I speak to you who are Gentiles. Inasmuch then 13
as I am an Apostle to Gentiles, I take pride in my ministry,
trying whether I can perhaps rouse my fellow-Jews to 14
jealousy and save some of them. For if their rejection 15
means the reconciliation of the world, what will their reception be but life from the dead ?

Gentiles warned not to be proud Now if the first piece is holy, so also is the 16
whole lump (Num. xv. 19–21) ; and if the root
is holy, so also are the branches. And if some 17
of the branches have been pruned away, and you, although
a wild olive, have been grafted in among them and have
become a sharer in the rich sap of the olive root, beware 18

---

4. *Have reserved*] The original Hebrew of 1 Kings xix. 18, means, ' I will
reserve.'
6. V.L. adds ' But if it is through works, it is no longer grace ; since work no
longer is work.'
12. *Enrichment*] Lit. ' riches.'
17. *Rich sap of the olive root*] Lit. ' root of the fatness of the olive.' V.L. ' root and
fatness of,' &c.

of glorying over the natural branches. Or if you glory, do not forget that it is not you who uphold the root : the root upholds you.

The Kindness and Severity of God 'Branches have been lopped off,' you will 19 say, 'for me to be grafted in.' True ; for 20 their unbelief they were lopped off, and you only stand through your faith. Do not be conceited. Tremble rather—for if God did not spare the 21 natural branches, neither will He spare you. Notice there- 22 fore God's kindness and His severity : on those who have fallen His severity comes, but upon you His kindness, provided that you continue responsive to that kindness. Otherwise you will be cut off also. Moreover, if they do 23 not persist in their unbelief, they too will be grafted in. For God is able to graft them in again ; and if you 24 were cut from that which by nature is a wild olive and contrary to nature were grafted into the good olive tree, how much more readily shall these natural branches be grafted on their own olive tree ?

God's Purpose one of Mercy to all alike There is a secret, brethren, of which I do 25 not wish to leave you in ignorance, for fear you should be conceited, namely, that partial blind- ness has fallen upon Israel until the great mass of the Gentiles has come in ; and so all Israel will be saved, 26 as is declared in Scripture,

'From Mount Zion a Deliverer will come :
He will remove all ungodliness from Jacob ;
And this is the Covenant I will grant them 27
(Isa. lix. 20, 21) ;
When I have taken away their sins ' (Isa. xxvii. 9).

In regard to the gospel they are God's enemies for your 28 sakes ; but in regard to God's election they are beloved for their fathers' sakes. For never does God repent of 29 His free gifts or of His call. Just as you were formerly 30 disobedient to Him, but now have received mercy when they are disobedient, so they also now have 31 been disobedient when you are receiving mercy ; so that they too may now receive mercy. For God has 32 imprisoned all in unbelief, that upon all alike He may have mercy.

26. *All ungodliness*] Lit. ' ungodlinesses.'
31. v.l. omits the second ' now.'

Oh the depth of the wealth both of the Wisdom and 33
The marvellous Wisdom of God's Methods Knowledge of God! How inscrutable His judgements, how trackless His footsteps! 'WHO HAS KNOWN THE MIND OF THE LORD, OR 34 SHARED HIS COUNSELS?' (Isa. xl. 13, 14).

'WHO HAS FIRST GIVEN GOD ANYTHING, AND THUS EARNED 35 A RECOMPENSE?' (Job xxxv. 7; xli. 11).

For all proceeds from Him, and exists by Him and for 36 Him. To Him be the glory for ever! Amen.

Practical Exhortations

12

Self-Surrender to the Love of God I plead with you therefore, brethren, by 1 the compassion of God, to present all your faculties to Him as a living and holy sacrifice acceptable to Him—a spiritual mode of worship. And do not conform to the present age, but be transformed 2 by the entire renewal of your minds, so that you may learn by experience what God's will is, namely, all that is good and acceptable to Him and perfect.

Union with the one Christ forbids Pride Through the grace given me I warn every 3 individual among you not to value himself unduly, but to aim at sober judgements in accordance with the degree of faith God has allotted to each one. Just as we have in the one body 4 many organs, and these organs have not all the same function; so collectively we form one body in Christ, 5 while individually we serve as organs for one another. But 6 since we have special gifts which differ according to the grace bestowed upon us, if it is prophecy, let it be in exact proportion to our faith; if administration, let our hearts 7 be in our ministry; the teacher's in his teaching; and the 8 pastor's in his exhortation. One who gives should be liberal; one who presides should be zealous; and one who gives help should do it cheerfully.

Brotherly Love and brotherly Conduct Let your love be sincere. Regard evil with 9 horror; cling to the right. Let your love 10 of the brethren be true mutual affection; in point of precedence defer to one another. Let not your zeal slacken. Have your spirits aglow as 11

1. *All your faculties*] Lit. ' your bodies.'
2. *Learn by experience*] Or ' habitually discriminate.'
7. *Administration*] Or perhaps 'deaconship.' But probably there were as yet no deacons in the Roman Church. Yet see xvi. 3, n.

the Lord's own servants, full of joyful hope, patient under 12
affliction, persistent in prayer. Relieve the necessities of 13
the saints ; always practise hospitality. Invoke blessings 14
on your persecutors—blessings, not curses. Rejoice with 15
those who rejoice ; weep with those who weep. Have full 16
sympathy with one another. Do not let your thoughts be
highflown, but accommodate yourselves to humble ways.
Do not be self-opinionated (Prov. iii. 7).

Pay back to no man evil for evil. TAKE THOUGHT FOR 17
WHAT IS RIGHT IN EVERY ONE'S ESTEEM (Prov. iii. 4 ; LXX).
If you can, so far as it depends on you, live at peace with 18
all the world. Never take revenge, my friends, but leave 19
it to God's wrath ; for it is written, '"REVENGE BELONGS
TO ME ; I WILL REPAY," says the Lord' (Deut. xxxii. 35).
On the contrary, IF YOUR ENEMY IS HUNGRY, GIVE HIM 20
FOOD ; IF HE IS THIRSTY, GIVE HIM DRINK. FOR BY DOING
THIS YOU WILL BE HEAPING BURNING COALS UPON HIS
HEAD (Prov. xxv. 21, 22). Do not be overcome by evil, 21
but overcome evil by goodness.

Our Duty in Relation to the State Let every individual be obedient to the 1 **13**
ruling authorities, for there is no authority
not under God's control, and under His con-
trol the existing authorities have been constituted. There- 2
fore the man who rebels against such authority is resisting
God's appointment ; and those who thus resist will incur
sentence. Judges and magistrates are no terror to right- 3
doers but to wrong-doers. You desire—do you not ?—to
have no reason to fear your ruler. Well, do what is right,
and he will commend you. He is God's servant for your 4
benefit. But if you do what is wrong, be afraid. He does
not wear the sword to no purpose : he is God's servant—
an avenger to inflict punishment upon the wrong-doer.
We must obey therefore, not only for fear of punishment, 5
but also for conscience' sake.

The prompt Payment of all Debts This indeed is the reason you pay taxes : 6
tax-gatherers are ministers of God, devoting
their energies to this very work. Pay to all 7
men what is due to them : tax to whom tax is due, toll

12. *The Lord's own servants*] V.L. ' servants of opportunity.'
16. *Accommodate, &c.*] Or ' associate freely with humble brethren.'
20. *Burning coals*] *i.e.* pangs of shame leading to repentance.
4. *Punishment*] Lit. ' wrath.'
6. *Tax-gatherers*] Not expressed in the Greek.
Ministers] The word here employed means service in sacred things.

to whom toll, respect to whom respect, and honour to whom honour.

True Love is perfect Obedience Leave no debt unpaid except the standing 8 debt of mutual love; for he who loves his fellow-man has fulfilled the Law. For the 9 commandments, 'THOU SHALT NOT COMMIT ADULTERY,' 'THOU SHALT DO NO MURDER,' 'THOU SHALT NOT STEAL,' 'THOU SHALT NOT COVET' (Exod. xx. 13–17; Deut. v. 17–21), and all other commandments, are summed up in this, 'THOU SHALT LOVE THY NEIGHBOUR AS THYSELF' (Lev. xix. 18). Love avoids wronging one's neighbour, and is 10 therefore the fulfilment of the Law.

The Nearness of the Day of Christ Live thus, realizing the situation, that it is 11 now high time to rouse yourselves from sleep; for our salvation is now nearer than when we first became believers. The night is far 12 advanced: day is about to dawn. Let us therefore lay aside the deeds of darkness, and put on the armour of light. As in the daytime, let us behave becomingly, not indulging 13 in revelry and drunkenness, nor in lust and debauchery, nor in quarrelling and jealousy. But put on as your 14 armour the Lord Jesus Christ, and make no provision for the passions of your lower nature.

Conscientious Differences of Opinion Welcome among you a man whose faith is weak, 1 **14** but not for the purpose of discussing opinions. One man's faith allows him to eat anything, 2 while a man of weaker faith eats only vegetables. Let not the 3 eater belittle the abstainer, nor the abstainer censure the eater, for God has accepted him. Who are you to find fault with 4 another man's servant? Whether he stands or falls is his own master's concern. But stand he will; for the Master can give him the power. One man esteems one day more 5 highly than another; another esteems all days alike. Let every one be convinced in his own mind. He who observes 6 the day observes it for the Lord's sake; and he who eats eats for the Lord's sake, for he gives thanks to God; and the abstainer abstains for the Lord's sake, and he also gives thanks to God.

We are all Servants of one Master For not one of us lives for himself, not one 7 dies for himself. If we live, we live for the 8 Lord: if we die, we die for the Lord, so whether we live or die we are the Lord's. For this was 9 the purpose of Christ's dying and coming to life, to be Lord both of dead and of living.

Individual Responsibility to God But you, why do you find fault with your 10 brother? Or you, why do you look down upon your brother? We shall all stand at the bar of God; for it is written, 11

' " As I LIVE," says the Lord, " TO ME EVERY KNEE SHALL BOW, AND EVERY TONGUE SHALL GIVE PRAISE TO GOD " ' (Isa. xlv. 23).

Therefore every one of us will give account of him- 12 self to God.

Hinder no one's Christian Progress Therefore let us no longer censure one another, 13 but rather do you come to this decision, not to put any obstacle or stumbling-block in your brother's path. I know and feel assured in 14 the Lord Jesus that in itself nothing is ' impure '; but if anyone regards anything as impure, to him it is so.

Brotherly Love limits Freedom of Action Still, if your brother is pained by the food 15 you are eating, you are no longer following the guidance of love. Do not by your food ruin a man for whom Christ died. Therefore 16 do not let what is a boon to you and others bring reproach. For the Kingdom of God does not consist in eating and 17 drinking, but in uprightness, peace, and joy in the Holy Spirit; and whoever in this way serves Christ, pleases God, 18 and is approved by men.

Therefore let us aim at whatever makes for peace and the 19 spiritual upbuilding of one another. Do not for food's sake 20 be throwing down God's work. All food is pure; but a man is in the wrong if his food is a stumbling-block to others. The right course is to forgo eating meat or drinking 21 wine or doing anything that tends to your brother's fall.

As to your faith, keep it to yourself and to God. Happy 22 the man who does not censure himself in the deeds he approves. But one who has misgivings stands self-con- 23 demned if he eats, because his act is not based on faith; for all action not so based is sin.

20. *All food*] Lit. ' everything.'
To others] Or perhaps ' to his own conscience.'
21. *Fall*] v.L. adds ' or stumbling or enfeeblement.'
22. *Happy, &c.*] This apparently means, ' Happy is he who feels no self-reproach for the freedom he allows himself.'

15 Our duty if we are strong is to bear with 1
the weaknesses of those who are not strong,
and not seek our own pleasure. Let each of 2
us endeavour to please his neighbour, aiming
at his spiritual upbuilding. For indeed Christ did not 3
seek His own pleasure, but exemplified that Scripture,
'THE REPROACHES OF THOSE THAT REPROACH THEE HAVE
FALLEN ON ME' (Ps. lxix. 9). All that was written of old 4
has been written for our instruction, that with patience
and the comfort derived from the Scriptures we may sustain our hope. And may the God of patience and of com- 5
fort grant you full sympathy with one another after the
example of Christ Jesus, that with oneness of heart and 6
voice you may glorify the God and Father of our Lord
Jesus Christ.

Christlike Sympathy and Unselfishness

Therefore welcome one another, just as 7
Christ has welcomed you, to promote the
glory of God. My meaning is that Christ has 8
become a servant to the circumcised in vindication of God's truthfulness—to fulfil the promises made
to our forefathers—and to make the Gentiles glorify God 9
for His mercy. So it is written,

Christ has welcomed Jews and Gentiles

' FOR THIS REASON I WILL PRAISE THEE AMONG THE
    GENTILES AND SING PSALMS TO THY NAME '
                                                    (Ps. xviii. 49).

And again the Psalmist says,   10
' BE GLAD, YE GENTILES, IN COMPANY WITH HIS PEOPLE '
                                                    (Deut. xxxii. 43).

And again,   11
' PRAISE THE LORD, ALL YE GENTILES,
    AND LET ALL THE NATIONS EXTOL HIM '
                                                    (Ps. cxvii. 1).

And again Isaiah says,   12
' THERE SHALL COME THE OFFSPRING OF JESSE,
    ONE WHO RISES UP TO RULE THE GENTILES.
  ON HIM SHALL THE GENTILES BUILD THEIR HOPES '
                                                    (Isa. xi. 1, 10).

May God, the giver of hope, fill you with 13
all joy and peace because you trust in Him
—so that you may be overflowing with hope
through the power of the Holy Spirit.

A Prayer for Joy, Peace, and Hope

Personal Explanation

The Apostle and his Readers But as to you, brethren, I am in my very 14 heart convinced that you yourselves are full of goodness, and equipped with all knowledge and competent to advise one another. But my letter is at times 15 rather bold, by way of stimulating your own recollection, because of God's grant to me in His grace, that I should 16 be a minister of Christ Jesus to the Gentiles, doing a priest's service to God's gospel, that the Gentiles consecrated by the Holy Spirit may prove an acceptable offering to Him. I have therefore my reason to boast of my relation to God 17 in Christ Jesus.

The Result of Paul's Ministry For I will not venture to say a word of 18 what Christ has not done through me in converting the Gentiles, by word and by deed, with 19 power manifested in signs and marvels, with the power of the Holy Spirit ; so that, beginning from Jerusalem and the surrounding districts, I have preached without reserve even as far as Illyricum the gospel of Christ. Herein I 20 made it my ambition not to preach the gospel where Christ's name was already known, for fear I should be building on another man's foundation. As Scripture says, 21

' THOSE WHO HAVE NOT BEEN TOLD ABOUT HIM SHALL SEE,
AND THOSE WHO HAVE NOT HEARD SHALL UNDERSTAND '
(Isa. lii. 15).

A Visit to Rome anticipated And it is really this which has again and 22 again prevented my coming to you. But now, 23 as there is no more opening in this part of the world, and I have for years past been eager to pay you a visit, I hope as soon as ever I proceed to Spain, to see you 24

---

18. *I will not venture, &c.*] The majority of commentators, in view of the following words ' so that I have preached,' would insert after ' not done through me ' the words ' but only of what he has done through me ' ; and this can be shortened to ' I will not venture to speak except of what Christ has done through me,' meaning that he will not speak of what Christ has effected through other apostles (cf. verse 20) ; or else, as some suppose, that he will not imitate the pseudo-apostles : in which case there is a touch of irony in his language (cf. 2 Cor. x. 12-15). There are other renderings of the passage, one of which is, that the apostle, aglow with the thought, ' What has Christ not done through me ! ' exclaims, ' I can hardly dare to tell what Christ has not done through me,' meaning that the wonder of the manifold display of Christ's power through him was unspeakable. The use of the redundant negative, assumed in this last interpretation, would be more permissible in Greek (cf. xiii. 8, 1 Cor. xiv. 5), in French, or in Old English, than in correct modern English ; which would require, ' I can hardly dare to tell all that Christ has done through me.'

19. *Beginning from Jerusalem, &c.*] Or perhaps simply ' over a region lying between Jerusalem and Illyricum.'

on my way and be helped forward by you, when I have first enjoyed being with you for a time.

The Collection for the Poor in Jerusalem But at present I am going to Jerusalem to 25 serve the saints, for Macedonia and Greece 26 have thought it good to contribute a certain sum in relief of the poor among the saints in Jerusalem. Yes, they have thought it good, and in fact it 27 was a debt they owed them. For seeing that the Gentiles have been admitted into partnership in their spiritual blessings, they in turn are bound to serve them with material benefits. So after discharging this duty, and 28 making sure that these gifts reach their destination, I shall start for Spain, visiting you on my way; and I 29 know that when I come to you it will be with rich blessing from Christ.

A Request for Prayer But I entreat you, brethren, in the name of 30 our Lord Jesus Christ and by the love which His Spirit inspires, to join with me in very earnest prayer to God on my behalf, that I may escape unhurt from 31 the unbelievers in Judaea, and that my service to Jerusalem may be well received by the saints there, in order that if 32 God be willing I may come to you with a glad heart, and may enjoy a time of rest with you. May the God of peace be 33 with you all ! Amen.

Conclusion

The Bearer of this Letter Herewith I introduce to you our sister 1 **16** Phoebe, who is a servant of the Church at Cenchreae, that you may receive her in the 2 Lord's name in a manner worthy of saints, and may assist her in any matter in which she may need help. For she has indeed befriended many, including myself.

Kindly Greetings Greetings to Prisca and Aquila, my fellow 3 labourers in Christ Jesus—friends who have 4 endangered their own lives for mine. I am grateful to them, and not I alone, but all the Gentile Churches also. Greetings, too, to the Church that meets 5 at their house.

1. *A servant*] Or perhaps ' deaconess.' v.l. ' also a servant.'
Cenchreae] The eastern port of Corinth.
5–15. None of these persons is mentioned elsewhere in the N.T., unless, possibly, Rufus (Mark xv. 21).

Greetings to my dear Epaenetus, who was the earliest convert to Christ in the province of Asia ; to Mary who 6 has laboured strenuously for you ; and to Andronicus and 7 Junia, my countrymen, who once shared my imprisonment. They are of note among the apostles, and have been Christians longer than I myself. Greetings to Ampliatus, dear 8 to me in the Lord ; to Urban, our fellow labourer in Christ, 9 and to my dear Stachys. Greetings to Apelles—that veteran 10 believer—and to the members of the household of Aristobulus. Greetings to my countryman, Herodion ; and to 11 the believing members of the household of Narcissus. Greetings to those Christian workers, Tryphaena and 12 Tryphosa ; also to dear Persis, who has laboured strenuously in the Lord's work. Greetings to Rufus, who is the 13 Lord's elect ; and to his mother, who has also been a mother to me. Greetings to Asyncritus, Phlegon, Hermes, 14 Patrobas, Hermas, and to the brethren associated with them ; to Philologus and Julia, Nereus and his sister and 15 Olympas, and to all the saints associated with them.

Salute one another with a holy kiss. 16

All the Churches of Christ send greetings to you.

But I beseech you, brethren, to keep a watch on those 17 who are causing divisions and occasions of stumbling among you, in defiance of the instruction which you have received ; and to shun them. For men of that stamp are 18 not servants of our Lord, but of their own appetites ; and by their plausible words and their flattery they deceive simple minds. Your fidelity to the truth is everywhere 19 known. I rejoice over you, therefore, but I wish you to be wise in what is good, and innocent in what is evil. And 20 before long, the God of peace will crush Satan under your feet. The grace of our Lord Jesus Christ be with you !

Timothy, my fellow worker, sends you greetings, and so 21 do my countrymen Lucius, Jason, and Sosipater. I, 22 Tertius, who write this letter, greet you in the Lord. Gaius, my host, who is also the host of the whole Church, 23

7. *Junia*] Or ' Junias.'
Countrymen] Or perhaps ' relatives.'
Of note, &c.] Or ' held in high esteem by the Apostles.' But others besides the Twelve are called Apostles in the N.T., *e.g.* Barnabas, see Acts, xiv. 14.
17. *To shun*] v.L. ' promptly to turn from.'
19. *Fidelity to the truth*] Lit. ' obedience.'
20. *The grace, &c.*] v.L. omits.

greets you. So do Erastus, the treasurer of the city, and Quartus our brother.

To Him who is able to make you strong, as declared in 25 the gospel I preach, and the proclamation concerning Jesus Christ, in harmony with the unveiling of the mystery shrouded in silence in past ages, but now brought to light, 26 and by the command of the eternal God made known through the writings of the Prophets among all the Gentiles to win them to obedience to the faith—to God, the only 27 wise, through Jesus Christ, even to Him be the glory through all the ages ! Amen.

23. After ' Quartus our brother ' v.l. inserts verse 24, ' The grace of our Lord Jesus Christ be with you all. Amen.'
26. *Obedience to the faith*] Lit. ' obedience of faith.'
27. *Even to Him*] Lit. ' to whom.'

THE FIRST EPISTLE OF PAUL
TO THE CORINTHIANS

There are two recorded visits of Paul to Corinth, one of eighteen months, the other of three (Acts xviii. 11 ; xx. 3). (But see Introduction to 2 Corinthians.) It appears from 1 Cor. xvi. 5–9 that this letter was written from Ephesus before the second visit. Its immediate occasion was a complacent letter of inquiry from Corinth as to certain perplexities of Christian conduct (vii. 1 ; viii. 1 ; xi. 2, 34). But Paul prefaces his reply with stern comments on matters which had been reported to him (i. 11 ; v. 1 ; vi. 1), while in xi. 2 to xiv. 40 he deals with excesses in public worship and ' spiritual gifts,' a theme which provokes the glorious hymn in praise of love as better than all ' gifts ' (xiii.).

Chapter xv. discusses, not the question of an after-life, but the resurrection of the body, in answer to some in the Church who denied its possibility. The letter closes with personal matters, ending with the Christian watchword ' Our Lord is coming.'

No other writing of Paul's gives so detailed and vivid a picture of Christianity at work in a heathen city. The thanksgiving of i. 4–9 is, in view of what is to follow, an amazing disclosure of Paul's invincible confidence in the power of the ' Grace of God.'

On an earlier letter referred to in v. 9 see Preface to 2 Corinthians.

THE FIRST EPISTLE OF PAUL
TO THE CORINTHIANS

Introduction

Greeting   Paul, called to be an Apostle of Christ Jesus 1 **1**
by the will of God, and our brother Sosthenes,
to the Church of God in Corinth, men and women 2
consecrated in Christ Jesus, called to be saints, with all
in any place who call on the name of our Lord Jesus Christ
—their Lord as well as ours: grace and peace be to you 3
from God our Father and the Lord Jesus Christ.

    I thank my God continually for the grace of 4
Reasons for God bestowed on you in Christ Jesus—that in 5
Thankfulness Him you have been enriched with everything,
with readiness of speech and fulness of knowledge. Thus 6
my testimony to Christ has been confirmed in your case, so 7
that there is no special gift in which you come short while
waiting for the revealing of our Lord Jesus Christ. He 8
will also confirm you to the end, so that you may be free
from reproach on the day of our Lord Jesus Christ. God 9
is ever faithful, and by Him you were called into fellowship
with His Son Jesus Christ, our Lord.

The Divisions in the Corinthian Church

An Appeal   I entreat you all, brethren, in the name of 10
for Unity our Lord Jesus Christ, to avoid disputes and
divisions, and be recalled to the same mind
and judgement. For I have been informed, my brethren, 11
by Chloe's people, that there are dissensions among you.
What I mean is that each of you says, ' I belong to Paul'; 12
' I belong to Apollos'; ' I belong to Cephas'; ' I belong to
Christ.' Is Christ split up? Was Paul crucified for you? 13
Or were you baptized into Paul's name? I am thankful 14

---

2. *Their Lord as well as ours*] Or ' their place and ours.'
12. *Cephas*] *i.e.* Peter.

that I did not baptize any of you except Crispus and Gaius
—for fear people should say that you were baptized into 15
my name. I did baptize Stephanas's household also: but 16
I do not know that I baptized any one else.

Christ did not send me to baptize, but to 17
The Message of the Cross preach the gospel; and not with merely clever
words—lest the cross of Christ should be frus-
trated. For the word about the cross is foolishness to 18
those who are on the way to perdition, but it is the power
of God to those whom He is saving. For so it is written, 19
' I WILL BAFFLE THE WISDOM OF THE WISE, AND THE ACUTE-
NESS OF THE ACUTE I WILL THWART ' (Isa. xxix. 14). Where 20
is your wise man? Where your scholar? Where your
disputant of this present age? Has not God stultified
the world's wisdom?

For when by God's wise ordinance the world by its 21
wisdom had failed to gain the knowledge of God, God was
pleased, by the foolishness of the preaching, to save those
who believe; seeing that Jews demand miracles, and 22
Greeks pursue wisdom, while we proclaim a crucified 23
Christ — to Jews a stumbling-block, to Gentiles foolishness, but to those who are called, whether Jews or Greeks, 24
Christ the power of God and the wisdom of God. Because 25
the foolishness of God is wiser than men, and the weakness
of God is stronger than men.

Facts as to the Church in Corinth For consider, brethren, your own calling. 26
Not many worldly-wise, not many influential,
not many of noble birth have been called. But 27
God has chosen the foolish things of the world in order to
shame its wise men; and God has chosen the weak things
of the world in order to shame its strong things; and the 28
mean and despised things of the world—things that are
nothing—God has chosen in order to bring to nothing
things that are; to prevent any mortal man from boast- 29
ing before God. But thanks to Him you are in Christ 30
Jesus: He has become our wisdom from God, which is

17. *Merely clever words*] Lit. ' wisdom of word ' : such arguments as contemporary
pagan rhetoricians used. The Corinthians are to trust not in human reasonings, but
in God's grace as manifested in a crucified Christ.
22. *Miracles*] Lit. ' signs,' as everywhere in John's Gospel.
26. *Not many . . have been called*] Or ' Not many of you are wise,' &c.
28. *That are nothing*] Slaves for example, of whom there were many in the early
Christian Church. According to the popular language of those days the slave was a
thing that was not.

righteousness and sanctification and redemption ; that it 31
may be as Scripture says, ' HE WHO BOASTS—LET HIS BOAST
BE IN THE LORD ' (Jer. ix. 24).

The Spirit in which Paul preached in Corinth   For my part, brethren, when I came to you, 1 **2**
it was not with superiority of speech or wisdom
that I came, announcing to you the testimony
of God. For I determined not to know any- 2
thing when among you, except Jesus Christ, and a crucified Jesus Christ. It was in weakness and fear and great 3
trepidation that I was among you. And my language and my 4
preaching were not armed with persuasive words of wisdom,
but with the convincing power of the Spirit ; so that your trust 5
might rest not on the wisdom of man, but on the power of God.

The true, Divine Wisdom   Yet there is a wisdom that we utter among 6
the mature ; a wisdom not belonging, however,
to the present age nor to the leaders of the
present age, whose power is on the wane. We speak a 7
wisdom of God in a mystery—that hidden wisdom which,
before the world began, God purposed for our glory ; a 8
wisdom which not one of the leaders of the present age has
learnt ; for if they had learnt it, they would not have
crucified the Lord of glory. But we speak—to use the 9
words of Scripture—of THINGS WHICH EYE HAS NOT SEEN
NOR EAR HEARD, and which have not entered the heart of
man : ALL THAT GOD HAS IN READINESS FOR THEM THAT
LOVE HIM (Isa. lxiv. 4). For to us God has revealed them 10
through the Spirit ; for the Spirit searches everything,
including the deeps of God.

The Teaching of the Holy Spirit   For who among men knows a man's thoughts, 11
except the man's own spirit within him ?
In the same way also only God's Spirit is
acquainted with God's thoughts. But we have not received 12
the spirit of the world, but the Spirit which comes from
God, that we may know what is freely given us by God.
This we also utter, not in language which man's wisdom 13
teaches us, but in that which the Spirit teaches, adapting
spiritual words to spiritual truths. The unspiritual man 14

1. *The testimony of God*] v.l. ' the mystery (or, secret truth) of God.'
7. *In a mystery*] *i.e.* not attainable by man's reason, but disclosed by divine
revelation.
13. *Truths*] Or ' men.'
14. *Unspiritual*] Lit. ' psychical.' In the psychical man ' the spirit being unvivified
and uninformed by the Spirit of God is overborne by the animal soul with its
desires—and is in abeyance, so that he may be said not to have it ' (Alford).

rejects the teachings of the Spirit of God; to him they are folly, and he cannot learn them, because they are spiritually measured. But the spiritual man takes the 15 measure of everything, although he is himself measured by no one. For WHO HAS LEARNT THE MIND OF THE LORD, 16 SO AS TO INSTRUCT HIM (Isa. xl. 13)? But we have the mind of Christ.

Divisions a sure Proof of Unspirituality And I myself, brethren, could not speak to 1 **3** you as to spiritual men: it had to be as to worldlings—mere babes in Christ. I fed you 2 with milk and not with solid food, since for this you were not yet strong enough. Why, even now you are not strong enough: you are still unspiritual. For so long 3 as there are jealousy and strife among you, are you not unspiritual and behaving like mere men? For when one 4 says, 'I am for Paul,' and another, 'I am for Apollos,' are you not mere men?

Human Teachers mere Instruments in God's Hands What then is Apollos? And what is Paul? 5 Men through whose ministry, and as the Lord granted power to each, you came to believe. I planted, Apollos watered; but it was God 6 who caused the growth. So that neither the 7 planter nor the waterer is anything, but God who causes the growth. Now in effect the planter and the waterer are 8 one; and yet each will receive his own reward, answering to his own work. We are fellow-workers, you are God's 9 field—God's building.

The Responsibility of Teachers In exercise of the grace given me by God, 10 I, like a competent master-builder, have laid a foundation, and others are building upon it. But let every one be careful how he builds. For no one 11 can lay any foundation other than that which is already laid, namely Jesus Christ. And whether the building which 12 any one erects on that foundation be of gold or silver or costly stones, or of timber or hay or straw—the character 13 of each individual's work will appear. For the Day will disclose it, because that Day is to reveal itself in fire, and it is the fire which shall test the quality of every one's work. If the work which any one has erected stands the test, he 14 shall be rewarded. If any one's work is burnt up, he will 15

---

2. *I fed you with*] Lit. ' I caused you to drink.'
9. *We*] *i.e.* Paul and Apollos.

suffer loss ; he will himself be rescued, but only, as it were, by escaping through the fire.

To injure God's People is an awful Sin Do you not know that you are God's Sanctuary, and that the Spirit of God dwells within you ? If any one destroys the Sanctuary of God, God will destroy him ; for the Sanctuary of God is sacred, and this Sanctuary you are. 16 17

Mere human Wisdom is worthless Let no one deceive himself. If any man among you imagines that he is wise with the wisdom of the present age, let him become 'foolish' so that he may be wise. This world's wisdom is foolishness to God ; for it is written, 'HE SNARES THE WISE WITH THEIR OWN CUNNING' (Job. v. 13). And again, 'THE LORD KNOWS THAT THE REASONINGS OF THE WISE ARE USELESS' (Ps. xciv. 11). Therefore let no one boast about men. For everything is yours—be it Paul, be it Apollos, be it Cephas, be it the world, be it life, be it death, be it the present, be it the future—everything is yours ; and you are Christ's and Christ is God's. 18 19 20 21 22 23

The Responsibility of Preachers is to God This is how men should think of us—we are Christ's servants, and stewards of God's secret truths. In this connection, further, what is required in stewards is to prove faithful. I, however, am very little concerned at undergoing your scrutiny, or that of any human tribunal ; in fact, I do not even scrutinize myself. Though I am not conscious of any fault, yet I am not thereby acquitted ; but He who scrutinizes me is the Lord. Therefore form no premature judgements, but wait until the Lord comes. He will both bring to light the secrets of darkness and will disclose the motives that have been in people's hearts ; and then each man's praise will come to him from God. 1 **4** 2 3 4 5

The Names of Party Leaders are not specified Now these considerations, brethren, I have specially applied to Apollos and myself, for your sakes, in order to teach you by our example the maxim not to exceed what is written ; so that you may not be arrogant champions of one teacher against another. 6

---

1. *Servants*] Or 'officers.' See Matt. xxvi. 58. The word occurs twenty times in all, but only here in the Letters of Paul.

6. *I have specially applied to, &c.*] 'By what I have said of Apollos and myself, I have shown what holds true of all Christian teachers' (Thayer).

The maxim, &c.] Text and sense are here somewhat uncertain.

Some keen Irony Why, who gives you your superiority, my 7 brother ? Or what have you that you did not receive ? And if you did receive it, why boast as if you had not ?

You all have already all you can wish ; already you have 8 grown rich : without us, you have ascended the throne ! Ay, would to God that you had ascended the throne, that we also might reign with you ! It seems to me that God 9 has exhibited us Apostles last of all, like men condemned to death ; for we have become a spectacle to all creation— alike to angels and to men. We rank as fools for Christ's 10 sake : you are shrewd men in Christ. We are weaklings : you are strong. You are in high repute : we are outcasts. To this very moment we endure both hunger 11 and thirst ; we are barely clad and roughly handled. Homes we have none. We tire ourselves out working 12 with our own hands. When reviled, we bless ; when persecuted, we bear it patiently ; when slandered, we try to 13 conciliate. We are regarded as the scum of the earth—the dregs of the world, even to this hour.

A loving Entreaty I am not writing this to shame you, but to 14 advise you as my beloved children. For even 15 if you were to have ten thousand tutors in Christ, yet you would not have several fathers. It is I who in Christ Jesus became your father through the gospel. I entreat you therefore to become like me. For 16, 1͟ this reason I have sent Timothy to you. He is my beloved and faithful child in the Lord. He will remind you of my conduct as a Christian teacher—the manner in which I teach everywhere in every Church.

The Reality of Apostolic Authority But some of you have grown arrogant, as 18 though I were not coming to you. But I shall 19 come to you soon if the Lord wills, and I shall discover not the fine speeches of these arrogant people, but their power. For God's Kingdom is not a thing of 20

7. With these three pointed questions Paul turns for a moment from the Church as a whole to rebuke some individual teacher unnamed, whom the flattery of a party has elated.

8. Ironical.

9. *Exhibited . . last of all*] Alluding ' to the custom of carrying into effect the sentence on men condemned to death as a fitting close to the day's sport, when less sanguinary exhibitions had palled on the spectators' appetite ' (T. C. Edwards).

10. *You*] ' Party leaders and party men ' (Alford).

17. *Have sent*] Or ' sent,' or ' send.'

Conduct as a Christian teacher] Lit. 'ways in Christ.'

words, but of power. What will you have? Shall I come 21
to you with a rod, or in a loving and tender spirit?

A Stern Rebuke

An Instance It is actually reported that there is licentious- 1 **5**
of gross ness among you, and of a kind unheard of even
Immorality among the Gentiles—a man has his father's
wife! And you, instead of mourning and removing from 2
among you the man who has done this deed, are self-
complacent! I for my part, present with you in spirit 3
although absent in body, have already, as though I were
present, judged him who has so acted. In the name of 4
our Lord Jesus, assembled in spirit with you, along with
the power of our Lord Jesus, I have handed over such a 5
man to Satan for the destruction of his body, that his spirit
may be saved on the day of the Lord Jesus.

The false It is no good thing—this boast of yours. 6
Attitude Do you not know that a little leaven leavens
of the the whole of the lump? Clear out the old 7
Corinthians leaven so that you may be a new lump; for in
fact you are free from that leaven. For our Passover Lamb
has been sacrificed—Christ! Therefore let us keep our 8
festival, not with old leaven nor with the leaven of villainy
and mischief, but with bread free from leaven—the bread of
sincerity and of truth.

A previous I wrote to you in that letter not to be 9
Warning associated with licentious people; not meaning 10
disregarded that you must wholly avoid the licentious of
this world, or the avaricious and grasping, or idolaters. For
then you would have to go out of the world altogether.
But what I actually meant was that you were not to be 11
associated with any one bearing the name of 'brother,' if
he was licentious or avaricious or idolatrous or scurrilous
or drunken or grasping. With such a man you ought not
even to eat. Is it my business to judge outsiders? Is it 12
not those who are within the Church whom you are to judge?
Those who are outside God will judge. Remove the 13
wicked man from among you (Deut. xxii. 24).

---

5. *Body*] Lit. ' flesh '; the word which Paul applies to the whole of man's earthly
nature.
6. *Boast*] Cf. iv. 8–10.
9. *In that letter*] *i.e.* one now lost. (See Introd. to 2 Cor.)

Litigation at Corinth

Litigation in heathen Law Courts If one of you has a grievance against an **6** 1 opponent, does he dare to go to law before wicked men and not before the saints ? Do 2 you not know that the saints shall judge the world ? And if you are the court before which the world is judged, are you unequal to these pettiest cases ? Do you not know 3 that we are to judge angels, not to mention matters of this life ? If therefore you have matters of this life to be 4 decided, is it men who have no standing at all in the Church whom you make your judges ? I say this to your 5 shame. Is there not then among you a single wise man competent to decide between brethren, but brother goes 6 to law with brother, and that before unbelievers ?

All Litigation between Christians discouraged Even now it is altogether a token of 7 your defeat that you have lawsuits with one another. Why not rather be wronged ? Why not rather be defrauded ? On the contrary, 8 you yourselves inflict wrong and fraud, and upon brethren too. Do you not know that wicked men will not inherit 9 God's Kingdom ?

Righteousness of Life absolutely indispensable Make no mistake. Neither the licentious, nor idolaters, nor adulterers, nor men guilty of unnatural crime, nor thieves, nor avaricious, 10 nor drunken, nor scurrilous, nor grasping people shall inherit God's Kingdom. And such were some of 11 you. But you have washed, you have been consecrated, you have been acquitted, in the name of our Lord Jesus Christ and through the Spirit of our God.

Christian Freedom no Excuse for Immorality Everything is allowable to me, but not 12 everything is profitable. Everything is allowable to me, but to nothing will I become enslaved. Food is for the stomach, and the 13 stomach is for food, and God will bring both of them to nothing. The body is not for licentiousness, but for the Lord, and the Lord is for the body ; and as God by His 14 power raised the Lord, so He will also raise us.

The awful Guilt of such Sins Do you not know that your bodies are 15 members of Christ ? Shall I then take the members of Christ and make them members

7. *Defeat*] Or ' lapse ' : defeat in the Christian life.
12. *To nothing, &c.*] Lit. ' I will not be brought under its power by anything.'

of a harlot? God forbid! Or do you not know that a 16
man who is tied to a harlot is one with her in body? For
God says, 'THE TWO SHALL BECOME ONE' (Gen. ii. 24).
But he who is tied to the Lord is one with Him in spirit. 17
Flee from licentiousness. Any other sin that a man com- 18
mits is outside the body; but the licentious man sins against
his own body. Or do you not know that your bodies are 19
a sanctuary of the Holy Spirit within you—the Spirit whom
you have from God? And you are not your own, for you 20
have been bought at a price. Glorify God, then, in your
bodies.

The Subject of Marriage

The Apostle's own View of the Matter Now as to the topics of your letter. It is 1 **7**
better for a man to abstain from marriage.
There is however so much licentiousness that 2
every man should have a wife of his own, and every
woman should have a husband of her own. Let the hus- 3
band pay his wife her due, and let a woman also pay her
husband his. A wife has not the control of her own 4
person, but her husband has. In the same way a husband
has not the control of his own person, but his wife has.
Do not deprive one another—unless by mutual consent 5
for a time, so that you may devote yourselves to prayer
and then associate again; otherwise Satan may tempt you
because of your incontinence.

I say this by way of concession, not of command. Yet I 6, 7
would have everybody be as I am; but each of us has his own
special gift from God—one of one kind and another of another.

Advice to Unmarried and Married But I say to the unmarried, and to widows, 8
that it is well for them to remain as I am. If, 9
however, they cannot control themselves, let
them marry; for marriage is better than the fever of
passion. But to those already married my instructions— 10
yet not mine, but the Lord's—are, that a wife is not to be
separated from her husband; or if she is separated, let her 11
either remain unmarried or be reconciled to him; and
that a husband is not to put away his wife.

Advice to those married to Unbelievers To the rest it is I who speak—not the Lord. 12
If a brother has a wife who is an unbeliever,
and she consents to live with him, let him not
put her away. And a woman who has an 13

unbelieving husband—if he consents to live with her, let her not put him away. For the unbelieving husband is 14 hallowed by union with a Christian woman, and the unbelieving wife is hallowed by union with a Christian brother. Otherwise your children would be unholy, but in reality they are holy. If, however, the unbeliever is 15 determined to separate, let him do so. In such circumstances the Christian man or woman is no slave ; God has called us to be at peace. For how do you know, O woman, 16 if you will save your husband ? Or how do you know, O man, if you will save your wife ?

Existing Relationships to be acquiesced in Only, whatever the condition which the 17 Lord has assigned to each individual—and whatever his condition when God called him — in that let him continue. This is what I enjoin in all the Churches. Was any one 18 already circumcised when he was called ? Let him not try to disguise it. Was any one uncircumcised when called ? Let him remain uncircumcised. Circumcision 19 is nothing, and uncircumcision is nothing : obedience to God's commandments is everything. Let each man 20 remain in the condition in which he was called. Were you 21 a slave when God called you ? Never mind. (And yet if you can get your freedom, you had better take it.) For 22 a slave who has received his calling in the Lord is the Lord's freed man, and in the same way a free man, if called, is the slave of Christ. You have been bought at 23 a price : do not become slaves to men. Where each one 24 was when he was called, there, brethren, let him still stand —close to God.

Concerning unmarried women I have no order from the 25 Lord ; but I give an opinion, as one who through the Lord's mercy is trustworthy. I think then that, in view 26 of the imminent distress, it is well for a man to remain as he is. Are you bound to a wife ? Do not seek to 27 become free. Are you free from a wife ? Do not seek for a wife. Yet if you get married, you have not sinned ; 28 and if a maiden gets married, she has not sinned. Such

16. *You will save*] Or possibly, ' you will not save.'

17. *Only*] Marking an exception to the ' is not a slave ' of verse 15. The Greek expression is limited in the N.T. to use after a negative, with the solitary exception of Acts xxvi. 32.

The condition] In the sense shown by the examples in verses 18, 21 ; not meaning ' trade ' or ' occupation.'

people, however, will have outward trouble. But I am for sparing you.

The transitory Character of all that is Earthly Yet this I tell you, brethren : the time has 29 been shortened : for the future let those who have wives be as though they had none, those 30 who weep as though they did not weep, those who rejoice as though they did not rejoice, those who buy as though they did not keep, and those who use 31 the world as though not using it to the full. For the form of this world is passing away. But I would have you free from 32 anxiety. An unmarried man's anxiety is about the Lord's business—how to please the Lord ; but a married man is 33 anxious about the concerns of the world—how to please his wife, and he is drawn two ways. And the unmarried woman 34 or maid is anxious about the Lord's business—to be holy both in body and spirit ; but the married woman is anxious about the concerns of the world—how to please her husband. This I say in your own interest ; not to put shackles 35 on you, but to promote seemliness and undistracted devotion to the Lord.

A Father's Duty to his unmarried Daughter If, however, any one thinks he is acting 36 unbecomingly towards his unmarried daughter if she be past the bloom of her youth, and so it must be, let him do what he desires ; he commits no sin ; she and her suitor should be allowed to marry. But the man who stands fixed in his mind, without 37 being compelled, and has a right to act as he pleases, and in his own mind has decided to keep his daughter unmarried, will do well. So that he who gives his daughter 38 in marriage does well, and yet he who does not give her in marriage will do better.

Should Widows marry again ? A woman is bound to her husband as long as 39 he lives ; but if he dies, she is free to marry whom she will, only in the Lord. But in my 40 judgement, she is happier if she remains as she is ; and I think that I also have the Spirit of God.

---

28. *Outward trouble*] Lit. ' affliction for the flesh.'
33, 34. v.L. 'please his wife. There is a difference between a married and an unmarried woman. She who is married,' &c.
36. *Unmarried daughter*] Lit. 'maiden': and so in verses 37, 38.
She and her suitor] Lit. ' they.'
36-38. It is possible that this passage treats not of a father and his unmarried daughter,' but of a man and woman living together for spiritual fellowship (a custom not unknown to the early Church).
39. *Dies*] Lit. ' shall have fallen asleep.'

Idol Sacrifices

Food that has been sacrificed to Idols

Now as to things that have been sacrificed 1 **8** to idols. We are aware that 'we all have knowledge.' Knowledge puffs up ; but love builds up. If any one imagines that he has any 2 knowledge, he never yet came to know as he ought to know ; but if any one loves God, that man is known 3 by God. Well now, as to eating things which have 4 been sacrificed to idols, we know that an idol is nothing whatever, and that there is no God but One. If, indeed, 5 there are so-called gods, either in heaven or on earth—and in fact there are gods many and lords many—yet for us 6 there is but one God, the Father, who is the source of all things, and for whom we exist, and but one Lord, Jesus Christ, through whom we and all things exist.

Brotherly Love must solve the Problem

But not every one has this knowledge. 7 Some, through being accustomed to idols hitherto, eat idol sacrifices as such ; and their consciences, being but weak, are polluted. It 8 is true that food will not bring us near to God ; we neither lose if we abstain, nor gain if we eat. But take care 9 lest this liberty of yours should prove any obstacle to the weak. For if any one sees you, who have that knowledge, 10 reclining at table in an idol's temple, will not his conscience (supposing him to be weak) be emboldened to eat the food which has been sacrificed to the idol ? Why, your know- 11 ledge is the ruin of the weak believer—your brother, for whom Christ died ! Besides, when you thus sin against 12 the brethren and wound their weak consciences, you are sinning against Christ. Therefore if food trips up my 13 brother, I will eat no flesh as long as I live, for fear I should trip up my brother.

Paul's own Example of Self-restraint

Am I not free ? Am I not an Apostle ? 1 **9** Have I not seen Jesus, our Lord ? Are you not yourselves the evidence of my work in the Lord ? If to other men I am not an Apostle, 2 yet at least I am to you ; for your conversion is the seal on my Apostleship. That is how I vindicate myself to my critics. 3

---

3. *Known by God*] And such a one will exhibit God's love in his life.

10. *Be emboldened*] Lit. ' be edified ' by your (supposed) good example.

11. *Your knowledge . . ruin of the weak believer*] **Lit.** ' the weak (believer) is ruined through (or, through acting on) your knowledge.'

2. *Your conversion, &c.*] Lit. ' the seal of my apostleship are you in the Lord.'

His Apostolic Position and Rights — Have we not a right to food and drink? 4 Have we not a right to take a Christian wife 5 about with us, as the rest of the Apostles do— and the Lord's brothers and Cephas? Or again, is it only 6 Barnabas and myself who have no right to give up working for our living? What soldier ever serves at his own cost? 7 Who plants a vineyard and yet does not eat the grapes? Or who tends a flock and yet does not taste their milk?

Am I saying merely what men say? Does not the Law 8 say the same? For in the Law of Moses it is written, 9 ' THOU SHALT NOT MUZZLE AN OX WHILE IT IS TREADING OUT THE GRAIN ' (Deut. xxv. 4).

Is God thinking about oxen? Or is it in our 10 interest that He speaks? Of course, it was written in our interest, because the ploughman is meant to plough, and the thresher to thresh, in the hope of sharing in the produce.

If we sowed the spiritual grain in you, is it a great thing 11 that we should reap a temporal harvest from you? If other 12 teachers share that right over you, do not we possess it much more? Yet we have not availed ourselves of the right, but we put up with anything rather than cause the least impediment to the gospel of Christ. Do you not know that 13 those who perform the sacred rites have their food from the sacred place, and that those who serve at the altar have their share of the altar-gifts? In the same way the Lord 14 also directed those who proclaim the gospel to get their living by the gospel.

Paul's Forbearance in the Exercise of his Rights — But I have not taken advantage of any of 15 these rights. Nor do I now write with that object so far as I am concerned, for I would rather die than have anybody make this boast of mine an empty one. If I preach the gospel, 16 that is nothing for me to boast of; for I feel compelled to do so; alas for me, if I fail to preach it! And if I do 17 it voluntarily, I have my reward; but if against my will, a stewardship has nevertheless been entrusted to me. What is my reward then? To make the gospel free of 18

---

4. *Right to food and drink*] At the expense of the Churches.
10. *The ploughman is meant, &c.*] Lit. ' the ploughman ought.' God's righteous, loving will is the ultimate criterion of human duty.
13. *The sacred place*] Or ' the Temple.' Cf. Matt. xxi. 12.

charge when I preach, so that I do not exhaust my privileges as a Christian preacher.

**His Motives:
(1) Eagerness to win Men to Christ**
Though free from all men, I have made 19 myself the slave of all, in the hope of winning as many converts as possible. To the Jews 20 I have become like a Jew in order to win Jews ; to men under the Law as if I were under the Law—although I myself am not—in order to win those who are under the Law ; to men without Law as if I were without Law— 21 although I am not without God's Law—being subject to Christ's Law—in order to win those who are without Law. To the weak I have become weak so as to gain the weak. 22 To all men I have become all things, in the hope that by all possible means I may save some. And all I do is for the 23 sake of the gospel, that I may get my share in it.

(2) His own Desire to secure the Crown of Life
Do you not know that in the foot-race, while 24 the runners all run, only one gets the prize ? Run so as to make sure. But every man in 25 training is temperate in all things. They indeed do this to win a fading wreath, but we an unfading one. I, then, so run, as with no uncertain aim. 26 I am a boxer who does not beat the air ; I bruise my 27 body and make it my slave, lest possibly, after being a herald to others, I myself should be rejected.

Israelites who for want of Self-mastery missed the Prize
For I would have you know, brethren, that 1 **10** our forefathers all had the protection of the cloud, and all got through the sea. All were 2 pledged to Moses by baptism in the cloud and the sea. All ate the same spiritual food, and all 3, 4 drank the same spiritual drink ; for they drank from the spiritual rock that went with them—and that rock was Christ. But with most of them God was not well pleased ; 5 for they were laid low in the desert.

The Lessons taught by their Example
And this serves as a warning to us, not to 6 hanker as they did after evil. And you must 7 not be idolaters, as some of them were, as it is written,

' THE PEOPLE SAT DOWN TO EAT AND DRINK, AND STOOD UP TO PLAY ' (Exod. xxxii. 6).

Nor may we be licentious, as some of them were, 8

27. *Being a herald, &c.*] Or 'preaching to others, I should myself not pass muster.'

3. *Spiritual*] Or, perhaps, ' miraculous.'

and on a single day twenty-three thousand of them fell. And let us not try the Lord's forbearance, as some of 9 them did, and they were destroyed by serpents. And 10 do not grumble, as some of them did, and they were destroyed by the Destroyer. All this happened to them 11 by way of warning; but it was recorded by way of admonition to us who live in the last days of the world.

Every Temptation may be successfully resisted So then let the man who thinks he stands 12 secure beware of falling. No temptation has 13 overtaken you but such as is common to men; and God is faithful and will not allow you to be tempted beyond your strength; but when the temptation comes, He will also provide the way out, so that you may be able to bear it.

Idolatry to be scrupulously shunned Therefore, my dear friends, keep clear of 14 idolatry. I speak as to men of sense; judge 15 for yourselves what I say. The cup of bless- 16 ing which we bless, does it not mean participation in the blood of Christ? The bread which we break, does it not mean participation in the body of Christ?

Since there is one bread, we, many as we are, are one 17 body; we all of us share in that one bread. Look at 18 Israel—the nation. Are not those who eat the sacrifices partakers in the altar? Do I mean that a thing sacri- 19 ficed to an idol is anything, or that an idol is anything? No, but what men sacrifice, they sacrifice to demons, 20 not to God; and I would not have you prove par- takers with demons. You cannot drink the Lord's cup 21 and the cup of demons: you cannot be partakers both in the table of the Lord and in the table of demons. Or are we arousing the Lord to jealousy? Are we 22 stronger than He is?

Brotherly Love limits Christian Freedom Everything is allowable, but not everything 23 is profitable. Everything is allowable, but everything does not edify. Let no one seek 24 his own good, but let each seek that of his fellow man.

Anything that is sold in the market eat, and ask no questions 25

---

13. *Temptation*] Or 'trial.'
17. Or, 'since, many as we are, we are one bread, one body; for—'
22. *To jealousy*] To be jealous of demon rivals. Cf. Deut. xxxii. 21. The verb here used is found elsewhere in the N.T. only in Rom. x. 19 (quoted from Deut.); xi. 11, 14.

for conscience' sake; for THE EARTH IS THE LORD'S, AND ALL 26
THAT IT CONTAINS (Ps. xxiv. 1). If an unbeliever invites 27
you and you consent to go, eat whatever is put before you,
and ask no questions for conscience' sake. But if any one 28
tells you, 'This food has been offered in sacrifice,' abstain
from eating it for the sake of him who warned you, and
for conscience' sake—I mean his conscience, not your 29
own. For why is my personal freedom to be decided by
another man's conscience? If I partake with a grateful 30
heart, why am I to be maligned in regard to a thing for
which I give thanks?

Whether, then, you eat or drink, or whatever you do, 31
let everything be done to the glory of God.

True Religion must inspire all our Actions Do not be causes of stumbling either to 32
Jews or to Greeks or to the Church of God.
That is how I too seek in everything the 33
approval of all men, not aiming at my own
profit, but at that of the many, in the hope
that they may be saved. Be imitators of me, as I myself 1 11
am an imitator of Christ.

Women at Meetings of the Church Now I commend you for remembering me in 2
everything, and for keeping my instructions just
as I delivered them to you. I would have you 3
know, however, that of every man Christ is the head, that
the head of a woman is her husband, and that the head of
Christ is God. A man who wears a veil when praying or 4
prophesying dishonours his head; but a woman who prays 5
or prophesies with her head uncovered dishonours her
head, for she is exactly the same as a woman who is
shorn.

If a woman will not wear a veil, let her also cut off her 6
hair. But since it is a dishonour to a woman to have her
hair cut off or to be shaved, let her wear a veil. For a 7
man ought not to have a veil on his head, since he is the
image and glory of God; while woman is the glory of man.
Man does not originate from woman, but woman from 8
man. For man was not created for woman's sake, but 9
woman for man's. That is why a woman ought to have on 10

---

28. *If any one*] Some Christian fellow-guest whose faith is weak.

29. *For why is my personal freedom, &c.*] In our idiom the whole question would more naturally be put in the second person—' Why should your personal freedom .. by another man's conscience? If you partake .. why are you .. you give thanks,?'

4. *Who wears a veil*] Or ' who wears long hair.' So Chrysostom. Lit. ' having (anything) hanging) from his head.'

her head a symbol of subjection, because of the angels. 11
Yet, in the Lord, woman is not independent of man nor
man of woman. For just as woman originates from man, 12
so also man has his birth through woman ; but everything
comes ultimately from God.

Judge for yourselves : is it seemly for a woman to pray 13
unveiled to God ? Does not nature itself teach you that 14
if a man has long hair, it is a dishonour to him ; but that 15
if a woman has long hair, it is her glory, because her hair
was given her for a covering ? But if any one is inclined 16
to be contentious on the point, we have no such custom,
nor have the Churches of God.

Matters relating to Christian Worship

Dissensions at Meetings of the Church   But while giving you this injunction I cannot 17
praise you, in that you meet together not for the
better but for the worse. In the first place, 18
I hear that when you meet as a Church there
are divisions among you ; and I partly believe it. For 19
there must be differences of opinion among you, in order
to show who are the men of worth among you.

Disorder at the Lord's Supper   When, however, you meet together, there 20
is no eating the Supper of the Lord ; for every 21
one seizes first his own supper, and one remains
hungry, while another drinks to excess. Why, have you no 22
homes in which to eat and drink ? Or would you show your
contempt for the Church of God and shame those who
are poor ? What shall I say to you ? Shall I praise
you ? In this matter I do not praise you.

The Facts as to the Origin of the Supper   For it was from the Lord that I received 23
what in turn I handed on to you—that the
Lord Jesus, on the night He was betrayed,
took bread, and after giving thanks, He broke 24
it and said,

' This is my body which is broken for you. Do this in
memory of me.'

---

10. *A symbol of subjection*] Lit. ' authority.' *I.e.* (a symbol of) her husband's
authority.
  Because of the angels] Who are conceived of as spectators.
11. *In the Lord*] In the Christian order of things.
14. *Nature itself, &c.*] A woman ' is instinctively conscious that Nature's gift of
long hair is for a covering ' (T. C. Edwards).
24. v.L. omits ' broken,' reading ' which is for your sakes.'

In the same way, when the meal was over, He also took 25 the cup.

' This cup,' He said, ' is the new Covenant as sealed with my blood. Do this, every time that you drink it, in memory of me.'

The Significance and Sacredness of the Meal

For every time that you eat this bread and 26 drink from the cup, you proclaim the Lord's death—until He comes. Whoever, therefore, 27 eats the bread or drinks from the cup of the Lord unworthily will be involved in sin against the body and blood of the Lord. Let a man examine 28 himself, and having done that, let him eat the bread and drink from the cup. For any one who eats and drinks, if 29 he fails to understand the body, eats and drinks to his own condemnation. That is why many among you are sickly 30 and out of health, and why not a few die. If, however, we 31 understood ourselves aright, we should not be judged. But when we are judged by the Lord, chastisement follows, 32 to save us from being condemned along with the world.

So then, brethren, when you come together for this meal, 33 wait for one another. If any one is hungry, let him eat 34 at home; so that your coming together may not lead to judgement.

The other matters I will deal with when I come.

Spiritual Gifts. The Need of Discrimination

Now about spiritual gifts, brethren, I would 1 **12** not have you ignorant. You know that when 2 you were heathens you went astray after dumb idols, wherever you might be led. For this 3 reason I inform you that no one speaking under the influence of the Spirit of God says, ' Jesus is accursed,' and that no one is able to say, ' Jesus is Lord,' except under the influence of the Holy Spirit.

Spiritual Gifts. Their Diversity

Now there are various kinds of gifts, but 4 there is the same Spirit ; various kinds of 5 official service, and yet the same Lord ; various 6 kinds of effects, and yet the same God who produces all the effects in each person. But to each a manifestation 7 of the Spirit has been granted for the common good. To 8 one the word of wisdom has been granted through the

---

25. *As . . blood*] Lit. ' in my blood.'
29. *Understand the body*] Or ' discern.' By failure to discern the body of Christ, Paul may possibly mean failure to recognize the unity and brotherhood of the Christian Church. 30. *Die*] Lit. ' fall asleep.'

Spirit ; to another the word of knowledge by the will of the same Spirit ; to one, in the same Spirit, special faith ; 9 to another various gifts of healing, in the one Spirit ; to 10 another the exercise of miraculous powers ; to another the gift of prophecy ; to another the power of discriminating between spirits ; to one varieties of the gift of ' tongues ' ; to another the interpretation of tongues. But 11 all these results are brought about by one and the same Spirit, allotting them to each individually as He pleases.

The organic Unity of the Church   For just as the body is one and yet has 12 many parts, and all its parts, many as they are, constitute but one body, so it is with Christ. In fact, in one Spirit all of us—whether Jews or Greeks, 13 slaves or free men—were baptized to form one body ; and we were all imbued with one Spirit.

Unity should make Jealousy impossible   The body does not consist of one part, but 14 of many. Were the foot to say, ' Because I 15 am not a hand, I am not a part of the body,' that would not make it any the less a part of the body. Or were the ear to say, ' Because I am not an 16 eye, I am not a part of the body,' that would not make it any the less a part of the body. If the whole body were 17 an eye, where would the hearing be ? If the whole body were an ear, where would the smelling be ? But, as it is, 18 God has arranged the parts in the body—every one of them—as He has seen fit. If they were all one part, 19 where would the body be ? But, in fact, there are many 20 parts and but one body.

Unity should exclude Pride and Contempt   It is also impossible for the eye to say to 21 the hand, ' I do not need you ' ; or again for the head to say to the feet, ' I do not need you.' So far from that, even those parts of the body 22 which seem somewhat feeble are yet indispensable ; and 23 those which we deem less honourable we clothe with additional honour ; and so our ungraceful parts come to have additional grace, while our graceful parts have no 24 need of it. No, God in building up the body, has bestowed additional honour on the part that came short, that there might be no disunion in the body, but that all the 25 members might entertain the same anxiety for one another.

---

13. *Imbued with*] Lit. ' made to drink.'
24. *Building up*] Lit. ' mixing together.'

And if one part suffers, every other part suffers with it, or 26 if one part is honoured, every other part shares in the joy.

Unity involves mutual Dependence

Now you are the body of Christ, and indi- 27 vidually members of it. And by God's appoint- 28 ment there are in the Church, first apostles, secondly prophets, thirdly teachers. Then come miraculous powers, and then ability to cure diseases or render assistance, or powers of organization, or varieties of the gift of tongues. Are all apostles? Are all prophets? Are all 29 teachers? Have all miraculous powers? Have all ability to 30 cure diseases? Do all speak in tongues? Do all interpret? But ever seek to excel in the greater gifts. 31

And still I have to show you a more excellent way.

Love is the supreme Gift

If I can speak with the tongues of men and 1 **13** of angels, but have not love, I am a blaring trumpet or a clanging cymbal. Or if I can 2 prophesy and am versed in all mysteries and all knowledge, and have such absolute faith that I can remove mountains, but have not love, I am nothing. And if I use all I have 3 to feed the poor, and give up my body to be burned, but have not love, it profits me nothing.

Love is forbearing and kind. Love knows no jealousy. 4 Love does not brag; is not conceited. She is not un- 5 mannerly, nor selfish, nor irritable, nor mindful of wrongs. She does not rejoice in injustice, but joyfully sides with 6 the truth. She can overlook faults. She is full of trust, 7 full of hope, full of endurance.

Love never fails. But if there are prophecies, they will 8 come to an end; if there are tongues, they will cease; if there is knowledge, it will come to an end. For our 9 knowledge is partial, and so is our prophesying; but when 10 that which is perfect is come, all that is partial will come to an end. When I was a child, I talked like a child, thought 11 like a child, reasoned like a child : now that I have become a man, I have put an end to childish ways. For at present 12 we see things as in a mirror, obscurely; but then we shall

---

26. *Shares in the joy*] *e.g.* ' the head is crowned with a garland, and the whole man is conscious of being glorified ; or the mouth pronounces an oration, and at once the eyes laugh and show their gladness ' (Chrysostom).

28. *By God's appointment there are*] Lit. ' God appointed some.' The voice (middle) of the verb intimates ' for Himself,' ' to do His will,' ' to render service to Him.'

Prophets] Or ' inspired teachers.' Cf. verse 10.

3. *To be burned*] v.L. ' that I may make a boast of it.'

12. *Obscurely*] Lit. ' in a riddle.' The brass mirror gave an imperfect reflection.

see face to face. At present I gain but partial knowledge, but then I shall know fully, even as I am fully known. And so there remain faith, hope, love—these three ; but 13 of these the greatest is love.

'Prophecy' superior to the Gift of Tongues Make love your quest, and be eager for 1 spiritual gifts, but chiefly for prophecy. For 2 he who speaks in a tongue is not speaking to men, but to God ; for no one understands him ; but in the Spirit he speaks divine secrets. But he who 3 prophesies speaks to men words of edification, encouragement, and comfort. He who speaks in a tongue edifies 4 himself, but he who prophesies edifies the Church. I 5 should like you all to speak in tongues, but yet more that you should prophesy. The man who prophesies is superior to him who speaks in tongues, except when the latter interprets in order that the Church may receive edification. But as things are, brethren, if I come to you speaking in 6 tongues, what good shall I do you, unless I address you with a revelation or knowledge or prophecy or teaching ?

If inanimate things—flutes or harps, for instance— 7 though they yield a sound, yet make no distinction in the notes, how shall the tune which is played on the flute or the harp be known ? If the bugle, again, gives an 8 uncertain sound, who will prepare for battle ? And so with 9 you ; if with the tongue you fail to utter intelligible words, how will people know what you are saying ? You will be talking to the winds.

There are, we will suppose, so many languages in the 10 world, and none without a meaning. If, then, I do not 11 know the meaning of the language, I shall seem to the speaker, and he to me, to be a foreigner. Therefore, seeing 12 that you are ambitious for spiritual gifts, seek to excel in them, so as to edify the Church.

So let a man who has the gift of tongues pray for the 13 power of interpreting them. For if I pray in a tongue, 14 my spirit prays, but my understanding is barren. What 15 then follows ? I will pray with my spirit, and I will pray with my understanding also. I will sing praise with my spirit, and I will sing praise with my understanding also. Otherwise, if you bless God in spirit only, 16 how shall any one who lacks the gift say 'Amen' to your thanksgiving when he does not know what you mean? You are giving thanks rightly enough, and yet 17 your neighbour is not edified. I speak in tongues, thank 18 God, more than all of you; but in the Church I would 19 rather speak five words with my understanding, so as to instruct others also, than ten thousand words in a tongue.

Brethren, do not be children in mind. As regards evil 20 indeed be babes, but in intelligence be mature. In the 21 Law it is written, '" BY MEN OF OTHER TONGUES AND BY THE LIPS OF OTHERS WILL I SPEAK TO THIS PEOPLE, BUT EVEN THEN THEY WILL NOT LISTEN TO ME " (Isa. xxviii. 11, 12), says the Lord.' This shows that the gift of tongues 22 is intended as a sign not for those who believe but for unbelievers, whereas prophecy is intended not for unbelievers but for those who believe. Accordingly, if the whole 23 Church has assembled together and all are speaking in tongues, and there come in some who lack the gift, or unbelievers, will they not say that you are mad? If, on the 24 other hand, every one is prophesying, and an unbeliever or one who lacks the gift comes in, he is convicted by all; he is sifted by all, and the secrets of his heart are brought to 25 light. And thus he will fall on his face and worship God, pronouncing that truly God is among you.

The orderly Exercise of spiritual Gifts
What then, brethren? Whenever you 26 assemble, there is not one of you who is not ready either with a song of praise, a sermon, a revelation, a tongue, or an interpretation. Let everything be done with a view to edification. If 27 there is speaking in a tongue, only two or at the most three should speak, one at a time, and one should interpret; or if there is no interpreter, let the speaker be 28 silent in the Church, speaking to himself and to God. Let 29 two or three prophets speak, and let the rest judge. And if 30 anything is revealed to some one else who is seated, let the first be silent. For you can all prophesy one by one, so 31 that all may learn and all be encouraged: the spirits of 32 prophets are under their own control. For God is not a 33 God of disorder, but of peace, as He is in all the Churches of the saints.

22. For unbelievers] i.e., apparently, 'to show who are unbelievers.'
33. Another punctuation connects the last clause with verse 34: 'As in all the Churches of the saints, let women be silent.'

Women at Meetings of the Church

Let women be silent in the Churches, for 34 they are not permitted to speak. They must be subordinate, as the Law also says ; and if 35 they wish to learn anything, they should ask their own husbands at home. For it is disgraceful for a woman to speak in Church.

No Power in Corinth to change Church Customs

Was it from you that God's word first went 36 forth, or is it to you only that it has come ?

Paul's Apostolic Authority

If any one reckons himself a prophet or a 37 man with spiritual gifts, let him recognize as the Lord's command what I am now writing to you. But if any one is ignorant, let him be ignorant. 38

Final Words as to spiritual Gifts

In conclusion, my brethren, be eager to 39 prophesy, and do not check speaking with tongues ; only let everything be done in a 40 becoming and orderly manner.

The Resurrection of the Dead

The Death and Resurrection of Jesus

Now let me recall to you, brethren, the 1 **15** gospel which I preached to you, which you accepted, and in which you stand ; through 2 which also you are saved, if you hold to the substance of my preaching—unless indeed your faith was mere caprice. I transmitted to you before all else 3 what had also been transmitted to me, that Christ died for our sins in accordance with the Scriptures ; that He was 4 buried ; that He rose on the third day in accordance with the Scriptures, and was seen by Cephas, and then by the 5 Twelve. Afterwards He was seen by more than five 6 hundred brethren at once, most of whom are still alive, although some of them have died. Afterwards He was 7 seen by James, and then by all the apostles. And last of 8 all He appeared to me also, to this abortion, so to speak, of an apostle.

Paul himself a Witness as to His Resurrection

For I am the least of the apostles, and am 9 not fit to be called an apostle, because I persecuted the Church of God. But by the grace 10 of God I am what I am, and the grace He bestowed upon me did not prove ineffectual. I laboured

---

36. This meets a supposed objection to receive Paul's directions.
38. *Let him be ignorant*] v.l. 'he is ignored,' or 'unknown,' *i.e.* probably, by God, and consequently, also by His people.

more strenuously than all of them : yet it was not I, but God's grace helping me. Whether, then, it is I or they, this 11 is the way we preach and the way that you came to believe.

The Denial of the Possibility of Resurrection But if we preach that Christ rose from the 12 dead, how is it that some of you say that there is no such thing as a resurrection of the dead ? If there is no such thing as a resurrection of 13 the dead, not even Christ has risen. And if 14 Christ has not risen, then our preaching is in vain, and your faith also is in vain. Further, we are shown to be bearing 15 false witness about God, because we have testified that God raised Christ, whom He did not raise, if in fact dead men do not rise. For if dead men do not rise, then Christ has 16 not risen ; and if Christ has not risen, your faith is of no 17 avail : you are still in your sins. It follows also that those 18 who have fallen asleep in Christ have perished. If in this 19 life we have had nothing more than a hope in Christ, we are the most pitiable of all men.

Christ's Resurrection a Pledge that all will rise But, in reality, Christ has risen from the 20 dead—the first of those who are asleep. For 21 seeing that death came through man, through man comes also the resurrection of the dead.

Just as in Adam all die, so also in Christ all 22 will be made alive again. But each in his own order— 23 Christ first, and afterwards Christ's people at His return. After that comes the end, when He is to surrender the 24 Kingship to God the Father, when He has abolished all other government and all other authority and power. For 25 He must be King until He has put all His enemies under His feet (Ps. viii. 6 ; cx. 1). The last enemy that is to be 26 abolished is death ; for God has put all things under His 27 feet. And when He says, 'All things are put under,' obviously this does not include Him who has put them all under Him. But when all things have been put under 28 Him, then the Son Himself will also come under Him who has put all things under Him, in order that GOD may be all in all.

Baptism for the Dead Otherwise what will those do who are 29 baptized for the dead ? If the dead do not rise at all, why are they baptized for them ?

29. *Otherwise*] *i.e.* if there is no resurrection of the dead.
Baptized for the dead] Apparently there were Christians who got themselves baptized for unbaptized departed friends in the belief that it would benefit them.

Why also do we apostles take such risks every hour ? I 30,31
risk death day by day. I affirm this, brethren, by my
glorying in you, as I justly do, in Christ Jesus our Lord.
If from merely human motives I have fought with wild 32
beasts in Ephesus, what profit is it to me ? If the dead do
not rise, let us eat and drink, for to-morrow we are to die
(Isa. xxii. 13). Do not deceive yourselves :   33
            ' Bad companionships spoil good morals.'
Return to a truly sober mind, and cease to sin ; for some 34
have no knowledge of God. I say this to your shame.

All Fruit But some one will say, ' How do the dead 35
differs from rise ? And with what kind of body do they
its Seed come back ? ' Foolish man ! the seed you 36
yourself sow does not come to life unless it dies ; and 37
what you sow is not the body which is to be, but a bare
grain of wheat (it may be) or of something else, and God 38
gives it a body as He pleases, and to each kind of seed a body
of its own. All flesh is not the same : there is human 39
flesh, and flesh of cattle, of birds, and of fishes. There are 40
celestial bodies and also earthly bodies, but the glory
of the celestial is one thing, and that of the earthly is
another. There is one glory of the sun, another of 41
the moon, and another of the stars ; star differs from
star in glory.

The earthly It is the same with the resurrection of the 42
and the dead. The body is sown perishable, it rises
spiritual imperishable ; it is sown in dishonour, it rises 43
Bodies in glory ; it is sown in weakness, it rises in
power ; it is sown an animal body, it is raised a spiritual 44
body. Just as there is an animal body, so there is also a
spiritual body. Thus too it is written, ' THE FIRST MAN 45
ADAM BECAME A LIVING BEING ' (Gen. ii. 7) ; the last Adam
a life-giving Spirit. Yet it is not the spiritual that 46
comes first, but the animal ; then the spiritual. The first 47
man is a man of earth, of dust ; the second man is from
heaven. What the man of dust is, that also are those who 48
are of dust ; and what the heavenly One is, that also are those
who are heavenly. As we have worn the likeness of the man 49
of dust, let us also wear the likeness of the heavenly One.

32. *Wild beasts*] Antagonists as ferocious as lions and tigers. Or, regarding the
wild beasts as literal ones, ' If I had fought . . what profit would it have been to
me ? '
49. *Let us*] v.L. ' we shall.'

The Change
which
awaits our
Bodies

But this I tell you, brethren, flesh and blood 50
cannot inherit the Kingdom of God, nor shall
the perishable inherit the imperishable. See, 51
I will tell you a secret : we shall not all sleep,
but we shall all be changed, in a moment, in the twinkling 52
of an eye, at the last trumpet call ; for the trumpet will
sound, and the dead will rise imperishable, and we shall be
changed. For this perishable nature must clothe itself 53
with the imperishable, and this mortality must clothe itself
with immortality. Now when this perishable nature has 54
put on the imperishable, and this mortality has put on
immortality, then shall the words of Scripture be fulfilled,
' DEATH HAS BEEN SWALLOWED UP IN VICTORY ' (Isa. xxv. 8).
' WHERE, O DEATH, IS THY VICTORY ? WHERE, O DEATH, 55
IS THY STING ? ' (Hos. xiii. 14). Now sin is the sting of 56
death, and the Law is the stronghold of sin ; but God be 57
thanked who gives us the victory through our Lord Jesus
Christ ! Therefore, my beloved brethren, be firm, immovable, abounding at all times in the work of the Lord, 58
knowing that your toil is not fruitless in the Lord.

The Poor in Jerusalem

The
Collection
for the Poor
in Jerusalem

As to the collection for the saints, what I 1 **16**
have directed the Churches of Galatia to do,
you must do also. On the first day of the 2
week, let each of you put by and keep any
profit he may have made ; so that there may be no collec-
tions made after I have come. And when I arrive, what- 3
ever brethren you approve I will send with letters to carry
your kind gift to Jerusalem. And if it is worth while for 4
me also to go, they shall go with me.

Personal Matters, and Farewell

The
Apostle's
Plans

I shall come to you after passing through 5
Macedonia ; for I am going to pass through
Macedonia ; and I shall make some stay per- 6
haps, or even spend the winter with you, in order that
you may help me forward, whichever way I travel. For 7
I do not wish to see you just now merely in passing ; if

---

56. Law is the stronghold of sin as defining and provoking sin.
2. *Any profit, &c.*] Lit. (the gain) ' whereinsoever he is prospered ' (by God).

the Lord permits, I hope to remain some time with you.
I shall remain in Ephesus, however, until Pentecost, for a 8, 9
door that offers wide and effective service stands open
before me, and there are many opponents.

Timothy If Timothy comes, see that his intercourse 10
with you may be free from fear ; for he is
engaged in the Master's work just as I am. Therefore 11
let no one slight him, but do you help him forward in
peace to join me ; for I am waiting for him with others
of the brethren.

Apollos As for our brother Apollos, I have repeatedly 12
urged him to accompany the brethren who are
coming to you ; but he is quite resolved not to do so at
present. He will come, however, when he has a good
opportunity.

Be alert ; stand firm in the faith ; acquit yourselves like 13
men ; be strong. Let all that you do be done from love. 14

Stephanas I beseech you, brethren—you know the 15
household of Stephanas, how they were the
earliest Greek converts, and have devoted themselves to the
service of the saints—do you show deference to such men, 16
and to every one who shares their work and toils hard. It 17
is joy to me that Stephanas, Fortunatus, and Achaicus have
arrived, because they have supplied what was wanting on
your part. They have refreshed my spirit, and yours. 18
Acknowledge such men as these.

Kindly Greetings The Churches of Asia send you greetings ; 19
and Aquila and Prisca send you hearty greetings
in the Lord, together with the Church which
meets at their house. The brethren all send greetings to 20
you. Greet one another with a holy kiss.

Conclusion The greeting of me—Paul—with my own 21
hand. If any one does not love the Lord, let him 22
be accursed. Maran atha (OUR LORD IS COMING).
The grace of the Lord Jesus be with you. My love be with 23,24
you all in Christ Jesus.

12. *He is quite resolved not*] Or perhaps ' it is by no means God's will,' &c.
17. *What was wanting on your part*] Or ' my lack of you.'
22. *Our Lord is coming*] Or ' Come, Lord.'

THE SECOND EPISTLE OF PAUL
TO THE CORINTHIANS

This letter is a very human document, throbbing with emotions of pain, thankfulness, and indignation.

Paul had sent Titus to Corinth with a letter so severe in tone that he dreaded lest its effect should be wholly to alienate the Church from himself. He hoped to receive an answer in Troas; but as Titus did not rejoin him there, he crossed over to Macedonia, where he learnt from Titus that the reception of his letter in Corinth was all that he could have wished, and sent this second Epistle back by the same messenger.

A close study of the Epistle raises several critical problems of interest.

1. The severe letter of chapters ii. and vii. can hardly be identified with 1 Corinthians. After the dispatch of that epistle things seem to have gone from bad to worse in Corinth, leading perhaps to an unrecorded visit of Paul from Ephesus, and then to an indignant letter remonstrating against the flouting of his personal claims on their loyalty.

2. In chapters i. to vii. we have the thankful calm after the mutterings of the departing storm, followed in chapters viii. and ix. by the discussion of Paul's collection for the poor at Jerusalem. But in chapters x. to xiii. the storm breaks out again in the fiercest invective to be found in all Paul's writings. This is not like the tactful and persuasive Apostle. It seems probable that these four chapters may really belong to the severe letter, and therefore precede chapters i. to ix.

3. A careful scrutiny of 2 Corinthians vi. 14 to vii. 1 suggests some dislocation. There is perfect connection between vi. 13 and vii. 2, and there is nothing in the previous part of the letter to prepare for the intervening paragraph. May it not be a fragment of the lost letter on the same theme referred to in 1 Corinthians v. 9? The conditions under which Paul's Epistles were preserved and subsequently edited makes such a combination of detached fragments quite possible.

THE SECOND EPISTLE OF PAUL
TO THE CORINTHIANS

The Apostle and his Readers

Greeting　　Paul, an Apostle of Christ Jesus by the will 1 **1** of God, and our brother Timothy, to the Church of God in Corinth, with all the saints throughout Greece: grace and peace to you from God our Father and the 2 Lord Jesus Christ.

Thanksgiving for Divine Comfort　Blessed be the God and Father of our Lord 3 Jesus Christ, the Father of mercies and God of all comfort. He comforts us in all our 4 affliction, so that we may be able to comfort those who are in any kind of affliction by the comfort with which we ourselves are comforted by God. For as we 5 have more than our share of suffering for Christ, so also through Christ we have more than our share of comfort. But if we endure affliction, it is for your comfort and salva- 6 tion; and if we receive comfort, it is for your comfort, which takes effect when patiently you endure the same sufferings as those which we also endure. And our hope 7 for you is firm; for we know that as you are sharers in the sufferings, so you are also sharers in the comfort.

Thanksgiving for Divine Deliverance　About our affliction which came upon us in 8 the province of Asia, we would have you know, brethren, that we were exceedingly depressed, quite beyond endurance, so that we renounced all hope even of life. Nay, we have had the presentiment 9 of death within ourselves, in order that our confidence may repose, not on ourselves, but on God who raises the dead. He rescued us from so imminent a death, and will 10 do so again; and we have a firm hope in Him that He

---

1. *Greece*] Greek 'Achaia,' *i.e.* the Roman province of Achaia, which roughly coincided with modern Greece. The capital was Corinth.
6. *For your comfort*] v.l. adds 'and salvation' to these words on their second occurrence here.
9. *Presentiment*] Lit. 'answer.'

will still rescue us, while you lend us your aid by 11
entreaty for us, so that thanksgivings may rise from
many on our behalf for the boon granted to us at the
intercession of many.

Paul's Motives had been disinterested The reason of our boasting is this—the 12
witness of our own conscience that it has been
in holiness and with pure motives before God,
not with worldly wisdom but by the grace
of God, that we have conducted ourselves in the world,
and above all in our relations with you. We write to you 13
nothing different from what you read, or indeed recognise as true, and will, I trust, recognise to the end; just 14
as you have partly recognised that we are your reason for
boasting, as you will be ours, on the day of Jesus our Lord.

Why Paul had post- poned his Visit It was with this confidence that I intended 15
to visit you first—so that you might receive a
twofold joy—and to come your way into 16
Macedonia and to return from Macedonia to
you, and so be helped forward by you to Judaea. Well, 17
did I show any levity in this? Or the plans which I form
—do I form them on worldly principles, so that it should
be, 'Yes, yes,' and then 'No, no' with me?

As certainly as God is faithful, our language to you is 18
not 'Yes' and 'No.' For the Son of God, Jesus Christ, 19
who was proclaimed among you by us—by Silvanus and
Timothy and myself—did not show Himself 'Yes' and
'No': it is always 'Yes' with Him. For all the promises 20
of God have their 'Yes' in Him; and therefore through
Him also we utter the 'Amen' to the glory of God. But 21
He who confirms us as well as you in union with Christ,
and has anointed us, is God, and He has also set His seal 22
upon us, and has put His Spirit into our hearts as a
guarantee.

But I call God as my soul's witness that it was to 23
spare you that I gave up my visit to Corinth. Not that 24
we would domineer over your faith; we would rather assist
your joy; for as to your faith you stand firm.

13. *What you read*] This is variously interpreted: (1) What I have previously
written. (2) What you understand me to mean. (3) What you read aloud (in church
meeting: in this last case Paul implies that he does not write private letters of different
tenour to individual church-members).

15. *Joy*] v.L. ' grace.'

18. Paul's argument in this and the following verses is that as faithful follower of
Christ, and preacher of His gospel, he is true to his promises; hence fickleness is not
the true explanation of his change of plan.

But I have resolved not to make a painful visit to you 1 **2**
again. For if I give you pain, who then is there to gladden 2
me, but the persons to whom I give pain? And I wrote 3
that in order that when I came I might not suffer pain from
those who ought to give me joy, confident as I am in all
of you that my joy is the joy of you all. For with many 4
tears I wrote to you, in deep affliction and anguish of spirit,
not in order to pain you, but in the hope of showing you
how brimful my heart is with love for you.

The penitent Offender to be received back

Now if any one has given pain, he has given 5
it not so much to me, as, in some degree—I
have no wish to exaggerate—to all of you.
For such a person the punishment inflicted by 6
the majority is enough. So that you may now take the 7
opposite course and forgive and comfort him, lest perhaps he be driven to despair by his excess of grief. I beg 8
you therefore fully to reinstate him in your love. For I 9
wrote with this object in view—to test whether you were
obedient in every respect. When you forgive a man an 10
offence I also forgive it; in fact what I have forgiven, if
I have forgiven anything, has been on your account, in the
presence of Christ, lest Satan should gain an advantage 11
over us. For we are not ignorant of his devices.

Personal Trials and Apostolic Success

Now when I came to Troas to spread the 12
gospel of Christ, even though in the Lord's
providence a door stood open before me, yet 13
I had no relief for my spirit, because I did not
find my brother Titus; so I bade them farewell and went on
into Macedonia. But to God be the thanks who in Christ 14
ever leads us in His triumphal procession, displaying everywhere through us the sweetness of the knowledge of Him.
For we are a fragrance of Christ grateful to God in those 15
being saved and in those perishing; to the one an odour 16
of death that leads to death, and to others an odour of life
that leads to life. And for such service as this who is
competent?—Unlike most teachers, we do not adulterate 17
God's word; but with sincerity, as sent by God, in God's
presence we speak in Christ.

3. *Wrote*] Or perhaps ' write.'
12. *Troas*] There was a district Troas, so called after the ancient city of Troy.
It formed the extreme north-west corner of Asia Minor. On its west coast was a
town named Troas, and it is probably the town that is here referred to.
16. The Apostle does not answer his question; but ' we are ' is implied.

Paul's Converts a Proof of his Divine Mission Do you say that we are beginning to commend ourselves once more ? Or do we need, as some do, letters of recommendation to you or from you ? Our letter is yourselves— written on our hearts and known and read by all men. For you show that you are a letter of Christ penned by us, written not with ink, but with the Spirit of the living God, not on tablets of stone, but on human hearts as tablets.

God alone fitted Paul for his Task Such is the confidence which we have through Christ toward God ; not that of ourselves we are competent to decide anything of our own judgement, but our competency comes from God. He has also made us competent servants of a new Covenant, which is not a written code but a Spirit ; for the written code kills, but the Spirit gives Life.

The Splendour of the new Faith But if the service that brings death—its code being engraved in writing upon stones—came with glory, so that the children of Israel could not look steadily on the face of Moses because of the brightness of his face—a vanishing brightness ; will not the service of the Spirit be far more glorious ? For if the service which pronounces doom had glory, far more glorious still is the service which offers righteousness. For, in fact, that which was so glorious (Exod. xxxiv. 30, LXX) has no glory at all in comparison with the surpassing glory. For if that which was to be abolished came with glory, much more is that which is permanent arrayed in glory.

With such a hope as this, then, we speak without reserve, unlike Moses, who used to throw a veil over his face to hide from the gaze of the children of Israel the end of the vanishing brightness. But indeed their minds had grown dense ; to this day during the reading of the Old Testament the same veil remains unlifted, because it is in Christ that it is to be abolished. Yes, to this day, whenever Moses is read, a veil lies upon their hearts. But whenever they return to the Lord, the veil is withdrawn (Exod. xxxiv. 34, LXX).

6. *Covenant*] Greek ' Diathēkē.' ' This word must be invariably taken in the sense of " covenant " in the N.T.' (Hatch). But Heb. ix. 16 is an exception.
7. *That brings death*] Lit. ' of death.' Cf. Rom. viii. 2.
9. *Had glory*] v.l. ' is glory.'

Now the Lord means the Spirit ; and where the Spirit 17
of the Lord is, freedom is. But all of us, as with un- 18
veiled faces we mirror the glory of the Lord, are transformed
into the same likeness, from glory to glory, even as the Lord
the Spirit inspires.

Therefore, while engaged in this service, 1 **4**
as we have experienced mercy we do not lose
heart. We have renounced the secrecy which 2
means shame. We do not deal in cunning,
nor do we adulterate God's word ; but by clear
statement of the truth we commend ourselves to every
human conscience before God. If, indeed, our gospel is 3
veiled, the veil is on the heart of those who are perishing,
in whom the god of this world has blinded their 4
unbelieving minds so as to shut out the radiance of the
gospel of the glory of Christ, who is the image of God.
For we do not proclaim ourselves, but Christ Jesus as 5
Lord, and ourselves as your servants for the sake of Jesus.
For the God who said, ' Out of darkness light shall 6
shine,' is He who has shone in our hearts to give the
light of the knowledge of the glory of God in the face
of Jesus Christ.

God's own Message declared with simple Fidelity

But we have this treasure in fragile earthen 7
pots in order that the surpassing greatness
of the power may be seen to be God's and
not to come from us. At all points we are 8
hard pressed, yet not hemmed in ; perplexed, yet not at
our wits' end ; pursued, yet not forsaken ; struck down, 9
yet not destroyed ; always carrying about in our bodies 10
the putting to death of Jesus, so that in our bodies the life
of Jesus also may be manifest. For we, alive though we 11
are, are continually surrendering ourselves to death for
the sake of Jesus, so that in our mortal nature the life of
Jesus also may be manifest. Thus death is at work in us, 12
but life in you.

Paul's Strength came wholly from God

But as we have that same Spirit of faith of 13
which it is written, ' I BELIEVED, AND THERE-
FORE I SPOKE ' (Ps. cxvi. 10), we too believe ;
therefore we also speak. For we know that He who 14
raised the Lord Jesus will raise us also with Jesus, and will
set us with you in His presence. For everything is for 15
your sakes, in order that grace may increase with the

The Hope of Eternal Life

increased number who receive it, and cause abundant
thanksgiving to the glory of God.

Transitory Pain may lead on to Eternal Glory
Therefore we do not lose heart, but, even 16
though our outward man does waste away,
yet our inward man is renewed day by day.
For our light and transitory affliction is achiev- 17
ing for us, beyond all proportion, an eternal
weight of glory—if we look not at the seen, but at the 18
unseen ; for the seen is temporary, but the unseen is eternal.

The spiritual and immortal Body
For we know that if the mere tent, which 1 **5**
is our earthly house, is taken down, we have
in heaven a building from God, a house not
made by human hands, but eternal. In this one, indeed, 2
we sigh, because we long to put on over it our dwelling
which comes from heaven—sure that, when we have put 3
it on we shall not be found unclothed. Yes, we who are 4
in this tent do sigh under our burdens, not that we wish to
lay aside our tent, but rather to put the other over it, so that
our mortality may be absorbed in Life. And He who 5
formed us for this very purpose is God, who has given us
His Spirit as guarantee.

The heavenly Home joyfully anticipated
We have therefore an unfailing confidence. 6
We know that while we are at home in the body
we are away from the Lord ; for we live our 7
life by faith, and not by sight. So we have con- 8
fidence, and we should be better pleased to leave
our home in the body and make our home with the Lord.
For this reason also we make it our ambition, whether 9
in our home or away, to please Him. For we must all of us 10
appear before Christ's judgement-seat in our true light,
in order that each may receive an award for his actions in
this life, in accordance with what he has done, whether it
be good or bad.

The Fear and Love of Christ
Knowing then what the fear of the Lord 11
means, we endeavour to win men ; and to God
our motives are clear, and I hope also to

17. *Our*] v.l. omits.
3. *Sure that*] v.l. ' if at least.'
4. *Absorbed in*] Lit. ' drunk down by.' The thought in this passage seems to be
that we are not immortal without the addition of the spiritual element (which is of
divine origin) to the natural elements. Cf. 1 Cor. xv. 44-46.
5. *Guarantee*] Or ' first instalment ' (of life). The same word occurs in i. 22 ;
Eph. i. 14. Some prefer to translate ' has given us a foretaste and pledge of
His Spirit ' ; implying that the Spirit itself in its fulness is the gift that is to be
bestowed hereafter. But tempting as this interpretation is, it seems hardly to
harmonize with Eph. i. 14. Cf. Rom. viii. 23.

you in your own consciences. We are not commending 12
ourselves again to you, but are furnishing you with a
ground of boasting on our behalf, so that you may have a
reply ready for those who boast openly but yet insincerely.
For if we have been beside ourselves, it has been 13
towards God ; or if we are in our senses, it is for your
good. For the love of Christ overmasters us, since 14
we have thus concluded, that One died for all, and
hence all died, and that He died for all in order that the 15
living may no longer live to themselves, but to Him who
for them died and rose again.

The new
View of Life Therefore for the future we know no one 16
which simply as a man. Even if we have known
results Christ simply as a man, yet now we do so
no longer. So if any one is in Christ, he is a 17
new creature : the old state of things has passed away ; a
new has come. And all this is from God, who has recon- 18
ciled us to Himself through Christ, and has appointed us
ministers of this reconciliation, to tell how in Christ God 19
was reconciling the world to Himself, not charging men's
transgressions to their account, and how He has deposited
with us the message of this reconciliation.

The Message As Christ's ambassadors therefore we 20
of Peace and speak, God, as it were, making entreaty
Friendship through us : we entreat you on Christ's behalf,
be reconciled to God. He has made Him who knew 21
nothing of sin to be sin for us, in order that in Him we
may become the righteousness of God. And as God's 1 **6**
fellow-workers, we entreat also that God's grace be not
received in vain by you. For He says, ' AT AN ACCEPTABLE 2
TIME I HAVE LISTENED TO YOU, AND ON A DAY OF SALVATION
I HAVE SUCCOURED YOU ' (Isa. xlix. 8). See, now is the
acceptable time ! Now is the day of salvation !

Apostolic We give no cause for stumbling of any sort, 3
Credentials lest our ministry should incur discredit. On 4
the contrary, we seek to commend ourselves
as God's servants in every way—by great endurance, by
afflictions; distresses, anguish ; in floggings, imprison- 5
ments, tumults ; by toil, sleeplessness, hunger and thirst ;
by purity, knowledge, patience, kindness, by the Holy 6
Spirit, by sincere love ; by truthful speech, by the power 7
of God ; by the weapons of righteousness in right hand

and left ; through honour and ignominy, through calumny 8
and praise : regarded as impostors, and yet true men ; as 9
unknown, yet well known ; as dying, and behold we are
yet alive ; as chastised, but not done to death ; as grieved, 10
but always joyful ; as poor, but enriching many ; as
having nothing, yet possessing everything.

An Appeal for personal Affection To you, Corinthians, we speak frankly : we 11
have opened our hearts to you. There is no 12
want of affection for you in us ; the want is
in your own affections. Then as a fair return—I speak as 13
to my children—let your hearts be opened also.

Intimate Friendship with Idolaters forbidden Avoid unsuitable connections with un- 14
believers. For what is there in common
between righteousness and lawlessness ? Or
what partnership has light with darkness ?
What harmony can exist between Christ and 15
Belial ? Or what participation has a believer with an
unbeliever ? And what compact has the Temple of God 16
with idols ? For we are the Temple of the living God ;
as God has said, ' I WILL DWELL AMONG THEM, AND HOLD
INTERCOURSE WITH THEM ; AND WILL BE THEIR GOD, AND THEY
SHALL BE MY PEOPLE ' (Lev. xxvi. 12 ; Ezek. xxxvii. 27).
Therefore, 17
' " COME OUT FROM AMONG THEM AND SEPARATE YOUR-
SELVES," SAYS THE LORD, " AND TOUCH NOTHING UNCLEAN ;
AND I WILL RECEIVE YOU, AND WILL BE A FATHER TO YOU, 18
AND YOU SHALL BE MY SONS AND DAUGHTERS," says the Lord
Almighty ' (Isa. lii. 11 ; Hos. i. 10 ; Isa. xliii. 6).

Having therefore these promises, beloved, let us cleanse 1 **7**
ourselves from all defilement of body and of spirit, and
attain to holiness through the fear of God.

Paul and his Converts Make room for us in your hearts. We have 2
wronged no one, we have ruined no one, we
have overreached no one. I do not say this 3
in condemnation, for, as I have already said, you have such
a place in our hearts that we would die with you or live
with you. I have great confidence in you : loudly do I 4
boast of you. I am filled with comfort : my heart over-
flows with joy amid all our affliction.

The timely Arrival of Titus For even after our arrival in Macedonia we 5
could get no relief for body or mind. We were
greatly harassed ; there were conflicts without

and fears within. But God, who comforts the downcast, 6
comforted us by the coming of Titus, and not by his coming 7
only, but also by the comfort he had found in you, as he
reported to us your eager affection, your grief, and your
jealousy on my behalf, so that I rejoiced more than ever.

Earnest Repentance in Corinth For if I did give you pain by my letter, I do 8
not regret it; if I did regret it (for I see that
that letter, if only for a time, gave you pain),
now I rejoice, not in your pain, but because the pain led to 9
repentance; for your pain was such as God accepts, so that
you received no injury from us in any respect. For the pain 10
God accepts produces repentance not to be regretted, leading to salvation; but the pain of the world finally produces
death. For mark this very pain that God accepts, what 11
earnestness it has called forth in you, what self-defence,
what indignation, what alarm, what longing affection, what
jealousy, what requital of wrong! You have completely
wiped away reproach from yourselves in the matter. So 12
then, though I wrote to you, it was not because of him
who did the wrong, nor him who suffered it, but in order
to make clear among you your earnest care for us in the
sight of God.

Paul's Hopes realized For this reason we feel comforted; and— 13
in addition to our own comfort—we have been
filled with all the deeper joy at the joy of Titus,
because his spirit has been set at rest by you all. For 14
however I may have boasted to him about you, I have not
been shamed; but as all we have said to you is true, so
also our boasting to Titus about you has proved true. And 15
his affection is all the more drawn to you when he calls
to mind the obedience of you all, how with fear and
trembling you received him. I rejoice that I have complete 16
confidence in you.

Help for the Poor in Jerusalem

Generous Gifts from Macedonia But, brethren, we desire to let you know of 1 **8**
the grace of God which has been bestowed on
the Churches of Macedonia; how, amid a trial 2
of great affliction, their abundant joy even in their deep

---

6. *Comforted*] Or 'has comforted,' if Wieseler is right in conjecturing, from
Paul's change of tone, that Titus arrived just when the early part of this chapter
was being written.
8. *For I see*] v.l. omits 'for.'

poverty has overflowed in the wealth of their liberality. I 3
testify that to the extent of their power, and even beyond
their power, they have of their own choice given help. With 4
earnest entreaty they begged from us the favour of sharing
in this service to the saints. They indeed exceeded our 5
expectations. First of all they gave themselves to the Lord,
and to us as God willed. This led us to urge Titus that, 6
as he had been the one who commenced the work, so he
should complete among you this act of beneficence also.
Well, as you are eminent in everything, in faith and speech 7
and knowledge and all zeal, and in your love for us, see that
this beneficent spirit also flourishes in you.

The Example of Jesus I am not saying this by way of command, 8
but to test by other men's earnestness the
genuineness of your love also; for you know 9
the grace of our Lord Jesus Christ—how for your sakes He
became poor, though He was rich, in order that you
through His poverty might become rich. But in this matter 10
I give my opinion; for this is to your advantage, seeing that
you were the first to begin, not merely to act, but even to
form the purpose a year ago.

Sympathy and Help to be mutual And now accomplish it also, in order that 11
your readiness of will may be matched by the
accomplishment in proportion to your means.
For if the readiness is forthcoming, the gift is acceptable 12
according to what a man has, and not to what he has not. Not 13
that others are to have relief while you are hard pressed, but 14
that by way of reciprocity, your surplus should at the
present juncture contribute to their deficiency, in order
that their surplus may in turn contribute to your deficiency,
so that there may be reciprocity. As it is written, 'HE 15
WHO GATHERED MUCH HAD NOT TOO MUCH, AND HE WHO
GATHERED LITTLE HAD NOT TOO LITTLE' (Exod. xvi. 18).

The new Mission of Titus But thanks be to God that He inspires the 16
heart of Titus with the same interest in you;
he welcomed our request, and being very 17
earnest comes to you of his own choice. And we send with 18
him the brother whose praises for his preaching of the
gospel are sounded throughout all the Churches. And more 19

---

4. *Favour of sharing*] Lit. ' favour and participation.'
7. *Your love for us*] v.L. ' our love to you.'
18. *Praises . . gospel*] Lit. simply ' praise in the gospel.' Whom the apostle refers
to in this verse (or in xii. 18) is uncertain.

than that, he was chosen by the vote of the Churches to travel with us in our administration of this generous gift, to promote the Lord's glory and gratify our own desire. For we are taking steps to prevent any one from blaming 20 us in respect to these liberal contributions which we are administering. We aim at appearing honourable in the 21 sight not only of God, but also of men.

And we send with them our brother, whom we have 22 often in many matters proved to be zealous, and now far more zealous through the strong confidence which he hàs in you.

A loving Welcome requested As for Titus, he is my partner and comrade 23 in my labours for you. And as for our brethren, they are apostles of churches, and are the glory of Christ. Exhibit therefore to the Churches 24 the evidence of your love and of our boasting to these brethren about you.

Contributions were to be ready when Paul came As to this service to the saints, it is really 1 **9** unnecessary for me to write to you. For I 2 know your readiness, of which I boast of you to the Macedonians, pointing out that for a whole year Greece has been ready ; and your ardour has stimulated the majority of them. Still, I send 3 the brethren in order that in this matter our boast about you may not prove hollow ; so that, as I told them, you may be ready ; for fear that if any Macedonians come with 4 me and find you unprepared, we—not to say yourselves—should be put to shame by this confidence of ours. I 5 have thought it necessary therefore to request these brethren to visit you first, and to make sure beforehand that your promised gift may be ready as a real act of grace, and not as something extorted from you.

We shall reap as we have sown But note this : he who sows thinly will also 6 reap thinly, and he who sows bountifully will also reap bountifully. Let each contribute as 7 he has decided in his own mind, and not with pain or constraint: 'IT IS A CHEERFUL GIVER THAT GOD LOVES' (Prov. xxii. 8 ; LXX). And God is able to bestow every 8 blessing on you in abundance, so that having in every case

---

19. *Vote*] Lit. ' show of hands.'
5. *Your promised gift*] Lit. ' blessing.' So the Heb. ' berāchah ' in Gen. xxxiii. 11 ; Joshua xv. 19.
6. *Bountifully*] Lit. ' with a view to blessings.'

all sufficiency at all times, you may have ample means for all good works. As it is written, 9

'HE HAS SCATTERED ABROAD;
HE HAS GIVEN TO THE POOR:
HIS RIGHTEOUSNESS REMAINS FOR EVER'
(Ps. cxii. 9).

The happy Results of Liberality And God, who supplies seed for the sower 10 and bread for eating, will supply you with seed and multiply it, and will increase the benefits wrought by your almsgiving. You will thus be enriched 11 in every way so as to show all liberality, such as through our instrumentality evokes thanksgiving to God. For the 12 service rendered in this ministry not only helps to relieve the wants of the saints, but it also has an overflow in many thanksgivings to God. By the evidence of this service 13 you procure glory to God for your loyalty to your profession of the gospel of Christ, and for the liberality of your contributions for them and for all, while they themselves also 14 in prayer on your behalf yearn towards you because of the surpassing grace of God which rests upon you. Thanks 15 be to God for His unspeakable gift!

Paul's Vindication of his Apostleship

Paul reluctant to assert his Authority Now I, Paul, entreat you by the gentleness 1 10 and reasonableness of Christ—I who (as you say) when present am humble among you, but when absent am bold towards you. I beg 2 that you will not force me, when I do come, to show my courage by the confidence with which I reckon I shall be bold against some who reckon that we are guided by worldly motives. For though we live in the world, it is 3 no worldly warfare that we are waging. The weapons of 4 our warfare are not of this world, but are mighty before God for overthrowing fortresses. For we overthrow 5 reasonings and everything raised aloft against the knowledge of God; and we lead every thought captive and bring it into obedience to Christ; while we hold ourselves in readi- 6 ness to punish all disobedience, as soon as you have fully shown your obedience.

9. See Matt. vi. 1-18, R.V.
15. *Gift*] The brotherly sympathy, generosity, and mutual kindness which were entirely due to the grace of God being in their hearts.

Paul's Vigour of Speech and Action Open your eyes to what is before your face. 7 If any man is sure of himself that he belongs to Christ, let him consider again that, just as he belongs to Christ, so also do we. If, indeed, 8 I were to boast too much of our authority, which the Lord has given that we may build you up, not cast you down, I should not be ashamed. My object is not to seem as if 9 I wanted to frighten you by my letters. For they say, ' His 10 letters are weighty and forcible, but his personal presence is feeble, and his speech is contemptible.' Let such 11 people take account of this, that whatever we are in word by our letters when absent, the same are we also in act when present.

Corinth included in Paul's Mission We do not venture to rank or compare 12 ourselves with certain persons who recommend themselves. Yet they are not wise in measuring and comparing themselves with one another. We, however, will not boast beyond our due 13 limits, but will keep within the limit of the field which God has assigned to us as a limit, which reaches even to you. There is no straining of authority on our part, as though it 14 did not extend to you. For we were the first to come to you with the gospel of Christ. We do not boast beyond our due 15 limits, nor of other men's labours ; but we entertain the hope that, as your faith grows, our field of activity among you may be enlarged till it goes beyond you, and we may 16 preach the gospel in the districts beyond you, not boasting in another man's field about work already done by him.

Credentials must be from God But ' WHOEVER BOASTS, LET HIS BOAST BE IN 17 THE LORD ' (Jer. ix. 24). It is not the man 18 who commends himself that is accepted, but the one whom the Lord commends.

Paul's Motive one of anxious Love I wish you could have borne with a little 1 **11** folly on my part : nay, do bear with me. I 2 am jealous over you with God's own jealousy. For I have betrothed you to Christ to present you like a faithful bride to her one husband. But I am afraid 3 that, as the serpent in his craftiness deceived Eve, so your

---

7. *Open your eyes to what is before your face*] Or, perhaps, ' You look (or, do you look ?) at outward appearances.'

14. *As though, &c.*] *i.e.* as there would be if our limit did not really extend to you. *We were the first to come to you*] Or, perhaps, ' We came even as far as you.'

1. *Folly*] Cf. verse 16.

thoughts may be perverted from their simplicity and their fidelity to Christ. If indeed a chance-comer proclaims 4 another Jesus whom we did not proclaim, or if you receive a Spirit different from the one you have received or a gospel different from that which you have welcomed, your toleration is admirable indeed! Why, I reckon myself in 5 no respect inferior to those pre-eminent apostles. And 6 if in speech I am no orator, yet in knowledge I am not deficient. Nay, we have in every way made that evident to you.

Paul's Reason for foregoing his Right to Maintenance Did I sin in abasing myself that you might 7 be exalted, in that I proclaimed God's gospel to you without reward? Other Churches I 8 robbed, receiving pay from them in order to do you service. And when I was with you 9 and my resources failed, I was a dead-weight on no one; for the brethren, when they came from Macedonia, fully supplied my wants; and I kept myself from being in the least a burden to you, and will do so still. It is Christ's 10 truth on my lips when I say that I will not be stopped from boasting of this anywhere in Greece. And why? 11 Because I do not love you? God knows that I do. What 12 I am doing I will still do, to cut the ground from under the feet of those who desire ground for being recognized as equal with us in the matters they boast about. Men of this stamp are sham apostles, dishonest workmen, 13 assuming the garb of apostles of Christ. And no wonder! 14 Satan himself assumes the garb of an angel of light. It is 15 therefore no great thing for his servants also to assume the garb of servants of righteousness. Their end will be in accordance with their deeds.

An ironical Defence of his own good Sense Again I say, let no one think that I am a fool. 16 Or if you must, make allowance for me even as a fool, in order that I too may boast a little. What I am now saying, I do not say 17 by the Lord's command, but as a fool in his folly in this confident boasting. Since many boast for merely 18 human reasons, I too will boast. Wise as you are, you 19 find pleasure in tolerating fools. For you tolerate it if 20 any one makes a slave of you, lives at your expense, makes off with your property, gives himself airs, or strikes you on the face!

Paul's Perils and Hardships I speak in self-disparagement as though 21 we had been feeble. Yet let who will be 'courageous' — I speak in folly — I too am courageous. Are they Hebrews? So am I. Are 22 they Israelites? So am I. Are they descendants of Abraham? So am I. Are they servants of Christ? (I 23 speak as if I were out of my senses.) Much more I; exceeding them in labours, exceeding them in imprisonments, quite surpassing them in floggings, with risk of life many a time. From the Jews I have five times received forty 24 lashes all but one. Thrice I have been beaten with rods, 25 once I have been stoned, thrice I have been shipwrecked, a whole night and day I have passed in the deep. I have 26 travelled much, amid dangers from rivers, dangers from robbers, dangers from my own people, dangers from Gentiles; dangers in the city, dangers in the desert, dangers by sea, dangers among false brethren; in labour 27 and toil, with many a sleepless night, in hunger and thirst, in frequent fastings, in cold and lack of clothing. And 28 apart from all else, there is that which presses on me daily—my anxiety for all the Churches. Who is weak, 29 and I not weak? Who is offended, and I not fired with anger?

If boast I must, it shall be of things which display 30 my weakness. The God and Father of our Lord Jesus 31 Christ—who is blessed for ever—knows that I am speaking the truth.

Paul's Escape from Damascus In Damascus the governor under King 32 Aretas had the city watched, in order to arrest me, but I was let down in a basket through a 33 window in the wall, and so escaped his hands.

Sublime Visions and humbling Infirmities I am obliged to boast. It is not profitable, 1 **12** but I will proceed to visions and revelations of the Lord. I know a man in Christ who four- 2 teen years ago—whether in the body or out of the body I know not; God knows—was caught up, this man, even to the third heaven. And I know that this 3 man—whether in the body or apart from the body I do not know; God knows—was caught up into Paradise and 4 heard unspeakable things which no human being is permitted to repeat. Of such a one I will boast; but of myself 5 I will not boast, except in my weaknesses. If indeed I 6 should choose to boast, I should not be a fool, for I should be speaking the truth. But I forbear, lest any one should esteem me more highly than by what he sees of me or hears from my lips. And because the revelations were of such 7 surpassing grandeur—therefore, lest I should be over-elated there was given me a thorn in the flesh, Satan's angel to deal blows at me, lest I should be over-elated. Concern- 8 ing this, three times have I besought the Lord that it might leave me ; but He has said to me, ' My grace suffices for you, 9 for power is perfected in weakness.' Most gladly therefore will I rather glory in my infirmities in order that the power of Christ may overshadow me. Hence I take delight in 10 infirmities, in insults, in distresses, in persecutions, in grievous difficulties—for Christ's sake ; for when I am weak, then am I strong.

The true Credentials of an Apostle I have descended to folly, but you have com- 11 pelled me. Why, you ought to have been my vindicators ; for in no respect have I been inferior to the pre-eminent apostles, even though I am nothing. The signs that mark the apostle 12 have been done among you, in unwearied persistence, with signs and marvels and mighty works. In what respect 13 have you been worse used than other Churches, except that I myself was not a dead-weight upon you ? Forgive this injustice !

An intended Visit to Corinth See, I am now for the third time prepared 14 to visit you, and I will not be a dead-weight on you. I desire not your money, but your-selves ; for children ought not to put by for their parents, but parents for their children. And I will most gladly 15 spend and be utterly spent for the good of your souls. If I love you so intensely, am I the less to be loved ? Be 16 that as it may, I was not a burden to you.

The unselfish Motives of Paul and Titus But I was cunning and entrapped you, they say ! Is there one of those I have sent to you 17 by whom I overreached you ? I begged Titus 18 to visit you, and sent our brother with him.

9. *Power*] Both the A.V. and the R.V. insert ' my.' But so important a word could hardly have been omitted here in the Greek, if such were the true meaning of the sentence. Cf. the A.V. with the R.V., John iii. 34.

15. *If I love you, &c.*] v.L. ' though the more intensely I love you, the less I am loved.'

16. *I was, &c.*] ' My opponents say that my very privation and poverty were means to some unworthy by-ends.' Paul disdains to give any other answer than that already given in verse 11. Cf. Rom. iii. 8.

Did Titus overreach you at all ? Were we not guided by the same Spirit, and did we not walk in the same steps ?

An Appeal to the great Judge of all You are thinking all this time that we are 19 making our defence to you. Really it is before God in Christ that we speak. But, beloved, it is all with a view to your upbuilding. For I am afraid 20 that perhaps when I come I may not find you what I desire, and that you may find me what you do not desire ; that perhaps there may be contention, jealousy, anger, party spirit, calumny, backbiting, and arrogance ; and that upon 21 re-visiting you I may be humbled by my God in your presence, and may have to mourn over many who formerly sinned, and who have not repented of the uncleanness, licentiousness, and sensuality which they have practised.

Coming Investigations and Punishments This is my third visit to you. 'ON THE EVI- 1 **13** DENCE OF TWO OR THREE WITNESSES EVERY WORD SHALL BE CONFIRMED ' (Deut. xix. 15). Those 2 who sinned formerly, and indeed the rest of you, I have forewarned and still forewarn, as when I was with you the second time, and now in my absence, that, when I come again, I shall not spare you ; since you want a proof 3 that Christ speaks by my lips. Christ is not feeble towards you, but powerful among you. Though He was crucified 4 through weakness, yet He lives through the power of God. And though we are weak in Him, yet with Him we shall live through the power of God to deal with you.

' Examine yourselves on the one vital Point ' It is your own selves you must test to dis- 5 cover whether you are true believers : examine yourselves. Or do you not know that Jesus Christ is within you, unless you cannot stand the test ? But I trust that you will recognize that we can 6 stand the test. And our prayer to God is that you may 7 do nothing wrong ; not in order that we may be shown to stand the test, but that you may do what is right, even though we may seem not to stand the test. For we 8 have no power against the truth, but only for the truth ; and we rejoice when we are feeble, but you are strong. 9 This we also pray for—your perfection. For this reason 10 I write thus while absent, that when present I may not have to act severely in the exercise of that authority

19. *That we speak. But, &c.*] v.L. ' that we say all this, dear friends, to promote your progress in goodness.'
4. *In Him*] v.L. ' with Him.'

which the Lord has given me for building up, and not for pulling down.

Finally, brethren, farewell; seek perfection, 11
Concluding Words take comfort, be of the same spirit, live in peace. And the God of love and peace shall be with you.

Salute one another with a holy kiss. All the saints salute 12,13 you.

The grace of the Lord Jesus Christ, the love of God, and 14 the fellowship of the Holy Spirit be with you all!

434

THE EPISTLE OF PAUL TO
THE GALATIANS

The uncertainty as to the situation of the ' Churches of Galatia ' (i. 2), and, consequently, as to the time when and the place whence this Epistle was written, has been noted in the general introduction to the Correspondence of St. Paul. But whether the letter was addressed to the cities of Northern Ethnic Galatia (Ancyra, Tavium, Pessinus) or to those of Southern Political Galatia (Pisidian Antioch, Iconium, Lystra, and Derbe), there is no doubt as to its occasion and message.

Hard on the heels of Paul's successful preaching of his gospel, other teachers had come, flouting his Apostolic standing, and insisting that his Gentile converts must submit to circumcision and other Jewish ritual. This provokes him to a passionate defence—(1) of his independence of the original Apostles ; (2) of his gospel of justification by faith.

The tension of feeling is evident all through the Epistle, not least in the unique omission of his customary thanksgiving (cf. Preface to 1 Corinthians, *ad fin.*).

Some details of the argument from Old Testament history may not appeal to the modern mind ; but the ' treasure ' is more than the ' earthen vessel.' A nobler or more enduring defence of Christian Freedom was never penned. Later on, when the conflict was past, the main theme of the Epistle was elaborated into the Epistle to the Romans.

THE EPISTLE OF PAUL TO
THE GALATIANS

Introduction

Greeting Paul, an Apostle — sent not from men nor 1 **1**
through any man, but through Jesus Christ and
God the Father who raised Him from the dead—and all 2
the brethren who are with me :

To the Churches of Galatia ; grace to you and peace 3
from God the Father, and from our Lord Jesus Christ, who 4
gave Himself for our sins in order to rescue us from the
present wicked world in accordance with the will of our
God and Father. To Him be the glory for ever and ever ! 5
Amen.

Paul vindicates his Apostolic Authority

The falling I am amazed that you are so readily deserting 6
away of the for a different gospel Him who called you by
Galatians the grace of Christ. For other gospel there is 7
none ; but there are some persons who are troubling you,
and seeking to distort the gospel of Christ. But even if we 8
or an angel from heaven should preach you a gospel contrary
to that which we have preached to you, let him be accursed.
What I have said before I say again now: if any one 9
preaches to you a gospel contrary to that which you have received, let him be accursed. Is it man's favour or God's 10
that I try to gain ? Or am I seeking to please men ? If I
were still a man-pleaser, I should not be Christ's servant.

Paul's I must tell you, brethren, that the gospel 11
Teaching which I preach bears no human impress. For
came direct indeed it was not from man that I received 12
from Christ or learnt it, but by a revelation from Jesus
Christ. You have heard of my early career in Judaism— 13
how furiously I persecuted the Church of God, and made

3. v.l. ' God our Father, and the Lord Jesus Christ.'
7. *For other, &c.*] Or ' This is nothing but that some persons ' &c.
10. ' Yes, I say accursed. Is that the language of a man-pleaser ? '

havoc of it ; and how in devotion to Judaism I out- 14
stripped many men of my own age among my people,
being far more zealous than they for the traditions of
my forefathers. But when He who set me apart even 15
from my birth, and called me by His grace, saw fit to 16
reveal His Son within me, in order that I might preach Him
among the Gentiles, I did not confer with any human being,
nor did I go up to Jerusalem to those who were Apostles 17
before me, but I went away at once into Arabia, and afterwards came back to Damascus.

Visits to Jerusalem, Syria, and Cilicia
Then, three years later, I went up to Jerusa- 18
lem to visit Cephas, and I spent a fortnight with
him. I saw none of the other Apostles, except 19
James, the Lord's brother. Be sure that in 20
writing this to you I am speaking the truth, as in the sight
of God. Afterwards I visited the districts of Syria and 21
Cilicia. But to the Christian Churches in Judaea I was 22
personally unknown. They only heard it said, ' He who 23
was once our persecutor is now preaching the faith of which
he formerly made havoc.' And they gave glory to God 24
on my account.

Paul's Divine Call recognized in Jerusalem
Then, after an interval of fourteen years, I 1 **2**
again went up to Jerusalem with Barnabas,
taking Titus also with me. I went up in 2
obedience to a revelation, and I put before them
the gospel which I proclaim among the Gentiles. I did this
in private to the leaders of the Church, for fear that I was
running or should have run in vain. But although my 3
companion Titus was a Greek, not even he was compelled
to be circumcised. My action was on account of the false 4
brethren secretly introduced, who had stolen in to spy out
the freedom which is ours in Christ Jesus, in order to
enslave us again. Not for an hour did we give way and sub- 5
mit to these, that the gospel might continue with you in its
purity. Further, from the reputed leaders I gained nothing. 6
Whether they were men of importance or not matters
nothing to me ; God recognizes no external distinctions.
To me, at any rate, the leaders imparted nothing new. So 7
far from that, when they saw that I was entrusted with the

18. *Cephas*] *i.e.* Peter.
4. *Freedom*] *i.e.* freedom from the Law of Moses.
7. *So far from that*] v.L. ' Nay, on the contrary.' But the exact contrary of
' imparting ' is actual ' taking away,' and of this there is no thought here.

preaching of the gospel to the Gentiles as Peter had been with that to the Jews—for He who had been at work in Peter 8 for an apostleship to the Jews had also been at work in me for the Gentiles—and when they perceived the grace which 9 was granted to me, the reputed pillars of the Church, James, Cephas and John, welcomed Barnabas and me to their fellowship, on the understanding that we were to go to the Gentiles and they to the Jews. Only they urged that we 10 should remember their poor—a thing which I myself was even eager to do.

Peter openly rebuked by Paul But when Peter visited Antioch, I opposed 11 him to his face, because his conduct condemned him. For until certain persons came from 12 James he would eat with Gentiles ; but when they came, he withdrew and separated himself for fear of the circumcision party. And along with him the other Jews also 13 concealed their real opinions, so that even Barnabas was carried away by their dissimulation. As soon as I saw that 14 they were not keeping to the true line of the gospel, I said to Cephas before them all,

' If you, though you are a Jew, live as a Gentile does, and not as a Jew, how can you make the Gentiles live like Jews ? ' We, though we are Jews by birth and not Gentile 15 sinners, know that a man is justified, not by keeping the Law, 16 but only through faith in Jesus Christ. So we too have believed in Christ Jesus, that we might be justified through faith in Christ, and not through keeping the Law. For through keeping the Law no human being shall be justified. But if while we are seeking in Christ acquittal from guilt 17 we ourselves are convicted of sin, is Christ then an agent of sin ? God forbid ! Why, if I rebuild that which I had 18 demolished, I thereby constitute myself a transgressor ; for 19 by the Law I died to the Law in order that I might live for God. I have been crucified with Christ, and it is no longer 20 I that live, but Christ lives in me ; and the life which I now live in the body I live by faith in the Son of God who loved me and gave Himself up for me. I do not nullify the grace 21 of God ; for if acquittal from guilt comes through the Law, then Christ died in vain.

9. *Grace . . granted*] Or ' divine favour . . shown.' See Rom. xii. 3, n.
12. *Eat with Gentiles*] Contrary to strict Jewish practice.
13. *Jews*] i.e. Jewish Christians.
17. *Convicted of sin*] For neglecting to keep the Law of Moses.

The Jewish Law far inferior to the Christian Faith

You foolish Galatians ! who has bewitched **1 3** you—before whose very eyes was portrayed Jesus Christ crucified ! This one question I **2** would ask you :

Is it on the ground of obeying the Law that you received the Spirit, or is it because you heard and believed ?

Are you so foolish ? Having begun by the spiritual, are **3** you now going to reach perfection by the external ? Have **4** you experienced so much to no purpose—if indeed it has been to no purpose ? He who gives you His Spirit and **5** works miracles among you—is it on the ground of your doing the Law, or of your having heard and believed ? Even as ABRAHAM BELIEVED GOD, AND IT WAS PLACED TO **6** HIS ACCOUNT AS RIGHTEOUSNESS (Gen. xv. 6).

You see then that those who rest on faith **7** are the true sons of Abraham. And the Scrip- **8** ture, foreseeing that in consequence of faith God would justify the Gentiles, foretold the Good News to Abraham, saying, ' IN YOU ALL THE NATIONS SHALL BE BLESSED ' (Gen. xii. 3 ; xviii. 18). So we see **9** that those who rest on faith are blessed with believing Abraham. All who depend upon obedience to the Law are **10** under a curse ; for it is written, ' CURSED IS EVERY ONE WHO DOES NOT ABIDE BY ALL THE PRECEPTS OF THE LAW AND PRACTISE THEM ' (Deut. xxvii. 26).

It is evident, too, that no one can be put right with God **11** by Law, because ' THE RIGHTEOUS SHALL LIVE BY FAITH ' (Hab. ii. 4), and the Law has nothing to do with faith. It **12** teaches that ' HE WHO DOES THESE THINGS SHALL LIVE BY THEM ' (Lev. xviii. 5). Christ purchased our freedom from the **13** curse of the Law by becoming accursed for us (for Scripture says, ' CURSED IS EVERY ONE WHO HANGS UPON A TREE ' [Deut. xxi. 23]), in order that in Christ Jesus the blessing of **14** Abraham might come upon the Gentiles, so that through faith we might receive the promised Spirit.

Brethren, I will take an illustration from **15** every-day life. Even a human covenant, when once ratified, no one can set aside or amplify. Now the promises were given to Abraham and **16** to his seed. It does not say 'and to seeds' referring to many, but 'and to your seed' (Gen. xii. 7) referring to one —and this is Christ. I mean that the Covenant which God 17 had ratified is not abrogated by the Law which was given four hundred and thirty years later—so as to annul the promise. For if the inheritance comes from Law, it no 18 longer comes from a promise. But God has granted it to Abraham by promise.

The real Place and Use of the Law Why then the Law? It was imposed later 19 on with a view to transgressions, until the seed should come to whom the promise had been made, and it was enacted by a mediator with the help of angels. But there cannot be a mediator for only one. 20 God, however, is only one. Is the Law then opposed to the 21 promises of God? God forbid! for if a Law had been given which could have conferred life, righteousness would certainly have come by the Law. But Scripture has im- 22 prisoned all under sin, in order that the promise depending on faith in Jesus Christ may be given to those who believe.

The Law prepares us to welcome the Saviour Before this faith came, we were imprisoned 23 under the Law, waiting in custody for the faith which was to be revealed. So that the 24 Law has proved a tutor to discipline us for Christ, that through faith we may be justified. But now 25 that this faith has come, we are no longer under a tutor. You are all sons of God through faith in Christ Jesus; for 26, 27 all of you who have been baptized into Christ have clothed yourselves with Christ. There cannot be Jew and Greek, 28 slave and free man, male and female; you are all one in Christ Jesus. And if you belong to Christ, then you are 29 indeed Abraham's offspring and are heirs in accordance with the promise.

Divine Sonship only possible through Faith in Christ Now I say that so long as an heir is a child, 1 **4** he in no way differs from a slave, although he is the owner of everything, but he is under 2 guardians and trustees until the time his father has appointed. So we also, when we were 3 minors, were kept like slaves under the world's rudimentary notions. But, when the time was fully come, God sent 4

---

19. *With a view to transgressions*] *i.e.* probably not to *check* transgressions, but to bring them into relief. Cf. Rom. vii. 8.
3. *World's rudimentary notions*] Cf. Col. ii. 8, n.

forth His Son, born of a woman, born subject to Law, in 5
order to ransom those who were subject to Law, so that we
might receive recognition as sons. And because you are 6
sons, God has sent out the Spirit of His Son to enter your
hearts and cry ' Abba ! Father ! ' Therefore you are no 7
longer a slave, but a son ; and if a son, then an heir also
through God's own act.

Mere external Observances worthless   But at one time you, having no knowledge 8
of God, were slaves to gods which were no gods
at all. Now, however, when you have come to 9
know God—or rather to be known by Him—
how is it you are turning back again to the weak and
worthless rudimentary notions to which you are once
more willing to be enslaved ? You observe days and 10
months, special seasons, and years. I am alarmed about 11
you, that I have perhaps bestowed labour upon you
to no purpose.

The once eager Affection of the Galatians   Brethren, become as I am, I beseech you ; 12
for I also became like you. I do not imply that
you have done me any wrong. As you know, 13
in former days it was on account of bodily
infirmity that I proclaimed the gospel to you, and 14
yet the physical condition which was such a trial to you, you
did not regard with contempt or loathing, but you received
me as an angel of God or Christ Jesus Himself ! What 15
then has become of that self-congratulation of yours ? For
I bear you witness that had it been possible you would
have torn out your own eyes and have given them to me.
Can it be that I have become your enemy by speaking 16
the truth to you ?

Paul's Anxiety for the Welfare of the Galatians   These men pay court to you, but not honour- 17
ably. They want to isolate you, so that you
may pay court to them. To be paid court to
in an honourable cause is an honourable thing 18
always, and not only when I am with you, my 19
children—you for whom I am again in birth-pangs, until
Christ is formed within you. Would that I were with you 20
just now and could change my tone, for I am perplexed
about you.

12. *Like you*] *i.e.* a Gentile—renouncing my traditional customs as a Jew.
13. *Bodily infirmity*] Some illness which detained him in Galatia, where he would
not otherwise have stayed so long.

Ishmael a slave, Isaac free

Tell me—you who want to be subject to Law 21 —will you not listen to the Law ? It is written 22 that Abraham had two sons, one by the slave-girl and one by the free woman. But whereas the child of 23 the slave-girl had an ordinary birth, the child of the free woman was born in fulfilment of God's promise. All this is 24 allegorical ; for the women represent two Covenants. One originates on Mount Sinai, and bears children destined for slavery. This is Hagar : for the name Hagar stands for 25 Mount Sinai in Arabia, and corresponds to the present Jerusalem, which is in bondage together with her children. But the Jerusalem which is above is free, and she is our 26 mother. For it is written : 27

' REJOICE, THOU BARREN WOMAN THAT BEAREST NOT,
BREAK FORTH INTO A JOYFUL CRY, THOU THAT DOST NOT TRAVAIL.
FOR THE DESOLATE WOMAN HAS MANY CHILDREN—
MORE THAN SHE WHO HAS A HUSBAND ' (Isa. liv. 1).

' Stedfastly maintain your Freedom '

But you, brethren, like Isaac, are the children 28 of a promise. Yet just as, at that time, the child 29 of ordinary birth persecuted the one born according to the word of the Spirit, so it is now. But what says the Scripture ? ' SEND AWAY THE SLAVE-GIRL 30 AND HER SON, FOR NEVER SHALL THE SLAVE-GIRL'S SON SHARE THE INHERITANCE WITH THE SON OF THE FREE WOMAN ' (Gen. xxi. 10). Therefore, brethren, we are not the 31 children of a slave-girl, but of the free woman. Christ has 1 **5** made us completely free ; stand fast then and do not again be hampered with the yoke of slavery.

Legalism leaves no Room for Christ

Mark, it is I Paul who tell you that if you 2 receive circumcision Christ will avail you nothing. I once more protest to every man 3 who receives circumcision that he is under obligation to keep the whole of the Law. You have lost 4 the good of union with Christ if you seek acquittal by Law : you have fallen from grace. For it is by the Spirit's help 5 and in faith that we wait for the hoped-for righteousness. In 6 Christ Jesus neither circumcision nor uncircumcision is of any avail ; but only faith working through love.

25. *For the name, &c.*] v.l. ' for Sinai is a mountain in Arabia ' ; omitting ' Hagar.' To this day the Arabs call Sinai ' Hajar,' with the *j* sounded as in the English ' jar.'
1. v.l. ' children of the free woman by the freedom with which Christ freed us.'
4. *You have lost, &c.*] Lit. ' you have been abrogated from Christ.' Cf. Rom. vi. 17.

You were running the race nobly ! Who has 7
A final Word of Protest got in the way of your obeying the truth ? That 8
persuasion does not come from Him who calls
you. A little leaven leavens the whole of the dough. For 9, 10
my part I am convinced about you in the Lord that you will
not think otherwise. But the man—be he who he may—
who is troubling you, will have to bear his sentence. As 11
for me, brethren, if I am still a preacher of circumcision,
why am I still suffering persecution ? Then the Cross has
ceased to be a stumbling-block ! Would to God that those 12
who are unsettling you would even mutilate themselves.

Moral and Spiritual Exhortations

Love restrains those free from Law You indeed, brethren, were called to freedom. 13
Only do not make your freedom an incentive to
your lower nature ; but serve one another in
love. For the entire Law is summed up in the 14
one precept, ' YOU ARE TO LOVE YOUR NEIGHBOUR AS YOUR-
SELF ' (Lev. xix. 18). But if you bite and devour one 15
another, beware lest you are destroyed by one another.

The Spirit and Man's earthly Nature I say then, let your lives be guided by the 16
Spirit, and then you will not fulfil the cravings
of your lower nature. For the cravings of the 17
lower nature are opposed to the Spirit, and the
Spirit is opposed to the lower nature, because these are
antagonistic to each other, so that you cannot do as you
would wish. But if guided by the Spirit, you are not 18
subject to Law.

The Outcome of Man's sinful Nature Now the doings of the lower nature are familiar 19
to you, namely, licentiousness, impurity, in-
decency, idol-worship, magic, animosity, strife, 20
jealousy, ill temper, intrigues, dissensions, factions, envy, 21
drunkenness, carousing, and the like. I forewarn you, as I
have already forewarned you, that those who practise such
things will not inherit the Kingdom of God. The Spirit, 22
on the other hand, brings a harvest of love, joy, peace ;
The Fruit borne by the Spirit forbearance, kindness, benevolence ; good
faith, meekness, self-restraint. Against such 23
things there is no law. Now those who belong 24
to Christ Jesus have crucified the lower nature with its

12. *Mutilate themselves*] Or ' cut themselves off,' *i.e.* from communication with you.
21. *Envy*] v.L. adds ' murders.'

passions and appetites. If we live by the Spirit, by the 25
Spirit also let us be guided. Let us not become vain- 26
glorious, challenging one another, envying one another.

Sympathy to be shown to the Fallen   Brethren, if anybody be detected in any mis- 1 **6**
conduct, you who are spiritual should restore
such a one in a spirit of meekness. And let each
of you keep an eye on himself, lest he also fall into temptation. Carry one another's burdens, and so fulfil the law of 2
Christ. For if any one thinks himself to be somebody when 3
he is nobody, he is deluding himself. But let every man 4
scrutinize his own conduct, and then he will have his reason for
boasting, not by comparison with another, but in regard to
himself. For every man will have to shoulder his own burden. 5

Let those who receive instruction in the word 6
Life's sure Harvest   share with their instructors all temporal blessings.
Do not deceive yourselves. God is not to be 7
mocked. For whatever a man sows, that he will also reap.
He who sows for his lower nature will from that nature reap 8
destruction; but he who sows for the Spirit will from that
Spirit reap Life eternal. Let us not lose heart in doing 9
what is right; for in due time we shall reap a harvest, if we
do not faint. So then, as we have opportunity, let us do 10
good to all, and especially to the household of the faith.

See in what large letters I am writing to you 11
Autograph Conclusion. Paul glories only in the Cross   with my own hand. All who desire to make a 12
good show outwardly try to compel you to
receive circumcision, but simply to escape being
persecuted for the Cross of Christ. For the 13
circumcised themselves do not really keep the Law, but they
would have you receive circumcision in order that they may
glory in your subjection to external rites. But God forbid 14
that I should glory in anything except in the Cross of our
Lord Jesus Christ, by which the world is crucified to me,
and I to the world. For neither circumcision nor uncircum- 15
cision is of any importance, but only a new nature. And all 16
who will regulate their lives by this principle—may peace
and mercy be upon them—and on the true Israel of God.

From this time onward let no one trouble me; for I bear 17
on my body the brand-marks of Jesus.

Farewell   The grace of our Lord Jesus Christ be with 18
your spirits, brethren. Amen.

15. *For*] v.l. adds ' in Christ Jesus.'

THE EPISTLE OF PAUL TO
THE EPHESIANS

The Book of Acts records a brief visit of Paul to Ephesus (xviii. 19–21), a ministry there of some three years (xix.), and the touching farewell at Miletus to the elders of the Church (xx.). This intimate personal relationship with Ephesus is hardly reflected in the Epistle. It is impersonal in its substance, in the absence of any greetings, and in the unique third person of the closing benediction (vi. 24). These features are emphasised by the omission, in a most important group of authorities for the text, of the words ' in Ephesus ' at i. 1 ; and it is now generally agreed that the Epistle was a circular letter addressed to the Churches of Asia. Paul sent from his Roman prison, by the same messengers, a private note to his friend Philemon at Colossae, and another to the Colossian Church. This latter, a controversial protest against heretical teaching, seems to have immediately suggested expansion into an uncontroversial treatise, very much as *Galatians* was expanded into *Romans*. Possibly a copy of *Ephesians* was taken by his messengers to Laodicea, with directions for interchange with Colossae, only a few miles away, which had a letter of its own (Col. iv. 16).

The two Epistles have much in common ; but the stress in *Colossians*, prompted by angelic rivalry to the supremacy of Christ, is on what Christ is to His Church : in *Ephesians* the theme is rather what the Church is to Christ : nothing short of one undivided body of redeemed humanity. (See Eph. i. 23, n.)

THE EPISTLE OF PAUL TO
THE EPHESIANS

Greeting Paul, an Apostle of Christ Jesus by the will **1** **1**
of God, to the saints who are in Ephesus—
faithful in Christ Jesus: may grace and peace be **2**
granted to you from God our Father and the Lord
Jesus Christ.

God's eternal Blessed be the God and Father of our Lord **3**
Purpose of Jesus Christ, who has crowned us with every
Love spiritual blessing in the heavenly realms in
Christ ; even as, in His love, He chose us as His own in **4**
Christ before the creation of the world, that we might be
holy and without blemish in His presence. For He pre- **5**
destined us to be adopted by Himself as sons through Jesus
Christ—such being His gracious will and pleasure—to the **6**
praise of the splendour of His grace with which He has
enriched us in the beloved One.

World-wide It is in Him, and through the shedding of His **7**
Redemption blood, that we have our deliverance—the for-
through giveness of our offences—so abundant was
Christ God's grace, the grace which He, the possessor **8**
of all wisdom and understanding, lavished upon us, when **9**
He made known to us the secret of His will. And this is in
harmony with God's merciful purpose for the government **10**
of the world when the times are ripe for it—the purpose
which He has cherished in His own mind of restoring the
whole creation to find its one Head in Christ ; yes, things
in heaven and things on earth, to find their one Head in
Him.

---

4. *He chose us as His own*] Lit. ' He chose us out (of the world) for Himself.'

7. *Deliverance*] Or ' redemption.' The Greek word, like its Latin equivalent
' redemption,' signifies by derivation the buying off by payment of a ransom. But
as the dominant O.T. usage of the noun and its cognate verb is in reference to the
deliverance of Israel from Egypt, where there was no question of a ransom, it may
be questioned whether, here and elsewhere in the N.T. (where the word occurs ten
times), the thought is not simply of *emancipation*, without reference to the means.
Cf. verse 14 ; iv. 30, and especially the crucial doctrinal passage Romans iii. 24,
with Sanday and Headlam's not very convincing note. Perhaps the best rendering
is *redemption*, a word which has become colourless as to the payment of a price.

The Holy Spirit a Pledge of future Glory In Him we Jews have been made heirs, having 11 been chosen beforehand in accordance with the intention of Him whose might carries out in everything the design of His own will, so that 12 we should be devoted to the extolling of His glorious attributes—we who were the first to fix our hopes on Christ. And in Him you Gentiles also, after listening to the word 13 of the truth, the gospel of your salvation—having believed in Him—were sealed with the promised Holy Spirit; that 14 Spirit being a pledge and foretaste of our inheritance, in anticipation of its full redemption—the inheritance which He has purchased to be specially His for the extolling of His glory.

Thanksgiving and Prayer For this reason I too, having heard of the 15 faith in the Lord Jesus which prevails among you, and of your love for all the saints, offer 16 never-ceasing thanks on your behalf while I make mention of you in my prayers. For I always beseech the God of our 17 Lord Jesus Christ—the Father most glorious—to give you the spirit of wisdom and penetration through an intimate knowledge of Him, the eyes of your heart being enlightened 18 so that you may know what is the hope which His call to you inspires, what the wealth of the glory of His inheritance in the saints, and what the transcendent greatness of His 19 power in us believers as seen in the working of His infinite might when He displayed it in Christ by raising Him from 20 the dead, and seating Him at His own right hand in the heavenly realms, high above all other government and 21 authority and power and dominion, and every title of sovereignty used either in this age or in the age to come. God has put all things under His feet, and has appointed 22 Him universal and supreme Head of the Church, which is 23 His Body, the completeness of Him who everywhere fills the universe with Himself.

14. *To be specially His*] See 1 Chron. xxix. 3, A.V. and LXX; and Mal. iii. 17, LXX and A.V. margin.
15. *Of your love*] v.l., omitting these three words, ' and of that (which you have) towards,' &c., the meaning of which is far from clear.
17. *Most glorious*] Cf. Acts vii. 2, n.
23. *The completeness, &c.*] *i.e.* without Christ the universe would be incomplete, and Christ would be incomplete without His Church. Cf. Col. i. 17, 18. Dean Armitage Robinson, *St. Paul's Epistle to the Ephesians*, argues strongly that the usage of the verb is decisive for the interpretation of the early versions and of some Greek commentators, which takes the meaning to be not ' fills (for himself) ' (middle voice), but ' is being filled ' (passive voice), *i.e.* the Church is the completion of the Christ, and in it the Christ is gradually moving to a completeness absolute and all-inclusive.

In Christ the Gentiles have Life

To you Gentiles also, who were dead through 1 **2** your offences and sins, which were once habitual 2 to you while you walked in the ways of this world and obeyed the Prince of the powers of the air, the spirits that are now at work in the hearts of the sons of disobedience—to you God has given Life.

Perfect Union with the risen and glorified Christ

Among them we too once all passed our 3 lives, governed by the inclinations of our lower nature, indulging the cravings of that nature and of our thoughts, and were in our original state deserving of anger like all others. But 4 God, being rich in mercy, because of the intense love which He bestowed on us, caused us, dead though we were through 5 our offences, to live with Christ—it is by grace that you have been saved—raised us with Him from the dead, and 6 enthroned us with Him in the heavenly realms as being in Christ Jesus, in order that, by His goodness to us in Christ 7 Jesus, He might display in the ages to come the transcendent riches of His grace. For it is by grace that you 8 have been saved through faith ; and that not of yourselves. It is God's gift, and is not on the ground of merit—so that 9 it may be impossible for any one to boast. For we are 10 God's own handiwork, created in Christ Jesus for good works which He has pre-destined us to practise.

The Gentiles made one with God's People

Therefore, do not forget that formerly you 11 were Gentiles as to your bodily condition. You were called the Uncircumcision by those who style themselves the Circumcised—a circumcision in the body made by hands. At that time you were 12 living apart from Christ, estranged from the commonwealth of Israel, with no share by birth in the covenants which are based on the promises, and you had no hope and no God, in all the world. But now in Christ Jesus you who once 13 were so far away have been brought near through the death of Christ.

Reconciliation with God and with Man

For He is our peace—He who has made 14 Jew and Gentile one, and in His own human nature has broken down the hostile dividing wall, by setting aside the Law with its commandments, 15

2. *Powers . . spirits that are*] Lit. ' power . . spirit that is.'
14. *Jew and Gentile*] Lit. simply ' both.'
The hostile dividing wall] The literal reference is to the stone wall in the Temple beyond which no Gentile might advance into the inner court. Josephus speaks of

expressed, as they were, in definite decrees. His design was to unite the two sections of humanity in Himself so as to form one new man, thus effecting peace, and to reconcile Jew and Gentile in one body to God, by 16 means of His cross—slaying by it their mutual enmity. So 17 He came and proclaimed the gospel of peace to you who were so far away, and peace to those who were near ; because it is through Him that Jew and Gentile alike have 18 access through one Spirit to the Father.

Humanity one City, one Family, one living Temple

You are therefore no longer mere foreigners 19 or persons excluded from civil rights. On the contrary you share citizenship with the saints and are members of His family. You are a 20 building which has been reared on the foundation of the Apostles and Prophets, the cornerstone being Christ Jesus Himself, in union with whom the whole fabric, 21 truly bonded together, is rising so as to form a holy sanctuary in the Lord ; in whom you also are being 22 built up together to become a fixed abode for God through the Spirit.

This wondrous Truth entrusted to Paul

For this reason I Paul, the prisoner of Christ 1 **3** Jesus on behalf of you Gentiles—if, that is, you 2 have heard of the work which God has graciously entrusted to me for your benefit, in 3 that by a revelation the truth hitherto kept secret was made known to me as I have already briefly explained it to you. By means of that explanation, as you 4 read it, you can judge of my insight into the truth of Christ, which in earlier ages was not made known to the human 5 race, as it has now been revealed to His holy Apostles and Prophets through the Spirit—I mean the truth that the 6 Gentiles are joint heirs with us Jews, and that they form one body with us, and have the same interest as we have in the promise which has been made good in Christ Jesus through the gospel, in which I have been appointed to serve, in 7 virtue of the word which God, in the exercise of His power within me, has graciously entrusted to me.

pillars upon this wall, bearing notices in Greek and Latin prohibiting entrance to non-Jews on pain of death. One of these inscriptions was discovered in 1871. In less than ten years after Paul saw that this barrier had already been done away with in Christ, ' in whom there cannot be Jew and Gentile.' it was actually razed for ever by the armies of Rome.

18. *Access*] Lit. ' our access,' or ' our introduction.'

2. *Work .. graciously entrusted*] Lit. ' the stewardship of the grace which was given.'

To me who am less than the least of all the 8
Paul's Apostleship to the Gentiles saints has this work been graciously entrusted— to proclaim to the Gentiles the gospel of the exhaustless wealth of Christ, and to show all men 9 in a clear light what my stewardship is. It is the stewardship of the truth which from all the ages lay concealed in the mind of God, the Creator of all things—concealed in order 10 that the Church might now be used to display to the powers and authorities in the heavenly realms the innumerable aspects of God's wisdom. Such was the eternal 11 purpose which He had formed in Christ Jesus our Lord, in whom we have this bold and confident access through 12 our faith in Him. Therefore I entreat you not to lose 13 heart in the midst of my sufferings on your behalf, for they bring you honour.

The Apostle's Prayer for his Readers For this reason, on bended knee I beseech 14 the Father, from whom the whole family in 15 heaven and on earth derives its name, to grant 16 you—in accordance with the wealth of His glorious perfections—to be strengthened by His Spirit with power penetrating to your inmost being. I pray that Christ 17 may make His home in your hearts through your faith ; so that having your roots deep and your foundations strong, in love, you may become mighty to grasp the idea, as it is 18 grasped by all the saints, of the breadth and length, height and depth—yes, to attain to a knowledge of the 19 knowledge-surpassing love of Christ, so that you may be filled unto all the fulness of God.

Praise to God through Christ Now to Him who, in the exercise of His 20 power that is at work within us, is able to do infinitely beyond all our highest prayers or thoughts—to Him be the glory in the Church and in Christ 21 Jesus to all generations, world without end ! Amen.

The Christlike Life and the Unity of the Church I, then, the prisoner for the Lord's sake, 1 **4** entreat you to live and act as becomes those who have received the call that you have received — with all lowliness of mind and 2

8. *Less than the least*] Cf. 1 Cor. xv. 9 ; 1 Tim. i. 15.
Exhaustless] Lit. ' untraceable.'
9. *All men*] v.l. omits.
15. *The whole*] Had the Apostle been writing Classical Greek, his words here would signify ' every family ' ; but the term ' family ' misses the word-play in the Greek, ' the Father (pater) from whom every family (patria) is named.' The English word ' family ' is not derived from ' father.' Perhaps the nearest paraphrase to the Greek in English would be ' the Father of whom all fatherhood is named.'

unselfishness, and with patience, bearing with one another lovingly, and earnestly striving to maintain, in the uniting 3 bond of peace, the unity given by the Spirit. There is but 4 one body and but one Spirit, as also when you were called you had one and the same hope held out to you. There is 5 but one Lord, one faith, one baptism, and one God and 6 Father of all, who rules over all, acts through all, and dwells in all.

Yet to each of us individually His grace was given, 7 measured out with the munificence of Christ.

Every Christian has some Gift from God For this reason Scripture says : 8

'HE ASCENDED ON HIGH,
HE LED CAPTIVE A HOST OF CAPTIVES,
AND GAVE GIFTS TO MEN ' (Ps. lxviii. 18).

(Now this ' ascended '—what does it mean but that He 9 had first descended into the lower regions of the earth ? He who descended is the same as He who ascended again, 10 far above all the heavens, in order to fill the universe.)

The Diversity of Gifts, and their Object And He Himself appointed some to be 11 apostles, some to be prophets, some to be evangelists, some to be pastors and teachers, in 12 order fully to equip His people for the work of serving— for the building up of Christ's body—till we all of us 13 arrive at oneness in faith and in the knowledge of the Son of God, and at mature manhood and the stature of full-grown men in Christ. So we shall no longer be babes 14 nor shall we resemble mariners tossed on the waves and carried about with every changing wind of doctrine according to men's cleverness and unscrupulous cunning, making use of every shifting device to mislead. But we shall 15 lovingly hold to the truth, and shall in all respects grow up into union with Him who is our Head, even Christ. Dependent on Him, the whole body—its various parts closely 16 fitting and firmly adhering to one another—grows by the aid of every contributory ligament, with power proportioned to

---

8. The quotation is freely paraphrased from the original, which addresses the victor of the newly-conquered heights of Sion as he ascends with his train of captives to *receive gifts among men*, offered either by his defeated foes or by others seeking his favour. Probably a traditional interpretation of the Psalm.

9. *The lower regions of the earth*] Or ' the world below.' Perhaps rather ' below the earth . . above the heavens,' *i.e.* throughout the whole universe.

10. *To fill the universe*] Cf. i. 23, n.

13. *At oneness in faith*] Lit. ' at the oneness of the faith.'

16. *Grows*] Lit. ' carries on for itself the growth of the body.'
Contributory ligament] Lit. ' connection of the supply,' that is constantly going on.

the need of each individual part, so as to build itself up in a spirit of love.

Old Gentile Vices must be renounced Therefore I warn you, and I implore you in 17 the name of the Lord, no longer to live as the Gentiles in their perverseness live, with 18 darkened understandings, having by reason of the ignorance which is deep-seated in them and the insensibility of their moral nature no share in the Life which God gives. Such men being past feeling have abandoned 19 themselves to impurity, greedily indulging in every kind of profligacy.

The new Christlike Nature must be sought But these are not the lessons which you have 20 learned from Christ ; if at least you have heard 21 His voice and in Him have been taught—and this is true Christian teaching—to put away, 22 in regard to your former mode of life, your original evil nature which is doomed to perish as befits its misleading impulses, and to get yourselves renewed in the temper 23 of your minds and to clothe yourselves with that new 24 and better self which has been created to resemble God in the righteousness and holiness which come from the truth.

Christian Virtues to be cultivated For this reason, laying aside falsehood, every 25 one of you should speak the truth to his fellow man ; for we are, as it were, parts of one another. If angry, beware of sinning. Let not your 26 irritation last until the sun goes down ; and do not leave 27 room for the devil. He who has been a thief must steal no 28 more, but, instead of that, should work with his own hands in honest industry, so that he may have something of which he can give the needy a share. Let no unwholesome words 29 ever pass your lips, but let all your words be good for benefiting others according to the need of the moment, so that they may be a means of blessing to the hearers. And 30 beware of grieving the Holy Spirit of God, in whom you have been sealed in preparation for the day of Redemption. Let all bitterness and all passionate feeling, all anger and 31 loud insulting language, be unknown among you—and also every kind of malice. On the contrary learn to be kind to 32

---

19. *Have abandoned*] The A.V., in inserting ‘ have,’ more truly represents the original Greek than the R.V., which omits it.
22. *Is doomed to perish*] Or ‘ is undergoing destruction.’ Cf. 2 Cor. iv. 16.

one another, tender-hearted, forgiving one another, just as
God in Christ has also forgiven you.

5 Therefore be imitators of God, as His dear **1**
'Be as loving as your heavenly Father is' children. And live and act lovingly, as Christ **2**
also loved you and gave Himself up to death on
our behalf as an offering and sacrifice to God,
yielding a fragrant odour.

Sins specially fatal to present Goodness and future Glory But fornication and every kind of impurity, **3**
or covetousness, let them not even be mentioned
among you, for they ought not to be named
among the saints. Avoid shameful and **4**
foolish talk and low jesting—they are all alike
discreditable—and in place of these give thanks. For be **5**
well assured that no fornicator or immoral person and no
profligate—or in other words idol-worshipper—has any
share awaiting him in the Kingdom of Christ and of God.

The Certainty of Retribution Let no one deceive you with empty words, for **6**
it is on account of these very sins that God's
anger is coming upon the disobedient. There- **7**
fore do not become sharers with them.

Darkness and Light contrasted There was a time when you were nothing but **8**
darkness. Now, as Christians, you are Light
itself. Live and act as sons of Light—for the **9**
effect of the Light is seen in every kind of goodness,
uprightness, and truth—and learn in your own experiences **10**
what is fully pleasing to the Lord. Have nothing to do **11**
with the barren unprofitable deeds of darkness, but, instead
of that, set your faces against them ; for the things which **12**
are done by these people in secret it is disgraceful even to
speak of. But everything can be tested by the light and **13**
thus be shown in its true colours ; for whatever shines of
itself is light. For this reason it is said, **14**

> ' Rise, sleeper ;
> Rise from among the dead,
> And Christ will shed light upon you.'

'Use your one short Life wisely' Therefore be very careful how you live **15**
and act. Let it not be as unwise men,
but as wise. Buy up your opportunities, for **16**

32. *Has . . forgiven you*] v.L. ' has . . forgiven us.'

5. *Profligate*] The cognate abstract noun is rendered ' profligacy ' at iv. 19, and
rightly. The root idea of ' having more ' extends from mere greed of money to an
entire disregard of others' rights, and is frequently linked, as here, with sins of impurity.

6. *Disobedient*] Lit. ' sons of disobedience ' ; a Hebraism.

11. *Set your faces against them*] Lit. ' convict them as evil.'

these are evil times. On this account do not prove your- 17
selves wanting in sense, but try to understand what
the Lord's will is.

'Be sober,   Do not indulge in much wine—a thing in 18
spiritual,   which excess is so easy—but drink deeply of
thankful,   God's Spirit. Speak to one another with 19
and humble' psalms and hymns and spiritual songs. Sing
and offer praise in your hearts to the Lord. Always and 20
for everything let your thanks to God the Father be presented in the name of our Lord Jesus Christ ; and submit 21
to one another out of reverence for Christ.

Wives   Married women, submit to your own hus- 22
bands as if to the Lord ; because a husband is 23
the head of his wife, as Christ also is the Head of the
Church, Himself the Saviour of the Body. And just as 24
the Church submits to Christ, so also married women
should be entirely submissive to their husbands.

Husbands   Married men, love your wives, as Christ also 25
loved the Church and gave Himself up to death
for her, in order to make her holy, cleansing her with the 26
baptismal water by the word, that He might present the 27
Church to Himself a glorious bride, without spot or wrinkle
or any other defect, but to be holy and unblemished. So 28
too married men ought to love their wives as much as they
love themselves. He who loves his wife loves himself. 29
For never yet has a man hated his own body. On the
contrary he feeds and cherishes it, just as Christ feeds and
cherishes the Church ; because we are, as it were, parts of 30
His Body.

' FOR THIS REASON A MAN IS TO LEAVE HIS FATHER AND 31
HIS MOTHER AND CLING TO HIS WIFE, AND THE TWO SHALL
BE AS ONE FLESH ' (Gen. ii. 24).

That is a great truth hitherto kept secret : I mean the 32
truth concerning Christ and the Church. Yet I insist that 33
among you also, each man is to love his own wife as much
as he loves himself, and let a married woman see to it that
she treats her husband with respect.

Children   Children, be obedient to your parents in 1 **6**
the Lord, for this is right. ' HONOUR YOUR 2
FATHER AND YOUR MOTHER '—this is the first Command-

---

18. *Drink deeply of*] Lit. ' fill yourselves with.'
26. *The baptismal water*] Lit. ' the laver of the water.'
1. *Be obedient to*] Or ' habitually obey.' The tense implies this.

ment which has a promise added to it—'SO THAT IT MAY 3
BE WELL WITH YOU, AND THAT YOU MAY LIVE LONG ON THE
EARTH' (Exod. xx. 12). And you, fathers, do not irritate 4
your children, but bring them up tenderly in the instruction
and admonition of the Lord.

Slaves Slaves, be obedient to your earthly masters, 5
with respect and eager anxiety to please and
with simplicity of motive as if you were obeying Christ.
Let it not be in acts of eye-service as if you had but to please 6
men, but as Christ's bondservants who are doing God's will
from the heart. With right good will be faithful to your 7
duty, as service rendered to the Lord and not to man. You 8
well know that whatever right thing any one does, he will
receive a requital for it from the Lord, whether he is a slave
or a free man.

Masters And you masters, act towards your slaves on 9
the same principles, and refrain from threats.
For you know that in heaven there is One who is your
Master as well as theirs, and that of merely earthly distinctions there are none with Him.

**We have
unseen
spiritual
Enemies** In conclusion, strengthen yourselves in the 10
Lord and in the power which His supreme
might imparts. Put on the complete armour 11
of God, so as to be able to stand firm against
all the stratagems of the devil. For ours is not a conflict 12
with mere flesh and blood, but with the despotisms, the
empires, the forces that control and govern this dark world
—the spiritual hosts of evil arrayed against us in the
heavenly warfare.

**' Arm before-
hand for the
coming
Conflict '** Therefore put on the complete armour of 13
God, so that you may be able to stand your
ground in the evil day, and, having fought to
the end, to remain victors on the field. Stand 14
therefore, first fastening round you the girdle of truth and
putting on the breastplate of uprightness as well as the 15
shoes of the gospel of peace—a firm foundation for your
feet. And besides all these take the great shield of faith, 16
on which you will be able to quench all the flaming darts
of the wicked one ; and take the helmet of salvation, and 17
the sword of the Spirit which is the word of God. Pray 18

4. *Irritate*] By vexatious commands and unreasonable blame and uncertain temper.
9. *Merely earthly distinctions there are none*] See Luke xx. 21, n.

with unceasing prayer and entreaty at all times in the Spirit,
and be always on the alert to seize opportunities for doing
so, with unwearied persistence and entreaty on behalf of all
the saints, and ask on my behalf that words may be given 19
to me so that, outspoken and fearless, I may make known
the truths (hitherto kept secret) of the gospel—to spread 20
which I am an ambassador in chains—so that when telling
them I may speak out boldly as I ought.

Tychicus But in order that you also may know how I 21
am doing, Tychicus our dearly-loved brother
and faithful helper in the Lord's service will tell you everything. I have sent him to you for the very purpose—that 22
you may know about us and that he may encourage you.

Farewell Blessing Peace be to the brethren, and love combined 23
with faith, from God the Father and the Lord
Jesus Christ. May grace be with all who love 24
our Lord Jesus Christ with perfect sincerity.

18. *Unceasing . . unwearied*] Lit. 'all . . all.'
24. *With perfect sincerity*] Lit. 'in incorruption,' possibly meaning 'undying.'

THE EPISTLE OF PAUL TO THE PHILIPPIANS

The story of Paul's first planting of Christianity in Europe is told in Acts xvi. Philippi was twice revisited by the Apostle (Acts xx. 2, 6). He had great satisfaction in his Macedonian converts. This letter brims over with confidence and affection. There is hardly a trace of misgiving, except, perhaps, in regard to the unity and humility of their Christian fellowship (ii. 1–18 ; iv. 2, 3 ; see notes).

It is the most intimate of all Paul's letters to his Churches. In acknowledging the gift sent to him in Rome by Epaphroditus, he reminds them that from them alone, because of the bond of love between them and him, could he bring himself to accept money for his needs (iv. 15, 16).

It appears from chapter i. that his trial before Nero was close at hand, if not actually begun, and that he was conscious that its issue was doubtful. Life and death are trembling in the balance. That does not trouble him, save for their sakes. His one concern is that their manner of life should be worthy of the gospel of Christ (i. 27). This religious and ethical appeal runs through the whole letter, and reaches its height in iv. 4–9, a passage not easily matched in the noblest literature of the ancient world. (See Phil. ii. 1–11, n.)

THE EPISTLE OF PAUL TO
THE PHILIPPIANS

Greeting Paul and Timothy, bondservants of Christ 1 **1**
Jesus, to all the saints in Christ Jesus who are
at Philippi, with the ministers of the Church and their
assistants: grace and peace to you from God our Father 2
and the Lord Jesus Christ.

The I thank my God at my every remembrance 3
Apostle's of you—always, when offering any prayer on 4
Thankfulness behalf of you all, finding a joy in offering it. I 5
and Joy thank my God, I say, for your co-operation in
spreading the gospel, from the time it first came to you
even until now. For of this I am confident, that He who 6
has begun a good work within you will go on to perfect it in
preparation for the Day of Jesus Christ. And I am justified 7
in having this confidence about you all, because, both during
my imprisonment and when I stand up in defence of the
gospel or to confirm its truth, I have you in my heart,
sharers as you all are in the same grace as myself. For 8
God is my witness how I yearn over all of you with tender
Christian affection.

Paul's And it is my prayer that your love may be 9
Prayer more and more accompanied by clear knowledge
for the and keen perception, for testing things that 10
Philippians differ, so that you may be men of transparent
character, and may be blameless, in preparation for the
Day of Christ, being filled with those fruits of righteous- 11
ness which come through Jesus Christ—to the glory and
praise of God.

1. *Ministers . . assistants*] Lit. 'bishops and deacons.'
3. *My every remembrance*] Or 'all my remembrance,' *i.e.* not all my separate
remembrances of you, but the aggregate of these as forming one delightful picture.
7. *Defence*] In the forensic, not the military, sense. So in verse 16.
10. *Testing things that differ*] Or 'approving things that are excellent.' Both
Greek words, rendered 'test' and 'differ,' are ambiguous. The prayer is either
for clear moral discernment between right and wrong, good and evil, or for ready
acceptance and practice of what is good. The same phrase occurs in Rom. ii. 18.

The happy Effects of his Imprisonment   Now I would have you know, brethren, that 12 what I have gone through has turned out to the furtherance of the gospel rather than otherwise. And thus it has become notorious among 13 all the Imperial Guards, and everywhere, that it is for the sake of Christ that I am a prisoner ; and the greater part of 14 the brethren, made confident in the Lord through my imprisonment, now declare God's word without fear, more boldly than ever.

Various Motives for preaching Christ   Some indeed actually preach Christ out of 15 envy and contentiousness, but there are also others who do it from goodwill. These latter 16 preach Him from love to me, knowing that I am here for the defence of the gospel ; while the others 17 proclaim Him from motives of rivalry, and insincerely, supposing that by this they are embittering my imprisonment.

Paul rejoices that Christ is preached   What does it matter, however ? In any case 18 Christ is preached—either perversely or in honest truth ; and in that I rejoice, yes, and will rejoice. For I know that it will result in my salvation 19 through your prayers and a bountiful supply of the Spirit of Jesus Christ, in fulfilment of my eager expectation and 20 hope that I shall never have reason to feel ashamed, but that by my perfect freedom of speech Christ will be glorified in me, now as always, either by my life or by my death.

Paul's Conflict of Feeling as to Life and Death   For, with me, to live is Christ and to die is 21 gain. But since to live means a longer stay on 22 earth, that implies more labour for me—and not unsuccessful labour ; and which I am to choose I cannot tell. I am in a dilemma, my 23 earnest desire being to depart and be with Christ, for that is far, far better. But for your sakes it is more important 24 that I should still remain in the body. I am convinced of 25 this, and I know that I shall remain, and shall go on working side by side with you all, to promote your progress and joy in the faith ; so that you may have additional reason 26 for glorying about me in Christ Jesus as the result of my being with you again.

(vv. 15–18.) See iii. 1, 2, n.

22. Lit. ' But if to live (is) to live in (the) flesh, that (is) for me fruit of labour.' Lightfoot is not far from this when he suggests as the meaning : ' If my living in the flesh will be fruitful through a laborious career.' See R.V. text and margin, and American R.V.

An Exhortation to noble Conduct and dauntless Courage
Only let the lives you live be worthy of the 27 gospel of the Christ, in order that, whether I come and see you or, being absent, only hear of you, I may know that you are standing fast in one spirit and with one mind, fighting shoulder to shoulder for the faith of the gospel. Never 28 for a moment quail before your antagonists. Your fearlessness will be to them a sure token of impending destruction, but to you it will be a sure token of your salvation — a token coming from God. For you have had the privilege 29 granted you on behalf of Christ—not only to believe in Him, but also to suffer on His behalf; maintaining, as you 30 do, the same kind of conflict that you once saw in me and which you still hear that I am engaged in.

An Appeal for mutual brotherly Love
If then I can appeal to you as the followers 1 **2** of Christ, if there is any persuasive power in love and any common sharing of the Spirit, or if any tender-heartedness and compassion, make 2 my joy complete by being of one mind, united by mutual love, with harmony of feeling giving your minds to one and the same object. Do nothing in a spirit of factiousness or 3 of vainglory, but in a humble spirit let every one regard the rest as being of more account than himself; each fixing 4 his attention, not simply on his own interests, but also on those of others.

The Humility and Self-Sacrifice of Jesus
Let the very spirit which was in Christ Jesus 5 be in you also. From the beginning He had the 6 nature of God. Yet He did not regard equality with God as something at which He should grasp. Nay, He stripped Himself of His glory, 7 and took on Him the nature of a bondservant by becoming a man like other men. And being recognized as truly 8 human, He humbled Himself and even stooped to die;

(vv. 1–11.) It is interesting to surmise that this noble appeal for unity and humility, under the compelling example of Christ, may have been evoked by some trivial disagreement between two women members of the Church, Euodia and Syntyche (see iv. 2).

6. *Had the nature*] Lit. ' was in the form.'

7. *He stripped Himself of His glory*] Lit. ' He emptied Himself ': Greek ' ekenosen.' Hence the *Kenosis* Doctrine of our Lord's humanity.

> ' The Lord of all things made Himself
> Naked of glory for His mortal change.'
> TENNYSON, *Holy Grail.*

8. *Being recognized as truly human*] Lit. ' being found in outward form as a man.'

and that too a death on the cross. It is because of 9
this also that God has so highly exalted Him, and has
conferred on Him the Name which is supreme above
every other name, in order that in the Name of JESUS 10
every knee should bow, of beings in the highest
heavens, of those on the earth, and of those in the
underworld, and that every tongue should confess that 11
JESUS CHRIST is LORD, to the glory of God the
Father.

Salvation to be strenuously worked out Therefore, my dearly-loved friends, as I have 12
always found you obedient, labour earnestly
with fear and trembling—not merely as though
I were present with you, but much more now
since I am absent from you—labour earnestly, I say, to
make sure of your own salvation. For it is God Himself 13
whose power creates within you both the desire and the
power to execute His gracious will.

Content-ment, Peace, Purity, and Joy Be ever on your guard against a grudging 14
and contentious spirit, so that you may always 15
prove yourselves to be blameless and spotless—
irreproachable children of God in the midst of
a crooked and perverse generation, among whom you are
seen as heavenly lights in the world, holding out to them 16
a word of Life. It will then be my glory on the Day of
Christ that I did not run my race in vain nor toil in vain.
Nay, even if my life is to be poured as a libation upon 17
the sacrificial offering of your faith, I rejoice, and I congratulate you all. And I bid you also share my gladness, 18
and congratulate me.

Timothy to be sent to Philippi But, if the Lord permits it, I hope before long 19
to send Timothy to you, that I, in turn, may be
cheered by getting news of you. For I have 20
no one likeminded with him, who will cherish a genuine
care for you: everybody concerns himself about his own 21
interests, not about those of Jesus Christ. But you know 22
Timothy's approved worth—how, like a child working with
his father, he has served with me in furtherance of the
gospel. So he it is that I hope to send as soon as ever 23
I see how things go with me ; but trusting, as I do, in 24
the Lord, I believe that I shall myself also come to you
before long.

16. *Holding out*] Like a blazing torch to dispel the darkness.

Epaphro-
ditus

Yet I deem it important to send Epaphroditus 25
to you now : he is my brother and comrade both
in labour and in arms, and is your messenger
who has ministered to my needs. I send him because he is 26
longing to see you all, and is distressed at your having heard
of his illness. For it is true that he has been ill, and was 27
apparently at the point of death ; but God had pity on him,
and not only on him, but also on me, to save me from having
sorrow upon sorrow. I am therefore all the more eager to 28
send him, in the hope that when you see him again you
may be glad and I may have the less sorrow. Receive him 29
therefore with all joy, and hold in honour men like him ;
because it was for the sake of Christ's work that he came 30
so near death, hazarding, as he did, his very life in
endeavouring to make good any deficiency that there might
be in your service to me.

The
comparative
Worthless-
ness of
external
Privileges

In conclusion, my brethren, be joyful in the 1 **3**
Lord. For me to write to you the same things
as before is not irksome to me, while so far
as you are concerned it is a safe precaution.
Beware of ' the dogs,' the dishonest workmen, 2
the self-mutilators. For we are the true circumcision—we 3
who render to God a spiritual worship and make our boast
in Christ Jesus and have no confidence in outward ceremonies ; although I myself might have some excuse for 4
confidence in outward ceremonies. If any one else claims
a right to trust in them, far more may I—circumcised, as I 5
was, on the eighth day, a member of the race of Israel and
of the tribe of Benjamin, a Hebrew sprung from Hebrews ;
as to the Law a Pharisee ; as to zeal, a persecutor of the 6
Church ; as to the righteousness which comes through
Law, blameless.

25. *Deem*] Or ' have deemed.'
26. *To see you*] Lit. ' for you.' v.l. ' to see you.'
1. *To write to you the same things*] What these ' same things ' are is doubtful.
Certainly there is nothing in the earlier part of the letter to prepare for the outburst
of verse 2. Many suppose some interruption at this point, and a sudden diversion of
thought and change of tone, by tidings of fresh activities on the part of the Judaisers.
The opposition mentioned in i. 15–18 may have come from a different quarter,
prompted not by Judaising propaganda, but by jealousy of the Apostle's influence in
Rome, on the part of old-standing members of the Church. Paul would hardly
have rejoiced in the preaching of the gospel by his Judaising opponents.
2. *Dishonest*] Cf. 2 Cor. xi. 13.
3. *Render to God a spiritual worship*] Lit. ' worship through the Spirit of God.'
Outward ceremonies] Lit. ' flesh.' ' The expression extends beyond circumcision
to all external privileges ' (Lightfoot).

Paul's Craving for complete Oneness with Christ Yet all that was gain to me, for Christ's sake 7 I have reckoned as loss. Nay, I even reckon all 8 things as pure loss because of the priceless privilege of knowing Christ Jesus my Lord. For His sake I have suffered the loss of everything, and reckon it all as mere refuse, in order that I may win Christ, and be found in Him, not 9 having a righteousness of my own, derived from the Law, but that which arises from faith in Christ—the righteousness which comes from God through faith. I long to know 10 Christ and the power which is in His resurrection, and to share in His sufferings and die even as He died ; in the hope that I may attain to the resurrection from 11 the dead.

Paul's Prize was still future I do not say that I have already won the race 12 or have already reached perfection. But I am pressing on, striving to lay hold of that for which I was also laid hold of by Christ Jesus. Brethren, 13 I do not imagine that I have yet laid hold of it. But this one thing I do—forgetting everything which is past and stretching forward to what lies in front of me, with my 14 eyes fixed on the goal I push on to secure the prize of God's heavenward call in Christ Jesus. Therefore let all of us 15 who are mature believers cherish these thoughts ; and if in any respect you think differently, that also God will make clear to you. But whatever be the point that we have 16 already reached, let us persevere in the same course.

Self-Indulgent Enemies of the Cross Brethren, vie with one another in imitating 17 me, and carefully observe those who follow the example which we have set you. For there are 18 many whom I have often described to you, and I now even with tears describe them, as being enemies to the cross of Christ. Their end is destruction, their 19 bellies are their God, their glory is in their shame, and their minds are devoted to earthly things. We, however, are free 20 citizens of heaven, and we are waiting with longing expectation for the coming from heaven of a Saviour, the Lord Jesus Christ, who, in the exercise of the power which 21

12. *Of that for which I was also laid hold of*] Or ' *because* I was also laid hold of.' This is the probable meaning of the same Greek expression in Rom. v. 12. The ' laid hold of,' ' arrested,' ' apprehended,' seems to refer to the arresting vision on the way to Damascus (Acts ix. 3–5). Cf. Gal. i. 16,
14. *Heavenward*] Lit. ' upward.'

He has even to subject all things to Himself, will transform this body of our humiliation until it resembles the body of His glory. Therefore, my brethren, dearly loved and 1 **4** longed for, my joy and crown, so stand firm in the Lord, my dearly-loved ones.

I entreat Euodia, and I entreat Syntyche, to 2 be of one mind, as sisters in Christ. Yes, and 3 I beg you also, my true yoke-fellow, to help these women, for they shared my toil in connexion with the gospel, together with Clement and the rest of my fellow labourers, whose names are recorded in the Book of Life.

Euodia and Syntyche

Always rejoice in the Lord : I will repeat it, 4 rejoice. Let your forbearing spirit be known 5 to every one : the Lord is near. Do not be 6 anxious about anything, but by prayer and earnest pleading, together with thanksgiving, let your requests be unreservedly made known before God. So 7 will the peace of God, which surpasses all power of thought, be a garrison to guard your hearts and minds in Christ Jesus.

'Be cheerful, unselfish, calm, prayerful'

Finally, brethren, whatever is true, whatever 8 wins respect, whatever is just, whatever is pure, whatever is lovable, whatever is of good repute —if there is any virtue or anything deemed worthy of praise—cherish the thought of these things. Let all that you learnt and received and heard 9 and saw in me fashion your conduct ; and the God of peace will be with you.

'Cherish beautiful Thoughts. Live noble Lives'

But I rejoice in the Lord greatly that now 10 at length you have revived your thoughtfulness for my welfare. Indeed you have always been thoughtful for me, although opportunity failed you. I do not refer to this through fear of privation, 11 for I indeed have learned, whatever be my outward experiences, to be content. I know both how to live in 12 straitened circumstances and how to live amid abundance. I am fully initiated into all the secrets both of fulness and

Personal Thanks for recent Kindness

---

3. *Yoke-fellow*] It is doubtful whom the Apostle addresses. Possibly Epaphroditus, the bearer of the letter.

If the Greek word for yoke-fellow occurred in the inscriptions as a proper name, it would be tempting to render it "Syzygus, truly so called," a word-play upon the name, for which we may compare Philem. 2. See note there.

8. To the six Greek adjectives used in this verse we have in English no six corresponding adjectives covering just the same ground.

of hunger, of abundance and of want. I have strength 13
for anything through Him who gives me power.

Sympathy and Service gratefully acknowledged Yet I thank you for taking your share in my 14
troubles. And you men and women of Philippi 15
also know that at the first preaching of the
gospel, when I had left Macedonia, no other
Church except yourselves held communication with me
about giving and receiving ; because even in Thessalonica 16
you sent several times to minister to my needs. Not that I 17
crave for gifts from you, but I do want to see a rich harvest
of service placed to your account. I have enough of every- 18
thing—and more than enough. My wants are fully satisfied
now that I have received from the hands of Epaphroditus
the generous gifts which you sent me : they are a fragrant
odour, an acceptable sacrifice, truly pleasing to God.
But my God—so great is His wealth of glory in Christ 19
Jesus—will fully supply every need of yours. And to our 20
God and Father be the glory for ever and ever ! Amen.

A loving Farewell My greetings in Christ to every saint. The 21
brethren who are with me send their greetings.
All the saints here greet you—especially the 22
members of Caesar's household.

The grace of our Lord Jesus Christ be with your spirits. 23

THE EPISTLE OF PAUL TO THE COLOSSIANS

(See also Preface to Ephesians.)

Paul had never visited Colossae (ii. 1), perhaps missing it by taking the shorter hill route from Pisidian Antioch to Ephesus, instead of the main road down the Lycus valley (Acts xix. 1, n.).

The Church had been founded by Epaphras (i. 7 ; iv. 12), probably Paul's missioner from Ephesus (Acts xix. 10). He could in many respects report well of his converts to the Apostle in Rome ; but there was grave trouble from false teachers. The ' Colossian heresy ' is hard to define. It appears to have been a complex of incipient Gnosticism, Judaism, and asceticism (see ii 8, n.) ; but the great Christological passage (i. 12–23) shows that in effect it deposed Christ from His supreme and sufficient place as Saviour. Evidently, too, these intellectual speculations had led to grievous moral laxity (iii. 5–17), and to domestic disturbances (iii. 18–iv. 1). Paul insists that unless the gospel builds up character, fashions conduct, and lifts the whole life to the ' things above ' (iii. 1), it is nothing, and worse than nothing.

THE EPISTLE OF PAUL TO
THE COLOSSIANS

Greeting Paul, by the will of God an Apostle of 1 **1**
Christ Jesus, and Timothy our brother, to 2
the saints and the believing brethren at Colossae who are
in Christ: may grace and peace be granted to you from
God our Father.

Thanksgiving to God for the Colossians We give thanks to God, the Father of our 3
Lord Jesus Christ, constantly praying for you as
we do, because we have heard of your faith in 4
Christ Jesus and of the love which you cherish
towards all the saints, on account of the hope treasured up 5
for you in heaven. Of this hope you have already heard
in the word of the truth of the gospel. For it has reached 6
you, and remains with you, just as it has also spread through
the whole world, yielding fruit there and increasing. It
has done so among you from the day when first you heard it
and came really to know the grace of God, as you learned 7
it from Epaphras our dearly-loved fellow servant. He
is to you a faithful minister of Christ in our stead, and 8
moreover he has informed us of your love, which is
inspired by the Spirit.

A Prayer for their spiritual Progress For this reason we also, from the day we 9
first received these tidings, have never ceased
to pray for you and to entreat that you may be
filled with a clear knowledge of His will accompanied by thorough wisdom and discernment in spiritual
things; so that your lives may be worthy of the Lord and 10
perfectly pleasing to Him, while you bear fruit in every
good work, and increase in the knowledge of God. Since 11
His power is so glorious, may you be strengthened with
strength of every kind, and be prepared for cheerfully
enduring all things with patience and long-suffering; and 12
may you give thanks to the Father who has made us fit to
receive our share of the inheritance of the saints in Light.

2. *To the saints and the believing brethren*] Or ' To the holy and faithful brethren
in Christ at Colossae.'

Christ is the 'Image of God' and the Lord of all Creation

It is God who has delivered us out of the dominion of darkness, and has transferred us into the Kingdom of His dearly-loved Son, in whom we have our redemption—the forgiveness of our sins. Christ is the visible representation of the invisible God, the Firstborn and Lord of all creation. For in Him was created the universe of things in heaven and on earth, things seen and things unseen, thrones, dominions, princedoms, powers—all were created, and exist, through and for Him. And HE IS before all things, and in and through Him the universe is one harmonious whole. 13 14 15 16 17

Christ is the divine Head of the Church

Moreover He is the Head of His Body, the Church. He is the Beginning, the Firstborn from among the dead, in order that He Himself may in all things occupy the foremost place. For it was the Father's gracious will that the whole of the divine perfections should dwell in Him. And God purposed through Him to reconcile the universe to Himself, making peace through His blood, which was shed upon the Cross—to reconcile to Himself through Him, I say, things on earth and things in heaven. 18 19 20

The Colossians had found Salvation in Christ

And you, estranged as you once were and even hostile in your minds amidst your evil deeds, He has now, in His human body, reconciled to God by His death, to bring you, holy and faultless and irreproachable, into His presence ; if, indeed, you are still firmly holding to faith as your foundation, without ever shifting from your hope that rests on the gospel that you have heard, which has been proclaimed in the whole creation under heaven, of which I Paul became a minister. 21 22 23

15. *Visible representation*] So Lightfoot. Or ' image.'
The Firstborn and Lord of all creation] Or ' of earlier birth than any created being,' ' born before anything was created.'
16. *In Him*] Not only by Him ; divine omnipotence, omniscience, and ubiquity being all implied.
Thrones, &c.] Names given to different grades of supposed angelic mediators between God and man ; a feature of the Colossian heresy. Paul says in effect, ' Call them what you will, they are subject to the all-inclusive and sufficient supremacy of Christ.' Cf. 1 Tim. ii. 5, and see Col. ii. 8, n.
And exist] This sense is contained in the tense (perfect) of the verb.
17. *HE IS*] There is here a manifest allusion to God's sublime declaration concerning Himself, ' I am because I am,' or ' I am that I am,' or ' I will be what I will be ' (Exod. iii. 14). Cf. John viii. 58.
22. *He has . . reconciled*] v.l. (not without grammatical difficulties) ' you have been reconciled.'

The
Sufferings
and Earnest-
ness of the
Apostle to
the Gentiles
Now I can find joy amid my sufferings for 24 you, and I fill up in my own person whatever is lacking in Christ's afflictions on behalf of His Body, the Church. I have been appointed to 25 serve the Church in the position of responsibility entrusted to me by God for your benefit, so that I may fully deliver God's word—the truth which has been kept secret 26 from all ages and generations, but has now been revealed to His saints, to whom it was His will to make known how 27 vast a wealth of glory for the Gentile world is implied in this truth—the truth that Christ is in you, the hope of glory. Him we preach, admonishing every one and instructing 28 every one, with all possible wisdom, so that we may bring every one into God's presence, made perfect through Christ. To this end, like an eager wrestler, I exert all my strength 29 in reliance upon the power of Him who is mightily at work within me.

Paul's
strenuous
Efforts for
the Welfare
of the
Colossians
For I would have you know in how severe a 1 **2** struggle I am engaged on behalf of you and the brethren in Laodicea and of all who have not known me personally, in order that their hearts 2 may be cheered, they themselves being welded together in love and advancing towards an abounding wealth of understanding, even to the knowledge of the secret of God. In Him all the treasures of wisdom and knowledge 3 are stored up, hidden from view.

His loving
Anxiety on
their Behalf
I say this to prevent your being misled by any 4 one's plausible sophistry. For although, as you 5 say, I am absent from you in body, yet in spirit I am present with you, and am delighted to witness your good discipline and the solid front presented by your faith in Christ.

His
Eagerness
for their
spiritual
Progress
As therefore you have received the Christ, 6 even Jesus our Lord, live and act in vital union with Him; having the roots of your being 7 firmly planted in Him, and continually build-ing yourselves up in Him, and always being increasingly confirmed in the faith as you were taught it, and abounding in it with thanksgiving.

---

5. *Discipline . . solid front*] Military terms. ' The enforced companionship of St. Paul with the soldiers of the Praetorian guard at this time may have suggested this image ' (Lightfoot).
6. *Live and act, &c.*] Lit. ' in Him walk.'
7. *In it*] v.L. ' abounding in thanksgiving.'

Christ's full Divinity re-asserted Take care lest there be any one who leads 8 you away as prisoners by means of his philosophy and idle fancies, following human traditions and the world's crude notions instead of following Christ. For it is in Christ that the fulness of God's nature 9 dwells embodied, and in Him you are made complete, and 10 He is the Lord of all princes and rulers. In Him also 11 you were circumcised with a circumcision not performed by hand, when you threw off your sinful nature in the circumcision of Christ; having been buried with Him in 12 your baptism, in which you were also raised with Him through faith produced within you by God, who raised Him from among the dead.

Christ's atoning Work and Victory over all Evil And to you—dead as you once were in your 13 transgressions and in the uncircumcision of your natural state—He has nevertheless given you Life with Him, having forgiven us all our transgressions. The bond, with its require- 14 ments, which was in force against us and was hostile to us, He cancelled, and cleared it out of the way, nailing it to His Cross. And the hostile princes and rulers He stripped 15 off from Himself, and boldly displayed them as His conquests, when by the Cross He triumphed over them.

8. *The world's crude notions*] Lit. ' the elements (or ' rudiments ') of the world.' This same phrase is translated in verse 20 and in Gal. iv. 3, ' the world's rudimentary notions ' (cf. Gal. iv. 9, ' weak and worthless rudimentary notions '). This interpretation takes the Greek word for ' elements ' in the sense which it undoubtedly bears in Heb. v. 12, of ' elementary teaching.' Relapse into observance of Jewish rites and ceremonies is a return to the very alphabet of knowledge. This is further characterised as ' of the world,' *i.e.* worldly, mundane, material. But the Hebrews parallel would suggest that ' of the world ' does not condemn certain elements, otherwise undefined, as ' worldly,' but gives the contents of these elements (cf. elements of music, of arithmetic, &c.). The phrase should naturally mean the material elements of which the universe is composed, and, apart from Heb. v. 12, this is the unvarying Biblical use. Cf. 2 Pet. iii. 10, 12, and O.T. Apocrypha. Hence Paul, perhaps, refers to these material things as tenanted by harmful spirits—a universal belief of the ancient world. Every ' handle not, taste not, touch not ' (ii. 21) had behind it the dread of demons. A study of the context in the passages quoted, with its contrast between the old pagan belief and the new-won Christian faith, does suggest a re-enslavement, not to impersonal teaching, but to personal beings—the ' Elemental Spirits ' (Moffatt). So interpreted, the phrase links on to the worship of the angels (ii. 18) ; cf. i. 16, n.

10. *Lord*] Lit. ' Head.'
Princes and rulers] Lit. ' authority and power.' So in verse 15, ' princes and rulers ' is literally ' authorities and powers.'

(vv. 14, 15.) There seems to be a change of subject from God, in verse 13, to Christ.
15. *Stripped off from Himself*] This is the proper meaning of the Greek voice (middle) ; but the difficulty of the conception, and the context, suggest an exceptional use of the middle for active, ' He stripped,' ' despoiled.' So A.V., American R.V. The ancient Latin interpretation of R.V. mg. is rightly omitted by the American R.V.

Triumphed over them] Or ' led them in triumph.' Cf. 2 Cor. ii. 14. ' The paradox of the crucifixion is thus placed in the strongest light—triumph in helplessness and glory in shame. The convict's gibbet is the victor's car ' (Lightfoot).

No Room left for Jewish Observances or angelic Mediation Therefore suffer no one to sit in judgement 16 on you as to eating or drinking or with regard to a festival, a new moon, or a Sabbath. These 17 were a shadow of things that were to come, but the substance belongs to Christ. Let no 18 one defraud you of your prize, priding himself on his humility and on his worship of the angels, and taking his stand on the visions he has seen, and idly puffed up with his unspiritual thoughts. Such a one does not keep his 19 hold upon Christ, the Head, from whom the body, in all its parts nourished and strengthened by its points of contact and its connexions, grows with a divine growth.

Obedience to outward Rules may leave Sin and Self unconquered If you have died with Christ and have escaped 20 from the world's rudimentary notions, why, as though your life still belonged to the world, do you submit to such precepts as, ' Do not handle this '; 21 ' Do not taste that '; ' Do not touch that other thing '—referring to things which are all intended to be used 22 up and to perish—in obedience to mere human injunctions and teachings ? These rules have indeed an appearance of 23 wisdom, where there is self-imposed worship and an affectation of humility and an ascetic severity. But not one of them is of any value in combating the indulgence of our lower natures.

Union with the risen and glorified Christ If, however, you have risen with Christ, seek 1 **3** the things that are above, where Christ is, enthroned at God's right hand. Give your minds 2 to the things that are above, not to the things that are on the earth. For you have died, and your life is 3 hidden with Christ in God. When Christ appears—He is 4 our true Life—then you also will appear with Him in glory.

Moral Results of Union with Christ Therefore put to death your earthward 5 inclinations — fornication, impurity, sensual passion, unholy desire, and all greed, for that is a form of idolatry. It is on account of 6 these very sins that God's wrath is coming, and you 7

18. *Priding himself on his humility*] ' Humility when it becomes self-conscious ceases to have any value ' (Lightfoot). ' The humility condemned is not Christian humility, but a false and perverted lowliness, which deemed God was so inaccessible that He could only be approached through the mediation of inferior beings ' (Ellicott). *Has seen*] v.L. ' has *not* seen '; idle and empty imaginings.

20. See ii. 8, n.

23. The latter part of this verse is of very uncertain interpretation. Possibly ' not of any value, but rather tending to the indulgence of the flesh.'

4. *Our true Life*] Lit. ' our life.' v.L. ' your life.'

6. *Is coming*] v.L. adds, ' upon the sons of disobedience.' Cf. Eph. v. 6.

also were once addicted to them, while you were living under their power.

Evil Habits must give Place to a new Nature But now you must rid yourselves of every 8 kind of sin—angry and passionate outbreaks, ill-will, evil speaking, foul-mouthed abuse—so that these may never soil your lips. Do not 9 lie to one another, for you have stripped off the old self with its doings, and have clothed yourselves with the new 10 self, which is being remoulded into full knowledge so as to become like Him who created it. In that new creation 11 there can be neither Greek nor Jew, circumcision nor uncircumcision, barbarian, Scythian, slave nor free man, but Christ is all and in all.

All Christlike Qualities to be appropriated Clothe yourselves therefore, as saints holy 12 and dearly loved, with tender-heartedness, kindness, lowliness of mind, meekness and long-suffering; bearing with one another, and readily 13 forgiving each other, if any one has a grievance against another. Just as the Lord has forgiven you, you also must forgive. And over all these put on love, which is the 14 perfect bond of union ; and let the peace which Christ 15 gives settle all questionings in your hearts, to which peace indeed you were called as belonging to His one Body ; and be thankful.

The Principles which are to regulate Conduct Let the word of Christ remain as a rich 16 treasure in your hearts. In all wisdom teach and admonish one another with psalms, hymns, and spiritual songs, and sing with grace in your hearts to God. And whatever you do, in word 17 or in deed, do everything in the name of the Lord Jesus, and through Him give thanks to God the Father.

Wives, Husbands, Children, Parents, Slaves, Masters Married women, be submissive to your hus- 18 bands, as is fitting in the Lord. Married men, 19 be affectionate to your wives, and do not treat them harshly. Children, be obedient to your 20 parents in everything ; for that is well pleasing in the Lord. Fathers, do not fret and harass your children, 21 or you may make them sullen and morose. Slaves, be 22 obedient in everything to your earthly masters ; not with

---

13. *The Lord*] Various readings are : Christ, God, God in Christ.

Forgiven] The word used emphasises the *grace* of forgiveness : the more usual word signifies release from a debt.

16. *In all wisdom*] Or these words may be connected with the preceding clause.

acts of eye-service, as aiming only to please men, but with
simplicity of purpose, because you fear the Lord. What- 23
ever you are doing, let your hearts be in your work, as a
thing done for the Lord and not for men. For you know 24
that it is from the Lord you will receive the inheritance as
your reward. Christ is the Master whose bondservants
you are. The man who perpetrates a wrong will find the 25
wrong repaid to him : with God there are no merely
earthly distinctions. Masters, deal justly and equitably with 1 **4**
your slaves, knowing that you too have a Master in heaven.

Prayerful-
ness and
Discretion
urged
Be earnest and unwearied in prayer, being 2
intent on it and on your giving of thanks.
And pray at the same time for us also, that God 3
may open to us a door for preaching, for us
to tell the truth concerning Christ for the sake of which
I am even a prisoner. Then I shall proclaim it fully, as 4
it is my duty to do. Behave wisely in relation to the outside 5
world, seizing your opportunities. Let your language be 6
always seasoned with the salt of grace, so that you may
know how to give every man a fitting answer.

Tychicus and
Onesimus
Tychicus, our much-loved brother, a trusty 7
assistant and fellow servant with us in the
Lord's work, will give you every information
about me. And for this very purpose I send him to you 8
that you may know how we are faring ; and that he may
cheer your hearts. And with him I send our dear and 9
trusty brother Onesimus, who is one of yourselves. They
will inform you of everything here.

Aristarchus,
Mark, and
Jesus Justus
Aristarchus my fellow prisoner sends greeting 10
to you, and so does Mark the cousin of Barnabas.
You have received instructions as to him ; if he
comes to you, give him a welcome. Jesus, called Justus, also 11
sends greeting. These three are Jewish converts. They
alone among such have worked loyally with me for the Kingdom of God : they are men who have been a comfort to me.

Epaphras,
Luke, and
Demas
Epaphras, who is one of yourselves, a bond- 12
servant of Jesus Christ, sends greeting to you,
always wrestling on your behalf in his prayers,

---

25. *No merely earthly distinctions*] See Luke xx. 21, n.
6. *A fitting answer*] Cf. Prov. xxvi. 4, 5 ; 1 Pet. iii. 15.
11. It will be observed that Luke is placed in a second group of salutations,
evidently from Gentiles. Cf. the greetings in the contemporary Epistle to Philemon
(verses 23, 24).

that you may stand firm, as men of ripe character and of clear conviction as to everything which is God's will. For I can bear witness to the deep interest he takes 13 in you and in the brethren at Laodicea and in those at Hierapolis. Luke, the dearly-loved physician, salutes 14 you, and so does Demas.

Greetings to the brethren at Laodicea, 15
The Church in Laodicea especially to Nymphas, and to the Church that meets at their house. And when this Letter 16 has been read among you, let it be read also in the Church of the Laodiceans, and you in turn must read the one I am sending to Laodicea. And tell Archippus to dis- 17 charge carefully the duties devolving upon him as a servant of the Lord.

I Paul add with my own hand this final greet- 18
Autograph Conclusion ing. Be mindful of me in my imprisonment. Grace be with you.

15. *The Church, &c.*] Cf. Rom. xvi. 5, n. ' There is no clear example of a separate building set apart for Christian worship within the limits of the Roman Empire before the third century, though apartments in private houses might be specially devoted to this purpose ' (Lightfoot).
16. *Among you*] Or ' in your hearing '; probably at a meeting expressly summoned with that object.
17. *Archippus*] Cf. Philem. 2, n.

THE FIRST EPISTLE OF PAUL TO
THE THESSALONIANS

For details of Paul's work in Thessalonica, the capital city of Macedonia, see Acts xvii. and notes. Luke seems to compress his narrative into a three weeks' preaching in the synagogue ; but this short Jewish ministry could hardly have resulted in the conversion of a large number of devout Greeks and chief women (Acts xvii. 4). The Epistle (i. 9) clearly points to a striking success among the Gentile population ; and, indeed, the picture drawn, in i. 6–ii. 14, of the tried faith and widespread renown of the converts, and of Paul's own conduct among them, suggests a sojourn of months rather than of weeks. The Jewish riot from which Paul had to flee (Acts xvii. 10) left him anxious for the infant Church exposed to bitter persecution. Twice he tried to revisit them, but for some reason, possibly because of the bond given by Jason, he could not (ii. 18). So he sent Timothy from Athens (iii. 1, 2), who rejoined him at Corinth (Acts xviii. 5) with reassuring news (iii. 6–10), to which this letter was the immediate response.

The pictorial description of the Second Coming (iv. 13–18), which Paul evidently expected in his own lifetime (verse 15), is unique in his writings. In v. 1–11 it passes into Christ's own repeated admonition to watchfulness, and in verses 12–22 to ethical precepts, which at their close are ' like a string of glittering diamonds.'

THE FIRST EPISTLE OF PAUL TO THE THESSALONIANS

Introduction

Greeting Paul, Silvanus, and Timothy, to the Church 1 **1** of the Thessalonians which is in God the Father and the Lord Jesus Christ: grace to you and peace.

Reasons for Gratitude and Thanksgiving We give thanks to God continually because 2 of you all, while we make mention of you in our prayers. For we never fail to remember your 3 works of faith and labours of love and patient hope in our Lord Jesus Christ before our God and Father; knowing as we do, brethren beloved by God, that He has 4 chosen you, since our gospel did not come to you in words 5 only, but also with power and with the Holy Spirit and with great conviction. You know indeed the sort of men we became among you for your sakes. And you followed our 6 example and the Lord's, after receiving the word amid severe affliction with the joy which the Holy Spirit gives, so 7 that you became a pattern to all the believers in Macedonia and Greece.

For from you the word of the Lord has sounded forth not 8 only in Macedonia and Greece; but everywhere your faith in God has become known, so that we have no need to say one word. Of their own accord people report the visit we 9 made to you, and how you turned from your idols to God, to serve a living and true God, and to await the return from 10 heaven of His Son, whom He raised from the dead—Jesus, our Deliverer from God's coming wrath.

The Apostles and their Converts

The Preaching of the Apostles in Thessalonica You yourselves, brethren, know that our visit 1 **2** to you did not prove useless. But, as you are 2 aware, after we had already met with suffering and outrage at Philippi, we found courage in our

1. *Silvanus*] Identical with Silas.
7. *Greece*] Lit. 'Achaia'; *i.e.* the Roman province of Achaia, of which Corinth was the capital; not the district which the Greek knew by that name.

God to tell you amid much opposition the gospel of God. Our appeal does not rest on delusion, nor on uncleanness, 3 and does not deal in fraud. But as God approved us to 4 entrust us with the gospel, so in what we say we seek to please not men but God, who tests our hearts.

Their Conduct while there As you know, we have never used the language 5 of flattery or pretexts for enriching ourselves : God is our witness. Nor did we seek glory 6 from men, either from you or any other, although we might have stood on our dignity as Apostles of Christ. And yet 7 we showed ourselves gentle when among you as a nursing mother cherishing her own children. With this tender 8 regard for you, we were ready to impart to you not only the gospel of God, but our very lives also, because you had become very dear to us.

For you remember, brethren, our labour and toil : how, 9 working night and day so as not to become a burden to any of you, we proclaimed to you the gospel of God. You are 10 witnesses—and God is witness—how holy and upright and blameless our dealings with you believers were. For you 11 know that we acted towards every one of you as a father towards his own children, encouraging and cheering you, and adjuring you to live lives worthy of the God who 12 invites you to share His own Kingdom and glory.

The Thessalonians' brave Endurance of Persecution For this reason we too render unceasing 13 thanks to God, that, when you received the word of God which you heard from us, you embraced it, not as men's word, but as—what it really is— God's word, which also is at work in you who believe. For you, brethren, followed the example of the 14 Churches of God in Christ Jesus which are in Judaea ; seeing that you endured the same ill-treatment from your own countrymen as they did from the Jews, who killed both the 15 Lord Jesus and the Prophets, and drove us out ; these men are displeasing to God, and enemies of all mankind ; for 16 they try to prevent our preaching to the Gentiles that they may be saved. They thus continually fill up the measure of their sins, and God's anger has overtaken them to the utmost.

7. *Gentle*] v.l. 'babes.'
8. *Lives*] Or 'souls.' So in Luke ix. 24.
9. *For*] Or the unemphatic 'Why.'
You remember] Or, as an imperative, 'remember.'
15. *Drove us out*] Or perhaps 'persecuted us harshly.'

Paul's
loving
Interest in
his Readers

But we, brethren, having been for a short 17 time taken from you—in person, not in spirit— endeavoured all the more with intense longing to see you face to face. And so we wanted to 18 come to you—I Paul again and again—but Satan hindered us. For what is our hope or joy, or the crown of which 19 we boast ? Is it not you yourselves in the presence of our Lord Jesus at His Coming ? Yes, you are our glory 20 and our joy.

The sending
of Timothy
to Thessa-
lonica

So when we could endure it no longer, we 1 **3** decided to remain behind in Athens alone ; and 2 we sent Timothy our brother and God's minister in Christ's gospel, that he might strengthen you and encourage you in your faith ; so that none of you 3 might be perturbed by these trials : for you yourselves know that they are our appointed lot. Even when we were with 4 you, we forewarned you that we were soon to suffer affliction ; and this has actually happened, as you know. For this reason I too, when I could no longer endure it, sent 5 to learn about your faith, lest perhaps the Tempter had tempted you, and our labour should prove to no purpose.

The Report
brought
back by
Timothy

But now that Timothy has come back to us 6 from you, and has brought us the good news of your faith and love, and that you cherish a constant and affectionate recollection of us, longing to see us as we also long to see you—for this reason 7 in all our distress and trial we have been comforted about you, brethren, through your faith. For now we live indeed, 8 if you stand fast in the Lord.

Paul's
intense
Gratitude
to God

What thanksgiving indeed can we offer to God 9 on your behalf in return for all the joy which we feel before our God for you, while night and day 10 with intense earnestness we pray that we may see your faces, and make good whatever may be lacking in your faith ?

The
Apostle's
Prayer for
his Readers

But may our God and Father Himself and our 11 Lord Jesus guide our way to you ; and may the 12 Lord make you increase and overflow in love to one another and to all men, as we do to you. Thus He will confirm your hearts blameless in holiness 13

2. *God's minister*] v.l. ' God's fellow worker,' or ' fellow worker for God.'
5. *I too*] Implies that there were others who ' could no longer endure it '—Timothy, and perhaps others of the Christian circle at Athens.

in the presence of our God and Father at the Coming of our Lord Jesus with all His holy ones.

Practical Exhortations

Lessons in the Christian Life — Further, brethren, we beg and exhort you in the name of the Lord Jesus, as you learnt from us how you ought to live so as to please God, as indeed you do live, so to do even more thoroughly. For 2 you know the commands which we gave you by the authority of the Lord Jesus.

Moral Purity — It is God's will that you be pure, that you 3 abstain from fornication ; that each of you 4 shall know how to procure himself a wife in purity and honour, not in lustful passion like the Gentiles 5 who have no knowledge of God ; and that in this matter 6 there be no trespass on a brother's rights and no over-reaching him. For the Lord is an avenger in all such cases, as we have already taught you and solemnly warned you. God has not called us to uncleanness, but to purity. 7 Therefore he who disregards this disregards not man but 8 God, who puts His Holy Spirit into your hearts.

Brotherly Love and honest Work — But about love for the brotherhood it is 9 unnecessary to write to you, for you yourselves have been taught by God to love one another ; and indeed you do love all the brethren throughout Mace- 10 donia. We exhort you, brethren, to do so more and more, and make a quiet life your ambition, and to mind your own 11 business and work with your hands, as we bade you to do ; so as to bear yourselves becomingly towards outsiders, and 12 to be independent.

The Re-appearing of the Lord Jesus

The Christian Dead are under no Dis-advantage — Now, concerning those who fall asleep we 13 would not have you ignorant, brethren, lest you should mourn, as do the rest who have no hope. For if we believe that Jesus died and rose again, 14 in the same way also through Jesus God will bring with Him those who have fallen asleep.

And this we declare to you on the Lord's own word—that 15

---

4. *Wife*] Or ' partner.' Lit. ' vessel.'
13, 14. *Fall asleep*] *i.e.* die.

we who are alive and survive until the Coming of the Lord
will have no advantage over those who have fallen asleep.
For the Lord Himself will come down from heaven with a 16
loud summons, with the voice of an archangel, and with the
trumpet of God, and the dead in Christ will rise first.
Afterwards we who are alive and survive will be caught up 17
along with them in the clouds to meet the Lord in the air.
And so we shall be with the Lord for ever. Therefore 18
encourage one another with these words.

The exact Date of the Lord's Coming unknown But as for times and dates it is unnecessary 1 **5**
that anything be written to you. For you your- 2
selves know perfectly well that the day of the
Lord comes like a thief in the night. While 3
they are saying ' Peace and safety,' then, in a
moment, destruction falls upon them, like birth-pains on a
woman who is with child ; and escape there is none. But 4
you, brethren, are not in darkness, that the day should surprise
you like a thief ; for all of you are sons of light and sons 5
of day. We belong neither to night nor to darkness.

The Need of a vigilant and sober Life So then let us not sleep like the rest, but let 6
us keep awake and be sober. For those who 7
sleep, sleep at night, and those who get drunk,
are drunk at night. But let us, since we belong 8
to the day, be sober, putting on the breastplate of faith and
love, and for a helmet the hope of salvation. God has 9
not destined us to incur His anger, but to obtain salvation
through our Lord Jesus Christ ; who died for us, so that 10
whether we wake or sleep we may share His Life. There- 11
fore encourage one another, building each other up, as in
fact you do.

Conclusion

Various Exhortations Now we beg you, brethren, to respect those 12
who labour among you and preside over you
in the Lord and counsel you, and to hold them 13
in the most affectionate esteem for their work's sake. Be at
peace among yourselves.

And we exhort you, brethren, admonish the unruly, 14
encourage the faint-hearted, sustain the weak, and keep your
temper with all men.

4. *Like a thief*] v.l. ' like thieves.'
12. *Respect*] Lit. ' know.'

See to it that no one repays another with evil for evil ; but 15 always aim at doing good both to one another and to all the world.

Be always joyful. Be unceasing in prayer. Always be 16, 17, thankful ; for this is God's will concerning you in Christ 18 Jesus. Do not quench the Spirit. Do not depreciate 19, 20 prophetic revelations ; but test them all, and hold fast to 21 the good. Keep yourselves aloof from every form of evil. 22

And may the God of peace Himself make you entirely 23 holy ; and may your spirits, souls, and bodies be preserved complete and be found blameless at the Coming of our Lord Jesus Christ. Faithful is He who calls you, and He will 24 also accomplish it.

Farewell Brethren, pray for us. Greet all the brethren 25, 26 with a holy kiss. I charge you in the Lord's 27 name to have this letter read to all the brethren.

The grace of our Lord Jesus Christ be with you. 28

THE SECOND EPISTLE OF PAUL TO THE THESSALONIANS

Very shortly after Paul's first letter, he seems to have written a second, also from Corinth (cf. 2 Thess. i. 1 with 1 Thess. i. 1), and very similar in contents. The tone is a little harder. We miss something of the warmth and glow of the earlier Epistle.

On various grounds the genuineness of 2 Thessalonians has been, and still is, a matter of keen debate. 'Is it likely,' it is asked, ' that one man writing to the same people at what must have been a very short interval of time, would repeat himself to so large an extent . . . especially a man so richly endowed, so fertile in thought as the Apostle Paul ? ' Perhaps the real motive of the letter is to be found in ii. 1–12. Paul had warned them (1 Thess. v. 1–11) of the *suddenness* of the Coming of Christ. This had been misinterpreted as *immediacy*, a mistake which the Apostle corrects by the curious apocalyptic section, unique in Paul, of ii. 3–8. It may be added, as a further reason for writing again, that the abuse of this expectation in the neglect of the duties and responsibilities of this life (1 Thess. iv. 11, 12) had become a grave scandal (2 Thess. iii. 6–15) ; and also that persecution had become more severe (i. 3–12).

On the whole, the difficulty of accounting for the Epistle, if it was not written by Paul, perhaps turns the scale in favour of its authenticity.

THE SECOND EPISTLE OF PAUL TO
THE THESSALONIANS

Introduction

Greeting

Paul, Silvanus, and Timothy, to the Church 1 **1**
of the Thessalonians in God our Father and the
Lord Jesus Christ: grace to you and peace from God our 2
Father and the Lord Jesus Christ.

Reasons for
Gratitude
and
Thanksgiving

We owe unceasing thanks to God on your 3
behalf, brethren. They are due because your
faith grows beyond measure, and the love of all
of you, without exception, one to another, goes
on increasing, so that we ourselves make you our boast among 4
the Churches of God because of your patience and faith amid
all the persecutions and afflictions which you are enduring.
For these are a plain token of God's righteous judgement, 5
which designs that you should be found worthy of the

The Coming
of Christ as
Vindicator
and Judge

Kingdom of God, for the sake of which, indeed,
you are sufferers; since it is a righteous thing 6
for Him to requite with affliction those who
afflict you; and to recompense with rest you 7
who suffer affliction—rest with us at the revelation of the
Lord Jesus from heaven with the angels of His power. He 8
will come in flames of fire to take vengeance on those who do
not acknowledge God and do not obey the gospel of our
Lord Jesus. They will pay the penalty of eternal destruc- 9
tion, away from the presence of the Lord and from the glory
of His might, when He comes to be glorified in His saints 10
and to be wondered at in all who have believed (for our
testimony to you was believed), on that Day.

It is with this in view also that we continually pray for 11
you, that our God will count you worthy of His call, and

---

1. *Silvanus*] Identical with Silas.
5. *A plain token of God's righteous judgement*] The persecutions are such a token
in their *sequel*, as shown in verses 6, 7.

The
Apostle's
Prayer for
his Readers

by His power accomplish every desire for goodness and every work of faith ; in order that 12
the name of our Lord Jesus may be glorified
in you, and you in Him, according to the grace
of our God and the Lord Jesus Christ.

The Re-appearing of the Lord Jesus

Events
which were
to precede
Christ's
Return

Now with respect to the Coming of our Lord 1 **2**
Jesus Christ and our gathering to meet Him, we
entreat you, brethren, not readily to become 2
unsettled in mind or troubled, either by any
spiritual revelation or by any word or letter
alleged to come through us, to the effect that the day of
the Lord is already here. Let no one in any way deceive 3
you, for it cannot come unless the apostasy comes first, and
the appearing of the man of sin, the son of perdition, who 4
sets himself against and exalts himself above every so-
called god or object of worship, and goes the length of
taking his seat in the temple of God, giving it out that he
himself is God.

The coming
Destruction
of the
Lawless one

Do you not remember that while I was still 5
with you, I told you this ? And now you know 6
what restrains him, that he may be revealed
only at his appointed time. For lawlessness is 7
already at work in secret ; but in secret only until the man
who now restrains it is removed, and then the lawless one 8
will be revealed, whom the Lord Jesus will slay with the
breath of His mouth, and overwhelm by the splendour of
His Coming.

An Outbreak
of awful
Wickedness

The appearing of the lawless one will be 9
attended by all sorts of miracles and signs and
delusive marvels—for so Satan works—and by 10
every kind of wicked deception for those who, because
they did not entertain the love of the truth so that they
might be saved, are on the way to perdition. And for 11
this reason God sends them a fatal delusion that they may
believe that lie ; in order that all may be judged who 12
have refused to believe the truth and have taken pleasure
in unrighteousness.

3. *The man of sin*] *i.e.* Antichrist.
6. *What restrains him*] Perhaps the Roman Empire. Cf. Rom. xiii. 1 ff.

Thanksgiving and Exhortations

Renewed
Thanks-
giving
But from us thanks are always due to God on 13 your behalf, brethren whom the Lord loves, because God from the beginning has chosen you for salvation through the Spirit's sanctifying influence and your belief in the truth. To this He has called you by 14 our gospel, so that you may attain to the glory of our Lord Jesus Christ.

An Exhorta-
tion and a
Prayer
So then, brethren, stand firm, and hold fast 15 to the teachings which you have received from us, whether by word of mouth or by letter. And may our Lord Jesus Christ Himself, and God our 16 Father who has loved us and has given us in His grace eternal consolation and good hope, comfort your hearts 17 and make you stedfast in every good work and word.

Finally, brethren, pray for us, that the Lord's 1 **3**
A Request
for Prayer
word may spread rapidly and be extolled, as it was among you ; and that we may be delivered 2 from perverse and wicked men. It is not everybody who has faith ; but the Lord is faithful, and He will make you 3 stedfast and will guard you from the evil one. And we 4 have confidence in you in the Lord, that you are doing and will do what we command. And may the Lord guide your 5 hearts into the love of God and into the patience of Christ !

The Duty of
quiet, honest
Work
But in the name of the Lord we command 6 you, brethren, to stand aloof from every brother whose life is disorderly and not in accordance with the teaching which you received from us. You your- 7 selves know that it is your duty to follow our example. There was no disorder in our life among you, nor did we get 8 bread to eat from any one without paying for it, but by labour and toil, working night and day in order not to be a burden to any of you. Not that we have not a right to such 9 support, but it was in order to set you an example—for you to imitate us. Even when we were with you, we gave you 10 this injunction : ' If a man does not choose to work, neither shall he eat.'

For we hear that there are some of you who live disorderly 11 lives and are mere idle busybodies. Persons of that sort we 12

1. *May spread rapidly*] So Alford. Or ' may hold its outward course ' (Conybeare).
6. *You received*] v.l. ' they received.'

call upon and command in the Lord Jesus Christ to work quietly and eat their own bread.

But you, brethren, must not grow weary in doing right. 13 If any one refuses to obey these our written instructions, 14 mark that man and hold no communication with him ; so that he may be ashamed. And yet do not regard him as an 15 enemy, but caution him as a brother. And may the Lord of 16 peace Himself continually grant you peace in every way. The Lord be with you all.

Conclusion

Farewell Blessing I Paul add a greeting with my own hand, 17 which is the credential in every letter of mine. This is my handwriting. The grace of our 18 Lord Jesus Christ be with you all.

THE PASTORAL EPISTLES

Three letters ascribed to ' Paul, an Apostle of Christ Jesus '—1 and 2 Timothy, and Titus—have a close resemblance one to another, and differ widely from the rest of the Pauline writings in substance, form, and historical standpoint.

They are addressed, not to Churches, but to assistant pastors whom he had left in charge of Churches in Ephesus and Crete. His one concern is now with Church order and discipline, and with pastoral efficiency. ' The essential mind of St. Paul is generally absent : the mystic has turned disciplinarian.' The vocabulary and diction are largely strange, and, as no place can be found in Acts for the historical data, the genuineness of the Pastorals involves Paul's release from imprisonment, and further missionary labours in the East (not in Spain as he had intended), a second imprisonment, and condemnation. Of course there is nothing impossible about all this, but the lack of corroborative evidence must throw doubt on the Pauline authorship. Many isolated sayings, and, indeed, whole paragraphs, notably 2 Tim. iv., may, without hesitation, be ascribed to Paul. Perhaps some tattered fragments of actual letters to Timothy and Titus were worked into a later elaboration of Church order and discipline, considered to be after the mind of Paul. There would in this case be, of course, no question of ' forgery,' but a reverent expedient for preserving what remained of Paul's words. The literary conscience of the first century is not to be judged by that of the twentieth.

THE FIRST EPISTLE OF PAUL
TO TIMOTHY

Written to Timothy, left in charge of the Church in Ephesus.

Its general aim is to encourage him, in spite of youth, timidity, and feeble health, to assert himself in his ministry, and remain stedfast in the faith.

THE FIRST EPISTLE OF PAUL
TO TIMOTHY

Greeting Paul, an Apostle of Christ Jesus by appoint- 1 **1**
ment of God our Saviour and Christ Jesus our
hope, to Timothy, my true son in the faith : grace, mercy, 2
and peace from God the Father and Christ Jesus our Lord.

Timothy's special Work in Ephesus When I was on my journey to Macedonia 3
I begged you to remain on in Ephesus that
you might caution certain persons against
erroneous teaching and attention to mere fables and endless 4
genealogies, such as foster discussions rather than acceptance
in faith of God's provision for salvation. Do so still.

Teachers who were false to Christian Truth The object to be secured by such caution is 5
the love which springs from a pure heart, from a
clear conscience, and from a sincere faith. From 6
these some have deviated, and have lost their way
in empty reasoning. They are ambitious to be 7
teachers of the Law, although they do not understand either
their own words or the things about which they make their
confident assertions.

The real Purpose of the Law Now we know that the Law is good, if a man 8
uses it in a lawful way, and remembers that a 9
law is not enacted for a righteous man, but for
the lawless and rebellious, the irreligious and sinful, the
godless and profane—for those who strike their fathers or
their mothers, for murderers, the licentious, sodomites, 10
slave-dealers, liars, and false witnesses ; and for whatever
else is opposed to the wholesome teaching of the glorious 11
gospel of the blessed God with which I have been entrusted.

The wonderful Mercy shown to Paul himself I am thankful to Christ Jesus our Lord who 12
gave me the needful strength—because He has
judged me faithful and has put me into His
service, though I was previously guilty of 13
blasphemy and persecution and wanton outrage. Yet mercy

4. *Genealogies*] Either (1) The genealogical registers belonging either to Israelitish
families, or to Rabbinical fables and fabrications ; or (2) spiritual myths, the ' aeons '
and ' emanations ' of the Gnostics ; or (3) the heathen mythologies. The last-
named seem least probable of all. Cf. Titus i. 14.

was shown me, because I had acted ignorantly, in unbelief ; and the grace of our Lord was more than abundant, 14 evoking faith and the love which centres in Christ Jesus.

Why so great a Sinner was forgiven True is the saying, and deserving of universal 15 acceptance, that Christ Jesus came into the world to save sinners ; among whom I am foremost. But mercy was shown me in order that 16 in me as the foremost Christ Jesus might display the fulness of His patience, as a striking example for those who would afterwards rest their faith on Him with a view to eternal Life.

An Outburst of Praise Now to the immortal, invisible, and eternal 17 King, who alone is God, be honour and glory for ever and ever ! Amen.

Timothy exhorted and warned This is the charge which I entrust to you, my 18 son Timothy, in accordance with the prophecies formerly uttered concerning you, that being equipped with them you may fight the good fight, holding 19 fast to faith and a clear conscience. This some have cast aside and they have made shipwreck of their faith : among 20 these are Hymenaeus and Alexander, whom I have delivered to Satan that they may be taught not to blaspheme.

The Church is to pray for all the World I exhort then, first of all, that supplications, 1 **2** prayers, petitions, and thanksgivings be offered on behalf of all men ; including kings and all 2 who are in high station, in order that we may live peaceful and tranquil lives with all godliness and gravity. This is right and pleasing in the sight of God our 3 Saviour, who wills all mankind to be saved and to come to a 4 knowledge of the truth. For there is one God and one 5 Mediator between God and men—Christ Jesus, Himself man ; who gave Himself as a ransom for all—a fact testified 6 to at its own appointed time. Of this fact I have been made 7 a herald and an Apostle (I speak the truth : it is not fiction), a teacher of the Gentiles in faith and truth.

Men were to lead in Prayer ; Women to dress modestly So then I would have the men in every place 8 of worship pray, lifting to God holy hands without anger or strife ; and I would have the 9 women dress becomingly, with modesty and sobriety, not with plaited hair or gold or pearls or costly clothes, but—as befits women making a claim to 10 godliness—with the ornament of good works.

20. *Taught*] By discipline. Cf. 1 Cor. v. 5.

Woman's Subordination to Man A woman should learn in silence with entire 11 submissiveness. I do not permit a woman to 12 teach, nor to have authority over a man, but she must remain silent. For Adam was formed first, and then 13 Eve ; Adam was not deceived, but his wife was thoroughly 14 deceived, and became involved in transgression. Yet 15 women will be saved through childbearing if they continue in faith and love and holiness, with self-restraint.

The Qualifications of a Christian Minister True is the saying, ' If any one is eager for 1 **3** the office of bishop, he desires a noble work.' A bishop then must be irreproachable, the 2 husband of one wife, temperate, sober-minded, well-behaved, hospitable, and with a gift for teaching ; not 3 a hard drinker nor given to blows, but gentle, not pugnacious, nor fond of money; one who manages his 4 own household well, keeping his children under control with true dignity. If a man does not know how to manage 5 his own household, how shall he take care of the Church of God ? He ought not to be a new convert, for fear he should 6 be blinded with pride and come under the same condemnation as the Devil. It is needful also that he bear a good 7 character with people outside the Church, lest he fall into reproach or a snare of the Devil.

The Qualifications of Deacons and their Wives Deacons, in the same way, must be men of 8 serious demeanour, not double-tongued, nor addicted to much wine, nor greedy of base gain, but holding the mysterious truths of the faith 9 with a clear conscience. And they must also undergo probation, and then, if they are of unblemished character, let them serve as deacons. Their wives, in the same way, must 11 be serious-minded women, not slanderers, but in every way temperate and trustworthy.

Let a deacon be the husband of one wife, and rule his 12 children and his own household well. For those who 13 have filled the deacon's office well gain for themselves an

---

15. It is not improbable that the writer is thinking here primarily of the birth of Christ by Mary.

2. *Bishop*] Lit. ' one who has the oversight.' The identity of ' bishops ' and ' elders ' in the early Church is shown by the fact that the qualifications here required from ' bishops ' are substantially the same as those required from ' elders ' in Titus i. 5–9, where indeed the word ' bishop ' occurs.

The husband of one wife] This was early interpreted to mean that a bishop must not be married more than once.

6. *The Devil*] Conceived as an angel, who from pride rebelled against the rule of the Most High.

honourable standing, and acquire great boldness of speech in their faith in Christ Jesus.

The Church of the ever-living God All this I write to you, though I am hoping 14 before long to come to see you. But, for fear I 15 may be hindered, I now write, so that you may know how to behave in God's household, which is the Church of the living God, the pillar and buttress of the truth. And 16 beyond controversy, great is the mystery of our religion —He who appeared in flesh, proved Himself righteous in Spirit, was seen by angels and proclaimed among Gentile nations, was believed on in the world, and received up into glory.

False Teachers on the Subjects of Marriage and Food Now the Spirit expressly declares that in later 1 **4** times some will fall away from the faith, giving heed to deceiving spirits and the teachings of demons ; and this through the hypocrisy of 2 men who teach falsely and have their own consciences seared as with a hot iron, forbidding people to 3 marry, and insisting on abstinence from foods which God has created to be partaken of with thankfulness by those who believe and know the truth. For everything that God has 4 created is good ; and nothing is to be rejected, if only it is received with thanksgiving : it is made holy by the word of 5 God and by prayer.

Error to be faithfully rebuked If you put this to the brethren, you will be a 6 good servant of Christ Jesus, nourished on the lessons of the faith and of the good teaching which you have faithfully followed. But profane stories, 7 fit only for old women, have nothing to do with.

Timothy urged to exercise spiritual Self-discipline Train yourself for godliness. Exercise for 8 the body is not useless, but godliness is useful in every respect, possessing the promise of the present and the future life. Faithful is this 9 saying and deserving of universal acceptance : and this is the motive of our toiling and wrestling, 10 that we have our hopes fixed on the living God, who is the Saviour of all mankind and especially of believers.

Command this and teach this. Let no one think slight- 11, 12 ingly of you because you are a young man ; but in speech, conduct, love, faith, and purity, be an example to your

16. This is the truth which the Church holds and defends.
10. *Wrestling*] v.l. ' bearing reproach.'

Noble Conduct and untiring Zeal needful
fellow Christians. Till I come, pay attention 13 to public reading, exhortation, and teaching. Do not neglect the gifts with which you are 14 endowed, which were conferred on you by prophetic revelation when the hands of the elders were placed upon you. Practise these duties and be absorbed in them ; 15 so that your progress in them may be evident to all. Take 16 pains with yourself and your teaching. Persevere in these things ; for by doing this you will secure your own and your hearers' salvation.

Gentleness in Rebuke
Never administer a sharp reprimand to an 1 **5** older man, but entreat him as if he were your father, and the younger men as brothers ; the 2 elder women too as mothers, and the younger women as sisters, with perfect modesty.

Directions as to widowed Women
Relieve widows who are really in need. But 3, 4 if a widow has children or grandchildren, let these learn first to show their piety at home and to make requital to their parents ; for this is acceptable in the sight of God. A widow who is really such, 5 actually desolate, has her hopes fixed on God, and continues at her supplications and prayers night and day ; but a 6 pleasure-loving widow is dead even while still alive. Press 7 these facts upon them, so that they may live lives free from reproach. But if a man makes no provision for his own 8 relations, and especially for his own household, he has disowned the faith and is behaving worse than an unbeliever.

No widow is to be put on the roll who is under sixty years 9 of age. She must have been the wife of but one man, and 10 well reported of for good deeds, as having brought up children, exercised hospitality, washed the feet of the saints, given relief to the distressed, and devoted herself to good works of every kind.

But younger widows you must not enrol ; for as soon as 11 their affections stray wantonly from Christ, they want to marry, and they incur the censure of having broken their 12 first plighted faith. And at the same time they also learn 13 to be idle as they go round from house to house ; and they are not only idle, but are gossips also and busybodies, speaking of things that ought not to be spoken of.

---

3. *Really in need*] Lit. ' really widows.' So in verse 16.
9. *Roll*] *i.e.* of the poor who received relief from the Church.

Unmarried Women I would therefore have the younger women 14 marry, bear children, manage the house, and furnish the adversary with no excuse for slander. For already some of them have gone astray, 15 following Satan. If a believing woman has widows 16 dependent on her, she should relieve them, and save the Church from being burdened—so that the Church may relieve the widows who are really in need.

Elders Let the Elders who preside well be held 17 worthy of double honour, especially those who labour in preaching and teaching. For the Scripture says, 18 ' You are not to muzzle the ox while it is treading out the grain ' (Deut. xxv. 4) ; and the workman deserves his pay.

Never entertain an accusation against an Elder except on 19 the evidence of two or three witnesses. Reprove in the 20 presence of all those who commit sin, so that the rest also may be afraid to sin.

A solemn Appeal, and personal Advice I solemnly call upon you, in the presence of 21 God and of Christ Jesus and of the elect angels, to carry out these instructions without prejudice, and to do nothing from partiality. Do 22 not lay hands upon any one hastily ; and do not be a partaker in the sins of others ; keep yourself pure. (No longer be a 23 water drinker ; but take a little wine for the sake of your stomach and your frequent ailments.)

Helps and Hindrances to a true Estimate of Character The sins of some men are obvious, going 24 before them to judgement, but the sins of others follow after them. So also the right 25 actions of some are obvious, and those that are not cannot remain for ever hidden.

Slaves Let all who are under the yoke of slavery hold 1 **6** their own masters to be deserving of all honour, so that the name of God and the teaching may not be spoken against. And those who have believing masters 2 should not be wanting in respect towards them because they are brethren, but should serve them all the more, because those who profit by the service are believers and beloved.

---

16. *If a believing woman*] v.l. ' If a believer, man or woman.'
22. *Lay hands upon*] Whether in ordination of presbyters, or (more probably) in restoration of penitents.
23. This verse has apparently become misplaced.

Thus teach and exhort. If any one teaches 3
False Teaching and its Results differently, and refuses assent to the wholesome instructions of our Lord Jesus Christ and the teaching that harmonizes with true godliness, he is blinded with conceit and really knows nothing, but 4 is crazy with discussions and controversies about words, which give rise to envy, quarrellings, revilings, ill-natured suspicions, and persistent wranglings on the part of people 5 perverted in mind and so deprived of the truth, who imagine that godliness means gain.

Godliness is indeed great gain when associated 6
A Warning against Greed with contentment ; for we brought nothing into 7 the world, nor can we carry anything out of it ; and if we have food and clothing, with these we should be 8 satisfied. But people who want to be rich fall into tempta- 9 tion and a snare, and into many unwise and pernicious cravings, which sink mankind in destruction and ruin. From love of money all sorts of evils arise ; and some 10 have so hankered after money that they have gone astray from the faith and have caused themselves many pangs of sorrow.

But you, O man of God, must flee from 11
A stirring Appeal these things, and strive for uprightness, godli- ness, faith, love, fortitude, and gentleness. Struggle your hardest in the good contest for the faith ; 12 seize hold of eternal Life, to which you were called ; you made the good confession before many witnesses. I 13 charge you—in the presence of God who gives life to all, and of Christ Jesus who at the bar of Pontius Pilate made the noble confession—that you keep God's commandment stain- 14 lessly and without reproach till the Appearing of our Lord Jesus Christ : this will be brought about at its appointed time 15 by the blessed and only Sovereign, the King of kings and Lord of lords ; who alone possesses immortality, and who dwells 16 in unapproachable light, and whom no man has seen or can see. To Him be eternal honour and power ! Amen.

Impress on those who are rich in the present 17
An Exhortation to the Rich world that they must not be haughty or set their hopes on an uncertain thing like riches, but on God who provides us richly with all things for our enjoyment. They must be beneficent, rich in good deeds, open-handed, 18 and liberal ; storing up for themselves what shall form a 19

solid foundation for the future, that they may lay hold of the Life which is life indeed.

O Timothy, guard the truths entrusted to 20
Conclusion and Blessing you, shunning irreligious and frivolous talk, and objections from what is falsely called ' knowledge '; which some have claimed to possess and they 21 have missed the true faith.

Grace be with you.

THE SECOND EPISTLE OF PAUL
TO TIMOTHY

Paul is again in his Roman prison, more closely confined than before (2 Tim. i. 17), deserted by his friends (i. 15 ; iv. 10, 11), sure of impending death (iv. 6–8), longing for the comfort of Timothy's presence, whom he summons from his charge in Ephesus (iv. 9–11, 21). Yet he finds in his own sufferings a last message of endurance and fidelity for that Church and its minister. ('The first defence' of iv. 16 does not necessarily imply a second imprisonment. It may refer to the first stage of the one trial, reflected in the suspense of Philippians i.).

THE SECOND EPISTLE OF PAUL
TO TIMOTHY

Greeting Paul, by the will of God an Apostle of Christ 1 **1**
Jesus, to proclaim the promise of the Life
which is in Christ Jesus, to Timothy my beloved child : 2
grace, mercy, and peace from God the Father and Christ
Jesus our Lord.

**An
Expression
of Gratitude** I thank God, whom I serve with a pure con- 3
science, as my fathers did, that night and day
I unceasingly remember you in my prayers,
longing, as I recall your tears, to see you, that I may be filled 4
with joy. For I recall the sincere faith which is in you— 5
a faith which dwelt first in your grandmother Lois and your
mother Eunice, and, I am convinced, dwells in you also.

**An
Exhortation
to fresh Zeal** For this reason let me remind you to rekindle 6
God's gift, which is yours through the laying on
of my hands. For the spirit which God has 7
given us is not a spirit of cowardice, but one of power and
of love and of sound judgement.

**An Exhorta-
tion to
Courage and
Fortitude** Do not be ashamed then of witnessing for our 8
Lord or of me His prisoner ; but rather share
suffering with me for the gospel, in reliance on
the power of God. For He saved us and called 9
us with a holy call, not in accordance with our deserts, but in
accordance with His own purpose and the grace which He
bestowed on us in Christ Jesus from all eternity, but which 10
has now been revealed through the Appearing of our Saviour,
Christ Jesus. He has put an end to death and has brought
life and immortality to light through the gospel, for which 11
I have been appointed a preacher, apostle, and teacher.
That indeed is the reason why I suffer as I do. But I am not 12
ashamed, for I know in whom I have trusted, and I am confident that He is able to keep what I have entrusted to Him
until that Day.

7. *Sound judgement*] Or ' discipline.'
8. *In reliance on*] Lit. ' according to.'
10. *Immortality*] Lit. ' incorruptibility.'
11. *Teacher*] v.L. adds ' of the nations.'
12. *That Day*] *i.e.* the Day of Judgement : and so in verse 18.

Christian Truth to be zealously guarded Hold to the pattern of the sound teaching 13 which you have heard from me, by means of the faith and love which are in Christ Jesus. That 14 precious truth which is entrusted to you guard through the Holy Spirit who has His home in our hearts.

Phygelus, Hermogenes, Onesiphorus Of this you are aware, that all the Christians 15 in Asia have deserted me : and among them Phygelus and Hermogenes. May the Lord 16 show mercy to the household of Onesiphorus ; for many a time he gave me fresh vigour and he was not ashamed of my chain. Nay, when he was here in Rome, he took great pains 17 to inquire for me, and found me. (The Lord grant that 18 he may obtain mercy at His hands on that Day !) And you yourself well know all the services which he rendered me in Ephesus.

Timothy urged to be diligent in Teaching You then, my child, must grow strong in the 1 **2** grace that is in Christ Jesus. What you have 2 been taught by me in the hearing of many witnesses, you must hand on to trusty men, who shall be competent to instruct others also.

Exhortation to Patience and Concentration of Purpose As a good soldier of Christ Jesus accept your 3 share of suffering. Every one who serves as a 4 soldier avoids becoming entangled in the affairs of civil life, so that he may satisfy the officer who enlisted him. And if any one takes 5 part in an athletic contest, he gets no prize unless he obeys the rules. The harvestman who labours must be the first 6 to get a share of the crop. Reflect on what I am saying : 7 the Lord will give you understanding in everything.

The Encouragement afforded by Christ's Resurrection Never forget Jesus Christ risen from the dead, 8 a descendant of David, as is declared in the gospel which I preach. For this I suffer, and am 9 even put in chains, as if I were a criminal : yet the word of God is not chained. And so I 10 endure all things for the sake of the elect ; that they also may obtain the salvation which is in Christ Jesus—and with it eternal glory.

The Cross and the Crown are inseparably connected True is the saying : 11

If we died with Him, we shall also live with Him ;

If we endure, we shall also reign with Him ; 12

If we disown Him, He will also disown us ;

If we are faithless, He remains faithful—He cannot 13
disown Himself.

Disputes about Words are to be avoided Bring this to men's remembrances, solemnly 14
charging them in the presence of God not
to wrangle about words, which is altogether
unprofitable and tends only to the ruin of
the hearers.

Hymenaeus and Philetus Earnestly seek to commend yourself to God 15
as a workman who, because of his straight-
forward dealing with the word of truth, has
no reason to feel any shame. But from irreligious and 16
frivolous talk hold aloof, for those who indulge in it will
proceed from bad to worse in impiety, and their teaching 17
will spread like a running sore. Hymenaeus and Philetus
are men of that stamp. As for finding the truth they 18
have gone astray, saying that the Resurrection is already
past, and they are upsetting the faith of some.

God's Church remains unshaken Yet God's solid foundation stands unmoved, 19
bearing this guarantee,

' THE LORD KNOWS THOSE WHO BELONG TO
HIM ' (Num. xvi. 5).

And this also,

' LET EVERY ONE WHO NAMES THE NAME OF THE LORD
RENOUNCE WICKEDNESS ' (Isa. xxvi. 13).

Two Sorts of Christians Now in a great house there are articles not 20
only of gold and silver, but also of wood and of
earthenware ; and some are for honourable,
and others for common use. If therefore a man keeps 21
himself clear of the latter, he will be for honourable use,
consecrated, fit for the Master's service, and equipped for
every good work.

Timothy to be scrupulously careful as to his own Conduct Curb the cravings of youth ; and strive for 22
integrity, faith, love, peace, in company with
all who pray to the Lord with pure hearts. But 23
decline foolish discussions with ignorant men,
knowing that these lead to quarrels ; and a 24
servant of the Lord must not quarrel, but must be inoffensive
towards all men, a skilful teacher, and patient under wrongs.
He must instruct his opponents with gentleness, in the hope 25
that God will some day grant them repentance leading to
knowledge of the truth, and that they may return from the 26

14. *God*] v.l. ' the Lord.'

Devil's delusion to a sober mind, though they are now
entrapped by him to do his will.

Grievous
Times were
coming But of this be assured : in the last days 1 3
grievous times will set in. For men will be 2
lovers of self, lovers of money, boastful, haughty,
profane. They will be disobedient to parents, thankless,
irreligious, hard-hearted, unforgiving, slanderers. They 3
will have no self-control, but will be brutal, opposed to
goodness, treacherous, headstrong, self-important. They 4
will love pleasure instead of loving God, and will keep up 5
a make-believe of piety and yet exclude its power. Turn
away from people of this sort.

False
Teachers
who would
meet with
some
Success Among them are included the men who make 6
their way into private houses and captivate weak
women—women who, weighed down by the
burden of their sins, are led by ever-changing
caprice, and are always learning, and yet never 7
able to arrive at knowledge of the truth.

Their
Hostility to
the Truth Just as Jannes and Jambres withstood Moses, 8
so also these withstand the truth—being men of
debased mind, and worthless so far as faith is
concerned. But they will have no further success ; for their 9
folly will be manifest to all men, just as that of the opponents
What Paul
had suffered
for Christ of Moses came to be. But you have faithfully 10
followed my teaching, life, aims, faith, patience,
love, fortitude, persecutions, and sufferings, all 11
the things which happened to me in Antioch, Iconium, and
Lystra, the persecutions I endured, and how the Lord
delivered me out of them all. And indeed every one who is 12
determined to live a godly life in Christ Jesus will be
persecuted. Bad men and impostors will go from bad to 13
worse, misleading and being misled.

Timothy
urged to be
faithful to
the Lessons
of his
Childhood But do you cling to the things which you 14
have learnt and of which you are convinced,
knowing who your teachers were, and that 15
from infancy you have known the sacred writings
which are able to make you wise to obtain
salvation through faith in Christ Jesus. Every Scripture 16

26. *Though, &c.*] Or ' being captured by him '—the Lord's bondservant—' in order
to do God's will.'
15. *And that*] Or ' and because.'
16. *Every*] Or ' all.'
Scripture] This word occurs about fifty times in the N.T.

is inspired by God and is useful for teaching, for reproof, for correction, and for instruction in right doing ; so that 17 the man of God may be complete, perfectly equipped for every good work.

An Appeal for Zeal and Self-Restraint I adjure you, in the presence of God and of 1 **4** Christ Jesus who is to judge the living and the dead, and by His Appearing and His Kingdom : preach the word, be zealous in season and out of 2 season ; reprove, rebuke, encourage, with the utmost patience and instruction. For a time is coming when men will not 3 tolerate wholesome instruction, but, wanting to have their ears tickled, they will find a multitude of teachers to satisfy their own fancies, and will close their ears to the truth and 4 will turn away to fables.

But do you be circumspect in all matters, and ready to 5 suffer ; do the duty of an evangelist and fully discharge the obligations of your office.

Paul's own Work was now at an End I am a drink-offering already being poured 6 out ; and the time for my departure is close at hand. I have fought the good fight ; I have run 7 the race ; I have kept the faith. Hereafter there 8 is reserved for me the crown of righteousness which the Lord, the righteous Judge, will award to me on that Day, and not only to me, but also to all who have loved the thought of His Appearing.

The lonely Apostle longs to see Timothy Make an effort to come to me speedily ; for 9, 10 Demas has deserted me—loving the present world—and has gone to Thessalonica ; Crescens has gone to Galatia, and Titus to Dalmatia. Luke alone is with me. Call for Mark and bring him with 11 you, for he is a great help to me in my ministry. Tychicus 12 I have sent to Ephesus.

When you come, bring the cloak which I left behind at 13 Troas at the house of Carpus, and the books, especially the parchments.

Alexander the Smith Alexander the smith did me much mischief : 14 the Lord will requite him according to his doings. You also should beware of him ; for 15 he has violently opposed our words.

At my first defence I had no one at my side ; all deserted 16 me : may it not be laid to their charge ! The Lord, 17

16. *Is . . and is*] Or ' being . . is also.'

Paul's first Trial before Nero however, stood by me and filled me with strength, that through me the Message might be fully proclaimed and that all the Gentiles might hear it ; and I was rescued from the lion's jaws. The Lord will deliver me from every malicious attack and will bring me safe to His heavenly Kingdom. To Him be the glory for ever and ever ! Amen. 18

Farewell Greetings Greet Prisca and Aquila, and the household 19 of Onesiphorus. Erastus stayed in Corinth ; 20 Trophimus I left behind me at Miletus, ill. Make an effort to come before winter. Eubulus greets you, 21 and so do Pudens, Linus, Claudia, and all the brethren.

The Lord be with your spirit. Grace be with you all. 22

22. *The Lord*] v.l. ' Lord Jesus ' or ' Lord Jesus Christ.'

THE EPISTLE OF PAUL TO TITUS

Of the founding of a Church in Crete we have no knowledge. Titus is not named in Acts, but appears prominently in 2 Corinthians as Paul's capable and trustworthy messenger in the difficult communications with Corinth. He might well be described as 'Paul's true son in their common faith ' (Titus i. 4).

He had been left in Crete to deal with a people and a situation which would make full demand upon his authority. This short letter bids him be firm, and unsparing in reproval of what is wrong in the Church.

THE EPISTLE OF PAUL TO TITUS

Greeting Paul, a servant of God and an Apostle of Jesus **1 1** Christ for furthering the faith of God's elect and a knowledge of the truths of religion, in hope of **2** eternal life, which God, who never deceives, promised from all eternity ; and at the appointed time He made **3** known His word in the preaching with which I was entrusted by the command of God our Saviour, to Titus **4** my own true child in our common faith : grace and peace from God the Father and Christ Jesus our Saviour.

The Qualifications of a Christian Minister I have left you behind in Crete in order that **5** you may set right the things which still require it and appoint Elders in every town, as I directed you ; wherever there is a man of **6** blameless life, the husband of one wife, having children who are believers and are free from every reproach of profligacy or of disorderliness. For, as God's steward, **7** a bishop must be blameless, not self-willed, not quick-tempered or a hard drinker, not given to blows or greedy of gain ; but hospitable, a lover of goodness, sober-minded, **8** upright, saintly, self-controlled ; holding fast to the trust-**9** worthy word as he has learnt it, so that he may be able both to encourage others with sound teaching and to refute opponents.

The Troublers of the Church at Crete For there are many disorderly persons given **10** to idle and misleading talk, who, for the most part, are adherents of the circumcision. You **11** must stop the mouths of such men, for they upset whole families, teaching what they ought not for the sake of making money. One of themselves—a prophet of **12** their own—has said,
' Cretans are always liars, noxious beasts, idle gluttons.'

7. *Bishop*] Lit. ' he who has the oversight.'
517

These False Teachers are to be denounced

This testimony is true. Therefore sternly 13 reprove them, that they may keep sound in their faith, and not give attention to Jewish legends 14 and the maxims of men who turn their backs on the truth. To the pure everything is pure. But to the 15 polluted and unbelieving nothing is pure ; on the contrary, their very minds and consciences are polluted : they profess 16 to know God, but in their actions they disown Him ; for they are detestable, disobedient men, for any good work useless.

Duties of the Aged

But do you speak in a manner that befits 1 **2** wholesome teaching. Exhort aged men to be 2 temperate, grave, sober-minded, and sound in their faith, their love, and their patience. In the same way 3 exhort aged women to be reverent in bearing, not slanderers nor enslaved to wine. They should school the young 4 women to be affectionate to their husbands and children, to be sober-minded, chaste, domesticated, kind, submissive 5 to their husbands, so that the word of God may not be exposed to reproach.

Duties of younger Men and of Slaves

In the same way exhort the younger men to 6 be self-restrained. And, above all, exhibit in 7 your own life a pattern of right conduct, in your teaching sincerity and seriousness and whole- 8 some language which no one can censure, so that our opponents may feel ashamed at having nothing evil to say against us. Exhort slaves to be obedient to their owners and 9 to give them satisfaction, not contradicting and not pilfering, 10 but manifesting perfect good faith, in order to do credit to the teaching of our Saviour, God, in all things.

The Necessity of a pure and noble Life

For the grace of God has displayed itself with 11 saving power to all mankind, training us to 12 renounce ungodliness and worldly desires, and to live sober, upright, and pious lives in the present world, awaiting fulfilment of our blessed hope—the 13 Appearing in glory of our great God and Saviour Jesus Christ ; who gave Himself for us to purchase our freedom 14 from all iniquity, and purify for Himself a people who should be His own, zealous for good works.

Thus speak, exhort, reprove, with all impressiveness. 15 Let no one make light of you.

6, 7. *Self-restrained. And, above all, exhibit, &c.*] Or ' self-restrained at all points. And exhibit,' &c.

13. *Appearing, &c.*] Or ' Appearing of the glory of the great God and our Saviour.'

TITUS III

Submission to Rulers Remind your hearers that they must submit **3** 1
to the rulers who are in authority, and obey
their rules ; they must be prepared for every
right action, not speak evil of any one, nor be contentious, 2
but be yielding and constantly manifest a gentle spirit
towards all men.

An Appeal to sublime religious Experiences For there was a time when we also were 3
unintelligent, obstinate, deluded, the slaves of
various cravings and pleasures, spending our
lives in malice and envy, hateful ourselves and
hating one another. But when the goodness of God our 4
Saviour and His love to man came to light, not in virtue of 5
any righteous deeds which we had done but in His own
mercy He saved us, by means of the bath of regeneration
and renewal by the Holy Spirit, which He poured out on us 6
richly through Jesus Christ our Saviour ; in order that 7
having been acknowledged righteous through His grace we
might become heirs to eternal life in fulfilment of our
hopes. These words are trustworthy. 8

A Demand for noble Living And on these points I would have you insist
strenuously, in order that those who have their
faith fixed on God may give careful attention to
the practice of good deeds ; for these are not only good in
themselves, but are also useful to mankind.

Useless Discussions But hold yourself aloof from foolish disputes 9
and genealogies and quarrels and wrangling
about the Law, for they are useless and vain.

Unteachable Offenders After a first and second admonition, have 10
nothing further to do with a man who causes
divisions, for, as you know, a person of that sort 11
has gone astray and is a sinner self-condemned.

Personal Requests After I have sent Artemas or Tychicus to you, 12
lose no time in joining me at Nicopolis, for I
have decided to pass the winter there. Help 13
Zenas the lawyer on his journey with special care, and Apollos,
so that nothing may be wanting to them. And let our people 14
too learn to follow honest occupations for the supply of
their necessities, so that they may not live useless lives.

Farewell Greetings Every one here sends you greeting. Greet 15
the believers who hold us dear.
May grace be with you all.

9. *Genealogies*] See note on 1 Tim. i. 4.

519

THE LETTER OF PAUL TO PHILEMON

Philemon and his family appear to have been prominent members of the Church at Colossae (Col. iv. 17; Philem. 1, 2, 23, 24). His conversion to Christianity by Paul (verse 19), possibly in Ephesus (Acts xix. 10), forged a bond of friendship, now to be strained and tested. Philemon's slave, Onesimus, had robbed his master and run away, incurring on recapture the summary penalty of death. Hiding himself in Rome (the suggestions of Caesarea or Ephesus are much less likely), he had somehow come into contact with the imprisoned Apostle, had repented, embraced the Christian faith, and had made himself dear and necessary to Paul. But Christian honour demanded that he must go back to his outraged owner and win forgiveness, if he might, through his new status, no longer merely a slave, a chattle at his wronged master's disposal, but ' a brother beloved.' So Paul brings himself to part with him, though it is parting with his ' very heart,' and gives him this letter of personal appeal to his friend on the slave's behalf. By common consent this private note—it is hardly more—saturated with the confidence of Christian faith, urged in a most difficult situation with tact and delicate humour, is a masterpiece, a little accidental letter which shows the Apostle, not as a theologian or an ardent missionary, but as a great Christian gentleman.

THE LETTER OF PAUL TO PHILEMON

Greeting   Paul, a prisoner for Christ Jesus, and Timothy 1
our brother :

To Philemon our dearly-loved fellow labourer—and to 2
our sister Apphia and our comrade Archippus—as well as
to the Church in your house. Grace to you all, and peace, 3
from God our Father and the Lord Jesus Christ.

Thanksgiving   I give continual thanks to my God while 4
making mention of you, my brother, in my
prayers, because I hear of your love and of the faith which 5
you have towards the Lord Jesus and which you manifest
towards all the saints ; praying as I do, that their partici- 6
pation in your faith may result in the full recognition of
all the right affection that is in us toward Christ. For I 7
have found great joy and comfort in your love, because
the hearts of the saints have been, and are, refreshed
through you, my brother.

Onesimus   Therefore, though I might with Christ's 8
authority speak very freely and order you to do
what is fitting, it is for love's sake that—instead of that— 9
although I am none other than Paul the aged, and now also
a prisoner for Christ Jesus, I entreat you on behalf of my 10

2. Probably father, mother, and son. For Archippus, cf. Col. iv. 17 ; and for
' Church,' Col. iv. 15, n.

6. *May result . . Christ*] Lit. ' may prove effectual in the recognition of every
good thing that is in us unto Christ.' The meaning may be that the sharing of
others in Philemon's faith may quicken and enlarge in us Christians the understanding of the manifold good in us which may be consecrated to the service of Christ (*e.g.*
Philemon's forgiveness of his runaway slave). It took the Christian Church eighteen
centuries to realize that the abolition of slavery was one of the good things in her
unto Christ.

That is in us] v.l. ' in you.'

7. *Joy*] v.l. with very insufficient authority, ' thankfulness.'

9. *Aged*] Greek ' presbutes ' ; another word ' presbeutes ' (*ambassador*) differs only
by a single letter, and there is evidence that *ambassador* was sometimes written
' presbutes.' Paul, at this time, was hardly aged in length of years, though,
perhaps, prematurely so by the kind of life he had lived : cf. 2 Cor. xi. 23–29.
' Ambassador and now also a prisoner ' (cf. R.V. mg.) yields a tempting correspondence with the expression in the contemporary Epistle to the Ephesians, vi. 20
(cf. 2 Cor. v. 20).

(vv. 10, 11.) A humorous word-play. Onesimus means ' useful,' ' profitable.'
The jest is carried on in the verb from the same root in verse 20, ' Let me have
profit.' See footnote.

own child whose father I have become while in my chains—
I mean, Onesimus. Formerly he was useless to you, but 11
now—true to his name—he is of great use to you and
to me.

I am sending him back to you, though in so doing I send 12
part of myself. It was my wish to keep him at my side for 13
him to attend to my wants, as your representative, during
my imprisonment for the gospel. Only I wished to do 14
nothing without your consent, so that this kind action of
yours might not be done under pressure, but might be of
your own free will. For perhaps it was for this reason he 15
was parted from you for a time, that you might receive him
back wholly and for ever yours ; no longer as a slave, but 16
as something better than a slave—a brother peculiarly dear
to me, and even dearer to you, both as a servant and as a
fellow Christian. If therefore you regard me as a comrade, 17
receive him as if he were I myself.

And if he was ever dishonest or is in your debt, debit 18
me with the amount. I Paul write this with my own hand 19
—I will pay you in full. (I say nothing of the fact that you
owe me even your own self.) Yes, brother, do me this 20
favour for the Lord's sake. Refresh my heart in Christ.

I write to you in the full confidence that you will meet 21
my wishes, for I know you will do even more than I say.
And at the same time provide a lodging for me ; for 22
I hope that through your prayers I shall be permitted
to come to you.

Farewell   Greetings to you, my brother, from Epaphras 23
my fellow prisoner for the sake of Christ Jesus ;
and from Mark, Aristarchus, Demas, and Luke, my fellow 24
workers.

May the grace of our Lord Jesus Christ be with the spirit 25
of every one of you.

19. *I Paul*] There is a touch of playfulness in the solemn use, in such a trivial
matter, of this impressive formula. Cf. 2 Cor. x. 1.
20. *Do me this favour*] Lit. ' let me have profit from you.' Cf. verse 10, n.
22. *A lodging*] Or ' hospitality.'

THE EPISTLE TO THE HEBREWS

In the R.V. we are still obliged to read as the title of this Book ' The Epistle of Paul the Apostle to the Hebrews.' This is unfortunate, and is hardly condoned by the statement in the Preface that the Revisers were not expressly directed to extend their revision to the titles of the New Testament Books ; for the one thing certain about the authorship is, that the Epistle was not written by Paul. There is no consistent ancient tradition of Pauline authorship, and both in form and substance it differs widely from his writings. Who wrote it, to whom, whence, and when, are all unsolved problems, for the discussion of which reference must be made to the Commentaries. The simple title ' To Hebrews ' (not original) may probably be accepted as correct. The Epistle seems to have been addressed to a small community of Jewish Christians, in danger of apostasy from the faith through persecution. The writer, who knows them intimately and is known by them, in turn argues, warns, and appeals to their former loyalty to Christ and to their brethren ; but argument predominates, the most sustained and eloquent in the New Testament. Its keynote is struck in ' God has spoken unto us in a Son ' (i. 2). As Son, He is superior to prophets, angels, and Moses ; but behind this apologetic ' better,' there sounds the absolute ' best.' Christianity is the final religion— substance in contrast to shadow. And as the argument proceeds, one feature of the contrast becomes predominant : man's persistent craving for a priest, a mediator and intercessor between him and God, and for an atoning sacrifice for his ignorance and error, is once and for all satisfied by the spiritual priesthood and atoning self-sacrifice of Christ (Jer. xxxi.). In Him, Jeremiah's great prophecy of the New Covenant, the crown of the Old Testament revelation, finds its fulfilment ; and the new has made the first old (viii. 8–13). It is noteworthy that in so ' theological ' a writing, the human name Jesus is very prominent. He is our brother, Himself tempted and suffering, and therefore has sympathy with us men and full understanding of our needs.

Independent of all question as to author, recipients, and details of argument, that message abides unchanging : ' Jesus Christ, the same yesterday and to-day—yea, and for ever.'

THE EPISTLE TO THE HEBREWS

Introduction. Christ's Superiority to Prophets and Angels

God has spoken to Man in and through Christ

God, who of old spoke to our forefathers 1 in many fragments and by various methods through the Prophets, has at the end of 2 these days spoken to us through a Son, who is the predestined Lord of the universe, and through whom He made the world. He brightly reflects 3 God's glory and is the exact representation of His being, and upholds the universe by His all-powerful word. After securing man's purification from sin He took His seat at the right hand of the Majesty on high, having become 4 as far superior to the angels as the Name He possesses by inheritance is more excellent than theirs.

Christ is the Son, Angels are mere Servants, of God

For to which of the angels did God ever say, 5 'MY SON ART THOU :

I HAVE THIS DAY BECOME THY FATHER '
(Ps. ii. 7) ;

and again,

'I WILL BE A FATHER TO HIM,

AND HE SHALL BE MY SON ' (2 Sam. vii. 14) ?

And again when He brings His Firstborn into the world, 6 He says,

1. *Spoke*] The word used (*laleo*) has reference rather to the sound of the uttered word than to the thought expressed (*lego*). Heaven's silence was broken, but only in a fragmentary and varying revelation. The Divine word to man was piecemeal and multiform, not complete and uniform. Cf. Browning's *Cleon* :
. . . ' those divine men of old time
Have reached, thou sayest well, each at one point
The outside verge that rounds our faculty.'

' But some . . . god descended here,
And, once for all, showed simultaneously
What, in its nature, never can be shown
Piecemeal or in succession.'

2. *World*] Lit. ' Ages.' The world in its time-aspect of successive eras of human history. The world as material is the Greek *cosmos*. The R.V. ' worlds ' is less probable.

6. *And again when He brings*] The position in the Greek of ' again,' and the proper force of the verb, ' when He shall have brought,' rather suggest ' when He once more brings,' a reference to the second Advent ; but this thought is strange and unexpected, and the rendering of the text may stand, the reference being to the Incarnation.

' AND LET ALL GOD'S ANGELS WORSHIP HIM '
(Deut. xxxii. 43, LXX ; Ps. xcvii. 7, LXX).

Moreover of the angels He says, 7
' HE CHANGES HIS ANGELS INTO WINDS,
AND HIS MINISTERING SERVANTS INTO A FLAME OF FIRE '
(Ps. civ. 4).

But of His Son, He says, 8
' THY THRONE, O GOD, IS FOR EVER AND EVER,
AND THE SCEPTRE OF THY KINGDOM IS A SCEPTRE OF
ABSOLUTE JUSTICE.

THOU HAST LOVED RIGHTEOUSNESS AND HATED LAWLESS- 9
NESS ;

THEREFORE GOD, THY GOD, HAS ANOINTED THEE
WITH THE OIL OF GLADNESS BEYOND THY FELLOWS '
(Ps. xlv. 6, 7).

It is also of His Son that God says, 10
' THOU, O LORD, IN THE BEGINNING DIDST LAY THE
FOUNDATIONS OF THE EARTH,

AND THE HEAVENS ARE THE WORK OF THY HANDS.
THE HEAVENS WILL PERISH, BUT THOU REMAINEST ; 11
AND THEY WILL ALL GROW OLD LIKE A GARMENT,
AND, AS A MANTLE THOU WILT ROLL THEM UP ; 12
YES, LIKE A GARMENT, AND THEY WILL UNDERGO
CHANGE.

BUT THOU ART THE SAME,
AND THY YEARS WILL NEVER COME TO AN END '
(Ps. cii. 25–27).

---

6. *And let, &c.*] The words occur in the LXX of Deut., but have nothing in the Hebrew to correspond. The Hebrew of the psalm is ' Worship Him all ye gods '; LXX ' all ye angels.'

7. A precarious tenure of existence is here attributed to the angels in contrast to the eternity of the life and reign of the Son of God. It was an ancient Jewish belief that angels sometimes lose their personality and are reduced to impersonal forces of nature. See A. S. Peake's excellent note in the *Century Bible.*

8. *O God*] Psalm xlv. is a Royal Marriage Song, and this translation involves the direct address of an earthly king by the title ' God.' The obvious difficulty has led to various conjectures :

(1) ' Thy throne is the *throne of* God ' (so R.V. mg. in the Psalm).
(2) Thy throne is God for ever and ever.'
(3) A corrupt Hebrew text, ' Yahweh ' (God), being a mistake for the almost identical Hebrew word meaning ' shall be '—' Thy throne shall be for ever and ever.' This conjecture is widely adopted, but the writer of the Epistle, in applying the words of the psalm to the Son, would not feel the difficulty ; and ' Thy throne, O God ' may stand.

Is for ever and ever, &c.] ' The angels are subject to constant change. He has a dominion for ever and ever ; they work through material powers ; He—the Incarnate Son—fulfils a moral sovereignty and is crowned with unique joy ' (Westcott).

A sceptre of absolute justice] Lit. ' the rod of straightness.'

9. *Therefore God, Thy God, has anointed*] Or, ' Therefore, O God, Thy God has anointed.'

To which of the angels has He ever said,   13
' Sit at My right hand
Till I make Thy foes a footstool for Thy feet ' ?
(Ps. cx. 1.)
Are not all angels spirits that serve Him—whom He 14
sends out to render service for the benefit of those who
are to inherit salvation ?

The Peril of Disobedience to the Saviour's Message

For this reason we ought to pay the more 1 **2**
earnest heed to the things which we have heard,
for fear we should drift away from them. For 2
if the message delivered through angels proved
to be true, and every transgression and act of
disobedience met with just retribution, how shall we 3
escape if we neglect a salvation as great as that now offered
to us ? This, after having first of all been announced by
the Lord Himself, had its truth made sure to us by those
who heard Him, while God corroborated their testimony 4
by signs and marvels and various mighty works, and by
gifts of the Holy Spirit distributed in accordance with
His own will.

Jesus, because of His Death, is crowned with Glory

It is not to angels that God has assigned 5
the sovereignty of that coming world of which
we speak. But, as we know, a Psalmist has 6
exclaimed,
' How poor a creature is man, and yet
Thou dost remember him,
And a son of man, and yet Thou dost come to him !
Thou hast made him only a little lower than the 7
angels ;
With glory and honour Thou hast crowned him,
And hast set him over the works of Thy hands.
Thou hast put everything in subjection under his 8
feet ' (Ps. viii. 4–6).
For this subjecting of the universe to man implies the
leaving nothing not subject to him. But we do not as
yet see the universe subject to him. But we do see Him 9

6. *As we know*] Or ' somewhere.'
7. *A little*] Or ' for a little while,' and so in verse 9. The Hebrew phrase in the
psalm refers to degree, the corresponding Greek phrase may be used either of degree
or of duration. The slight degree of the inferiority of man to the angels is very
pertinent in the psalm, but is less relevant in the application to Jesus. Hence many
prefer a reference to the duration of the humiliation of His earthly life ; so A.V.
mg. ; R.V. mg.
And hast set Him over the works of Thy hands] v.l. omits this clause.

who was made a little lower than the angels—even Jesus
—because of His suffering of death crowned with glory
and honour, that by God's grace He might taste death
for every man.

Man's divine Brother made perfect through Suffering For it was fitting that He for whom and 10
through whom all things exist, in bringing
many sons to glory, should perfect by suffering the Prince Leader of their salvation. For 11
both He who sanctifies and those whom He
is sanctifying have all one Father ; and for this reason
He is not ashamed to speak of them as His brothers ; as 12
when He says :

' I WILL PROCLAIM THY NAME TO MY BROTHERS ;
IN THE MIDST OF THE CONGREGATION I WILL HYMN
THY PRAISES ' (Ps. xxii. 22) ;

and again, 13

' I WILL BE ONE WHOSE TRUST REPOSES IN GOD '

(Ps. xviii. 2 ; Isa. xii. 2) ;

and again,

' HERE AM I, AND HERE ARE THE CHILDREN GOD HAS
GIVEN ME ' (Isa. viii. 18).

Our High Priest Himself suffered and died Since then the children referred to are all 14
alike sharers in perishable human nature, He
Himself also, in the same way, took on Him a
share of it, in order that through death He
might render powerless him who had authority over death,
that is, the Devil, and might set at liberty all those who 15
through fear of death had been subject to lifelong slavery.
For assuredly it is not to angels that He reaches a helping 16
hand, but it is to the descendants of Abraham. And for 17
this purpose it was necessary that in all respects He should

9. *A little lower*] The author of the psalm speaks of the *exaltation* of man : this
writer applies the words to the *humiliation* of Jesus.
That by God's grace, &c.] This clause does not naturally link on to ' crowned with
glory and honour.' Nor can it well be attached (as in former editions of this
book) to ' made lower than the angels,' in order that He might taste death. The
order of the Greek forbids. Either the clause is loosely appended without strict
logical sequence, or perhaps the writer means to say, ' with a view to the suffering
of death crowned,' &c. ; *i.e.* the crowning was in the pre-incarnate state : the con-
templated death for every man was not humiliation, but glory and honour—
' crowned for death.' In this case the writer's view-point differs from that of Paul in
Phil. ii. 6–11, a view of the Cross shared also by this writer (Heb. xii. 2).
10. *In bringing*] R.V. mg. ' having brought,' a supposed reference to the O.T.
saints ; but the tense of the Greek participle (*Aorist*) does not necessitate this rendering, and the thought is quite inappropriate to this context.
Prince Leader] Or ' pioneer '; A.V. ' captain '; R.V. ' author.' The word may
be studied in its various contexts (Heb. xii. 2 ; Acts iii. 15 ; v. 31).
14. *Perishable human nature*] Lit. ' blood and flesh.'

be made to resemble His brothers, so that He might prove Himself a compassionate and faithful High Priest in things relating to God, in order to atone for the sins of the people. For inasmuch as He has Himself felt the pain 18 of temptation and trial, He is also able to help those who are tempted and tried.

Christ's Superiority to Moses Therefore, holy brethren, sharers with others 1 **3** in a heavenly calling, fix your thoughts on Jesus, the Apostle and High Priest whose followers we profess to be. How faithful He was to Him 2 who appointed Him, just as Moses also was faithful in all God's house ! For Jesus has been counted worthy of 3 greater glory than Moses, in so far as he who has built a house has higher honour than the house itself. For every 4 house has a builder, the Builder of all things being God.

Moses was only a faithful Servant Moreover, Moses was faithful in all God's 5 house as a servant in delivering the message given him to speak ; but Christ was faithful as 6 a Son having authority over God's house, and we are that house, if we hold firm to the end the boldness and the hope which we boast of as ours.

A Warning against Unbelief and Disobedience For this reason—as the Holy Spirit warns us, 7 ' TO-DAY, IF YOU SHOULD HEAR HIS VOICE, DO NOT HARDEN YOUR HEARTS AS IN THE 8 TIME OF THE PROVOCATION

ON THE DAY OF THE TEMPTATION IN THE DESERT, WHERE YOUR FATHERS TEMPTED AND TESTED ME, AND 9 THEY SAW ALL THAT I DID DURING FORTY YEARS. THEREFORE I WAS GREATLY 10 GRIEVED WITH THAT GENERATION,

17. *High Priest*] The first hint of a theme soon to dominate the Epistle.
18. *Temptation and trial*] Both these thoughts are included in the Greek word, as in Jas. i. 2.
2. *Just as Moses also*] Cf. Exod. xl. 16–32 ; Num. xii. 7.
3. *He who has built a house*] Or ' he who founded (or established) a household.' The Greek word used here three times for ' build ' denotes not only the putting up of an edifice, but also the supplying it with every material and personal requisite.
6. *Hope which, &c.*] Lit ' boast—*i.e.* thing boasted of—of our hope.'
7. *To-day, &c.*] Or ' Oh that to-day you would but listen to His voice ! ' So in verse 15 and iv. 7 ; but though this is probably the meaning of the Hebrew in the psalm (so R.V. text), the context here seems to point to ' if you should hear ' rather than to the elliptical use of ' if,' ' If only you would hear ! '
8. *Provocation*] Hebrew, ' Meribah.' Exod. xvii. 7.
Temptation] Hebrew ' Massah.' Exod. xvii. 7.
10. *Therefore*] An insertion by this writer in order to connect the ' during forty years ' with ' all that I did,' instead of, as in the psalm, with ' I was grieved.' Perhaps he intends a glance at the long period of God's patience with Jewish unbelief since the Crucifixion, a period now nearing its close in the impending destruction of Jerusalem (A.D. 70). In verse 17 the true connection is recovered.

AND I SAID, " IN THEIR HEARTS THEY ARE EVER ASTRAY :
THEY HAVE NOT LEARNT TO KNOW MY PATHS."
WHILE I SWORE IN MY ANGER,   11
THEY SHALL NOT BE ADMITTED TO MY REST '
          (Ps. xcv. 7–11).

See to it, brethren, that there is never in any one of you—as 12
perhaps there is—a sinful and unbelieving heart, manifesting
itself in revolt from the ever-living God.

The Necessity of Fidelity to the very End On the contrary encourage one another, 13 day after day, so long as ' to-day ' lasts, so that not one of you may be hardened through the deceitful character of sin. For we have, 14 all alike, become sharers with Christ, if we really hold our first confidence firm to the end ; seeing that the warning 15 still comes to us,

' TO-DAY, IF YOU SHOULD HEAR HIS VOICE,
  DO NOT HARDEN YOUR HEARTS AS YOUR FOREFATHERS
    DID IN THE TIME OF THE PROVOCATION '
          (Ps. xcv. 7).

A Lesson from Jewish History For who were they that heard, and yet 16 provoked God ? Was it not the whole of the people who had come out of Egypt under the leadership of Moses ? And with whom was God so greatly 17 grieved for forty years ? Was it not with those who had sinned, and whose dead bodies fell in the Desert ? And to 18 whom did He swear that they should not be admitted to His rest, if it was not to those who were disobedient ? And 19 so we see that it was owing to lack of faith that they could not be admitted.

We enter the heavenly Canaan through Faith Therefore let us be on our guard lest perhaps, 1 **4** while He still leaves us a promise of being admitted to His rest, some one of you should be found to have fallen short of it. For the 2 gospel has been brought to us as truly as to them ; but the word they heard failed to benefit them, because they were not united by faith with those who gave heed to it. We who have believed are to be admitted to 3 the true rest ; as He has said,

2. *Those who gave heed to it*] *i.e.* Joshua and Caleb ; but these trifling exceptions are ignored in iii. 16. The v.L. seems preferable, though not so well attested, ' because *it* (the word) was not united by faith with those who heard it ' (*i.e.* the whole congregation of Israel) ; or ' because it was not mixed with faith for those who heard it.' The two readings differ only by a single letter.

'WHILE I SWORE IN MY ANGER,
THEY SHALL NOT BE ADMITTED TO MY REST' (Ps. xcv. 11);
although God's works were completed from the creation
of the world. For, as we know, when speaking of the 4
seventh day He has used the words, 'AND GOD RESTED
ON THE SEVENTH DAY FROM ALL HIS WORKS' (Gen. ii. 2);
and He has also declared, 'THEY SHALL NOT BE ADMITTED 5
TO MY REST' (Ps. xcv. 11).

The Possession of Palestine did not exhaust the Promise Since, then, it is still true that some will be 6
admitted to that rest, and that because of
disobedience those who formerly had the
gospel proclaimed to them were not admitted,
He again definitely mentions a certain day, 7
'to-day,' saying long afterwards, by David's lips, in the
words already quoted,

'TO-DAY, IF YOU SHOULD HEAR HIS VOICE,
DO NOT HARDEN YOUR HEARTS' (Ps. xcv. 7).

For if Joshua had given them the true rest, God would 8
not have continued to speak later about another still future
day. It follows that there still remains a Sabbath-Rest for 9
the people of God. For whoever has been admitted to 10
His rest, has rested from his works as God did from His.

An Appeal to the Warnings contained in the Word of God Let it then be our earnest endeavour to be 11
admitted to that rest, so that no one may
perish through following the same example of
unbelief. For the word of God is full of life 12
and power, and is keener than the sharpest
two-edged sword. It pierces even to the severance of soul
from spirit, and penetrates between the joints and the
marrow, and it can discern the secret thoughts and purposes of the heart. And no created thing is able to escape 13
its scrutiny; but everything lies bare and completely exposed
before the eyes of Him with whom we have to do.

The keen Sympathy of our great High Priest Inasmuch, then, as we have in Jesus, the Son 14
of God, a great High Priest who has passed
into heaven itself, let us hold firmly to our
profession of faith. For we have not a High 15
Priest who is unable to feel for us in our weaknesses, but

13. *Completely exposed*] The word is obscure but seems to mean, 'like the victim
whose neck is bent back for the knife.'
With whom we have to do] Or 'to whom we are responsible.'
14. *Into heaven itself*] Lit. 'through the (lower) heavens'; to the highest heaven
—into the very presence of God. The lower and higher heavens of Jewish theology;
three or even seven. Cf. 2 Cor. xii. 2.

one who was tempted in every respect, just as we are tempted, and yet did not sin. Therefore let us come 16 boldly to the throne of grace, that we may receive mercy and find grace to help us in our time of need.

High Priests must themselves be human For every High Priest, chosen as he is from 1 **5** among men, is appointed to act on behalf of men in matters relating to God, in order to offer both gifts and sin-offerings, and he must 2 be one who is able to bear patiently with the ignorant and erring, because he himself also is beset with infirmity. And 3 for this reason he is required to offer sin-offerings not only for the people but also for himself.

High Priests are appointed by God And no one takes this honourable office upon 4 himself, but only accepts it when called to it by God, as Aaron was. So Christ also did not 5 claim for Himself the honour of being made High Priest, but was appointed to it by Him who said to Him,

‘ MY SON ART THOU :
I HAVE TO-DAY BECOME THY FATHER ’ (Ps. ii. 7) ;
as also in another passage He says, 6
‘ THOU ART A PRIEST FOR EVER,
BELONGING TO THE ORDER OF MELCHIZEDEK ’ (Ps. cx. 4).

The Prayers and Tears of the Man Jesus For Jesus during His earthly life offered up 7 prayers and entreaties, crying aloud and weeping as He pleaded with Him who was able to save Him from death, and He was heard for His godly fear. Although He was God's Son, yet He 8 learned obedience from the sufferings which He endured ; and so, having been made perfect, He became to all who 9 obey Him the source and giver of eternal salvation. For 10 God Himself addresses Him as a High Priest for ever, belonging to the order of Melchizedek.

These Hebrew Christians had gone backward Of Him we have much to say, and much 11 that it would be difficult to make clear to you, since you have become so dull of apprehension. For although, considering the long time you 12 have been believers, you ought now to be

4. *Honourable office*] Lit. ‘ honour,’ or ‘ dignity.’
7. *Death*] Cf. Mark xiv. 36 ; or, possibly, ‘ bring Him to safety through and out of death.’
11. *Of Him*] *i.e.* Melchizedek or Christ : but more probably the pronoun is neuter, ‘ of which matter,’ *i.e.* Christ, a Priest after the order of Melchizedek.
So dull of apprehension] Lit. ‘ hard of hearing.’

teachers of others, you really need some one to teach you over again the very rudiments of the truths of God, and you have come to require milk instead of solid food. By 13 people who live on milk I mean those who are imperfectly acquainted with the doctrine of righteousness. Such persons are mere babes. But solid food is for adults 14 —that is, for those who through constant practice have their spiritual faculties carefully trained to distinguish good from evil.

An Appeal for manly Progress   Therefore leaving elementary instruction 1 **6** about the Christ, let us advance to mature manhood, and not be continually re-laying a foundation of repentance from lifeless works and of faith in God, or of teaching about ceremonial washings, the 2 laying on of hands, the resurrection of the dead, and the last judgement. And advance we will, if God permits 3 us to do so.

A solemn Warning   For it is impossible, in the case of those who 4 have once for all been enlightened, and have tasted the sweetness of the heavenly gift, and have been made partakers of the Holy Spirit, and have 5 realized how good the word of God is and how mighty are the powers of the coming age, and then fall away—it is 6 impossible, I say, to bring them back to a new repentance, since, to their own undoing, they are crucifying the Son of God afresh and exposing Him to open shame. For land which has drunk in the rain that often falls 7 upon it, and brings forth vegetation useful to those for whose sakes it is tilled, has a share in God's blessing. But if it only yields a mass of thorns and thistles, it 8 is considered worthless, and is in danger of being cursed, and in the end will be destroyed by fire.

A confident Expectation of better Things   But we, even while we speak in this tone, 9 have a happier conviction concerning you, my dearly-loved friends—a conviction of things which point towards salvation. For God is 10 not unjust so as to be unmindful of your labour and of the love which you have manifested towards Himself in having rendered services to His people and in still rendering

---

13. *Doctrine*] Lit. ' word.'
2. *Ceremonial washings*] Lit. ' baptisms,' including Jewish ablutions (cf. Mark vii. 3, 4), the baptism of John and Christian baptism.

them. But we long for each of you to continue to mani- 11
fest the same earnestness, with a view to your enjoying
fulness of hope to the very end ; so that you may not 12
become half-hearted, but be imitators of those who through
faith and patient endurance are heirs to the promises.

God's   For when God gave the promise to Abraham, 13
Promises since He had no one greater to swear by, He
inspire   swore by Himself, saying,   14
infinite Hope   ' ASSUREDLY I WILL BLESS YOU,

AND I WILL INCREASE YOU ' (Gen. xxii. 16, 17).

And so, as the result of patient waiting, our forefather 15
obtained what God had promised. Men swear by what 16
is greater than themselves ; and with them an oath in
confirmation of a statement always puts an end to a dispute.
In the same way, since it was God's desire to display more 17
convincingly to the heirs of the promise how unchangeable
His purpose was, He added an oath, in order that, through 18
two unchangeable things, in which it is impossible for Him
to prove false, we may possess mighty encouragement—we
who, for safety, have hastened to lay hold of the hope set
before us. That hope we have as an anchor of the soul— 19
an anchor that can neither break nor drag. It passes in behind
the veil, where Jesus has entered as a fore-runner on our be- 20
half, having become, like Melchizedek, a High Priest for ever.

Jesus   This Melchizedek, King of Salem, priest of 1 **7**
a High   the Most High God, who met Abraham as
Priest like he was returning from the slaughter of the
Melchizedek kings and blessed him, to whom also Abraham 2
assigned a tenth part of all the spoil, was in the first place,
as his name means, King of righteousness, and besides that,
King of Salem (that is, King of peace). Being without 3
father or mother or ancestry, having neither beginning of
days nor end of life, but made like to the Son of God, he
remains a priest in perpetuity (Gen. xiv. 18–20 ; Ps. cx. 4).

Now think how great this man must have been, 4

18. *Two unchangeable things*] God's promise and God's oath.

(vv. 1–3.) The punctuation adopted preserves the simple sequence of the clauses
which describe the unique greatness of Melch'zedek—leading up to the culmination.
He retains a perpetual priesthood. In verse 3, and in the 'he lives' (of verse 8), the
silence of the Genesis narrative is pressed into the argument, as often by Philo. This
mysterious meeting of Melchizedek and Abraham is a striking episode in the history :

'Ships that pass in the night and speak each other in passing.'

And this writer's combination of Gen. xiv. and Psalm cx., to prove the superiority
of the Priesthood of Christ, though some of the detail of his exegesis may seem
strange to us, shows bold imagination and fine insight.

Melchizedek's Greatness. His Superiority to Abraham

to whom Abraham, the Patriarch, gave a tenth part of the best of the spoil. Those 5 of the descendants of Levi who receive the priesthood are indeed authorized by the Law to take tithes from the people, that is, from their brethren, though these have sprung from Abraham. But, in this 6 instance, one who does not trace his origin from them takes tithes from Abraham, and blesses him to whom the promises belong! And beyond all dispute it is always 7 the inferior who is blessed by the superior.

Levi, as it were, paid him Tithes

Moreover, here mortal men receive tithes: 8 there one receives them about whom it is witnessed that he lives. And even Levi—if I may so 9 speak—pays tithes through Abraham: for Levi was yet in 10 the loins of his forefather when Melchizedek met Abraham.

The Imperfection of the Jewish Priesthood

If then perfection was attainable by means of 11 the Levitical priesthood—for on this basis the people received the Law—what further need was there for a priest of a different kind to be raised up belonging to the order of Melchizedek instead of being said to belong to the order of Aaron? For when the priest- 12 hood changes, a change of Law also of necessity takes place.

Jesus did not belong to the Tribe of Levi

He of whom all this is said is connected 13 with a different tribe, not one member of which has anything to do with the altar. For 14 it is undeniable that our Lord sprang from Judah, a tribe of which Moses said nothing about priests. And this is still more abundantly clear when we read that 15 it is as belonging to the order of Melchizedek that a priest of a different kind is to arise, and to hold His office not 16 in obedience to any temporary Law, but by virtue of an indestructible Life. The words indeed are in evidence, 17

' THOU ART A PRIEST FOR EVER, BELONGING TO THE ORDER OF MELCHIZEDEK ' (Ps. cx. 4).

The Jewish Priesthood superseded

On the one hand we have here the abrogation 18 of an earlier code because it was weak and ineffective—for the Law made nothing perfect; 19 on the other hand we have the bringing in of a new and better hope by means of which we draw near to God.

---

8. *Here*] *i.e.* in the regulations of the Levitical priesthood as contrasted with that of Melchizedek.

11. *What further, &c.*] Why change the priest, unless, indeed, that means change of the Law?

Christ's
Priesthood
has been
made sure
to Him
by God

And since this was effected not without an 20
oath—for those others became priests apart 21
from any oath, but He entered upon an office
confirmed by an oath from Him who said to
Him, 'THE LORD HAS SWORN AND WILL NOT
RECALL HIS WORDS, THOU ART A PRIEST FOR EVER' (Ps.
cx. 4)—so much the more also is the Covenant of which 22
Jesus has become the guarantor, a better covenant.

Christ the
one Priest
who never
dies

And they have been appointed priests many in 23
number, because death prevents their continuance in office : but He, because He continues 24
for ever, has a priesthood which does not pass
to any successor. Hence too He is able to save to the utter- 25
most those who come to God through Him, seeing that He
ever lives to make intercession on their behalf.

The sinless
and perfect
Son of God

Such a High Priest as this was exactly suited 26
to our need—holy, guileless, undefiled, far
removed from sinful men, and exalted above
the heavens ; who, unlike other High Priests, is not under 27
the necessity of offering up sacrifices day after day, first for
His own sins, and afterwards for those of the people ;
because this He did once for all when He offered up Him- 28
self. For the Law constitutes men —men with all their
infirmity as High Priests ; but the word of the oath, which
came later than the Law, constitutes as High Priest a Son
who has been made for ever perfect.

Christ's High Priesthood, and the new Covenant

A heavenly,
not an
earthly
Priesthood

Now of what we have been saying the main 1 **8**
point is this. We have a High Priest who
has taken His seat at the right hand of the
throne of God's Majesty in the heavens, and 2
ministers in the Holy place and in the true tabernacle built
by the Lord and not by man.

The Mosaic
System a
dim Shadow
of spiritual
Realities

Every High Priest, however, is appointed to 3
offer both bloodless gifts and sacrifices. Therefore this High Priest also must have some
offering to present. If then He were still on 4
earth, He would not be a priest at all, since
there are already those who present the offerings in

21. *Recall His words*] Lit. ' regret it.'
22. *Guarantor*] Or ' surety.' Cf. Job xvii. 3, R.V.

obedience to the Law, and do service to a copy and type of 5
things heavenly, just as Moses was divinely instructed
when about to build the tabernacle. God said, ' SEE THAT
YOU MAKE EVERYTHING AFTER THE PATTERN SHOWN YOU
ON THE MOUNTAIN ' (Exod. xxv. 40). But, as a matter of 6
fact, the ministry which Christ has obtained is all the nobler
a ministry, in that He is at the same time the negotiator of
a sublimer covenant, based upon sublimer promises.

A new and spiritual Covenant was promised For if that first Covenant had been free 7
from imperfection, there would have been no
occasion to introduce a second. But Scripture 8
says that God was dissatisfied with His people :

" " THERE ARE DAYS COMING," SAYS THE LORD,
" WHEN I WILL ESTABLISH WITH THE HOUSE OF ISRAEL
AND WITH THE HOUSE OF JUDAH A NEW COVENANT—
A COVENANT UNLIKE THE ONE WHICH I MADE WITH 9
THEIR FATHERS
ON THE DAY WHEN I TOOK THEM BY THE HAND TO
LEAD THEM OUT FROM THE LAND OF EGYPT ;
FOR THEY WOULD NOT REMAIN FAITHFUL TO MY
COVENANT."
" SO I TURNED FROM THEM," SAYS THE LORD.
" BUT THIS IS THE COVENANT THAT I WILL MAKE WITH 10
THE HOUSE OF ISRAEL
AFTER THOSE DAYS," SAYS THE LORD :
" I WILL PUT MY LAWS INTO THEIR MINDS
AND WILL WRITE THEM UPON THEIR HEARTS.
AND I WILL INDEED BE THEIR GOD
AND THEY SHALL BE MY PEOPLE.
AND THERE SHALL BE NO NEED FOR THEM TO TEACH 11
EACH ONE HIS FELLOW CITIZEN
AND EACH ONE HIS BROTHER, SAYING, KNOW THE LORD.
FOR ALL WILL KNOW ME
FROM THE LEAST OF THEM TO THE GREATEST ;
BECAUSE I WILL BE MERCIFUL TO THEIR WRONG- 12
DOINGS,
AND THEIR SINS I WILL REMEMBER NO LONGER " '
(Jer. xxxi. 31–34).

By using the words, ' a new Covenant,' He has made 13
the first one obsolete. But whatever is decaying and
showing signs of old age is not far from disappearing
altogether.

A Description of the earthly Sanctuary

Now even the first Covenant had regulations 1 **9**
for divine worship, and had also its sanctuary
—a sanctuary belonging to this material world.
A sacred tent was constructed—the outer one, 2
in which were the lamp and the table and the presented
loaves ; and this is called the Holy Place. And behind the 3
second veil was a sacred tent called the Holy of Holies.
This had a golden altar of incense, and the ark of the 4
Covenant completely covered with gold, and in it there
were a gold vase holding the manna, and Aaron's rod
which budded, and the tables of the Covenant. And above 5
the ark were the Cherubim of the glory overshadow-
ing the Mercy-seat. But I cannot now speak about
all these in detail.

The innermost Sanctuary of Heaven was not yet open

These arrangements having been completed, 6
the priests, when conducting the divine services, continually enter the outer tent. But 7
into the second the High Priest goes only on one
day of the year, and goes alone, taking with
him blood, which he offers both on his own behalf and on
account of the sins which the people have ignorantly committed. The lesson which the Holy Spirit teaches is 8
this—that the way into the true Holy Place is not yet open
so long as the outer tent still stands. And this is a figure 9
—for the time now present—answering to which both
gifts and sacrifices are offered, unable though they are
to give complete freedom from sin to him who worships.
For they relied only on meats and drinks and various 10
washings, regulations for the body, imposed until a time
of reformation.

But our great High Priest was already behind the Veil

But when Christ appeared as a High Priest 11
of the blessings that are to come through the
greater and more perfect Tabernacle (a tent
which has not been built with hands—that
is to say, which does not belong to this material

4. *Altar of incense*] So R.V. mg. ; Amer. R.V. text ; or ' censer ' (A.V. and R.V. text ; Amer. R.V. mg.) ; but there is no evidence that a golden censer was part of the furniture of the Holy of Holies ; and the writer could not have omitted to include in the furniture of the Tabernacle the far more important altar of incense ; see Exod. xxx. 1–10. It is true that the altar was not within the Holy of Holies, but its position before the second veil, and its importance in the ritual of the Day of Atonement (Lev. xvi. 12), may warrant the similar statement of 1 Kings vi. 22, that it ' *belonged* ' to the Oracle.

8. *Holy Place*] So in verses 12, 24, 25, evidently signifying in these instances the most Holy Place.

11. *That are to come*] v.l. ' that have (already) come.'

creation) and through His own blood, not through the blood 12
of goats and calves, He once for all entered the Holy
Place ; thus securing an eternal redemption.

The cleansing Power of Christ's Blood For if the blood of goats and bulls and the 13
ashes of a heifer sprinkling those who have
contracted defilement make them holy so as
to bring about ceremonial purity, how much 14
more certainly shall the blood of Christ, who
through eternal Spirit offered Himself to God, free from
blemish, purify your consciences from lifeless works to
serve the living God ?

The new Covenant owes its Validity to Christ's Death And because of this He is the mediator of 15
a new Covenant, in order that, since a life has
been given in atonement for the offences committed under the first Covenant, those who
have been called may receive the eternal
inheritance which has been promised to them. For where 16
there is a legal ' will,' there must also be a death brought
forward in evidence—the death of him who made it. And 17
a will is only of force in the case of a deceased person, being
never of any avail so long as he who made it lives.

Sin requires the Surrender of some Life Accordingly we find that the first Covenant 18
was not inaugurated without blood. Thus when 19
Moses had proclaimed to all the people every
commandment contained in the Law, he took
the blood of the calves and of the goats and with them water,
scarlet wool and hyssop, and sprinkled both the book itself
and all the people, saying, 20
' THIS IS THE BLOOD WHICH CONFIRMS THE COVENANT
THAT GOD HAS MADE BINDING UPON YOU ' (Exod. xxiv. 8).

In the same way he also sprinkled blood upon the 21
Tent of worship and upon all the vessels used in the

12. *The blood*] ' The Scriptural idea of blood is essentially an idea of life and not of
death ' (Westcott).
13. *Ceremonial purity*] Lit. ' the purity of the flesh '; not the act of purification,
but the state of legal cleanness which results.
14. In this verse occurs a textual tragedy. The greatest of all manuscripts, the
Codex Vaticanus (fourth century), comes to an end in the middle of the Greek verb
' purify,' and is wanting for the rest of the N.T.
Your] V.L. ' our.'
16, 17. *Legal ' will ' . . will*] In the N.T. this word is usually rendered ' Covenant,'
as in verses 15, 18. Here the mention of the inheritance, in verse 15, seems to remind
the writer of another meaning of the word ; and in verses 16, 17 he glides from the
one sense into the other, in order to suggest a fresh reason for the necessity of the death
of Christ. The attempt of some Commentators to retain throughout the passage
the one sense ' Covenant ' leads to forced interpretation. Verses 16, 17 are little
more than an aside, or passing illustration.
17. *Being never of any avail*] Or, ' doth it ever avail, &c. ? '

ministry. Indeed we may almost say that in obedience 22
to the Law everything is sprinkled with blood, and
that apart from the shedding of blood there is no
remission of sins.

Christ's one Sacrifice does away with Sin It was needful therefore that the copies of the 23
things in heaven should be cleansed in this way,
but that the heavenly things themselves should
be cleansed with more costly sacrifices. For 24
not into a Holy Place built by men's hands—a mere copy
of the reality—did Christ enter, but He entered heaven
itself, now to appear in the presence of God on our behalf.
Nor was it for the purpose of many times offering Himself 25
in sacrifice, as the High Priest enters the Holy Place,
year after year, taking with him blood not his own. In 26
that case Christ would have needed to suffer many times,
from the creation of the world onwards ; but as a matter
of fact He has appeared once for all, at the close of
the ages, in order to do away with sin by the sacrifice
of Himself.

Death is always followed by Judgement And since it is reserved for all mankind 27
once to die, and afterwards to be judged ;
so the Christ also, having been once offered in 28
sacrifice in order that He might bear the sins
of many, will appear a second time, separated from sin,
to those who are eagerly expecting Him, to make their
salvation complete.

The Mosaic Sacrifices were of small Value Now, since the Law exhibits only an outline of 1 **10**
the blessings to come and not a perfect repre-
sentation of the realities, the priests can never,
by repeating the same sacrifices which they
continually offer year after year, give complete freedom
from sin to those who draw near. For then would not the 2
sacrifices have ceased to be offered, because the consciences
of the worshippers, in that case cleansed once for all,
would no longer be burdened with sins ? But in those 3
sacrifices sins are recalled to memory year after year.
It is impossible for the blood of bulls and goats to take 4
away sins.

---

22. *Shedding*] Or ' outpouring ' ; but the stress of the whole argument is on the
death of the victim rather than on the sprinkling with the blood. The whole verse
refers to the requirements of the Levitical Law.
28. *Separated from sin*] Having done with sin for ever.
1. *The priests*] v.l. ' it.'

It is the
Surrender
of Man's
Will that
God wants That is why, when He comes into the world, 5
He says,

'SACRIFICE AND OFFERING THOU HAST NOT
DESIRED,
BUT A BODY THOU HAST PREPARED FOR ME.

IN WHOLE BURNT-OFFERINGS AND IN SIN-OFFERINGS THOU 6
HAST TAKEN NO PLEASURE.

THEN I SAID, "I AM COME—IN THE ROLL OF THE BOOK 7
IT IS WRITTEN CONCERNING ME—
TO DO THY WILL, O GOD "' (Ps. xl. 6–8).

After saying the words I have just quoted, ' SACRIFICES 8
AND OFFERINGS OT WHOLE BURNT-OFFERINGS AND SIN-OFFER-
INGS THOU HAST NOT DESIRED OR TAKEN PLEASURE IN ' (all
such being offered in obedience to the Law), He then adds, 9
' I AM COME TO DO THY WILL.' He does away with the first
in order to establish the second. It is through that divine 10
will that we have been set free from sin, through the offering of Jesus Christ as our sacrifice once for all.

Christ's one
Sacrifice is
of eternal
Efficacy And while every priest stands ministering, 11
day after day, and constantly offering the same
sacrifices—though these can never rid us of
our sins—this Priest, on the contrary, after 12
offering for sins a single sacrifice of perpetual efficacy,
took His seat at God's right hand, waiting from that time 13
onward until His enemies be put as a footstool under 14
His feet. By one single offering He has for ever perfected the sanctified.

The new
Covenant
is written
on Men's
Hearts And the Holy Spirit also gives us His testi- 15
mony ; for when He had said,

' " THIS IS THE COVENANT THAT I WILL MAKE 16
WITH THEM
AFTER THOSE DAYS," SAYS THE LORD :

" I WILL PUT MY LAWS UPON THEIR HEARTS
AND WILL WRITE THEM ON THEIR MINDS "' ;
He adds,   17

' AND THEIR SINS AND OFFENCES I WILL REMEMBER NO
LONGER ' (Jer. xxxi. 33, 34).

But where these have been forgiven no further offering 18
for sin is required.

---

5. *But a body*] A notable variation of the LXX from the Hebrew, ' Mine ears hast
Thou opened,' *i.e.* for the Psalmist to listen to the Divine voice. See Ps. xl. 6,
R.V. mg.

11. *Priest*] v.L. ' High Priest.'

Exhortations based on the new Covenant

The Privilege of entering God's immediate Presence — Since then, brethren, we have free access to 19 the Holy Place through the blood of Jesus, by 20 the new and living way which He opened up for us through the veil—that is to say, His flesh—and since we have a great Priest who has 21 authority over the house of God, let us draw near with 22 sincerity and unfaltering faith, our hearts sprinkled clean from consciences oppressed with sin, and our bodies bathed in pure water. Let us hold firmly to an unflinching 23 avowal of our hope, for He is faithful who gave us the promises. And let us bestow thought on one another 24 with a view to arousing one another to brotherly love and right conduct ; not neglecting—as some habitually do— 25 to meet together, but encouraging one another, and doing this all the more since you can see the Day of Christ drawing near.

The awful Guilt of deliberate Apostasy — For if we wilfully persist in sin after having 26 received the knowledge of the truth, there no longer remains in reserve any other sacrifice for sins. There remains nothing but a certain 27 awful expectation of judgement, and the fury of fire which is to consume the enemies of God. Any one who 28 bids defiance to the Law of Moses is put to death without mercy on the testimony of two or three witnesses. How 29 much severer punishment, think you, will he be held to deserve who has trampled under foot the Son of God, has not regarded as holy that Covenant-blood with which he was set free from sin, and has insulted the Spirit from whom comes grace ? For we know who it is that has 30 said, ' VENGEANCE BELONGS TO ME : I WILL PAY BACK ' (Deut. xxxii. 35) ; and again, ' THE LORD WILL BE HIS PEOPLE'S JUDGE ' (Deut. xxxii. 36). It is an awful thing 31 to fall into the hands of the living God.

A cheering Appeal to the Past — But recall to mind the days now past, when 32 on being first enlightened you went through a great conflict and many sufferings. This 33 was partly through allowing yourselves to be made a public spectacle amid reproaches and persecutions, and partly

---

20. He had to die, to remove, for Himself and for us, the barrier which shuts out from the Holy Place.
25. *Meet together*] Lit. ' not leaving in the lurch our own assembly ' ; perhaps by occasional attendance at other more attractive churches in the same city.

through coming forward to share the sufferings of those who were thus treated. For you not only showed sympathy 34 with those who were imprisoned, but you even submitted with joy when your property was taken from you, being well aware that you have in your own selves a more valuable possession and one which will remain.

The Nearness of Reward or Retribution — Therefore do not cast from you your confident 35 hope, for it will receive a vast reward. You 36 stand in need of patient endurance, so that, as the result of having done the will of God, you may receive the promised blessing. There is still but a 37 short time, and then

'THE COMING ONE WILL COME AND WILL NOT DELAY.

BUT IT IS BY FAITH THAT MY RIGHTEOUS SERVANT SHALL 38 LIVE;

AND IF HE SHRINKS BACK, MY SOUL TAKES NO PLEASURE IN HIM' (Hab. ii. 3, 4, LXX).

We however are not the ones to shrink back and perish, 39 but are of those who believe and so win possession of their souls.

Faith and its ancient Heroes

The Nature of Faith — Now faith is a confident assurance of that 1 **11** for which we hope, a conviction of the reality of things which we do not see. By it the 2 saints of old won God's approval. Through faith we under- 3 stand that the world came into being by the command of God, so that what is seen does not owe its existence to that which is visible (Gen. i. 1).

Abel — Through faith Abel offered to God a more 4 acceptable sacrifice than Cain, and through this faith he had witness borne to him that he was righteous, God bearing witness by accepting his gifts (Gen. iv. 4); and through his faith, though he is dead, he still speaks.

Enoch — Through faith Enoch was taken from the 5 earth so that he did not see death, and he could

34. *Your own selves*] Or 'that you yourselves have'; v.L. 'You have for yourselves.'

38. *Faith*] *i.e.* fidelity, stedfastness, nearer to the meaning of the Hebrew word than in Paul's use of the same passage (Rom. i. 17; Gal. iii. 11).

3. *Visible*] Cf. Rom. i. 20.

4. *More acceptable*] Lit. 'more abundant,' 'richer.' Why, the Genesis record does not say.

God bearing witness, &c.] The Greek text in this clause is uncertain; see R.V. mg.

Though he is dead, he still speaks] Or 'even after he was dead, he still spoke'; a reference to 'the voice of Abel's blood' (Gen. iv. 10). Cf. xii. 24.

not be found, because God took him; for before he was taken he had witness borne to him that he pleased God (Gen. v. 22, 24). Where there is no faith it is impossible 6 truly to please Him; for the man who draws near to God must believe that there is a God, and that He proves Himself a rewarder of those who seek after Him.

Noah Through faith Noah, being divinely warned 7 about things as yet unseen, reverently gave heed and built an ark for the safety of his family (Gen. vi. 13–22); and by this act he condemned the world, and became an heir of the righteousness which depends on faith.

Abraham Through faith Abraham, called to leave 8 home and go into a land which he was to receive for an inheritance, obeyed; and he went out, not knowing where he was going (Gen. xii. 1, 4). Through 9 faith he came and made his home for a time in a land which had been promised to him, as if in a foreign country, living in tents together with Isaac and Jacob, sharers with him in the same promise; for he was looking forward to 10 the city which has the foundations, whose architect and builder is God.

Sarah Through faith even Sarah herself received 11 strength to become a mother—although she was past the time of life for this—because she judged Him faithful who had given the promise (Gen. xxi. 1, 2). And 12 thus there sprang from one man, one practically dead, a nation like the stars of the sky in number, and like the sands on the sea shore which cannot be counted.

It was
Heaven that
they looked
forward to
All these died in the possession of faith. 13 They had not received the promised blessings, but had seen them from a distance and had greeted them, and had acknowledged themselves to be foreigners and strangers here on earth: men who 14 acknowledge this make it manifest that they are seeking elsewhere a country of their own. If they had cherished 15 the remembrance of the country they had left, they would have found an opportunity to return; but, as it 16 is, we see them eager for a better land, that is to say, a

5. *Pleased God*] The LXX translation of the Hebrew phrase, 'walked with God.'
11. *To become a mother*] Or ' to found a posterity.' The reference to Sarah's faith is difficult in view of Gen. xviii. 12. Perhaps the writer means ' in spite of her earlier incredulity.' The like incredulous laughter is attributed also to Abraham (Gen. xvii. 17), and when Isaac (*laughter*) is born, Sarah laughs in exultation over her neighbours (Gen. xxi. 6).

heavenly one. For this reason God is not ashamed to be called their God, for He has prepared a city for them.

The supreme Trial of Abraham's Faith

Through faith Abraham, when he was being 17 put to the test, offered up Isaac (Gen. xxii.). Yes, he who had joyfully welcomed the promises was ready to sacrifice his only son with regard 18 to whom he had been told, ' IT IS THROUGH ISAAC THAT YOUR POSTERITY SHALL BE TRACED ' (Gen. xxi. 12). For 19 he reckoned that God is even able to raise a man up from the dead, and, figuratively speaking, it was from the dead that he received Isaac back again.

Isaac, Jacob, Joseph

Through faith Isaac blessed Jacob and Esau, 20 even as to things yet to come (Gen. xxvii. 27-40). Through faith Jacob, when dying, 21 blessed each of Joseph's sons, and, bowing upon the top of his staff, worshipped God (Gen. xlviii. 8-20). Through 22 faith Joseph, when he was near his end, made mention of the exodus of the sons of Israel, and gave orders about his own body (Gen. l. 24, 25).

Amram and Jochebed

Through faith the child Moses was hid for 23 three months by his parents, because they saw his rare beauty ; and the king's edict had no terror for them (Exod. ii. 2).

Moses

Through faith Moses, when he grew to 24 manhood, refused to be known as Pharaoh's daughter's son, preferring rather to endure ill-treatment 25 along with the people of God than to enjoy the short-lived pleasures of sin ; because he deemed the reproaches 26 which he might meet with in the service of the Christ to be greater riches than all the treasures of Egypt ; for he fixed his gaze on the coming reward. Through faith he left 27 Egypt, not being afraid of the king's anger ; for he held

19. *Figuratively speaking*] Lit. ' in a parable,' since he did not actually die. Some suppose that the writer means ' he received him back again ' by what is a parable of the Resurrection of Christ.

21. *Top of his staff*] i.e. in the attitude of worship. The O.T. has ' upon the head of the bed,' the same word as ' staff ' in unpointed Hebrew. The incident (Gen. xlvii. 29-31) records a pledge exacted from Joseph, and is earlier than the blessing upon Joseph's sons, Ephraim and Manasseh (Gen. xlviii. 8-20).

22. *Made mention of*] Or, simply, ' thought of.'
His own body] Lit. ' his bones.'

23. *His rare beauty*] Lit. ' that the boy was beautiful.'

26. *The reproaches which he might meet with in the service of the Christ*] Lit. simply ' the reproach of the Christ.' Cf. xiii. 13.

27. *Not being afraid of*] The writer corrects the impression which the Genesis narrative might give, that the flight into Midian was prompted by fear. ' Not so,' he says ; ' it was due to the faith of Moses that God, in His own good time, had yet a mission for him to fulfil. It is the later exodus from Egypt which is attributed in verses 28, 29 to the like faith.'

on his course as seeing the unseen One (Exod. ii. 14, 15).
Through faith he instituted the Passover and the sprinkling 28
of the blood so that the destroyer of the firstborn might
not touch the Israelites (Exod. xii. 21, 22).

The
Israelites

Through faith they passed through the Red 29
Sea as though they were passing over dry land,
but the Egyptians, when they tried to do the
same, were swallowed up (Exod. xiv. 22–28).

Through faith the walls of Jericho fell to the ground after 30
being surrounded for seven days (Josh. vi. 20).

Rahab

Through faith Rahab the harlot did not 31
perish along with the disobedient, because she
had welcomed the spies and had sheltered them (Josh.
ii. 1 ; vi. 23).

Other
Heroes of
Faith

And why need I say more ? For time will 32
fail me if I tell the story of Gideon, Barak,
Samson, Jephthah, and of David and Samuel
and the Prophets ; men who, through faith, conquered 33
whole kingdoms, executed true justice, obtained promises,
shut the mouths of lions (Dan. vi. 22), quenched the power 34
of fire (Dan. iii.), escaped the edge of the sword, out of
weakness were made strong, became mighty in war, put to
flight foreign armies. Women received back their dear 35
ones alive from the dead (1 Kings xvii. 23 ; 2 Kings iv. 37) ;
and others were put to death with torture, refusing the
deliverance offered to them—that they might secure a better
resurrection. Others again were tested by cruel mockery 36
and by scourging ; yes, and by chains and imprisonment.
They were stoned (2 Chron. xxiv. 20, 21), they were sawn 37
asunder, they were tried by temptation, they were killed
with the sword (1 Kings xix. 14 ; Jer. xxvi. 20–23). They
went from place to place in sheepskins or goatskins, enduring want, oppression, and cruelty—men of whom the 38
world was not worthy : they wandered across deserts

32. *Gideon*] Judges vi. 11.
Barak] Judges iv. 6.
Samson] Judges xiii. 24, &c.
Jephthah] Judges xi. 1–xii. 7.
David] 1 Sam. xvi. 1, &c.
Samuel] 1 Sam. i. 20, &c.
35. *Put to death*] Probably by beating. In illustration of this verse see 2 Macc. vi.
18–31 ; vii. 9, 11, 14, 29, 36.
37. *Sawn asunder*] The traditional fate of Isaiah.
Tried by temptation] So general an assertion seems out of place in this context of
specific persecutions. A slight emendation of the Greek verb gives the meaning ' they
were burned ' ; or the word may be an intrusion into the text from a marginal note.

and mountains, or hid themselves in caves and in holes in the ground.

Apart from Christ and His Church their Blessedness was incomplete   And although by their faith they all won 39 God's approval, none of them received the fulfilment of His great promise ; for God 40 had provided for us something better, so that apart from us they were not to be perfected.

Renewed Exhortations

Jesus Himself the chief Hero of Faith   Therefore, surrounded as we are by such a 1 **12** vast cloud of witnesses, let us fling aside every encumbrance and the sin that so readily entangles our feet. And let us run with patient endurance the race that lies before us, simply fixing our 2 gaze upon Jesus, the Leader and Perfecter of faith. He, for the sake of the joy which lay before Him, patiently endured the cross, looking with contempt upon its shame, and is now seated at the right hand of the throne of God.

Our Sorrows are far less than His were   Therefore, if you would escape becoming 3 weary and faint-hearted, compare your own sufferings with those of Him who endured such hostility directed against Him by sinners. In 4 your struggle against sin you have not yet resisted to the shedding of blood ; and you have quite forgotten the 5 encouraging words which are addressed to you as sons,

' MY SON, DO NOT THINK LIGHTLY OF THE LORD'S DIS-
    CIPLINE,
AND DO NOT FAINT WHEN HE CORRECTS YOU ;
FOR THOSE WHOM THE LORD LOVES HE DISCIPLINES :   6
AND HE SCOURGES EVERY SON WHOM HE ACCEPTS '
             (Prov. iii. 11, 12 ; Job v. 17).

Pain is an Evidence of God's Love   The sufferings that you are enduring are for 7 your discipline. God is dealing with you as sons ; for what son is there whom his father

1. *Witnesses*] Not merely spectators, but such spectators as were qualified by their own experience to judge of our faith.
2. *The Leader . . faith*] See ii. 10, n.
3. *Against Him*] v.L. ' against themselves.' Cf. Num. xvi. 38 (' sinners against their own souls ').
4. *The shedding of blood*] Lit. ' resisted unto blood.' If this means that no martyrdoms had yet occurred, the address of the Epistle either to Jerusalem or Rome would be excluded. And the cause of martyrdom was hardly resistance against sin. Probably the expression is metaphorical, ' Your moral conflict has not yet been in deadly earnest. No blood has been drawn in this spiritual fight against sin.'

does not discipline ?   And if you are left without discipline, 8
of which all have had a share, that shows that you are
bastards, and not sons.

Besides this, our earthly fathers used to 9
Our Father brings Nobility of Character out of Pain discipline us and we treated them with respect, and shall we not still more be submissive to the Father of our spirits, and live ?   They dis- 10
ciplined us for a few years according as they
thought fit ; but He does it for our certain good, in order
that we may become sharers in His own holy character.
Now, at the time, discipline seems to be a matter not 11
for joy, but for grief ; yet it afterwards yields to those
who have passed through its training the peace of a
righteous life.

Therefore strengthen the drooping hands 12
' Be cheerful, peaceable, and always on your Guard ' and paralysed knees, and make straight paths 13
for your feet, so that what is lame may not be
put entirely out of joint but may rather be
restored.   Ever strive for peace with all men, 14
and for that sanctification apart from which no one
will see the Lord.   Carefully see to it that there be 15
no one falling short of the grace of God ; that no root
bearing bitter fruit spring up and cause trouble among
you, and through it the whole brotherhood be defiled ; and 16
that there be no fornicator, and no ungodly person like
Esau, who, in return for a single meal, parted with his
birthright.   For you know that even afterwards, when 17
he wished to secure the blessing, he was rejected ; he
found no opportunity for repentance, though he sought
the blessing earnestly with tears.

The Difference between the Inauguration of the earthly and the heavenly Kingdoms of God

No, you have not come near to something 18
The Contrast between Sinai and Mount Zion material all ablaze with fire, and to gloom and darkness and storm and trumpet-blast and the 19
sound of words—a sound such that those who
heard it entreated that no further word should be added.

9. *Our earthly, &c.*] Lit. ' we had the fathers of our flesh (as) chastisers.'
15. *The whole brotherhood*] Lit. ' the many.'
17. *The blessing*] Lit. ' it,' possibly, though not probably, referring to repentance.
18. *Material*] Lit. ' which could be touched.'

For they could not endure the order which had been given, 20 'EVEN A BEAST, IF IT TOUCHES THE MOUNTAIN, SHALL BE STONED TO DEATH ' (Exod. xix. 12, 13) ; and so terrible was 21 the scene that Moses said, 'I TREMBLE WITH FEAR ' (Deut. ix. 19). No ! you have come to Mount Zion, and to the 22 city of the living God, the heavenly Jerusalem, to countless hosts of angels, to the festal gathering and Church of the first- 23 born, whose names are recorded in heaven, and to the God of all as Judge, and to the spirits of righteous men made perfect, and to Jesus the mediator of a new Covenant, and 24 to the sprinkled blood which speaks in more gracious tones than that of Abel.

The Necessity for scrupulous Obedience See to it that you do not refuse to listen to 25 Him who is speaking to you. For if they of old did not escape unpunished when they refused to listen to Him who spoke on earth, much less shall we escape who turn a deaf ear to Him who now speaks from heaven. His voice then shook the earth, 26 but now we have His promise, ' YET AGAIN I WILL, ONCE FOR ALL, CAUSE NOT ONLY THE EARTH TO TREMBLE, BUT HEAVEN ALSO ' (Hag. ii. 6). Here the words ' Yet again, 27 once for all ' denote the removal of the things which can be shaken—created things—in order that the things which cannot be shaken may remain.

A Reason for Gratitude Therefore, receiving a kingdom which 28 cannot be shaken, let us cherish thankfulness, so that we may offer to God an acceptable service with godly reverence and awe. For our God is 29 indeed a consuming fire (Deut. iv. 24).

Final Exhortations

Brotherly Love and Purity urged Let brotherly love continue. Do not neglect 1,2 **13** to show hospitality to strangers ; for, by being hospitable, some, without knowing it, have had angels as their guests (Gen. xviii., xix. ; Judges xiii.). Remember prisoners, as if you were in prison with them ; 3 and remember those suffering ill-treatment, for you yourselves also are still in the body. Let marriage be held in 4 honour among all, and let the marriage bed be unpolluted ; fornicators and adulterers God will judge.

Your lives should be untainted by love for money. Be 5
content with what you have ; for God Himself
'Be
contented. has said,
GOD will   ' I WILL NEVER LET YOU GO :
never fail   I WILL NEVER FORSAKE YOU '
you '
     (Gen. xxviii. 15 ; Deut. xxxi. 6–8 ; Josh. i. 5).
So that we fearlessly say, 6
' THE LORD IS MY HELPER ; I WILL NOT BE AFRAID :
WHAT CAN MAN DO TO ME ? ' (Ps. cxviii. 6).

Christ and   Remember your former leaders—it was they 7
Christian who brought you the word of God. Bear in
Truth do mind how they ended their lives, and imitate
not change their faith. Jesus Christ is the same yesterday 8
and to-day—yes, and for ever. Do not be drawn aside by 9
all sorts of strange teaching ; for it is well to have the
heart strengthened by grace, and not by meats, from
which those who place dependence upon them have
derived no benefit.

Our Altar,   We Christians have an altar from which 10
Sacrifice, those who serve the Tabernacle have no right
and true to eat. For the bodies of those animals of 11
Home which the blood is carried by the High Priest
into the Holy Place as an offering for sin are burned outside the camp (Lev. xvi.). And for this reason Jesus also, 12
in order, by His own blood, to set the people free from sin,
suffered outside the gate. Therefore let us go to Him 13
outside the camp, bearing the same reproach as He. For 14
we have no abiding city here, but we seek the city which
is to come.

(vv. 8–14.) A short and tentative paraphrase of this very difficult and much discussed passage is all that can be here attempted.
  ' Jesus does not change, and in His teaching there is no place for " meats." Do
we thereby suffer loss ? On the contrary, we surpass the Jewish ritual. There was
one supreme yearly sacrifice of which the priests might not, indeed could not, be,
partake ; for it was burned outside the camp. So our Sacrifice is one with which no
" meats " can be associated. As the bullock and the goat for the sin-offering, after
the presentation of their blood in the Holy of Holies, were burned outside the camp,
so Jesus suffered outside the gate, that He might present His atoning blood in the
heavenly Holy of Holies. Let us, then, gladly go forth to Him, away from the
camp of Judaism, and, disdaining participation in any actual sacrificial meal, feed on
Him in our hearts by faith, with thanksgiving.'
  9. *Meats*] Apparently less general than in ix. 10, where the ritual distinction of
clean and unclean would be included. Here the reference seems to be limited to
the sacrificial meats of verse 10, by partaking of which the heart of the worshipper was
supposed to be strengthened.
  10. *Altar*] Perhaps specifically the Cross. Or the thought may be more general :
' We Christians, it is true, are without an actual altar, but we possess in the Cross all
that the altar and its sacrifices stood for, and far more.'
  12. *Outside the gate*] Cf. John xix. 20, ' near the city.'

' Give Thanks in Words and by Unselfishness ' Through Him, then, let us continually lay on 15 the altar a sacrifice of praise to God, that is, the fruit of lips that give thanks to His Name. And do not forget to be kind and liberal ; for 16 with sacrifices of that sort God is greatly pleased.

' Be loyal to your religious Leaders ' Obey your leaders and be submissive to them, 17 because they are keeping watch over your souls as those who will have to give account ; so that they may do this with joy and not with lamentation—for that would be of no advantage to you.

A Request for Prayer Pray for us ; for we are sure that we have 18 clear consciences, and we desire to live honourably in every respect. I specially urge 19 this upon you all the more, that I may the sooner be restored to you.

A farewell Blessing Now may the God of peace who brought up 20 from the dead the great Shepherd of the sheep with the blood of the eternal Covenant, even Jesus our Lord, equip you with every good for the 21 doing of His will, effecting in us that which is pleasing in His sight through Jesus Christ. To Him be the glory for ever and ever. Amen.

Conclusion Bear with me, brethren, when I thus exhort 22 you ; for, in fact, it is but a short letter that I have written to you.

You will rejoice to hear that our brother Timothy has 23 been set at liberty. If he comes soon, I will see you with him. Greet all your leaders and all the saints. The 24 brethren from Italy send you greetings.

Grace be with you all. Amen. 25

15. *Fruit of lips*] Cf. Hos. xiv. 2, ' the calves of our lips.'
23. *You will rejoice to hear*] Lit. ' know ' (imperative) ; or, possibly, ' You know.'
24. *The brethren from Italy send*] Probably this implies that the writer is out of Italy, accompanied by Italian Christians who send greetings to their friends at home, presumably in Rome. But the Greek phrase may mean, ' the brethren send you greetings from Italy,' in which case Rome would be, not the destination, but the origin of the Epistle.

THE CATHOLIC EPISTLES

The New Testament contains a group of seven Epistles, to five of which—James, 1 and 2 Peter, 1 John, and Jude—in A.V. and R.V. the title ' general,' the English rendering of the Greek ' catholic,' is prefixed. The remaining two, 2 and 3 John, naturally link on to 1 John.

Eusebius (c. A.D. 310) is the first to speak of the seven so-called Catholic Epistles. The meaning and history of the term are obscure. Probably the term was suggested by the very wide address of each of the seven, except 2 and 3 John. They are also marked off from Paul and *Hebrews* as less personal and less creative in theological thought. Most of them had to struggle hard and long for admission into the New Testament Canon, and they still raise difficult critical problems.

THE EPISTLE OF JAMES

The author describes himself as 'James, a servant of God, and of the Lord Jesus Christ.' As James, the son of Zebedee, had met an early death (Acts xii. 1), the only N.T. James to write with apostolic authority would be James, the Lord's brother, head of the Church in Jerusalem, who had now learnt to think of himself, not as brother of Jesus, but as 'a servant of the Lord Jesus Christ.' (Similarly another brother of the four (Mark vi. 3) styles himself, if the Epistle of Jude is his, as 'a servant of Jesus Christ and brother of James.') This authorship is confirmed by the strikingly Jewish character of the Epistle. Its ethical teaching is finely Christian ; many of its sayings sound like words of Christ ; but from so prominent a leader of the Church, the distinctive Christian note is strangely lacking— not Jesus but Job is chosen as type of patient endurance (v. 11 ; contrast 1 Peter ii. 21–25). The name of Jesus Christ occurs only twice (i. 1 ; ii. 1) ; and, in the latter case, occasions Greek all but impossible of translation. An attractive hypothesis of the late Professor J. H. Moulton deserves attention as solving conspicuous difficulties of this unique writing. He suggests that the Epistle was addressed not to Christians, but to non-Christian Jews, by one whom they would respect. To name 'Jesus' would be to prejudice his message ; but he conveys much of His teaching to make its own appeal. The two passages (i. 1 and ii. 1), would then originally have run, in Old Testament phraseology, 'James, a servant of God.' 'Hold the faith of the Lord of glory.'

The question of date is too intricate to be here discussed.

THE EPISTLE OF JAMES

1 1

Greeting   James, a servant of God and of the Lord
Jesus Christ, to the twelve tribes of the
Dispersion: greeting.

The Testing   Reckon it nothing but joy, my brethren, 2
of Faith and whenever you find yourselves hedged in by
Character various trials. Be assured that the testing of 3
your faith leads to power of endurance. Only let endurance 4
do its full work, so that you may become perfect and
complete, deficient in nothing. If any one of you is 5
Wisdom to deficient in wisdom, let him ask God, who
be sought gives with open hand to all men and without
from God upbraiding; and it will be given him. But let 6
him ask in faith and have no doubts; for he who has doubts is
like the surge of the sea, driven by the wind and tossed about.
A person of that sort must not expect to receive anything 7
from the Lord, being a man of two minds, undecided in 8
every step he takes.

Outward Cir-   Let a brother in humble life rejoice when 9
cumstances he is promoted; but a rich man should rejoice 10
do not last in being brought low, for like flowers of the field
he will pass away. The sun rises with his scorching heat 11
and dries up the herbage, so that its flowers drop off and the
beauty of its appearance perishes; and in the same way rich
men in the midst of their occupations will fade away.

Sin: its   Blessed is he who endures trials; for when he 12
real Origin has stood the test, he shall gain the crown of life
and final which the Lord has promised to those who love
Harvest Him. Let no one say when passing through trial, 13
'My temptation is from God'; for God is incapable of being
tempted by evil, and He Himself tempts no one. But when 14
a man is tempted, it is his own passions that carry him

---

1. *The twelve tribes, &c.*] Apparently this includes not simply Jewish Christians,
but Christians in general, as the true people of God.
2. *Trials*] Or ' temptations.' Cf. Heb. ii. 18, n.
13. *Trial*] Or ' temptation '; and so seven times in verses 2–14.

away and serve as a bait. Then the passion conceives, and 15 becomes the parent of sin ; and sin, when fully matured, gives birth to death.

Only what is good comes from God Do not be deceived, my beloved brethren. 16 Every good gift and every perfect boon is from 17 above, and comes down from the Father, who is the source of all Light. In Him there is no variation nor the shadow of change. In accordance with His will He made us 18 His children through the word of the truth, so that we might, in a sense, be the first fruits of the things which He has created.

Self-control in Speech and Temper urged You know this, my beloved brethren. But 19 let every one be quick to hear, slow to speak, and slow to be angry. A man's anger does 20 not accomplish God's righteousness. Ridding 21 yourselves, therefore, of all that is vile and of the overflow of malice, welcome in a humble spirit the word implanted within you, which is able to save your souls.

The Necessity and Blessed- ness of Obedience But prove yourselves obedient to the word, 22 and do not be mere hearers of it, deluding your- selves. If any one listens but does not obey, 23 he is like a man who carefully looks at his own face in a mirror ; but although he looks carefully 24 at himself, he goes away and immediately forgets what sort of man he was. He however who looks closely into the perfect 25 law of freedom and continues looking, being not a hearer who forgets, but an obedient doer, will in the act of his obedience be blessed.

Brotherly Love and Purity of Life are essential If a man thinks that he is religious, although 26 he does not curb his tongue but deceives his own heart, his religion is worthless. The religion 27 which is pure and stainless in the sight of our God and Father is to visit orphans and widows in their time of trouble, and to keep one's own self unspotted from the world.

' Do not court the Rich and slight the Poor ' My brethren, while holding to your faith 1 **2** in our Lord Jesus Christ who is the Glory, do not exhibit partiality. Suppose a man 2 comes into one of your meetings wearing gold rings and fine clothes, and there also comes in a poor man wearing shabby clothes, and you pay regard to the 3

15. *The passion*] Whatever passion it may be.
26. *Thinks that he is*] Or ' is regarded as.'

one who wears the fine clothes, and say, ' Sit here ; this is a good place ' ; while to the poor man you say, ' Stand there, or sit on the floor at my feet '—is it not plain that in your hearts you have little faith, seeing that you have become judges full of wrong thoughts ? 4

Some poor Men are rich. Some rich Men are wicked Listen, my beloved brethren. Has not God chosen those whom the world regards as poor to be rich in faith and heirs of the Kingdom which He has promised to those that love Him ? 5

But you have put dishonour upon the poor man. Yet is it not the rich who grind you down ? Are not they the people who drag you into the law courts ? the people who speak evil of the noble Name by which you are called ? If, however, you perform the royal law, in obedience to the Scripture ' YOU ARE TO LOVE YOUR NEIGHBOUR AS YOU LOVE YOURSELF ' (Lev. xix. 18), you act rightly. But if you show partiality you commit sin, and are convicted by the law as offenders. 6 7 8 9

The Law demands perfect Obedience A man who keeps the law as a whole, but fails in a single point, has become guilty of violating all. For He who said, ' DO NOT COMMIT ADULTERY,' also said, ' DO NOT COMMIT MURDER ' (Exod. xx. 13, 14 ; Deut. v. 17, 18) ; and if you are a murderer, although not an adulterer, you have become an offender against the law. Speak and act as those should who are to be judged by the law of freedom. For he who shows no mercy will incur judgement without mercy ; but mercy triumphs over judgement. 10 11 12 13

A lifeless Faith is useless What good is it, my brethren, if a man professes to have faith, and yet his actions do not correspond ? Can such faith save him ? Suppose a brother and a sister are poorly clad or lack daily food, and one of you says to them, ' Fare you well ; keep yourselves warm and well fed,' and yet you do not supply their bodily needs ; what is the use of that ? So also faith, if it is unaccompanied by obedience, is dead in itself. 14 15 16 17

Even evil Spirits ' believe ' Nay, some one will say, ' You have faith, I have actions : prove to me your faith apart from corresponding actions and I will prove mine to you by my actions. You believe that God is one, 18 19

4. *You have little faith*] Or, perhaps, ' are divided in your own minds ' ; or (less probably) ' make distinctions among yourselves.'
19. *God is one*] v.L. ' there is one God.'

and you are quite right : evil spirits also believe this, and shudder.'

Abraham's Faith, and Rahab's But, idle boaster, are you willing to be taught 20 that faith apart from obedience is worthless ? Was it not because of his actions that Abraham 21 our father was declared to be righteous when he had offered up his son Isaac upon the altar ? You notice that his faith 22 was co-operating with his actions, and that by his actions his faith was perfected ; and the Scripture was fulfilled 23 which says, ' AND ABRAHAM BELIEVED GOD, AND HIS FAITH WAS CREDITED TO HIM AS RIGHTEOUSNESS ' (Gen. xv. 6), and he received the name of ' God's friend ' (2 Chron. xx. 7 ; Isa. xli. 8). You see that it is because of actions that a 24 man is pronounced righteous, and not simply because of faith. In the same way also was not the harlot Rahab 25 declared to be righteous because of her actions when she welcomed the spies and sent them off another way ? For just as a human body without a spirit is lifeless, so also 26 faith is lifeless without obedience.

The urgent Need for Self-control in Speech Not many of you, my brethren, should 1 **3** become teachers, knowing as you do that we teachers shall undergo severer judgement ; for 2 all of us often stumble and fall. If any one never stumbles in speech, he is a perfect man, able to curb even his whole nature. Now if we put the horses' 3 bits into their mouths to make them obey us, we can turn them wholly round. Look, again, at the ships : great 4 as they are, and driven along by strong gales, yet they can be steered with a very small rudder in whatever direction the will of the man at the helm determines. In the same 5 way the tongue is an insignificant part of the body, but utters great boasts. Remember how a mere spark may set a vast forest in flames.

The Mischief the Tongue can do And the tongue is a fire. The tongue shows 6 itself the world of wickedness within us, soils our whole nature, and sets the whole round of our lives on fire, being itself set on fire by Gehenna. All 7 kinds of beasts and birds, reptiles and fishes, can be and have been tamed by human nature. But the tongue no man can 8 tame : it is a restless mischief, full of deadly poison. With 9

22. *You*] Singular, as addressed to some individual. Not so in verse 24.
5. *Forest*] Or ' mass of fuel.'
6. *Our lives*] Or perhaps ' creation.'

it we bless the Lord and Father, and with it we curse men, who are made in God's likeness. Out of the same mouth 10 there proceed blessing and cursing. My brethren, this ought not to be. Does a fountain send forth fresh water 11 and bitter from the same opening? Can a fig-tree, my 12 brethren, yield olives, or a vine yield figs? No; nor can salt water yield sweet water.

True Wisdom shows itself in noble Living Which of you is a wise and well-instructed 13 man? Let him by a right life show his conduct to be guided by a wise gentleness. But if in 14 your hearts you have bitter envy and rivalry, do not speak boastfully and falsely, in defiance of the truth. That is not the wisdom which comes down 15 from above : it belongs to earth, to the unspiritual nature, and to evil spirits. For where envy and rivalry are, there 16 also are unrest and every vile deed. The wisdom from 17 above is first of all pure, then peaceful, courteous, compliant, full of compassion and kind actions, free from vacillation and from insincerity. And righteousness is the 18 fruit of the seed that is sown in peace by the peacemakers.

The real Cause of Strife and of War What causes wars and contentions among 1 **4** you? Is it not the passions which are ever at war in your natures? You covet things and 2 cannot get them ; you commit murder ; you are envious and cannot gain your end ; you fight and make war. You have not, because you do not pray ; you ask 3 and yet do not receive, because you pray wrongly, your object being to waste on your pleasures what you acquire.

We must definitely choose between God and the World You wantons, do you not know that friendship 4 with the world means enmity to God? Therefore whoever is bent on being friendly with the world makes himself an enemy to God. Or do 5 you suppose that it is to no purpose that the Scripture says, ' The Spirit which He has caused to dwell in us yearns jealously over us ' ? And He gives more abundant 6 grace. Hence He says, ' GOD SETS HIMSELF AGAINST THE HAUGHTY, BUT TO THE LOWLY HE GIVES GRACE ' (Prov. iii. 34). Submit therefore to God : resist the devil, and he will flee 7

5. *The Spirit . . yearns jealously*] Other possible renderings are (1) He longs jealously for the Spirit which He made to dwell in us ; (2) Do you think that the Scripture speaks to no purpose? Does the Spirit which He made to dwell in us long jealously ?

He has caused to dwell] v.L. ' has dwelt.'

Over us] Implied, but not expressed in the Greek.

from you. Draw near to God, and He will draw near to 8 you. Cleanse your hands, you sinners, and make your hearts pure, you double-minded. Afflict yourselves and 9 mourn and weep; let your laughter be turned into grief, and your gladness into shame. Humble yourselves in the 10 presence of the Lord, and He will exalt you.

All evil Speaking is forbidden Do not speak evil of one another, brethren. 11 The man who speaks evil of a brother or judges his brother speaks evil of the Law and judges the Law. And if you judge the Law, you are no longer one who obeys the Law, but a judge. The only Lawgiver and 12 Judge is He who is able to save or to destroy. Who are you to be judging your neighbour?

The awful Uncertainty of Life Come, you who say, 'To-day or to-morrow 13 we will go to this or that city, and spend a year there and carry on a successful business,' when 14 you do not know what will happen to-morrow. For what is your life? Why, it is but a mist, which appears for a short time and then disappears. Instead of that you ought to say, 15 'If it is the Lord's will, we shall live and do this or that.' But, as it is, you boast in your presumption: all such boast-16 ing is evil. If, then, a man knows what is right and does not 17 do it, he commits a sin.

Ill-gotten Gains bring a Curse Come now, you rich men, weep and howl for 1 **5** the woes which will soon be upon you. Your 2 treasures are rotten, and your clothes are moth-eaten; your gold and silver are covered with rust, and their 3 rust will give evidence against you, and will eat your flesh like fire. You have hoarded up wealth in these last days. See, the pay of the labourers who have reaped your fields— 4 pay which you have kept back—is crying out; and the outcries of your harvesters have entered into the ears of the Lord of the hosts of heaven. Here on earth you have lived 5 self-indulgent and profligate lives. You have gratified your appetite with a day of slaughter! You have condemned—you 6 have murdered—the righteous man: he offers no resistance.

The Nearness of Christ's Return should inspire Fortitude Be patient therefore, brethren, until the 7 Coming of the Lord. Notice how a farmer awaits a precious crop! He is patient over it till it has received the early and the latter rain. So you also must be patient, keeping up your 8 courage; for the Coming of the Lord is at hand. Do not 9 cry out against one another, brethren, lest you come under judgement. See, the Judge is standing at the door. In 10 illustration, brethren, of persecution patiently endured, take the Prophets who have spoken as messengers from the Lord. Remember that we call those blessed who endured. You 11 have also heard of Job's endurance, and have seen the issue of the Lord's dealings with him—how full of tenderness and pity the Lord is.

Simple Truthfulness of Speech But above all things, my brethren, do not 12 swear, either by heaven or by the earth, or with any other oath. Let your ' yes ' be simply ' yes,' and your ' no ' be simply ' no '; that you may not come under condemnation.

What to do when sad, happy, ill Is any one of you suffering ? Let him pray. 13 Is any one in good spirits ? Let him sing praise. Is any one ill ? Let him send for the Elders 14 of the Church, and let them pray over him, anointing him with oil in the name of the Lord. And the prayer of faith 15 will restore the sick man, and the Lord will raise him up ; and if he has committed sins, they shall be forgiven him.

Confession and Intercession to be mutual Therefore confess your sins to one another, 16 and pray for one another, so that you may be cured. Powerful is the heartfelt supplication of a righteous man. Elijah was a man with 17 a nature similar to ours, and he earnestly prayed that there might be no rain : and no rain fell on the land for three years and six months. Again he prayed, and the sky 18 gave rain and the land yielded its crops (1 Kings xvii., xviii.).

The Blessedness of saving even one from Sin and Death My brethren, if one of you strays from the 19 truth and some one brings him back, let him 20 know that he who brings a sinner back from his wrong road will save the man's soul from death and throw a veil over a multitude of sins.

16. *Heartfelt*] Or ' inwardly prompted,' by the Holy Spirit ; or, perhaps, ' when it shows its activity.'
20. *Let him know*] v.L. ' be assured.'

THE FIRST EPISTLE OF PETER

Both James and Peter addressed their readers as those of the Dispersion, a Jewish term transferred by them to scattered communities of Christians, as God's true Israel. This letter is practically one to all the Churches of Asia Minor. The order of the provinces named in i. 1 perhaps indicates the route which would be taken by its bearers. It was almost certainly written from Rome (the ' Babylon ' of v. 13). These Asiatic Christians were exposed to persecution, probably at the hands of the State (i. 6, 7; ii. 12; iii. 14–17; iv. 12–19).

The letter is mainly a letter of encouragement to stand fast. The Petrine authorship, which there is really no serious reason to doubt, would best fit in with the persecution of Nero (A.D. 64), in which both Peter and Paul probably suffered martyrdom. It has been doubted, however, whether this attack upon the Christian Church spread from Rome to the provinces, as it did in the later persecution under Domitian; and some think that the expression ' suffer as a Christian ' (iv. 16) even points to the time of Trajan, when the mere profession of Christianity was made a capital offence. The argument is inconclusive. If Peter and Paul were at this time together in Rome, the letter, in Peter's name, to the Pauline Churches of Asia would come as a vivid and stimulating witness to unity in loyalty to Christ.

THE FIRST EPISTLE OF PETER

Greeting

Peter, an Apostle of Jesus Christ, to 1 God's elect of the Dispersion in Pontus, Galatia, Cappadocia, Asia, and Bithynia, chosen in 2 accordance with the foreknowledge of God the Father, through the sanctifying work of the Spirit, with a view to obedience and to sprinkling with the blood of Jesus Christ: may more and more grace and peace be granted to you.

Thanksgiving for the Hope and Promise of Heaven

Blessed be the God and Father of our Lord 3 Jesus Christ, who in His great mercy has begotten us anew to a living hope through the resurrection of Jesus Christ from the dead, to 4 an inheritance imperishable, undefiled, and unfading, reserved in heaven for you, who are kept by God's 5 power through your faith for a salvation that is ready to be unveiled at the end of the world. Exult in the 6

The earthly Cross tests and perfects Faith

prospect of this, even if now, for a short time, you are compelled to sorrow amid various trials. These happen in order that the testing of your 7 faith—being more precious than that of gold, which perishes but yet is proved by fire—may be found to result in praise and glory and honour at the revelation of Jesus Christ. You love Him, though you have never seen Him. In Him, 8 though at present you do not see Him, you yet trust, and triumph with a joy unspeakable and crowned with glory, while you are securing as the outcome of your faith the 9 salvation of your souls.

About that salvation Prophets made earnest inquiry and 10 search, and they spoke beforehand of the grace which was to come to you. They investigated the time which the 11

1. v.L. omits ' Asia.'   Another v.L. omits ' and Bithynia.'
6. *Exult*] Or ' you exult.'
For a short time] Or ' to some extent.'
7. *Precious*] ' It is not "the testing" which is precious, though the literal construction at first sight seems to be this, but the faith itself ' (Alford). For ' than that of gold ' is lit. ' than gold.'
8. *You have never seen Him*] v.L. ' not knowing Him.'

Spirit of Christ within them kept indicating, or its characteristics, when He solemnly made known beforehand the

Prophets and Angels keenly interested in our Salvation sufferings that were destined for Christ and the glories which would follow. To them it was 12 revealed that they were serving not themselves but you, in predicting the things which have now been announced to you by those who, through the Holy Spirit sent from heaven, brought you the gospel. Angels long to see into these things.

Alertness, Self-control, Obedience, Consecration Therefore prepare your minds, and fix your 13 hopes calmly and unfalteringly upon the boon that is soon to be yours at the revelation of Jesus Christ. And, like obedient children, do 14 not shape your lives by the cravings which were formerly yours in the time of your ignorance, but, in imitation of 15 the holy One who has called you, do you also be holy in all your behaviour; since it is written, ' You are to 16 be holy, because I am holy ' (Lev. xi. 44 ; xix. 2).

'Redeemed at infinite Cost, love and fear God' And if you address as your Father the One 17 who judges impartially in accordance with each man's actions, then spend in fear the time of your stay, for you know that it was not with 18 perishable wealth, silver or gold, that you were ransomed from the futile habits of life inherited from your forefathers, but with the precious blood of 19 Christ—as of an unblemished and spotless lamb. He was pre-destined indeed to this work, even before the creation 20 of the world, but has been manifested in these last days for your sake ; through Him you are faithful to God, who raised 21 Him from the dead and gave Him glory, so that your faith and hope are resting upon God.

The Gospel gives Birth to a Life of brotherly Love Now that, through your obedience to the 22 truth, you have prepared your souls by purification for sincere brotherly love, you must love one another heartily and fervently. For 23 you have been begotten again by God's living and enduring word not from perishable, but imperishable seed. For

24

' All mankind is like grass,
    And all their beauty is like its flowers.
    The grass dries up,

21. *Your faith and hope, &c.*] Or ' your faith is also hope towards God.'

And its flowers drop off;
But the word of the Lord remains for ever'   25
                   (Isa. xl. 6–8).
And that means the message which has been proclaimed
to you in the gospel.

How brotherly Love must manifest itself

Rid yourselves therefore of all ill-will and all 1 **2**
deceitfulness, of insincerity and envy, and of all
evil speaking. Thirst, like newly-born infants, 2
for pure milk for the soul, that by it you may
grow up to salvation; if you have had any 3
taste of the goodness of the Lord.

Christ a Cornerstone, or a Rock to stumble over

Come to Him, the living Stone, rejected 4
indeed by men, but in God's esteem chosen
and valuable. And yourselves also like living 5
stones be built up into a spiritual house, as a
holy priesthood to offer spiritual sacrifices
acceptable to God through Jesus Christ. For it is con- 6
tained in Scripture,
  'See, I am placing in Zion a Cornerstone, chosen
    and valuable,
  And he whose faith rests on Him shall never be
    ashamed' (Isa. xxviii. 16).
You believers, therefore, feel His value; but for unbelievers 7
—'A Stone which the builders rejected has been made
the Cornerstone' (Ps. cxviii. 22), and 'A Stone to trip 8
over, and a Rock to stumble at' (Isa. viii. 14). They trip
over it because they are disobedient to God's message, and

Consecrated Christians are the true Israel

to this they were destined. But you are a 9
chosen race, a royal priesthood, a holy nation,
a people belonging to God, that you may make
known the perfections of Him who called you
out of darkness into His marvellous light. Once you were 10
not a people, but now you are the people of God. Once
you had not found mercy, but now you have.

The Foe within us is to be strenuously resisted

Beloved, I entreat you as strangers and 11
foreigners to restrain the cravings of your lower
natures which wage war upon the soul. Live 12
honourable lives among the Gentiles, in order
that, although they speak against you as evil-
doers, from your good deeds they may witness your character,
and may glorify God on the day of scrutiny.

11. *Strangers*] *i.e.* in this (evil) world.

The Duty of Obedience to earthly Rulers Submit, for the Lord's sake, to every 13 authority set up by man, whether it be to the Emperor as supreme, or to governors as sent 14 by him for the punishment of evil-doers and the encouragement of well-doers. For it is God's will that 15 by doing well you should thus silence the ignorant talk of foolish persons. Be free men, and yet do not make your 16 freedom a screen for base conduct, but be God's servants. Honour every one. Love the brotherhood, fear God, 17 honour the Emperor.

Servants were to be faithful, even if ill-treated Servants, be submissive to your masters, 18 with the utmost respect—not only if they are kind and thoughtful, but also if they are unreasonable. For it is acceptable with God, if, 19 from a sense of duty to Him, a man bears wrong when treated unjustly. If you do wrong and receive a blow 20 for it, what credit is there in your bearing it patiently? But if when you do right and suffer for it you bear it patiently, this is acceptable with God.

The Example of Jesus, who bore our Sins It is to this you were called; because Christ 21 also suffered on your behalf, leaving you an example so that you should follow in His steps. He never sinned, and no guile was ever heard 22 from His mouth. When He was reviled, He did not answer 23 with reviling; when He suffered, He did not threaten, but left His cause in the hands of the righteous Judge. Our 24 sins He Himself bore in His own body on the cross, so that we, being alienated from our sins, may live righteous lives. By His wounds you have been healed. For you were astray 25 like lost sheep, but now you have come back to the Shepherd and Guardian of your souls.

Wives were to live nobly and dress simply Married women, in the same way, be submis- 1 **3** sive to your husbands, so that even if some of them disbelieve the word, they may, apart from the word, be won over by the daily life of their wives, after seeing your daily lives so chaste and reverent. 2 Yours ought not to be the outward adornment of plaiting 3 the hair, putting on jewels of gold, or wearing various

14. *Him*] *i.e.* the Emperor. Or ' Him,' *i.e.* God.
15. *Silence*] Lit. ' muzzle ' or ' gag.'
25. *Guardian*] Lit. ' Overseer ' ; it is the word from which ' bishop ' is derived.
1. *Be submissive*] Lit. ' being submissive.' Cf. ii. 18.
Disbelieve] Or ' are disobedient to.' But cf. iv. 17.
Apart from the word] Or ' without a word being spoken.'

dresses, but an inward beauty of nature, the imperishable 4
ornament of a gentle and peaceful spirit, which is indeed
precious in the sight of God. For this is how of old the 5
holy women who set their hopes upon God used to adorn
themselves, being submissive to their husbands. Thus 6
Sarah obeyed Abraham, calling him master. And you have
become Sarah's children if you do right and permit nothing
whatever to terrify you.

Husbands were to manifest tender Thoughtfulness
Husbands, in the same way, live with your 7
wives with a clear recognition of the fact that
they are weaker than you. Yet, since you are
heirs with them of God's free gift of Life, treat
them with honour ; so that your prayers may
not be hindered.

Unity, mutual Affection, Humility, and a forgiving Spirit urged
In conclusion, all of you should be har- 8
monious, sympathetic, kind to the brethren,
tender-hearted, lowly-minded, not requiting 9
evil with evil nor abuse with abuse, but, on
the contrary, giving a blessing, because a
blessing is what you have been called by God
to inherit. For 10

' HE WHO WISHES TO ENJOY LIFE
AND SEE HAPPY DAYS—
LET HIM RESTRAIN HIS TONGUE FROM EVIL,
AND HIS LIPS FROM DECEITFUL WORDS ;
LET HIM TURN FROM EVIL, AND DO GOOD ; 11
LET HIM SEEK PEACE AND PURSUE IT.
FOR THE EYES OF THE LORD ARE UPON THE RIGHTEOUS, 12
AND HIS EARS ARE OPEN TO THEIR SUPPLICATION ;
BUT THE FACE OF THE LORD IS SET AGAINST EVILDOERS '
(Ps. xxxiv. 12–16).

The happy Results of Enthusiasm for Righteousness
And who will harm you, if you show your- 13
selves zealous for what is good ? But even if 14
you suffer for righteousness' sake, you are to be
envied. So do not be alarmed by their threats,
nor troubled ; but in your hearts consecrate 15
Christ as Lord, being always ready to make your defence

---

4. *An inward beauty of nature*] Lit. ' the hidden man of the heart.'
7. *With a clear recognition . . that they are weaker than you*] Lit. ' according to knowledge, as with the weaker vessel (or sex).'
8. *Sympathetic*] Whether in sorrow or in joy. Cf. Rom. xii. 15.
10, 11. *Let him restrain . . turn from . . do . . seek . . pursue*] All aorists impera-tive, enjoining what is to be done promptly, and once for all.
14. *Their threats*] Lit. ' their fear.'

to any one who asks from you a reason for the hope which you cherish. Yet argue gently and cautiously, keeping 16 your consciences clean, so that, when you are spoken against, those who slander your good Christian lives may be put to shame.

Blessings which followed the Sufferings of the sinless Jesus — For it is better that you should suffer for doing 17 right, if such be God's will, than for doing evil ; because Christ also once for all died for sins, 18 the innocent One for the guilty many, in order to bring us to God. He was put to death in the flesh, but made alive in the spirit, in which He also went 19 and preached to the spirits that were in prison, who in 20 former times had been disobedient, when God's longsuffering patiently waited in the days of Noah during the building of the Ark, in which a few persons—eight in number—were brought safely through the water. And, corresponding to 21 that figure, baptism now saves you—not the washing off of material defilement, but the craving of a good conscience after God—through the resurrection of Jesus Christ, who is at God's right hand—He has gone into 22 heaven, and angels, authorities, and powers have been made subject to Him.

Christ's Example should inspire Fortitude and Purity of Life — Since, then, Christ has suffered in the flesh, 1 **4** you also must arm yourselves with the same disposition—because he who has suffered in the flesh has done with sin—that henceforth 2 you may spend the rest of your earthly lives, governed not by human passions, but by the will of God. For you have given time enough in the past 3 to the things which the Gentiles delight in—pursuing, as you did, a course of licence, debauchery, hard drinking, revelry, carousing, and unholy idolatry. In regard to this 4 they are astonished that you do not run into the same excess of profligacy as they do ; and they abuse you. But they 5 will have to give account to Him who is ready to pronounce judgement on the living and the dead. For it is to this end 6 that the gospel was proclaimed even to dead men, that they may be judged as men in the body, but may live as God lives in the spirit.

18. *Died*] v.l. ' suffered.'
21. *The craving, &c.*] Or ' the demand for a good conscience towards God.'
1. *Suffered*] v.l. ' suffered for us.'

'The End is at Hand. Live accordingly'

But the end of all things is at hand : therefore 7 be sober-minded and temperate, that you may give yourselves to prayer. Above all love one 8 another fervently, for love veils a multitude of faults. Extend ungrudging hospitality towards one another. 9 Whatever be the gifts which each has received, you must 10 use them for one another's benefit, as good stewards of God's manifold kindness. If any one preaches, let it be 11 as uttering God's oracles ; if any one renders a service, let it be in the strength which God supplies ; so that in everything glory may be given to God through Jesus Christ, to whom belong the glory and the might for ever and ever. Amen.

To suffer for Christ is a glorious Privilege

Beloved, do not be surprised at the fiery 12 ordeal coming among you to put you to the test—as though some exceptional thing were happening to you. No, in the degree that you 13 share in the sufferings of Christ, rejoice, so that at the unveiling of His glory you may also rejoice with exultation. Blessed are you if you are reproached for bearing the name 14 of Christ ; for the Spirit of glory—even the Spirit of God —is resting upon you. But let not one of you suffer as 15 a murderer or a thief or an evil-doer, or as a busybody. If however any one suffers because he is a Christian, let him 16 not be ashamed, but let him glorify God for that name.

The Awful-ness of the Judgement which was now beginning

For the time has come for judgement to 17 begin at the house of God ; and if it begins with us, what will be the end of those who reject God's gospel ? And if it is difficult for a 18 righteous man to be saved, what will become of irreligious men and sinners ?

So then, let those who suffer in accordance with the 19 will of God entrust their souls in well-doing to a faith-ful Creator.

Pastors urged to live exemplary Lives

Now I exhort the Elders among you—I who 1 **5** am their fellow Elder and an eye-witness of the sufferings of Christ, and also a sharer in the glory which is to be revealed : be shepherds 2

14. *Even the Spirit of God*] v.l. ' even the Spirit of power and of God.' Another v.l. adds at the end of the verse, ' So far as they are concerned He is spoken against, but so far as you are concerned He is glorified.'
16. *Christian*] This word only occurs here and in Acts xi. 26, xxvi. 28.
For that name] v.l. ' in that respect.'

of God's flock which is among you. Exercise the oversight not reluctantly but voluntarily, in accordance with the will of God; not for base gain but readily; not lording it over 3 your charges but proving yourselves patterns to the flock. And then, when the chief Shepherd appears, you will 4 receive the never-withering wreath of glory.

Young Men exhorted to Humility and quiet Faith In the same way you younger men must 5 submit to your elders; and all of you must gird yourselves with humility towards one another, for God sets Himself against the proud, but gives grace to the humble. Humble yourselves there- 6 fore under the mighty hand of God, so that at the right time He may set you on high. Throw the whole of your 7 anxiety upon Him, because He cares for you.

'Be on the alert. Strenuously resist the Tempter' Be restrained, and be on the alert. Your 8 enemy, the Devil, is going about like a roaring lion to see whom he can devour. Withstand 9 him, firm in your faith; knowing that the same sufferings are imposed on your brethren in all the world. And the God of all grace, who has called you 10 to share His eternal glory, through Christ, after you have suffered for a short time, will Himself make you perfect, firm, and strong. His is the power for ever and ever! Amen. 11

Farewell Greetings I have written you this short letter by the 12 hand of Silvanus, our faithful brother—for such I regard him—in order to encourage you, and to bear witness that such is the true grace of God. In it stand fast. The Church in Babylon, elect like yourselves, 13 sends greetings, and so does Mark my son. Greet one 14 another with a kiss of love. Peace be with all of you who are in Christ.

2. *Exercise the oversight*] v.L. omits these words (it is only one word in the Greek). Lit. ' being bishops,' an indication that in the early Church the office of bishop was identical with that of elder or presbyter. Cf. Phil. i. 1, n.; 1 Tim. iii. 2, n.

3. *Your charges*] Lit. ' the portions ' (of the Lord's flock), over each of which an overseer presided.

5. *Gird yourselves*] The Greek word denotes ' as with the apron of one who waits upon others.' See especially John xiii. 3-5; Phil. ii. 6, 7.

9. *That the same, &c.*] Or ' how to undertake the same burden of suffering as your brethren,' &c.

11. *Power*] Or ' dominion.'

12. *Such is, &c.*] Lit. ' this,' *i.e.* the grace which has been illustrated throughout the letter.

13. *The Church*] Lit. ' She.'

Babylon] Either (1) the literal Babylon, on the Euphrates; or (2) Rome; or—if the Babylon of Rev. xiv. 8; xvi. 19; xviii. was Jerusalem—(3) Jerusalem. But see Preface, p. 568.

THE SECOND EPISTLE OF PETER

By general consent of scholars this is the most doubtful book of the New Testament. In this judgement modern criticism endorses the verdict of the early Church. Only after long suspicion and rejection did it win entrance, at the close of the fourth century, into the New Testament Canon.

It presents itself as an Epistle of Peter, witness of the Transfiguration (i. 16–18), and author of an earlier Epistle (iii. 1); but the style and substance differ markedly from 1 Peter.

Chapter ii. incorporates virtually the whole Epistle of Jude (for the priority of Jude hardly admits of reasonable doubt), and the reference to a collection of Paul's Epistles already ranking as Scriptures (iii. 15, 16) certainly points to a post-apostolic date. Yet many of the sayings of the letter have become Christian watchwords, of which no absurd charge of ' forgery ' can deprive the Church. The literary conscience of the second century was not that of the twentieth, and, authorship apart,—

> ' All who speak truth to me commissioned are ;
> All who love God are in my Church embraced.'

THE SECOND EPISTLE OF PETER

Greeting **Simon Peter, a servant and Apostle of Jesus 1 1
Christ**, to those to whom there has been allotted
a faith of equal privilege with ours through the righteousness
of our God and of our Saviour Jesus Christ: may more 2
and more grace and peace be granted to you in the knowledge of God and of Jesus our Lord, seeing that His 3
divine power has given us all things that are needful for
life and godliness, through the knowledge of Him who
called us by His own glory and perfection.

'Rely upon
God's
Promises
and grow
more and
more
Christlike'

Thereby He has granted us His exceeding 4
great and precious promises, in order that
through them you may become sharers in the
divine nature, having escaped the corruption
which is now in the world by reason of earthly
cravings. And for this very cause—adding, 5
besides, all earnestness—with your faith, exhibit also a noble
character: with a noble character, knowledge; with know- 6
ledge, self-control; with self-control, endurance; with
endurance, godliness; with godliness, love to the brethren; 7
and with love to the brethren, love. If these things exist in 8
you, and increase, they prevent your being either idle or
unfruitful in advancing towards a full knowledge of our
Lord Jesus Christ. For the man in whom they are lacking 9
is blind, short-sighted, forgetful that he has been cleansed
from his old sins.

For this reason, brethren, be all the more in earnest 10

---

1. *Simon*] Lit. 'Symeon.'
Of our God and of our Saviour] Or, perhaps, 'of our God and Saviour.'
(vv. 3, 4.) These two verses ought perhaps to be connected with verse 5, the paragraph beginning at verse 3: 'Seeing that . . . . glory and perfection, whereby He has granted . . . . through earthly cravings, even for this very cause,' etc.
5. *With*] Lit. 'in.' So throughout verses 6, 7.
Exhibit] Lit. 'supply' (as your contribution to the glory of God and the honour of His Church).
A noble character] Lit. 'virtue'; a general word, inclusive of every moral excellence; so in the Greek philosophers, mostly or always. The primary meaning ('manhood,' 'courage,' 'prowess') does not suit any of the five passages in which the word occurs in the N.T. See verse 3; Phil. iv. 8; 1 Pet. ii. 9.

to make certain of your calling and election; for, so
long as you practise these things, you will
never stumble. And so the admission into 11
the eternal Kingdom of our Lord and Saviour
Jesus Christ shall be richly accorded to you.

The Need for persistent Faithfulness

For this reason I shall always persist in re- 12
minding you of these things, although you know
them and are stedfast believers in the truth
which you possess. But I think it right, so long 13
as I sojourn in this body, to arouse you by such
reminders. For I know that soon my body must be laid 14
aside, as indeed our Lord Jesus Christ revealed to me.
So on every occasion I will also do my best to enable you 15
to recall these things after my departure.

Peter's Earnestness in view of his approaching Death

For when we made known to you the power 16
and Coming of our Lord Jesus Christ, we were
not following cleverly devised legends, but we had
been eye-witnesses of His majesty. He received 17
honour and glory from God the Father, and out
of the wondrous glory words such as these were
conveyed to Him, 'This is My beloved Son, in whom I take
delight.' And we ourselves heard these words conveyed 18
from heaven, when we were with Him on the holy mountain.

Christ's Transfiguration a Pledge and Foretaste of His Advent

So we have the word of prophecy confirmed; 19
to which you do well to pay attention—as to a
lamp shining in a dark place—until day dawns
and the morning star rises in your hearts. But, 20
above all, remember that no prophecy in Scrip-
ture is a matter of private interpretation; for never did any 21
prophecy come by human will, but men sent by God spoke
as they were impelled by the Holy Spirit.

The ancient Scriptures also testify to His glorious Advent

But there were also false prophets among the 1 **2**
people, as there will be teachers of falsehood
among you also, who will cunningly introduce
fatal heresies, disowning even the Lord who
has redeemed them, and bringing on themselves
swift destruction. And in their immoral ways 2
they will have many disciples, through whom the true
way will be brought into disrepute. Greedy for riches, they 3
will trade on you with their canting talk. From of old their

False Teachers were coming, foredoomed to Destruction

---

10. *Make certain of*] v.l. ' make sure by means of your noble actions.'
21. *Men sent by God*] Lit. ' men from God.' v.l. ' holy men of God.'

condemnation has not been in abeyance, and their destruction has not been slumbering.

Ancient Examples of Retribution and Deliverance For if God did not spare angels when they 4 had sinned, but hurled them down to Tartarus and consigned them to caves of darkness, keeping them in reserve for judgement ; and if He 5 did not spare the ancient world, although He preserved Noah, that herald of righteousness, with seven others, when He brought a deluge on the world of the ungodly ; if He reduced to ashes the cities of Sodom and 6 Gomorrah, and condemned them to overthrow, making them an example to people who should thereafter live godless lives, but rescued righteous Lot, who was sore distressed by 7 the dissolute conduct of lawless men (for their lawless deeds 8 were torture, day after day, to the righteous soul of that righteous man—all that he saw and heard in their midst), then the Lord knows how to rescue godly men from 9 temptation, and on the other hand how to keep the unrighteous under punishment for the Day of Judgement, and especially those who are abandoned to sensuality— 10 craving for polluted things, and scorning control.

A Description of the False Teachers. Their sure Ruin Audacious and self-willed, they do not tremble when speaking evil of glorious beings ; while angels, though greater than they in might 11 and power, do not bring any railing accusation against these in the presence of the Lord. But 12 these men, like brute beasts, born with such natural instincts that they are only to be captured or destroyed, in their ignorance are abusive, and in their corruption they will perish receiving injury in retribution for the injuries 13 they do. They reckon it pleasure to roll in luxury in broad daylight. They are spots and blemishes, while feeding luxuriously at their love-feasts, as they banquet with you. Their eyes are full of adultery, eyes such as cannot 14 cease from sin. These men set traps for unstedfast souls, their own hearts being trained in covetousness—an accursed

3. *Has not been slumbering*] Lit. ' not lying idle.'
4. *Caves*] v.L. ' bonds ' or ' chains.'
11. Cf. Jude 9.
In the presence of the Lord] v.L. omits.
13. *Receiving injury, &c.*] v.L. 'receiving retribution for,' &c.
Love-feasts] v.L. ' delusions ' or ' deceits ' ; their love-feasts being delusions and nothing more.
14. *Their eyes are full of adultery*] Lit. ' having eyes full of an adulteress.'
Covetousness] Or, possibly, ' seduction.' Cf. Eph. v. 3.

race ! Forsaking the straight road, they have gone astray, 15
having followed in the steps of Balaam, the son of Beor, who
preferred the wages of unrighteousness. He however was re- 16
buked for his transgression: a dumb beast of burden spoke
with a human voice and checked the madness of the prophet.

They corrupt and enslave their fellow Men These people are wells without water, mists 17
driven along by a storm, men for whom the
densest darkness has been reserved. For, 18
while they pour out their frivolous and arrogant
talk, they use earthly cravings—various kinds of immorality
—as a trap for men who are just escaping from those who
live in error. And they promise them freedom, although 19
they are themselves the slaves of corruption. For a man
is the slave of anything by which he has been overcome.

Backsliders: their Misery and Degradation For if, after escaping from the pollutions of 20
the world through knowledge of our Lord and
Saviour Jesus Christ, people are once more
entangled in these pollutions and are overcome,
their last state is worse than their first. It would have 21
been better for them not to have known the way of
righteousness, than, after knowing it, to turn back from
the holy commandment which was delivered to them.
Their case is that described in the true proverb, ' A DOG 22
RETURNS TO WHAT HE HAS VOMITED ' (Prov. xxvi. 11), and
' A sow when washed falls to rolling in filth.'

The Object of this Letter This is the second letter which I have now 1 **3**
written to you, beloved. In both I seek to
revive in your sincere minds certain memories,
so that you may recall the words spoken beforehand by the 2
holy Prophets, and the commandment of our Lord and
Saviour given through your Apostles.

Men would come ridiculing Warnings as to Judgement First, remember that, in the last days, men 3
will come with their mockery—men governed
by their own passions, and asking, 4
' Where is His promised Return ? For from
the time our fathers fell asleep all things continue as they have been ever since the creation.'

---

15. *Forsaking*] v.l. ' Having forsaken.'
19. *They promise them freedom*] The Gnostics asserted that they were free to live
as they pleased.
Anything by which] Or ' any one by whom.'
22. *In filth*] ' Gnostic teachers said that they " might wallow in the mire as
much as they pleased," and that—such was their spiritual virtue—they could not be
perverted by it any more than gold by mud ' (Wordsworth).

They are wilfully blind to the fact that there were 5
heavens of old, and an earth composed from water and
by water, by the word of God ; and that, by means of 6
these, the then existing world was overwhelmed with
water and perished. But the present heavens and 7
earth are, by the same word, stored up, reserved for
fire against a day of judgement and of destruction
for the ungodly.

The Day of Christ. Its Certainty and sudden Coming
But this one thing, beloved, you must not 8
forget. With the Lord one day is as a
thousand years, and a thousand years are as
one day. The Lord is not slow about His 9
promise, as some men count slowness. He
bears patiently with you, His desire being that no one
should perish but that all should come to repentance.
But the day of the Lord will come like a thief, on which the 10
heavens will pass away with a rush and a roar, the elements
be destroyed in the fierce heat, and the earth and all its
works will vanish.

'Live nobly in preparation for that Day'
Since all these things are thus on the verge 11
of dissolution, what sort of men ought you
to be in all holy living and godly conduct,
expecting and helping to hasten the coming 12
of the day of God, by reason of which the heavens,
all ablaze, will be dissolved, and the elements will
burn and melt ? But in accordance with His promise 13
we expect new heavens and a new earth, in which
righteousness dwells.

Absolute Perfection to be striven for
Therefore, beloved, as you are expecting 14
this, earnestly seek to be found by Him,
free from blemish or reproach, in peace. And 15
regard the forbearance of our Lord as salvation,
as our beloved brother Paul also has written to you in
virtue of the wisdom granted to him. That is what he 16
says in all his letters, when speaking in them of these
things. In those letters there are some statements hard
to understand, which ill-taught and unstable people
pervert, just as they do the rest of the Scriptures, to
their own ruin.

10. *Vanish*] v.L. ' be burnt up.'
11. *Since*] v.L. ' Since then,' omitting ' thus.'
13. *New heavens, &c.*] To this ' reconstitution of all things ' Peter possibly alludes
in Acts iii. 21.

You, therefore, beloved, being warned beforehand, must 17
be on your guard so as not to be led away by
the errors of lawless men nor fall from your own
stedfastness. But grow in the grace and know- 18
ledge of our Lord and Saviour Jesus Christ.
To Him be the glory, both now and to the day of
Eternity !

A final
Warning
and
Exhortation

THE FIRST EPISTLE OF JOHN

This Epistle has from early times been confidently ascribed to the Apostle John ; and it may be here assumed that it comes from the author of the Fourth Gospel.

The Epistolary form is wanting, but there are signs of intimate relationship between the writer and his readers. It is not simply a homily or pastoral to the Church at large.

No very definite plan can be traced : an old man's musings take shape in affectionate counsel and warning. But two themes stand out in prominence :—

(1) Insistence upon the real humanity of Jesus Christ. The early Gnostic heresy of Docetism, which made Him only seeming man, and separated the redeeming work of the Son of God from the earthly life of Jesus, echoes in the opening words of chapter i., and is directly attacked at ii. 22 ; iv. 2, 3 (see R.V. mg.) ; iv. 15 ; v. 1, 5, 6. There is also repeated warning that these intellectual subtleties lead to a light estimate of sin. This apologetic motive is also apparent in the Fourth Gospel, which is at once an interpretation of the Christ and a human life of Jesus. The historical framework is fundamental to the writer's purpose ; it is this which he fills with the glory of the Eternal Word, the Incarnate Son of God.

(2) Only love is true churchmanship ; for 'God is love' (iv. 8, 16).

THE FIRST EPISTLE OF JOHN

Introduction

Eternal Life has been manifested in Jesus What was from the beginning, what we have 1 **1** listened to, and have seen with our own eyes, what we once beheld and our own hands handled concerning the Word of Life—the Life 2 was manifested, and we have seen and bear witness, and we declare unto you the Life eternal which was with the Father and was manifested to us—what we have seen and listened 3 to we announce to you also, in order that you also may have fellowship with us, our fellowship being with the Father and with His Son Jesus Christ. We write these things 4 in order that our joy may be made complete.

Some vivid Contrasts

'Live in the Light and confess your Sins' This is the Message which we have heard 5 from Him and report to you—God is Light, and in Him there is no darkness. If, while we 6 are living in darkness, we profess to have fellowship with Him, we speak falsely and do not carry out the truth. But if we live in the light as He is in the light, we 7 have fellowship with one another, and the blood of Jesus, His Son, cleanses us from all sin. If we claim to be free 8 from sin, we deceive ourselves and the truth is not in us. If we confess our sins, He is so faithful and just that He 9 forgives us our sins and cleanses us from all unrighteousness. If we deny that we have sinned, we make Him a liar, and 10 His word is not in us.

The Saviour of the World. Only the Obedient really know Him My dear children, I write thus to you that 1 **2** you may not sin. If any one does sin, we have an Advocate with the Father—Jesus Christ the righteous ; and He is Himself the propitiation 2 for our sins, and not for ours only, but also for the sins of the whole world. And by this we may know 3

4. *Our*] v.l. ' your.'
5. *Message*] The word is found elsewhere in the N.T. only in iii. 11.
2. *The sins of*] The English idiom requires the insertion of these words.

that we know Him—if we obey His commands. He who 4
professes to know Him, and does not obey His commands,
is a liar, and the truth is not in him. But whoever obeys 5
His word, in him love for God has reached perfection. By
this we can know that we are in Him. The man who 6
professes to continue in Him is himself also bound to
live as He lived.

Those who
disobey the
Law of
brotherly
Love are in
Darkness
Beloved, it is no new command that I am 7
writing you, but an old command which you
have had from the beginning. By the old
command I mean the word which you have
heard. And yet I am writing you a new com- 8
mand, for such it really is, so far as both He and you are
concerned ; because the darkness is passing away and the
true light is already shining. Any one who professes to be 9
in the light and hates his brother is still in darkness. He 10
who loves his brother continues in the light, and there is no
stumbling-block in him. But he who hates his brother is in 11
darkness and walks in darkness ; and he does not know
where he is going, because the darkness has blinded his eyes.

Reasons
why this
Letter was
written
I am writing to you, dear children, because 12
your sins are forgiven you for His sake. I am 13
writing to you, fathers, because you know Him
who has existed from the beginning. I am
writing to you, young men, because you have overcome
the Evil one.

I have written to you, children, because you know the
Father. I have written to you, fathers, because you know 14
Him who has existed from the beginning. I have written
to you, young men, because you are strong and God's
word continues to be in you, and you have overcome
the evil one.

Love for this
passing
World
cannot co-
exist with
Love for God
Love not the world, nor the things in the 15
world. If any one loves the world, there is no
love in him for the Father. For all that is in 16
the world—the desire of the flesh, the desire
of the eyes, the show and pride of life—
comes not from the Father, but from the world. And 17
the world, with its desire, is passing away, but he who does
God's will continues for ever.

---

8. Or perhaps ' a new command,' *i.e.* ' what is realized in him and you.'
10. *No stumbling-block in him*] Whether to himself or to others.

Warnings against Backsliders and false Teachers

Apostasy a Sign that the End of the Age was at Hand Dear children, the last hour has come ; and 18 as you have heard that antichrist is coming, so even now many antichrists have appeared. By this we may know that the last hour has come. They have gone forth from our midst, 19 but they did not belong to us ; for had they belonged to us, they would have remained with us. But they left us that it might be manifest that none of them belongs to us. As for you, you have an anointing from the holy One 20 and you all have knowledge. I have written to you, 21 not because you are ignorant of the truth, but because you do know it, and that no lie comes from the truth.

The Denial or Acknowledgement of Jesus as the Christ Who is the liar but he who denies that Jesus 22 is the Christ ? He who disowns the Father and the Son is the antichrist. No one who 23 disowns the Son has the Father. He who acknowledges the Son has also the Father. For 24 yourselves, let the teaching which you have heard from the beginning abide within you. If that teaching does abide within you, you also will abide in the Son and in the Father. And this is the promise which He Himself has 25 given us—the life eternal.

'Taught by the Spirit, maintain Union with Christ' I have thus written to you concerning those 26 who try to lead you astray. But the anointing 27 which you yourselves received from Him remains within you, and you have no need for any one to teach you ; but as His anointing gives you instruction in all things—and is true and is no falsehood—you are abiding in Him, even as it has taught you to do.

And now, dear children, abide in Him ; so that, if He 28 appears, we may have confidence, and may not shrink away in shame from Him at His Coming. Since you 29 know that He is righteous, be assured that every one also who acts righteously is a child of His.

20. *You all*] v.l. ' have all knowledge.'
27. *You are abiding*] Or (imperative) ' abide.'
28. *If He*] Or, perhaps, ' when He.'

God's Children and the Devil's Children

God's wondrous Love inspires with Hope and makes us pure
See what love the Father has bestowed upon 1 **3** us, that we should be called God's children : and that is what we are. For this reason the world does not recognize us, because it did not recognize Him. Beloved, we are now God's 2 children, but what we are to be has not yet been manifested. We know that if He appears we shall be like Him, because we shall see Him as He is. And any one who has this hope 3 fixed on Him, purifies himself as He is pure.

Sin cannot co-exist with Union with Christ
Every one who commits sin also commits 4 lawlessness ; for sin is lawlessness. And you 5 know that He appeared in order to take away sins ; and in Him there is no sin. No one who 6 abides in Him sins : no one who sins has seen Him or knows Him.

Righteousness impossible apart from a righteous Life
Dear children, let no one lead you astray. 7 The man who acts righteously is righteous, just as He is righteous. He who commits 8 sin belongs to the devil, because the devil has been a sinner from the beginning. The Son of God appeared for the purpose of undoing the work of the devil.

Sin cannot co-exist with divine Sonship
No one who is a child of God commits sin. 9 A divine germ remains in him, and he cannot sin—because he is a child of God. By this 10 are distinguished God's children and the devil's children : no one who fails to act righteously is a child of God, nor he who does not love his brother. For this is the 11 message you have heard from the beginning—that we are to love one another. We are not to resemble Cain, who 12 was a child of the evil one and killed his brother. And why did he kill him ? Because his own actions were wicked and his brother's righteous.

Love for Man, as Man, a Sign that we already have eternal Life
Do not be surprised, brethren, if the world 13 hates you. We know that we have passed out 14 of death into life—because we love the brotherhood. He who does not love abides in death. Every one who hates his brother is a 15 murderer ; and you know that no murderer has eternal life abiding in him.

2. *If He*] Or ' when He.' Cf. ii. 28.
5. *To take away*] The same verb as in John i. 29.
9. *A divine germ, &c.*] Or possibly ' God's offspring remains in him.'

True Love is defined, and measured, by Christ's Cross We know what love is—because He laid down 16 His life for us ; and we ought to lay down our lives for our brethren. But if any one has this 17 world's goods and sees that his brother is in need, and yet closes his heart against him— how can love for God continue in him ? Dear children, 18 let us not love in word only and with the lips, but in deed and truth.

Obedience brings us Peace and renders Prayer effective In this way we shall come to know that 19 we are loyal to the truth, and shall reassure our hearts in His presence in whatever matters our 20 hearts condemn us—because God is greater than our hearts and knows everything. Be- 21 loved, if our hearts do not condemn us, we address God with confidence ; and whatever we ask for we obtain from 22 Him, because we obey His commands and do what is pleasing in His sight. And this is His command—that we 23 are to believe in the name of His Son Jesus Christ and love one another, as He has commanded us to do. The man 24 who obeys His commands abides in God, and God in him ; and through His Spirit which He has given us we can know that He abides in us.

The Conflict between Truth and Falsehood

'Discriminate between true and false Teaching' Beloved, do not believe every spirit, but test 1 **4** the spirits to see whether they are from God ; for many false prophets have gone out into the world. The test by which you may recognize 2 the Spirit of God is that every spirit which acknowledges that Jesus Christ has come in the flesh is from God, and that no spirit is from God which does not 3 acknowledge this about Jesus. Such is the spirit of the antichrist ; you have heard that it is to come, and now it is already in the world.

God's Spirit delivers us from false Teaching You, dear children, are God's children, and 4 have overcome them ; for greater is He who is in you than he who is in the world. They 5 are the world's children, and so their language is that of the world, and the world listens to them. We 6

23. *Believe, &c.*] 'Equivalent to "believe as true the message which the name conveys"' (Westcott).

are God's children. The man who knows God listens to us, but he who is not a child of God does not listen to us. By this test we can distinguish the Spirit of truth from the spirit of error.

The Duty of Brotherly Love

There is no divine Sonship apart from brotherly Love Beloved, let us love one another; for love 7 comes from God, and every one who loves is a child of God and knows God. He who does 8 not love has no knowledge of God; because God is love. God's love for us has been mani- 9 fested in that God has sent His only Son into the world so that we may have life through Him. Here is the love— 10 not that we loved God, but that He loved us and sent His Son to be a propitiation for our sins.

Union with God is impossible apart from brotherly Love Beloved, if God so loved us, we also ought 11 to love one another. No one has ever seen 12 God. If we love one another, God abides in us, and His love is perfect in us. We can 13 know that we abide in Him and He in us, by the fact that He has given us a portion of His Spirit. And we have seen and bear witness that the Father has 14 sent the Son to be the Saviour of the world. Whoever 15 acknowledges that Jesus is the Son of God—God abides in him, and he abides in God. And we know and we 16 trust the love which God has for us.

God's great Love inspires us with Confidence and Love God is love, and he who abides in love abides in God, and God abides in him. In 17 this will love in its perfection be displayed in us, in our being fearless on the day of judgement; because what He is, that we also are in this world. Love has in it no fear; but perfect love 18 drives away fear, because fear involves punishment, and if a man fears, there is something imperfect in his love. We 19 love because He first loved us. If any one says that he 20 loves God, while he hates his brother, he is a liar; for he who does not love his brother whom he has seen, cannot love God whom he has not seen. And this command 21 we have from Him, that he who loves God must love his brother also.

9. *Only*] Lit. ' only begotten.'
20. *Cannot*] v.l. ' how can he ? '

Sure Proofs of divine Sonship follow Faith Every one who believes that Jesus is the 1 Christ is a child of God ; and every one who loves the Father loves Him who is the Father's Child. The fact that we love God, and obey 2 His commands, is a proof to us that we love God's children. Love for God means obedience to His commands ; and 3 His commands are not irksome. For every thing that is 4 born of God overcomes the world ; and the victory which has overcome the world is our faith. Who over- 5 comes the world but the man that believes that Jesus is the Son of God ?

God's threefold Testimony as to His Gift of eternal Life in Christ Jesus Christ is He who came with water and 6 blood ; not with the water only, but with the water and with the blood. And it is the 7 Spirit who gives witness—because the Spirit is the truth. For there are three that give 8 witness—the Spirit, the water, and the blood ; and the three have the same purport. If we accept 9 the witness of men, God's witness is greater : for God's witness is what He has testified about His Son. He who 10 believes in the Son of God has the witness in himself : he who does not believe God has made Him a liar, in that he has refused to believe the witness which God has given about His Son. And that witness is to the effect that 11 God has given us the eternal life, and that this life is in His Son. He who has the Son has the life : he who has 12 not the Son of God has not the life.

Conclusion

The Certainty of eternal Life. Prayer for ourselves and others I write all this to you who believe in the 13 name of the Son of God, that you may know for certain that you have eternal life. And 14 this is the confidence which we have in Him, that whenever we ask anything in accordance with His will, He listens to us. And since we know that 15

1. *Jesus is the Christ*] The Cerinthians denied the identity of Jesus with the Messiah. The former, they said, was a man on whom the latter as a Power of God descended.
Is a child of God] Lit. ' has been begotten by God.'
6. *With the water and with the blood*] The article is used as referring to the definite incident concerning water and blood which must have been familiarly known to the readers of John's Gospel, and to all who received oral instruction from this Apostle. Cf. John xix. 34, n.
7. *Because, &c.*] ' Just as Christ is the Truth (John xiv. 6), so the Spirit sent in Christ's name is the Truth ' (Westcott).

He listens to us, whatever we ask, we know that we have the requests which we have asked from Him. If any one 16 sees his brother committing a sin which is not mortal, he shall ask and God shall give him life—for any who do not sin mortally. There is such a thing as mortal sin ; for that I do not bid him make request. Any kind of wrongdoing 17 is sin ; but there is sin which is not mortal.

The great Facts of the Christian Faith We know that no one who is a child of God 18 sins, but He who was born of God keeps him, and the evil one cannot touch him. We know 19 that we are children of God, and that the whole world lies in the power of the evil one. And we know that 20 the Son of God has come, and has given us understanding to know the true One, and we are in the true One, in His Son Jesus Christ. This is the true God and eternal life.

Dear children, guard yourselves from idols. 21

18. *But He, &c.*] v.l. ' but he who has been begotten by God keeps himself.'
19. *In the power of the evil one*] Lit. ' in the evil one.'

THE SECOND EPISTLE OF JOHN

The Second and Third Epistles of John are ascribed to the 'Elder,' who may well be identified with the author of the First Epistle and of the Gospel. He writes here to the 'elect lady,' probably a symbolic designation of some Church, to which the members of a sister Church send greetings (verse 13). The teaching of this short letter is the same as that of 1 John.

THE SECOND EPISTLE OF JOHN

Greeting The Elder to the elect lady and her children, 1 whom I truly love, and not I alone, but also all who know the truth, for the sake of the truth which 2 abides in us and will be with us for ever : grace, mercy, and 3 peace will be with us from God the Father, and from Jesus Christ the Son of the Father, in truth and love.

Commenda-tion and Warning I am overjoyed to have found some of your 4 children living true lives, in obedience to the command which we have received from the Father. And now, lady, I pray you—writing to you no 5 new command, but the one which we have had from the beginning—let us love one another. The love I mean con- 6 sists in our living in obedience to His commands. God's command is that you should live in love, as you have been taught from the beginning. For many deceivers have gone 7 out into the world—men who do not acknowledge Jesus Christ as coming in the flesh. Such a one is ' the deceiver ' and ' the antichrist.'

The Need of simple Fidelity to Christ Look to yourselves, so that you may not lose 8 the result of your deeds, but may receive a full reward. No one has God who, instead of 9 remaining true to the teaching of Christ, goes beyond it : but he who remains true to that teaching has both the Father and the Son. If any one who comes to 10 you does not bring this teaching, do not receive him under your roof nor greet him ; for he who greets him is a sharer 11 in his evil deeds.

Conclusion I have a great deal to write to you, but will 12 not write it with paper and ink. I hope to come to see you and speak face to face, so that your happiness may be complete.

The children of your elect sister send greetings to you. 13

1. *To the elect lady*] Whether this was an individual or a Church has been much debated. Some render ' to the lady Electa ' ; others again ' to the elect Kyria.'
4. *I am, &c.*] Or, perhaps, ' I was.'
12. *Your*] v.L. ' our.'

Salutation 1 The Elder to the elect lady and her children,
whom I truly love, and not I alone, but also
2 all who know the truth, for the sake of the truth which
abides in us and will be with us for ever: grace, mercy, and 3
peace will be with us, coming from God the Father, and from Jesus
Christ the Son of the Father, in truth and love.

Commends 4 I am overjoyed to have found some of your
and children living true lives in obedience to the
Warns Father's command which we have received from the 5
Father; and now I ask—I pray you—unless to you as a
new command, but the one which we have had from the
beginning—let us love one another. The love I mean is 6
that in our lives we obedience to His commands. This is
command is that you should live in love, as you have been
taught from the beginning. For many deceivers have gone 7
out into the world—men who do not acknowledge Jesus
Christ as coming in the flesh. Such a one is the
deceiver and the antichrist.

The head of 8 Look to yourselves, so that you may not lose 8
the false the fruit of our labour, but may receive a full
teachers reward. No one who goes too far, instead of 9
abiding in the teaching of Christ, possesses God;
he who abides in the teaching, he it is who possesses
both the Father and the Son. If any one who comes to you 10
does not bring this teaching, do not receive him under
your roof nor give him a greeting; for he who gives him a greeting 11
shares in his evil deeds.

Caution 12 I have a great deal to write to you, but I will 12
not write it with paper and ink. I hope to
come to see you and speak face to face, so that your
happiness may be complete.

13 The children of your elect sister send greetings to you.

THE THIRD EPISTLE OF JOHN

The Elder sent a private letter to one Gaius, by Demetrius (verse 12). If the Church of verse 9 is the one addressed in 2 John, an interesting reconstruction is possible. The messengers who brought that letter were welcomed by Gaius ; but Diotrephes, an arrogant officer of the Church, resenting the Elder's tone of authority, would not himself receive the messengers, and turned out of the Church all who did. The absolute use of ' the Name ' (verse 7) is noteworthy. Cf. Acts v. 41.

THE THIRD EPISTLE OF JOHN

Greeting and Commendation The Elder to his dearly loved Gaius, whom I 1 truly love.

Dearly loved one, I pray that you may in all 2 respects prosper and keep well, as your soul prospers. For 3 I am overjoyed when brethren come and bear witness to your fidelity to the truth, how you live in obedience to the truth. I have no greater joy than to hear that my children 4 are living in the truth.

Beloved, you are acting faithfully in all your behaviour 5 towards the brethren, particularly when they are strangers to you. They have testified, in the presence of the Church, 6 to your love ; and you will do well to help them on their journey in a manner worthy of your fellowship with God. For it is for the Name's sake that they have gone forth, 7 accepting nothing from the Gentiles. It is therefore our 8 duty to entertain such men, so that we may be fellow workers with the truth.

Diotrephes I wrote to the Church ; but Diotrephes, who 9 loves to have the foremost place among them, refuses to listen to us. For this reason, when I come, I 10 shall call attention to his conduct, his idle and mischievous talk against us. And not content with this, not only will he himself not receive the brethren, but those who desire to do this he hinders, and excludes them from the Church.

Dearly loved one, do not copy evil, but good. He who does 11 good is a child of God : he who does evil has not seen God.

Demetrius Demetrius has a good word from all men, 12 and the witness of the truth itself. We also give our witness, and you know that our witness is true.

---

3. *I am . . come . . bear*] Or ' It was . . came . . bore.' Cf. 2 John 4, n.
4. *Joy*] v.L. ' grace,' *i.e.* favour from God.
6. *In a manner worthy of your fellowship with God*] Lit. ' worthily of God.'
9. *I wrote*] Or ' I wrote a few lines.' Lit. ' I wrote something.'

3 JOHN

Conclusion I had a great deal to say to you, but I do not ¹³ wish to write to you with ink and pen. But I ¹⁴ hope to see you very soon, and then we will speak face to face.

Peace be with you. Our friends send greetings to you. Greet our friends one by one.

THE EPISTLE OF JUDE

This is a compact little letter, much more likely to have been incorporated in 2 Peter than to have been a later expansion of parts of that Epistle. Opinions as to the undoubted literary interdependence differ; but the priority of Jude seems to hold the field. Probably the Epistle is ascribed in verse 1 to the Jude who was brother of Jesus (see Preface to 2 Peter). The one theme is denunciation of false teaching, of Gnostic type, a pretended deeper knowledge combined with moral laxity. Curious appeal is made to two Jewish Apocryphal writings, the Assumption of Moses (verse 9) and the Book of Enoch, ascribed to the Patriarch (vv. 14, 15)! A not very edifying Scripture is redeemed by the singularly beautiful doxology (vv. 24, 25).

THE EPISTLE OF JUDE

Greeting Jude, a servant of Jesus Christ and a brother 1
of James, to those saints who are beloved as
God the Father's, and kept for Jesus Christ: may mercy, 2
peace, and love be abundantly granted to you.

An Encouragement to defend Christian Truth Beloved ones, while I was eager to write to 3
you on the subject of our common salvation, I
find myself constrained to write and urge you
to defend the faith delivered once for all to
the saints. For certain persons have crept 4
in unnoticed—men for whom in ancient writings this condemnation was foretold—ungodly men, who pervert the
grace of our God into immorality, and disown Jesus Christ,
our only Sovereign and Lord.

Ancient Examples of Retribution for Disobedience I desire to remind you—although the whole 5
matter is sufficiently familiar to you—that the
Lord saved a people out of the land of Egypt,
but afterwards destroyed those who had no
faith. And angels who did not keep their own 6
primacy, but deserted their proper abode, He reserves in
everlasting bonds, in darkness, for the judgement of the
great day. So also Sodom and Gomorrah and the neigh- 7
bouring towns, having in the same manner been guilty of
gross immorality and pursued unnatural vice, are now
before us as an example of eternal fire in the punishment
which they are undergoing. Yet in just the same way 8
these dreamers also pollute the body, while they set authority
at naught and speak evil of dignities.

False Teachers. Their Insolence and Greed But Michael the Archangel, when contending 9
with the devil and disputing with him about
the body of Moses, did not dare to pronounce
judgement on him in abusive terms, but said,
' The Lord rebuke you.' Yet these men are 10
abusive in matters of which they know nothing, and in
things which, like the brutes, they do understand in-

1. *A brother of James*] Cf. Matt. xiii. 55.
Beloved as God the Father's] Cf. 1 John v. 20.

stinctively—in all these they become depraved. Woe to 11
them ! for they have followed in the steps of Cain : for
the sake of gain they have rushed headlong in the
errors of Balaam, and have perished in the rebellion of
Korah.

Their selfish, useless, shameful Lives These are the men—sunken rocks—who in 12
your love-feasts are not afraid to feast with
you, caring only for themselves ; clouds without water, driven along by the winds ; trees in
autumn, fruitless, doubly dead, uprooted ; wild waves of 13
the sea, foaming out their own shame ; wandering stars,
for whom is reserved dense darkness for ever.

The Prediction of Enoch It was also about these that Enoch, the 14
seventh from Adam, prophesied, saying,
' The Lord comes with myriads of His people, 15
to execute judgement upon all, and to convict all the
ungodly of all the ungodly deeds which they have committed, and of all the hard words which they, ungodly
sinners, have spoken against Him.'

These men are murmurers, complaining of their lot. 16
Their lives are guided by their evil passions, and
their mouths are full of big and boastful words, while
they defer to persons for the sake of the advantage
they may gain.

The Prediction of the Apostles But do you, beloved, remember the words 17
that before now were spoken by the Apostles
of our Lord Jesus Christ—how they declared 18
to you, ' In the last times there shall be scoffers, obeying
only their own ungodly passions.' These are those who cause 19
divisions : they are men of the world, devoid of the Spirit.

The Readers' Duties to themselves and the false Teachers But do you, beloved, building yourselves up 20
on your most holy faith and praying in the
Holy Spirit, keep yourselves in the love of 21
God, waiting for the mercy of our Lord Jesus
Christ which issues in eternal life. On some 22
who are in doubt, you should have pity ; others you must 23

10. *They become depraved*] Or ' they are perishing.'
11. *Rebellion*] Lit. ' contradiction.'
Korah] ' Some of the Gnostics professed even to regard Korah with admiration ' (Wordsworth).
12. *Are not afraid, &c.*] Or ' feast with you, fearlessly caring for themselves.'
15. *Comes*] Or ' came.' Anticipative. Cf. verse 11.
19. *Men of the world*] Greek ' psychical,' for which ' we have no English word ; and our biblical psychology is, by this defect, entirely at fault ' (Alford). See Heard's *Tripartite Nature of Man*, pp. 88–90, Hatch's *Biblical Greek*, iii., and Mayor's *James*, pp. 120, 121.

save, snatching them out of the fire ; and on others have pity mingled with fear, while you hate even the garment stained by the flesh.

All Glory ascribed to God Now to Him who is able to keep you from stumbling, and cause you to stand in the presence of His glory free from blemish and exultant—to the only God our Saviour through Jesus Christ our Lord—be glory, majesty, might, and authority, before all time, now, and to all time ! Amen. 24 25

THE REVELATION OF JOHN

THE REVELATION OF JOHN

The Book of Revelation is the only specimen in the New Testament of what is now known as Apocalyptic Literature. The object of this literature (of which many books have been discovered—or at any rate re-edited during recent years) is to unveil the future and describe the drama which is to be enacted when God breaks into human history and sets up His Kingdom. The Book of Revelation is an attempt to Christianize the Apocalyptic Faith of Judaism.

The book was probably written in the reign of Domitian (81–96) to meet a grave crisis in the history of the Christian Church. Fierce persecution had broken out. The writer himself had been exiled to Patmos. Martyrdoms had occurred. A systematic attempt was being made in Asia to establish Emperor-worship on a large scale. All who refused to take part in this worship suffered social ostracism. They were boycotted in the market-place and excluded from social life. The strain was becoming intolerable, and it looked as if Christianity were in danger of being crushed out of existence. It was to meet this situation—to comfort and strengthen Christians in the hour of their peril—that the Book was published.

We know very little about the author except that his name was John, and that he was a Prophet. The traditional view which identified him with John the Apostle (the reputed author of the Fourth Gospel) has now been abandoned by the majority of modern scholars.

The interpretation of the Book has always been an enigma. The most important types of interpretation are :

(1) *The Futurist*, which holds that the prophecies in the Book refer to the future and will not be fulfilled till the end of the world.

(2) *The continuous historical*, which maintains that the Book is a diagram of history. Part of it has already been fulfilled—part is now in course of fulfilment—and part still belongs to the future.

(3) *The poetic*, which holds that the Book portrays under

various symbols (which are not to be taken literally) the eternal conflict between good and evil.

(4) The method generally accepted by modern scholars and known as the *Preterist*, which maintains that the writer had in view only the needs and circumstances of his own time. The drama belongs to the first century. The author could see no escape from the situation that confronted the Church except in a great Divine intervention which would mean the end of the age. That was the only outlook possible to a Jewish Christian in the first century.

THE REVELATION OF JOHN

Introduction

The Book and its Writer The revelation given by Jesus Christ, which **1** **1** God granted Him, that He might make known to His servants certain events which must shortly come to pass. He sent His angel and communicated it to His servant John; who now is making **2** a faithful record of the Word that came from God and the truth revealed by Jesus Christ and all the things that he saw in his vision. Blessed is he who reads, and blessed are **3** those who listen to the words of this prophecy and lay to heart what is written in it; for the time for its fulfilment is now close at hand.

Greeting John sends greetings to the seven Churches in **4** the province of Asia. May grace be granted to you, and peace, from Him who is and was and is to be; and from the seven Spirits which are before His throne; and **5** from Jesus Christ, the truthful witness, the first of the dead to be born to life, and the Ruler of the kings of the earth.

Ascription of Praise To Him who loves us and has freed us from our sins with His own blood, and has formed us **6** into a Kingdom, to be priests to God, His Father

---

1. *The revelation*] The writer obviously expects that his meaning, so far from being obscured by the strange figures of speech and symbols which he employs, will be thereby illustrated, enforced, and brought home to the mind, with greater than ordinary power (Milligan).

Given by] Lit. 'of.'

Shortly] *i.e.* soon after this book was written. Cf. i. 3, 19; xxii. 6, 10.

2. *The truth . . Jesus Christ*] Lit. 'the testimony of Jesus Christ.'

3. *The time for its fulfilment, &c.*] Lit. simply 'the time is near'; *i.e.* was near when this book was written. Cf. i. 1, 19; xxii. 6, 10.

4. *Seven Churches*] The seven Churches mentioned by name in chapters ii. and iii. Cf. verse 11.

The province of Asia] Cf. Acts ii. 9, n.

Seven Spirits] A startling expression. We should expect a reference to the Holy Spirit, as in the benediction in 2 Cor. xiii. 14. Many scholars suppose that the writer uses this expression to describe the Holy Spirit in His plenitude and perfection, and to signify that each of the seven Churches has its special impartation.

5. *Freed us from*] v.l. 'washed us from.'

6. *Formed us into*] v.l. 'made for us.'

God, His Father] Lit. 'God and His Father.' Cf. Jas. i. 27. Or 'His God and Father.'

—to Him be ascribed the glory and the power for ever and ever. Amen.

Lo, He is coming in the clouds, and every eye will see 7 Him, and so will those who pierced Him ; and all the nations of the earth will gaze on Him and mourn. Even so. Amen.

' I am the Alpha and the Omega,' says the Lord God, 8 ' He who is and was and is to be—the Ruler of all.'

The Coming of the Message I John, your brother, and a sharer with you 9 in the sorrows and the Kingdom and the patient endurance of Jesus, found myself in the island of Patmos, for my loyalty to the Word of God and the truth told us by Jesus. On the Lord's day I was inspired by the 10 Spirit, and I heard behind me a loud voice like the blast of a trumpet. It said, 11

' Write your vision in a book, and send it to the seven Churches — to Ephesus, Smyrna, Pergamum, Thyatira, Sardis, Philadelphia, and Laodicea.'

A Vision of the glorified Redeemer I turned to see who it was that was speaking 12 to me ; and then I saw seven golden lampstands, and in the centre of the lampstands 13 One resembling the Son of Man, clothed in a robe which reached to His feet, and with a girdle of gold across His breast. His head and His hair were white, 14 like white wool—as white as snow ; and His eyes were like a flame of fire. His feet were like silver-bronze when it 15 is white-hot in a furnace ; and His voice was as the sound of many waters. In His right hand He held seven stars, 16 and a sharp, two-edged sword was seen coming from His mouth ; and His face was like the sun shining in its full power.

6. *For ever and ever*] Lit. ' until the Ages of the Ages.'

7. *So will those who pierced Him*] An indication that the Seer expected the Saviour to return in the lifetime of those who crucified Him. Cf. Matt. xxvi. 64 ; John i. 51.

10. *Lord's day*] i.e. the day consecrated to the Lord—the first day of the week— the day of Resurrection ; cf. Acts xx. 7 ; 1 Cor. xvi. 2. This is the first occurrence of the name ' Lord's day ' in Christian literature ; but it occurs in the *Teaching of the Apostles* (written a little later), ' Every Lord's day come together and break bread.'

12. *Who . . that*] Lit. ' the voice which.'
Then] Lit. ' having turned.'
Seven] In the earthly temple there was only one lampstand (Exod. xxv. 31 ; Heb. ix. 2).

15. *White-hot*] The whiteness is expressed by the second half of the Greek word ' chalcolibanus.' The participle in the Greek here has the full force of the perfect tense. Contrast the present participle passive of the same verb in the *Martyrdom of Polycarp*, xv. The case here is the genitive absolute. v.L. ' as if they (the feet) were glowing in a furnace.'

When I saw Him, I fell at His feet as if dead. 17
But He laid His hand upon me and said,
' Do not be afraid : I am the First and the
Last, and the ever-living One. I died ; but 18
I am now alive for evermore, and I have the keys of the
gates of Death and of Hades ! Write down therefore the 19
things you have just seen—the things which are and the
things which are to be hereafter : the secret meaning of 20
the seven stars which you have seen in My right hand,
and of the seven lampstands of gold. The seven stars are
the angels of the seven Churches, and the seven lampstands
are the seven Churches.

The Letters to the seven Churches

' To the angel of the Church in Ephesus 1 **2**
write :
' " These are the words of Him who holds the
seven stars in His right hand and walks to and fro among
the seven lampstands of gold. I know your doings and 2
your toil and your endurance. And I know that you
cannot tolerate wicked men, but have put to the test those
who call themselves Apostles but are not, and you have
found them to be liars. And you endure patiently and 3
have borne burdens for My sake and have never flagged.
Yet I have this against you—that you no longer love Me 4
as you did at first. Be mindful, therefore, of the height 5
from which you have fallen. Repent at once, and act as
you did at first, or else I will surely come and remove your
lampstand out of its place—unless you repent. Yet this 6
you have in your favour : you hate the doings of the
Nicolaitans, which I also hate.
' " Let all who have ears give heed to what the Spirit 7
is saying to the Churches. To the victor I will give the

18. *For evermore*] Lit. ' until the Ages of the Ages.'
20. *Angels*] This term has often been taken to refer to the ' presbyters ' or
' bishops ' of the Churches. But such an interpretation is against the usage of the
term in this book. The word ' angel ' occurs sixty times and always denotes a
superhuman being employed in the service of God or Satan.
1. *Angel*] See note on i. 20.
Stars . . lampstands] See i. 20.
4. *You no longer love*] Lit. ' You have lost your first love.' The interpretation is
doubtful. Some scholars would translate ' You no longer love one another.'
6. *Nicolaitans*] Probably an Antinomian sect who divorced ethics from religion
and held that conduct did not matter so long as belief was correct.

privilege of eating the fruit of the Tree of Life, which is in the Paradise of God."

The Letter to Smyrna ' To the angel of the Church at Smyrna 8 write as follows :

' " These are the words of Him who is the First and the Last—who died and has returned to life. Your 9 sufferings I know, and your poverty—but you are rich— and the evil name given you by those who say that they themselves are Jews, and are not, but are Satan's synagogue. Dismiss your fears concerning all that you are about to 10 suffer. I tell you that the Devil is about to throw some of you into prison that you may be put to the test, and for ten days you will have to endure persecution. Be faithful, even if you have to die for it, and then I will give you the Crown of Life.

' " Let all who have ears give heed to what the Spirit is 11 saying to the Churches. The victor shall be in no way hurt by the Second Death."

The Letter to Pergamum ' To the angel of the Church at Pergamum 12 write as follows :

' " These are the words of Him who has the sharp, two-edged sword. I know where you dwell. 13 Satan's throne is there ; and yet you are true to Me, and did not deny your faith in Me, even in the days of Antipas My faithful witness, who was martyred among you, in the place where Satan dwells. Yet I have a few things against 14 you, because you have with you some that cling to the teaching of Balaam, who taught Balak to put a stumbling-block in the way of the descendants of Israel—to eat what had been sacrificed to idols, and commit fornication. So 15 even you have some that cling in the same way to the teaching of the Nicolaitans. Repent at once ; or else I 16 will come to you quickly, and will make war upon them with the sword which is in My mouth.

---

7. *Tree of Life*] See and cf. xxii. 2.
8. *Angel*] See note on i. 20.
10. *Even if you have to die*] Lit. ' up to (the point of) death ' ; not meaning ' so long as life shall last.' Cf. Phil. ii. 8, where ' stooped to die ' is literally ' becoming obedient up to (the point of) death.'
11. *The Second Death*] Cf. verse 7, n. ; xx. 6, 14 ; xxi. 8.
12. *Angel*] See note on i. 20.
Sharp . . sword] See i. 16.
13. *Satan's throne*] Pergamum was the headquarters of Emperor-worship in the province of Asia, and Emperor-worship was regarded as the special enemy of Christianity at the time when this book was written.
14. *Balaam and Balak*] See Numbers xxii.–xxv. ; xxxi. 16.

' " Let all who have ears give heed to what the Spirit is 17
saying to the Churches. As for the victor—to him I will
give some of the hidden manna, and a white stone
with a new name inscribed upon it known only to him
who receives it."

The Letter to Thyatira ' To the angel of the Church at Thyatira 18
write as follows :

' " These are the words of the Son of God
who has eyes like a flame of fire, and feet resembling silver-
bronze. I know your doings, your love, your faith, your 19
service, and your patient endurance ; and that of late you
have toiled harder than you did at first. Yet I have this 20
against you, that you tolerate the woman Jezebel, who calls
herself a prophetess and by her teaching leads astray My
servants, so that they commit fornication and eat what has
been sacrificed to idols. I have given her time to repent, 21
but she is determined not to repent of her fornication. I tell 22
you that I am about to cast her upon a bed of sickness, and
I will severely afflict those who commit adultery with her,
unless they repent of conduct such as hers. Her children 23
too shall surely die ; and all the Churches shall come to
know that I am He who searches into men's inmost
thoughts ; and I will requite each of you in accordance
with his deeds. But to you, the rest of you in Thyatira, 24
all who do not hold this teaching and have not learnt the
' deep things,' as they call them (the deep things of
Satan !)—to you I say that I lay no other burden on you.
Only hold fast to what you possess until I come. 25
' " And to the victor, the one who obeys My commands 26
to the very end, I will give authority over the nations.
And he shall be their shepherd, ruling them with a rod of 27
iron, just as potter's ware is dashed to atoms ; and his power
over them shall be like that which I Myself have received
from My Father ; and I will give him the Morning Star. 28

17. *Hidden manna*] According to 2 Macc. ii. 1–8 the Ark, which contained a pot
of manna (Exod. xvi. 34), was hidden away by Jeremiah till the Messiah should
appear.
White stone] The symbol of citizenship in the Kingdom of heaven.
A new name] Cf. verse 7, n. ; iii. 12 ; xiv. 1 ; xxii. 4.
19. *Of late, &c.*] Lit. ' your last works are more numerous than your first.'
20. *Jezebel*] The reference is probably to some woman who had been advocating
the doctrines of the Nicolaitans.
24. ' *Deep things* '] The followers of Jezebel undertook to lead the people into what
they regarded as the profounder or deeper truths of Christianity—and by this they
probably meant the doctrine that ' everything is allowable.' Cf. 1 Cor. ii. 10, vi. 12.
28. *The Morning Star*] Christ Himself, xxii. 16.

Let all who have ears give heed to what the Spirit is saying 29
to the Churches."

The Letter to Sardis ' To the angel of the Church at Sardis write 1 **3**
as follows :

' " These are the words of Him who has the
seven Spirits of God and the seven stars. I know your
doings—you are supposed to be alive, but in reality you
are dead. Rouse yourself and keep awake, and strengthen 2
what still remains though it is on the point of death ; for I
have found no doings of yours perfect in the sight of My
God. Be mindful, therefore, of the lessons you have 3
received and heard. Continually lay them to heart, and
repent. If, however, you fail to rouse yourself and keep
awake, I shall come upon you suddenly like a thief, and you
will certainly not know the hour at which I shall come to
judge you. Yet you have in Sardis a few who have not 4
soiled their garments ; and they shall walk with Me in
white ; for they are worthy.

' " And thus the victor shall be clothed in white garments ; 5
and never will I erase his name from the Book of Life, but
will acknowledge him in the presence of My Father and
His angels. Let all who have ears give heed to what the 6
Spirit is saying to the Churches."

The Letter to Philadelphia ' To the angel of the Church at Philadelphia 7
write as follows :

' " These are the words of Him who is Holy
and True—He who has the key of David—He who opens
and no one shall shut, and shuts and no one shall open. I 8
know your doings. I have put a door wide open in front of
you, which no one can shut ; because you have but a little
power, and yet you have kept My word and have not disowned me. I will cause some belonging to Satan's syna- 9
gogue who say that they themselves are Jews, and are not,
but are liars—I will make them come and prostrate themselves before your feet and know for certain that I have
loved you. Because you have kept the word for which I 10
suffered, I in turn will keep you from that hour of trial
which is soon coming upon the whole world, to put to the

1. *Angel*] See note on i. 20.
5. *Book of Life*] Cf. ii. 7, n. ; xiii. 8 ; xvii. 8 ; xx. 12, 15 ; xxi. 27 ; xxii. 19.
7. *Angel*] See note on i. 20.
The key of David] Cf. Isa. xxii. 22 where the key of David is given to Eliakim as
the symbol of office.
10. *You have kept the word*] Lit. ' You kept the word of my patience.'

test the inhabitants of the earth. I am coming quickly : 11
hold fast to that which you already possess, so that your
crown of victory be not taken away from you.

' " As for the victor—I will make him a pillar in the 12
sanctuary of My God, and he shall never go out from it
again. And I will write on him the name of My God, and
the name of the city of My God, the new Jerusalem, which
is to come down out of heaven from My God, and My own
new name. Let all who have ears give heed to what the 13
Spirit is saying to the Churches."

The
Letter to
Laodicea
' And to the angel of the Church at Laodicea 14
write as follows :
' " These are the words of Him who is the
Amen—the true and faithful witness, the Beginning of
God's Creation. I know your doings—you are neither 15
cold nor hot ; I would that you were cold or hot ! So, 16
because you are lukewarm and neither hot nor cold, before
long I will vomit you out of My mouth. You say, I am rich, 17
and have wealth stored up, and I stand in need of nothing ;
and you do not know that if there is a wretched creature it
is you—pitiable, poor, blind, naked. Therefore I counsel 18
you to buy of Me gold refined in the fire that you may
become rich, and white robes to put on to hide your
shameful nakedness, and eye-salve to anoint your eyes
with, so that you may be able to see. All whom I hold 19
dear, I reprove and chastise ; therefore be in earnest and
repent. See, I am now standing at the door and knocking. 20
If any one listens to My voice and opens the door, I will
come in to him and feast with him, and he shall feast
with Me.

' " To the victor I will give the privilege of sitting down 21
beside Me on My throne, as I also have won the victory and
have sat down beside My Father on His throne. Let all 22
who have ears give heed to what the Spirit is saying to
the Churches." '

12. *New Jerusalem*] Cf. xxi. 2.
14. *Angel*] See note on i. 20.
The Amen] See Isa. lxv. 16, ' the God of the Amen.'
The Beginning] Cf. Col. i. 15, ' the first-born of all creation.' The phrase does
not mean merely that Christ was the first to be created—but that He was the
Lord of Creation.

A Vision of God on His Throne

A Door into Heaven stood open After all this I looked and saw a door in 1 **4** heaven standing open; and the voice that I had previously heard, like the blast of a trumpet, again spoke to me and said,

' Come up here, and I will show you things which are to happen in the future.'

Immediately I found myself in the Spirit, and saw a 2 throne in heaven, and One sitting on the throne. The 3 appearance of Him who sat there was like jasper or sardius ; and encircling the throne was a rainbow, in appearance like an emerald. Surrounding the throne there were also 4 twenty-four other thrones, on which sat twenty-four Elders clothed in white robes, with golden crowns upon their heads.

The Beings and Things around the Throne Out from the throne there came flashes of 5 lightning, and voices, and peals of thunder, while in front of the throne seven blazing lamps were burning, which are the seven Spirits of God. And in front of the throne there seemed to be a sea 6 of glass, resembling crystal. And round about the throne between it and the Elders were four living creatures, full of eyes in front and behind. The first living creature re- 7 sembled a lion, the second an ox, the third had a face like that of a man, and the fourth resembled an eagle flying. And the four living creatures had each of them six wings, 8 and all round their bodies and under their wings they are full of eyes ; day after day, and night after night, they never cease saying,

' Holy, holy, holy, Lord God, the Ruler of all, who wast and art and art to be.'

God's Power and Glory proclaimed And whenever the living creatures give glory 9 and honour and thanks to Him who is seated on the throne and lives for ever and ever, the 10 twenty-four Elders fall down before Him who sits on the

---

1. *Previously heard*] Cf. i. 10.

3. *Like jasper*] Cf. xxi. 11, ' a stone most precious—clear as crystal.' As this description does not apply to the modern jasper some scholars think that the reference is to the opal. Note the absence of anthropomorphism. ' The seer's eye is arrested by the flashing of gemlike colours but he sees no form ' (Swete).

Sardius] A deep red stone, probably our cornelian.

4. *Twenty-four Elders*] Probably angels of the highest rank. The term Elder was often used of angels ; cf. Isa. xxiv. 23.

5. *There came*] Lit. ' come.'

6. *Four living creatures*] Probably cherubim or seraphim. Cf. Ezek. i. 5 ; Isa. vi. 2.

10. *For ever and ever*] Lit. ' unto the Ages of the Ages.'

throne and worship Him who lives for ever and ever, and
they cast their crowns down in front of the throne, saying,

'Worthy art Thou our Lord and God to receive glory 11
and honour and power ;
For Thou didst create all things,
And it was by Thy will that they came into existence,
and were created.'

The breaking of the seven Seals

The Book of coming Events And I saw in the right hand of Him who 1 **5**
sat on the throne a book written on both sides
of the page and closely sealed with seven seals.
And I saw a mighty angel who was exclaiming in a loud 2
voice,

'Who is worthy to open the book and break its seals ?'

But no one in heaven, or on earth, or under the earth, 3
was able to open the book or look into it.

Only the Redeemer could open the Book And while I was weeping bitterly, because 4
no one was found worthy to open the book or
look into it, one of the Elders said to me, 5
'Do not weep. The Lion which belongs to
the tribe of Judah, the Root of David, has won the right to
open the book and break its seven seals.'

A Vision of the Lamb of God Then I saw, between the throne (with the 6
four living creatures) and the Elders, a Lamb
standing, looking as if it had been slain. And
it had seven horns and seven eyes, which are the seven
Spirits of God who have been sent far and wide into
all the earth, and it came and took the book out of the 7
right hand of Him who is seated on the throne. And when 8
He had taken the book, the four living creatures and the
twenty-four Elders fell down before the Lamb, having each
of them a harp and golden bowls full of incense, which
represent the prayers of the saints. And now they sing 9
a new song, saying,

1. *A book*] *i.e.* a scroll, or roll of parchment or papyrus.
5. *The Lion*] Cf. Gen. xlix. 9, 'Judah is a lion's whelp,' which was interpreted messianically.
The Root of David] Cf. Isa. xi. 1.
6. *Between*] Lit. 'in the midst of.' The Hebrew preposition denoting this is always repeated ; and this may be regarded as a Hebraism.
A Lamb] Strange and unlooked for. The Seer had been told of a lion, and he beholds a lamb, the emblem of patience and innocence, and a lamb, too, which had been sacrificed (Milligan).

' Worthy art Thou to take the book
And break its seals ;
Because Thou hast been slain,
And hast purchased for God with Thine own blood
Men out of every tribe and tongue and people and
nation,
And hast formed them into a Kingdom to be priests 10
to our God,
And they shall reign over the earth.'

His Power and Glory proclaimed And I looked, and heard the voices of many 11
angels on every side of the throne, and of the
living creatures and the Elders numbering
myriads of myriads and thousands of thousands, and in 12
loud voices they were singing,

' Worthy is the Lamb which has been slain to receive all
power and riches and wisdom and might and honour and
glory and blessing.'

And I heard every created thing in heaven and on earth 13
and under the earth and on the sea (and all that is therein)
saying,

' To Him who is seated on the throne,
And to the Lamb,
Be ascribed all blessing and honour
And glory and might,
For ever and ever ! '

Then the four living creatures said ' Amen,' and the 14
Elders fell down and worshipped.

The first Seal And when the Lamb broke one of the seven 1 **6**
seals I saw it, and I heard one of the four living
creatures say, as if in a voice of thunder,
' Come.'

And I looked and a white horse appeared, and its rider 2
carried a bow ; and a crown was given to him ; and he went
out conquering and to conquer.

The second Seal And when the Lamb broke the second seal, I 3
heard the second living creature say,
' Come.'

---

10. *Shall reign*] Some MSS. read the present tense instead of the future. In this case the reign of the saints must be regarded as having already commenced.

14. *Worshipped*] v.L. ' worshipped Him who lives until the Ages of the Ages.'

2. *White horse . . and its rider*] Many commentators hold that this phrase refers to Christ. Cf. xix. 11, where one whose name is called ' the Word of God ' is represented as riding on a white horse. But this interpretation ignores the fact that the white horse is connected with the other three which are depicted as scourges of humanity. The white horse represents ' conquest ' or ' triumphant militarism.'

And out came another horse—a fiery-red one ; and 4 power was given to its rider to take peace from the earth, and to cause men to kill one another ; and a great sword was given to him.

The third Seal When the Lamb broke the third seal, I heard 5 the third living creature say,

' Come.'

I looked, and a black horse appeared, its rider carrying a balance in his hand. And I heard what seemed to be a 6 voice speaking in the midst of the four living creatures, and saying,

' A whole day's wage for a loaf of bread, a whole day's wage for three barley cakes, but do not damage the oil or the wine.'

The fourth Seal When the Lamb broke the fourth seal I 7 heard the voice of the fourth living creature say,

' Come.'

I looked and a pale-coloured horse appeared. Its rider's 8 name was Death, and Hades came close behind him ; and authority was given to them over the fourth part of the earth, to kill with the sword or with famine or pestilence or by means of the wild beasts of the earth.

The fifth Seal When the Lamb broke the fifth seal, I saw 9 at the foot of the altar the souls of those whose lives had been sacrificed because of the word of God and of the testimony which they had given. And 10 now in loud voices they cried out, saying,

' How long, O Sovereign Lord, the holy One and the true, dost Thou delay judgement and the taking of vengeance upon the inhabitants of the earth for our blood ? '

And there was given to each of them a long white robe, 11

---

4. *Fiery-red*] Emblematic of great slaughter.

5. *A black horse*] Indicating famine.

6. *A whole day's wage*] Lit. ' a quart of wheat for a denarius, and three quarts of barley for a denarius.' A denarius was the regular pay for a day's work in Palestine, and the phrase indicates that a man's utmost earnings would scarcely suffice to procure the bare necessities of life.

The oil or the wine] The meaning of this clause is obscure. Perhaps the allusion is to what seems to have been a recognized military practice of refraining from injuring vines and olive-trees. The contrast between this clause and the former seems to indicate the approach of a time when the necessities of life would be at famine prices while luxuries would be abundant.

7. *The voice*] Not ' a ' voice, although there is no article in the Greek.

10. *Now*] When the fifth seal was broken—implied by the tense.

and they were bidden to wait patiently for a short time longer, until the full number of their fellow bondservants should also be complete—namely of their brethren who were to be killed just as they had been.

The sixth Seal When the Lamb broke the sixth seal, I looked, 12 and there was a great earthquake, and the sun became as dark as sackcloth, and the whole disc of the moon became like blood. The stars in the sky also 13 fell to the earth, as when a fig-tree, shaken by a gale of wind, casts its unripe figs to the ground. The sky too 14 passed away, as if a scroll were being rolled up, and every mountain and island was removed from its place. The 15 kings of the earth and the great men, the military chiefs, the wealthy and the powerful—all, whether slaves or free men—hid themselves in the caves and in the rocks of the mountains, while they called to the mountains and the rocks, 16 saying,

' Fall on us and hide us from the presence of Him who sits on the throne and from the anger of the Lamb ; for the 17 day of His Wrath—that great day—has come, and who is able to stand ? '

The Safety of God's true Servants After this I saw four angels standing at the 1 **7** four corners of the earth, and holding back the four winds of the earth so that no wind should blow over the earth or the sea or upon any tree. And I saw another angel ascending from the east and carry- 2 ing a seal belonging to the ever-living God. He called in a loud voice to the four angels whose work it was to injure the earth and the sea.

' Injure neither land nor sea nor trees,' he said, ' until 3 we have sealed the bondservants of our God upon their foreheads.'

The 144,000 When the sealing was finished, I heard how 4 many were sealed out of all the tribes of the descendants of Israel. They were 144,000.

Of the tribe of Judah, 12,000 were sealed ; 5
Of the tribe of Reuben, 12,000 ;

---

13. *Unripe figs*] Or ' winter figs.'
(vv. 15, 16.) Cf. Luke xxiii. 30. The limestone hills of Palestine are honeycombed with caves which from time immemorial have afforded shelter to robbers and fugitives. It is a significant fact that upon the fall of Jerusalem these caves formed the last hiding-place of vast numbers of the Jews (Josephus, *Wars*, vi. 7 ; vi. 9 ; vii. 2). In Acts iv. 26, the phrase ' kings of the earth ' (or, land) is applied by Peter to the rulers of Palestine.

Of the tribe of Gad, 12,000 ;
Of the tribe of Asher, 12,000 ; 6
Of the tribe of Naphtali, 12,000 ;
Of the tribe of Manasseh, 12,000 ;
Of the tribe of Symeon, 12,000 ; 7
Of the tribe of Levi, 12,000 ;
Of the tribe of Issachar, 12,000 ;
Of the tribe of Zebulun, 12,000 ; 8
Of the tribe of Joseph, 12,000 ;
Of the tribe of Benjamin, 12,000.

A vast Throng of gloriously triumphant Saints After this I looked, and a vast host appeared 9 which it was impossible for any one to count, gathered out of every nation and from all tribes and peoples and languages, standing before the throne and before the Lamb, clothed in long white robes, and carrying palm-branches in their hands. In loud voices they cried, 10

' To our God seated on the throne, and to the Lamb, we owe our salvation ! '

All the angels were standing in a circle round the throne 11 and round the Elders and the four living creatures, and they fell on their faces in front of the throne and worshipped God.

' Even so ! ' they cried : 12
' The blessing and the glory
And the wisdom and the thanks
And the honour and the power and the might
Be ascribed to our God,
For ever and ever !
Amen ! '

Though martyred, full Salvation was now theirs through the Lamb Then, addressing me, one of the Elders said, 13 ' Who are these people clothed in the long white robes ? And where have they come from ? '

' My lord, you know,' I replied. 14

' They are those,' he said, ' who have just come out of the great distress, and have washed their robes and made them white in the blood of the Lamb. For 15 this reason they stand before the very throne of God, and render Him service day and night in His sanctuary, and He who is sitting upon the throne will shelter them in His tent. Nevermore shall they hunger, nevermore 16 shall they thirst, nevermore shall the sun smite them nor any scorching heat. For the Lamb who is before the 17 throne will be their Shepherd, and will guide them to the water-springs of Life, and God will wipe every tear from their eyes.'

8 When the Lamb broke the seventh seal, there 1
The seventh Seal was silence in heaven for about half an hour.

The sounding of the seven Trumpets

The Prayers of the Saints. Their Enemies punished Then I saw the seven angels who are in the 2 presence of God, and seven trumpets were given to them. And another angel went and 3 stood close to the altar, carrying a censer of gold; and abundance of incense was given to him that he might place it with the prayers of all the saints upon the golden altar in front of the throne. And 4 the smoke of the incense rose into the presence of God from the angel's hand, and mingled with the prayers of His people. So the angel took the censer and filled it with 5 fire from the altar and flung it to the earth; and there followed peals of thunder, and voices, and flashes of lightning, and an earthquake.

Then the seven angels who had the seven trumpets made 6 preparations for blowing them.

The first Trumpet The first blew his trumpet; and there came 7 hail and fire, mixed with blood, falling upon the earth; and a third part of the earth was burnt up, and a third part of the trees and all the green grass.

The second Trumpet The second angel blew his trumpet; and 8 what seemed to be a great mountain, all ablaze with fire, was hurled into the sea; and a third part of the sea was turned into blood. And a third part of 9

1. *Silence in heaven*] Charles takes this verse in close connection with verses 3–5, ' The praise and thanksgiving of all the mighty hierarchies in heaven are hushed in order that the prayers of the suffering saints on earth may be heard before the throne of God.'
Half an hour] This phrase is not to be taken literally; as Swete says, ' Half an hour is a long interval in a drama.'
2. *Seven trumpets*] Rev. viii. to xi. describes over again substantially the same events as those seen in the Vision of the Seven Seals (Rev. v. to viii.). The several divisions of the Apocalypse are not really consecutive, but run, as it were, parallel to one another, and merely give different aspects and varied representations of the same set of events. Others, however, regard the Visions of the Apocalypse as following one another in their fulfilment.
4. Lit. ' The smoke of the incense went up to help (lit. ' for ') the prayers of the saints.'

the living creatures that were in the sea died ; and a third part of the ships were destroyed.

The third angel blew his trumpet ; and there 10 **The third Trumpet** fell from heaven a great star, blazing like a torch. It fell upon a third part of the rivers and upon the springs of water. The name of the star 11 is ' Wormwood ' ; and a third part of the waters were turned into wormwood, and many people died from drinking the water, because it had become bitter.

Then the fourth angel blew his trumpet ; and 12 **The fourth Trumpet** a third part of the sun was smitten, a third part of the moon, and a third part of the stars, so that a third part of them might be darkened, and for a third of the day, and also of the night, there might be no light.

Yet more fearful Woes to come Then I looked, and I heard a solitary eagle 13 crying with a loud voice, as it flew across the sky, ' Alas, alas, alas, for the inhabitants of the earth, because of the trumpet blasts which the three angels are about to blow ! '

The fifth angel blew his trumpet ; and I 1 **9** **The fifth Trumpet** saw a Star which had fallen from heaven to the earth ; and to him was given the key of the depths of the bottomless pit, and he opened the depths 2 of the bottomless pit. And smoke came up out of the pit like the smoke of a vast furnace, so that the sun and the air were darkened by the smoke of the pit.

The Locusts And from the midst of the smoke there came 3 locusts on to the earth, and power was given to them like the power which earthly scorpions possess. And they were forbidden to injure the herbage of the 4 earth, or any green thing, or any tree. They were only to injure human beings who have not the seal of God on their foreheads. Their mission was not to kill, but to cause 5 awful agony for five months ; and this agony was like that which a scorpion inflicts when it stings a man. And at 6 that time people will seek death, but will not find it, and they will long to die, but death evades them.

The appearance of the locusts was like that of horses 7 equipped for war. On their heads they had a kind of

---

11. *Wormwood*] Lit. ' Absinthe.' The term is always used in the O.T. to denote the bitterness of injustice or the Divine retribution. See Prov. v. 4.
13. *Eagle*] v.L. ' angel.'
1. *Star*] The star represents a person—probably Satan.

crown which looked like gold. Their faces seemed human 8
and they had hair like women's hair, but their teeth
resembled those of lions. They had breastplates which 9
seemed to be made of steel ; and the noise caused by their
wings was like that of a vast number of horses and chariots
hurrying into battle. They had tails like those of 10
scorpions, and also stings ; and in their tails lay their
power of injuring mankind for five months.

The locusts had a king over them—the angel of the 11
bottomless pit, whose name in Hebrew is ' Abaddon,' while
in Greek he is called ' Apollyon.' The first woe is past ; 12
two other woes have still to come.

The sixth Trumpet The sixth angel blew his trumpet ; and I heard 13
a single voice speaking from the four horns of
the golden altar which is in the presence of God.
It said to the sixth angel—the angel who had the trumpet, 14
' Set at liberty the four angels who are prisoners near
the great river Euphrates.'

And the four angels who had been kept in readiness 15
for that hour, day, month, and year, were set at liberty,
so that they might kill a third part of mankind. The 16
number of the squadrons of their cavalry was two hundred
millions ; I heard their number.

The Horses and Horsemen And this was the appearance of the horses 17
and their riders as I saw them in my vision.
The riders had breastplates which were red
as fire, blue as jacinth, and yellow as sulphur ; and the
horses' heads were like those of lions, while from their
mouths there came fire and smoke and sulphur. By these 18
three plagues a third part of mankind were destroyed—by
the fire and the smoke, and by the sulphur which came
from their mouths. For the power of the horses is in their 19
mouths and in their tails ; their tails are like serpents :
they have heads, and it is with these that they do the damage.

The People whose Lives were spared refused to repent But the rest of mankind who were not killed 20
by these plagues, did not even then repent and
leave the things they had made, so as to cease
worshipping the demons, and the idols of gold
and silver, bronze, stone, and wood, which can
neither see, nor hear, nor move. Nor did they repent of 21

11. *Abaddon*] A Hebrew word meaning ' destruction '; cf. Job. xxvi. 6 ; xxviii.
22 ; Ps. lxxxviii. 11 ; Prov. xv. 11.
Apollyon] The Greek equivalent of Abaddon—meaning ' destroyer.'

their murders, their practice of magic, their fornication,
or their thefts.

Then I saw another strong angel coming 1
down from heaven. He was robed in a cloud,
and over his head was the rainbow. His face
was like the sun, and his feet resembled pillars
of fire. In his hand he held a small scroll 2

*A glorious
Angel and
the seven
Peals of
Thunder*

unrolled; and, planting his right foot on the sea and his
left foot on the land, he cried out in a loud voice like the 3
roar of a lion. And when he had cried out, each of the
seven peals of thunder uttered its own message. And when 4
the seven peals of thunder had spoken, I was about to
write down what they had said; but I heard a voice from
heaven saying, 'Keep secret what the seven peals of
thunder have spoken, do not write it.'

*God's
Purposes
to be now
fully
realized*

Then the angel that I saw standing on the sea 5
and on the land, lifted his right hand toward 6
heaven. And in the name of Him who lives for
ever and ever, the Creator of heaven and all that
is in it, of the earth and all that is in it, and of
the sea and all that is in it, he solemnly declared,

'There shall be no further delay; but in the days 7
when the seventh angel blows his trumpet, when he
begins to blow, then is the secret purpose of God fulfilled
according to the message which He gave to His servants
the Prophets.'

*The Seer
eats the
Angel's
Scroll*

Then the voice which I had heard speaking 8
from heaven once more addressed me, saying,
'Go and take the scroll which lies open in
the hand of the angel who is standing on the
sea and on the land.'

So I went to the angel and asked him to give me the 9
small scroll.

'Take it,' he said, 'and eat the whole of it. It will give
you great pain when you have eaten it, although in your
mouth it will taste as sweet as honey.'

So I took the small scroll out of the angel's hand and ate 10
the whole of it; and in my mouth it was as sweet as honey,
but when I had eaten it it gave me great pain. And a 11
voice said to me,

'You must prophesy yet further concerning peoples,
nations, languages, and many kings.'

11 1 'Measure the earthly Temple, and count the Worshippers,' Then a reed was given me to serve as a measuring rod ; and a voice said,

'Rise, and measure God's sanctuary—and the altar—and count the worshippers who are in it. But as for the court which is outside the 2 sanctuary, pass it over. Do not measure it ; for it has been given to the Gentiles, and for forty-two months they will trample the holy city under foot. And I will authorize My 3 two witnesses to prophesy for 1260 days, clothed in sackcloth.

The two Witnesses for God 'These witnesses are the two olive-trees, 4 and they are the two lamps which stand in the presence of the Lord of the earth. And if any 5 one seeks to injure them—fire comes from their mouths and devours their enemies ; and if any one shall seek to injure them, he will in this way certainly be killed. They have 6 power given to them to seal up the sky, so that no rain may fall so long as they continue to prophesy ; and power over the waters to turn them into blood, and to smite the earth with various plagues whenever they choose to do so.

The Murder of the two Witnesses 'And when they have fully delivered their 7 testimony, the Wild Beast which is to rise out of the bottomless pit will make war upon them and overcome them and kill them. And their dead bodies 8 are to lie in the broad street of the great city which is mystically called " Sodom " and " Egypt," where indeed their Lord was crucified. And men belonging to all 9 peoples, tribes, languages, and nations gaze at their dead bodies for three days and a half, but they refuse to let them be laid in a tomb. The inhabitants of the earth rejoice 10 over them and are glad and will send gifts to one another ; for these two Prophets had greatly troubled the inhabitants of the earth.'

---

2. *Forty-two months*] Equivalent to the 1260 days of verse 3 and the three years and a half of Dan. vii. 25 ; xii. 7. The period represents the actual duration of the persecution under Antiochus Epiphanes (from the spring of 168 B.C. to the autumn of 165 B.C.)—when the temple was profaned, and a pagan altar erected. This event invested the period of three years and a half with special significance, and it became the standard figure for the length of the persecution under Antichrist ; cf. Rev. xii. 6, 14 ; xiii. 5.

4. *The two olive-trees*] Cf. Zech. iv. 1-6. They 'represent the Holy Spirit bestowing His gifts and His grace through the Old and New Testaments.'

7. *The Wild Beast*] This is the first of thirty-seven passages where some fierce, hell-born power is so described in this book. See xiii. 1.

8. *Sodom*] Applied to Jerusalem as a term of reproach in Isa. i. 10. 'Egypt' is also used as a term of reproach.

9. *Three days and a half*] 'Day' is here used as equivalent to year—and the period is identical with the forty-two months of verse 2.

They come back to Life and ascend to Heaven But at the end of the three days and a half 11 the breath of life from God entered into them, and they rose to their feet; and all who saw them were terrified. Then they heard a loud 12 voice calling to them out of heaven, ' Come up here '; and they went up to heaven in the cloud, and their enemies saw them go. And just at that time there was a great earth- 13 quake, and a tenth part of the city was overthrown. Seven thousand people were killed in the earthquake, and the rest were terrified and gave glory to the God of heaven. The 14 second Woe is past; the third Woe will soon be here.

The seventh Trumpet The seventh angel blew his trumpet; and there 15 followed loud voices in heaven which said,
' The sovereignty of the world now belongs to our Lord and His Christ; and He will be King for ever and ever.'

Then the twenty-four Elders, who sit on thrones in the 16 presence of God, fell on their faces and worshipped God, saying, 17
' We give thee thanks, O Lord God, the Ruler of all,
Who art and wast,
Because Thou hast exerted Thy power, Thy great power, and hast become King.
The nations grew wrathful, 18
And Thy Wrath has come,
And the time for the dead to be judged,
And the time for Thee to give their reward to Thy servants the Prophets and to Thy people,
And to those who fear Thee, the small and the great,
And to destroy those who destroy the earth.'

Then the doors of God's sanctuary in heaven were 19 opened, and the Ark, in which His Covenant was, was seen in His sanctuary; and there came flashes of lightning, and voices, and peals of thunder, and an earthquake, and a storm of hail.

A Series of Marvels

The Sun-clad Woman And a great marvel was seen in heaven—a 1 **12** woman who was robed with the sun and had the moon under her feet, and had also a crown of twelve stars round her head, was with child, and she was 2 crying out in the pains and agony of childbirth.

The great Dragon And another marvel was seen in heaven—a 3 great fiery-red Dragon, with seven heads and ten horns ; and on his heads were seven kingly crowns. His tail was drawing after it a third part of the 4 stars of heaven, and it dashed them to the ground. And in front of the woman who was about to become a mother, the Dragon was standing in order to devour the child as soon as it was born. She gave birth to a son—a male child, destined 5 before long to rule all nations with an iron sceptre. But her child was caught up to God and His throne, and the woman 6 fled into the Desert, there to be cared for, for 1260 days, in a place which God had prepared for her.

The Dragon is cast down from Heaven to Earth And war broke out in heaven, Michael and 7 his angels engaging in battle with the Dragon. The Dragon fought and so did his angels ; but 8 they were defeated, and there was no longer any room found for them in heaven. The great Dragon, the 9 ancient serpent, he who is called ' the Devil ' and ' Satan ' and leads the whole earth astray, was hurled down : he was hurled down to the earth, and his angels were hurled down with him.

The Triumph of Christ and His People Then I heard a loud voice speaking in heaven. 10 It said,

' Now is come the salvation and the power and the Kingdom of our God, and the sovereignty of His Christ ; for the accuser of our brethren has been hurled down—he who, day after day and night after night, was wont to accuse them in the presence of God. But they have 11 gained the victory over him because of the blood of the Lamb and of the testimony which they have borne, and because they held their lives cheap and did not shrink even from death. For this reason be glad, O heaven, and you 12 who live therein ! Alas for the earth and the sea ! For the Devil has gone down to you full of fierce anger, because he knows that his appointed time is short.'

The Dragon persecutes the Woman And when the Dragon saw that he was hurled 13 down to the earth, he went in pursuit of the woman who had given birth to the male child.

---

3. *Seven heads and ten horns*] The frequent occurrence of similar terms in the Book of Daniel makes it clear that the writer uses them to denote Kings or Kingdoms. The reference here is to Roman Emperors.

6. 1260 *days*] Three years and a half. The length of the Jewish war. Cf. xi. 2, 3 ; xiii. 5.

7. *Michael*] The guardian angel of Israel ; cf. Dan. x. 13 ; xii. 1.

Then, the two wings of a great eagle were given to the woman 14
to enable her to fly away into the Desert to the place assigned
her, there to be cared for, for a period of time, two periods
of time, and half a period of time, beyond the reach of the
serpent. And the serpent poured water from his mouth—a 15
very river it seemed—after the woman, in the hope that she
would be carried away by its flood. But the earth came 16
to the woman's help; it opened its mouth and drank up
the river which the Dragon had poured from his mouth.
This made the Dragon furiously angry with the woman, and 17
he went elsewhere to make war upon her other children—
those who keep God's commandments and hold fast to the
testimony of Jesus. And he took up a position upon the 1 **13**
sands of the sea-shore.

Then I saw a Wild Beast coming up out of
The first Wild Beast the sea, and he had ten horns and seven heads.
On his horns were ten kingly crowns, and in-
scribed on his heads were names full of blasphemy. The 2
Wild Beast which I saw resembled a leopard, and had feet
like the feet of a bear, and his mouth was like the mouth of
a lion ; and it was to the Dragon that he owed his power and
his throne and his wide dominion.

I saw that one of his heads seemed to have been mortally 3
wounded ; but his mortal wound was healed, and the whole
world was amazed and followed him. And they offered 4
worship to the Dragon, because it was to him that the
Wild Beast owed his dominion ; and they also offered
worship to the Wild Beast, and said,

' Who is there like him ? And who is able to engage
in battle with him ? '

And there was given him a mouth full of boastful and 5
blasphemous words ; and liberty of action was granted
him for forty-two months. And he opened his mouth 6
to utter blasphemies against God, to speak evil of His

14. *A period of time, two periods . . and half a period*] *i.e.* three years and a half :
the length of the Jewish war. See verse 6, n. ; xi. 2, 3 ; xiii. 5.
1. *He took up*] v.L. ' I took up.'
Upon] Or ' overlooking,' ' facing.'
Wild Beast] Probably the Roman Empire.
Ten horns] Roman Emperors probably beginning with Augustus and ending with
Vespasian. An alternative view regards the ' seven heads ' as the Emperors
(Augustus to Titus) and the ten horns as provincial governors or dependent kings.
Names . . blasphemy] The Emperors assumed titles (*e.g.* Augustus=' worthy of
worship,' Dominus et Deus=' Lord and God ') which claimed Divine rights.
2. *Leopard, &c.*] The imagery is derived from Dan. vii. 4–6.
3. *One of his heads*] The reference here is to the Emperor Nero ; see xvii. 8.
5. *Forty-two months*] See note on xi. 2.

name and of His dwelling-place—that is to say, of those who dwell in heaven. And permission was given him 7 to make war upon God's people and conquer them; and power was given him over every tribe, people, language, and nation. And all the inhabitants of the 8 earth will be found to be worshipping him: every one whose name is not recorded in the Book of Life—the Book of the Lamb offered in sacrifice from the creation of the world.

Sure Retribution will come upon all Persecutors

Let all who have ears give heed. If any one 9, 10 is eager to lead others into captivity, he must himself go into captivity. If any one is bent on killing with the sword, he must himself be killed by the sword. Here is an opportunity for endurance, and for the exercise of faith, on the part of the saints.

The second Wild Beast

Then I saw another Wild Beast, coming up 11 out of the earth. He had two horns like those of a lamb, but he spoke like a dragon. And 12 the authority of the first Wild Beast—the whole of that authority—he exercises in his presence, and he causes the earth and its inhabitants to worship the first Wild Beast, whose mortal wound had been healed. He also works 13 great miracles, so as even to make fire come down from heaven to earth in the presence of human beings. And 14 his power of leading astray the inhabitants of the earth is due to the marvels which he has been permitted to work in the presence of the Wild Beast. And he told the inhabitants of the earth to erect a statue to the Wild Beast who had received the sword-stroke and yet had recovered. And power was granted him to give breath 15 to the statue of the Wild Beast, so that the statue of the Wild Beast could even speak and cause all who refuse to

8. *Worshipping him*] *i.e.* Nero—a reference to the Emperor-worship which was so prevalent at the time.

From the creation] It is uncertain whether this phrase should be connected with 'the Lamb offered in sacrifice,' or with the Book of Life as in xvii. 8.

9, 10. The meaning of these verses is uncertain. An alternative rendering is 'If any man is doomed to captivity, into captivity he goes. If any man is doomed to the sword, with the sword he is killed.'

11. *Another Wild Beast*] The spirit of paganism and the priestly system which was organized to enforce Caesar-worship.

14. *Sword-stroke, &c.*] An allusion to the legend of Nero redivivus. Cf. xvii. 8.

15. *Give breath*] An allusion to the pretended miracles wrought by the priests, like the later so-called miracles of the Middle Ages by which a stone image was made to move and act like a living person.

Statue] A statue of the Emperor used in Caesar-worship.

worship it to be put to death. And he causes all, small 16
and great, rich and poor, free men and slaves, to have
stamped upon them a mark on their right hands or on their
foreheads, in order that no one should be allowed to buy 17
or sell unless he had the mark—either the name of the
Wild Beast or the number which his name represents.

*The Name
of the
Wild Beast
indicated*

Here is scope for ingenuity. Let people of 18
shrewd intelligence calculate the number of
the Wild Beast ; for it indicates a certain man,
and his number is 666.

*The Joy
of the
Redeemer
and His
People*

Then I looked, and I saw the Lamb stand- 1 **14**
ing upon Mount Zion, and with Him 144,000
people, having His name and His Father's name
written on their foreheads. And I heard music 2
from heaven which resembled the sound of many
waters and the roar of loud thunder ; and the music which
I heard was like that of harpists playing upon their harps.
And they were singing what seemed to be a new song, in 3
front of the throne and in the presence of the four living
creatures and the Elders ; and no one was able to learn
that song except the 144,000 people who had been redeemed
out of the world.

*The
Firstfruits
of Mankind.
Their spot-
less Purity*

These are those who had not defiled them- 4
selves with women : they are as pure as virgins.
They follow the Lamb wherever He goes. They
have been redeemed from among men, as firstfruits to God and to the Lamb. And no lie has 5
ever been found upon their lips : they are faultless.

Four Voices from Heaven

*The first
Voice*

And I saw another angel flying across the 6
sky, carrying the eternal gospel to tell to every
nation, tribe, language, and people, among those
who live on the earth. He said in a loud voice, 7
' Fear God and give Him glory, because the time of His
judgement has come ; and worship Him who made heaven
and earth, the sea and the water-springs.'

16. *Mark on their right hands*] An allusion to the fact that Christians were boycotted in the market-place.
18. 666] Many guesses have been made as to the solution of the riddle—most of
which are incredible. It is practically certain that the reference is to Nero.
2. *Music, Sound, Roar, Music*] Lit. ' voice ' (four times).

And another, a second angel, followed, ex- 8
claiming,

The second Voice

'Fallen, fallen is Babylon the great—she who made all the nations drink the wine of the anger provoked by her fornication.'

And another, a third angel, followed them, 9
exclaiming in a loud voice,

The third Voice

'If any one worships the Wild Beast and his statue, and receives a mark on his forehead or on his hand, he shall drink the wine of God's wrath which stands 10 ready, undiluted, in the cup of His anger, and he shall be tormented with fire and brimstone in the presence of the holy angels and of the Lamb. And the smoke of their 11 torment goes up for ever and ever ; and the worshippers of the Wild Beast and of his statue have no rest day or night, nor has any one who receives the mark of his name. Here is an opportunity for endurance on the part of 12 the saints who carefully keep His commandments and the faith of Jesus !'

And I heard a voice speaking from heaven. 13
It said,

The fourth Voice

'Write as follows :

'"Blessed are the dead who die in the Lord from this time onward. Yes, says the Spirit, let them rest from their labours ; for what they have done goes with them."'

Then I looked, and a white cloud appeared, 14
and sitting on the cloud was One resembling the Son of Man, having a crown of gold upon His head and in His hand a sharp sickle. And 15 another angel came out of the sanctuary, calling in a loud voice to Him who sat on the cloud, and saying,

The Coming of the Son of Man. He reaps the Grain Harvest

'Thrust in your sickle and reap the harvest, for the hour for reaping it has come : the harvest of the earth is overripe.'

Then He who sat on the cloud flung His sickle on the 16 earth, and the earth had its harvest reaped.

---

8. *Babylon*] There can be no doubt that Babylon here stands for Rome.

10. This description of the punishment of the pagan world is based on the imagery of Psalm lxxv. 8 ; Isa. xxx. 33 ; li. 22, ff.

12. *An opportunity, &c.*] Or ' the secret of the endurance of the saints.' Cf. xiii. 9, 10.

13. *Let them rest*] Lit. (they die) ' in order to get rest.'

14. *Cloud*] The imagery is borrowed from Dan. vii. 13. ff.

The Vintage is gathered, and is trodden in fierce Anger

And another angel came out from the 17 sanctuary in heaven, and he too carried a sharp sickle. And another angel came from 18 the altar—he who has power over fire—and he spoke in a loud voice to him who had the sharp sickle, saying,

‘ Thrust in your sharp sickle, and gather the bunches from the vine of the earth, for its grapes are now quite ripe.’

And the angel flung his sickle down to the earth, and 19 reaped the vine of the earth and threw the grapes into the great winepress of God's wrath. And the winepress was 20 trodden outside the city, and out of it came blood reaching the horses' bridles for a distance of 200 miles.

The seven Plagues

The Plagues are brought by seven Angels

Then I saw another marvel in heaven, great 1 **15** and wonderful — there were seven angels bringing seven plagues. These are the last plagues, because in them the wrath of God has reached its climax.

The redeemed sing Songs of glad Triumph to God

And I saw what seemed to be a sea of glass 2 mingled with fire, and those who had gained the victory over the Wild Beast and over his statue and the number of his name, standing by the sea of glass with harps of God in their hands.

And they were singing the song of Moses, God's servant, 3 and the song of the Lamb. Their words were,

‘ Great and wonderful are Thy works,
O Lord God Omnipotent.
Righteous and true are Thy ways,
O King of the nations.
Who shall not be afraid, O Lord, and glorify Thy 4
name ?
For Thou alone art holy.
All nations shall come and shall worship Thee,
Because Thy righteous acts have been made manifest.’

---

19. *Winepress*] Cf. Isa. lxiii. 1–6.
20. 200 *miles*] A possible reference to the geographical length of Palestine—from north to south. In the Jewish war the whole country was deluged with blood.
2. *Statue*] See xiii. 15.
Number of his name] See xiii. 18.
By the sea] Lit. (with their faces) ‘ towards the sea.’
3. *The nations*] v.l. ‘ the Ages.’   Another v.l. is ‘ saints.’

The Plagues come unmistakably from Heaven and God After this I looked and the sanctuary of the 5 tent of witness in heaven was thrown open ; and there came out of the sanctuary the seven 6 angels with the seven plagues, clad in pure, bright linen, and wearing girdles of gold across their breasts. And one of the four living creatures gave 7 the seven angels seven bowls of gold, full of the wrath of God who lives for ever and ever. And the sanctuary was 8 filled with smoke from the glory of God and from His power ; and no one could enter the sanctuary till the seven plagues brought by the seven angels were at an end.

16

The first Plague Then I heard a loud voice from the sanctuary 1 say to the seven angels,

' Go and pour on to the earth the seven bowls of the wrath of God.'

So the first angel went away and poured his bowl on to 2 the earth ; and it brought noisome and grievous sores upon the men who had on them the mark of the Wild Beast and worshipped his statue.

The second Plague The second angel poured his bowl into the 3 sea, and it became blood, like a dead man's blood, and every living creature in the sea died.

The third Plague The third angel poured his bowl into the 4 rivers and springs of water, and they became blood. And I heard the angel of the waters say, 5

' Righteous art Thou, who art and wast, the holy One, because Thou hast thus executed judgement. For they 6 poured out the blood of Thy people and of the Prophets, and in return Thou hast given them blood to drink. And this they deserved.'

And I heard a voice from the altar say, 7

' Even so, O Lord God, the Ruler of all, true and righteous are Thy judgements.'

The fourth Plague Then the fourth angel poured his bowl on 8 to the sun, and power was given to it to scorch men with fire. And the men were burned by 9

---

5. *The tent of witness*] Cf. xi. 19. As in the Epistle to the Hebrews, the tabernacle rather than the later Temple is the symbol of the Divine presence.

6. *The seven angels, &c.*] See ch. xvi.

v.l. followed by the R.V. reads ' arrayed in precious stone pure and bright.' The Greek words for ' linen ' and ' stone ' only differ in a single letter. If ' stone ' is the right reading, it must be interpreted in the light of Ezek. xxviii. 13.

2. *It brought*] Lit. ' it became.' Or we might render ' a bad and painful sore broke out upon.'

3. *Every living creature*] Lit. ' every soul of life.'

a fierce heat; and yet they spoke evil of God who had power over the plagues, and they did not repent so as to give Him glory.

The fifth Plague The fifth angel poured his bowl on to the 10 throne of the Wild Beast; and his kingdom became darkened. People gnawed their tongues in anguish, and yet they spoke evil of the God in heaven 11 because of their pains and their sores, and did not repent of their deeds.

The sixth Plague The sixth angel poured his bowl into that 12 great river, the Euphrates; and its stream was dried up in order to clear the way for the kings who are to come from the east. Then I saw three foul 13 spirits, resembling frogs, issue from the mouth of the Dragon, from the mouth of the Wild Beast, and from the mouth of the false Prophet. For they are the spirits of 14 demons working miracles—spirits that go out to control the kings of the whole earth, to assemble them for the battle which is to take place on the great day of God, the Ruler of all.

('I am coming like a thief. Blessed is the man who 15 keeps awake and guards his raiment for fear he walk about naked and men see his shame.')

And assemble them they did at the place called in Hebrew 16 'Har-Magedon.'

The seventh Plague Then the seventh angel poured his bowl 17 into the air; and a loud voice came out of the sanctuary from the throne, saying, 'It is all accomplished.'

Flashes of lightning followed, and loud blasts, and peals 18 of thunder, and an earthquake more dreadful than there had ever been since there was a man upon the earth—so terrible was it, and so great! The great city was split into three 19 parts; the cities of the nations fell; and great Babylon

---

10. *The throne of the Wild Beast*] The city of Rome itself. Cf. Josephus, *Wars*, iv. ii. 3 and 4.

12. *To clear the way*] To make it easier for the forces in the Far East to attack the Roman Empire.

16. *Har-Magedon*] *i.e.* the mountain of Megiddo (or slaughter). 'It rises from the famous plain of Esdraelon or Jezreel, which was the great battlefield of Palestine. "Two kings perished on its soil; some of Israel's chief victories were won here: and also two of the saddest dirges of the Jewish nation were evoked by the defeats of Gilboa and Megiddo"' (Dr. J. Brown). See Judges v. 19; 2 Kings ix. 27; xxiii. 29, 30; 2 Chron. xxxv. 22. The plain of Esdraelon is described by G. A. Smith as 'the classic battleground of Scripture.'

19. *Babylon*] The name given to Rome throughout the Book of Revelation.

came into remembrance before God, for Him to make her drink from the wine-cup of His fierce anger. Every island 20 fled away, and there was not a mountain anywhere to be seen. And heavy hail, that seemed to be a talent in weight, 21 fell from the sky upon the people ; and they spoke evil of God on account of the plague of the hail—because the plague of it was exceedingly severe.

The great Harlot

An Angel addresses the Seer Then one of the seven angels who were 1 **17** carrying the seven bowls came and spoke to me.

' Come with me,' he said, ' and I will show you the doom of the great Harlot who sits upon many waters. The kings of the earth have committed fornication with 2 her, and the inhabitants of the earth have been made drunk with the wine of her fornication.'

A Vision of the great Harlot So he carried me away in the Spirit into 3 a desert, and there I saw a woman sitting on a scarlet-coloured Wild Beast which was covered with names of blasphemy and had seven heads and ten horns. The woman was clothed in purple and 4 scarlet, and was brilliantly attired with gold and jewels and pearls. She held in her hand a cup of gold, full of abominations and the impurities of her fornication. And 5 on her forehead was a name written which is symbolical of

' Babylon, the great mother of the harlots and of the abominations of the earth.'

And I saw the woman drinking herself drunk with the blood 6 of the saints, and with the blood of the witnesses of Jesus. And when I saw her I was filled with utter astonishment.

Then the angel said to me, 7

The Meaning of the Vision explained ' Why are you so astonished ? I will explain to you the secret meaning of the woman and of the seven-headed, ten-horned Wild Beast which carries her.

1. *Who sits . . waters*] The description comes from Jer. li. 13 and refers to the world-wide dominion of the Roman Empire. See xvii. 15.

2. *Committed fornication*] The sin of these kings ' consisted in purchasing the favour of Rome by accepting her suzerainty and with it her vices and idolatries ' (Swete).

3. *Woman*] The woman symbolises Rome, and the Wild Beast the Empire of which Rome was the centre.

Names of blasphemy] The Imperial titles which claimed Divine honours for the Emperor.

Seven heads] See note on xii. 3.

' The Wild Beast which you have seen was, and is not, 8
and yet is destined to re-ascend, before long, out of the
bottomless pit and go his way into perdition. And the
inhabitants of the earth will be filled with amazement—all
whose names have not been inscribed in the Book of Life
from the foundation of the world—when they see the Wild
Beast : because he was, and is not, and yet is to come. Here 9
is scope for the exercise of a mind that has wisdom ! The
seven heads are the seven hills on which the woman sits.
And they are seven kings : five of them have fallen, and 10
one is still reigning. The seventh has not yet come,
but when he comes he must continue for a short time.
And the Wild Beast which once existed but does not now 11
exist—he is an eighth king and yet is one of the seven and
he goes his way into perdition.

' And the ten horns which you have seen are ten kings 12
who have not yet come to the throne, but for a single hour
they are to receive authority as kings along with the Wild
Beast. They have one common policy, and they are to 13
give their power and authority to the Wild Beast. They 14
will make war upon the Lamb, and the Lamb will
triumph over them ; for He is Lord of lords and King
of kings. And those who accompany Him—called, as
they are, and chosen, and faithful—shall share in the
victory.'

He also said to me,   15
' The waters which you have seen, on which the Harlot
sits, are peoples and multitudes, nations and languages.
And the ten horns that you have seen—and the Wild Beast 16
—these will hate the Harlot, and they will make her desolate and will strip her bare. They will eat her flesh, and
burn her up with fire. For God has put it into their 17
hearts to carry out His purpose with one intent, and to
give their kingdom to the Wild Beast until God's words
have been fulfilled.   And the woman whom you have 18

8. *Was, and is not*] The legend that Nero was about to reappear ; Tacitus says
' Greece and Asia were greatly alarmed by a false report that Nero was about to
reappear . . and many pretended that he was alive, and even believed it.'

9. *Here is scope, &c.*] Lit. ' Here is the mind that hath wisdom.'
Rome has been described as the ' city of the seven hills.'

10. *Seven kings*] The five who ' have fallen ' are the Emperors Augustus, Tiberius,
Caligula, Claudius, and Nero. The one ' still reigning ' is Vespasian—and the
seventh is probably Titus, and the eighth Nero redivivus in the person of Domitian.
See xii. 3.

12. *Ten horns*] Possibly the allies of Rome in the Jewish war.
16. *Hate*] Cf. Josephus, *History*, v. 1 ; *Wars*, ii. 18.

seen is the great city which reigns over the kings of the earth.'

The Downfall of Babylon

After these things I saw another angel coming 1 **18** down from heaven, armed with great power. The earth was illumined with his splendour, 2 and with a mighty voice he cried out, saying,

'Fallen, fallen is Babylon the great,

She has become the haunt of demons
And the abode of every kind of foul spirit
And every kind of foul and hateful bird.

For all the nations have drunk of the wrath-provoking 3 wine of her fornication,
And the kings of the earth have committed fornication with her,
And the merchants of the earth have grown rich through her excessive wantonness.'

Then I heard another voice from heaven, 4 which said,

'Come out of her, My people,
That you may not become partakers in her sins,
Nor receive a share of her plagues.

For her sins are piled up to the sky, 5
And God has called her misdeeds to mind.

Give back to her as she has given; 6
Render unto her double for all her crimes;
In the bowl that she has mixed, mix twice as much for her.

As she has exulted and revelled in wantonness; 7
Pay back to her an equal measure of torment and woe.

For in her heart she boasts, saying, "I sit enthroned as Queen:
No widow am I: I shall never know sorrow."

'For this reason calamities shall come thick 8 upon her on a single day—
Death and sorrow and famine—
And she shall be burned to the ground.
For strong is the Lord God who has judged her.

The Wickedness and the Overthrow of the City

Christ's People are bidden to leave the City

The Grief and Terror of her Friends. But there is Joy in Heaven

---

18. *Great city*] Jerusalem is so described in xi. 8.
Kings of the earth] See Acts iv. 26. The words are there applied to the rulers of Palestine.
Earth] Or 'land.' So in xviii. 3, 9, 11, 23.
8. *The Lord*] v.L. omits these words.

The kings of the earth who have committed fornication 9
    and acted wantonly with her,
Shall weep aloud and lament over her
When they see the smoke of her burning,
While they stand afar off because of their terror at her 10
    doom,
And say, " Alas, alas, thou great city, O Babylon, the
    mighty city !
For in one short hour thy doom has come ! "
And the merchants of the earth weep aloud and lament 11
    over her,
Because now there is no sale for their cargoes—
Cargoes of gold and silver, 12
Of jewels and pearls,
Of fine linen, purple, and silk, and of scarlet stuff ;
All kinds of rare woods, and all kinds of ivory goods
And articles of costly wood,
Of bronze, steel, and marble.
Also cinnamon and balsam ; 13
Odours to burn as incense or for perfume ;
Frankincense, wine, oil ;
Fine flour, wheat, cattle, and sheep ;
Horses and carriages and slaves ;
And the lives of men.
The dainties that thy soul longed for are gone from thee, 14
And all thine elegance and splendour have perished,
And never again shall they be found.
Those who traded in these things, who grew wealthy 15
    through her,
Will stand afar off, through terror at her doom,
Weeping and wailing, and saying, 16
" Alas, alas, for this great city,
Which was brilliantly arrayed in fine linen, and purple
    and scarlet stuff,
And richly adorned with gold, jewels, and pearls ;
Because in one short hour all this great wealth has been 17
    swept away ! "
And every shipmaster and every passenger by sea

---

13. *The lives of men*] Lit. ' the souls of men.' The writer is alluding to the
traffic in human life whether in the form of slavery—or immorality—or the brutal
sports of the amphitheatre.
14. *Dainties, &c.*] Lit. ' and the ripe fruit of the desire of thy soul is gone from
thee.'

And the crews and all who ply their trade on the sea
Stood afar off, and cried aloud   18
When they saw the smoke of her burning. And they
said,
" What city is like this great city ? "
And they threw dust upon their heads,   19
And cried out, as they wept and wailed.
" Alas, alas," they said, " for this great city,
Where all shipowners made rich profit through her
wealth ;
Because in one short hour she has been laid waste ! "
Rejoice over her, O heaven,   20
· And you saints and Apostles and Prophets ;
For God has taken vengeance upon her because of you.'
Then a strong angel took a stone like a huge millstone, 21
The Ruin of and hurled it into the sea, saying,
the City is   ' So shall Babylon, that great city, be violently
complete   hurled down and never again be found.
No harp or song, no flute or trumpet, shall ever again 22
be heard in thee ;
No craftsman of any kind shall ever again be found in
thee ;
Nor shall the grinding of the mill ever again be heard
in thee.
Never again shall the light of a lamp shine in thee,   23
And never again shall the voice of a bridegroom or of a
bride be heard in thee.
For thy merchants were the great men of the earth,
And with the magic of thy spells all nations were led
astray.
And in her was found the blood of Prophets and of the 24
saints
And of all who had been put to death on the earth.'
The   After this I seemed to hear the far-echoing 1 **19**
Inhabitants voices of a great multitude in heaven, who
of Heaven said,
give Thanks   ' Hallelujah !
Salvation and glory and power
Belong to our God.

1. *Hallelujah*] Praise the Lord. This term only occurs here in the N.T. The
Hebrew original is found in several of the Psalms, but it is always translated in the
version. The word itself is first found in the Apocrypha in Tobit xiii. 18, ' All her
streets shall say " Hallelujah." '

True and just are His judgements, **2**
Because He has judged the great Harlot who was corrupting the whole earth with her fornication,
And He has taken vengeance for the blood of His bondservants which her hands have shed.'

And a second time they said, **3**
' Hallelujah !
For her smoke ascends for ever and ever.'

And the twenty-four Elders and the four living **4**
creatures fell down and worshipped God who sits upon the throne.

' Even so,' they said ; ' Hallelujah ! '

And from the throne there came a voice which said, **5**
' Praise our God, all you His bondservants—
You who fear Him, both small and great.'

Their Joy at the Coming of Christ's Kingdom, and of His Marriage Feast And I seemed to hear the voices of a great **6** multitude and the sound of many waters and of loud peals of thunder, which said,

' Hallelujah !

Because our God the Lord Omnipotent has begun His reign.

Let us rejoice and triumph **7**
And give Him the glory ;
For the marriage day of the Lamb has come,
And His Bride has made herself ready.'

She has been allowed to robe herself in fine linen of **8** dazzling purity—the fine linen being the righteous actions of the saints. And he said to me, **9**
' Write as follows : " Blessed are those who have been invited to the Marriage Banquet of the Lamb." '

And he added, still addressing me,
' These are truly the words of God.'

Then I fell at his feet to worship him. But he exclaimed, **10**
' Do not do that. I am a fellow servant of yours and a fellow servant of your brethren who hold fast the truth revealed by Jesus. Worship God.'

For the truth revealed by Jesus is the inspiration of all prophecy.

---

4. *Elders . . creatures*] See iv. 4 and 6.
10. Lit. ' for the testimony of Jesus is the spirit of prophecy.' Prophecy in this connection means ' preaching ' rather than ' prediction.'

A glorious
Vision of
our great
Redeemer
and King

Then I saw a door open in heaven, and a 11
white horse appeared. Its rider was named
'Faithful and True'—One who in righteousness executes judgement and wages war. His 12
eyes were like a flame of fire, and on His head
were many kingly crowns, and He has a name written upon
Him which no one knows but He Himself. He is clad in 13
raiment which had been dipped in blood, and His name is
THE WORD OF GOD. The armies in heaven followed 14
Him—mounted on white horses and clothed in fine linen,
white and spotless. From His mouth there comes a sharp 15
sword with which He will smite the nations ; and He will
Himself be their Shepherd, ruling them with a sceptre of
iron ; and it is His work to tread the winepress of the
fierce anger of God, the Ruler of all. And on His raiment 16
and on His thigh He has a name written,

KING OF KINGS AND LORD OF LORDS.

The
complete
Destruction
of His
human
Enemies

And I saw a single angel standing in the full 17
light of the sun, who cried in a loud voice to all
the birds that flew across the sky,
'Come and be present at God's great banquet, that you may feast on the flesh of kings 18
and the flesh of generals and the flesh of mighty men, on
the flesh of horses and their riders, and on the flesh of all
mankind, whether free men or slaves, great or small.'

And I saw the Wild Beast, and the kings of the earth, and 19
their armies, all assembled to make war against the Rider
upon the horse and against His army. And the Wild 20
Beast was captured, and with him the false Prophet who had
done the miracles in his presence with which he had led
astray those who had received the mark of the Wild Beast,
and worshipped his statue. Both of them were thrown
alive into the Lake of fire that was all ablaze with sulphur.
But the rest were killed with the sword that came from the 21
mouth of the Rider on the horse. And the birds all fed
ravenously upon their flesh.

13. *The Word of God*] This phrase is used in the same sense as in the Fourth Gospel
of John. Cf. John i. 1.
19. *The Wild Beast*] The last reference to the Roman Empire and Nero as the
wild beast.
20. *Done the miracles*] See note on xiii. 13.
Mark of . . Beast] See xiii. 16.
Lake of fire] See xx. 10, 14 ; xxi. 8. The phrase is parallel to the Gehenna of
Fire of the Gospels ; cf. Matt. v. 22 ; Mark ix. 43.

The Devil is put into Prison Then I saw an angel coming down from 1 **20** heaven with the key of the bottomless pit, and in his hand a great chain. He laid hold of the 2 Dragon—the ancient serpent—who is the Devil and Satan, and bound him for a thousand years, and hurled him into 3 the bottomless pit. He shut it up and sealed it over that he might not lead the nations astray any more until the thousand years were at an end. Afterwards he is to be set at liberty for a short time.

Martyrs and Saints rise to Life and to kingly Power And I saw thrones, and people seated on 4 them, to whom judgement was entrusted. And I saw the souls of those who had been beheaded on account of the testimony that they had borne to Jesus and on account of the word of God, and also the souls of those who had not worshipped the Wild Beast or his statue, nor received his mark on their foreheads or their hands ; and they came to life and shared Christ's Kingdom for a thousand years. The rest 5 of the dead did not come to life until the thousand years were at an end. This is the First Resurrection. Blessed 6 and holy are those who share in the First Resurrection. The Second Death has no power over them, but they shall be priests to God and to Christ, and shall reign with Him for the thousand years.

Satan is set at Liberty for a Time. His Destruction But when the thousand years are at an end, 7 Satan will be released from his imprisonment, and will go out to lead astray the nations in all 8 the four corners of the earth, Gog and Magog, and assemble them for war, in number like the sand on the seashore. And they went up over the 9 whole breadth of the earth and surrounded the encampment of the saints and the beloved city. But fire came down from heaven and consumed them ; and the Devil, who had been 10 leading them astray, was thrown into the Lake of fire and sulphur where the Wild Beast and the false Prophet were, and day and night they will suffer torture for ever and ever.

2. *A thousand years*] The idea of a millennial reign of Christ on earth is derived from the Slavonic Book of Enoch, which was written between 1 and 50 A.D. The idea originated from a combination of Gen. ii. 3 and Ps. xc. 4. Six millennia of labour were to be succeeded by a millennium of rest. The Book of Revelation simply incorporates an idea which was current at the time, and Christianizes it.
6. *The Second Death*] Cf. verse 14 ; ii. 7, 11 : xxi. 8.
8. *Gog and Magog*] See Ezek. xxxviii. (R.V.).
9. *Beloved city*] Jerusalem.
10. *For ever and ever*] Or ' until the Ages of the Ages.'

Then I saw a great white throne and One 11
The world-wide Resurrection and Judgement who was seated on it, from whose presence earth and sky fled away, and no place was found for them. And I saw the dead, the 12 great and the small, standing in front of the throne. And books were opened ; and so was another book —namely, the Book of Life ; and the dead were judged by the record in the books according to their deeds. Then 13 the sea yielded up its dead, Death and Hades yielded up their dead, and each man was judged according to his deeds. Then Death and Hades were thrown into the Lake of fire : 14 this is the Second Death—the Lake of fire. And if any 15 one's name was not found recorded in the Book of Life he was thrown into the Lake of fire.

The new Heaven and the new Earth

And I saw a new heaven and a new earth ; 1 **21**
Heaven and God descend into human Nature for the first heaven and the first earth had passed away, and the sea no longer existed. And 2 I saw the holy city, the new Jerusalem, coming down out of heaven from God and made ready like a bride attired to meet her husband. And I heard a 3 loud voice from the throne, saying,

'Lo, God's dwelling place is among men
And He will dwell among them
And they shall be His peoples.
Yes, God Himself will be among them.
He will wipe every tear from their eyes. 4
Death shall be no more ;
Nor sorrow, nor wail of woe, nor pain ;
For the first things have passed away.'

Then He who was seated on the throne said, 5
The Result is an entirely new Creation 'See, I am making everything new.'
And He added,
'Write down these words, for they are trustworthy and true.'

13. *Hades*] The abode of the dead, not the place of punishment. Death and Hades are here personified.

1. *A new heaven . . earth*] The conception is derived from Isa. lxv. 17 and is common in Apocalyptic literature.

The sea] 'To the Apostolic age the ocean spoke of separation and isolation. . . For this element of unrest, this fruitful cause of destruction and death, this divider of nations and churches, there could be no place in a world of social intercourse, deathless life, and unbroken peace ' (Swete).

2. *The new Jerusalem*] Cf. iii. 12.

He also said,   6
'They have now been fulfilled. I am the Alpha and the
Omega, the Beginning and the End. It is I who will give
the thirsty man the right to drink of the fountain of the
Water of Life without cost. All this shall be the victor's 7
heritage, and I will be his God and he shall be a son to Me.
But as for cowards and the unfaithful, and the polluted, 8
and murderers, fornicators, and those who practise magic
or worship idols, and all liars—the portion allotted to them
shall be in the Lake which burns with fire and sulphur.
This is the Second Death.'

The Bride, the heavenly Jerusalem

A Description of the new Jerusalem   Then there came one of the seven angels 9
who were carrying the seven bowls full of the
seven last plagues.
'Come with me,' he said, 'and I will show
you the Bride, the Lamb's wife.'
So in the Spirit he carried me to the top of a vast, lofty 10
mountain, and showed me the holy city, Jerusalem, coming
down out of heaven from God, and bringing with it the 11
glory of God. It shone with a radiance like that of a very
precious stone—such as a jasper, bright and transparent.
It had a wall, massive and high, with twelve large gates, 12
and in charge of the gates were twelve angels. And over-
head, above the gates, names were inscribed which are those
of the twelve tribes of the descendants of Israel. There 13
were three gates on the east, three on the north, three on
the south, and three on the west. The wall of the city 14
had twelve foundation stones, and engraved upon them
were twelve names—the names of the twelve Apostles
of the Lamb.

The Length and Breadth and Height of the City   Now he who was speaking to me had a 15
measuring-rod of gold, with which to measure
the city and its gates and its wall. The plan 16
of the city is a square, the length being the
same as the breadth ; and he measured the city furlong by
furlong, with his measuring-rod—it is fifteen hundred

8. *The Second Death*] See Heb. x. 27 ; Rev. ii. 11 ; xx. 6, 14.
9. *Seven angels . . bowls*] Cf. ch. xvi.
16. *Furlong by furlong*] Lit. ' over furlongs,' to indicate the exactness of the
measure. There were Rabbinical writers who supposed that at some future time
God would lift Jerusalem to a height of twelve miles.
Fifteen hundred] Lit. ' 12,000 stadia or furlongs,' *i.e.* nearly 1500 English miles.

miles long, and the length and the breadth and the height of
it are equal. And He made the measure of the wall seventy- 17
two yards according to human, that is, angelic measurement.

The Wall, the Gates, and the Street of the City   The solid fabric of the wall was jasper ; and 18
the city itself was made of gold, resembling
transparent glass. The foundation-stones of 19
the city wall were adorned with all kinds of
precious stones, the first was of jasper, the
second of sapphire, the third of chalcedony, the fourth
of emerald, the fifth of sardonyx, the sixth of sardius, the 20
seventh of chrysolite, the eighth of beryl, the ninth of topaz,
the tenth of chrysoprase, the eleventh of jacinth, the
twelfth of amethyst.

And the twelve gates were twelve pearls ; each of them 21
consisting of a single pearl. And the main street of the
city was made of pure gold, resembling transparent glass.

The City's Sanctuary and Sun   I saw no temple in the city, for the Lord 22
God, the Ruler of all, is its temple, and so is
the Lamb. Nor has the city any need of the 23
sun or of the moon, to give it light ; for the glory of God
has illumined it and its lamp is the Lamb. By its light 24
the nations will walk ; and into it the kings of the earth
are to bring their glory. And in the daytime (for there 25
will be no night there) the gates will never be closed ; and 26
the glory and honour of the nations shall be brought into
it. And no unclean thing shall ever enter it, nor any one 27
who is guilty of base conduct or tells lies, but only they
whose names are registered in the Lamb's Book of Life.

The River of Life and the Tree of Life   Then he showed me the river of the Water of 1 **22**
Life, bright as crystal, issuing from the throne
of God and of the Lamb. On either side of 2
the river, midway between it and the main
street of the city, was the Tree of Life. It produced twelve
kinds of fruit, yielding a fresh crop month by month, and
the leaves of the tree served as medicine for the nations.

---

17. *Seventy-two yards*] Lit. ' 144 cubits ' or about 216 feet=72 English yards.
These figures are not to be taken literally. ' Such dimensions defy imagination and
are permissible only in the language of symbolism ' (Swete).
    19-21. *Precious stones*] There is some difficulty in identifying these stones. Probably the sapphire is our lapis-lazuli, the chalcedony our onyx, the sardonyx our
onyx, the sardius our cornelian, the chrysolite a golden-yellow stone—probably
amber or topaz, the topaz our chrysolite but of a paler yellow, the jacinth our
sapphire. The emerald, beryl, and amethyst are the same as ours. (See C. A.
Scott, Century Bible.)
    2. *Midway between*] See iv. 6, n. ; vii. 17, n.

The eternal Throne and the eternal Light 'Nothing accursed will be there,' he said; 3 'but the throne of God and of the Lamb will be in that city. And His servants will render Him holy service and will see His face, and His 4 name will be on their foreheads. And there will be no 5 night there; and they have no need of lamplight or sunlight, for the Lord God will illumine them, and they will be kings for ever and ever.'

Conclusion

The Certainty of the speedy Fulfilment of the Book And he said to me, 6 'These words are trustworthy and true; and the Lord, the God of the spirits of the Prophets, sent His angel to make known to His servants the things which must soon happen. "I am coming quickly." Blessed is he who is 7 mindful of the prophecies contained in this book.'

I John heard and saw these things; and when I had 8 heard and seen them, I fell at the feet of the angel who was showing me them—to worship him. But he said to me, 9 'Do not do that. I am a fellow servant of yours, and a fellow servant of your brethren the Prophets and of those who are mindful of the teachings of this book. • Worship God.'

'Make no secret,' he added, 'of the meaning of the 10 prophecies contained in this book; for the time for their fulfilment is now close at hand. Let the dishonest man act 11 dishonestly still; let the filthy make himself filthy still; let the righteous practise righteousness still; and let the holy keep himself holy still.'

The Nearness of the Time of our Lord's Return 'Lo, I am coming quickly; and My reward 12 is with Me, that I may requite every man according to his deeds. I am the Alpha and 13 the Omega, the First and the Last, the Beginning and the End. Blessed are those who 14 wash their robes clean, that they may have a right to the Tree of Life, and may enter the gates of the city. The 15 unclean are shut out, and so are all who practise magic,

4. *His name . . on their foreheads*] Cf. vii. 3, and contrast the mark on the right hand or the foreheads of those who worshipped the beast, xiii. 16.
10. *Make no secret*] Lit. 'Do not seal up.' Contrast the instructions to the Seer in x. 4 and to Daniel in Dan. xii. 4.
14. *Wash their robes clean*] v.L. 'obey His commands.'
15. *Unclean*] Lit. 'dogs.' Cf. Phil. iii. 2; Matt. vii. 6.

all fornicators, all murderers, and those who worship idols, and every one who loves falsehood and tells lies.

A gracious Invitation ' I Jesus have sent My angel for him solemnly 16 to declare these things to you among the Churches. I am the Root and the offspring of David, the bright Morning Star. The Spirit and the Bride 17 say, " Come " ; and whoever hears, let him say, " Come " ; and let those who are thirsty come. Whoever will, let him take the Water of Life, without payment.

This Book to be neither added to nor taken from ' I solemnly declare to every one who hears 18 the words of the prophecy contained in this book, that if any one adds to those words, God will add to him the plagues spoken of in this book ; and that if any one takes away from the 19 words of the book of this prophecy, God will take from him his share in the Tree of Life and in the holy city—the things described in this book.

The Lord was at hand ' He who solemnly declares all this says, 20 ' " Yes, I am coming quickly." ' Amen. Come, Lord Jesus.

Benediction The grace of the Lord Jesus be with the 21 saints.

16. *Morning Star*] Cf. ii. 28.
18. Cf. Deut. iv. 2 ; xii. 32. Such imprecations are customary in Apocalyptic literature ; cf. the ending of the letter of Aristeas, which says that after the LXX translation was completed ' the whole company . . bade them pronounce a curse in accordance with their custom upon any one who should make any alteration either by adding or changing or omitting anything.'

APPENDIX

ADDITIONAL NOTES ON THE EPISTLE TO THE ROMANS

i. 7. There is important textual evidence for the omission here, and in verse 15, of the words 'in Rome.' Further, at the close of the Epistle, as the R.V. mg. notes at xiv. 23, many authorities insert at this point the doxology of xvi. 25-27. On this and other textual evidence of chapters xv., xvi. there is general agreement that in the second century there was in existence a shorter edition of the Epistle, omitting the last two chapters and all mention of Rome, and probably ending with the doxology after xiv. 23. Various explanations are given. Did Paul himself issue both editions ? If so, did he expand an earlier *general* Epistle into our *Epistle to the Romans* ? Or did he adapt the original Roman letter for wider circulation ? Or did the heretic Marcion, for dogmatic reasons, cut out chapters xv. and xvi. ? These and other hypotheses raise problems far too intricate to be here discussed. See the Commentaries, and the additional note on chapter xvi.

i. 16, 17. Paul's announcement of his theme. The leading ideas may be briefly summarized : (1) *Salvation.* The word and the aspiration were as common to the Pagan as to the Christian world. The Greek desired and interpreted it, for the most part, as material safety and well-being in this world and the next, and sought to obtain it by vows and sacred rites. The Jew had a more moral conception, and made it a salvation to be gained through obedience to the Law ; a tragic failure, recorded in Paul's self-revelation of Romans vii. (cf. ix. 31, 32). (2) *Power of God.* The theoretical ethic of the ancient world, Pagan or Jewish, however noble, was ' weak through the flesh '—lacked the moral motive power which would make the ideal actual. Paul has discovered in faith in Jesus Christ a new relation to God which will set free His dynamic to pardon and to save. (3) *A righteousness of God.* Better, perhaps, so rendered than ' a righteousness which comes from God.' It is His own righteousness which He also imparts. (4) For the quotation from Habakkuk cf. Heb. x. 38, n. Habakkuk is assured that if he will wait he shall see the oppressor overthrown, and the righteous living on through his ' constancy ' or ' faithfulness.' It is the LXX rendering of the Hebrew word by ' faith ' which enables Paul to use this text.

ii. 13. *Will be pronounced righteous*] Or ' acquitted,' or ' justified.' The word, which occurs here for the first time in the Epistle, has reference to a verdict pronounced by a judge. In this instance Paul seems to concede for a moment that righteousness may be secured by obedience to the Law. Contrast iii. 20, Gal. ii. 16, and see Introduction. Cf. also the use of the word in Luke x. 29 and xviii. 14.

iii. 24. *Ransom*] Perhaps, rather, ' redemption.' See Eph. i. 7, n.

iv. 25. *Because of . . for*] The Greek preposition here repeated with the same case may be either retrospective (*because of*) or prospective (*with a view to*). There can be little doubt, in view of Isa. liii. 12, LXX, ' And He was delivered up because of their acts of lawlessness,' that the former clause is retrospective, ' because of our trespasses.' If the second clause must have the same meaning, then, ' was raised up because of the acquittal secured.' But this is not necessary, and the clause may be prospective, ' with a view to our acquittal.' Note how one meaning of a Greek word slips into another in Heb. ix. 15-18, and the same double use of the preposition in Rom. xi. 28.

v. 12-21. The argument is ' Because of this (*i.e.* of all that Christ has wrought for mankind) it follows that just as one man brought death, so one man brought life.' But though Paul begins with a *parallel*, his thought ascends to a *contrast*, the *just as* is exchanged for a *much more* (vv. 15-17). This leads to the broken construction, indicated in the R.V. of verse 12. Then in verse 18 Paul starts afresh and completes the interrupted parallel.

v. 12. *In that all sinned*] To interpret this of individual sin and therefore of individual death to all Adam's descendants is difficult in view of verses 13 and 14. Nor can ' all sinned ' well mean ' all inherited a sinful tendency.' Exegesis, theological implication apart, seems to demand ' all sinned in Adam's sin.' The Apostle repeats and expands his earlier parallel, ' For as in Adam all die, so also in Christ shall

all be made alive ' (1 Cor. xv. 22 ; cf. verse 45). These references to the consequence of Adam's transgression for the race are little more than incidental and for the sake of the contrast. The real stress of Paul's thought is on the second member of the comparison, the mystical identification of the believer with the death and resurrection of Christ, and on the surpassing benefits which this bestows (vv. 15-19 ; Rom. vi. 1-11 ; 2 Cor. v. 14 ; Col. ii. 20, iii. 1, &c.).

vi. 1-vii. 25. Paul defends the bearing upon conduct and character of his central doctrine against four possible objections :

(1) Persistence in sin will enhance the power of grace. vi. 1-14 (cf. iii. 5).
(2) Emancipation from the Law permits sin. vi. 15-vii. 6.
(3) If the Law was the instrument of sin, it was itself sin. vii. 7-12.
(4) The Law, good in itself, did nevertheless work death. vii. 13-25.

Then there follows in chapter viii. the triumphant description of Life in the Spirit.

viii. 15. ' Abba ! Father ! ' The same repetition of ' Father,' first in Aramaic and then in Greek, occurs also in Mark xiv. 36 and Gal. iv. 6. The emotional tension of prayer in each case forbids the supposition that the Greek term was added as an *interpretation* of the Aramaic. Perhaps our Lord, under impulse of strong feeling, used both words, as in Mark xiv. 36, and His disciples caught the habit. Or perhaps His single word ' Abba ' became something like a sacred proper name ' God,' to which the Greek ' Father ' was added as an appellative, ' O God, our Father ! '

viii. 23-27. For this thought of the sharing of the human soul in the expectancy and striving of creation towards an undefined goal, compare Wordsworth's *Ode on Intimations of Immortality*. In contrast to the clear-cut, glad visions of childhood, he speaks of a yet higher worth in life.

> ' Not for these I raise
>   The song of thanks and praise ;
> But for those obstinate questionings
> Of sense and outward things,
> Fallings from us, vanishings ;
> Blank misgivings of a Creature
> Moving about in worlds not realised,
> High instincts before which our mortal Nature
> Did tremble like a guilty thing surprised :
>   But for those first affections,
>   Those shadowy recollections,
>   Which, be they what they may,
> Are yet the fountain light of all our day,
> Are yet a master light of all our seeing ;
>   Uphold us, cherish, and have power to make
> Our noisy years seem moments in the being
> Of the eternal Silence.'

Paul solves the poet's paradox of *shadow* which is yet master *light*, by interpreting the mysteries of the haunting sense of God that will not let us go, the perplexities of conscience, thought, and will which baffle the instinct to pray, as the ceaseless pleading and striving of the Spirit of God.

viii. 33, 34. For alternative punctuation of these verses see R.V. text and mg. The parallel structure of Isa. l. 7-9 rather suggests that *assertion* is followed by *question*.

ix. 5. ' The interpretation of Rom. ix. 5 has probably been discussed at greater length than that of any other verse of the N.T.' (Sanday and Headlam). It is perhaps a little unfortunate that S. and H. endorse the R.V. text with its three marginal notes as constituting ' four main interpretations.' That is to confuse the issue. There are really only two ' main interpretations,' as the American R.V. rightly sees, by omitting two of the R.V. margins and improving the third. The question is between :

(a) The *Christological* interpretation, predicating of Christ, in antithesis to the human aspect ' as concerning the flesh,' the divine attributes ' He who is over all, God,' and ascribing to Him the doxology, ' blessed for ever.'

(b) The *Doxological*, which supposes a break after ' as concerning the flesh,' and makes the rest a doxology to God.

This note can only touch on the fringe of a great matter.

The salient considerations seem to be these :

(1) It may be allowed that the Christological reference gives a smoother and more natural interpretation of the Greek. On the other hand, the attempt to rule out on linguistic grounds the rival interpretation fails. Both are quite possible.

(2) The difficulty felt with regard to the reference to Christ is not due to doctrinal bias, but to Pauline usage, and indeed to that of the N.T. writers generally. It is true that Paul freely transfers to Christ O.T. language used of Jehovah. He regards Him as the cause and goal, the unifying principle, of all created things (*e.g.* Col. i. 15-17) ;

APPENDIX

but he never calls Him 'God,' still less 'God over all' (contrast Eph. iv. 6), and elsewhere his doxologies are addressed to God the Father.

(3) Possibly, in an isolated instance, Paul might, in adoration of the divine Jesus Christ of his experience, transcend his self-imposed limits. But here he is speaking of the Messiah promised to the Jews. Was *this* Christ 'God over all'? Surely in an argument meant to be conciliatory such an assertion would exasperate the deep-rooted monotheism of his countrymen.

(4) So there is at least room for the doxological interpretation, widely adopted. Paul enumerates the privileges of Israel and their tragic failure, leading up to the climax 'from whom is sprung the Christ according to the flesh, '—'! Then he breaks off in an emotion which overmasters him, to find refuge in the all-wise but inscrutable purpose of Almighty God. 'Well, He who is over all, God, blessed be He for ever' (cf. xi. 33-36).

xvi. 1. In the Introduction to the Epistle the possibility is noted that part at least of this chapter (vv. 1-20) may have been a letter of commendation of Phoebe addressed to the Church in *Ephesus*. The reasons for this suggestion are briefly as follows:

(1) The long list of salutations, unexampled in other Epistles, marked by an intimate knowledge of those saluted. And this to a Church Paul had never visited! Of course, 'all roads lead to Rome,' and converts from his Asiatic Churches may have drifted to the Capital; but this suggestion hardly removes the doubt.

(2) The personal appeal and claim of verses 1 and 2 and the admonition of verses 17-20, not prepared for by anything that precedes, seem alien to the studiously impersonal character of the Epistle.

(3) 'Epaenetus, the first fruits of Asia' (verse 5) has more point if he is singled out as the earliest member of the Church addressed. The A.V. 'first fruits of Achaia' is a harmonizing correction, and contradicts 1 Cor. xvi. 15.

(4) 'Prisca and Aquila, and the Church that is in their house' (vv. 3-5). They were expelled from Rome and found by Paul in Corinth (Acts xviii. 2), went with him to Ephesus, and were left there (Acts xviii. 18, 19). They were still in Ephesus, with a Church in their house, at the writing of 1 Cor. (1 Cor. xvi. 19). At a later date, 2 Tim. iv. 19 involves at least a tradition of continued residence there. Thus, apart from Rom. xvi. 3, all the evidence points to a permanent settlement in Ephesus. Of course, they may shortly after 1 Cor. have returned to Rome, and made their home a Church-centre, and again returned to Ephesus. Such wandering to and fro is not impossible, but is, perhaps, hardly probable.

ADDITIONAL NOTES ON 1 AND 2 CORINTHIANS

1 Cor. ii. 13. There are three words in the Greek, of which only one, 'spiritual things,' is unambiguous. A.V. 'comparing spiritual things with spiritual.' So R.V. text, with mg., 'combining spiritual things with spiritual,' or 'interpreting spiritual things to spiritual men.' The American R.V. text has the rendering here adopted, 'combining spiritual things with spiritual *words*,' and omits mg. 18.

Perhaps Paul's thought is of a consistency and unity in spiritual truth, 'combining, or comparing, spiritual things with spiritual.'

v. It is now generally agreed that the offender of this chapter is not to be identified with the one for whom, after he had been punished by the majority of the Church, Paul asks forgiveness in 2 Cor. ii. 5-11. Paul would not write in that indulgent way about one who had committed so gross a sin, nor insist that he had demanded punishment for it in order to test the Church's loyalty to himself. Probably the offence of 2 Cor. is a personal attack upon the Apostle, subsequent to the writing of 1 Cor., and resented with hot indignation in the 'severe letter,' part of which perhaps survives in 2 Cor. x.–xiii. The majority of the Church respond to Paul's appeal for loyalty (2 Cor. ii. 9, vii. 12) and punish the offender with such severity that he himself, the 'one who suffered the wrong' (2 Cor. vii. 12), interposes with a plea for mercy on the wrongdoer. Thus the too easy reconstruction of Paul's correspondence with Corinth (viz. 1 Cor., the meeting with Titus in Macedonia, 2 Cor.) breaks down. (See Introduction to 2 Cor.)

vii. 21. It is curious that the Greek is ambiguous as between two diametrically opposed interpretations. 'You received your call while a slave! Never mind. Yet if a chance of freedom comes your way, take it.' So the translation adopted here with A.V. and R.V. text and American R.V. mg. Or, 'even if the chance of freedom comes, neglect it; the time is so short that whether you are a slave or free matters nothing.' So R.V. mg. and American R.V. text; and so Mr. A. S. Way (*The Letters of St. Paul*). Perhaps the tense of the imperative 'use it' as well as intrinsic probability is decisive for 'take advantage of the chance of freedom.'

APPENDIX

vii. 36–38. The R.V. by inserting *daughter* (not in the Greek) in verses 36, 37, 38 interprets of a father giving or withholding his daughter in marriage. In accordance with this the 'let them marry' of verse 36 is to be explained as in the text here. But it is possible that the passage refers to an ascetic Christian association of men and women, a practice of which in the second century there is clear evidence. In some cases human nature proved too strong for the celibate vow to the service of the Church. Then, says Paul, 'let the "spiritual bride" be taken to wife.' In this case the alternative translation of verse 36 would run, 'But if any man feels that he is acting unfairly to the maid who is his "spiritual bride," if his passions are strong, and it must be so, let him do what he wishes : he does not sin. Let them marry.' This custom of spiritual marriage was found to be perilous, and after the fourth century gradually disappeared.

viii. 1–xi. 1. A noble treatment of a delicate subject and a real difficulty. In a heathen city like Corinth it was practically impossible to avoid meat from an animal which had been consecrated to some god, if only by the ritual burning of a few hairs. Probably some phrases in chapter viii. are quoted from the Corinthian letter, seeking a pronouncement from the Apostle in favour of the man of strong conscience and enlightened mind (vv. 1, 4, 7, 10). Paul accepts the claim of 'knowledge.' But what if it be exercised without consideration for the weaker conscience ? The complacent suggestion that the example of the strong would fortify the weak (verse 10) provokes the crushing retort of verse 11. What a success ! The weak, who deserved all consideration, is ruined by your 'knowledge'—your brother, for whom Christ died ! (cf. Rom. xiv., especially vv. 20–23). In chapter ix. Paul points to his own surrender of freedom for the gospel's sake, then passes on to a warning against a false confidence in the protection afforded by the Christian sacraments. In the sequel he absolutely forbids participation in the heathen temple feasts, rules out any question of conscience in the purchase of meat, and draws a delightful little picture of the Christian guest of an unbelieving host.

xi. 23–25. This is, of course, the earliest record of the institution of the Lord's Supper. There are slight differences, with substantial agreement, in Mark xiv., Matt. xxvi., Luke xxii. The Fourth Gospel is silent as to the Institution, but interprets the Christian Eucharist in the discourse on 'the bread of Life' (John vi. 51–59). It is to Paul and Luke alone that we owe the aspect of a perpetual memorial service—'This do in remembrance of me.' But commemoration does not exhaust the meaning of the Lord's Supper. There is also communication (1 Cor. x. 16, John vi. 51–59) and proclamation, 'You proclaim the Lord's death until He come' (1 Cor. xi. 26). That is a fine paradox, the Christian challenge to a world waiting for a saviour. 'Dead, yet the Lord'; 'Dead, therefore Lord.' It is these three aspects—Commemoration, Communication, Proclamation—which blend in the Eucharist, *i.e.* the supreme service of Thanksgiving.

2 Cor. i. 15–23. In 1 Cor. xvi. 5 Paul's projected route from Ephesus was simply through Macedonia to Corinth. This plan was actually carried out (Acts xx. 1, 2 Cor. ii. 13). But subsequently to the intimation of 1 Cor. xvi. 5 the Apostle had apparently changed his purpose for the route—Ephesus, Corinth, Macedonia, Corinth again —and had abandoned the double visit because of disaffection towards him in the Corinthian Church.

ii. 1. The Greek clearly indicates a previous *painful* visit, unrecorded in Acts. Such a visit from Ephesus seems to be confirmed by 2 Cor. xii. 14, xiii. 1. See Introduction.

ii. 5–11. See additional note on 1 Cor. v.

vi. 14–vii. 1. See Introduction.

x.–xiii. See Introduction.

xii. 14, xiii. 1. See note on ii. 1.

ADDITIONAL NOTES ON GALATIANS

i. 15–ii. 14. This bit of Paul's autobiography, as compared with the narrative of Acts, raises questions of great importance, too intricate to be here fully discussed. Some salient points of a still unsettled controversy may be briefly indicated.

(1) The retirement into Arabia (i. 17) is not mentioned in Acts. Perhaps it was a brief sojourn in Northern Arabia, immediately adjacent to Damascus, and subject to King Aretas, not a prolonged seclusion in the wilderness of Sinai, on which Luke could hardly have been silent.

(2) It is doubtful whether the fourteen years of ii. 1 are included in, or are additional to, the three years of i. 18. The point is of importance for the chronology of Paul's life, but not for the main purpose of this autobiography.

(3) Paul is here asserting his complete independence of the original Apostles by an

APPENDIX

account of his visits to their headquarters in Jerusalem. He names only two—a private visit of a fortnight to Peter, and a later visit with Barnabas and Titus ; this too was private. 'To me at any rate the leaders imparted nothing new.' These two visits have usually been identified with those of Acts ix. and xv., but there are difficulties.

(a) Paul, with Barnabas, paid an intermediate visit to Jerusalem, taking aid for the famine-stricken Church (Acts xi. 30, xii. 25). Of this Paul seems to make no mention, though his argument surely requires a complete list of the opportunities he had of consulting the older Apostles.

(b) While there are resemblances between Gal. ii. 1–10 and Luke's account of the Council of Acts xv., the careful reader will discover notable differences. If Paul really accepted as binding upon his Gentile Churches the Apostolic decree of Acts xv. 29, it is a little astonishing that he should affirm that from the leaders he received nothing new.

(c) Peter perhaps is a man full of surprises, but, after the liberal attitude he had taken at the Council, we are hardly prepared for the incident of Gal. ii. 11–14. Hence some scholars fit Gal. ii. 1–10 into the convenient gap left by Luke's mere references to the beginning and close of the *second* visit (Acts xi. 30, xii. 25). This makes it possible to place Peter's action (ii. 11–14) *before* the Council, and to suppose that Paul's silence as to a third visit is due to the fact that he wrote this Epistle before that visit had taken place. For the early date thus given to *Galatians* see the General Introduction to the Correspondence of St. Paul.

iv. 12–16. The Greek of verse 13 here rendered ' in former days ' has also been interpreted as the former of two visits, with the inference that *Galatians* was subsequent to Acts xviii. 23 (cf. xvi. 6), see Introductions. If the Churches in question were those of North Galatia, it is a little difficult to understand why illness should cause Paul to turn aside from his main route eastward into less civilised regions. On the South Galatian theory we may perhaps surmise, with Sir Wm. Ramsay, that on the first missionary journey Paul intended from Perga to evangelize Pamphylia, but was attacked on that unhealthy coast by some illness (malaria or ophthalmia), which drove him to seek the invigorating uplands of Antioch, some 3600 feet above sea-level. Mark, not prepared for this extended journey over the Taurus range, returned to his mother's house in Jerusalem (Acts xiii. 13, 14). The distressing physical condition of the Apostle might well have been repulsive to these Galatians : it evoked instead sympathy and loving care. The more wonder then that they so quickly abandoned the gospel which they had gladly received from the Apostle (Gal. iv. 13–15, i. 6, 7).

vi. 11. *In what large letters*] The A.V. ' how large a letter ' is impossible. Paul dictated his letters (Rom. xvi. 22), sometimes adding an authenticating signature (2 Thess. iii. 17, 18 ; i. Cor. xvi. 21 ; Col. iv. 18 : cf. Philemon 19). It is just possible that in this severe letter to the Galatians Paul may have chosen not to employ an amanuensis. So R.V. text ' In what large letters I have written,' but mg. ' write,' and so American R.V. text. Probably only at this point Paul himself takes up the pen for a final admonition. The ' large letters ' may be those of a hand which wrote only with difficulty, in comparison with the neat caligraphy of the professional scribe. Other suggestions are that they call attention to the importance of what Paul is to write. Or possibly, as Deissmann suggests, it is a playful touch to relieve the tension, ' You are only children ! See, I write these final words in big characters such as children can decipher.'

ADDITIONAL NOTES ON 1 AND 2 THESSALONIANS

1 Thess. iv. 13–18. It is indisputable that this picturesque prophecy of the ' coming of the Lord ' was not fulfilled in Paul's own lifetime, and has not been fulfilled yet. But the Christian hope remains. Two imperishable sayings (vv. 14, 17) disclose the treasure in the earthen vessel. The Apostle's assurance of a blessed after-life flames out against the dark hopelessness of the pagan world in the presence of death. A touching papyrus letter of consolation from a lady to a friend and her husband bereaved of a child has the sad phrase, ' But against these things one can do nothing,' and adds, ' Wherefore comfort one another '—Paul's very words, but lacking the addition which makes all the difference ' with these words.'

2 Thess. ii. 1–12. ' The meaning of this section has been keenly and voluminously debated. The two points which have to be decided before the passage can be rightly interpreted are : (a) Who is the ' Man of Sin ' ? (b) What is the ' power that restrains ' ? Probably the most satisfactory answer to these questions is : (a) the ' Man of Sin ' represents Antichrist, who is expected by Paul to arise out of the Jewish nation. Hitherto, it must be remembered, opposition to Christianity had come almost entirely from the Jews, and it was quite natural for Paul to think that the intense

APPENDIX

hatred of Judaism would embody itself in the person of some Jewish antagonist. Just as the spirit of love had become incarnate in Jesus Christ, so the spirit of hate would embody itself in Antichrist. This view seems on the whole more satisfactory than the theory that the ' Man of Sin ' will emanate from the pagan world, though the phrase ' he sitteth in the Temple of God, setting himself forth as God ' would be very applicable to Caligula's attempt to profane the Temple and the later cult of Caesar worship which deified the Roman Emperor. (b) The ' power that restrains ' on this theory is the Roman Empire, which had always hitherto protected Christianity against lawless attacks from the Jews.

In plain English the passage seems to mean : The Parousia will not come without signs and warnings. Antichrist must appear first, and Antichrist will embody the Jewish hostility to the Christian faith. At present the Roman Empire is holding this hostility in check. The time will come, however, when this restraint will be withdrawn. Then Antichrist will be let loose and Christ will reappear to challenge and destroy him.' [Prof. H. T. Andrews, D.D., in Peake's *Commentary*.]

ADDITIONAL NOTES ON THE CATHOLIC EPISTLES

JAMES

James ii. 1. It is noted in the preface to the Epistle that the Greek of this verse is all but impossible of translation. The rendering ' who is the glory of God,' or ' who is our glory,' is an *explanation* of a phrase which, if this interpretation is correct, simply says, ' who is the Glory ' (so Moffatt). In point of grammar this rendering of a very difficult phrase is the simplest. It applies yet another abstract term to Him who is the Word, the Way, the Truth, and the Life. He is the manifested glory of God (cf. John i. 14). If this is rejected, we are left with a choice between the all but impossible A.V. and R.V. ' our Lord Jesus Christ, the *Lord* of glory,' and a Christian insertion into a Jewish letter. See Introduction.

ii. 14–26. There seems to be a difference, almost amounting to contradiction, between the insistence of this paragraph on justification by *works* and Paul's great doctrine of justification by *faith*. This led Luther to dismiss *James* as a ' right strawy epistle.' Possibly James, if the Epistle is late, is correcting some perversion of Paul's teaching. But the contradiction is really only on the surface. James means by ' faith ' the orthodox acceptance of a *creed*, and declares that this, apart from fruits in character and conduct, is valueless. Paul means by ' faith ' *trust*, and urges that only by the new relation to God created by this faith in Jesus Christ the moral ' works ' acceptable to God, on which both writers equally insist, can be prompted and sustained.

1 PETER

i. 7. *Testing*] A.V. ' trial.' R.V. ' proof.' This was the only known meaning of the Greek word, until papyri showed that, in addition to its proper meaning of process or instrument of testing, as gold is refined by fire, it had come to take on the meaning of the result of the process, ' proved worth,' ' genuineness.' So Moffatt, ' to prove your faith is sterling.' Obviously the ' more precious ' applies not to the testing, but to its result.

iii. 19–21, iv. 6. It must be admitted that these thoughts—the preaching to the dead who were disobedient in the days of Noah, and the parallel between Noah's safety through the flood and the saving water of Christian Baptism—are unexpected and strange. Of course, the descent of Christ into Hades, *i.e.* the grave, was a commonplace of Christian belief (cf. 1 Cor. xv. 4, Acts ii. 27–31 ; also the Apostles' Creed, ' He descended into hell,' with its equivalent in the Nicene Creed, ' He suffered and was buried '). But these references have no hint of a *ministry* in Hades. Perhaps the earliest suggestion of this is in the fragment of the apocryphal gospel according to St. Peter (about 130 A.D., recovered in 1892). There we read, among the wonders attending the crucifixion, the question, ' Hast thou preached to those who have fallen asleep ? ' And an answer was heard from the Cross, ' Yes.' But it is difficult to find place for this legend in an authentic epistle of St. Peter. Relief may perhaps be sought in the brilliant conjectural emendation of the text by Dr. Rendel Harris. In the apocryphal book of Enoch, quoted by Jude (v. 14), Enoch visits the underworld and seems to promise to antediluvian sinners a time of repentance before the final judgement and ' there was great joy among them, because the name of the Son of Man was revealed unto them.' Now, if the words of our text ' in which also ' (enōk) were originally followed by the almost identical proper name (Enōk, Enoch), then, by one of the commonest sources of corruption of the text, the second com-

APPENDIX

bination of letters may have fallen out (cf. Acts xx. 28, n.), and we may read, ' in which (spirit) Enoch also went and preached.'

iv. 15, 16. The word here rendered ' busybody ' (A.V. ' busybody,' R.V. ' meddler in other men's matters ') is not found elsewhere and is of doubtful meaning. The reference may be to conduct which does not befit a Christian *citizen*, repeating the admonition of ii. 13 (so Moffatt, ' revolutionary,' cf. Romans xiii. 1–7). Or it may be a falling into heathen practices alien to the Christian character. But it is perhaps more probable that the Apostle has in mind the temptation to Christian zeal, untempered by discretion and tact, to introduce dissension into family relationships. The phrase ' suffer as a Christian ' does not necessarily point to the edict of Trajan making the mere profession of Christianity a penal offence, so involving a post-Petrine date for the Epistle. Probably the suffering is not from the State, but from the dislike and hostility shown to the Christian by his neighbour, Jewish or Pagan.

2 PETER

i. 19. The plain meaning is that the word of prophecy is a surer witness than the spoken word on the ' Holy Mountain.' Then follows a warning against individual predilection in the interpretation of prophecy. The Spirit gave it : by the Spirit alone can it be understood.

1 JOHN

v. 6–8. In the A.V. we read in verse 7, ' for there are three that bear record in heaven, the Father, the Word, and the Holy Ghost.' This reference to the three heavenly witnesses is an audacious interpolation, of Latin origin, into the Greek text. It is uncertain what the Apostle means by saying that Jesus Christ came with water and blood. Possibly the reference is to the initial and the closing acts of His ministry—the Baptism and the Crucifixion. But it is perhaps even more probable that the writer is thinking of the Christian sacraments—Baptism and the Eucharist. It is these which sustain the Christian experience of what Christ is perpetually to His Church. Neither can be lightly let go if the Church is to preserve loyalty to her Lord.

So interpreted, the statement links on to the mystic utterance of St. John xix. 34, 35. From the riven side of Jesus ' there came out blood and water,' a record to which solemn emphasis is given by the appended declaration that it is the true testimony of an eye-witness on which belief itself depends. Evidently not a mere statement of phenomenal fact, but of symbolized truth. From the riven side there came *blood*, the life sacrificed that it might be imparted, a truth commemorated and apprehended in the Eucharist ; and *water*, the power of the Spiritual life of which Baptism is the symbol. In the present passage these two sacraments naturally revert to their order in the experience of the Church.

PRINTED IN GREAT BRITAIN BY NEILL AND CO., LTD., EDINBURGH.

A Selection of Personal Opinions and Press Notices
of Previous Editions of

THE NEW TESTAMENT IN MODERN SPEECH

" Full of instruction and interest."—Rev. Principal A. M. Fairbairn, LL.D., D.D., Mansfield College, Oxford.

" I never felt the sacred writings so near to me before."—Most Rev. Bishop Welldon, formerly Headmaster of Harrow.

" I have been much interested in reading Dr. Weymouth's book. Such efforts to popularize the Bible without vulgarizing it must always command one's sympathy."—Right Rev. Bishop J. J. S. Perowne, D.D.

" I am struck by the symmetry and often rhythmical beauty of its phraseology, and how entirely it succeeds in reconciling to modern ears so startling a departure from the familiar style of the Authorized Version."—Very Rev. E. C. Maclure, D.D., Dean of Manchester.

" It makes the New Testament interesting and intelligible to a modern reader without sacrificing dignity or reverence."—Very Rev. Principal Alexander Stewart, D.D., St. Mary's College, St. Andrews.

" Dr. Weymouth seems to have carried out his idea with great skill and judgment."—Mr. R. Y. Tyrrell, Litt.D., LL.D., D.C.L., Regius Professor of Greek, Trinity College, Dublin.

" Based on the best available Greek text and rendered into English with scholarly accuracy."—Rev. Principal W. F. Adeney, M.A., D.D., Manchester.

" The quiet and simple style reproduces very truly that of the original Greek."—Mr. E. V. Arnold, Litt.D., Professor of Latin, University College, Bangor.

" An admirable piece of work. Will come as a new revelation to most readers. Not only the ordinary reader, but also the scholar will be struck with the freshness and vigour with which the old truths are presented through their translation into modern speech. I should be glad to learn that there was a copy of it in every home, and that it, or some similar work, was used at Family Prayer, especially in the case of the Epistles, which in many passages are all but unintelligible in the Authorized and Revised Versions."—Rev. R. H. Charles, D.D., Professor of Biblical Greek, Dublin.

" I have used it in Public Worship on several occasions with great advantage. It is not only accurate, but full of freshness and life."—Rev. John Clifford, M.A., D.D.

" Has been done with a careful and painstaking hand."—Very Rev. G. W. Kitchin, D.D., Dean of Durham.

"The arguments of St. Paul's Epistles are brought out in a most masterly manner."—Rev. Principal McClellan, M.A., Cirencester.

"I welcome this translation heartily, as I think every generation is entitled to have the New Testament put in their own speech, as well as Homer and Virgil."—Rev. Professor A. Menzies, D.D., St. Andrews.

"A most careful, scholarly, and sagacious piece of work, worthy of Dr. Weymouth's well-earned reputation. Can always be relied on for accuracy and penetration. A real help not only to the general reader but also to the student of the Greek original."—Rev. Principal S. D. F. Salmond, D.D., U.F.C. College, Aberdeen.

"It is a brave experiment—carried out with delicacy and skill."—Very Rev. E. C. Wickham, D.D., Dean of Lincoln.

Opinions of the Press

"Is very useful and handy, and will help the English reader to realize what the various books really say, and to some extent how they say it."—*Athenæum*.

"This undertaking, which under less-cultured hands might have given an impression of irreverence, has come from the late Dr. Weymouth and his able editor as a valuable and elucidating piece of work. The language is simple and dignified."—*Bookman*.

"In rendering the meaning into idiomatic, modern, and not undignified English, Dr. Weymouth rarely if ever fails."—*British Weekly*.

"Luminous and illuminating. It is remarkable how much clearness characterizes the New Testament when it is relieved of its Oriental formalism in language."—*Brooklyn Eagle* (U.S.A.).

"Every intelligent reader of the New Testament should profit by this careful and correct translation. Indeed, none can afford to ignore it unless he is able to read with ease the original Greek."—*Examiner*.

"As a commentary on the older versions it may be heartily commended. It is attractive not only in substance but in outward form. The general effect is pleasing and musical."—*Guardian*.

"In dignity and clearness, holds its own remarkably well in a comparison with the King James' version."—*New York Sun*.

"A work of sound and exact learning."—*Scotsman*.

"Dr. Weymouth was an accomplished scholar, and his translation, which is neither too familiar nor too pedantic, will be found really valuable as—to use his own words—'a compressed running commentary (not doctrinal).'"—*Times*.

THE RESULTANT GREEK TESTAMENT

Exhibiting the Text in which the majority
of modern Editors are agreed

Crown 8vo, Cloth Boards, **4s.** net

A Selection of Personal Opinions and Press Notices

" Your most carefully executed volume will help to educate public opinion, and be welcomed by all the higher class of students."—Right Rev. C. J. Ellicott, D.D., Bishop of Gloucester and Bristol.

" The intelligent care and the independence which it shows throughout are not too common in textual criticism."—Rev. F. J. A. Hort, D.D., Hulsean Professor of Divinity, Cambridge.

" Admirable clearness and compactness."—Rev. W. F. Moulton, D.D., Cambridge.

" I have been able to go over somewhat minutely three separate portions taken respectively from the Gospels, the Epistles, and the Apocalypse. I cannot express too emphatically my admiration of the wonderful accuracy of your work, and of the labour and care by which that accuracy has been secured."—Rev. Samuel Newth, D.D., Principal of New College, London.

" This is a very useful work. The basis of Dr. Weymouth's comparison is wider than that of those who have preceded him in the same field. The work has been done with the most conscientious care, and, so far as my observation has extended, with remarkable accuracy."—Right Rev. J. J. Stewart Perowne, D.D., Bishop of Worcester, in the *Churchman*.

" Your edition occupies a ground of its own, and fairly represents the general consensus of critical editors. It must have cost you a vast amount of labour, and deserves the support of all critical students of the Greek Testament."—Rev. Philip Schaff, D.D., New York.

" You have a right to speak with authority about the readings, for you give us the benefit of your prolonged and anxious study."—Rev. F. H. A. Scrivener, D.C.L., LL.D., Prebendary of Exeter.

" The work has been executed with the greatest care. It is much pleasanter to work with a text to which all the best modern critics would in most cases assent, than with one from which nearly every one would be perpetually dissenting."—*Classical Review*.

" Occupies a place of its own, and will certainly prove most convenient for all who wish to see the net result of modern textual criticism."—*Expositor*.

" A convenient book. In compact and intelligible form. The printing is a matter of great moment : we can commend that of the volume before us as very clear and very accurate."—*Guardian*.

" Unquestionably a work of the highest value. The work really comprehends a library in a single volume."—*Methodist Times*.

ON THE RENDERING INTO ENGLISH
OF THE GREEK AORIST AND PERFECT

With Appendices on the New Testament
use of ΓΑΡ and of OYN

Price **1s. 3d.** net

" Your arguments strike me as unanswerable."—The Rev. H. A. Holden, LL.D.

" I have found Dr. Weymouth's careful investigation of the Greek Tenses a great assistance in studying the Greek Testament."—Rev. Joseph B. Mayor, Litt.D., Emeritus Professor, King's College, London : Editor of the *Classical Review.*

" The main principle for which you contend is convincingly supported."—Rev. G. B. Stevens, Ph.D., D.D., Professor of New Testament Criticism, Harvard.